W9-AYE-787

A BOOK IN THE SERIES

RADICAL PERSPECTIVES: A *RADICAL HISTORY REVIEW* BOOK SERIES

Series editors: Daniel J. Walkowitz, New York University

Barbara Weinstein, New York University

History, as radical historians have long observed, cannot be severed from authorial subjectivity, indeed from politics. Political concerns animate the questions we ask, the subjects on which we write. For over thirty years the *Radical History Review* has led in nurturing and advancing politically engaged historical research. Radical Perspectives seeks to further the journal's mission: any author wishing to be in the series makes a self-conscious decision to associate her or his work with a radical perspective. To be sure, many of us are currently struggling with the issue of what it means to be a radical historian in the early twenty-first century, and this series is intended to provide some signposts for what we would judge to be radical history. It will offer innovative ways of telling stories from multiple perspectives; comparative, transnational, and global histories that transcend conventional boundaries of region and nation; works that elaborate on the implications of the postcolonial move to "provincialize Europe"; studies of the public in and of the past, including those that consider the commodification of the past; histories that explore the intersection of identities such as gender, race, class, and sexuality with an eye to their political implications and complications. Above all, this book series seeks to create an important intellectual space and discursive community to explore the very issue of what constitutes radical history. Within this context, some of the books published in the series may privilege alternative and oppositional political cultures, but all will be concerned with the way power is constituted, contested, used, and abused.

A central objective of this series is to broaden the range of issues that can be addressed and reinterpreted from a radical perspective; this volume is therefore a very welcome addition. *The Making of the Middle Class: Toward a Transnational History* challenges longstanding assumptions about middle-class formation and identity construction and deepens our understanding of the middle class as a historical agent in locations ranging from South Asia, Africa, the Middle East, and Europe, to Latin America, Canada, and the United States. These essays and commentaries by historians and historically minded scholars invite us to reflect on the ways a segment of society designated as middle class has shaped—and been shaped by—the historical construction of modernity. Taken together, they allow us to conceptualize middle-class formation as a transnational historical process occurring in multiple places across the globe, rather than simply as a phenomenon that begins in Western Europe and radiates outward from there. It also traces the genealogy of a category that has become the standard of social existence in a remarkable range of cultural and economic settings. Hence the (deliberately ironic) title of the introduction—"We Shall Be All"—a phrase historically associated with the struggles of laboring peoples, but which may now more accurately reflect the seemingly endless celebration and promotion of middle-class lifestyles and "values" even in a world where "the middle" threatens to disappear.

The Making of the Middle Class

The Making of the MIDDLE CLASS

Toward a Transnational History

A. Ricardo López and Barbara Weinstein, editors

Afterword by Mrinalini Sinha

DUKE UNIVERSITY PRESS | DURHAM AND LONDON | 2012

© 2012 Duke University Press
All rights reserved
Printed in the United States of America on acid-free paper ∞
Designed by Kristina Kachele Design, LLC
Typeset in Chaparral Pro by Keystone Typesetting, Inc.
Library of Congress Cataloging-in-Publication Data appear on the last printed page of this book.

CONTENTS

Part III Middle-Class Politics in Revolution

Part IV Middle-Class Politics and the Making of the Public Sphere

ACKNOWLEDGMENTS

This volume has been long in the making. The project has its roots in two panels on the history of the middle class organized by Robert Johnston and Iñigo García-Bryce for the 2004 annual meetings of the American Historical Association and the Conference on Latin American History. Those two stimulating panels on the middle class around the world made it evident that there was a pressing need for a deeper and wider scholarly conversation about the history of the middle class.

With this concern in mind, we organized a conference at the University of Maryland's Miller Center for Historical Studies, in the spring of 2006, that brought together scholars from a variety of locations and specializations. Titled "'We Shall Be All': Toward a Global History of the Middle Class," this three-day symposium extended and amplified the conversation begun by the previous panels as scholars researching a variety of historical contexts reflected on the ways in which members of the middle class have shaped—and been shaped by—the historical construction of modernity. Since then there has been a steady stream of publications about the middle class, and we can now say with confidence that it has become a central part of scholarly discourse and political debate. As is argued in the introduction to this volume, so many of the political, social, and economic hopes associated with modernity have been defined by the notion of the middle class. It is no accident that the economic crisis of the last few years has been measured in terms of how much the middle class around the globe has suffered, which partly explains the robust production of movies, books, museum exhibits, and symposia on the role of the middle class in the consolidation of a new social order. In Latin America, Africa, India, Europe, and the United States, there is a continuous conversation about the middle class. When we initiated this project, little did we know that the publication of this volume would be so timely.

The conference that gave birth to this volume was generously sponsored by the Department of History, the Nathan and Jeanette Miller Center for Historical Studies, the International Activity Fund, and the Designated Research Initiative Funds at the University of Maryland, College Park. The Humanities Initiative at New York University and the Office of Research and Sponsored Programs at Western Washington University offered financial support for the materialization of this volume.

Given our strong sense that the writing of transnational histories requires truly collective endeavors, it is no surprise that we have accumulated more debts to our colleagues than can properly be acknowledged. Gary Gerstle, Mary Kay Vaughan, Sonya Michel, Daryle Williams, Robyn Muncy, David Parker, and Brian Owensby lent support, ideas, and inspiration at various stages of this process. We are also very grateful to all those who participated in the conference, whether or not their specific contributions appear in this volume. Special thanks go to Emily Ades, Leandro Benmergui, Thomas Castillo, Paula Halperin, Thanayi Jackson, and Shari Orisich, who helped make the original conference possible. We are particularly indebted to Claire Goldstene, for her many efforts on behalf of the conference and for many lively discussions about the history of the middle class.

We are grateful to the anonymous readers who took the time to offer detailed comments and thoughtful criticisms that improved the manuscript significantly. It is a special pleasure to thank Valerie Millholland, Gisela Fosado, and Miriam Angress at Duke University Press for their support, advice, and encouragement. We also want to offer our thanks to Rebecca L. Fowler for her careful reading of the manuscript. Finally, we want to thank all the contributors to this volume for their patience, their good-natured responses to suggestions and criticisms, and their crucial role in making this volume a reality.

A. Ricardo López wishes to thank the institutional support offered by the Department of History at Western Washington University. He is indebted to his stimulating colleagues—particularly Johann Neem, Chris Friday, Kevin Leonard, Steve Garfinkle, Laurie Hochstetler, Amanda Eurich, and Kathleen

Kennedy—who have made Western a very welcoming place for discussions about teaching and research. Ricardo is also grateful to Mauricio Archila, Gisela Cramer, John W. Green, Oscar I. Calvo, Marta Dominguez, Mario Barbosa, Brian Owensby, and Gregorio Saldarriaga, as well as attendees at the Social History Research Group of the Universidad de Antioquia for their critical comments on earlier drafts of this book's introduction. Ricardo wants to acknowledge as well his very productive discussions with Susana Romero-Sánchez and Rob Karl. He thanks Abel Ignacio López, Miriam Pedreros, Sandra Lucia López (Teté), Gerardo Parra, Sandra Cortés, Matilde Zamora, Juanita Parra, and Hector Cortés for their emotional or material support, and for the constant reminders of what is important in life. He is very grateful to Maria Isabel Cortés-Zamora for her critical thinking and the countless ways in which she contributed to the completion of this volume. Likewise, Valentina López-Cortés has also been part of this volume, as she has constantly asked: is the middle class so important?

Barbara Weinstein wishes to thank her former colleagues and students at the University of Maryland, as well as her current colleagues and students at New York University, for providing an intellectual community that is both supportive and challenging. Daniel Walkowitz has been a particularly welcome source of ideas and encouragement throughout this process. As always, she is immensely grateful to Erich Goode for the many ways in which he makes everything in her life possible. And finally, she thanks Sarah and Danny for keeping her on her toes, and for making the more conventional version of middle-class life utterly impossible.

A. Ricardo López
Bellingham, Washington

Barbara Weinstein
New York City
June 2011

INTRODUCTION

We Shall Be All

TOWARD A TRANSNATIONAL HISTORY OF THE MIDDLE CLASS

A. Ricardo López with Barbara Weinstein

It is hardly coincidental that the middle class—as a concept and as a practice—is at the center of current political discussions about globalization. Spokespersons for international organizations and US government officials, technocrats, journalists, politicians, and scholars across the political spectrum and around the world are talking about the middle class. With intense social interest and political anxiety, we now witness the organization of conferences, the promotion of publications, the making of documentaries, and, not least important, the institutionalization of nonprofit and governmental initiatives that foreground the middle class. But what exactly is at stake in all this talk about the middle class? For some commentators, it is clear that a consolidation of a "middle-class consensus" could become a fundamental conduit to global economic prosperity and political stability. Resurrecting and modifying some of the major arguments of 1950s modernization theory, both scholarly studies and policy programs propose the creation of a "global middle class" that would eventually legitimize globalization and neoliberalism. Some scholars seem to argue that once every society around the world promotes the creation of a worldwide middle class, neoliberal and global social orders would be beyond question. Indeed, these prophets of neoliberal globalization contend that this global middle class would (finally) abolish the "age of politics" by promoting stable and socially integrated societies on a global scale—a political call that seeks to perpetuate a global middle class as an algorithm for a post-class, postpolitical and postindustrial global society.[1]

Others have suggested that the creation of this global middle class would counter the hegemony of globalization and its need to erase the role of the state. A global middle class would, on the one hand, resuscitate the crucial regulatory role of the state for national and local economies and, on the other hand, discipline capitalists to promote worldwide democratic development.[2] In a context of an ongoing economic crisis, these calls have been further appropriated by policy experts who have insisted that dedicating US foreign policy to the promotion of a global middle class would do far more for US "security and future prosperity" than prolonged military actions across the globe.[3] In fact, Sherle R. Schwenninger contends that this putatively new foreign policy would make the United States "relevant again to the lives of millions of people—from Latin America to Africa to the Middle East to the Pacific."[4] In short, a promotion of a global middle class would help reconstitute what is considered to be a much-needed US economic supremacy and political leadership in the international sphere.

Although subscribing to the same overall framework, others beg to differ. As the United States is facing competition beyond its borders as well as a major economic crisis at home, they claim, the US middle class is "turning out to be the loser of globalization,"[5] as other parts of the world (specifically India and China) are catching up with the "American way of life." In the process, the American middle-class standard of living could disappear as international economic competition pushes prices up, thus forcing the US middle class to struggle to maintain its middle-classness. Indeed, the current economic crisis has been defined that way in the United States precisely because the middle class—"the backbone of the country," as Vice President Joe Biden has called it—might disappear.[6] And if this middle class were to disappear, some worry that the very primacy and distinctiveness of the United States on the world stage as a middle-class nation could vanish. The journalist Gabor Steingart has anxiously speculated that, if this scenario becomes a reality, the United States, as an empire in decline, could soon begin to resemble a third world country.[7] Consequently, some wonder whether the US government should stop setting up the "American way of life" as an example for the world and should instead focus on reviving the American middle class at home.[8] In order to do so, these policymakers and commentators conclude, it is imperative to draw on what has historically distinguished the United States from other modern, industrialized, and advanced societies during the twentieth century: a uniquely middle-class past.[9]

Despite serious disagreements over the significance and political implications of the middle class, these discussions all treat the middle class as a foundational requirement for either restraining or advancing the process of globalization. The narratives point to a specific way of understanding the world in which the middle class is constantly talked about as *the* solution for whatever political, economic, or social problems we face in this globalized present. Indeed, the middle class is now the common currency of nearly all normative constructions of current politics, and ignoring it is equivalent to writing oneself out of the political conversation. Take, for example, the economic growth initiative of the New American Foundation, in which politicians, journalists, policy advisors, and scholars across the political spectrum have actively promoted "the American and European models of building a middle class in the twentieth century [as] the key to both international political stability and world economic growth in the decades ahead."[10]

We are well aware that normative understandings of modernity have been challenged by postmodern and postcolonial theorists alike, and that contemporary scholars as a rule are wary of the tendency to couple progress with Westernization. Yet we would contend that some widely shared assumptions about political normativity persist. Thus, for many policymakers, the constitution of a global middle class is seen as potentially effacing economic inequalities, political instability, and, above all, social dissent. In the neoliberal imagination, societies are spatially envisioned as advancing toward a one-class society—that is, the global middle class—which is seen as a political foundation for an always-becoming postclass global society.[11] This narrative, moreover, not only rehabilitates elements of a much-criticized modernization theory paradigm, but it also simultaneously reverts to the alleged exceptionalism (and, by implication, superiority) of the West. In this politically powerful narrative, the history of middle-class modernity is spatially understood as a differential and sequential process moving from the *local* (usually associated with the lack or absence of a middle class, or the failure of a "flawed" one, in the non-Western societies) to what is described as the *global* (frequently coupled with the genuine consolidation of a middle class in the North Atlantic societies). Thus, "in an era that likes to imagine itself as characterized by ever-expanding connection and communication,"[12] the project for a global middle class is a political vision through which the so-called postindustrialized nations spatially maintain their hierarchical differences from the rest of the world. Middle-classness thus serves as the criterion by which different locales can be hierarchically situated, according to how much they approximate the prescribed features of a global middle class. In the process, the middle class has emerged as both a problem and a model in political debates on how we should live in a globalized world. And this political option—typically seen as the only acceptable option—invites those geographical locations that are defined as the Global South (Africa, Asia, and Latin America) to transcend their multiple, different, and particular modernities by becoming global—that is to say, by aspiring to an American or European way of life. Thus, political legitimacy in what is considered a new global order or "civilization" is associated with the very possibility of creating—or maintaining—a middle class.

What, then, should world histories of the middle class look like, now that we are asked to celebrate the formation of a global middle class? What light can careful, critical historical investigation shed on these claims regarding such a class? And how can historians contribute to debates over globalization by offering more-nuanced accounts of a social formation so politically and ideologically central to this complex process? With some of these questions in mind, the editors of this volume invited scholars studying various locations around the globe to participate in an international conference at the University of Maryland, College Park, in 2006. The main goal of the conference was to enunciate a historiographical moment through which we could rethink the formation, contributions, and complex roles of middle-class people in the making of modern societies since the mid-nineteenth century in a variety of places throughout the world. Several discussions and revisions later, this conference has now been translated into a volume that seeks to intervene in a broader political discussion about the middle class. Our intent is to offer a historical critique to understand why the middle class as an idea and as a practice of modernity is yet again implicated in the current definitions of the world order. In doing so, this book proposes a history of the middle class that is more properly transnational than global. To this end, the chapters contained here examine the creation of multilayered, translocal repertoires of political struggle, economic interest, gendered discourses, religious practices, and racial categorizations that have defined certain historical subjects and experiences as pertaining to a collective middle class. By looking at middle-class lives in South Asia, Africa, Latin America, the Middle East, Canada, Europe, and the United States, the volume sets out to understand the projects of class politics through which middle-class men and women shaped—and were shaped by—modernity since the mid-nineteenth century.

The remainder of this introduction will be divided into three parts. First, we will provide a brief critique of recent historiographical trends, to clarify how this volume departs from previous historical analyses of the middle class and thereby challenges our current understandings of modernity. Second, we will introduce the different rereadings of modernity to be found in the subsequent parts of the volume. And we will finish by offering a provocation on how transnational histories of the middle class are crucial for understanding our present.

Modernity and the Predicament of the Middle Class

The historical trope of a steadily expanding global middle class is by no means new. The originating narratives of the middle class have long been associated almost exclusively with North Atlantic societies, where "white, male, and middle class" became the hegemonic identity.[13] Thus, middle-class modernity is seen as originating *first* in Europe and the United States, and then moving out to the rest of the globe. To be sure, the model of a modern, democratic, progressive middle class dismantling the feudal and authoritarian conditions of premodern Europe has been called into question by scholars of both Europe and its colonial projects.[14] Nevertheless, some scholars continue to argue that, distinct from other parts of the world, in Europe the middle class triumphed over traditional and feudal conditions to make modernity, precisely because of the specific historical unfolding of the Enlightenment in that geographical location.[15] This presumed specialness of Europe—in terms of culture, historical process, and emerging paradigms—meant that Europe alone would develop a fully realized middle class, which could be, at best, emulated elsewhere.

Even among scholars sensitive to the particularities of historical developments beyond the West, such interpretive assumptions have proved remarkably resilient. To cite just one example, in her recent study of the rural middle classes in East Asia and Latin America, Diane Davis constructs a sociological and historical argument that relies heavily on a model of modernity that she associates with what she calls "early industrializers" in Europe and North America, and she analyzes the successes or failures of the East Asian and Latin American cases—the "late developers"—almost exclusively in terms of this previous modernizing paradigm.[16] Despite cautioning that it would be a mistake to use models drawn from "early industrializers" to understand "late developers," Davis understands East Asia and Latin America only through a model of modernity and development associated with North Atlantic societies, so that incongruencies end up being highlighted and understood not just as variations but as deviations. Late developing countries, she claims, transitioned to modernity with rural middle classes that were nonexistent or politically marginal, often as a result of colonial and traditionalist legacies. It is crucial to note that the latter are understood as a historical effect of a colonialism experienced only by late developers (not by their colonizers), and therefore whatever harmful effects these legacies bequeath are absent in the consolidation of modernity in the early industrializing (that is, the colonizing) nations. And it is these legacies that reputedly spawned markers of backwardness, such as regional (urban/rural) differences, rigid class distinctions, and ethnic divisions between urban and rural inhabitants. These obstacles, she insists, prevented the consolidation of a modern middle class capable of disciplining capital and labor.[17] This Davis contrasts to the experience of Western early industrializers, whom she characterizes as enjoying strong forward and backward linkages between city and countryside, "a situation which also helps eliminate the likelihood of stark regional or urban/rural inequalities."[18] Unlike Max Weber, who located the holy grail of the capitalist spirit in Protestant religious mores, Davis identifies agrarian values of self-sufficiency, order, discipline, and hard work that infused the early industrializing societies, both urban and rural centers, with a truly modern middle-class sensibility. In short, precisely because Euro-American societies are historicized as having unique conditions that allowed for the formation of the desirable model of the middle class, the historical and sociological study of middle-class modernity elsewhere is fated to be conducted through notions of failure, or at best, frustrated emulation.

Some scholars have sought to revise such narratives by adopting a global approach to the middle class. We suggest, however, that such studies still tend to reproduce dominant historical understandings of modernity and middle-class formation. Linda Young, for example, argues that the formation of the middle class in the United States, Britain, and Australia during the nineteenth century should be analyzed as a transnational phenomenon, but she confines her analysis to locales that present little challenge to normative conceptualizations of middle-class identity. Young argues that the creation of a culture of gentility was a shared practice that defined the formation of a unified and fully modern middle-class identity in Australia, America, and Britain; in other words, her point of reference is invariably "the Anglo world, the English-speaking middle class," or, even more problematically, "the Anglos."[19] Young makes her argument regarding the universal significance and homogeneity of the middle class by ignoring those who fall outside the charmed circle of the Anglo world and its predominantly white "settler" offspring. Thus, even those who seek to understand modernity from a global perspective may end up effectively reproducing the assumption that the middle class is, after all, a

Euro-American invention. As with other studies, Young's efforts to avoid oversimplification ends up reinforcing a narrative of "first here, then there." According to Young, there were inevitable geographical variations precisely because middle-class formation occurred in each location but on "different time scales . . . a different process but with similar results."[20] Analogous and unified on both sides of the Atlantic, it was a process that began first, or at least earlier, in Britain, where certain conditions—shifts in work patterns, urbanization and industrialization, new styles of organizing the family and social networks, and unprecedented opportunities to develop relative wealth and stability—allowed the emergence of a middle class that could devote itself to the practices of consumption and the production of a culture of gentility. In contrast, slavery in the United States and convict transports to Australia delayed the formation of a culture of gentility in those locales. Young argues that, eventually, Australia and America were able to catch up with Britain and develop the necessary geographical and historical conditions. Freed from the remnants of colonial society, "Anglos" could begin to take advantage of their shared cultural capital—family strategies of distinction, consumption practices, patterns of class behavior, and religious beliefs—to create a fully modern culture of middle-class gentility. As a result, a unified and homogeneous sensibility flourished and spread throughout the English-speaking world, becoming the "ideal and then the norm as the standard of desirable lifestyle."[21]

It is this ideal or norm associated with the Anglo world that historians typically refer to as the model even when analyzing other cases within the geographical location called Europe. In *The Myth of the French Bourgeoisie*, Sarah Maza contends that there was no bourgeoisie or middle class in France during the late eighteenth to early nineteenth century.[22] No group, she argues, calling itself bourgeois or middle class had emerged at the time to assert political claims for status and cultural distinctions within French society. One of her main historical explanations for the nonappearance of this bourgeoisie or middle class is precisely "the near total absence of industrial capitalism in France before 1850."[23] Only with the development of industrial capitalism in the late nineteenth century, concludes Maza, could "a bourgeois or middle class consciousness finally [be] crystallized."[24] Implicit throughout her historical narrative is an Anglo-American model through which the French case needs to be historically understood. The lack of a bourgeoisie or middle class in France is explained precisely as a result of its failure to follow or replicate the historical conditions of what is considered the Anglo model. Maza writes: "It is high time . . . to stop projecting the Anglo-American model with its inevitable linking of capitalism, liberal democracy and middle-class individualism onto

Continental societies. It may be time to start wondering whether that Anglo-American model does not constitute the exception rather than the norm in the development of Western culture."[25] The subtle negative in this statement suggests the problem: even when denied, the so-called Anglo American model is understood as both universal and unique—indeed, a universal exception—through which other historical cases, even those within Europe, can be historicized and always found wanting. Furthermore, as French bourgeois or middle-class modernity did not follow the development of industrial capitalism à la Anglo, it could only be historicized in terms of what it lacked.

Thus, what is considered the Anglo model of modernity and its association with an exemplary middle-class formation has been further parsed to particularize the yet more exceptional case of the United States. Take, for example, a volume edited by Olivier Zunz, Leonard Schoppa, and Nobuhiro Hiwatari, which seeks to examine comparatively the middle class in what one reviewer called "the core countries of the capitalist West."[26] As a whole, this edited volume coalesces one of the major narratives of the formation of the middle class since the Second World War. Beginning in the late 1930s and early 1940s, the argument goes, the United States created the necessary structural conditions to expand its welfare state, to provide unprecedented access to stable and well-paid jobs, and, not least important, to advance specific policies to fight inequality. Coordinated mass production promoted the growth of a class of white-collar workers, while expanding factory employment compensated with middle-class wages. The basic narrative suggests that these structural changes—historicized as not being found elsewhere in the world—diminished the social differences between blue- and white-collar workers. Simultaneously, US government projects successfully consolidated a social pact that created a modern society in which economic cooperation and political consent made class conflict obsolete.

Although recognizing the gender and racial biases in the US social contract during the second half of the twentieth century, several authors in this edited volume argue that Americans were committed to an open class structure and worked toward an ever-expanding middle class that could become the key to the realization of a modern middle-class social contract. Framed as a comparative historical study of the middle class in "advanced nations," the volume as a whole explains "the rise of a [new] middle class" as a specific consequence of the role of the United States in the world.[27] In this narrative, the United States—rather than Europe or, more specifically, Britain—now appears as the unique and exceptional model through which the history of middle-class modernity during the twentieth century must be understood. It was the United

States, this volume argues, that first initiated a "social contract" that allowed people "of widely different cultural and national traditions as well as of different wealth, status, and power, including workers" to be grouped as belonging to a "broad middle class in a society that was [already] predominantly middle class."[28] Celebrating the putative particularities of the United States, these authors implicitly view all other historical or sociological cases of the advanced industrialized nations—Germany, Britain, France, the countries of Eastern Europe, Italy, and Japan—through the lens of what has been referred to as the "American century."[29] The authors, then, attempt to measure the historical and spatial gap between these other national paths and what they consider the uniqueness (and, implicitly, the desirability) of the ever-expanding middle-class modernity of the United States. Mike Savage, for example, presents Britain—the model of middle-classness and Victorian modernity in the nineteenth century—as a failure in the twentieth century. Contrary to the development of an "American ideal of a middle class society in which most people can aspire toward middle class status" during the second half of the twentieth century, the middle class in Britain "developed as an essentially fractured class" defined by rigid class boundaries.[30] Moreover, says Savage, the twentieth-century middle class in Britain has kept the more prosperous members of the working class from aspiring to middle-class status, effectively preventing Britain from being the standard-bearer of modernity and democracy during the last one hundred years.[31] In a similar vein, Patrick Fridenson historicizes the French case not against an Anglo-American model, but more specifically in relation to the United States. Given the "peculiar French [social] make up," the middle classes in France still "prefer to perpetuate their own privileged arrangements rather than allow the creation of a market based, middle class society of the American model."[32] The good news, the authors conclude, is that "finally the middle class is opening up" in some geographical locations, to create a "middle class contract" that follows the American model. Japan, the argument goes, is the quintessential example of how following the US model of middle-classness could pay off. Indeed, Zunz argues, the "Japanese constructing their own version of a middle class contract could be seen as the ultimate victory of the Americans."[33] In short, it is now the United States that is narrativized as the "irresistible" leader, indeed the signifier, of modern change in the twentieth century through the development of its middle class.[34]

These influential studies indicate that, in the world of scholarship, two major overlapping narratives of modernity and middle-class formation have emerged as hegemonic. The important texts by Young, Maza, and the contributors to Zunz, Schoppa, and Hiwatari's edited volume are emblematic of a broader explanation of modernity among scholars on both sides of the Atlantic.[35] The universalization of Euro-American modernity and, more recently, the particularization of a uniquely US modernity have perpetuated a teleological narrative of an intrinsically Western modernity in which divergent historical experiences can be understood only as deviations, failures, or, at best, close emulations. Despite the proliferation of scholarly production on historical comparisons and transnationalism, our historical understanding of the middle class and modernity remain limited by the analytical tendency to privilege the English-speaking world as the unique but universal model through which all other cases must be historically understood.

Recent studies of the middle class have tried to disrupt this teleological narrative by historicizing the local experiences of the middle class outside the West.[36] In many senses, much of what is argued in this book builds on these recent historical works, which have sought to question this deeply embedded Euro-American centrism in the study of the middle class.[37] By looking beyond Europe and the United States, these works have made it abundantly clear that the formation of the middle class was not a development limited to Europe and the United States. As a whole, however, the book seeks to put forward a larger historical argument about modernity and to take a somewhat different tack from the studies of the middle class informed by postcolonial theory and subaltern studies that have recently questioned a Euro-Anglo-US-centric understanding of modernity.[38] These studies have called on scholars to analyze what is historically understood as the local cases of modernity formation—indeed, the need to historicize the multiple experiences of modernity outside Europe and the United States.[39] It is increasingly common to argue that, in order to see how different modernities took shape, we need to understand them according to the historical conditions of each geographical location rather than imposing a priori conceptions of historical processes.[40] In so doing, scholars whose work is informed by subaltern studies and postcolonial theory have tended to attach their historical interrogations of modernity to geographical region or national space—that is to say, to understand these multiple modernities strictly in relation to what is historically understood as "local conditions." Arturo Escobar, for instance, has recently argued that it is necessary to produce a new conceptualization of modernity, a modernity that, he contends, "allows one to see how local histories of European modernity have, since the conquest of America, produced global designs within which subaltern groups have had to live." A new conceptualization of modernity "also makes understandable the emergence of subaltern knowledge and identities in the cracks of the modern colonial world system. These knowledges point at both a reappropriation of *global designs by subaltern local histories* and the possible reconstruction of *local* and *regional* worlds on different logics, in their networked potential, may get to constitute narratives of alternatives to modernity."[41]

Despite Escobar's reference to Europe as another local space, whose global designs could later be reappropriated by what is seen as subaltern local histories, his approach still situates Europe as a locality that can be globalized, whereas the local histories of the subaltern can produce only local alternatives of—or to—modernity. Although this has been a crucial move to challenge the triumphalist narrative of an exclusively Western modernity, these studies have nonetheless tended to reinscribe the very dichotomy that has for so long reduced the world outside Europe and the United States to the status of a second-order term. In what are considered local contexts, study after study narrativizes modernity as vernacular, particular, alternative, hybrid, fractured, and, above all, authentically subaltern in comparison to those places where modernity is understood as original, prior, and unfractured. Europe, the Anglo world, and the United States appear as places where modernity is first and most fully experienced.[42] Then, within specific local contexts, subaltern groups are able to appropriate this original modernity to creatively produce alternative political orders to—or constitute multiple counter-hegemonic projects of—modernity. Thus, it seems that the United States and Europe are now credited with being not only the original source of modernity but also, indirectly, the generators of alternative modernities.

The Shape of the Volume

Although very much indebted to and in dialogue with these recent historical interrogations, this volume seeks to engage, extend, and question this enduring and dominant understanding of modernity by historicizing the formation of the middle class since the early nineteenth century. Precisely because we seek to go beyond a widening of the geographical compass, the volume suggests a specific narrative that invites the reader to think about the historical formation of the middle class in a comparative, connective, and transnational framework. The task must involve more than organizing the narrative according to putatively homogeneous regions—a section on the middle class in the United States, the middle class in Europe, and the middle class in the rest of the world. Although tempting, such an organization would force us to dichotomize the world between what is considered the modern West and what is often defined as the alternative version of modernity for the rest of the world. In this context, we would merely be demonstrating that those societies outside Europe and the United States also had a middle class. Instead, the book proposes four main, interlocking historical problems through which we seek to rethink the historical formation of the middle class across the world—the practices of modernity; the experiences of professionalization, state rule, and class formation; the politics of revolution; and the making of a public sphere.

To be sure, no chapter by itself makes the case. Taken together, however, the chapters suggest a historical understanding of modernity as an integrated—indeed, entangled—transnational process. Thus, the arguments put forward here by the different contributors are to be understood neither as particular instances lacking universal relevance, nor as a specific version of a universal case. Rather we seek above all to understand modernity as an integrated and connected formation, historically unfolding in the same temporal frame on a transnational terrain. Thus, and contrary to several recent studies, we argue that middle-class modernities were not originally European, uniquely North American, homogeneously Anglo, alternatively Indian, genuinely African, or differently Latin American, but rather transnational historical formations through which the meanings, subjectivities, and practices of being middle class were mutually—and coevally—constituted across the globe. In this framework, we argue that colonial practices, gender hierarchies, class segmentations, racial categorizations, and religious projects were indeed constitutive of—rather than opposed or marginal to—the historical experiences of modernity *throughout the world*.

The Making of the Middle Class and Practices of Modernity

The first part opens the volume by offering both historiographical discussions and historical examples of the pivotal role played by the middle class in defining what it meant to be modern in different geographical locations. The part proposes that the best way to provincialize Europe is by historicizing the very contradictory character of modernity itself. By drawing some historical comparisons between the formation of the middle class in colonial northern India and the formation of the middle class in Western Europe, Sanjay Joshi specifically argues that those actors who thought of themselves as middle class shaped the production—as much as they were the product of—a fractured modernity. On the one hand, specific ideas and institutions that came with British imperial rule allowed these men to question the older, aristocratic, and traditional paradigm of class distinction and respectability. On the other hand, this very same project of middle-class modernity shaped specific self-definitions based on religious categories, gender hierarchies, and class distinctions.

Similarly, Michael West argues that the middle class was at the center of colonial relations in Zimbabwe. During the late nineteenth and early twentieth centuries, the middle classes appropriated colonial Christian educational discourses of civilization, social mobility, meritocracy, intellectual labor, and respectability as a way to distinguish themselves from those who were defined as part of an uncivilized Africa. West argues, however, that starting in the 1940s the middle class underwent a process of political radicalization that both questioned colonial power and forged a modern political body through nationalism.

These historical contradictions and fractures were not unique to India or Africa. Quite the contrary, these fractured experiences were at the very center of the middle-class formation in those cases that we still imagine as unfractured, original, and, above all, ideal. Echoing some of Joshi's arguments, Simon Gunn's contribution questions the long-standing convention by which the English middle class is seen as the prototype through which to understand societies as modern or traditional. Furthermore, Gunn historicizes the very tension that underpins what we may call English historiography on the formation of the middle class. In so doing, he deconstructs the widely held assumption by which the middle class in the nineteenth century consolidated a modernity that was unique to England and a mandatory model for the rest of the world to follow. In a similar vein, Marina Moskowitz questions the approach that positions the United States as the example of modern social change precisely because of the unique development of its middle class. Instead of perpetuating this narrative, she asks how and why a cohesive middle-class identity—based on notions of cultural capital, luxury, material aspiration, and credit—became so compelling as to define what it meant to be modern in the United States during the twentieth century. Moskowitz engages a critical debate on how these ideas, practices, and representations of the middle class have historically been pivotal to defining values in the conceptualization of the United States as a cohesive, "one-class society."[43]

Finally, Franca Iacovetta explores the role played by middle-class gatekeepers in defining notions of citizenship in Canada during the Cold War. As part of their self-identification as middle class, these professional social workers, mental health experts, and government officials developed campaigns—dealing with everything from food customs and child rearing to anti-Communist activism—to transform immigrants from Europe into full members of what the gatekeepers imagined was a truly modern, capitalist Canadian society. Like the practices of modernity taking shape in India, the United States, and Zimbabwe, this project of modernization was characterized by ironies, ambiguities, and contradictions. In the context of a strong postwar economy that expanded the role of the welfare state, these middle-class gatekeepers changed Canada into a more pluralized, multiethnic society. However, in a period of deeply ingrained political fear, the gatekeepers defined themselves as the embodiment of modern Canadian society by creating gendered and racialized notions of national belonging—a project that sought to exclude and eliminate those definitions of modernity that were seen as questioning their bourgeois notions of morality, proper behavior, and citizenship.

Labor Professionalization, Class Formation, and State Rule

It is this gatekeeping role performed by the middle class that the second part of the book analyzes further. Taken together, the chapters in this part address two related weaknesses that we perceive in much of the recent literature influenced by poststructuralist theory. As historians and social scientists alike have sought to relocate historical explanations to the realm of the political and cultural, class as an identity linked to labor has become nearly obsolete as a useful category for explaining important major historical processes. And when labor is reclaimed as a legitimate site of historical interpretation, it is usually associated with the project of historicizing the consolidation of the industrial sector and social experiences of the working class. In contrast, this part provides critical insights for understanding one of the major structural transformations of the labor market across the world in the twentieth century: the expansion of the service sector and its concomitant implications for the relationship between labor, state rule, and class formation. Furthermore, the section demonstrates how experiences of professional workers closely intersected with notions of cultural capital, practices of governance, and political meanings to define middle-class identities in several geographical locations.

By looking at the participation of the professional managerial workers in the folk dance movement in English Country Dance, Daniel Walkowitz questions the dominant national ideology in the United States through which class is understood as an "Old World problem that Americans have escaped." Specifically, he offers a case study to illustrate how material conditions and subjective meanings shape what it means to belong to the liberal sectors of the middle class. Although these professional and managerial workers critically develop an alternative to mainstream liberalism, they claim certain kinds of cultural capital—on the dance floor and in their musical tastes—to distinguish themselves from those (black and Latino) people whom they see as performing more sexually evocative dances and favoring uncultured musical styles. As part of their self-identification as middle class, these liberals claim to belong to a distinctive class sector, "affluent yet not quite elite, alternative but also bourgeois." Such a middle-class liberal project, concludes Walkowitz, is thus defined as white, heterosexual, and sharply distinguished from the working people and racial minorities in US society.

During the first decades of the twentieth century in colonial Bombay, a variety of professionals—from doctors and lawyers to journalists and teachers—also claimed cultural capital as a way to struggle for a place in an educated middle class. Seizing educational opportunities provided by British colonial rule, these professionals assumed the role of new arbiters of appropriate social conduct for the society at large. Equally important, Prashant Kidambi explains how the economic conditions of these middle-class actors as professional workers affected their discourse of middle-classness as they were, in a moment of economic and political anxiety, striving to distinguish themselves from those seen as poor, uncivilized, and in need of improvement.

During the second half of the twentieth century, these liberal discourses of uplift and civilization played a crucial role in shaping US imperial projects of development in Latin America. By looking at transnational social programs implemented through different US governmental offices, multilateral organizations, and private associations, A. Ricardo López discusses how middle-class professionals as workers became embedded in a specific form of democratic state rule in the context of US imperial expansion. Like the middle-class gatekeepers in Canada or the cultural arbiters of colonial Bombay, these Colombian development workers were conscripted to become the best governors for a democracy—ready to educate both the elites and the working classes to live in a peaceful and hierarchical society.

Through a similar experience of professionalization, Michael Ervin argues, middle-class agronomists shaped the impact of the revolution of 1910 on Mexican society. As part of their middle-class politics, these agronomists carried out the agrarian reform that the revolutionary government wanted to implement in the rural areas. On the one hand, these professional workers attempted to persuade the elites to cooperate with the programs of land distribution. On the other hand, the agronomists urged the peasant classes to participate in economic plans for expanded production to advance the goals of national progress and modernity. Although this political project of middle-class redemption failed, Ervin argues that during the 1930s these class struggles and negotiations would shape the educational efforts of the postrevolutionary state that sought to nationalize and modernize rural society.[44]

Middle-Class Politics in Revolution

Although policymakers celebrate the middle class as constitutive of democratic practice, historians usually view it as, at best, a passive political force and, at worst, politically apathetic. Taken together, the last two parts of the volume—middle-class politics in revolution and the making of the public sphere—question such widely held assumptions by illuminating how the middle class defined its identities through different political experiences.

Iñigo García-Bryce opens the third part by arguing that the middle class played a crucial role in one of the most enduring multiclass political parties in Latin America—the American Popular Revolutionary Alliance (APRA). By exploring the rhetoric and practices of APRA in Peru since the 1930s through the 1960s, he analyzes this movement and its revolutionary agenda not as a representation of a preexisting middle class, but rather as a party that itself contributed to the creation of a new middle-class political identity. As was the case with the middle class in colonial Lucknow or Canada, this identity was shaped by ambiguities and contradictions. Although the middle class critically engaged political discourses that advocated class alliances between manual and intellectual workers, the persistence of class and racial divides in Peruvian society and the hierarchical organization of the party itself were powerful obstacles that worked against APRA's revolutionary ideals.

In close dialogue with Michael Ervin's arguments, Susanne Eineigel explores how the residents of a self-identified middle-class neighborhood in Mexico City experienced and influenced the consequences of the Mexican Revolution during the first decades of the twentieth century. Eineigel demonstrates how, in the process of becoming middle class, these residents reclaimed some of the political promises of the Mexican Revolution, calling on the revolutionary state to deliver various rights and goods of modernity—urban services, housing programs, and better transportation systems. Likewise, Keith David Watenpaugh explores the rise of a middle class during the first decades of the twentieth century in the Arab Middle East, and the ways its members created a civil society, new forms of revolutionary politics during the Young Turk Revolution, and new styles of engagement with colonialism throughout the establishment of the French Mandate for Syria. Drawing on the experiences of Edmond Rabbath, a Sorbonne-educated Arab lawyer, Watenpaugh argues that the middle class played a crucial—if contradictory—role in these political events. They created institutions of civil society and promoted ideas of equality as well as political accountability. At the same time, middle-class participation was weakened by bonds of religion, ethnicity, and family that proved to be stronger than the bonds that middle-class members created in civil society. Like the contradictions explored by Joshi for colonial India or Iacovetta in the case of Canada, Watenpaugh concludes that these ambiguities were at the very center of middle-class politics in revolution.

Middle-Class Politics and the Making of a Public Sphere

The last part further reveals middle-class engagement with the public sphere. By discussing cases in Peru, Chile, Argentina, France, and Germany, these chapters historicize the massive proliferation and on-the-ground manifestations of middle-class politics—voluntary associations, religious teachings, public opinion, and party membership. Joining a vibrant and growing body of scholarship on the public sphere, understood as shaped by power relationships, the chapters in this part explore the formation of middle-class identities as effects of specific class struggles, racial categorizations, gender representations, political negotiations, and continuous contestation. Indeed, rather than merely the reproduction of structural locations, this part shows how certain historical subjects became middle class *through* different sites of activism and participation in a changing public sphere. Gisela Mettele shows that, during the nineteenth century, women critically participated in a variety of voluntary civic associations to constitute themselves as middle-class subjects. Despite the fact that the public sphere was already defined by a gender privilege that promoted the middle-class male as the embodiment of German citizenship, women shaped civil society by creating their own political associations and forging a notion of civic motherhood. These women became middle class by promoting certain codes of gendered social conduct and class-based notions of distinction.

Carol Harrison questions what may be one of most enduring narratives of modernity. By critically reading feminist historiography on postrevolutionary France, Harrison challenges the tendency to locate "religiosity and class society on opposite sides of the division marked by the French Revolution and the advent of modernity." Indeed, Harrison observes that the post-Enlightenment notion of public sphere, as defined by Habermas, usually connotes a space defined by secularity, masculinity, and rationality, where religiosity has no role to play.[45] In contrast, Harrison proposes to understand religiosity and bourgeois class identities in the same analytical framework, and she demonstrates how in postrevolutionary France, families of the bourgeoisie—daughters, sons, fathers, and mothers—appropriated Catholicism as a political tool to forge an identity in the public sphere as middle-class women and men.

Echoing Watenpaugh's arguments about the Arab middle class, Harrison concludes that in postrevolutionary France, religious practices played a constitutive role in middle-class participation in the public sphere.

David Parker's contribution discusses the constant public contestation in defining social boundaries between the upper class and the middle class in Chile and Peru, from the latter half of the nineteenth century to the middle of the twentieth. Parker shows how a vibrant public discussion of the competing, and sometimes incompatible, images, insults, descriptions, and anecdotes about the social climber constructed this figure. Such public discussion—usually in the form of essays, novels, plays, and memoirs—established a class struggle between those favored by society, who fought to maintain the exclusivity of their ranks, and others who challenged it. Parker concludes that these class struggles were at best contradictory since they "embodied and betrayed the contradictions of an arbitrary" social hierarchy.

Enrique Garguin moves the analysis to Argentina and historicizes how specific notions of the public sphere intersected with the emergence of a political middle-class identity. During the first decades of the twentieth century, argues Garguin, participation in the public sphere and representations of the nation were closely associated with being European and white. Such definitions of legitimate political participation were drastically challenged during the 1940s, with the emergence of Peronism as a populist movement. Now, a "popular public sphere" was celebrated as a political space where the working class could be the legitimate force for social change. Confronting what they considered to be an invasion of their space, certain historical subjects tried to restructure the public sphere and, in doing so, defined themselves as a racialized middle class. The Peronist working class thus became the racialized other—embodied in the notion of the *cabecita negra* (little black head). The middle class, in turn, claimed a "deep sense of whiteness" that would sort out who could or could not participate in the public sphere and genuinely belong to the Argentinean nation.

As this organization of the book suggests, one of our principal objectives is to criticize modernity itself as a transnational phenomenon, and to do so by historicizing what it meant to be middle class.[46] It is in this context that the commentaries for each part reflect the objectives of this volume. Starting with the premise that local detail must surely form the basis of any significant historical account of the middle class, these comments seek to explore transnational connections of locally rooted processes of middle-class formation. In so doing, Barbara Weinstein, Mary Kay Vaughan, Brian Owensby, and Robyn Muncy show that modernity was a process of constant translation, citation, and contestation, in which the idea and the meanings of being middle class were continually formed historically and re-formed transnationally. By making specific comparisons and connections across geographical locations, they explore how a variety of discourses, ideas, meanings, and practices allowed some historical actors to create a sense of modern collective belonging to a middle class. Taken together, these commentaries conclude that such creations were facets of a single—yet complex and variegated—historical formation occurring over most of the globe from the nineteenth century on.

Likewise, we invite our readers to engage with these pieces as *critical* commentaries. Following a specific request, the commentators approached the formation of the middle class as an open historical question that can provoke further theorization, scholarly analysis, and political innovation. Indeed, these part-concluding essays are offered as a counternarrative to a current tendency —cited at the beginning of this introduction—to foreclose historiographical and political debate by making the middle class *the* answer to the putative problems of modernity, globalization, and neoliberalism. Thus, along with the afterword by Mrinalini Sinha, the commentators connect the different chapters in each part in a critical manner, as a way to envision what conceptual approaches we may follow and which historical questions we may want to ask to further analyze the transnational formation of the middle class.

The Fuzziness of the Middle Class

Scholars have long debated the question of how to understand the historical formation of the middle class. In recent decades, historians and other academics concerned with culture have eschewed a positivist social-science approach that measured middle-classness through occupational categories, income levels, or consumption patterns. But the sharp turn away from these objective definitions of the middle class has created other problems. Perhaps the best indication of the difficulties involved is the quotation marks that are now usually attached to the concept: "middle class."[47] Despite an important historiographical literature on social class (mostly based on the experiences of the working class), we still harbor the assumption that the middle class—unlike the elites and working classes that appear as representing homogenous and clear-cut political and social interests—has been historically characterized by an "overabundance of meanings," which makes the concept too amorphous, fuzzy, "imprecise and unhelpful" as a category of historical analysis.[48] Since now the important question, presumably, is how a middle class is signified and spoken of in language, we may be condemning the middle class to historical nonexistence precisely because, given its fuzziness, there was no "unified and pivotal middling or upper middling group" that could acknowledge in language and discourse their middle-classness.[49] With no collective social or political formation of its own, the middle class, some authors have recently concluded, should be understood as a mere abstraction, a discourse, a metaphor, a rhetorical device, with too many political agendas that prevent—or disqualify—any specific class project. Underlying this narrative is precisely the tendency to claim that, since the middle class has no real ideology or real coherent identity, it is futile to historicize it as a social formation. Taken to its logical conclusion, this argument calls for a total abandonment of the very concept as a category of historical analysis.

At the same time, these approaches have tended to accept middle-class identity (if not an actually existing middle class) as yet another given.[50] Perhaps because of this recurring fuzziness, historical discussions of "the middle" seem to snare us in riddles that defy the disciplinary reflex to categorical clarity, making it prudent simply to take the term at face value. Hence, if for some the best option is to abandon the concept of the middle class altogether, other scholars are content to go no further than historical representations of middle-class identity. As a response to these historiographical debates, other scholars have anxiously sought definitional precision regarding what counts as a real social formation of the middle class. Although this may seem a compelling historical approach, once we begin identifying those particular (a)historical features to label some groups as middle class, we are engaging in a complicated but ultimately self-defeating task in which certain ascriptions, attributions, and characteristics have to be found in different historical or geographical contexts. Or, in the best case, we are entering an analytical circuit in which any social, cultural, or political trait that we attribute to the middle class is inevitably subjected to many exceptions. Whether too fuzzy or too precise, the middle class as a concept seems to preclude, rather than provoke, historical interpretation.

This volume invites a more thoroughgoing historical analysis. Neither turning away from what Hannah Arendt called "the wild confusion of historical terminology,"[51] nor presuming historical practices and meanings, nor going back to a real social definition of the middle class suitable to an encyclopedia entry, the volume proposes that we open genuine venues of critical inquiry by staying close to the formative power of language or discourse, while interrogating the different historical material practices of middle-class subjectivity.[52] We contend that such an approach will allow historians and social scientists alike to rethink the two poles of historical interpretation of the middle class: either as a self-evident description of social reality, or a mere rhetorical or metaphorical tool with no real purchase in everyday practice. This volume seeks to challenge and question these two poles of interpretation by radically moving the historical analysis from fixed categories and preconceived definitions to the historical practices of what it meant to be—and live—the middle class in a variety of geographic locations. The volume proposes, moreover, to understand the middle class as a working social concept, a material experience, a political project, and a cultural practice—all of which acquire meaning only within specific historical experiences and discursive conditions. We argue that historical analysis has to move from a priori suppositions to the terrain of ongoing historical practices and contingent processes, within which historical actors have come to think of themselves as belonging to a collective middle class.

Provocations

Critical historical work over the last two decades has developed sophisticated analytical perspectives that privilege microhistories of everyday life to explore how a variety of historical actors elaborated, experienced, and responded to various forms of domination at different moments in time. As will become apparent in this volume, all authors fully endorse such crucial historiographical approaches by historicizing the practices of being middle class across different geographical locations.[53] Echoing Mrinalini Sinha's call in the afterword, however, we want to invite the reader to consider the possibility—however tentative it may be—that a transnational study of the middle class can offer crucial opportunities to relocate grand historical narratives as a central part of our historical inquiries into modernity. As Sinha argues, "there could be no better model to follow in constructing such a narrative than the connected history of middle-class formations." The effort, it should be clear by now, does not seek a return to grand historical narratives as they were once written—Eurocentric, imperialistic, masculinist, and exclusionary. Instead, it is an invitation to ask fundamental questions about capitalism, imperialism, postcolonialism, and modernity. From this perspective, the volume tackles a provocative question recently posed by the historian Gabrielle Spiegel. In commenting on recent studies of transnationalism, she asks: "If not from nation, society or domicile, from where does social identity derive its shape? If we are at once citizens of the world and citizens and subjects of specific nations, how are the contradictions implicit in this form of multilocality negotiated on both the individual and the collective level?"[54] Broadly speaking, we wish to propose that, across the world and over the last two centuries, class—and, more specifically, the middle class—has been one of the major transnational political projects of modernity through which historical actors have struggled to define themselves as belonging to a social collectivity.

The chapters collected here, furthermore, provide what we hope is a political provocation for a critical conversation about the transnational formation of the middle class. Unsurprisingly, the reader will not find a unified voice about how middle-class social identities have been shaped since the nineteenth century. The book as a whole asks readers to think about how the historical analysis of the middle class can offer critical opportunities to question our present, which has been described as "an age of abolition of politics."[55] If we continue to treat the middle class as something natural, as a self-evident reality, or as a pure manifestation of a worldwide postclass society—indeed, as the expression of a society where material equality can be potentially attained—our opportunities to understand and question the neoliberal order will remain incomplete.

As historians of the present, we want to invite, even provoke, our readers to consider whether we can still talk of the middle class as *the* foundational answer for our political situation. If, as this volume should make clear, the modern historical formation of the middle class has been transnationally constituted through changing, unequal relationships and shifting racial and gender hierarchies, colonial practices, and religious divisions across the world in the last two centuries, is there any political sense in the conceit that makes a global middle class the prerequisite for a so-called postclass globalized society? Or, to put it more succinctly: Shall we be all? In discussing these questions, and many more that the reader will find in the pages of this volume, we, as a collective research group, hope the historical critique offered herein can suggest new political languages and practices that we might not otherwise have been able to envision for our futures.

Notes

This introduction is the result of a collective endeavor. The ideas and arguments contained herein have been thought through and discussed extensively with Barbara Weinstein.

1. Everybody is talking about the middle class. Here I can cite only two titles: Mead and Schwenninger, *The Bridge to a Global Middle Class*, and Easterly, "The Middle Class Consensus and Economic Development."

2. Davis, *Discipline and Development*.

3. Schwenninger, "Reconnecting to the World," 13; Davis, *Discipline and Development*.

4. Schwenninger, "Reconnecting the World," 14. For similar arguments see Schwenninger, "Democratizing Capital"; Lind, *The American Way of Strategy*, 21 and 151; Dawisha and Dawisha, "How to Build a Democratic Iraq"; Estache and Leipziger, *Stuck in the Middle*.

5. Steingart, "A Super Power in Decline."

6. Middle Class Task Force (http://www.whitehouse.gov/strongmiddleclass).

7. Similarly, Arianna Huffington has warned that unless "we [the United States] do not correct our course, contrary to our history and to what has always seemed to be our destiny, we could indeed become a Third World Nation—a place where there are only two classes: the rich and . . . everyone else" (*Third World America*, 3). See also Beban, "India Rising"; Lind, "Are We Still a Middle Class Nation." For a critical analysis, see Fernandes, *India's New Middle Class*; Mark Lietchty, *Suitably Modern*; Cohen, *Searching for a Different Future*; School for Advance Research Seminar, "Middle Classes—a Global Perspective," March 28–April 3, 2009, Santa Fe, New Mexico.

8. Perhaps the best example is President Obama's Middle Class Task Force (http://www.whitehouse.gov/strongmiddleclass). See also Hacker, *The Great Risk Shift*; Acemoglu and Robinson, *Economic Origins of Dictatorship and Democracy*; Glassman, *The New Middle Class and Democracy in Global Perspective*.

9. Hartmann, *Screwed*.

10. New America Foundation, "New America on Trade and Globalization" (http://www.newamerica.net/programs/global_middle_class/about_this_program). See also Ravallion, *The Developing World's Bulging (but Vulnerable) "Middle Class"*; Krugman, *The Return of Depression Economics*.

11. Inglehandt and Welzel, *Modernization, Cultural Change and Democracy*.

12. Ferguson, "Decomposing Modernity," 179. See also Weinstein, "Developing Inequality."

13. C. Hall, *White, Male and Middle Class*.

14. See the chapter by Sanjay Joshi in this volume for a historiographical discussion of those works that challenge the standard view of European middle class. For other works that historicize the relationship between colonialism and European identity see Davidoff and Hall, *Family Fortunes*; Cooper and Stoler, *Tension of Empire*; Mehta, *Liberalism and Empire*; Hall, *Civilising Subjects*.

15. Kocka, "The Middle Class in Europe," 807. See also Gay, *Schnitzler's Century*.

16. Davis, *Discipline and Development*.

17. Ibid., 20.

18. Ibid., 21.

19. L. Young, *Middle Class Culture in the Nineteenth Century*, 7, 10, 33.

20. Ibid., 42.

21. Ibid. See also 26, 188, 189. For a critical history of whiteness as a global identity, see Lake and Reynolds, *Drawing the Global Colour Line*.

22. Maza, *The Myth of the French Bourgeoisie*. For a critical understanding of the middle class or bourgeoisie in France, see the chapter by Carol Harrison in this volume.

23. Maza, *The Myth of the French Bourgeoisie*, 4.

24. Ibid., 203.

25. Ibid., 204.

26. Beckert, "Review of *Social Contract under Stress*," 1116; in Zunz, Schoppa, and Hiwatari's *Social Contracts under Stress*, there is little, if any, historical analysis of the practices of those who called themselves middle class.

27. Zunz, "Introduction," 4, 8, in Zunz, Schoppa and Hiwatari, *Social Contracts under Stress*.

28. Ibid., 2, 3.

29. Zunz, *Why the American Century*.

30. Savage, "Individuality and Class," 54.

31. Ibid. See also 49, 56.

32. This is how Olivier Zunz summarizes the argument by Fridenson. Zunz ("Introduction," 6). See also Fridenson, "Could Postwar France Become a Middle Class Society?," 90.

33. Zunz, "Introduction," 7. See also A. Gordon, "The Short Happy Life of the Japanese Middle Class."

34. Victoria de Grazia explains how during the twentieth century the United States triumphed over the "bourgeois European civilization." The latter, she explains, was a traditional society waiting to be modernized by the advancement of a US market empire. In the process, she argues, Europe was able to become a middle-class society by following the modern manifestations brought by the United States and its irresistible empire: mass consumption, pluralism, participation and freedom. De Grazia does not unpack the practices of middle class either for Europe or for the United States. See Victoria de Grazia, *Irresistible Empire*. For alternative interpretations, see the chapters by Daniel Walkowitz and Marina Moskowitz in this volume.

35. Among many others, see Adamovsky, "Acerca de la relación entre el Radicalismo argentino y la 'clase media.'"

36. See Owensby, *Intimate Ironies*; D. Parker, *The Idea of the Middle Class*; Ervin, "The 1930s Agrarian Census in Mexico"; Barr-Melej, *Reforming Chile*; O'Dougherty, *Consumption Intensified*; Gilbert, *Mexico's Middle Class in the Neo-Liberal Era*; Joshi, *Fractured Modernity*; Jimenez, "The Elision of the Middle Classes and Beyond"; D. Parker and Walker, *Latin America's Middle Class*; Watenpaugh, *Being Modern in the Middle East*.

37. See the chapters by Sanjay Joshi, A. Ricardo López, Iñigo García-Bryce, Michael Ervin, David Parker, and Keith David Watenpaugh in this volume.

38. Dipesh Chakrabarty, *Provincializing Europe*. There have been several works that question the so-called exceptionality of the United States. This exceptionality, some argue, is very much part of the historical formation of the United States as an imperial nation. See, among others, Kaplan and Pease, eds., *Cultures of U.S. Imperialism*; G. Joseph, Legrand, and Salvatore, *Close Encounters of Empire*; Kaplan, *The Anarchy of Empire and the Making of U.S. Culture*; Stoler, McGranahan, and Perdue, *Imperial Formations*; Stoler, *Haunted by Empire*.

39. Chatterjee, *Our Modernity* and *The Politics of the Governed*; Guha, *History at the Limit of World History*; G. Joseph and Nugent, eds., *Everyday Forms of State Formation*; Mallon, *Peasant and Nation*; Mignolo, *Local Histories/Global Designs*; García Canclini, *Hybrid Cultures*. Even in recent studies of Latin American history, Latin American

middle classes appear as "hybrid"—that is, presumably, both modern and traditional. See Thurner and Guerrero, *After Spanish Rule*.

40. See the chapter by Sanjay Joshi in this volume.

41. Escobar, *Territories of Difference*, 162 (my emphasis).

42. For these criticisms we have found inspiration in Krishnaswamy and Hawley, *The Post-Colonial and the Global*; Harry Harootunian, "Some Thoughts on Comparability and the Space-Time Problem"; and Bhambra, *Rethinking Modernity*. Bhambra's notion of "connected histories" has been very helpful in understanding the transnational formation of the middle class. And we have found the discussion about "space-time" by Harootunian quite insightful in rethinking modernity.

43. See also Johnston, *A Radical Middle Class*; Hornstein, *A Nation of Realtors*; Bledstein and Johnston, *The Middling Sorts*.

44. See also Mary Kay Vaughan, *Cultural Politics in Revolution*.

45. Habermas, *The Structural Transformation of the Public Sphere*. See also Piccato, "Public Sphere in Latin America"; Enke, *Finding the Movement*.

46. We have found inspiration in recent studies on transnationalism. Among others, see Shukla and Tinsman, *Imagining Our Americas*; Seigel, *Uneven Encounters*; Sinha, *Specters of Mother India*; Palmié, *Wizards and Scientists*; Lake and Reynolds, *Drawing the Global Colour Line*; Krishnaswamy and Hawley, *The Post-Colonial and the Global*.

47. Some social scientists refer to the middle class as "middle sectors" precisely because they argue that the middle class could not be a class. See John J. Johnson's influential *Political Change in Latin America*. See also Adamovsky, *Historia de la clase media en Argentina*, 4.

48. Maza, *The Myth of the French Bourgeoisie*, 4. Unsurprisingly, most theorization of class is historically based on working-class experiences. See Joyce, *Class*; J. Hall, *Reworking Class*.

49. Maza, *The Myth of the French Bourgeoisie*, 4. For authors who argue that the middle class was only a discursive creation, see Wahrman, *Imagining the Middle Class*; Adamovsky, *Historia de la clase media en Argentina*.

50. Among several others, see Klubock, *Contested Comunities*; Bederman, *Manliness & Civilization*; Burton, *Burdens of History*; de Grazia, *Irresistible Empire*.

51. Arendt, *The Origins of Totalitarianism*, 212.

52. See especially the chapters by Daniel Walkowitz and David Parker in this volume. See also Eley, *A Crooked Line*; Eley and Nield, *The Future of Class in History*.

53. Some of these ideas have been discussed with Claire Goldstene

54. Spiegel, "The Task of the Historian," 14. See also Goswami, "Remembering the Future."

55. Mendieta, "The Liberation of Politics," vii.

PART I

The Making of the Middle Class and Practices of Modernity

Thinking about Modernity from the Margins

THE MAKING OF A MIDDLE CLASS IN COLONIAL INDIA

Sanjay Joshi

As inhabitants of a world structured by modernity, it is absolutely vital that we better understand the middle class. Not only in India, but in most parts of the world, the middle class has played a crucial role in defining what it means to be "modern." Broadly defined, modernity in this sense refers to new models of organizing social, political, and economic relations, which, we are told, draw their inspiration from the ideas of the Enlightenment and material circumstances following from the triumph of industrial capitalism. These models, in turn, have become yardsticks or standards, against which many parts of the world—particularly the non-Western world—are judged and found wanting. It is this apparent lack of modernity characterizing non-Western middle classes that I seek to explore in this chapter.

In colonial Lucknow, the middle class was both a product and the producers of modernity. It was the product of modernity because without the new professions, new institutions, or new notions of the importance of a category called the "public," all of which came with British rule to Lucknow, well-to-do Indian men from so-called service communities—social groups and families who had traditionally served in the courts of indigenous rulers and large landlords—could never have fashioned themselves into a middle class. The power they acquired in colonial Lucknow was derived from their being champions of modernity, and it was their efforts that created newer, modern forms of politics, culture, domesticity, and religion. In that sense, the middle class was also the producer of much of what came to define modernity. To highlight cultural projects as central to middle-class formation is not to deny the significance of either economic structure or, indeed, the historical context of changes in the nature of legal and economic regimes that accompanied the transition to colonialism. The one objective factor that distinguished most of the people who came to be termed middle class in colonial India was the fact that they belonged to the upper strata of society, without being at the very top.[1] Most of them were upper-caste Hindus or *ashraf* (high-born) Muslims, and many belonged to the so-called service communities. For the most part they came from families that were financially comfortable, but not so rich that they did not have to earn a living. This was one factor that distinguished them from the richest strata of Indian society, such as the major hereditary landlords or the remnants of the indigenous aristocracy. It also clearly put them well above the vast majority of India's poor.

Examining the rise of a middle class in colonial Lucknow, however, necessarily takes us beyond simple economic indicators of income and occupation in defining this social category. Though members of the middle class had certain commonalities of social and economic background, it was not simply their similarities in education, occupation, or profession that made them a middle class in colonial India. Nor was it traditional status alone that upper-caste Hindus or ashraf Muslim men deployed to make distinctions between themselves and other social groups in colonial India. Rather, it was by transforming traditional cultural values and the basis of social hierarchy that a distinctive middle class emerged. It was not simply the objective circumstances of their existence that made a hitherto less significant group of intellectuals and bureaucrats into key political and social figures. Rather, efforts of cultural entrepreneurship made the middle class a significant player in the social and political life of colonial India.[2] In colonial India, as elsewhere around the world, a middle class emerged from processes through which intellectuals and activists created a new and distinctive social category through a "self-conscious interposition between people of rank and the common people."[3]

The sort of imaginations the middle class in India drew on derived a great deal from models originating in Victorian Britain. Yet in the circumstances they found themselves in, Indian constructions of the modern could not be identical with the ideal types of modernity established by European philosophers or advocates of the middle class in England. A close investigation of the construction of an Indian middle class in a local milieu reveals multiple, often

contradictory, pressures constituting middle-class pol
certainly demonstrates the extent to which traditior
the construction of modern ideas about religion, com
and the nation, propagated by the Indian middle
ideas about politics contained elements drawn fro
political and social organization. Their belief in mo
the reinforcing of older hierarchies, their nationali
has been termed "communalism," and their belie
their advocacy of tradition.

The contradictions of their politics emerged from the contrary pulls of their social situation. On the one hand, ideas and institutions that came with colonial rule allowed them to represent themselves as enlightened representatives of public opinion, through which they sought to replace the older, aristocratic paradigm of respectability in Lucknow. But on the other hand, it was equally important for men who were traditionally a part of respectable society to also clearly distinguish themselves from the lower orders. Therefore they were compelled to use a more traditional vocabulary, with which they were quite familiar given their respectable status in precolonial Lucknow, thus emphasizing the inherent inferiority of the lower classes. Although this duality certainly allowed them to emerge as the opinion makers in Lucknow, it also limited their agenda in that middle-class politics continued to retain a profound ambivalence about popular politics, which it sought to "discipline and mobilize" rather than persuade and include in its political endeavors.[4]

Taking into account new ideas about gender relations makes the social origins of the contradictions in middle-class positions even more apparent. Middle-class interventions constructed a new ideology of gender relations that deployed new ideas about the equality of the sexes and the importance of education and modern training for women, but they also used a much older vocabulary drawn from the ideology of *stridharma*, which can best be defined as husband worship. This stitching together of older and newer ideas created a modernity full of tensions and different possibilities. Although this modernity allowed for a certain disciplining of women, it also provided opportunities for critiques of patriarchy. However, limits framed by their own middle-class lifestyles also prevented middle-class women from breaking completely with the discourse on gender relations created by a fractured modernity. Middle-class feminist politics therefore continued to maintain a relationship with modernity and tradition that was at least as ambivalent as that of the men's.

Middle-class contradictions evident in Indians' ideas about religion and the nation equally reflect the contrary pulls arising from the circumstances of e rather than any conscious effort at duplicity or deception. The osity of the middle class was not a guise or cover for some other, olitical interest. However, the modern religiosity they sought to con- t revealed the opposing forces underlying their social, political, and intel- ctual agenda. Similarly their oscillation between secular and religious nationalism was not simply a political tactic, but a product of the fact that in the 1920s, both secular and religious imaginings were equally critical to middle-class nationalism. These contradictions both enabled and limited middle-class politics, giving middle-class Indians a more significant presence in the political arena, yet circumscribing how far they could take their reformist, nationalist, or revivalist agenda.

Middle-class activists sought to be modern, but their social positions meant that they would use the resources of tradition to construct their modernity. This was not simply the product of being a colonized people, though colonialism undoubtedly inflected their modernity. Looked at from the perspective of an ideal-typical modernity, the politics of the middle class of colonial Lucknow would be found wanting. They were not egalitarian enough to perceive the lower social orders as equal citizens. They were not liberal enough to allow even women from their own class equality within the home. They were not secular enough to keep away from Hindu nationalist imaginings of the nation. How are we to understand these contradictions, especially given that they existed in a class that so consciously copied the model of a progressive, egalitarian, liberal, secular middle class?

Writing about the history of the middle class in India, one is necessarily and always confronted by a series of questions about the nature of modernity: What is it? How do we understand modernity? And why must "our modernity" be different from "theirs"?[5] It is, of course, interesting that it is those who write about the non-Western world who feel compelled to engage with and address these questions. Similar contradictions, as we shall see, abound in the history of the heart of Western modernity, but seldom do these create the same degree of angst among their chroniclers.[6] For the moment, rather than decrying the differences between Western and non-Western histories, I will simply argue that engaging with these questions from the margins can help us better understand the meaning of modernity.

One way of trying to understand these contradictions of middle-class politics is to point to the impossibility of a true modernity in a world peopled by *Homo hierarchicus*, as Louis Dumont's work suggested, echoing the sentiments of many generations of Orientalist scholars and colonial administrators before him.[7] Do these contradictions, alternatively, prove right those critics who argue against using the category of middle class in Indian history at all? Colonial India never had an Industrial Revolution, which these scholars assume is a necessary precondition for a strong and vibrant middle class.[8] Or, should we follow the lead of Partha Chatterjee, along with some other scholars of the Subaltern Studies collective, and trace the contradictions of the middle class to the colonial milieu that compelled the Indian middle class to define its modernity in ways very different from those used in the West?[9] Underlying all these questions, ostensibly about the peculiarities of the Indian case, are comparisons between the failures, lacks, or deviations of that case and certain supposedly originary models of middle-classness. To try to answer such questions, then, we too need to undertake a comparative exercise, to contrast the Indian experience with the metropolitan middle class, which operates as the standard against which the Indian case is being judged.

Even a cursory examination of the literature on the middle class in England, for instance, reveals significant variation between a messy and complicated historical reality and the model of a progressive, enlightened middle class that emerged "like the rising sun" out of the Industrial Revolution.[10] Such scholarship questions the causal connection between rapid industrialization and the emergence of a middle-class society. But it also reveals that public-sphere interventions were critical in establishing certain myths about middle-class formation, which now stand as models used to judge non-Western historical developments.[11] Moreover, general surveys of European history reveal that, much as in Lucknow, hierarchy was very much a part of domestic as well as public life for the European bourgeoisie of the mid- to late nineteenth century. Eric Hobsbawm notes that ideas about representative government, civil rights, and liberties were part of the political vocabulary of the middle class, but only so long as they were "compatible with the rule of law and with the kind of order which kept the poor in their place." If we take into account attitudes toward women, children, and servants, then "the structure of the bourgeois family flatly contradicted that of bourgeois [public] society."[12] In fact, Hobsbawm goes on to argue that a sense of superiority was central to the constitution of the bourgeois man, and "the monopoly of command—in his house, in his business, in his factory—was crucial to his self-definition."[13]

These are, of course, fairly well-known facts about nineteenth-century European history, and they could well be elaborated on. The model of a liberal, democratic, progressive middle class that seizes power from a decadent, enfeebled, feudal elite to reorder society and politics along the lines suggested by the *philosophes* of the Enlightenment is a myth that has been undermined repeatedly by historians of Europe.[14] The really interesting part about all of this is that even masses of counterfactual examples have not dented the power and persistence of the model of an ideal-typical modernity. Thus, despite recognizing differences between different European middle classes; despite acknowledging the importance of self-constitution in the making of the middle class; and despite surveying literature that points to the persistence and power of older ideas, institutions, and classes in European society in what is known as the long nineteenth century, a review article on the subject concludes that the existence of the middle classes in Europe depended on "certain historical constellations, among them the tradition of the Enlightenment," which were specific to European history. "It is not very likely," Jürgen Kocka concludes, "that they will be found in many other parts of the world."[15]

One can dismiss this as yet another example of Eurocentric historiography, but the issues that such reviews raise are of greater significance simply because of the assumptions that underlie this understanding of history, and its implications for those of us who happen to work on non-European histories. If the import of such essays was simply to point to the specificity of historical experience in different parts of the world, there would be no reason to disagree. However, despite recognizing the regional variations within Europe, the different meanings and political connotations that equivalent words carry in different European languages, and even the fact that the category has been used "as a polemical or affirmative code word in public debates," Kocka affirms the existence of a pan-European middle class.[16] What allows him to do this—despite plenty of evidence to the contrary even from the authors he reviews in this essay—is the notion of a shared liberal tradition to be traced back to the European Enlightenment, which apparently makes industrialists and professionals, living under different economic and political circumstances across a large continent, "a middle class." Implicit in this formulation, however unintentionally, is the assumption that other social groups that constitute themselves as middle classes in other parts of the world must ultimately also be judged by these standards.

This is exactly the point Dipesh Chakrabarty makes in his thoughtful, much-cited essay discussing the impact of modern historical categories on subaltern histories.[17] Chakrabarty argues that in the world of scholarly knowledge, only "Europe"—by which he means a model of modernity derived from Western history—is "*theoretically* (i.e., at the level of the fundamental categories that shape historical thinking) knowable."[18] Dominance of the West over the rest of the world has meant that models derived from the history of this "Europe" are universalized, so that histories of the aptly termed non-Western regions of the world are always compared to supposedly universal models, and found wanting. The universalization of Western modernity perpetuates the dominance of "Europe" over others through what Gyan Prakash calls "the representations of all histories as History."[19] Perhaps even more problematically, the universalization of modernity means that historical developments that are different can be evaluated only as emulations, deviations, or failures. Chakrabarty's approach certainly helps us rethink solutions to one of the central problems in understanding Indian middle-class projects—namely, the persistence of the ideal-typical model. Or, to paraphrase a famous song, why couldn't the Indian middle class be more like the English? Chakrabarty's analysis helps explains how Kocka can confidently assert the middle-classness of Europe, while denying its "exportability." It also explains why historians of the non-Western world find it impossible to do the same. Even while pointing out the limits of European modernity, I cannot but engage extensively with the history of Europe, thus pointing to the strength of Chakrabarty's argument.

Acknowledging the impossibility of escaping modernity, or of constructing a historical discourse outside of these categories of modernity, Chakrabarty rejects the possibility of a history framed by "indigenous" or nativist categories and instead asks historians to "provincialize Europe," by showing "the ambivalences, contradictions, the use of force, and the tragedies and ironies" that necessarily form a part of the universalization of modernity.[20] As one part of establishing the "provinciality" of the claims of modernity, Chakrabarty demonstrates aspects of radical difference between constructions of a modern domesticity in colonial Bengal and the ideal type of bourgeois modernity. This is a theme he takes up in more detail in a parallel essay, in which he shows the Bengali modern, exemplified here by the neologism *grihalakshmi* (to translate this as "goddess of the home" would be to undermine the point that Chakrabarty wishes to make). This modern construction, he argues, is constituted by tensions as it seeks to incorporate both the historical and modern, as defined by the ideal type of Western modernity, and the antihistorical modern, which is "tied to mythico-religious time" that "escapes and exceeds bourgeois time."[21] There is much in the Bengali modern that is derivative of the modernity brought by colonialism, he argues, but Bengali modernity also seeks to evoke "formations of pleasure, emotions and ideas of good life that associated themselves with models of non-autonomous, non-bourgeois and non-secular personhood."[22]

In pointing to both the complicity and difference of Indians with the ideal types of modernity, Chakrabarty reflects the orientation of the current Subaltern Studies project, in which—to cite Prakash again—a "notion of the subalterns' radical heterogeneity with, though not autonomy from, the dominant remains crucial."[23] Let me call attention to a wonderful lecture by Partha Chatterjee, which sums up his position on the subject of modernity. Chatterjee begins by making the unimpeachable argument for acknowledging different modernities. "The forms of modernity will have to vary between different countries, depending upon specific circumstances and social practices," he says. "If there is any universally acceptable definition of modernity, it is this: that by teaching us to employ the methods of reason, universal modernity enables us to identify the forms of our own particular modernity."[24] Within this particular modernity Chatterjee, like Chakrabarty, identifies important points of difference, including profound ambivalence toward the modernist enterprise itself. The reasons for this ambivalence? "There must have been something in the very process of becoming modern that continues to lead us, even in our acceptance of modernity, to a certain skepticism about its values and consequences."[25] The answer, in other words, is colonialism. He writes: "Ours is the modernity of the once-colonized. The same historical process that has taught us the value of modernity has also made us the victims of modernity. Our attitude to modernity, therefore, cannot but deeply be ambiguous . . . But this ambiguity does not stem from any uncertainty about whether to be for or against modernity. Rather the uncertainty is because we know that to fashion the forms of our modernity, we need to have the courage at times to reject the modernities established by others."[26] The presupposition through this entire lecture, and in fact through much of the formally postcolonial writings of the Subaltern Studies collective, is the essential difference in "our modernity."

But was "our modernity" really that different from "theirs"? The history of Lucknow certainly does not suggest that the colonial context created a middle class and a modernity that was so different from that of the West as to forbid comparative exercises all together. One important similarity that we can note between the Indian and English middle classes is that in both cases, a small and relatively privileged group of men—and, later, women—made their distinctions from other social strata, by virtue of being representatives of a modern social order. There is no doubt that middle-class visions of modernity in India were contradictory. Thus, modern politics unleashed by the middle class in colonial India simultaneously spoke in the voice of reason and of sentiment, about the need to preserve tradition and initiate radical change, and in favor of liberty and authoritarianism, equality and hierarchy, often at the same time. All the public-sphere projects of the middle class were shot through with these inconsistencies and contradictions, and these were constitutive of middle-class politics, indeed of the modernity that the projects initiated in colonial India. Yet such anomalies were not unique to the Indian case.

There is little doubt that in excluding the lower orders of society from participating in the public sphere, as in many other aspects of the modern that were created by the middle class in Lucknow, members of the class drew on assumptions based on an older hierarchical tradition of social relations. Their European counterparts too had little room for women or the lower classes in the public they represented. Like the European bourgeois public sphere examined by Habermas, the public sphere of colonial north India was theoretically a forum open to all. Yet practically, both public spheres were the province of literary adepts who set or could follow new norms of public conduct.[27] Given the class and gender exclusions of bourgeois practice, Habermas's model of the public sphere has been assessed "as an ideal of critical liberalism that remains historically unattained."[28] "The formation of Birmingham's later-eighteenth-century associational networks, the creation of an elite club in early-nineteenth-century German small towns, and the creation of literary societies in mid-nineteenth century Bohemia," as much as the associations, clubs, and societies of colonial Lucknow, "all involved questions of *interest*, *prestige*, and *power*, as well as those of rational communication."[29] A contradictory historical practice, at odds with the ideology of egalitarianism that it propagated, remained at the heart of the public sphere in both cases. For many of the same reasons as their European counterparts, members of the Indian middle class also initially excluded subaltern groups and based this exclusion on the presumed natural inferiority of these groups, or on account of their lack of education on matters of public import. Both in Europe and India, the public sphere thus became the site where, for the most part, educated professional men constructed a highly gendered, exclusive, and hierarchical middle class.

The exclusion, marginalization, and recasting of women through institutions of the public sphere is yet another instance of the way in which this quintessentially modern institution worked in comparable ways in India and Europe. Joan Landes makes a forceful case for the fact that the public sphere was gendered at the moment of its production in revolutionary France. Though there were certainly important differences created by time and place, one can see, for instance, a parallel in the marginalization of the courtesans of Lucknow and the aristocratic women of the salons of prerevolutionary France, as a new gendered public sphere emerged in both contexts.[30] Leonore Davidoff and Catherine Hall's work also demonstrates some important parallels in the way the emergence of public associations "increased the confidence of middle-class men and contributed to their claims to political power," and deliberately excluded women from this public world. In fact, these authors argue that the power and confidence of middle-class men was predicated on their position "as heads of households, representing their wives, children, servants, and other dependents."[31] This rich study of the making of a middle class in nineteenth-century England has as its main focus family life and new ideologies of domesticity, which became an integral part of the formation of a gendered middle-class world. Parallels between the domestic ideals articulated in Indian domestic manuals[32] and the didactic literature aimed at the inculcation of new ideas of domesticity in nineteenth-century England are quite striking.

The point of these comparisons is not, of course, to suggest an identity between two quite dissimilar contexts. There were important differences in historical and cultural context between the groups who constituted themselves as middle class in Birmingham and Lucknow, as indeed there were between the middle classes of Lucknow and, say, Calcutta, Madras, or Surat, which did not have quite the same history of British occupation or, indeed, the recent history of an indigenous ruling elite. The important position occupied by merchants in Surat as opposed to the historically low profile of the richer merchants in Lucknow is just one instance of these differences.[33] The objective then, is not to claim that middle classes across the world are identical, but to point to the similarities in the nature of middle-class modernities constructed in different parts of the world; to point to the extent to which all such politics deviated from the ideal type usually attributed to a hyper-real Europe.[34]

Rather than reinforce the binary oppositions between the West and the rest, these comparisons suggest that we take into account the extent to which serious social historians of Western modernity themselves point out that middle-class ideas involved a "jostling together of the concepts of liberty with those of patronage and deference . . . [and] the contradictory ways in which purer discourses of philosophers and ideologues are reworked within common sense."[35] We also need to take into account the extent to which the ideas about domesticity and separate spheres that Davidoff and Hall see as purely modern phenomena in fact had a much longer history.[36] Following this critique of Davidoff and Hall, it seems that, like the middle-class men of colonial Lucknow, the English middle class too reworked existing, older ideas about patriarchy, and also no doubt patronage and deference, to produce a modernity in which the old and new "jostled together."

Perhaps the best instance of such jostling comes when we consider the role of religion in the formation of a modern class and the modern nation. The presence of religion in politics of the public sphere is normatively regarded as a failure or lack of modernity. Religion—almost by its modern definition, if we follow Talal Asad[37]—should remain confined to the private realm. When religion refuses to play its appointed role, it is usually dismissed with labels like "fundamentalism" or "communalism," which question the modernity if not the morality (are they really that different?) of the practitioners of such politics.[38] Western commentators on Indian history or politics have found it easy to dismiss politics that include religion as the result of "primitive" or "primordial" attachments of non-Western peoples, and such ahistorical stereotypes have been reinforced by representations in the contemporary media.[39] This of course is the ideal type of modernity. The lived reality has been considerably different. Davidoff and Hall point to the centrality of the church in the production of middle-class identities in Britain and identify "religious belonging" as "a central plinth of middle class culture."[40] Though the narrative of modernization emphasizes the decline of religion and the growing secularization of society as an essential part of the emergence of the modern West, recent scholarship questions such assumptions. There is, for example, José Casanova's work on the place of religion in modern society, which points out that "deprivatized" religion can, under certain circumstances, have a formative role to play in modern politics.[41] Bruce Lincoln's recent study shows the parallels between the speeches of Osama bin Laden and George W. Bush.[42] Peter van der Veer has warned against accepting the secularization thesis too easily, pointing to the important role played by evangelical Christianity and the revival of Roman Catholicism in producing the modern subject and shaping political culture in Victorian Britain. In fact, van der Veer makes a case for arguing that modernity was "sacralized" at the moment of its production, not just in India but also in Europe.[43]

Once we accept the fact that modernity in the West, despite its ideal-type representations, did not automatically usher in a new secular order but indeed was constituted by existing religious discourses, then the case for Indian exceptionalism—whether based on backwardness and primordialism, or guided by the intent of demonstrating the radical heterogeneity of a colonial modernity—becomes weaker. Rather than understand the religiosity of the Lucknow middle class as a lack or failure, a case of striving for and ultimately failing to achieve the secular-modern ideal, we can look at the members of the middle class as both active producers and products of a sacralized modernity that in turn produced a modernized religiosity in colonial India. This was a modernity shaped by their own concerns and contexts, and their rhetoric and politics were in turn shaped by it. Religion, or rather self-definitions based on religious categories, became a critical part of the modern self created by the colonial middle class. This self-definition also helped shape the later political commitment to a more militant anti-Muslim Hindu nationalism. Yet the contrary impulses at the heart of the middle-class agenda also prevented the members of the class from articulating a full-throated Hindu chauvinism. The identities produced by modern politics were thus protean and impermanent. Rather than a lack of modernity, therefore, there is a good case to be made for understanding the sort of impermanent identities that we see in colonial Lucknow as the products of a fractured modernity the members of its middle class shared with their counterparts in Europe and other parts of the world.

Based on this comparison then, it seems that neither India nor the West actually lives up to the ideal-typical model of modernity. Given the similarities between the experience of historical modernities in India, the West, and other parts of the world as well, it seems that we do need to reconceptualize this model. Starting from our study of the middle class of Lucknow and then comparing the contradictions in their politics with similar phenomena elsewhere suggests that despite a more or less singular ideal type of modernity derived from a very selective reading of a Western historical experience, in practice, modern politics and social relations always reveal their fractures and disarticulations. It was a fractured modernity that created the circumstances for and set limits to the various cultural and political projects of the middle class in colonial India. Looking at how the middle class was constituting itself and the world around it in colonial India therefore not only presents an opportunity to better understand the nature of modernity in India, but also helps formulate a category to comprehend this phenomenon in other parts of the world.

This is not to say that the idea of a fractured modernity is absolutely novel. Traditionalism, even antimodernism, has been recognized as very much a part of the making of the modern in the United States, and a valorization of "the simple life," as well as a fascination with the traditional and the primitive, was an important component of this middle-class ideology.[44] Marshall Berman, whose work is one of the best-known celebrations of modernity, submits that modernity, as it is experienced, is full of contradictions, dissonance, and conflict.[45] It should come as no surprise, however, that it is primarily historians and scholars of colonized or subaltern groups, often struggling to define and sometimes defend the modernity of the societies they study, who are more alert to these fractures in the practice of modernity, its variations from the ideal type, and attempts to rethink the category. Writing about the middle class in Brazil, Brian Owensby observes: "The changes generally thought to be characteristic of modernity have been deeply intertwined with what are usually called traditions. In Brazil, thus, the market mentalities, meritocracy and egalitarianism, professionalization, consumer culture, and social identities typically connected with the notion of the middle class are inseparable from a disdain for manual labor, an insistence on social hierarchy, and the presumed naturalness of patronage, time-tested values and practices constantly renewed and folded into modern social life."[46]

Of course, at least two generations of nationalist, Marxist, and now Saidian scholarship have made us aware of the ways in which the self-styled representatives of Western modernity in the colonies revealed the illiberal stratum of ideas, practices, and institutions that comprised their modernity. It is, however, only more recently that these histories are being used to question the categories on which so much of colonialism itself rested. Frederick Cooper and Ann Stoler argue that colonial projects "showed up the fundamental contradictions inherent in bourgeois projects and the way universal claims were bound up in particularistic assertions."[47] In his fascinating study of the "Black Atlantic," Paul Gilroy suggests a more fundamental reconsideration of the category, one that would put slavery and terror at the very heart of any definition of modernity.[48] Ann Stoler's own work on colonialism and sexuality, like the work of many others, demonstrates that a large part of modern bourgeois identities was formed in relation to colonial encounters in which ideas of racial distinctions were central.[49] Uday Mehta goes as far as to argue that ideas about race were built into the philosophy behind eighteenth-century liberalism itself.[50] Middle-class Englishmen excluded women as well as nonwhite people from the benefits of liberalism, which they clearly deployed for their own empowerment.[51] Antoinette Burton's work, however, shows us the extent to which British feminism, which drew on the legacy of liberalism and modernity to shape its concerns, was deployed to empower middle-class British women at the expense of Indian women.[52] In all of these cases, a close examination of the discourse of modernity reveals its illiberal and perhaps nonmodern substrata.

The point of this comparative exercise is to argue that if our goal is to destabilize the categories derived from a selective reading of Western history—in other words, to provincialize Europe—we do not have to abandon comparative history completely. We do not necessarily have to dichotomize the historical experience of the West and the rest, because this strategy itself may reinforce ideas of an originary, unfractured, and monolithic Western modernity, and its derivative and hence necessarily lesser non-Western counterparts. This chapter suggests an alternative. Closely examining the construction of modernity in a specific context, it shows that far from being a totalizing or monolithic ideology, modernity in colonial India was built on an existing set of ideas, which it transformed in new ways. Emerging through the public sphere, this modernity was very much the product of middle-class activists and reflected the contrary pressures of the constitution of that class. Deploying their cultural capital to maximum effect, middle-class men were able to transform existing ideas of social conduct, cultural preferences, and politics in ways that allowed them to emerge as the representatives and leaders of Indian society. Middle-class ideas, though they were certainly novel, were not monolithic. Not only were there competing opinions on issues among the middle class, but a close examination of middle-class ideas reveals a number of contradictions. Thus their modern ideas about politics contained elements drawn from much older and hierarchical ideas about political and social organization. Their belief in secularism coexisted with the importance of religious identities, their belief in progress was simultaneous with their advocacy of tradition, and their nationalism was complicit with what has been termed "communalism."

A comparison with the modernities of the Western and other parts of the non-Western world suggests that similar though not identical fractures, contradictions, and anomalies were constitutive of modern ideas, institutions, and practices there as well. In Lucknow, as in other parts of the world, modernity was built with a variety of resources, including much that modernity labels either traditional or nonmodern. Whether in the form of patriarchal ideas, racism, notions of patronage and deference, or religion, the traditional or nonmodern never quite disappears, but it does become a resource for the modern. Moreover, if, following the example of Lucknow, we recognize the deployment of the ideal-typical modernity more as a strategy of empowerment over various others than a reflection of lived reality, then we can also better understand its evident contradictions. To enforce or maintain power over subordinate groups—whether it was the middle class over lower classes in the public sphere of Lucknow, Europeans over colonized natives or indeed their "own" working classes, the Hindu middle class over Muslims, or British feminists over their Indian sisters—it became necessary in certain situations to also resort to the darker side of the discourse of modernity, to have recourse to the language of race, hierarchy, and "communalism" rather than that of egalitarianism, improvement, liberal nationalism, or global sisterhood.

In contrast to the dichotomizing of modernities, I suggest that a better way of "provincializing Europe" is by highlighting the fractured nature of modernity itself. I argue that modernity in India was neither inadequately modern nor a special-case scenario of a colonial modernity. The middle-class shapers of modernity in colonial India worked in ways that were similar to those used by their counterparts in other parts of the world, including the West. Cultural projects of becoming middle class ensured that Indians used a variety of resources to construct notions of being modern that emulated but also varied from the ideal type. In other words, their modernities were inherently fractured. Examining the emergence of a middle class in India and wrestling with modernity from the margins, therefore, not only allows us to comprehend the apparent inconsistencies of middle-class politics in the colonial milieu but may also suggest a theoretical framework to better understand the working of modern politics in much of the world today.

Notes

1. Misra, *The Indian Middle Classes*.

2. For details, see Joshi, *Fractured Modernity*.

3. Williams, *Keywords*, 63.

4. Ranajit Guha, "Discipline and Mobilize."

5. Chatterjee, *Our Modernity*.

6. Chakrabarty, *Provincializing Europe*, and "The Difference-Deferral of a Colonial Modernity."

7. Louis Dumont, *Homo Hierarchicus*. See also Appadurai, "Putting Hierarchy in Its Place"; Nicholas Dirks, "Castes of Mind"; van der Veer, "The Foreign Hand."

8. Michelguglielmo, "'Westernized Middle Class'"; Oberoi, *The Construction of Religious Boundaries*.

9. Chatterjee, *Our Modernity*.

10. Wahrman, *Imagining the Middle Class*, 1. See Simon Gunn's chapter in this volume for a discussion on how the stories of the middle class in England have been told.

11. Owensby, *Intimate Ironies*.

12. Hobsbawm, *The Age of Capital*, 287, 280.

13. Ibid., 288.

14. Mayer, *The Persistence of the Old Regime*; Blackbourn and Eley, *The Peculiarities of German History*; Maza, *The Myth of the French Bourgeoisie*. See also the introduction to this volume by López.

15. Kocka, "The Middle Class in Europe," 806.

16. Ibid., 783.

17. Chakrabarty "Postcoloniality and the Artifice of History."

18. Ibid., 3.

19. Prakash, "Subaltern Studies as Postcolonial Criticism," 1484.

20. Chakrabarty, "Postcoloniality and the Artifice of History," 21.

21. Chakrabarty, "The Difference-Deferral of (A) Colonial Modernity," 81.

22. Ibid., 84–85.

23. Prakash, "Subaltern Studies as Postcolonial Criticism," 1482.

24. Chatterjee, *Our Modernity*, 8–9.

25. Ibid., 14.

26. Ibid.

27. La Vopa, "Conceiving a Public."

28. Eley, "Nations, Publics, and Political Cultures," 289.

29. Ibid., 307.

30. Landes, *Women and the Public Sphere in the Age of the French Revolution.*

31. Davidoff and Hall, *Family Fortunes*, 416.

32. For example, see S. Gupta, *Strisubodhini.*

33. Haynes, *Rhetoric and Ritual in Colonial India*; Oldenburg, *The Making of Colonial Lucknow*; Sahai, *Family Structure and Partition.*

34. Chakrabarty, *Provincializing Europe.*

35. Davidoff and Hall, *Family Fortunes*, 16.

36. Vickery, "Shaking the Separate Spheres."

37. Asad, *Genealogies of Religion.*

38. See the chapter by Carol E. Harrison in this volume.

39. Asad, *Genealogies of Religion.*

40. Davidoff and Hall, *Family Fortunes*, 73.

41. Casanova, *Public Religions in the Modern World.*

42. Lincoln, *Holy Terrors.*

43. Van der Veer, "The Moral State."

44. Lears, *No Place of Grace*; Hinsley and Wilcox, *The Southwest in the American Imagination.* For India, see Ghosh, "A Market for Aboriginality."

45. Berman, *All That Is Solid Melts into Air.*

46. Owensby, *Intimate Ironies*, 7. See also Abu-Lughod, *Remaking Women.*

47. Cooper and Stoler, "Between Metropole and Colony," 3.

48. Gilroy, *The Black Atlantic.*

49. Stoler, *Race and the Education of Desire.* See also A. Burton, "Introduction."

50. Mehta, "Liberal Strategies of Exclusion."

51. Hall, *White, Male and Middle Class.*

52. A. Burton, *Burdens of History.*

The African Middle Class in Zimbabwe

HISTORICAL AND CONTEMPORARY PERSPECTIVES

Michael O. West

The African middle class in Zimbabwe has its origins in the colonial project, which was part of the larger European scramble for Africa in the late nineteenth century. Like everywhere else in Africa and beyond, colonialism in Southern Rhodesia, which became Zimbabwe at independence in 1980, centered on expropriation. That is, the expropriation of natural, mineral, and agricultural resources and the human labor needed to exploit those resources. This was not an enterprise that proceeded with the consent of the colonized. Colonialism, the point bears emphasizing, was a violent process. Like African slavery in the Americas, on which it was partly modeled, colonialism in Africa was imposed and maintained by violence.[1] The whip, that most potent of symbols of African slavery in the Americas, reemerged as a favored instrument of colonial oppression in Africa, deployed early and often on the colonized body in locations as varied as the work site, the prison, the schoolhouse, and the church. This was in many respects colonial slavery, as some took to calling it.

Such were the unpromising foundations that would eventually give rise to indigenous middle classes in Africa as a whole. The struggle for social mobility began as a struggle against terror, the systemic terror and violence of colonialism. In the Southern Rhodesian case, the struggle was all the more vexed because the territory experienced colonialism of a special kind: settler colonialism. The influx of relatively large numbers of white settlers (individuals who left Europe to settle in Africa permanently, not just the more itinerant administrators, soldiers, businessmen, and missionaries) into the colony magnified the horrors of colonialism. White settler colonialism amplified the level of the expropriation, inflated the violence and terror, enlarged the humiliation visited on the colonized, imposed cruder racist practices, and increased the burdens of women.[2]

The correlation between the violence of the colonizer and the resistance of the colonized was much in evidence in Southern Rhodesia, resulting in two major uprisings during the first decade of white rule.[3] The swift and bloody suppression of both risings left a deep imprint on the colonized and called forth alternate, mainly nonviolent, forms of resistance. In this new dispensation, the agrarian producers and wage laborers, who formed the great bulk of the colonized, struggled within the context of work and community. Such forms of resistance ranged from withholding labor to holding up produce, from deserting to striking.[4]

Concurrently, a new social class was beginning to emerge among the colonized, a group variously called middle class, elite, or *evolue*.[5] Unlike the agrarian producers and wage laborers—loosely dubbed peasants and workers—who were indispensable to the colonial political economy, this middle class was not part of the colonizers' master plan. In Southern Rhodesia the African middle class emerged out of the contradictory interstices of the colonial project. The Rhodesian settlers and the colonial state, which normally did their bidding, especially on "native policy," generally opposed the rise of an African middle class. State policy tended toward social leveling of the colonized as a whole. All the colonized, that is, should be kept at the same level—the level of hewers of wood and drawers of water. Seen from this angle, the African middle class arose in spite of the colonial state, even in opposition to it.

At the same time, the African middle class was very much a product of colonialism. Above all, its emergence was made possible by Christian missionary education, the principal means of upward social mobility in Southern Rhodesia and colonial Africa generally. This was more by accident than by design. Conceptually, the European missionaries, Bible in hand and following closely on the heels of the armies that imposed colonial rule at the point of the Maxim gun, had no more intention of creating an indigenous elite than did the colonial state. The missionaries had joined the colonial undertaking to swell the ranks of the followers of the Cross, and they soon discovered that literacy in the European tongue (English in the case of Southern Rhodesia) was among the more surefire means of conversion. The link between Christianity and education, between church and school, an enduring colonial symbiosis everywhere in Africa and beyond, had been made. It did not take the colonized peoples very long to size up the situation: colonial education offered an escape from the life of hewer of wood and drawer of water. By going to a mission school, one could possibly avoid the drudgery, poverty, and misery that were the lot of the peasantry and the proletariat. Soon the demand of the colonized for literacy and numeracy far exceeded the capacity of the missionaries to provide them.[6]

The African middle class emerged because of the opportunities provided by missionary education and the exertions and ingenuity of its own members, individual and collective. Ultimately, though, elite Africans managed to reproduce as a class because of the demand for their skills and knowledge. Small in numbers, and largely ignorant of the languages and cultures of those they sought to convert, the European missionaries depended on native intermediaries to staff their schools and churches, few of which could have existed without African teachers and preachers. Colonial capital, too, employed an ever-increasing number of indigenous clerks, salesmen, and bookkeepers. Similarly, despite the fear and loathing of elite Africans, whom the Southern Rhodesian white settlers saw as a long-term existential threat, the bureaucracy of the colonial state remained dependent on native clerks and interpreters, and, in due course, other Africans with even more specialized skills, like social workers, nurses, and doctors.

Still, the Southern Rhodesian state, especially in the years between the two world wars, attempted to interdict, or at least retard, the growth of the African middle class. European colonial policy in Africa, most notably in British colonies like Southern Rhodesia, evolved against the backdrop of the Indian experience. For the British, India was the great bellwether of colonialism, for good and for ill. And among the worst features of colonialism in India, it seemed to the guardians of empire, was the rise of a socially frustrated native middle class, with the intelligentsia in the vanguard. British officials attributed this state of affairs to inappropriate education, or miseducation, and they were determined to avoid a repetition of the problem in Africa.

In Africa, even more so than in India, where the foreign Christian presence was less conspicuous, the colonial authorities saw miseducation as a direct outgrowth of missionary education. Accordingly, in the years after the First World War, the colonial state in Southern Rhodesia (and elsewhere in British-ruled Africa) embarked on a project of social engineering—a project that sought to reorient African education. The missionaries, the colonial state alleged, were offering Africans an education that was altogether unsuited for subjects of empire. Instead of literary education, which they imagined the missionary schools to be dispensing, colonial officials insisted on industrial training. Industrial institutes, the reasoning went, would not produce very many intellectuals—men, and they were mostly men, who not only harbored aspirations above their assigned station but also, and far worse, articulated such outsize aspirations in public and often mobilized politically around them. In fact, the campaign for industrial, as opposed to literary, education amounted to an attempt at social underdevelopment—the underdevelopment of the emerging African middle class. Industrial education would be the antidote to *babus*, the name given to educated natives in the state bureaucracy and elsewhere in India.

In the attempt to protect their African colonies from the Indian contagion, the British colonialists, once again, looked across the Atlantic for an archetype. They found it in the post–Civil War, post-Reconstruction United States, with its coterie of industrial schools for the freed African Americans and their descendants, now returned to a status not far removed from slavery. In particular, British colonial social engineers developed a fondness for Tuskegee Institute (now Tuskegee University), which was founded by the ex-slave turned educator and man of affairs Booker T. Washington.[7] Washington appeared dramatically on the US national stage in 1895, when he gave a famous speech at the Atlanta Exposition offering to help reconcile the ex-slaves and their scions to the political and social disabilities of Jim Crow, the peculiar name for American apartheid, in return for giving African Americans an opportunity to participate more fully in the nation's economic life. This offer, dubbed the Atlanta Compromise by his critics, made Washington the black darling of the American ruling class, North as well as South. Soon he also became an international sensation, his approach to the development of black folk in the United States bruited about by colonizers and colonial subjects alike, though for different reasons.

In this way, the Tuskegee model of development, as interpreted by the colonialists, became a blueprint for the underdevelopment of the African middle class in Southern Rhodesia and elsewhere in colonial Africa during the interwar years. The Booker T. Washington whom the colonialists imported into Africa was a caricatured figure, the Washington of the Atlanta Compromise fame. That is, the champion of industrial over literary education and the liquidator of black political and social rights—in sum, a collaborator of Jim Crow. For their part, middle-class Africans in Southern Rhodesia, who had built their own transatlantic connections to African Americans and had been much inspired by the postslavery black experience in the United States, were not about to repudiate Washington. Instead, they reinterpreted him and his work. In the Tuskegee Institute, the African middle class in Southern Rhodesia saw not so much a center of industrial education as a shining testament of black achievement, and in Booker T. Washington not so much a vacillator before the demigod of white supremacy as a vindicator of independent black capacity—the very possibilities denied by colonial racist ideology.[8]

As the debate over the true meaning of the Tuskegee model of development went on, the Southern Rhodesian authorities drew up various blueprints to frustrate African middle-class formation at its source. The most ambitious plans called for replacing the mission schools with government-run industrial institutes modeled on the Tuskegee Institute. As with most such plans directed at the colonized, however, this one foundered on the bedrock of parsimony. Despite railing against the mission schools, the government was not prepared to assume the cost of replacing them. In the end, just two government-run schools were built. Instead, the state used its legislative and regulatory might to bludgeon the mission schools into line, by requiring them to do what most had been doing all along: include industrial education in their curricula. Meanwhile, the economic and social development of the colony, a project that mainly benefited the white settlers, dictated the training of more and more African educators, technicians, and professionals. As they exhausted the limited training facilities in Southern Rhodesia, Africans increasingly sought education outside the colony, first in South Africa and later in Britain and the United States. On returning home, many of these individuals assumed leading roles in various struggles to expand African rights. The settler fear was not unfounded, for the African middle class would in time metamorphose into a direct political threat to white colonial rule.

The African middle class in Southern Rhodesia emerged as a self-conscious entity in the era after the First World War, at the very time that the government was busy trying to thwart its development. Consistent with its social origins, the politics of the African elite were highly ambiguous. One faction among the elite, the more radical one, opted for what may be called the mass line. These individuals were schooled in the postwar radical political culture, especially trade unionism and black internationalism. In this regard, two organizations were especially important—namely, the Industrial and Commercial Workers Union of Africa, a trade union movement founded in South Africa in 1919, and the Universal Negro Improvement Association, a group headed by Marcus Garvey and headquartered in the United States. With trade unionism and black internationalism as their standard, the radical faction of Southern Rhodesia's emerging African middle class reached out to the urban workers and, more tentatively, to the peasants, seeking to build an alliance, an all-African alliance. The alliance centered on grievances concerning education, urban housing, political rights, wages, and land.

The colonial state did not take kindly to the notion of an all-African alliance. In fact, the colonialists embarked on a policy of repression. They placed radical organizations under surveillance and variously harassed, fired, prosecuted, imprisoned, rusticated, and deported leading radicals. But the radicals, who were a small faction within a small elite, did not speak for the African middle class as a whole. A majority of the elite—or, to be more precise, a majority of the elite leadership—consisted of individuals who wished to operate within parameters acceptable to the colonial state. That meant, above all, eschewing trade unionism and black internationalism on the one hand, while steering clear of an all-African alliance on the other hand. Loyalty became the watchword of those members of the emerging African middle class who favored cooperation rather than confrontation with the authorities.

Yet for all their denunciations of the radicals, the loyalists had precious little to show for their loyalty. The colonial state made few concessions to the loyalists, whose agenda included some of the same items as those found in the radicals' platform—namely education, urban housing, and political rights. Unlike the radicals, however, the loyalists were spared state harassment and repression, which enabled them to better weather the Depression years of the 1930s. Indeed, in the midst of the Depression the loyalists took the lead in forming a new organization, the Southern Rhodesia Bantu Congress, which soon became the major voice of African aspirations in the colony.

Then came the Second World War. In Africa, the second great global conflict of the twentieth century changed everything. Colonial subjects, who in many cases had helped to save their colonizers from defeat, emerged from the war with a new consciousness and a new self-confidence.[9] Politically, the new mood was best expressed in the numerous labor and popular actions that gripped Africa in the immediate postwar era, of which the railway strike was an especially noteworthy example.[10] One such railway strike descended on Southern Rhodesia in 1945. Important segments of the African middle-class leadership rallied in support of the strike, and the workers won relatively significant concessions. Three years later, in 1948, an even more massive worker action, this one a general strike, the first in the colony's history, happened in Southern Rhodesia.[11]

The 1948 all-sector walkout was a central event in the making of the African middle class in Southern Rhodesia. The period between the two strikes, the railway strike of 1945 and the general strike of 1948, witnessed an emerging African *national* consciousness, which is not to be confused with an African *nationalist* consciousness. The one signified a sense of togetherness and national belonging among Africans in Southern Rhodesia, while the other maintained that sovereign independence was the logical outcome of African togetherness and national belonging. An African national consciousness was not necessarily antithetical to continued foreign rule, but an African nationalist consciousness, with its militant opposition to colonialism, most assuredly was.

African national consciousness deepened in Southern Rhodesia in the years between the two great postwar strikes. During this period, which may be called a national moment, elite African leaders renewed attempts to form an alliance with the urban workers, a compact that had its origins in the 1945 railway strike. Significantly, this alliance was more solid than the one attempted in the period after the First World War. Then the elite leaders were deeply divided; now they were far more united.

It was against this backdrop that elite Africans offered themselves as representatives of the workers during the 1948 general strike. In the spirit of the national moment, and in view of the fact that a visible proletarian leadership had not yet emerged, the workers accepted the offer, even though they had gone on strike in defiance of the wishes of the African middle-class leaders. All the elements for deception were in place, and deception there was. In the end, the middle-class leaders double-crossed the workers, helping the state and employers to break the strike. It was a historic defeat for the working class.

The disastrous end of the general strike of 1948 doubled as a huge setback for African nationalism in Southern Rhodesia, and ultimately for the political aspirations of the African middle class. It was a setback that ensured that in Southern Rhodesia, unlike in many other parts of Africa, the national moment would not, willy-nilly, lead to the nationalist moment. That is to say, the elite betrayal of the working class interdicted the maturation of an alliance of the elite, workers, and peasants—an alliance that everywhere in Africa formed the social base of nationalism.

The nationalist template having collapsed in the 1948 general strike, Southern Rhodesia's colonized middle class was in no position to follow the general political trend in Africa. Elsewhere on the continent, anticolonial alliances demanded self-government and independence, most famously in the Gold Coast under Kwame Nkrumah, with his biblically derived slogan, "Seek ye first the political kingdom, and all other things shall be added unto you."[12] Eschewing Nkrumah's admonition, Southern Rhodesia's African middle class went on an entirely different odyssey—namely, one in search of political partners among the more liberal elements of the white settlers. African nationalism was out; racial partnership was in.[13]

In the era of racial partnership, Southern Rhodesia's elite Africans revived an old slogan: "equal rights for all civilized men," a mantra as old as the African middle class itself, but one that had been largely abandoned during the national moment of 1945–48. Paradoxically this trope was a riff on Cecil Rhodes, the British diamond magnate (he founded De Beers) and one of the most notorious figures in the history of European colonialism in Africa. A towering presence in southern Africa, Rhodes had two colonies named after him, Southern Rhodesia and the neighboring Northern Rhodesia (now Zambia). No friend of the natives, and certainly not of the African middle class, Rhodes, in an apparent attempt to appease white workers and thwart labor solidarity across racial lines, is reputed to have advocated "equal rights for all civilized *white* men." Embracing the colonizers' civilizationist discourse, but rejecting its racist connotations, elite Africans in Southern Rhodesia and elsewhere in the region offered their own nonracial rejoinder to Rhodes: they called simply for "equal rights for all civilized men." That is to say, those Africans who had attained European standards of culture and education—in a word, the elite—should be accorded the same rights as whites. Using the playbook of the classical European bourgeoisie, but modifying it to suit colonial conditions, the African middle class was bidding for a society in which careers would be open to talent regardless of race.

When the national moment gave way to a search for racial partnership with white liberals, the notion of equal rights among civilized men regained currency among the African middle class. Citizenship would be determined by education and lifestyle, not by race and phenotype. Equality would reign among the reputed civilized, black and white alike. It was a plea for integration—the integration of the African middle class into white settler society. Naturally, racial partnership made no provision for the unwashed colonized masses, the peasants and the workers, and certainly not the women among them, all of whom would have to fend for themselves, politically and otherwise.[14]

But racial partnership failed. The great bulk of the Rhodesian settlers rejected integration for Africans, whether "civilized" or not. Indeed, so far as most settlers were concerned, civilization and Africanity were mutually exclusive. Consequently, Southern Rhodesia's African middle class rediscovered the idea of the all-African alliance and, simultaneously, discovered African nationalism. Henceforth, the trope of equal rights for all civilized men would be banished from the political lexicon. In its place came a new slogan: "one man, one vote." The demand for universal franchise would cement the political marriage between the elite, peasants, and workers—or rather the political *ménage à trois*, since the elite had no real long-term commitment to the union.

The nationalist moment had begun. Politically, the process of African middle-class formation in Southern Rhodesia now entered a new phase—the phase of African nationalism. Organizationally, the African nationalist dispensation dawned in 1957, with the formation of the Southern Rhodesian African National Congress.[15]

Decolonization turned out to be a much more fraught process in Southern Rhodesia than it did in Ghana and other parts of Africa with relatively few white settlers. In 1965, after Northern Rhodesia became the independent nation-state of Zambia, the Southern Rhodesian settlers undertook a somewhat similar nomenclatorial makeover, albeit one that did not dethrone Cecil Rhodes: they changed the name of the country from Southern Rhodesia to just Rhodesia. In that same year, the Rhodesian white settler regime rebelled against British colonial authority and made its infamous Unilateral Declaration of Independence (UDI). (This was the first such act of white settler insurrection in the British Empire since the United States made its bid for independence nearly two centuries earlier. Indeed, the Rhodesian independence document cited the US Declaration of Independence as a precedent.) The UDI was, above all else, a rude rejection of African nationalism, now the dominant ideology of the African middle class. Like white settlers everywhere in Africa—Algeria, Kenya, Namibia, South Africa, and the Portuguese colonies—the Rhodesians refused to treat with African nationalism, and they eventually outlawed it. The African nationalist recourse was armed struggle. After a brutal and bloody guerrilla war lasting some fifteen years, a struggle in which the Rhodesians elevated crimes against humanity to the level of state policy, Zimbabwe was at length wrested from the claws of Rhodesia.[16]

The triumph of African nationalism in Zimbabwe was a triumph for the African middle class. For a generation, from independence in 1980 till the turn of the century, Zimbabwe's black elite prospered, socially and economically, if unevenly. Refugees—professional men and women trained in Africa, Europe, and North America, among other places—returned home to staff the state bureaucracy, the media, the university, the medical and legal infrastructures, even the middle and upper echelons of the largely white-owned corporate sector. The former whites-only suburbs became increasingly interracial, and the African elite assumed the lifestyle and manner of the white settlers, complete with the *brie* (barbeque) around the swimming pool, the retinue of servants, and the requisite colonial-style disdain for those servants. Arriving for the first time in Zimbabwe in 1987 to do research on the African middle class, and initially bunking with members of that class, I was especially struck by the treatment they meted out to domestic servants. On my first day in the country, I confided to my diary: "My most striking impression today was the way the various domestic workers that I came across appear to be cowed by and under the complete sociocultural hegemony of the African middle class." This first impression of an uninitiated researcher, fresh off the plane, underestimated the resistance and moral resiliency of the domestic workers, but it fairly caught the attitude and demeanor of the greater part of the African middle class. I later added to my diary in respect to the treatment of house servants: "They [elite Africans] don't even practice paternalism. It is sheer exploitation without responsibility."

As the interaction between middle class and masses in independent Zimbabwe partly demonstrated, colonialism had been a bad school in which to learn democratic norms. The postcolonial state, like the postcolonial domestic workplace, reproduced all the authoritarian features of colonialism, despite the existence of a constitution and a parliament. Indeed, independent Zimbabwe has had but one chief executive: Robert Mugabe. A schoolteacher by profession, Mugabe lived for several years in early independent Ghana before returning home to Southern Rhodesia in 1960 with a determination to replicate the Ghanaian experiment. An articulator of the prevailing political line rather than a natural leader, he was appointed press secretary of the then-dominant African nationalist formation. In effect, he became the chief mouthpiece of African nationalism in Southern Rhodesia. Over time, as the front-rank leaders were eliminated—by defections, purges, and deaths—Mugabe gradually made the ascent from spokesman to helmsman. In this way, he assumed power at independence in 1980.

During his first two decades in office, Mugabe governed largely to the acclamation of the Western world, despite initial wariness about his reputed Marxism—an ideological amalgam in which he, like so many other rebels of the 1960s and 1970s, had dabbled, not least to obtain international sponsorship, from Soviet or Chinese Communists. That Mugabe's government, as part of a furious military campaign against so-called dissident African nationalists, had massacred thousands of peasants, did not seem to unduly perturb the ruling circles of the Western world. Certainly there was little talk of sanctions against the regime. The reason was self-evident: despite his unsavory behavior, Mugabe, quite literally, was taking care of business. His stewardship, of course, had been good to the African middle class. More important from the Western standpoint, Mugabe had shown due respect for private property, which was largely white-owned, all the while courting foreign investment. Newly converted to the Gucci brand of Marxism—or, perhaps more accurately, dispensing with old leftist ideological baggage—he was hailed in the West as a moderate and responsible statesman, despite the occasional rhetorical excess deployed to placate his populist flank.[17]

Then came the turning point, beginning in 2000. For the African middle class, the consequences of that turning point have been disastrous, resulting in decreased standards of living and massive immigration. It all started with the regime's determination to cling to power, no matter the cost. Since independence, Mugabe had been loquacious about the need for land redistribution. His actions, however, never matched his rhetoric. Whatever land the government had acquired had been disproportionately turned over to well-connected members of the government and the ruling party. Far from revolutionizing the patterns of landownership inherited from the colonial era, the Mugabe regime pursued a policy of building up a black propertied class, seeking to deracialize rather than abolish the white landed gentry.[18]

All the while, the peasants waited in vain for the promised land reform, even as the country slipped into economic crisis amid rampant corruption and mismanagement. Unemployment soared into the stratosphere, and most of the population lived below the poverty level. Basic commodities, including gas, became scarce. The AIDS pandemic continued its destructive march, largely uncontested by the state. The elections of 2000 coincided with this economic and social debacle. His regime increasingly unpopular, Mugabe needed a trump card, which he conveniently found in the unresolved land question. In a move opposed by many within his own government and ruling ZANU-PF party, he decided to hold a referendum ahead of the elections. Among other things, the referendum would strengthen an already imperial presidency and empower the government to forcibly acquire land from the white landed gentry.

The referendum would be the first real test of the Movement for Democratic Change (MDC), the first really important opposition to Mugabe's ZANU-PF since independence. With the ruling party divided and failing to mobilize its base in the rural areas, where most Zimbabweans still live, the MDC focused on the urban centers, where the government was most unpopular. A low voter turnout in the countryside, coupled with a high turnout in the cities, led to the defeat of the referendum. Mugabe soon turned his wrath on the white landed gentry, an important source of money for the MDC.[19] This was not the first time he had inveighed against white farmers: he had previously lashed out at them, especially during elections, even as they prospered under his rule. But this time, Mugabe's heated rhetoric convinced a group of ex-guerrillas, one of the few popular constituencies to remain loyal to his ZANU-PF, that he was ready to settle the land question once and for all. Most of the ex-guerrillas came from the ranks of the land-hungry peasantry, and they had joined the anticolonial struggle largely on the strength of its promise to return the land to the tillers. In short order, white farms were occupied and many of their owners rudely evicted. Newly righteously indignant over the loss of white property and propriety, the Western world, led by Britain, placed Mugabe and his regime beyond the pale.

If Western sanctions were aimed at dislodging Mugabe from power, they have failed. Though not unscathed by it, at this writing (summer 2010) the regime has weathered a decade of economic and diplomatic isolation. The African middle class has not been as fortunate, and the masses have fared worse still. For them, Mugabe's continued reign has come at a high price. A prolonged economic crisis—complete with capital flight, runaway inflation, currency devaluation, and commodity shortages—has made daily living a severe struggle. It has certainly removed much of the material foundation of the middle-class lifestyle. Accordingly, Africans with skills to sell in the international marketplace—bankers, doctors, nurses, academics, and others—have fled the country in droves, the favorite destinations being South Africa, Britain, the United States, Australia, and New Zealand. For some of these individuals, this is a second stint of exile, a condition they endured before independence. Except for a limited and privileged category closely allied with the state and the ruling party, the process of middle-class formation in Zimbabwe has virtually ground to a halt. In this sense, the present moment resembles the dawn of the colonial era, when the struggle for social mobility was, in the first instance, a struggle against the tyranny of state power. For the Zimbabweans as a whole, including the middle class, the past is indeed prologue.

Notes

This chapter draws, in part, on M. West, "The Struggle for Zimbabwe, Then and Now."

1. Frantz Fanon would make this point with particular poignancy for a new generation of activists in *The Wretched of the Earth*.
2. Samkange, *Origins of Rhodesia*; Chamunorwa Mutambirwa, *The Rise of Settler Power in Southern Rhodesia*; Schmidt, *Peasants, Traders, and Wives*.
3. Ranger, *Revolt in Southern Rhodesia*.
4. Palmer, *Land and Racial Discrimination in Rhodesia*; van Onselen, *Chibaro*.
5. M. West, *The Rise of an African Middle Clas*.
6. Ibid., 36–67.

7. Harlan, *Booker T. Washington: The Making of a Black Leader* and *Booker T. Washington: The Wizard of Tuskegee*.

8. M. West, "The Tuskegee Model of Development in Africa."

9. Killingray, *Fighting for Britain*.

10. Cooper, *Decolonization and African Society*.

11. D. Johnson, *World War II and the Scramble for Labour in Colonial Zimbabwe*.

12. Nkrumah, *Ghana*.

13. For personal accounts, see Shamuyarira, *Crisis in Rhodesia*; Vambe, *From Rhodesia to Zimbabwe*. For an overview, see Hancock, *White Liberals, Moderates, and Radicals in Rhodesia*.

14. Barnes, *"We Women Worked So Hard."*

15. Significantly, this was also the year of Ghana's independence, with Nkrumah leading the first country in sub-Saharan Africa to formally emerge from under the colonial yoke.

16. Martin and Johnson, *The Struggle for Zimbabwe*; Kriger, *Zimbabwe's Guerrilla War*; Horne, *From the Barrel of a Gun*.

17. Auret, *From Liberator to Dictator*; Compagnon, *Robert Mugabe and the Destruction of Zimbabwe*.

18. Horace Campbell, *Reclaiming Zimbabwe*.

19. Raftopoulos and Savage, *Zimbabwe*.

Between Modernity and Backwardness

THE CASE OF THE ENGLISH MIDDLE CLASS

Simon Gunn

England is often taken to be the birthplace of a modern middle class. Although other early modern states possessed significant urban populations of merchants, officials, and independent tradespeople, none could approach the proportionate scale and substance of the "middling sort" of eighteenth-century England, with historians variously estimating its size at upward of a quarter of English society.[1] Moreover, the term "middle class" first entered the language as part of a new lexicon of class in late-eighteenth-century England, as Asa Briggs has noted in a classic article, or even earlier according to recent historians.[2] A well-established narrative of English (and British) history also placed the middle class at the center of the nation's precocious entry to economic and political modernity: as the progenitors of the Industrial Revolution; and as a vital force in the successive movements for parliamentary reform, culminating in the Reform Act of 1832, which is seen as launching Britain on the road to parliamentary democracy.[3] It is a narrative, indeed, that has a pedigree almost as long as the events it describes, stretching back through the *History of England* by G. M. Trevelyan (1926) to the work of the same title written by his great uncle, Thomas Babington Macaulay, between 1848 and 1855.[4] The period between the American Revolution and the Reform Act of 1832 have thus become identified in the historiography of modern Britain with the "making of the middle class," a development set alongside Edward Thompson's "making of the English working class."[5]

There are dangers in emphasizing the uniqueness and precocity of England's middle class in the period, as I shall indicate; it can easily lead to a neglect of what such a class shared with similar groups elsewhere and to its construction as an ideal type, against which other equivalent formations can be misleadingly seen as a deviation or weak imitation. But one can nevertheless ask the question, in what precisely was its modernity seen to consist? One needs to be mindful of the very different intellectual traditions in which "modernity" has been understood.[6] Yet the narrative I have just outlined provides some clues as to how modernity and the English middle class have been articulated within a historical framework. The middle class is thus identified with three specific "breaks": the economic transformation associated with the onset of industrial capitalism; the political changes connected with liberalism, including representative government at both local and national levels and reform of the state in general; and the emergence of a modern social structure, no longer organized as a graded hierarchy but on a tripartite or occasionally bipolar class model.[7] These historical developments can be seen to mesh with a number of more explicitly theoretical perspectives on modernity. Marx and Engels's apocalyptic vision of the bourgeoisie in 1848 as a revolutionary class, "constantly revolutionizing the instruments of production, and thereby the relations of production, and with them the whole relations of society," made the middle class the engineers as well as the villains of modernity.[8] Despite the universal terms in which the theory of *The Communist Manifesto* was necessarily couched, its portrait of the bourgeoisie corresponds closely with the English experience of which Marx and Engels were such attentive observers, associated with "Free Trade," "Modern Industry," imperial expansion, and dominance of the urban over the rural. It was likewise late-seventeenth- and eighteenth-century Britain (specifically England) that formed the model case for the emergence of a modern public sphere, in Jürgen Habermas's account. Of particular significance here, according to Habermas, was the existence of a relatively free and flourishing press, capable of acting as a focus for public opinion, and of "those bourgeois strata of the Protestant middle class, involved in business and commerce," which "formed something like a steadily expanding pre-parliamentary forum."[9] Indeed, seen from Continental Europe, the English middle class has appeared to be the pivot around which a smooth and successful transition to modernity was effected. The combination of an evolutionary parliamentary system and a socially integrated nation-state, in the words of the historian of Germany Geoff Eley, can suggest "a view of British history in which the British bourgeoisie is endowed with a kind of superior political intelligence. Having restructured its relations with the old 'pre-industrial ruling stratum' between 1640 and 1832, redefined the function of the Church, and established certain civil rights under the law, it then proceeded to integrate the new working class into the socio-political order. In this way British history becomes the privileged site of fundamental evolutionary processes of social and political 'modernization.' "[10]

From different vantage points, therefore, England has been viewed as home to a prototypical and uniquely powerful middle class that was itself the catalyst for bringing into being the economic, social, and political conditions of modernity. Or so went the established story. Those acquainted with the historiography of modern England will be aware that over the last quarter-century or so, this story has been challenged and effectively overturned. Briefly, the attack has come from four directions, several of which bear little direct relationship to the others. In the first place, the English middle class has been seen as subordinated, politically and above all culturally, to the established authority of the landed aristocracy and gentry. After the highpoint of the repeal of the Corn Laws in 1846, the middle class forsook its mission to overturn the inherited power of land, a historical volte-face that was to have baleful long-term consequences both for the nation's political culture and its economic performance.[11] Second, following the extensive research on wealth holding by W. D. Rubinstein, the nineteenth-century middle class has been viewed as divided between, on the one hand, a commercial and financial elite centered on the City of London and closely allied to elements of the landed class, and a manufacturing component centered on the Midlands and the north, socially isolated and in every sense the "poor relation" of its metropolitan cousins.[12] Third, in line with the lengthening of the time scale of industrialization and the attention to the eighteenth-century consumer revolution, historians have questioned the idea of a new middle class in the early nineteenth century, arguing that an equivalent social formation had long been in place in the "middling sort" of post-Restoration England.[13] Finally, and most radically, there is the interpretation of Dror Wahrman and others, which sees the middle class as a rhetorical device, invented and deployed for various political ends in the debates about political reform and English society in the decades between the French Revolution and the Reform Act of 1832. In this interpretation, the middle class was merely a convenient political invention of the early nineteenth century that was subsequently transformed into an essential prop in the narrative of modern British history.[14]

Collectively, these revisionist interpretations (which have in turn been established as a new orthodoxy) represent the obverse and to some extent the mirror image of the established narrative that preceded it. Far from being in the vanguard of modernity, the English middle class is depicted as backward—or, more precisely and variously, as subordinated, fractured, amorphous, and mythical. Contrary to its international reputation, the English middle class has come to be seen as weak, divided, or imagined, not a source of power or a model to be emulated on the path to a modern state and society. Not surprisingly, the revisionist position has, in turn, been the object of sustained critique.[15] Here, however, I do not wish to reenter what has become a long-running and multifaceted debate. Instead, I want to suggest that the two poles of modernity and backwardness, which appear as products of the recent historiographical debate, have in fact a much longer pedigree: they have emerged at different points in public discussions of the English middle class over the last 150 years. The modernity-backwardness dispute is in fact a trope of discourse about the middle class in England, and it is one that has come to limit how we understand this particular historical formation and, indeed, class itself. In attending to these limitations, I shall also propose in the last section of this chapter some ways of moving the debate forward, indicating how the history of the English middle class can be reconnected with newer themes in the historiography of class, nation, and empire.

The Backwardness of the English Middle Class

There have been at least three significant moments since the mid-nineteenth century when the English middle class became the object of heightened criticism and concern. The first occurred in the 1850s, following what historians traditionally viewed as the high point of middle-class power, the repeal of the Corn Laws in 1846.[16] It was in the immediate aftermath of the repeal that Richard Cobden, leader of the Anti-Corn Law League, wrote to the prime minister, Lord Peel, famously challenging him: "Do you shrink from governing through the *bona fide* representatives of the middle class? . . . The Reform Bill decreed it; the passing of the Corn Bill has realised it."[17] Moreover, the triumph of 1846 came after an era during which a string of influential commentators such as Edward Baines, John Bright, and Robert Vaughan portrayed the middle class as the backbone of the nation and the agents of civilization.[18] Repeal of the Corn Laws was indeed part of the circumstances that led Marx and Engels to proclaim the revolutionary role of the bourgeoisie.

Within a matter of years, however, many of the same commentators were viewing the middle class very differently. In the light of the persisting political and social ascendancy of the landed upper class, Marx had been led by 1854 to decry the "servile" character of the middle class and to predict that "the feudalism of England will not perish beneath the scarcely perceptible dissolving processes of the middle class."[19] Failure to continue the political momentum of the Anti-Corn Law League and the catastrophic electoral defeats in the heartlands of radical Liberalism, Birmingham and Manchester, in 1857, led Cobden and his ally John Bright to similar conclusions. "The snobbishness of the monied classes in the great seats of manufacture is a fearful obstacle to any effectual change in the system," wrote Cobden. "The truth must be that people in Lancashire grow conservative and aristocratic with their prosperous trade."[20] Nor was the failure temporary; it came to be seen as part of an inexorable social process. Writing in the aftermath of Conservative victories at the 1868 elections, Cobden's biographer, the Lancashire manufacturer John Morley, asserted that "the new feudalism is beginning to assert itself . . . The man who began life as a beggar and a Chartist softens down into a radical when he got credit enough for a weaving shed; a factory of his own mollifies him into what is called a strong Liberal; and by the time he owns a mansion and a piece of land he has a feeling of blue blood tingling in his veins, and thinks of a pedigree and a motto in old French."[21] Although Lancashire was not England, its identification by Marx and others as the epitome of the new class society based on industry appeared to make its politics especially telling. What became clear here, as elsewhere, to commentators on all sides of the political spectrum, including perceptive conservatives like Disraeli, was that the middle class was by no means committed to its alleged historical destiny of overthrowing the rule of land and aristocracy but was content, on the contrary, to become "re-feudalised," a bulwark against change rather than an agent of modernity.[22]

I am less interested here in the status and accuracy of this diagnosis than in the existence of the public discourse that highlights the assumed weaknesses of the English middle class, failings that often appear to be measured against some putative but unnamed national "other." The second historical moment of significant public debate about the English middle class was of a rather different nature and occurred around the First World War. Concern here focused not on the merchants and manufacturers of the industrial north but on owners of small businesses and "black-coated workers," the latter identified with clerical and professional occupations and with London. From the early 1900s to the mid-1920s, this group was consistently represented as squeezed between organized labor and big business. A lead editorial in *Cassell's Saturday Journal* in August 1914 caught the mood: "Society tends ever to divide itself into two main sections—those of Capital and Labour, with a smaller but important section, that of the hard-working Middle Classes between, which runs the risk of being ground to powder in the coming impact of the upper and nether millstones of the two big sections."[23] This discourse of the "small man" was reflected in consumer issues as well as those to do with the workplace; immediately after the war, it was typically represented in fears of middle-class pauperization, caused by rising prices that were seen as benefiting only the very rich, and declining real incomes among the salaried classes and small business.[24] The result was the idea of a "crisis" of the middle class, encapsulated in the work of the Liberal journalist Charles Masterman, who depicted the group as the "New Poor," harassed and with their way of life under threat.[25] It was also promulgated by the number of short-lived but vociferous associations formed in the period, from the Middle Class Defence Organisation (1906) to the Middle Classes Union (1919). The crisis, however, passed. In 1923 financial stability returned, and material conditions until the outbreak of the Second World War were in fact favorable to middle-class life, amounting to what was to appear in retrospect as a golden age.[26] The keynote of this period, in the view of historians like Raphael Samuel and Alison Light, was a "conservative modernity," linked to an essentially domestic ideal of expanding suburbia, a middle-class England of gardeners and housewives.[27] It was a modernity, for instance, with hardly a trace of the zeal for modernist experimentation and planning that was widely if differentially displayed in North America and Continental Europe in the interwar years.[28]

The third and final moment when the English middle class was perceived to be in crisis occurred in the 1970s. In this case the class was less immediately visible, since its predicament was enmeshed with Britain's larger economic and political crisis, which was triggered by the oil shortage of 1973 but soon seen as the culmination of a much longer process of industrial and imperial decline.[29] The "decline" of the middle class was deemed by some to be part or even a central component of this and to be caused by a complex of factors. As in the period after the First World War, middle-class families claimed to be suffering from the combined effects of high taxation and escalating inflation; likewise, complaints were voiced that the middle class was losing out to organized labor and the working class in general in terms of income, welfare, and political influence.[30] It was certainly the case that white-collar and professional occupations were affected by unemployment in the 1970s, and that the economic recession accelerated changes in middle-class career structures, symbolized at the time by the "end of organisation man."[31] Moreover, as women began to move into what were previously all-male careers, starting in the late 1960s, not only did the composition of the workplace change but so did the organization of the middle-class family, previously predicated on a sexual division of labor that had seen married women overwhelmingly identified with the home.[32] Although in some quarters the middle class and its institutions were seen as threatened and in need of defending, in others they were viewed as one of the sources of Britain's malaise. Inadequate training, lack of entrepreneurial zeal, inefficient management, and "restrictive practices" among the professions were all blamed for poor economic performance. Still more radically, elements in the Conservative party, traditionally the party of business, adopted the view that middle-class failure was a historical reason for Britain's plight. According to Keith Joseph, the intellectual architect of "New Right" Conservatism, writing in 1975, Britain had "never had a capitalist ruling class or stable *haute bourgeoisie* . . . capitalist values have never shaped thought and institutions as they have in some countries."[33] What was required was a proper bourgeois revolution to reverse Britain's failed modernity. Consequently, when the Thatcher government came to power in 1979, it quickly set about sweeping away the privileges of professional groups such as doctors, civil servants, and academics. The middle class was to be saved by being recast in the image of the enterprise culture and the private sector.[34]

The revisionist historiography of the English middle class, which I described earlier, was not therefore the product of neutral, self-contained academic research. It derived directly from a period perceived as one of crisis for the middle class, linked to national and economic decline both in public discourse and in the historiography itself.[35] In this sense it can be understood as a component of a much longer discursive tradition, stretching back to at least the mid-nineteenth century, in which the English middle class has been viewed alternately as a harbinger of modernity or as in some way flawed, weak, or backward. In the same manner, one needs to understand the ideas of the modernity and backwardness of the middle class, its success or failure, not as somehow antithetical but as integral parts of the same discourse. If they are not the mirror image of one another, to mix metaphors, they are two sides of the same coin. Thus, the claims of one side frequently called the other into existence.[36]

What was it that triggered these periodic debates about the crisis of the middle class? Were they linked to specific material circumstances—economic downturn, social tension, political turbulence—or were they independent of these, merely a discursive or rhetorical construction, much as some of the recent literature would have us think about the middle class as a concept? Looking at what the three instances have in common, I would argue that the answer lies neither wholly with one nor the other side; they are comprehensible neither as an unmediated reflection of reality nor simply through the lens of representation. Clearly, the discourse of backwardness, like that of modernity, was discursively constituted, those who engaged in it often having a clear ideological stake in the outcome. It would be perverse to see matters of public debate otherwise. But this does not mean that the successive crises were merely self-referential, or that they had no real goal. On the contrary, they all occurred at periods of national—and international—pressure, when the stability of English society and Britain's place in the world had been called into question. Although this may be relatively obvious around the First World War and in the 1970s, it also applied in the 1850s, following the "condition of England" debate of the 1840s and the Crimean War of 1854–56, which provoked questions about the country's security and its military capacity. Talking about the middle class was a way of talking about the nation, its internal coherence as well as its external power.[37] Moreover, the successive debates also reflected the changing social formation of the middle class. In the 1850s and 1860s, the focus was on large industrial employers, with their increasing wealth and social conservatism. By the First World War, the issue was rather the rise of the white-collar salaried classes, symbolized in Charles Masterman's term the "Suburbans."[38] By the 1970s, the focus was not merely the changing configuration of the middle class, but also its potential dissolution in the face of economic competition and a demanding state.[39]

However, there are distinct drawbacks in following convention and framing the historiography of the English middle class between the poles of modernity and backwardness. Configuring history in this manner has had at least two effects. One is to limit the understanding of the middle class to a relatively narrow spatial frame, that of the nation-state, at a period when Britain was developing as an imperial and world power. Indeed, the middle class in Britain has often been studied on the still smaller stage of the individual town or city.[40] The second effect is the relative neglect of issues to do with social reproduction in the middle class—that is, how specific components of the middle class reproduced themselves materially, socially, and culturally over time. Oddly, our understanding of this sociological process is very limited because studies of the middle class so often operate at a higher level of abstraction and generality. In the penultimate section of this chapter, therefore, I shall look briefly at the international dimensions of the subject and issues to do with the transmission of economic and cultural capital across generations as a way of suggesting different ways of approaching the history of the English middle class.

Beginning in the eighteenth century, if not earlier, the English middling sort (as well as elements of the aristocracy and gentry) was bound into economic and social networks at an international level, from the slave trade and the Jamaican plantation system to the East India Company and colonial administration. By the 1850s, the upper echelons of the Indian army and the Indian civil service had become a "large, vested interest of the educated [British] upper middle class," the two institutions taking up 65 percent of the total expenditure of the government of India by the time of the First World War.[41] English identities, especially masculine identity, were importantly reshaped in the colonial encounter, as were European bourgeois identities more generally—French and Dutch as well as British. As Ann Laura Stoler has written, "colonialism was not only about the importation of middle-class sensibilities to the colonies, but about the *making* of them." And they were remade by a set of complex interactions with "native" populations in which gender and sexuality crisscrossed with "race" and class.[42] Nor was insertion in international and colonial networks unusual for middle-class families, even in northern English cities apparently distant from metropolitan and imperial connections. Analysis of the kinship patterns of the Fenton and Oates clans in nineteenth-century Leeds, prosperous but by no means front-rank families in the textile industry, reveals something of this imbrication. The Fentons' connections spread outward to London, Riga, and Belfast, through interests in the manufacture and trade of flax; to Brussels and St. Petersburg, where a daughter married the British consul; and to India, where a grandson entered the Indian Civil Service. The Oates family was linked to London ("a family member in London was always an asset," Bob Morris observes)[43] and to Bristol, and thence to the Jamaica sugar plantations; other Oates family members settled in Seville, Spain, and New South Wales, Australia. All this did not imply that those branches of the family living in Leeds were any the less rooted in local, urban life.[44] Yet the existence of these extended clan networks indicate something of the geographical range of the English middle class, even at relatively modest levels. Indeed, the socioeconomic resources that such networks could provide were vital at a time when the family remained a primary source of capital and business partners.[45]

As this evidence also suggests, association with the middle class of other European states was closer than is often assumed, given Britain's apparent detachment from European affairs in the period 1815–1914 and its increasing orientation to "Greater Britain" overseas. Victorian industrial cities beyond

London took a full part in what might be termed a pan-European bourgeois culture, epitomized by the rise of classical music to the apex of the cultural hierarchy.[46] If Birmingham shared Mendelssohn with Leipzig, Manchester had its Hallé concerts from the 1850s, Leeds its triennial music festivals from the 1870s, featuring specially commissioned works by composers such as Dvořák and Gounod.[47] The presence of German families in such cities, as manufacturers and merchants, contributed significantly to this cultural life. Germans were the largest foreign minority in England before 1891. The German population peaked at 56,000 in 1911, with almost half of the Germans based in London and the rest in major industrial centers like Bradford and Manchester.[48] These figures represented only the German-born population, excluding second- and third-generation children as well as the many German women who married into English middle-class families and thus became British citizens. Consequently, it is mistaken to see the English middle class as somehow sealed off from its Continental counterparts, either culturally or socially. Looking in a different direction, Linda Young has recently argued that a code of gentility came to be shared across the English-speaking world of Britain, North America, and Australia in the course of the nineteenth century, representing a "transnational cultural system" that effectively defined middle-class status. It was a highly elaborated code, according to Young, which allowed for the expression of minute social differences while its complexity meant that it could be mastered only over time. Yet it made middle-class identity recognizable across cultural space, from Philadelphia to Manchester and Melbourne, because it was based on a common understanding of ritual practice and bodily performance: "in *doing* they came to *be* middle class."[49] Thinking about the middle classes in various parts of the world as basically similar (with significant variations) rather than—as has tended to be the case—basically different (with some shared features) alters the principal coordinates, notably the boundaries of the nation-state, which have conventionally anchored the historiography of the middle class. Were the meanings and practices of *Bürgerlichkeit*, *bourgeois*, and middle-classness fundamentally divergent? Recent studies suggest that they were not. But we are only at the beginning of the attempt to understand the insertion of the English middle class in wider crossnational networks of culture and connectivity.[50]

Finally, it is important to consider questions of social formation and social reproduction. This dimension has tended to get lost in recent years, as historians focused on discourse and consumption as the principal means of investigating the middle class. Yet the durability of a particular social formation over time is integral to any meaningful concept of class, together with the understanding that it involves a patterned inequality in the distribution of resources, reproduced by specific strategies as well as by the impersonal forces of the market and the state. How, one can ask, does middle-classness get passed on from one generation to the next and become a central part of the inheritance process itself? In thinking about these themes in relation to the English middle class in the later nineteenth and twentieth centuries, I have found Pierre Bourdieu's concept of capital helpful in explaining how different categories of resource—economic, social, cultural, and symbolic—can serve as forms of "capital," capable of being transmuted from one to another, within groups and across time.[51] It helps to illuminate, for example, the strategies pursued by upper-middle-class clans and extended families in the later nineteenth century, with some branches remaining closely connected to the family business while others accumulated social and cultural capital through attendance at public school, entry into the church or civil service, and intermarriage with "significant others."[52] Family was the essential unit of middle-class social formation, but in the form of extended networks of kinship, not simply in its nuclear form, and to understand the stability and reproduction of the class—especially the upper middle class—it is necessary to understand that resources were often spread deep and wide across branches of the family and across generations. This is the formation that the journalist Neal Ascheson described in apocryphal terms in 1976 as dwellers in substantial houses, "passed on from generation to generation, living sometimes austerely but after good rains with a mysterious ease and opulence":

> To call on Charles and Melissa Heigho wouldn't have told you much. Rush matting, a few nice rugs, one or two small but very good bits of antique furniture, a "daily woman," quite likely no car "because we can't afford one" . . . "Wealthy" is obviously the wrong word . . . Yet this is where the English ruling class is reproducing itself, discreetly ensuring another generation of security and privilege within the Secret Garden whose key no fumbling socialist Chancellor has yet discovered. The bulge under Melissa's gingham smock is another little Public Schoolboy, destined for the administrative grade of the Civil Service, a place in a merchant bank or a Headship of Chancery in some embassy.[53]

The key to the continuity of this upper middle class, in Ascheson's analysis, is the elaborate system of trusts and investments that might yield little in the short term, but that provides a foundation of capital that ensures stability and the inheritance of wealth across the generations.

In the transmission of middle-class capital, women were of special importance. This was not only in relation to economic capital, where recent historians have found women to have had a much more active stake than has previously been allowed in family finance, and especially in inheritance processes.[54] It was also the case with regard to cultural capital, where they were the principal transmitters of gentility, signifying to the outside world the status of the household, and to class taste. This influence was strongly evident in the nineteenth century, as numerous studies have testified, and it persisted into the late twentieth.[55] A sociological survey of culinary taste among the middle classes between 1968 and 1988 concluded that "it is women who are the principal inheritors of class taste . . . and it is their behaviour that most strongly underpins class-based patterns of consumption."[56] Education, as Bourdieu has noted, was likewise critical to cultural capital and social reproduction. In the English context, attention here is normally drawn to the role of the major public schools—Eton, Harrow, and so on—in the training of upper-middle-class men.[57] But it was no less significant further down the social pecking order, where access to secondary education was central to family strategies. From the late-nineteenth-century perspective, this meant investing in children's acquisition of educational credentials and encouraging them to enter stable white-collar occupations such as teaching and office work. Following the First World War, access to grammar or direct grant school was understood to be a passport to middle-class status, extended also to a tiny proportion of working-class scholarship children, since it signaled entry into the world of "mental work" and escape from a life of manual labor.[58] Secondary schooling was central to the idea of a "social ladder" that gained ground after 1918, facilitating the idea of limited class mobility, especially between skilled manual and white-collar groups. It was evidence of upward social mobility through education that led to the relatively optimistic conclusions of studies such as the Oxford Mobility Project of 1972 that the expansion of secondary schooling in the early and mid-twentieth century was leveling out the inherited effects of cultural capital on class differences.[59] More recent studies, however, have been considerably less sanguine about the impact of education on the life chances of different groups or on social mobility overall.[60] There are in fact very few detailed studies of family strategies over several generations. Yet where they have been carried out, as in the case of an oral history undertaken by Paul Thompson, the results suggest that among all social classes, families used cultural and other forms of capital to preserve the family situation, rather than to modify it.[61] Despite periodic crises and upheavals, economic strategies within the families, inheritance, and education appear to have enabled the English middle class to reproduce itself effectively and to maintain a relative stability over time.

Conclusion

I have argued in this chapter that the recent historiography of the English middle class has been cast within a trope of modernity and backwardness, an antithesis that replicates in certain respects the dual vision evident at earlier historical moments over the last century and a half. In trying to move beyond this simple duality, is it necessary to dispense with the notion of modernity altogether? My answer is a qualified no. Even were it desirable to do so, the ideas of modernity and middle class are so mutually implicated that it is almost impossible to disentangle them. At the same time, to make the linkage viable, we have to acknowledge several qualifications. First, as Craig Calhoun has observed, we require a notion of modernity that is not predicated on epochal rupture and that accommodates historical continuity.[62] Recent historical studies have emphasized that although the middle class is integral to the notion of a modern social structure, it has a long prehistory in England. What "middle class" means is historically as well as geographically variable, and this very continuity is in part a retrospective construction, but the historical longevity of the social "middle" also demands recognition. Second, it is helpful to understand the middle class as the product as much as the agent of modernity, not the hero or villain of the piece, but merely one component among many in what "modernity" might mean. Indeed, to speak of the middle class at all as a historical actor is problematic in the light of the cultural turn. Yet I have also argued that we need to know more about the social formation of this group historically, and in particular the mechanisms that enabled its reproduction and transformation over time. Attempting to understand the middle class purely in discursive terms is insufficient, not least because it leaves intact and unquestioned certain enduring sources of socioeconomic inequality.[63] Finally, and by extension, it is important to locate the English middle class in an international context, in relation to networks and flows that were European, imperial, and ultimately global in scope. Arguably, the real myth of the middle class is not so much its invention as a product of political discourse, as the idea of its immaculate conception, emerging sui generis in late-eighteenth-century England and developing in splendid isolation within the confines of the nation-state to stand as the exemplar of a modern society and modern polity for the rest of the world. "First here, later elsewhere": it is this logic, with which this chapter began, that needs to be challenged in the case of the

English middle class, no less than in the version of modernity—and history—with which it is so intimately bound up.[64]

Notes

I have chosen to focus on England rather than Britain. Not only is the former too often made to stand for the latter (an effect of hegemony itself), but Wales and Scotland differed in their social and religious structure. Scotland also has a distinctive legal and educational system. All this makes generalizations about the middle class across Britain more hazardous than historians sometimes assume.

1. The figures vary widely between historians and are never better than approximate; they also include independent yeoman farmers in the definition of the "middling sort." See, for example, Barry and Brooks, "Introduction," 3; Seed, "From 'Middling Sort' to Middle Class," 116–17; Weatherill, *Consumer Behaviour and Material Culture in Britain*, 235.

2. Briggs, "The Language of Class in Early Nineteenth-Century England"; Corfield, "Class by Name and Number in Eighteenth-Century Britain"; Wallech, "Class Versus Rank"; Keith Wrightson, "Estates, Degrees and Sorts."

3. The two classic examples of this narrative in the last half of the twentieth century are Briggs, *The Age of Improvement*, and Perkin, *The Origins of Modern English Society*.

4. Trevelyan, *History of England*; Macaulay, *History of England*.

5. E. Thompson, *The Making of the English Working Class*. A host of other works have upheld this view from a variety of analytical perspectives over the last twenty years. See, for example, Davidoff and Hall, *Family Fortunes*; Hobsbawm, "The Example of the English Middle Class"; Koditschek, *Class Formation and Urban Industrial Society*; B. Lewis, *The Middlemost and the Mill Towns*. From yet another (Weberian) direction, R. J. Morris arrived at a similar conclusion, albeit with a slightly different time frame in his *Class, Sect and Party*.

6. It is important to distinguish between different, albeit overlapping, definitional traditions of modernity: the tradition of history of science, which seeks to locate (or deny) modernity in the scientific revolution; its identification, following Weber, with the Enlightenment and the division of knowledge into autonomous spheres; the notion that modernity represents the moment when Europe and the West became aware of the rest of the world as its "other"; and the idea that modernity is both a historical epoch and an experience of the world linked to the spread of urban industrial capitalism. See, for example, Bayly, *The Birth of the Modern World*; Berman, *All That Is Solid Melts into Air*; Habermas, *The Philosophical Discourse of Modernity*; Latour, *We Have Never Been Modern*.

7. For an extensive commentary on this last point, see Cannadine, *Class in Britain*, chapters 2 and 3.

8. Marx and Engels, *The Communist Manifesto*, 83. Although there are significant conceptual differences between the notions of bourgeoisie and middle class, it is note-

worthy that Marx and Engels often used them interchangeably in their writings, including *The Communist Manifesto*.

9. Habermas, *The Structural Transformation of the Public Sphere*, 57–67.

10. Eley, "The British Model and the German Road," 71.

11. The classic statement of this thesis is Wiener, *English Culture and the Decline of the Industrial Spirit*. For the argument at a European level, see Mayer, *The Persistence of the Old Régime*. For a Marxist variant, see Anderson, "The Origins of the Present Crisis." Anderson's position changed in a later essay, "The Figures of Descent," in which he sought to incorporate the views of W. D. Rubinstein on the "divided" middle class.

12. Rubinstein, *Men of Property*. See also Cain and Hopkins, *British Imperialism*; Lee, "Regional Growth and Structural Change in Victorian Britain." The views of Rubinstein were extensively challenged in the 1980s.

13. See for example, Barry and Brooks, *The Middling Sort of People*; Earle, *The Making of the English Middle Class*; Hunt, *The Middling Sort*; Smail, *The Origins of Middle-Class Culture*.

14. Wahrman, *Imagining the Middle Class*. Similar arguments can be found in Joyce, *Democratic Subjects*, 161–64. See the discussion of this point in the introduction to this volume.

15. See, for example, Martin Daunton, "'Gentlemanly Capitalism' and British Industry 1820–1914," 119–58; Gunn, "The 'Failure' of the Victorian Middle Class." See also the essays in the two volumes edited by Alan Kidd and David Nicholls, *The Making of the British Middle Class?* and *Gender, Civic Culture and Consumerism*.

16. See, for instance, Briggs, *The Age of Improvement*, 324; Perkin, *The Origins of Modern English Society*, 350. For a more recent, nuanced account, see Tyrell and Pickering, *The People's Bread*.

17. Cobden to Peel, 23 June 1846, quoted by John Morley in Morley, *The Life of Richard Cobden*, 397.

18. Baines Junior, *On the Social, Educational and Religious State of the Manufacturing Districts*; R. Vaughan, *The Age of Great Cities*; George Barnett Smith, *The Life and Speeches of John Bright*.

19. Marx, "The English Middle Class," 664–65.

20. Quoted in Morley, *The Life of Richard Cobden*, 1.

21. John Morley, "The Chamber of Mediocrity," *Fortnightly Review*, December 1868, 690.

22. P. Smith, *Disraelian Conservatism and Social Reform*.

23. *Cassell's Saturday Journal*, August 1, 1914.

24. Hilton, *Consumerism in Twentieth-Century Britain*, 48–51; McKibbin, *Classes and Cultures*, 50–59.

25. Masterman, *The Condition of England* and *England after the War*.

26. McKibbin, *Classes and Cultures*, 59.

27. Light, *Forever England*, 211; Samuel, "The Middle Class between the Wars." See also Mandler, "The Consciousness of Modernity?"

28. For further comments on the idea of Britain's "failed" or "deferred" modernity at this period and after the Second World War, see Barnett, *The Audit of War*.

29. Standard works that set the 1970s in the context of a longer "decline" include Dintenfass, *The Decline of Industrial Britain*, and Gamble, *Britain in Decline*.

30. The classic expression of these views is Hutber, *The Decline of the Middle Class—and How It Can Fight Back*.

31. "The Coming Entrepreneurial Revolution," *Economist*, November 25, 1976, 41–65.

32. The proportion of economically active women in the United Kingdom increased from 56 percent to 72 percent between 1970 and 1999, according to the Office of National Statistics, *Social Trends* (London, 2000), 68. For a wider perspective on changes in the middle class during this period, see Butler and Savage, *Social Change and the Middle Classes*; Gunn and Bell, *Middle Classes*, chapter 7.

33. K. Joseph, "Is Beckerman among the Sociologists?," 501.

34. H. Young, *One of Us*, 227–29; Perkin, *The Rise of Professional Society*, 485–90.

35. For works that link the history of the middle class with economic decline, see Ingham, *Capitalism Divided?*; Rubinstein, *Capitalism, Culture and Decline in Britain*; F. Thompson, *Gentrification and the Enterprise Culture*.

36. An example is the way in which memories of the crisis of the middle class after the First World War—combined with the threat of socialism, provoked by the advent of the Attlee Labour government in 1945—led to strong assertions of the modernizing impulses of the middle class among postwar commentators. See, for instance, Lewis and Maude, *The English Middle Classes*.

37. For similar arguments on this theme, see Wilson, *The Island Race*, especially chapter 1.

38. Masterman, *The Condition of England*.

39. For further discussion of this point, see Gunn, "The Public Sphere, Modernity and Consumption."

40. Gunn, "Class, Identity and the Urban."

41. Cain and Hopkins, *British Imperialism*, 329–30.

42. Stoler, *Race and the Education of Desire*, 99. See also Sinha, *Colonial Masculinity*.

43. Morris, *Men, Women and Property in England*, 125–26.

44. Ibid., 318–46.

45. Other studies of middle-class family networks can be found in Benwell Community Project, *The Making of a Ruling Class*; Davidoff and Hall, *Family Fortunes*; Gunn, "The Manchester Middle Class"; Joyce, *Work, Society and Politics*, chapter 1.

46. On this theme, see Gay, *The Naked Heart* and *Pleasure Wars*; Kaschuba, "German *Bürgerlichkeit* after 1800"; Kocka, "The Middle Class in Europe."

47. Gunn, *The Public Culture of the Victorian Middle Class*, especially chapter 6. See also Pieper, "The Making of a Middle-Class Cultural Identity."

48. Panayi, *Immigrants, Ethnicity and Racism in Britain* and *German Immigrants in Britain during the Nineteenth Century*.

49. L. Young, *Middle-Class Culture in the Nineteenth Century*, 10. See also the discussion on this point in the introduction to this volume.

50. Recent studies that begin to step outside the national frame and look at cross-national connections in instructive ways include C. Hall, *Civilising Subjects*; Rich, "Bourgeois Consumption"; Rodgers, *Atlantic Crossings*.

51. The fullest account and application of the notion of multiple "capitals" is in Bourdieu, *Distinction*. See also Gunn, "Translating Bourdieu."

52. For an illuminating discussion of nonconformist extended families in the nineteenth century, see Binfield, *So Down to Prayers*.

53. Ascheson, "The English bourgeoisie" in Neal Ascheson, *Games with Shadows*, 31–35.

54. Combs, "Wives and Household Wealth."

55. See, for example, Banks, *Prosperity and Parenthood*, 86–102; Davidoff, *The Best Circles*, especially chapter 3; E. Gordon and Nair, *Public Lives*; J. Walkowitz, *City of Dreadful Delight*.

56. Warde and Tomlinson, "Taste among the Middle Classes," 254.

57. See, for instance, Berghoff, "Public Schools and the Decline of the British Economy."

58. See the interviews with former grammar school pupils in Gunn and Bell, *Middle Classes*, chapter 6. This dividing line remained socially critical with the introduction of the "eleven plus" examination and the division between grammar and secondary modern schools, following the Butler Education Act of 1944. See Simon, *Education and the Social Order, 1940–1990*.

59. Halsey, Heath, and Ridge, *Origins and Destinations*.

60. See, for example, the study by Gordon Marshall, Adam Swift, and Stephen Roberts, *Against the Odds?*, which claims to reach similar conclusions for Britain as the Oxford Project, but which interprets them much less positively.

61. P. Thompson, "Family Myth, Models, Myths and Memories in the Shaping of Individual Life-Paths."

62. Calhoun, "Postmodernism as Pseudohistory," 90.

63. In *The Hidden Injuries of Class*, coauthored with Jonathan Cobb, Richard Sennett has provided a fine example of the way in which issues of class and enduring social inequality can be pursued through studies of identity, urban space, and narrative.

64. As this implies, we need to reread the history of the English and European middle class within the context of postcolonial history. For important arguments about history, modernity, and class from a postcolonial perspective, see Chakrabarty, *Provincializing Europe*.

"Aren't We All?"

ASPIRATION, ACQUISITION, AND THE AMERICAN MIDDLE CLASS

Marina Moskowitz

The American middle class is both large and invisible. Large, unquestionably, because over the generations since the 1940s, an overwhelming majority of Americans have claimed membership in the middle class. Invisible, because what meaningful spectrum can be divided in such a way that its "middle" constitutes the vast majority of its whole? The polling statistics that document the breadth of the middle class in the United States also seem to uphold the limits to which class is a useful category in delineating American society. Still, perhaps this elephant in the room in fact demands that we consider what class means to this broad middle, rather than ignoring, or even dismissing, its monolithic presence.[1]

In 1940, *Fortune* magazine published, and publicized, a poll in which 79 percent of its representative sample identified themselves as belonging to the middle class. In more recent surveys, upward of 90 percent have considered themselves to constitute this expanding group.[2] Debates arise over the validity of self-identification as a means of classification along socioeconomic lines. For example, Robert Lynd, coauthor of the landmark survey of American society, *Middletown*, cautioned against "subjective self-rating" as the basis for class delineation, but nonetheless cited the *Fortune* statistics as fodder for social scientists.[3] In his 1935 study of the American middle class, Alfred Bingham defends self-evaluation as the criterion for categorization, writing: "We are what we think we are. And if the bulk of the people, in a modern capitalist country like the United States, thinking of themselves as being of the middle class, having interests between those of 'capital' and 'labor,' then there is such a middle class or middle group of classes."[4] In this chapter, I am less interested in whether or not self-identification results in "valid" patterns of class status recognized by traditional theorists and social analysts, than in what the term "middle class" represents to those who claim membership in it. Certainly, the prevalence of this assertion of middle-class identity is revealing in terms of social experience and as such has provided the impetus for varied studies of the middle class, from Lynd's postwar lectures on the topic, to John Gilkeson's 1986 community study of Providence, Rhode Island, in the nineteenth and early twentieth centuries, to Jeffrey Hornstein's recent study of realtors and the meaning of property in twentieth-century America.[5]

If the *Fortune* survey was the bellwether for a twentieth-century trend of middle-class affiliation, it can also be seen as the culmination of a generation spent representing the middling sorts, particularly in the realm of print culture. Over the course of the early twentieth century, a broad cross-section of American authors, writing for literary, popular, and academic audiences, set out to describe the American middle class. They often saw themselves as part of this central group, existing, in socioeconomic terms, between those who financed the nation's industrial productivity and those who tended the production lines. Indeed Sherwood Anderson, author of the acclaimed *Winesburg, Ohio* (1919), wrote in a letter to his future wife, "Surely in this situation, capital on one side and labor on the other, there should be a place for the artist who wants merely to be open-eyed, to receive impressions and make his pictures, wanting to serve only the central inner story and not one side or the other."[6]

The social relationships of the industrial era had been a growing concern in the United States, particularly in the years following the Civil War. Many Americans held ambivalent views about the course of industrialization, on the one hand benefiting from the seemingly secure footing for the national economy and material comforts, while on the other hand, hoping to contain its physical presence and social influence. The widening gap between the richest and poorest strata of the country, and their access to political influence, economic security, and consumer goods, was increasingly apparent to the reformers of what is now known as the Progressive Era. Characterized broadly as an "age of reform" or "search for order" by historians, the first generation of the twentieth century saw a rise in the civic concern of the managerial classes.[7] They sought to apply the mediating and managerial roles they had learned in industrial settings to everyday life. Starting in the last quarter of the nineteenth century and continuing into the twentieth, middle-class reformers and statisticians studied budgets, costs of living, housing, and domestic relationships, particularly of the American working classes.

In their initial aim of documenting the society that they hoped to improve, progressive reformers' work was underpinned by the burgeoning work of the social sciences. Early studies, such as Helen Campbell's *Prisoners of Poverty* (1887), Walter Wyckoff's *The Workers* (1897), and Robert Chapin's *The Standard of Living of Workingmen's Families in New York* (1909), concentrated on the working class, but by the 1910s and 1920s, studies of middle-class living standards and household budgets were common in sources ranging from Robert S. Lynd and Helen Merrell Lynd's classic text, *Middletown*, to women's magazines. Social scientists began using the methods of observation and analysis that they had developed while studying other nations, cultures, and classes for projects closer to home. Anthropologists, sociologists, and economists grew more likely to turn their trained eyes on groups similar to themselves, sometimes at very close range, such as Jessica Peixotto's groundbreaking study *Getting and Spending at the Professional Standard of Living*, which focused on academics at her own institution, the University of California, Berkeley.[8] It is perhaps not surprising that as the middle class grew, it would also become the object of academic study, but this trend did raise a challenge for those completing the research; as Lynd said, tacitly assuming the middle-class status of his peers, "in trying to think about [the] mid[dle] class objectively—all of us have to try to achieve a stance outside ourselves."[9]

Analyses and representations of the middle class were not confined to academic journals and textbooks but were mirrored in popular forms of print culture as well, whether articles on the family budget in domestic magazines, prescriptive literature such as household management or etiquette manuals, or in fiction. The early twentieth century also witnessed a huge boom in the American publishing industry, which produced copious numbers of magazine stories and novels depicting middle-class life. This "social fiction" followed the lives of male and female clerks, managers, professionals, and their families through their daily routines.[10] Authors who had trained as journalists to observe and report, much as their counterparts in the social sciences had, joined with those of the realist literary tradition to create what one contemporary critic called "the literature of national introspection."[11]

All of these texts helped to identify and unite the middle class at the beginning of the twentieth century; at the beginning of the twenty-first, they encourage a recasting of class as a category of social experience rather than measurable status. Writing what Anderson called "the central inner story," these authors describe the experience of class status from within rather than limn it from without. Thus, a backward glance at these authors provides a useful model. Reading the varied literature of the early twentieth century, three themes emerge: class was understood as a cultural designation, not just a strictly economic one; class could be cohesive rather than stratifying; and class was understood on a national scale, as much as in local communities. By considering class in these ways, we can begin to understand how and why so many Americans wish to come together under the umbrella of the middle class. In order to make sense of this group, the category of class must be considered in terms beyond its link to measurable socioeconomic conditions, just as recent cultural history and theory have reconsidered the categories of race and gender beyond the biological or physiognomic characteristics that originally defined them.[12] Looking at class as a social and cultural construct as well as a financial or political one, we may begin to capture not only how class is defined but also how it is experienced.

Although class is certainly a socioeconomic categorization, writings of the early twentieth century look beyond measurable financial criteria to describe the affinities of groups united by class status. Of course, economic attainment is a factor, but not an exclusive one; in particular, annual income based on wages or salary is a limited measure for assigning class status. As the sociologist Robert Chapin, an expert on the different living standards of Americans, wrote: "It goes without saying that the standard of living attained does not depend simply upon income."[13] In seeking a more useful measure, some critics looked to occupational groupings as a basis for class status. For example, in *Middletown* the Lynds drew one primary class distinction between what they termed the working class and the business class: "Members of the first group, by and large, address their activities in getting their living primarily to things, utilizing material tools in the making of things and the performance of services, while the members of the second group address their activities predominantly to people in the selling or promoting of things, services, and ideas."[14] Still, although the working class and business class were categorized by their modes of work, these terms were in essence a shorthand reference to two different systems of organizing daily life.

The authors were as concerned with how income was spent as how it was earned. Lynd himself discussed the limitations of both income and occupation as "a sure basis for class identity in our society."[15] In his view, varied and variable costs of living required a more refined measure than income, while occupational designations encompassed too broad a range of earnings and experience. Shared income level could also mask diversity in consumer choice that might betray significant differences in the ways in which daily life was carried out. In descriptions of household contents and décor, the Lynds showed how different priorities between families of the same income level might be encapsulated in their material surroundings: "There is less likely to be a radio than in the more prosperous working class home, but one may come upon a copy of Whistler's portrait of his mother or a water-color landscape and a set of Dickens or Irving in a worn binding; the rugs are often more threadbare than those in the living room of a foreman, but text-books of a missionary society or of a study section of the Woman's Club are lying on the mission library table."[16] Here, the Lynds seem to pit the technology and home furnishings of the working class against the cultural expressions and continuing education of the business class as priorities for expenditure. The Lynds' emphasis on books in particular as material and intellectual markers of the business class suggests that they saw their readers as members of this numerically small but culturally significant group, in which the authors themselves were placed by means of their occupational status, among other possible traits.

The authors of such studies could see themselves reflected not just in their projected audience but even in their subjects. As a community study of a professional group, Jessica Peixotto's work on her fellow Berkeley professors separated studies of their actual family budgets from the standard of living they hoped to achieve. Although she did chart the former, she found that salaries in the field were not a good indication of the growing expectation for academics to share the quality of life of a more general professional culture. Peixotto believed that academics were culturally valued in American society, writing: "Not only does the public want the class; it wants the members of the profession to look like other people; to behave like other people; to take their place on even terms with other professionals."[17] In short, academics were expected to share markers of class status with other professional or middle-class groups, but their earnings were almost always outpaced by other fields. As among the lowest paid of the salaried professionals, academics proved to be the perfect test case for explaining class distinctions based on organization of daily life, rather than income.[18]

If income and occupational grouping, traditional markers of economic distinction, were not enough to designate class, what needed to be added to the mix? Peixotto showed that her peers' middle-class status stemmed from cultural rather than financial capital. The budgetary, social, and literary studies of the early twentieth century suggest that class is formed from the sharing of cultural attributes, as much as it is informed by the differentiation of economic, social, and political position. Although culture can be as slippery a term as class itself, I (and the authors on whom I draw) refer to the myriad productions—material life, domestic organization, foodways, print, technology, art, religion, legal codes, to name some important examples—that a group creates to express itself and its beliefs. The creation, consumption, prioritizing, and ordering of these cultural productions provide means of expressing affinities among groups of people and, thus, ways of establishing communities that are identified as classes. The cultural markers of daily life are ways to "look like" or "behave like" other people and therefore identify oneself as a member of a particular class. Thus, the relationships of production, on which class distinction can rest, encompass cultural production. The middling sort did not always have control over others' labor; they were not always political leaders; nor were they the wealthiest echelon of any given community. Increasingly, however, the middling sort claimed access to cultural productions that were also important, if perhaps less obvious, as avenues to power.

If class is recast as a socioeconomic group defined by the cultural productions its members share, then identification with a particular class status becomes more accessible than it might otherwise be. This model of class consolidation is based on the connective tissue that binds a group together rather than the circumstances that set it apart from other groups. Thinking about a class in terms of cohesion rather than distinction (though perhaps somewhat counterintuitive) helps to explain why such a large swath of the American population claims a place in the middle. Clearly, many Americans have chosen to prioritize the bonds they do share rather than the admitted internal disparities that such a large group would of necessity display. The emergence of this sense of cohesion, of a widely shared American pattern of daily life and access to the cultural markers that defined class status, was born, ironically, out of an era of discord stretching from the Civil War into the early twentieth century. The Gilded Age and Progressive Era witnessed a variety of conflicts, often along the fault lines of class, race, ethnicity, and gender, which at their core focused on issues of access to and achievement of a shared quality of life. Whoever the agents of these struggles, whether large-scale labor uprisings or conflicts over Jim Crow laws, the varied sides shared a conviction that an American standard of living did exist.

In the early twentieth century, many cultural critics commented on this increasingly shared ideal of the expectations of daily life, which encompassed not only material goods but also access to education, leisure activities, the ability to save, and numerous other facets of social and economic standing. This ideal was not perceived as the pinnacle of attainment but as a middle-class standard.[19] In trying to explain the level or degree of this status, social scientists categorized different strata of daily life in the United States; although different authors used slightly different rhetoric, a common scheme enumerated four planes of daily life: subsistence, convenience, comfort, and luxury. The essayist F. Spencer Baldwin defined these terms as early as 1899: "A necessary is something indispensable to physical health; a convenience is something that relieves from slight pain or annoyance . . . ; a comfort . . . is a common and inexpensive means of enjoyment; a luxury . . . is an unusual and expensive means of enjoyment."[20] Middle-class life was said to correspond to the level of comfort. Peixotto referred to the "comfort standard" as the "new single standard" in the United States.[21] The economist Simon Patten concurred, considering the middle class as the standard bearers for normative American consumption patterns.[22] Thus, the comfort attained by the American middle class was widely represented as a national way of life.

Still, in referring to the "comfort standard" as a national ideal, Baldwin, Peixotto, Patten, and their peers were certainly not saying that the majority of Americans lived in the same degree of comfort. The ideal of a comfortable quality of life was widely shared, even if the attainment of that ideal was not; these shared expectations were enough to provide cohesion to a broad group of people. All of these authors pointed to aspiration as the key to consolidating the American middle class. Although of course a small percentage of the population lived well above the comfort standard, and another larger percentage lived at a plane so far below it as to not have sensed its existence, this notion of aspiration made middle-class ideals available to many. As the economist Ira Wile explained: "It is but natural that aspiration, imitation, and emulation should serve as incentives to raise the lower standards to the higher levels."[23] Wile's contemporary Frank Streightoff agreed, noting the "inborn spirit of emulation" that Americans possessed.[24] Even if they exhibited a wide variety in material, financial, and social attainment, Americans would be drawn together in agreement on what they were hoping to attain. During the twentieth century, representations of middle-class life were broadcast through a variety of media, starting with print culture and extending to other communications media, such as radio, film, and television, in both programming and advertising. Whatever their level of consumer spending, ratio of work to leisure time, or domestic organization, many Americans had some access to these representations and thus were able to share in the broad understanding of what it meant to be middle class. The economist Hazel Kyrk noted that the spectrum of Americans' spending habits was in quantity rather than type, showing that many had the same vision of what items should be included in the household budget, even if their purchasing power varied. As she wrote in *Economic Problems of the Family*: "Another marked characteristic of American consumption habits is their similarity from class to class. Variations are not in kind, merely in degree. This is the result of a democratization process that is the product not only of the social and political structure but of an educational system which was to some extent deliberately planned for this purpose."[25] Although Kyrk pointed to American education as the mechanism for inculcating a middle-class standard of living, many of her peers looked to a more tangible mechanism: the widespread acceptance and availability of credit. If Wile pointed to "aspiration, imitation, and emulation" as one means of identifying with the middle class, he also recognized the influence of credit arrangements. As he explained to a national conference on home economics in 1913, "the installment business has made possible the acquisition of well-furnished homes that would otherwise be impossible."[26] The Lynds also commented on the trend toward paying by installment, "which turns wishes into horses overnight."[27] Although networks of credit had existed in local contexts for generations, these systems gradually became codified business practices rather than individual, face-to-face arrangements between buyers and sellers.[28] The twin cultural and financial mechanisms of emulation and credit explain how aspiration enables a broad swath of the population, with potentially limited financial resources, to consider themselves members of the middle class.

But what about the "upper" end of the broad middle? Why does aspiration explain a desire to claim middle-class status, but not a desire to achieve an elite status? I believe there are two answers to these questions. The first stems from the planes of living described above. Building on a long-standing skepticism of luxury, many Americans seem uncomfortable admitting to the "unusual and expensive means of enjoyment" that Baldwin outlined. The concern with the increased social and economic stratification in the United States that found such a receptive audience in the Progressive Era has not abated, nor has that stratification. Claiming membership in the middle class and a cohesive relationship with a broad sector of the American population prioritizes a shared cultural influence over a disparity in economic and political power. At the same time, a claim to middle-class status is justified because the shared ideal of the standard of living is dynamic, and usually pitched just ahead of broad attainment. As Wile wrote: "Standards level upwards. The luxuries of yesterday are the necessities of today . . . There is no absolute standard of living save as an ideal; and when the highest standards of today are realized, they will fall short of the standards that will then be used."[29] Thus, the upper reaches of the middle class may always stretch the boundaries of their community and retain their place within it. For these reasons what binds the group together is as important as what sets it apart from others, and helps explain the overwhelming self-identification of the middle class.

The broad self-identification of middle-class status that blossomed in the twentieth century had one additional precondition: the ability for Americans to understand their place in a national context. For many Americans, the multiple small settings of daily life did not (and do not) provide exposure to the socioeconomic diversity of the nation. In their attempt to characterize "typical" Americans in *Middletown*, the Lynds in fact struggled with how the middle class was defined. They used a binary class division, between the business and working classes, as the central distinction in Muncie's population. The Lynds avoided the tripartite designations of lower, middle, and upper class as not truly representing the experience of daily life in Muncie. Their rejection of the tripartite class divisions, despite encouragement from their advisors to use them, stemmed primarily from their belief that in a town the size and stature of Muncie, there was no true upper class, as might have existed in a metropolitan area.[30] In order to perceive of themselves as residing in the middle of a larger socioeconomic and cultural spectrum, the citizens of Muncie would also need to take a broader, perhaps national, view of the community they inhabited. Since the beginning of the twentieth century, Americans have turned to the myriad examples of national culture that they do encounter daily in order to establish their sense of being "in the middle."

Cultural markers of American life, such as dress, domestic organization, working patterns, leisure activities, or even local legal codes, began to transcend regional variation due to national media outlets, transportation technology, and internal migration. This increasingly national culture allowed Americans to see themselves in a broader context than previous generations had. In particular, the distinctions between urban and rural societies were eroding. The home economist Christine Frederick discussed this fluidity in terms of consumer behavior, writing in 1924: "The farm woman once wore little else but gingham and alpaca. She buys copies of Fifth Avenue models today, and her daughter, whose face was innocent of aught but freckles, now possesses the standard female laboratory of toilet articles."[31] As before, these cultural changes were charted not only in academic texts but also in popular fiction. The popular writer Edna Ferber conveyed the same sentiment as Frederick's in her depiction of the fictional town of Winnebago, a "little Mid-Western town." Ferber described the residents: "The Winnebagoans seem to know what is being served and worn, from salad to veilings, surprisingly soon after New York has informed itself of those subjects."[32] In a variety of media Americans were being told that they were increasingly alike from coast to coast. These shared patterns of daily life were particularly important in providing a sense of middle-class identity in the towns and small cities in which the majority of Americans lived, where the gradations of socioeconomic status may have been less apparent. Widespread self-identification as members of the middle class arose from association and comparison on a national level.

The broad self-identification of middle-class status that has characterized American society in the twentieth century also may betray a pride in how that status compares to other nations. Again, Americans have tended to choose not the pinnacle but the average of American life to hold up as an example. As early as 1907, the essayist Joseph Jacobs envisioned how such national comparisons of quality of life could be made. Writing in the *American Magazine*, Jacobs imagined "The Middle American," whose typicality derived from the median of every measurable facet of life, from personal statistics such as height and weight, to residential location within the United States, to income. Jacobs explained his purpose in carrying out such an exercise: "The value of such a figure, if we could obtain it, is great, especially for comparative purposes . . . To compare the bulk of one nation with another, our only method seems to be to compare the Middle Man of each nation with that of the other."[33] Jacobs's essay showed one more appeal of middle-class identity: the opportunity to represent the nation. In a very recent representation of American life, the television series *The West Wing*, the fictional politicians debate whether or not the term "average American" will be perceived as "pejorative." One character insists: "This may come as a shock to you, but 80 percent of the people in this country would use the word 'average' to describe themselves. They do not find the term deprecating. Indeed being considered an average American is something they find to be positive and comforting."[34] Whether or not the screenwriter Aaron Sorkin based these lines on actual polls, they do ring true in a nation in which such a large majority identifies with the middle class. Fifty years earlier, Robert Lynd pointed to this satisfaction with a middling lot in life as an American characteristic. He wrote of the middle class: "We Americans have never been wont to regard it as a term of reproach, our feeling being: 'Aren't we all?' "[35] Clearly, the vast majority of Americans agree.

Notes

This chapter was previously published in *Considering Class: Essays on the Discourse of the American Dream*, edited by Kevin Cahill and Lene Johannessen (Berlin: LitVerlag, 2007).

1. My use of the term "elephant in the room" refers specifically to the middle class and its dominant, but often unconsidered, presence in American society. For a broader discussion of the category of class itself as the "elephant in the room," an unexplored terrain in social and cultural analysis of the United States, see bell hooks, *Where We Stand*.

2. "The Fortune Survey," *Fortune* 21 (February 1940), 14. J. Anthony Lukas cites a 1991 survey in which 93 percent of Americans polled perceived of themselves as members of the middle class; see *Big Trouble*, 13. See also, Igo, *The Averaged American*.

3. Robert S. Lynd, Lecture Notes, "Role of the Middle Class in Contemporary Social Change," John Reed Society, Harvard University, November 3, 1947, 5, Container 2, Reel 1, File: Lectures, outlines, notes, Robert and Helen Merrell Lynd Papers, Manuscript Division, Library of Congress, Washington, DC. (In subsequent references, this archival collection will be designated "LP.")

4. Bingham, *Insurgent America*, 47.

5. Lynd, Lecture Notes, 5; John S. Gilkeson Jr., *Middle-Class Providence, 1820–1940*; Hornstein, *A Nation of Realtors*.

6. Anderson, *Sherwood Anderson's Love Letters to Eleanor Copenhaver*, 37.

7. I take these terms from two classic works on the Progressive Era: Hofstadter, *The Age of Reform*, and Wiebe, *The Search for Order, 1877–1920*.

8. Peixotto, *Getting and Spending at the Professional Standard of Living*, vii. Similar studies of other universities include Y. Henderson and Davie, *Incomes and Living Costs of a University Faculty* and John H. McNeely, *Salaries in Land-grant Universities and Colleges*.

9. Lynd, Lecture Notes, 3.

10. I have borrowed the useful term "social fiction" from the historian and bibliographer Archibald Hanna; his *Mirror for the Nation* is an invaluable tool for locating fiction documenting the middle class. For additional background on the publishing industry, the middle class, and the culture of books and reading, see Minter, *A Cultural History of the American Novel*; Rubin, *The Making of Middlebrow Culture*; J. West, *American Authors and the Literary Marketplace*.

11. Maxwell Lerner, review of *Middletown*, clipping, Container 12, File: Middletown Reviews, LP.

12. See, for example, J. Scott, *Gender and the Politics of History*; Riley, *"Am I That Name?"*; Bederman, *Manliness & Civilization*; Carnes and Griffen, *Meanings for Manhood*; Omi and Winant, *Racial Formation in the United States*; Jacobson, *Whiteness of a Different Color*.

13. Chapin, "The Influence of Income on Standards of Life," 638.

14. Lynd and Lynd, *Middletown*, 22. The organization of *Middletown* is the first clue to the place that work experience occupied in the Lynds' estimation. Although "Getting a Living" was the starting point for the book, it was only one of six major categories of daily life experience that defined the community; the others were: "Making a Home," "Training the Young," "Using Leisure," "Engaging in Religious Practices," and "Engaging in Community Activities."

15. Lynd, Lecture Notes, 7.

16. Lynd and Lynd, *Middletown*, 101–2.

17. Peixotto, *Getting and Spending at the Professional Standard of Living*, 21.

18. Ibid., viii–ix. Mary Hinman Abel ("Community and Personal Standards") discusses teachers, clerks, and ministers in this same category. See also, Kirkpatrick, *The Farmer's Standard of Living*, 202–3.

19. I have discussed this emergence of the standard of living in much greater depth in Moskowitz, *Standard of Living*.

20. Baldwin, "Some Aspects of Luxury," 155. For strikingly similar categorizations of the planes of living, see Kyrk, *Economic Problems of the Family*, 372, 387; Streightoff, *The Standard of Living among the Industrial People of America*, 2; Moran, "Ethics of Wealth," 824; Donham, "Conscious Standards," 477–78.

21. Peixotto, *Getting and Spending at the Professional Standard of Living*, viii–ix.

22. Patten, "The Standardization of Family Life," 194–95.

23. Wile, "Standards of Living," 410; Eliot, Introduction to "The Standardization of Family Life," 194; Patten, "The Standardization of Family Life," 194–95; Kyrk, *Economic Problems of the Family*, 381.

24. Streightoff, *The Standard of Living among the Industrial People of America*, 2.

25. Kyrk, *Economic Problems of the Family*, 381.

26. Wile, "Standards of Living," 417. See also Kyrk, *Economic Problems of the Family*, 424–25; Peixotto, *Getting and Spending at the Professional Standard of Living*, viii–ix.

27. Lynd and Lynd, *Middletown*, 82. See also 81–82, especially note 18.

28. For a more thorough discussion of consumer credit, see Calder, *Financing the American Dream*; and Olney, *Buy Now, Pay Later*.

29. Wile, "Standards of Living," 410–11. See also, Baldwin, "Some Aspects of Luxury," 155; Kyrk *Economic Problems of the Family*, 376; Streightoff, *The Standard of Living among the Industrial People of America*, 2; Abel, "Community and Personal Standards," 183.

30. Lynd and Lynd, *Middletown*, 22–23 (see especially note 3). See also Galen Fisher, "Notes on Small City Manuscript," May 6, 1927, and S. Went, "General Comments," May 5, 1927, both in Container 7, File: Comments on Manuscript, LP.

31. C. Frederick, "New Wealth, New Standards of Living and Changed Family Budgets," 79. See also Kirkpatrick, *The Farmer's Standard of Living*, 6–8 and passim.

32. Ferber, *Fanny Herself*, 52–53.

33. Jacobs, "The Middle American," 526.

34. *The West Wing*, season 1, episode 21, "Lies, Damn Lies, and Statistics." written by Aaron Sorkin, directed by Don Scardino.

35. Lynd, Lecture Notes, 3.

The Gatekeepers

MIDDLE-CLASS CAMPAIGNS OF CITIZENSHIP IN EARLY COLD WAR CANADA

Franca Iacovetta

In anticipation of and then in response to the huge volume of immigration into Canada after the Second World War, especially from war-torn Europe, and the rise of the Cold War, a wide variety of mostly middle-class Canadians mobilized resources to integrate a mass of embattled, stateless, and impoverished people into the Canadian mainstream. They developed strategies and ran campaigns aimed at transforming these "new Canadians," to use a popular term of the era, into what they envisioned as fit and proper democracy-practicing citizens ready for life in a modern capitalist society. These citizenship gatekeepers included professional social workers, mental health experts, and government officials as well as journalists, nutritionists, public health nurses, teachers, and the civic-minded volunteers of the country's many women's groups, male service clubs, youth troupes, settlement houses, and other community organizations.

In the push particularly to have the Europeans conform to "Canadian ways," the emphasis was on everything from food customs, child rearing, marriage, and family dynamics to participatory democracy, kitchen consumerism, and anti-Communist activism. The gatekeepers' varied activities occurred in a highly charged postwar context, where social optimism and rising expectations based on Canada's strong postwar economy and expanding welfare state were mixed with deep-seated fears of Communism and nuclear fallout, and rising anxiety about unemployment, poor marriages, fragile families, juvenile delinquency, failing health, mental illness, and an increase in sexual deviance of all kinds. A pluralist ideology that showed a certain respect for immigrant cultural customs and contributions to the Canadian "mosaic" also gained considerable traction in these years. Together, mass migration and the Cold War transformed Canada into both a more decidedly multiethnic, or pluralist, society and a national security state that was on high alert and poised to contain or eliminate variously defined threats to the nation's political, social, and moral order. The promotion of a bourgeois construction of citizenship within a capitalist democracy characterized by such opposing trends deeply informed Canadian nation building during the early Cold War.[1]

This essay focuses on the discourses of Canada's gatekeepers, those mostly middle-class individuals and groups—especially in English Canada—who in multiple and complex ways sought to modify the newcomers' behavior and values so that they better reflected Canadian bourgeois ideals. It draws most directly on Gramsci's concept of hegemony, Foucault's work on the role of knowledge-based professionals in normalizing bourgeois codes, and the now-extensive North American social, women and gender, gay/lesbian, and Left historical scholarship documenting the Cold War's repressive domestic side—that is, the raced, classed, and heterosexist politics of "domestic containment."[2] I have taken up the call for more carefully conducted historical excavations of the middle classes in specific times and places by providing an empirically rooted analysis of how certain historical contingencies mobilized a large segment of the Canadian bourgeoisie to make common cause in the years immediately after the Second World War.[3] Notwithstanding the differences among them, these middle-class gatekeepers shared a broad understanding of citizenship work in this period, one that considered the bodily, moral, sexual, psychological, and cultural—as well as political and ideological—features involved. Their approaches and efforts reflected and reinforced the paradoxical mix of optimism, fear, and sense of urgency that characterized the era. Canadians were influenced by the global scene, including Canada's participation in NATO and the United Nations, and also, more particularly, by their relationship to two countries: Britain, still a major source of immigrants to Canada and the inspiration for Canada's social welfare policies; and the mighty neighbor to the south, the United States, now one of the world's two superpowers, and a nation to which Canada was increasingly tied, economically and militarily, and whose culture exerted an ever-growing influence on Canada. In fact, some of the much-heralded "Canadian ways" closely resembled American models, though there were some important distinctions. An analysis of the gatekeepers' discourses of immigrant integration and citizenship sheds light on their constructions of modernity, capitalism, and democracy; on the connections between the political, social, gender, sexual, and immigrant histories of early Cold War Canada; and on the ironies, hypocrisies, and corrupted democracy of the day. I combine an analysis of what were often national discourses with a look at how they played out in a particular locale, Toronto, the single most popular immigrant destination and the site of much gatekeeper activity.

Like other immigrant-receiving nations, Canada had closed its doors to most immigrants during the Depression and the Second World War. A combination of factors—including economic self-interest; labor shortages in resource and other industries, which prompted employer demands for cheap immigrant labor; international pressures, especially from Britain, to help with the refugee crisis in Europe; and pro-refugee lobbies led by both liberal Canadians and ethnic Canadian groups—eventually convinced Canada's Liberal government to open the country's doors to some of the millions of people in Britain, Continental Europe, and elsewhere eager to emigrate after the war. Immigration into Canada after 1945 reached mass proportions. Into a geographically vast country whose population in 1941 had been only 11.5 million people, more than 2.1 million newcomers, the great majority of them whites from Britain and Europe, entered Canada between 1946 and 1962. For Canada, the early postwar era was one of almost continuous immigration. During the 1950s, the ratio of net immigration to total population growth was the largest of any decade in Canadian history, save for the 1901–11 years of mass migration to western Canada. Between 1951 and 1971, the foreign-born in Canada increased twentyfold, from a hundred thousand to about two million people. Across the country, but especially in big cities like Montreal, Vancouver, Winnipeg, and especially Toronto, which alone drew fully one-quarter of the newcomers as a whole, the Europeans attracted the lion's share of attention.

The men, women, and children who left Europe's bombed-out cities, churned up countryside, and Displaced Persons camps for Canada were part of the wider emigration to various parts of the world and represented a diverse group of refugees and volunteer immigrants. The early arrivals included 165,000 Displaced Persons (DPs)—a group that included Jews who had toiled in Nazi slave labor camps or been in the death camps but had managed to survive the Holocaust—as well as the different Slavic nationals (such as Poles and Ukrainians) and Baltic nationals (including Latvians and Lithuanians) who had refused repatriation to homelands now under Communist control. Both groups were recruited from the DP camps between 1947 and 1953 to fill labor shortages in Canadian industry. By 1965, they had been joined by another 1.5 million Continental Europeans, a group that included volunteer immigrants from West Germany (a number of whom had earlier been refugees from East Germany), war-ravaged Holland, and the impoverished rural regions of Greece, Italy, and Portugal. Another notable group of newcomers was the more than 37,000 Hungarian refugees from the failed 1956 revolt against the Communist regime in their country. A final group was the Iron Curtain or East bloc refugees who had escaped from Communist states such as Poland and Czechoslovakia and then made their way to Canada. With an average age of 24.9 years, the newcomers were a youthful group. Men initially outnumbered women, but by the early 1960s the sex ratio had grown more balanced. Because immigration often coincided with marriage and having children—though older youth like the Jewish orphans also came—the immigrant population was full of young families.[4]

Although they shared certain experiences, the European newcomers were not a homogeneous group. Most of the war brides of Canadian servicemen were British, but there were some women from Holland, Italy, and other European countries. There were the Balts, Ukrainians, Poles, and others who had suffered under both Russian and German occupation, many of them having toiled in the German-controlled factories or in the private homes of German officers and other privileged Nazis; others having been collaborators. Jewish Holocaust survivors had endured the Nazi slave labor camps, concentration camps, and death camps. There were refugee women, both Jews and gentiles, who had lost families to war and had formed surrogate families with others. Some of them were among the millions of wartime rape victims and those who had been forced to exchange sex for food in order to feed starving children or to save lives. There were class differences that distinguished the minority of the Eastern European DPs, Jews and gentiles alike, who were urban professionals, artists, and intellectuals, from the majority of the European newcomers, who came from overwhelmingly humble backgrounds, most from rural Southern and Eastern Europe. Overall, the refugee streams included a mix of people, from farmers to tradesmen and tradeswomen (such as lab technicians) and professionals, but the elites would attract a disproportionate amount of attention in Canada, and their political significance was greater than their actual numbers might suggest. Most of the newcomers were unsympathetic or opposed to Communism, a pattern reinforced by Canada's political screening procedures for potential immigrants. But there were differences even among the Eastern European DPs, between those generally opposed to Communism and the core of right-wing political émigrés who were highly aggressive cold warriors.[5]

There were plenty of Canadians who feared or balked at the growing presence of Europeans in their midst, and there were bigots who denounced the immigrants as so many traumatized, diseased, and dangerous foreigners who would destroy the country. But there were also large numbers of Canadians, including middle-class individuals and groups, who called for proactive efforts to help the newcomers with jobs, English classes, and emergency support, and to guide their adjustment to modernity and mainstream society, through "Canadianization" programs. The gatekeepers differed in their training, expertise, experience, and sensitivity; in their status, material wealth, and political clout; and in ethnicity (there were ethnic Canadians, largely of European origins, and some newcomers, who joined the gatekeepers' ranks).[6] Protestant and Catholic gatekeepers might also differ on certain matters. But although the various groups may have had some different reasons for getting involved, they generally agreed on the major aims of reception work. For example, there were obvious differences of emphasis between the urgent pleas of veteran liberal Jewish Canadian social workers like Joseph Kage of the Jewish Immigrant Aid Society in Montreal, who implored Canadians to show patience and tolerance to the "frightened strangers" from "war-torn Poland, Austria, Germany, Italy, Hungary, or Czechoslovakia" as they recovered and made their transition to a better life,[7] and the moral judgments of conservative moralists like Rev. G. Stanley Russell, a United Church minister and religious columnist for the popular *Toronto Star* newspaper, who railed against alcohol and the new women's beverage rooms, sexually candid pulp fiction from the United States, the spread of sexual promiscuity, and the *Kinsey Report*, but who also called for modern reforms in labor conditions and housing, especially for immigrants, as well as job placements, increased training opportunities, and more unemployment benefits, because the "human misery" resulting from such ills created recruits for Communism and were thus "much more menacing than anything Karl Marx ever wrote or Stalin ever said."[8] But they reached a similar conclusion about the importance of reception and citizenship work for the immigrants.

By the 1950s, social work, psychology, and the older and more prestigious field of psychiatry had made some critical gains, carving out a niche for themselves within penal, educational, and welfare institutions and family court, and now each field sought to protect and expand its influence. Professional self-interest also mattered: social workers and psychologists recognized the fragility of their new status, especially compared to psychiatrists, and both their alarmist warnings and bold claims as problem solvers partly reflected this status anxiety. Still, the different experts agreed on the major aims of reception and citizenship work.

The gatekeepers' various campaigns reflected a shared set of assumptions. One of them was the view that—in the words of the Canadian Association of Adult Education, a progressive adult literacy group—"the newcomers can make their full contribution to Canadian life only if they are happy and well-adjusted in their new surroundings."[9] The corollary was equally important: a failure to contain, guide, and incorporate the frightened, ill, vulnerable, or potentially explosive or self-destructive newcomer would produce individual anomie and social disorder. In addition, overly anxious mothers might produce defective children; alienated young men might become sexual predators, lashing out against women; psychosomatic symptoms left untreated could produce permanent mental misfits; and perennially unemployed or brutally exploited workers could become vulnerable to the seductions of Communists, especially ethnic Canadians who shared the newcomers' culture and language and plied them with Communist newspapers. Thus a shared desire for a healthy body politic—in physical and emotional as well as political, moral, and sexual terms—fueled the middle-class gatekeepers' activism. Many of the reform campaigns aimed at the newcomers were also part of wider nation-building projects to "uplift," "modernize" (as in improving medical, moral, and homemaking standards), and "contain" (as in regulating sexual behavior and children's leisure time) the whole Canadian population, though, invariably, the gatekeepers isolated the Europeans as special cases requiring more heroic remedies. Both men and women were targeted, but women, as in the past, were more vulnerable to moral blame.

Of course, immigration alone would have generated Canadianization programs, but the Cold War added great urgency to the citizenship cause. Citizenship as a construct and process does not merely confer political and legal status on individuals, who are then permitted to enjoy certain social entitlements. It also operates as ideology and requires citizens and potential citizens to engage in self-discipline and self-censorship, not only out of a fear that transgressing dominant social or moral norms will invite censure or punishment, but also out of a desire to belong and to reap the rewards that come with obedience and conformity to the rules.

Many of Canada's postwar experts operated within a dominant paradigm that normalized conventional bourgeois ideals of proper gender roles, the family, and sexual behavior and that sought to cultivate good citizens who would be as cognizant of their civic duties to the state and wider society as of their individual rights and social benefits. The Canadian state adopted an expansive welfare system after the Second World War as a way of cushioning the many inequities produced by capitalism. The list of compensatory rights and social security entitlements was increased in the greater interest of encouraging continuing obedience to the needs and demands of the economic order and its ruling elites. The tensions inherent in a conception of modern citizenship that contained the contradictory pulls of individual rights and social welfare guarantees, as well as a principle of participatory democracy, were much in evidence in early postwar Canada, as its gatekeepers sought to politically incorporate a large foreign and, in the case of those from peripheral rural Europe, "backward" population. Paradoxically, the middle-class gatekeepers both envisioned the ideal citizen as a thinking person, warning against the dangers of a complacent citizenry, and also subscribed to the era's Cold War consensus, which discouraged political criticism and, in its right-wing version, dubbed criticism of the government treason. A handful of leftist (social democrat) and left-liberal groups stood against the tide and argued that repressing dissent posed the greatest danger of all to democracy, though they too were anti-Communist. There was a tiny minority of radical gatekeepers, particularly some social workers involved in child resettlement and other programs, but they had no appreciable impact on their profession's paradigms, which largely associated conformity to mainstream norms with being well adjusted.

The paradoxical mix of optimism and anxiety was a hallmark of the gatekeepers' discourses. In their speeches, news reports, and government publications, they stressed the huge gap between a postwar Europe "in ruins" and, in the east, "under red slavery," and the abundance and freedom of Western capitalist countries like Canada, but they worried about the newcomers' lack of experience with participatory democracy. They applauded the Europeans for choosing democracy over totalitarianism, whether of the Right (as in Italian or German fascism) or the Left (Communism), but they worried about the additional burdens that a mass of war-weary or impoverished people would add to the already daunting task of national reconstruction. They boldly declared that the newcomers' access to Canada's expanded social welfare services and to the experts' latest problem-solving remedies would permit their full recovery and facilitate their full integration and citizenship. But they also fretted about the newcomers' physical, mental, and sexual morality and their capacity for modern marriage and parenthood and warned that their failure to adapt would threaten Canadian values and mores and compound the challenging task of affecting a "return to normalcy"—a phrase that came to represent the efforts to "return" people, especially women who had worked during the war or enjoyed some independence, back into the family fold, and back to a supposedly more simple and moral way of life. How did this dialectical brew of optimism, anxiety, and contradiction play itself out in the gatekeepers' approaches and efforts to reshape the lives of newcomers along more bourgeois models? Even a brief look at some of the major arenas of activity captures some of the complex and competing dynamics produced.

Let me turn first to the issue of democratic citizenship. The political gatekeepers included senior officials and frontline liaison officers in the federal government's newly created Canadian Citizenship Branch, as well as volunteer groups like the Imperial Order Daughters of the Empire (IODE), a patriotic middle-class women's group that pushed for more-stringent citizenship requirements and organized elaborate citizenship ceremonies, the better to mark the importance of these events for the newly enfranchised. The leading citizenship official was Vladimir Kaye, a Ukrainian-Canadian academic who was an active leader of the nationalist, anti-Communist Ukrainian Canadian organizations, a committed cold warrior, and the chief liaison officer and head of the foreign-press section of the Citizenship Branch. Kaye and his colleagues in the branch portrayed themselves as enlightened liberal integrationists who, unlike earlier assimilationists, would guide, not dictate, newcomers' adaptation to Canadian society. In speeches and publications, Kaye offered many versions of an ideal integration scenario, which in fact contained a good dose of the old assimilationist impulse. He insisted, for example, that each newcomer, regardless of class, cultural, or political background, "must go through a change which affects his body and soul—changes of climate, diet, change of culture, change of . . . his whole behaviour to the new system of values."[10]

The branch's many publications also revealed the ideological agenda of the ruling elite, which encouraged new groups to display their cultural differences as long as they adapted to Canadian political and social norms and accepted established authority. When discussing citizenship, senior branch officials like R. Alex Sim were fond of making lofty claims, asserting, for instance, that the superior Canadian approach to integrating immigrants reflected a continuing commitment to the liberal principles of freedom, tolerance, and understanding that had made Canada a society capable of such "highly civilized accomplishments." He also asserted the right of the dominant majority to enrich itself by mining the best of the immigrants' cultures and declared that the new groups "could flourish and grow" as long as they did so in a manner that "does not alter the larger dominant group in a destructive way."[11]

Canada's citizenship officials worked with ethnic Canadian organizations, except Communist ones, on the grounds that already Canadianized groups, especially those led by accomplished or influential leaders, could ease the acculturation process by providing war-weary or emotionally damaged newcomers with information in their own language, material aid, and psychological and social support. Branch officers worked with and gave support to mainstream ethnic groups like the Canadian Polish Congress and the Ukrainian Canadian Committee. The branch supplied these groups with "democratic" Canadian material for their newspapers, such as immigrant success stories and social service information, and helped create an ethnic press club than enhanced the editors' clout. Such efforts also helped to provide a defense against alienation or disorder that could endanger Canada's social fabric and entail huge health costs. Although these were not solely Cold War goals, this activity fit in well with the state's national security aim of ensuring a contented and conformist citizenry. It also enhanced the status of the mostly European ethnic elites, whose later claims to represent the country's "third force" (after the English and French founding nations) influenced the adoption of official multiculturalism in 1971.

There were also overtly ideological campaigns carried out by the Citizenship Branch, the Royal Canadian Mounted Police security forces, and a variety of willing civilian groups in the name of integration and democratic citizenship. During the war, Kaye worked in the precursor to the Citizenship Branch, the wartime Nationalities Branch, which had engaged in political surveillance of the ethnic left-wing press as well as in efforts to rally ethnic Canadians to the war effort. After the war, he continued with these activities. The Citizenship Branch worked with the mostly male elites in both the older ethnic Canadian organizations and the new immigrant mainstream, and with anti-Communist groups and communities, in an effort to combat Communism and undermine and discredit left-wing ethnic Canadian groups and their newspapers. Many of these papers had been established in the early twentieth century by Ukrainian, Jewish, and other immigrants and were now being run by these aging radicals or their Canadian-born successors. Kaye especially railed against the infiltration techniques of Slavic Communists. In response, the branch, with the help of journalists, openly denounced the Communist press, directly encouraged the anti-Communist newcomers, especially well-educated Eastern European refugees, to start their own newspapers and then sought to bolster their role as "democratic tools" of integration by, again, supplying editors with appropriately Canadian "democratic" material. In 1950, Kaye happily reported that Toronto, which had become home to "practically the whole Communist Foreign Language press" after the war, was already witnessing a rapid increase of anti-Communist papers; there had been thirteen Communist papers, but they were now outnumbered by twenty-five new, mostly anti-Communist publications, whose presence Kaye attributed to the concentration of postwar newcomers in the province.[12] The branch's translation service tracked the ethnic press in order to monitor political trends and manipulate the bitter ideological battles that occurred, especially within deeply polarized ethnic groups like the Ukrainians. The charges of collaboration that Communist Ukrainians hurled at certain Ukrainian DPs fuelled explosive intra-ethnic debates as well as tensions between Jews and Ukrainians.

Canadian middle-class women's groups, such as the IODE and the Catholic Women's League, and business organizations, such as the Chambers of Commerce, joined in these campaigns. They funded reception projects and the *Canadian Scene*, the press repository of Canadian news clippings and stories meant to counteract the heavily European content of the ethnic newspapers and ensure that they were promoting democracy in appropriate ways; helped the police with the blacklisting of Canadians suspected of being Communists; entered into anti-Communist alliances with politically active Eastern European refugees; and helped to run the Communist Alert Services, which printed and distributed fliers and pamphlets informing ordinary citizens about nefarious Communist activities at home and abroad. They created platforms for the testimonials of refugee newcomers, who delivered heart-wrenching stories of living conditions in Communist regimes and warned Canadians away from all progressive causes. In this way, the gatekeepers forged alliances with some of the most right-wing émigrés in the country, some of whom belonged to nationalist governments in exile and were primarily interested in using Canada as a base from which to regroup, defeat Communism with the help of the West, and return home to regain political power. These refugees took every opportunity given them as "new Canadians" to tell Canadians that they knew from firsthand experience, or from loved ones who had been imprisoned or murdered back home, how evil Communism was, and to impress on them the necessity of quashing any views and activities that even remotely resembled Communist ones. They offered a mix of compelling stories of Communist oppression and right-wing critiques of freedom of speech. Nor were they afraid to use violent language: the Ukrainian, Byelorussian, Hungarian, Slovak, Croatian, and Latvian speakers who took the stage at a major rally held in Toronto in 1950 for one of these groups, the Anti-Bolshevik Block of Nations, declared they would not rest until they had annihilated the Russians and liquidated every Bolshevik who got in their way. Such politicized refugees could influence Canada's democratic culture by carrying out their own anti-Communist activities. Citizenship and Cold War agendas converged, as evidenced by the many citizenship ceremonies at which Canadian judges praised the refugees of Communism as best appreciating the rights and freedoms they now enjoyed.

The IODE was especially eager to rally Canadian women, native-born and newcomer alike, to the anti-Communist cause, calling it essential democratic work. A politically conservative but reform-oriented middle-class women's group, the IODE upheld the family values ideology and heightened domesticity of the era while calling on all women, including housewives, to become involved in campaigns to help the immigrants. The IODE's members supported immigrant agencies and occasionally "adopted" a struggling immigrant family and paid all their bills. They also aimed to create a more informed and active female citizenry, urging women to vote against Communist and other leftist candidates in all elections, to spy and report on their neighbors, and to denounce the Canadian peace movement and the women—variously described as naive or dangerous—who supported this Soviet front. The group's magazine, *Echoes*, offers some striking female images, including that of a Canadian housewife with a broom sweeping Communism out of her kitchen and the entire globe.[13]

The cultural arena, another site of much activity, was where liberal pluralism flourished most. Culture was a highly charged political terrain, but in this era it was also a comparatively safe one on which Canadians could respect "difference" without challenging class and racial hierarchies. As integrationists, many gatekeepers advocated a pluralist approach that encouraged immigrants to celebrate their cultural distinctiveness, and these gatekeepers ran cultural events and programs meant to encourage mutual understanding and cultural exchange between established and new Canadians. For government officials like Kaye, a key concern was to find ways of fostering a sense of national unity within the context of an increasingly ethnically diverse population. In recognition of this challenge, the ruling Liberal Party had passed a Canadian Citizenship Act in 1947 that defined Canadian citizenship not in terms of (English or French) founding races or blood ties but as a set of "Canadian" values—including tolerance and mutual respect—that everyone could be loyal to.

The International Institute of Toronto, a multilingual immigrant social agency organized many interethnic cultural events. These included carnivals where one could sample foods from different lands and Old World fairs that sold ethnic handicrafts, as well as international musical concerts with Lithuanian and Hungarian choral groups, Polish and Greek pianists, Italian opera singers; and the folk-dancing shows where colorfully costumed troupes demonstrated their national dances and got the spectators to join in. By the early 1960s, the institute was helping to organize "musical extravaganzas" and international folk festivals that, as its director put it, were "major multicultural events . . . celebrating the Canadian mosaic."[14] To attract the desired mix of immigrant, ethnic, and Anglo-Canadians to their events, the institute's staff spoke of the value of bringing immigrants out of their isolation to perform for and mingle with other Canadians, of making better citizens of old and new Canadians alike, and of encouraging in everyone a more cosmopolitan form of global citizenship, this last comment reflecting a United Nations–style liberal internationalism. Indeed, the staff declared that by facilitating "greater mutual understanding and co-operation between Canadians and newcomers," they were building an international community, or local United Nations, in Toronto that would also serve as a model for a more multiethnic postwar Canada.[15] These events drew some impressive audiences in the 1960s although, ironically, never enough of the key people: Anglo-Torontonians. Aware that a sense of belonging was a necessary part of inculcating patriotism and citizenship, the Citizenship Branch worked with the institute and other groups to organize immigrant exhibits, concerts, and folk fairs showcasing the newcomers' art, handicrafts, dance, and music for Canadian audiences. As gatekeepers, all of these groups also well understood that cultural strategies for celebrating individual talents or mounting cultural performances celebrating colorful diversity did not challenge existing power structures or mainstream society. The strategies offered a form of cultural containment: the newcomers' colorful cultures were put on display for the greater enrichment of Canada as a whole.

Another major area of cultural activity was food. Canada's liberal-minded food writers and nutritional experts, for example, encouraged newcomer mothers to adapt to certain Canadian (read, modern) food ways, such as the three-meal pattern most appropriate for nine-to-five, urban industrial life, and also encouraged Canadian mothers to surprise their families by experimenting with some modified ethnic ingredients or recipes. In large cities like Toronto—which, though still staunchly British before the postwar immigrant "invasion," had experienced earlier migrations—many newcomer mothers could reproduce traditional meals because of the presence of ethnic food shops and markets established by earlier European immigrants. Also, dieticians like those on the Toronto Nutrition Committee, which studied ethnic food customs and recommended improvements, recognized the generally healthful nature of the newcomers' one-pot stews, lasagnas, cabbage rolls, and goulashes, which involved stretching a modest amount of meat with some vegetables and starch (potatoes, rice, or pasta). Indeed, this fit with the dieticians' own advice about producing nutritious but inexpensive meals. Of course, there was always room for improvement, especially in the case of the rural Eastern and Southern European mothers, who, if they had learned to cook at all during the war, had used "primitive" wood stoves and outdoor ovens and now needed to modernize and be introduced to nutritious Canadian items, like enriched white bread. By the early 1960s, the mainstreaming of ethnic foods grew apace, led in part by food columnists and Canada's premier woman's magazine, *Chatelaine*, which began publishing ethnic recipes (but with greatly reduced quantities of garlic, paprika, and other pungent spices) and profiles of immigrant women with family recipes. One such article, on an Italian family in one of Toronto's "Little Italies," first introduced readers to radicchio—"a bitter tasting" salad green that is reportedly "very good for the blood."[16]

A desire to modernize and reshape the families of the European newcomers provided the impulse for the greatest amount of gatekeeper activity. Family specialists spoke of the need to respect cultural differences in marital and family relations. Leading social workers called for pluralist methods that, for example, would help staff appreciate rather than dismiss or pathologize the seemingly overly emotional or aggressive manner with which European men and women expressed their problems.[17] Nevertheless, one of the most hegemonic of bourgeois models was the much-vaunted middle-class nuclear family, in which breadwinner fathers, homemaker mothers, and well-adjusted (and rapidly Canadianizing) children performed their appropriate roles. Family and child experts worked hard to encourage stateless, working-class or impoverished newcomers to aspire to life in "proper" single-family households, preferably in suburbia, with its restrictive gender roles. A Toronto school principal's approach to teaching English classes well illustrates how this bourgeois ideology, and sense of Canadian superiority, informed even the gatekeepers' efforts at all levels: he explained that in teaching his adult European students a new language, he was also introducing them to such enlightened concepts and institutions as the "Canadian democratic family." In invoking this image, J. G. Johnson was drawing a contrast between his idealized image of the middle-class Canadian family and a commonly held view among many Canadians that the European family was a more deeply patriarchal and authoritarian institution, which was in urgent need of reforming.[18] He also issued the familiar warning that if newcomer parents did not adapt to Canadian standards, they would face the "possibilities of family conflict and heart-ache."

The caseworkers, marriage counselors, teachers, and family and child clinicians working with European families drew similar conclusions. Even while they fully recognized that immigrants, both men and women, had fulfilled their expected laboring role by filling the ranks of the industrial workforce, and that many would remain in the working class, the experts stressed the importance of aspiring to upward social mobility and expected to see it in the next generation. In this regard, the Canadian middle class, as represented by the gatekeepers, promoted a North American capitalist ideology of an open class structure without expecting that most immigrant workers, particularly former peasants and fishers, would enter the middle class themselves.

In the effort to encourage newcomers to aspire to the middle-class markers of Canadian modernity, social workers, counselors, and volunteers in the settlement houses and community-based organizations like the YWCA, the Local Councils of Women (Toronto), and International Institute of Toronto used promotional materials and films that celebrated individual men's (and, less frequently, women's) entrepreneurial, professional, or artistic achievements. Teaching tools for women, including films produced by Canada's esteemed National Film Board, featured consumer images of the ideal homemaker and the many modern conveniences—such as refrigerators and stoves in model kitchens—that defined the Canadian way of life. These materials presented an image of the Canadian homemaker as a white, slim, attractive, well-dressed and well-coifed middle-class woman, pushing an overflowing grocery cart down store aisles with well-stocked shelves. At home, she is at work in a well-appointed modern kitchen, using canned, frozen, and other items from her well-stocked pantry shelf, refrigerator, and freezer.[19]

Cold War ideology informed the discourses surrounding this resurgence of the nuclear family and the homemaker ideal, which the gatekeepers presented as symbols of the stability and superiority of Western democratic families. Just as the anti-Communist alerts and fact sheets often emphasized the contrast between Soviet claims about the quality of life under Communism and the difficult realities of workers' lives in Communist countries, the Cold War versions of the homemaker ideology stressed the huge gap in quality of life between North America and the Soviet Union. In Canada, as in the United States (and Canadians were regularly exposed to American propaganda), mothers were portrayed as the beneficiaries of an economic system that ensured them a decent standard of living, good health, the resources to raise children, and opportunities for personal and cultural fulfillment. In contrast, Soviet women were depicted as beasts of burden brutalized by heavy work and acute scarcity, and denied the opportunity to ensure "a wholesome family life" for their children.[20] Not merely rhetorical devices, such propaganda materials were carefully constructed and gendered ideological weapons meant to promote Western capitalism's superiority and to cultivate loyalty and conformity to North American ideals.

The huge gap between these images and the overcrowded (and often kitchenless) flats or multiple-family houses in which many newcomers initially lived reflected the working-class realities of men and women who had been recruited from the DP camps or admitted from various European countries to fill labor shortages in largely low-skilled jobs. The fact that many men who toiled in resource industries, factories, and construction or other outdoor jobs failed to earn a breadwinner's wage prompted many women to enter the workforce to keep family finances afloat. They were in addition to the original DP women who had been recruited to immigrate with domestic service labor contracts. In response, the gatekeepers tried to help immigrant women workers, especially because the government-supported training programs for the manufacturing sector and other low-skilled jobs where so many immigrant women could be found were inadequate. But just as the DP domestics were expected to marry eventually and raise families, the main message to immigrant women workers was to strive for a domesticity largely defined by bourgeois standards, even if their husbands remained workers.[21]

Just as the discourses of integration did not entirely eliminate older assimilationist impulses, it did not displace the experts' presumption that they were authorized to intervene in the lives of newcomers who transgressed Canadian norms. As Benjamin Schlesinger put it, experts like himself carried out "the community's right to protect children, to regulate family disorganization, and to interfere with difficult family relations."[22] Often ignoring the patriarchal character of Canadian families—one of the great ironies or hypocrisies of the much exalted "companionate marriage model" is the suggestion that women can enjoy egalitarian relations within a patriarchal institution—the family and child experts invoked stereotypes of domineering European fathers and submissive mothers as explanations for poorly adjusted children, juvenile delinquency, and other ills among immigrant youth. To help remedy the situation, the settlement houses ran mothers' clubs, and the public health nurses ran baby classes promoting "Canadian" child-rearing methods that, among other things, introduced modern regimens of formula feeding. These groups also ran a variety of well-intentioned but intrusive frontline programs, such as inner-city school-lunch programs, which also required the mothers to enroll in "Canadian" cooking and nutrition classes, reflecting the goal of reducing immigrant parents' influence on their children. Social agency staff who introduced immigrant mothers to available social services to help them deal with sick or disabled children, or who assisted a couple in resolving a family crisis, frequently dismissed women's customary healing rituals as dangerously backward and the family's suspicion toward them as a manifestation of outmoded values that had to be overcome. In an effort to improve parenting skills, they employed familiar social work approaches, such as home visits and help with creating family budgets, meant to expose mothers but also fathers to modern child-rearing practices.[23]

At the other end of the spectrum were the frontline caseworkers, counselors, and mental health experts who dealt with some of the severest casualties of the war and the most marginal of newcomers: adults suffering from depression and various post-traumatic symptoms, angry and alienated young men, abused wives, young wartime rape victims, unwed mothers, and families on welfare who were categorized as highly dysfunctional or as "multiple problem families." Men got more public attention than women, and the press coverage of the occasional sexual assault or murder involving a newcomer fueled long-standing stereotypes of Europeans as volatile people more prone to crimes of passion or violence than white Canadians. A sensational case that engendered much bigoted discourse about mentally diseased foreign men ruining the country involved the murder of two refugee women in Toronto in 1956; police, journalists, and certain members of the general public dubbed the murderer the DP strangler.

The gatekeepers drew on their repertoire of diagnoses, theories, and treatments to deal with the admittedly small number of immigrant clients they considered sexually delinquent or mentally ill. Without disparaging genuine efforts to treat or cure clients, my reading of more than a thousand case files and other materials reveals that here, too, there was a gap between claims and efficacy, a few cruel ironies, and some gender differences. For example, the International Institute counselors and caseworkers viewed most of their sexually delinquent women as textbook cases of how the war and the supposed amorality of liberated Europe—where, some argued, everyone was "on the make" and women "shacked up" with Allied soldiers in the hopes of gifts and a ticket to North America—had loosened morals among women. Thus the institute staff categorized most of these women as clinging vines, women who attached themselves to men, usually of the wrong sort, out of loneliness, desperation, poverty, or self-interest. The staff used a number of overlapping labels: gullible girls (especially those who moved in with married men, some with family still in Europe, who promised to get divorced and marry the gullible girls); poor judges of men; amoral women unschooled in the proper mores of courtship and marriage; and the easy prey of manipulative men. Such moral judgments had real repercussions on the women, given that Canada's welfare regulations, like those in other welfare states, expected women to meet standards of the morally fit and proper mother—standards that were unrealistic for many struggling or poor immigrants. An unkempt house drew negative assessments by home visitors, for example, while having a man in the house disqualified an unmarried woman from collecting the mother's allowance. Although caseworkers hoping to reform such women tried to develop the sort of ongoing therapeutic relationship central to casework practice, sometimes, out of frustration over disobedient clients, they threatened deportation. But one of cruelest ironies was that the commitment to the much-exalted family paradigm was so strong that caseworkers commonly advised abused women, desperate to get rid of a brutal husband, to remain with him while the caseworker treated and reformed the husband, to stabilize the family dynamics along more modern, or companionate, lines. Few abusers ever showed up for treatment, and frustrated wives often gave up on their caseworkers and disappeared. Only rarely did a caseworker support a woman's request for help with a divorce, and that was only after witnessing some of the husband's cruel or bizarre behavior.[24]

Psychiatric approaches influenced the staff of social agencies and clinics in the 1950s, sometimes with alarming results: caseworkers with little training in psychiatry applied diagnoses (neurosis, persecution complex) to clients, especially men, who might then be committed to psychiatric wards or hospitals. Yet the same mental health experts who laid claim to the requisite expertise (and who also issued alarmist claims that mental illness was spreading rapidly) also admitted to diagnosing immigrants without the appropriate language skills or with inadequate translators. They admitted that staff were prejudiced against these clients and froze up when the man spoke "foreign." Also, when it came to non-English-speaking clients, the experts might more quickly eschew the more progressive talk therapies of the era for medications and hospital committals.

None of this is to say that Canada's middle-class gatekeepers ruled with an iron hand, or that there were not plenty of cracks in the containment approach. It must be said, if only briefly, that the European newcomers were hardly passive pawns in the processes described. Nor was the Canadian model of integration simply assimilation by another word. For all of the heavy-handedness, even hypocrisy, involved in these campaigns, European newcomers were not subjected to the sort of ruthless assimilation policies that, for example, were aimed at Aboriginal Canadians. Moreover, the newcomers did talk back, declaring, for example, that Canadian children were too indulged and spoiled. Impressed by the abundance of food, they were appalled by Canadian portions and waste, noting that a restaurant's scraps could feed refugees in a DP camp for a week. In addition, many of the adults and even youth found ways to resist or, more commonly, modify external pressures to adopt Canadian ways. When immigrants resisted an intrusion, or negotiated its terms, they were exercising some choice and agency over the pace and degree of acculturation, and this process of adaptation led to various hybrid patterns in parenting styles, children's play, family relations, and so forth. Although it took many years to recover from the ravages of war and genocide, many—perhaps most—of the women and men who had been suffering from crippling emotional and psychological burdens when they arrived in Canada eventually remade their lives. This was true even for those who continued to carry deep emotional scars that could never be fully healed. Moreover, in the long term, the postwar Europeans changed Canadian society and influenced national discourses of democracy—and, later, multiculturalism—even as their own customs were being modified.

Certainly, the newcomers differed in their capacity to reestablish themselves, and we should not discount the class distinctions that, for example, differentiated middle-class refugees who rebuilt professional careers or businesses from the much larger number of impoverished peasants and workers who remained more firmly within the Canadian working class. In Toronto, many of the former quickly moved to the suburbs, while most Italian and Portuguese immigrants, for example, remained far longer in the city's inner-city neighborhoods. Still, immigrants across the class divide exhibited significant rates of citizenship and homeownership, and their children and grandchildren would experience upward social mobility. The cultural pluralism of the postwar era, however limited, encouraged the European immigrants to transplant cherished cultural forms that helped them to rebuild meaningful lives, families, and communities that also made a mark on the Canadian landscape. Talented and ambitious poets, artists, and dancers fueled Canada's postwar high-brow art culture. Ethnic foodways helped to transform cultural landscapes, especially in cities like Toronto and Montreal that received many immigrants, which witnessed an expansion in the number and range of ethnic shops and restaurants and various forms of culinary experimentation and hybrid diets in both immigrant and Canadian households.[25] The critical presence of the anti-Communist Europeans also allowed the Canadian state to meet its long-standing objective of undermining the influence of the left-wing ethnic press, though the 1956 revelations about Stalin, the crushed Hungarian revolt, and other international events also had an impact. The 1950s and 1960s saw not only the incorporation of some 2.5 million immigrants from Europe, Britain, and elsewhere into the Canadian polity without massive societal rupture or institutional crisis, but also a more decidedly multicultural (if not more egalitarian) society, which emerged out of the many dynamic interactions, conflicts, and accommodations—over food, family, rituals, politics, folk culture, and more—that took place between new and old Canadians.

In conclusion, the social, political, and women's and gender history of early Cold War Canada was refracted through the prism of immigrant reception and citizenship work, and a constellation of bourgeois ideals and norms deeply informed the gatekeeper's discourses. In stressing that the postwar immigrant campaigns exhibited a contradictory mix of liberal discourses of tolerance, respect, and cultural pluralism and intrusive tactics reflecting a certain continuity with earlier immigrant campaigns that demanded high levels of conformity to Canadian models, as well as a domestic Cold War against all perceived threats to mainstream society, I have challenged easy generalizations about Canada as a kinder, gentler nation fated to become a multicultural one. That upbeat image is perhaps most easily captured in the postwar newspaper images of classrooms filled with smiling new Canadians. That liberal bias partly reflects the tendency to separate two phenomena—mass migration and the Cold War, or pluralism and repression, that were so intimately intertwined in these years. This was a terrain that upheld bourgeois norms, trampled on civil rights in the name of protecting them, and sought to contain immigrant families, sexualities, cultures, and communities. The so-called war on terror of the new century has displayed similarly disturbing elements, such as equating certain family values and the uncritical acceptance of the national security state with respectability, loyalty, and democracy. Again in step with the United States, Canada's mostly middle-class gatekeepers, including the liberals who extol the virtues of a multicultural society, demonize the Muslim terrorist who, like the Communist or deviant before him or her, is everywhere.

Notes

1. I provide a detailed documentation and treatment of these themes in Iacovetta, *Gatekeepers*.

2. Gramsci, *Letters from Prison*; Foucault, *Discipline and Punishment*. A tiny sample of this literature, which uses the concept of domestic containment to highlight links between the US-led policy of containing Communism abroad and the efforts at home to contain and remove perceived threats to the body politic, includes: Whitaker and Marcuse, *Cold War Canada*; Kinsman, Buse, and Steedman, *Whose National Security?*; Cavell, *Love, Hate, and Fear in Canada's Cold War*; Adams, *The Trouble with Normal*.

3. Davidoff and Hall, *Family Fortunes*; Cooper and Stoler, *Tensions of Empire*. See also the introduction and afterword in this volume.

4. Hayes, *Historical Atlas of Canada*, 1720; Whitaker, *Double Standard*, 12–13; Kelley and Trebilcock, *The Making of the Mosaic*, chapter 8.

5. Iacovetta, *Gatekeepers*, introduction.

6. Farhni, *Household Politics*.

7. Joseph Kage, "Immigration and Social Service," *Canadian Welfare* 24, no. 3 (January 1949), 34.

8. G. Stanley Russell, "A Clergyman Looks at the World," *Toronto Star*, April 9, 1949; March 11, 1950. See also February 28, 1948.

9. Canadian Association for Adult Education, Introduction, *Food for Thought* 13, no. 4 (January 1953), special issue, "Newcomers to Canada."

10. Vladimir Kaye, July 4, 1952, Report. MG 31 D69, vol. 11, File: Kaye, Department of Citizenship and Immigration, Liaison Officer, Report of Liaison Work (1952), National Archives, Ottawa. (In subsequent references, this archival collection will be designated "NA.")

11. R. Alex Sim, "The Concept of Integration in Canada's Treatment of Ethnic Groups," Nationitizenship Seminar, Minaki, Ontario, August 24–28, 1958. Record Group 26, vol. 84, File 1–24–107 Pt 2, NA.

12. Kaye, Report of Trip to Toronto and Hamilton, September 27–October 2, 1950. MG31 D69, vol. 12, CB, File: 1950, NA.

13. See, for example, the spring 1948 edition of *Echoes*. See also, Marjorie Lamb, *The Canadian Peace Congress and the World Peace Movement* (published by The Alert Service, Box 464, Terminal "A" Post Office, Toronto, spring 1958). RG 26, vol. 12, File: Ligue Anticommuniste Canadiene, NA. The pamphlet also bears a stamp saying it was distributed by the "Latvian Distribution Centre, PO Box 285, Terminal 'A,'" Toronto.

14. H. C. Forbell, Memo, October 26, 1961, "Re: Establishment of an Annual Cultural Festival." Archives of Ontario, Toronto, MU6413, collection of the International Institute of (Metropolitan) Toronto, File: Cultural Festival 1961.

15. Mrs. W. E West, director, to Controller Jean Newman, City Hall, Toronto, March 28, 1957. MU6413, File: Ethnic Occasions, 1957.

16. Edna Steabler, "The Other Canadians," *Chatelaine*, March 1965, 32.

17. Katz, "How Mental Illness Is Attacking Our Immigrants," 3–4, 7.

18. J. G. Johnson, "Immigrant Meets Teacher," *Food for Thought*, vol. 13, no. 4 (January 1953).

19. Korinek, *Roughing It*; Iacovetta and Korinek, "Jello Salads"; Clarke, *Tupperware*; National Film Board Archives, File 57–327, *Women at Work*, 1958, produced for Department of Citizenship and Immigration (Gordon Sparling, producer and director).

20. US State Department pamphlet quoted in Belmonte, "Mr and Mrs America." My thanks to the author for a copy of her paper, which is based on her PhD dissertation.

21. Iacovetta and Korinek, "Jello Salads"; Harzig, "MacNamara's DP Domestics."

22. Benjamin Schlesinger, "The Social-Cultural Elements in Casework—the Canadian Scene," *Social Worker*, January 1, 1962.

23. Martz, *Open Your Hearts*; Iacovetta, *Gatekeepers*, chapter 7; Adams, *The Trouble with Normal*, 68–69, 101–15; Gleason, *Normalizing the Ideal*; Caralee Daigle, "They Carry Their Books Home."

24. See Iacovetta, "'Making New Canadians.'"

25. C. Smith, "Stepping Out," chapter 7.

Commentary on Part I

THE MAKING OF THE MIDDLE CLASS AND PRACTICES OF MODERNITY

Barbara Weinstein

Several decades of scholarship since the cultural turn have put to rest the notion of the middle class as an entity that emerged "like the rising sun" (to quote Sanjay Joshi quoting Dror Wahrman)[1] from the Industrial Revolution, and that could be identified by "objective" material and cultural coordinates situating it as a stable quantity in historical time and sociological space. Each of the chapters in this part of the volume proceeds from the premise that there is no a priori middle-class identity and goes beyond this starting point to explore the way in which modernity made the middle class, and created expectations about the role of the middle class (both among those who identified with it and those who stood outside of it) in a modernizing society, as well as how middle-class actors shaped what modernity meant in a particular historical and cultural context.

Having said that, it is daunting to generalize any further; these five chapters demonstrate most cogently what a moving target the middle class can be, and how tricky it is to try to focus on the common transnational elements of middle-classness. But as both Simon Gunn and Sanjay Joshi indicate, highlighting variations in middle-class identities in historical contexts outside the Western "core" does not necessarily challenge the notion of a paradigmatic European middle class; the latter's normative status is by no means undermined by lengthening the list of variations. As the introduction to this volume makes clear, the diversity of historical and cultural settings in this part (and in the volume as a whole) is not an exercise in multiculturalism, or a showcasing of middle-class formation around the globe. Rather, the objective is to highlight the transnational formation of modernity and the crucial role that the middle class has played in shaping our very notion of what modernity is (and vice versa). My goal in the brief comments that follow is to consider how well and in what ways the chapters by Gunn, Joshi, Moskowitz, West, and Iacovetta address and illuminate the principal mission of this volume.

Before turning my attention to the individual chapters, it might be useful to consider common patterns or characteristics that could be described as symptomatic of the middle-class identities these authors discuss. After all, the middle class is not an entirely floating signifier—nowhere in this volume are factory workers designated as quintessentially middle class (though many factory workers may identify themselves as such). And certain attributes—for example, sensuality—rarely if ever appear in the list of qualities ascribed to or claimed by the middle class. In other words, the meaning of "middle class" may not be stable, but it is not infinitely expandable—even in the United States—and we can at least venture to identify some characteristics that are often (if not always) associated with middle-classness, particularly traits that have been embraced by emerging middle classes to solidify their identity and to advance their position as legitimate participants in the public sphere. Perhaps the most widely claimed (and acclaimed) middle-class marker is the concept of merit or achieved status—the idea that what sets the middle class apart from the so-called upper and lower orders is that its members have risen in society, rather than inherited a station in life. Their relative social mobility is attributed to talent and effort, qualities that prepare the middle class to serve as the engine of innovation and change.

The second theme that appears with frequency is the notion of the middle class as a buffer, the "balance wheel of social orders fractured by class differences,"[2] the golden mean that can maintain social peace in a society that might otherwise be rent apart by the extremes of wealth and poverty. Here, the point is not so much the middle class as the key to modernity, but as the key to an *orderly* modernizing process.

Then there is the middle class as the thinking class: freed from the dulling effects of manual labor but not corrupted by a leisured existence, its members can maintain a sense of taste and discernment, and both introduce new modern ways of living and guard traditional values even as their society is undergoing a transition to modernity. A variation of the above is the middle-class professional—the educated, modern individual whose knowledge is power, and who plays an indispensable role in pressing the elite to meet their responsibilities and in teaching the laboring classes proper discipline in the workplace and good hygiene at home.

This is not an exhaustive list of middle-class qualities, and none of the above constructions is the sine qua non of middle-classness, but a historian would be hard-pressed to find a society where a self-proclaimed middle class did not deploy at least one of these identity traits to advance its political prestige or material interests. To be sure, these discourses should not be seen as literally making the middle class, but they indicate why it is difficult to conceptualize the middle class apart from the question of modernity.

If a crucial objective of this volume is to destabilize Eurocentric assumptions about degrees of middle-class modernity, there is no better way to start than with Simon Gunn's cogent rethinking of the history of the English middle class. Far from having been consistently regarded as a paragon of modernity and enlightenment, the English middle class, Gunn shows us, has been periodically accused of backwardness—of failing to live up to a paradigm that, even in the English case, was a prescriptive, not descriptive, notion of middle-classness. In key moments of crisis, the English middle class came under fire for precisely the same flaws that have been lamented in locations distant from the European "core." These include taking on the aristocratic airs of the landed elite, or settling into a self-satisfied "conservative modernity," phrases that would be familiar to anyone who has studied the middle class in what we now call the Global South.

Returning to the bundle of middle-class traits outlined above, I would argue that embedded in each quality associated with a "successful" middle class (that is, one that fulfills its supposed historical destiny) is another tendency that could be cited to explain its limitations or failures. Thus the quintessentially modern English middle class (at least in the classic historical narrative) that spearheaded the repeal of the Corn Laws could both decry inherited privilege and unearned wealth, and disdain the lower orders for lacking the superior talents and abilities of the bourgeoisie. Such disdain might be denounced as aristocratic airs, but it could also be seen as perfectly compatible with a modernizing discourse of equal opportunity and its intrinsic assumption of unequal outcomes.[3]

The second historical moment that Gunn cites—the period following the First World War—sees a salaried, suburbanized middle class performing the role of buffer between capital (now moved out of the middle class and into the elite position formerly monopolized by the landed gentry) and a burgeoning labor movement. Neither fish nor fowl, the middle class could be seen by contemporaries as crucial to preventing society from being pulled to extremes, but also as "run[ning] the risk of being ground to powder in the coming impact of the upper and nether millstones."[4] Finally there is the crisis of the 1970s, with the middle class now appearing mainly in the guise of professional experts, a cohort that had thrived with the rise of the welfare state but then found itself floundering—both in terms of material conditions and political legitimacy—as demands for a universalization of certain standards of consumption and leisure came to be seen as undermining the solvency of the state and the vigor of the economy. Indeed, merit and talent would soon be revived as key middle-class traits, with the rise of Thatcherite neoliberalism.

In other words, the so-called failings of the middle class are not—as contemporaries and historians have often assumed—about a gap between discourse and practice. To quote Gunn, "one needs to understand the ideas of the modernity and backwardness of the middle class, its 'success' or 'failure,' not as somehow antithetical but as integral parts of the same discourse." I would only add that the guises and discourses of the middle class are multiple and can shift both in response to a changing cast of characters, as well as to challenges that cannot be deflected by a particular discursive position. Thus, an emerging Bengali middle class became a problem precisely because of its energetic engagement with the meritocratic construction of middle-class identity. In effect, the Bengalis became more middle class than the British, compelling representatives of the imperial order (as Mrinalini Sinha observes) to emphasize intangible aspects of middle-classness—especially a certain disciplined, masculine self-confidence—that were presumed to be beyond the reach of effeminate colonial subjects.[5]

In the interests of keeping these remarks brief, I cannot discuss all of the significant contributions that Simon Gunn's chapter makes to the debates over the history of the middle class, but I would like to highlight his extended critique of the notion that there was no actual socioeconomic group in the early nineteenth century that corresponded to the category of middle class, and thus it was purely a rhetorical device. Gunn makes a two-pronged criticism of this revisionist approach, first noting that rhetoric about the middle class was not exclusively self-referential but rather reflected, at least in part, shifting meanings of middle-classness connected to changes in economic activity and occupations. The other is that "attempting to understand the middle class purely in discursive terms is insufficient, not least because it leaves intact and unquestioned certain enduring sources of socioeconomic inequality." Gunn sees the "middle class as rhetorical device" argument as leading to a neglect of issues such as how middle-class families reproduced their social and economic status—and by implication, made it inaccessible to other segments of the population at home and abroad.[6] It is ironic that those who have made discourse most central to their argument have ignored the Foucauldian insistence that we not separate discourse from practice.

Sanjay Joshi's "Thinking about Modernity from the Margins" flips the coin and considers how a historical study of the middle class in a "marginal" (that is, colonized, not European) region might inform our guiding concepts of middle-class history. In other words, colonial India is offered not as a variation on a theme but as a case that allows us to rethink our narrative of the middle class and modernity. According to Joshi, middle-class identity in colonial India was emblematic of a "fractured modernity," and the middle class's experiences and struggles with modernity and tradition are far more illuminating of actually existing middle-class formations than the ideal type of the Eurocentric imagination. In effect, he is eschewing an emphasis on the "peculiarities of the Indian case" in favor of an approach that sees the tension between tradition and modernity as symptomatic of middle-class politics and culture everywhere. That would, of course, include the case of Britain—as Joshi notes, "the model of a liberal, democratic, progressive middle class that seizes power from a decadent, enfeebled, feudal elite to reorder society and politics along the lines suggested by the *philosophes* of the Enlightenment is a myth that has been undermined repeatedly by historians of Europe." Similar to Gunn, Joshi sees debunking the classic narrative of the English middle class as useful but insufficient, suggesting instead that we consider how middle classes engaged with modernity in different ways due to their particular historical experiences.

There are two possibly generalizable features of the middle class in India—especially colonial Lucknow—that Joshi foregrounds in this chapter. One is the class's ambivalent relationship with modernity, a project so closely associated with colonialism, a point often featured in the writings of the Subaltern Studies Collective. Joshi takes this argument in a different direction, contending that this ambivalence is not "peculiar" but rather a general feature of middle-class engagement with modernity. The second (and related) feature is the middle class's "profound ambivalence about popular politics, which it sought to 'discipline and mobilize' rather than persuade and include in its political endeavors." Here, Joshi's claim about the nonpeculiarity of the Indian middle class seems even more persuasive, given the spotty track record of the European middle classes in willingly sharing the public sphere with workers or even women of their own social class. But this point also raises some issues that I offer more as questions than as criticisms.

In discussing the conundrum of middle-class men who were "not egalitarian enough to perceive the lower social orders as equal citizens" and "not liberal enough to allow even women from their own class equality within the home," Joshi first acknowledges that such exclusions "drew on assumptions based on an older hierarchical tradition of social relations." But he then reminds us that this was hardly unusual for men of the middle class in any locale: "For many of the same reasons as their European counterparts, members of the Indian middle class also initially excluded subaltern groups and based this exclusion on the presumed natural inferiority of these groups, or on account of their lack of education on matters of public import." It is the second half of this latter sentence that especially intrigues me because it treats as equivalent what we might regard as two rather distinct bases for exclusion. Does it make a difference in politics, policies, and protest if exclusion is based primarily on a discourse of innate—and irredeemable—inferiority (such as race or caste) or remediable inferiority (for example, illiteracy)? Or is one always inflected with the other? And does one reflect a modern concept of merit-based hierarchies (which could be just as pernicious in its representation of superiority as entirely earned and deserved) while the other relies on traditional notions of natural difference? I would favor avoiding the term "traditional" except as a discursive category, given how much meanings can be altered—even if related to a venerable caste system—when deployed in a novel political and cultural context (such as the heyday of "scientific racism," in the late nineteenth century). Ultimately, I worry that it becomes too easy to fall into a way of thinking that defines one position, typically associated with the West, as insufficiently liberal, and the other, associated with more "traditional" societies, as illiberal, even backward.

Another point that I think needs more explicit consideration (and not just in Joshi's chapter) is the question of material constraints. The aspirations stirred by modernity may vary, but I would argue that in some respects, they vary surprisingly little; everywhere they hypothetically include roads, communications, basic services, medical care, education, and a certain capacity to consume. In other words, modernity does not come cheap, so we might ask whether the degree of ambivalence of a particular middle class can be understood, in part, through perceptions of material possibilities and limitations. Does the capacity to see "the lower social orders as equal citizens" have any relationship to the economic capacity of the nation to accommodate new demands?[7]

In that regard, it was refreshing to see that at least one of the sources cited in Marina Moskowitz's chapter, "Aspiration, Acquisition, and the American

Middle Class," identified easy credit as one explanation for the expanding US middle class in the early twentieth century. Differing from the other chapters in this part, which emphasize the way middle-class identity constructs exclusions, Moskowitz addresses the intriguing question of how the middle class in the United States has become so inclusive. Because critical scholars have dedicated most of their efforts to debunking the notion of the almost infinitely expandable US middle class—an understandable concern when a candidate for president with seven houses and a multimillionaire spouse could joke that an annual income of $5 million is the upper boundary of the middle class—we have devoted far too little attention to the opposite end of the question: how did a middle-class identity become so capacious in the United States?[8]

Focusing on the first decades of the twentieth century, Moskowitz cites the emerging idea of class as a cultural designation and sees this as broadening the definition of what it meant to be middle class, incorporating a wide range of occupations and incomes (though apparently not the erstwhile bourgeois industrialists, now firmly rooted in the upper class). Similarly, the increasing means—through novels, the press, and civic organizations—by which local groups could define themselves in national terms also made possible the expansion of a national middle class. Interestingly, the various studies about the middle class that Moskowitz cites put little emphasis on mobility and merit; rather, these discourses of middle-class identity tended to cluster around notions of the middle class as a source of cohesiveness and stability, and as cultural experts whose vision of civic life and domestic order could potentially define the nation. According to Moskowitz, members of the middle class "sought to apply the mediating and managerial roles they had learned in industrial settings to everyday life." But it is also apparent that the category of middle class was very much a moving target, with studies about lower-paid professionals emphasizing taste and refinement, while other research, focused on the widespread availability of credit, sought to explain an increasingly common standard of comfort that indicated higher levels of consumption.

As intriguing and original as Moskowitz's approach may be, I think her arguments would be sharpened by some comparative thinking. Given the many instances in which a certain cultural perspective is seen as essential to a middle-class identity, why in the US case does this translate into an unusually expansive middle-class category? In effect, we need to consider why the US case was, in this regard, exceptional—the definition of "middle class" does seem unusually elastic in the US context—without resorting to a notion of exceptionalism, which dispenses with analysis. Here I would particularly cite Moskowitz's argument regarding the relative lack of aspiration to rise to the upper class, which she tentatively attributes to an aversion to luxury. But that alleged aversion is something that needs to be explained, not an explanation by itself. Perhaps it reflects a historical moment, associated with the rise of the large corporation, when Americans aspiring to positions of prestige and respectability perceived that previous routes to positions of wealth, power, and independence had been shut down. But rather than be seen as marks of failure, these constraints on the "managerial classes" could then be deployed as a positive condition that allowed the middle class to perform its balancing-wheel function, even as the Gilded Age magnates and labor agitators threatened to widen the tears in the social fabric.

Again, Moskowitz's objective in her chapter is less to deconstruct claims about middle-classness than to understand how "middle class" became an appealing, useful, and malleable category. Accordingly, her emphasis is on inclusion, not exclusion. Nonetheless, I would suggest that the one always implies the other, and that exclusion can tell us a great deal about how the included are defining themselves. And here I would argue that whatever the approach, it is impossible to ignore the way in which whiteness operated to expand the middle class, as well as to fix certain boundaries that ensured the allure (to the white majority) of middle-class identity. As for the increasingly national sense of what it meant to be middle class, it is interesting to note that none of Moskowitz's examples come from the South, a region where one might expect very different assumptions (among whites) about what it meant to be middle class, including the questions of domestic servants and the proper roles for women in the middle-class household.

The subject of servants looms large in Michael West's searingly critical history of the middle class in Zimbabwe (or Southern Rhodesia, prior to independence). West recalls his own distress—on first visiting Zimbabwe—at the way his middle-class hosts treated their servants, and this recollection serves as a way to introduce the idea that colonialism was a poor school in which to learn democratic attitudes. Here he seems to be echoing Joshi's remark about the Indian middle class being considered "not egalitarian enough to perceive the lower social orders as equal citizens," but whereas Joshi sees this as neither peculiar to the Indian middle class, nor entirely attributable to the experience of colonialism, West frames the issue entirely within the oppressive legacy of colonial rule, "the unpromising foundations that would eventually give rise to indigenous middle classes in Africa as a whole."

Elsewhere greeted as a healthy sign of modernity and mobility, the emerging middle class in Southern Rhodesia provoked quite a different response from the ruling white elites, who regarded any sign of upward mobility among black Africans as a potential threat to their rule. Brought into existence, according to West, by a missionary project that promoted literacy and encouraged black preachers and, secondarily, by the needs of a colonial bureaucracy, the very existence of a middle class in Southern Rhodesia is an excellent example of the fragmented character, and hence the indeterminate effects, of even the most oppressive white-supremacist regime. To quote West, "this middle class was not part of the colonizers' master plan," but his own evidence indicates that there may not have been any one single plan.

Although West sometimes indicates that he regards what happened in Southern Rhodesia as generalizable to Africa as a whole, at other times the fact that Southern Rhodesia had been a settler colony seems the crucial feature, especially when he discusses the indigenous middle class's delayed embrace of a nationalist position. This raises questions about the specificity of the Southern Rhodesian case. It is well established that British colonial rule in other parts of Africa relied heavily on indigenous structures of authority (though often in modified form), and that local notables could become quite influential as intermediaries between the colonial regime and the colonized population. These figures in the middle, however, did not necessarily see themselves as middle class. After all, their authority stemmed from their claims to represent traditional order and hierarchy, not modernity or a collectivity of near-equals.

Surely there were areas of Southern Rhodesia with precolonial hierarchies and authority structures. Did the influx of settlers obviate the need for rule by intermediaries? Did the emerging indigenous middle class see itself as linked to such traditional authorities, or as breaking with past forms of power and prestige? It might also be useful to consider how the white settlers saw themselves. Did they take on the airs of a landed gentry? Was the classic tripartite model of class stratification irrelevant to them, given the enormous chasm they tried to insert between themselves and anyone not of European descent? West shows that the indigenous middle class periodically colluded with white supremacists to suppress the demands of the popular classes. In short, we have a fairly clear picture of how the members of the middle class in Southern Rhodesia, and later Zimbabwe, saw themselves (more modern, more civilized, more entitled to political power and material comforts) vis-à-vis the workers and peasants. Less in focus is the way they saw themselves vis-à-vis the white settler population. The indigenous middle class derived notions of proper, civilized culture and behavior from a gamut of transnational sources, including Booker T. Washington's gospel of racial uplift, but did they also take the white population's self-representation as civilized and superior at face value? And was one legacy of this an assumption that it was modern and civilized, rather than crude and autocratic, to treat one's servants with disdain?

Franca Iacovetta's chapter on "gatekeepers" in Cold War Canada analyzes the middle class in perhaps its most familiar (and hegemonic) guise—that of tutors and pedagogues of populations regarded as inadequately trained in good citizenship practices and domestic management. In sharp contrast to the unwanted and unintended indigenous middle class of Southern Rhodesia, here we have a robust white middle class made even more influential through its crucial role in shaping expectations for the wave of postwar European immigration to Canada. Iacovetta cites both Gramsci and Foucault as theoretical influences in her own work, but I think Gramsci is of relatively little relevance in this context, given how many of the immigrants already brought fiercely anti-Communist attitudes with them. On the other hand, the discourses of various Canadian politicians and social commentators are a virtual banquet for Foucauldian analysis. Hence the statement of one federal official that each newcomer, regardless of class, cultural, or political background, "must go through a change which affects his body and soul—changes of climate, diet, change of culture, change of . . . his whole behaviour to the new system of values."[9]

I think it would be difficult to find another Cold War enterprise more focused on the microphysics of power than the Canadian campaign to integrate (rather than assimilate) the new immigrants into the citizenry. One ramification of this was the prominent role of women as gatekeepers, though I think we should ask to what extent middle-class women's eagerness to carve out a safe place in the public sphere shaped the gatekeeping enterprise and shifted it toward a more domestic and bodily orientation. Wielding their special knowledge of skilled household management (that they could "naturally" claim as middle-class wives and mothers), female gatekeepers sought to transform how immigrants cooked, ate, organized their homes, raised their children, pursued sexual relationships, and worked out marital disputes. And because this pedagogy took place within the framework of the Cold War anti-Communist campaign, it allowed them to claim a political identity that might otherwise have eluded them.

I also suspect that another factor facilitating the prominent role of middle-class women as gatekeepers in this era was the Europeanness of the immigrant population. The immigrants arriving on Canadian shores after the Second World War may not yet have had the full complement of traits that would allegedly make them good Canadian citizens, but their whiteness meant that they were not too foreign or too threatening, particularly sexually. Of course, there are always shades of white, and it is interesting to note that immigrants from peripheral regions of Europe intermittently sparked fears of sexual predation.

Toward the end of her chapter, Iacovetta briefly notes what I think any historian familiar with such programs would predict: that there was extensive noncompliance on the part of the immigrants who were the target of these social, cultural, and hygienic programs. What might be more intriguing to consider is to what extent the gatekeeping role, and encounters with uncooperative immigrant men and women, reshaped middle-class identities and undermined, even if only a little, the self-confidence that middle-class representatives radiated at the outset of the Cold War. And anyone familiar with the transformation of the Canadian population since the 1970s—when the government lifted racial restrictions on immigration—cannot but imagine a fascinating comparison of integration programs during the earlier and later Cold War decades, as the sources of immigration shifted to the Global South.

To conclude, I want to return to my earlier point about the different attributes or guises that have situated the middle class as crucial shapers of modernity. These five chapters beautifully illustrate the fact that middle-class identities—who can claim to be middle class, and what political, social, and cultural advantages and disadvantages come with that designation—can vary dramatically from one context to the next, even as certain themes regularly reappear. But one issue that I think is somewhat underdeveloped in these chapters is the source of images or ideas about the middle class. Only Moskowitz makes this a central issue in her chapter, though Gunn also notes that particular moments of crisis have been productive of new scholarly interpretations of the middle class. We might ask what difference it makes if the academic or the opinion maker (as in the case of Jessica Peixotto, the Berkeley professor) is situating him- or herself within the middle class, or (as in the case of the Brazilian academics interviewed by Maureen O'Dougherty in the 1980s) firmly locating him- or herself outside, and morally above, the middle class.[10] It is not enough to know what was being said about the middle class; we also need to consider more carefully who was in a position to produce knowledge about the middle class, and what they were up to when they did so.

Notes

1. Wahrman, *Imagining the Middle Class*, 1. Of course, Wahrman was using the phrase facetiously.

2. See the commentary by Brian Owensby in this volume.

3. For a fascinating discussion of the discourse of equal opportunity, see Goldstene, "'America Was Promises.'"

4. *Cassell's Saturday Journal*, August 1, 1914.

5. Sinha, *Colonial Masculinity*, 109–15.

6. I discuss the need to focus on the reproduction and widening of material inequalities in Weinstein, "Developing Inequality."

7. I don't mean to reduce the question to one of economic constraints; for one thing, that would do little to explain the exclusion of middle-class women from the public sphere.

8. *Newsweek*, "McCain's '$5 Million' Mistake," August 18, 2008, http://www.newsweek.com/blogs/stumper/2008/08/18/mccain-s-5-million-mistake.html.

9. Vladimir Kaye, July 4, 1952, Report. MG 31 D69, vol. 11, File: Kaye, Department of Citizenship and Immigration, Liaison Officer, Report of Liaison Work (1952), National Archives, Ottawa.

10. O'Dougherty, *Consumption Intensified*.

PART II

Labor Professionalization, Class Formation, and State Rule

The Conundrum of the Middle-Class Worker in the Twentieth-Century United States

PROFESSIONAL-MANAGERIAL WORKERS' (FOLK) DANCE AROUND CLASS

Daniel J. Walkowitz

Two characteristics of identity in history taken from the rich work of the last two decades are starting points for this reflection on the history and historiography of the middle class in United States. First, people have multiple, historically contingent identities that they draw on in different combinations under different historical circumstances—for instance, as woman, Italian-American, senior citizen, white, Midwestern, and middle or working class. This observation reminds us that middle class can have different meanings in combination with other identities, as a black middle class may imagine itself and be imagined by others differently than a white middle class. But it is the second principle, that all identities are oppositional, that highlights the current middle-class muddle in the United States. People declare an identity only to distinguish themselves from someone or some other group, and any "middle" presumably sits between two stools, one above and one below it.

In the United States, the middle class as a twentieth- and twenty-first century social identity is usually a part of a narrative of social mobility, a stage in a vertical hierarchy from a lower and presumably lesser social position. Consensus historiography from the Cold War era may have waned, but it continues to cast a long shadow that misshapes the language and subjective meanings of class in the modern era. The dominant national ideology continues to insist that abundance (all those "fruited plains") and democracy-understood-as-opportunity make class an Old World problem that Americans have escaped. So the historian Joan Scott's question about gender needs to be asked of the middle class: is it a useful historical category?[1] If it is, then locating the middle class as a material and subjective experience requires it be located both against others above and below it and, at the same time, against the ideological baggage that denies the existence of social class in America.[2]

I have argued elsewhere that I am not sanguine about the scholarly application of the term "middle class." Social analysts (not exempting historians) and pundits have used the term—and continue to do so—promiscuously, with either no definition or with countless vague usages.[3] Three fairly mainstream examples from the last decade suggest the analytic paucity yet descriptive complexity presented in contemporary work. David Brooks, the omnipresent neoconservative commentator for PBS and the *New York Times*, parodies—often with humorous insight—the cultural pretensions of the urban liberal fraction of the middle-class Bohemian-bourgeoisie ("bobos") in his 2000 book, *Bobos in Paradise*. Brooks refreshingly seems to presume more than a homogenized middle, locating bobos in the "New Upper Class." He is more intent on exposing their hypocrisies and contradictions, however, than on illuminating the language of class. In contrast, the PBS program "People Like Us: Social Class in America"[4] focuses on a vast middle class. This program does acknowledge the complexity of social positions in contemporary America. Distinguishing between a black and a white middle class (that is, using race as a marker of difference), it examines the plight of "white trash" (rather than that of the usual black underclass) and recognizes the ambiguity of changes in contemporary work and identity in a section it calls "Blue Collar Workers in a White Collar World." But, like Brooks's book, the program fails to define its subject, and through lively anecdotal cases that make good television but poor social analysis, it focuses on many middle classes, largely as self-defined status groups that locate themselves between the "middle" and an "upper middle."

The third study, "Class Matters," a 2005 series in the *New York Times*—and subsequently a best-selling paperback much ballyhooed by social scientists—both acknowledges the problem of class in modern America and replicates it in its reporters' own analysis. The report tells readers at one point that "through it all, one thing was certain: a factory job was [the] . . . ticket to the middle class," yet in almost the same breath, a bold subheading proclaims, "Diploma's Absence Strands Many in the Working Class."[5]

Fortunately, historians have treated the historical emergence of the middle class through the nineteenth century with relatively greater clarity. When they trace the rise of the middle class in Tudor and Stuart England (i.e., the gentry controversy), historians root it in the capitalist development of a merchant class that resembles a classic bourgeoisie. In the United States, the making of the middle class in the first half of the nineteenth century follows that general line—Paul Johnson's shopkeepers are cradled inside Mary Ryan's bourgeois domestic family.[6] More recently, a comparable but unique Southern bourgeoisie has also been nicely delineated by Jonathan Daniel Wells and Stephen P. Rice.[7] Indeed, the nineteenth-century American middle class described by these historians—and similarly by Leonore Davidoff and Catherine Hall in their monumental study of England at this time, *Family Fortunes*, corresponds generally to the "Old Middle Class" described in the sociologist C. Wright Mills's classic study, *White Collar*: it is a group defined in classical Marxist terms in relation to the means of production. It consists of independent professionals and farmers, and it is oppositional to both the working class below it and to the plantation and merchant capitalist class above it.

I think it is not coincidental that much of the writing on the nineteenth-century middle class has come from social and labor historians. These historians, who cut their teeth writing the history of the working class as informed by British Marxists such as Edward Thompson and Eric Hobsbawm, have long been concerned with class relations more generally. Thompson's cultural Marxism stimulated for this generation an expansive notion of class, informed as much by his sense of himself as a socialist humanist as by his Marxism. In the oft-cited preface to *The Making of the English Working Class*, Thompson defines class not as a structure, but as a "historical relationship" embedded in how people identified their common interests in on-the-ground experiences: "Class happens when some men [*sic*], as a result of common experience (inherited or shared), feel and articulate the identity of their interests as between themselves and as against other men [*sic*] whose interests are different from (and usually opposed to) theirs." Class, he continues, is "largely determined by productive relationships," but, prefiguring the cultural turn, he adds: "Class consciousness is the way these experiences are handled in cultural terms."[8] Indeed, in my salad days as a New Left labor historian over thirty years ago, the emphasis on historical relationships that happen shaped my understanding of the emergence of an ethnic middle class in Troy, New York: when Irish ironworkers went out on strike in the 1860s and 1870s, local grocers and saloonkeepers—identifying as part of the Irish working class—acted as "men of the community" and gave them credit. By the 1880s, when strikes erupted again, ethnicity no longer reinforced class identity but served a cross-class identity: a new generation of Irish shopkeepers and merchants, now constituted as an Irish middle class in opposition to the working-class Irish, aligned themselves with capital as "men of commerce."[9]

The insights from these historical studies of the middle class in the nineteenth-century United States have not, however, been well suited to the study of the middle in the twentieth and twenty-first centuries. The reasons for this disconnect are many and I can only begin to hint at them here, but I think they are fundamentally about the inapplicability of the nineteenth-century category to changing patterns of work and labor in the twentieth century. There are lessons from the Thompsonian historiographic moment about the class as a relationship that reflects attitudes, values, and traditions as much as productive relations that remain pertinent to those of us who began our careers in labor history studying blue-collar industrial workers, but equally important are the theoretical contributions of the last quarter-century, especially in the work of feminist scholars and the development of cultural theory. We now seek to bring the histories of the nineteenth-century working class forward into the twentieth and twenty-first centuries, and I hope to suggest in what follows how we can begin to confront the question I asked in the introduction to my 1999 study of social workers and the politics of middle-class identity, *Working with Class*: how do you write the history of the working class when all the people think they are middle class?[10]

Mills suggested the first of two fundamental shifts in work in the twentieth century: the rise of white-collar work early in the century, typically associated with education and professional status. As work shifts from production to service, sales, distribution, and management, new professional technical workers arise to train, nurse, and adjust the Organization Man through the psychic traumas of corporate life. This is Mills's "New Middle Class"—salaried, dependent white-collar workers, who increasingly imagine themselves as middle class and fight to win professional status to mark out their occupational (and profoundly gendered) turf against other trades (for example, nurses versus doctors, and social workers versus psychiatrists). Class for this group has an "other" against which it struggles.

Unfortunately, the history of the middle class has been less well served by the second shift in work occurring in last quarter-century. The middle dramatically changes in the last half of the twentieth century, and the class "other" central to identity becomes increasingly unclear. The geographer David Harvey has provided one useful explanation for the expansion and changed sense of the middle. The crisis of overaccumulation that Harvey notes began in the 1960s resulted in a new wave of drives by capital to reduce labor costs. What distinguished this transformation from others was its effect on the New Middle Class, which faced downsizing layoffs of the sort long familiar to industrial workers, but from which engineers and managers had historically been insulated. At the same time as these middle-class workers faced a job crisis (of production and money), a vast outpouring of goods accentuated both the volatility and ephemeral quality of the consumption to which their identity as middle class was tied in two ways: people consumed more (increasingly on credit), yet as industry increasingly moved to create new markets, work further shifted from production into services, most notably in the rise of a robust leisure industry. The result is the vexed cultural mass of consumers and producers that provided what David Harvey has noted was "yet another layer to that amorphous formation known as the 'middle class.' "[11]

The sociologist David Halle has provided an analytic lever to begin to unpack this "amorphous formation" of the last half-century. His interviews, conducted during the 1980s with workers in a New Jersey chemical plant and their spouses, give voice to the complex experiences and subjectivities that differently shaped how each person understood his or her class position as working class at work and middle class at home. Equally important, Halle shows how their views of the class position of managers, clerical workers, and wives not working outside the home differed from how these people imagined themselves.[12] This hybrid construction suggests how working people can embrace the oxymoronic location of the working middle, nicely capturing the ambiguity of class subjectivity at a particular moment for particular skilled industrial workers. Unfortunately, Halle focuses on the workers in the chemical industry rather than the changing routines, computerization, or capital flight that increasingly characterized late-twentieth-century work, and he only begins to explain what workers mean by these categories and what prompts their use of them.

Still, Halle's hybrid formulation of dual identities suggests the virtue of a dual analytic track that combines a focus on subjectivity with the study of the material conditions of labor and consumption. In an earlier essay on the future of social history, I suggested how we might build on work by geographers like Harvey and historical sociologists such as Halle to resuscitate class as a useful category. Paying tribute to the insights of feminist scholarship and poststructuralist theory, I have urged that what is generally known as the cultural turn needs to be combined with some of the materialist, empirical concerns of the new social history.[13]

What follows is a case study of folk dancers in the United States, a recreation practice of mostly professional-managerial workers, to illustrate how one might navigate the material and subjective worlds in which modern folk who identify as middle class establish a language of class. This case continues my interest in the middle-class subjectivity of a class fraction where middle class is more about style and status claims—cultural capital—than about political or economic power. But in examining how the language of class and, most especially, middle class functions, this case also affords an opportunity to examine the role of liberalism in the shaping or reshaping of the meaning of class.

The remainder of this essay, following the cultural critic Patrick Joyce, examines the cultural dimension of liberalism as embodied in the folk dancer as liberal subject. For Joyce, the liberal subject, with its own internal logics, reflexes, and ordinances of self-regulation, administers Foucault's governmental understanding of freedom as a way of making the reality of the city thinkable, rational. Around the beginning of the twentieth century, liberal subjects imagined what they termed the sanitary city though what Joyce calls techno-social solutions; the folk dance revivals in English country dance (ECD)—the subject of what follows—similarly looked at bodily solutions. As we shall see, ECD dancers perform liberalism with the governance of space as a moral project, creating and moving in a space to make it knowable, stable, and dependable. Judith Stein, in her work on restructuring in the steel industry and the emphasis of liberal social policy on opportunity rather than structural change, has highlighted how race has been a salient feature of American social life as well as liberalism. Indeed, the liberal subject in America has been especially racialized, and the study that follows calls particular attention to these inflections.[14]

This chapter examines only one fraction of the middle.[15] The liminality of this group, however, makes it unusually evocative of the tensions and contradictions in class identity at the center of this amorphously muddled middle. Folk dancers, especially those in the international dance movement who move into ECD after the 1960s, self-identify as liberal and left-wing (or radical). The stories that follow suggest the extent to which liberalism penetrates a cadre of professional-managerial workers who, from the Left, are themselves most invested in finding an alternative to liberalism.

This study, then, focuses on the subjectivity of a self-identified liberal fraction of the middle class, a group for which ECD is an especially compelling window. In the last half of the twentieth century, my survey of several hundred dancers across the United States found that four out of five identified themselves as "liberal" or "left wing." Equally interesting, more than 70 percent of English country dancers came to the dance through the countercultural movements of the 1960s and 1970s, such as international folk dance or American country dance (contra- or square-dancing);[16] others came through folk song, which also tends to be an international tradition. The international core provides an especially good point of entry into left-liberal political culture, for outside the national folk traditions, "folkies" tend to be countercultural. So the history of ECD in America is not just a way into the politics of the folk, it also permits a reexamination of left-liberal political culture in America at the end of the twentieth century.

The Folkie Middle

In 1967, the weeklong Newport Folk Festival announced that it would, for the first time, dedicate two days to folk dance. The director, George Wein, explained the festival had chosen the Country Song and Dance Society of America—the "oldest such organization in the country" and the lineal descendant of the American branch of the English Country Dance Society—to demonstrate the "significant role" that folk dance had played in the "urban dance revival in this country."[17] Dancers from the Boston branch of the Country Dance and Song Society performed a representative sample of what they imagined to be the English tradition: Morris dances, which originated among West Country village people in the medieval era; a "rapper" dance, which originated among pit miners in nineteenth-century Northumberland and was performed with flexible steel swords; round dances, rooted in medieval villages; and, finally, country dances from the seventeenth and eighteenth centuries, which had been danced in assemblies by the English gentry. In these country dances (amply displayed in recent dramatizations of Jane Austen novels), men and women dancing as a couple faced one another and lined up in "longways sets" for "as many as will." The top two couples and each set of couples after them danced together for thirty-two bars of music, and then each couple, progressing up or down the set, repeated the pattern with another couple. Although some of the reels, jigs, and hornpipe dances from the North Country were playful and rambunctious, most of the longways assembly dances were courtly, elegant, and restrained, performed on the ball of the foot with a forward-moving walking, a relatively flat waltz step, or a skipping step. Cecil Sharp, the Englishman most responsible for the folk revival in Edwardian England, deliberately did not try to figure out what steps went with each figure, but in the twentieth century the walking step became predominant. The dances were sociable, with opportunities for flirtatious looks or for small talk when not dancing; physical contact was limited to hands. Moreover, the music encouraged what Sharp called "gay simplicity." Choreographed to tunes from classical and baroque composers such as Purcell and Handel, the music and its dance were lyrical, not pulsating or atonal. Although the full range of these dances performed at Newport shaped the imaginings of the English country dance in twentieth-century America, the longways country dances—published in seventeen editions by John Playford and his son, starting in 1651, which were then being done by the gentry—predominated at local dance venues of previous centuries and shaped the imaginings of participants then.

The emerging professional-technical class (managers were notably absent then) took up English country dance as an expression of folk culture in the "revival" that swept Northern Europe, England, and the United States early in the twentieth century, and the movement's history reflects how such people built a decidedly urban cultural form through ethnic, gender, and class imaginings of country life. The stately posture, gestures, attire, and conventions of the English country dance were in such ways markers of the class fraction that promoted the dance and did it as a recreational adjunct of life. As the historian James Cook has observed, the increasing difficulty of reading who was respectable in the "anonymous environment of the antebellum metropolis" was multiplied in the industrial, immigrant city of the early twentieth century. Building on the French sociologist Pierre Bourdieu's analysis of the material markers of class identity in the second half of the twentieth century, Cook reminds us that the "middle class created elaborate new systems of significance and distinction (their heads, wardrobes, gestures, homes and urban landscapes served as the raw materials), all with the same basic impulse to fix one's social status rigidly and unambiguously."[18]

The Newport Folk Festival demonstration of English Country Dance by the Boston branch of the Country Dance and Song Society of America aptly represented the left-liberal character of the dance community, a community revitalized by infusions of New Left enthusiasts caught up in the postwar second folk revival. Folk music was an organizing tool within the civil rights and antiwar movements, in the words of the cultural historian George Lipsitz, making "musical expression an organic part of the political process."[19] Folk music and country dance, especially American contradances and square dances, were embedded in the alternative and sometimes oppositional countercultures that thrived in and around rural communes. As noted earlier, over 60 percent of dancers questioned in 2003 characterized themselves as "liberal" and another 20 percent described themselves as "left wing." Only eight people (5.3 percent) described themselves as "conservative" or "right wing." About half of this group did not regularly do ECD. They were members of the Society for Creative Anachronisms, a group that does historical reconstructions, mostly of medieval fairs and jousts and patriotic and military events such as US Civil War and Revolutionary War commemorations.[20]

Complicating the matter of the folk dancer's subjectivity is the mixed heterogeneous origins of the dance among village people and gentry. Indeed, this confusion of origins and the idea of the folk process complicate the dancer's sense of him- or herself in the dance. At the same time, it makes body language potentially the more revealing: people dissemble when they speak, but they perform identity when they dance. Each person's behavior is layered with distancing techniques, such as irony and play. But on video, unconscious (at least on some level) mannerisms expose nonverbal feelings: people open or enfold arms and legs, hesitate or grow silent, and so forth; dancers express attitudes. The embodied voice may confirm stated senses of the self or be in dialogue with stated views. Such mannerisms are not self-evident, but they are deep cultural cues, best used, I would argue, with complementary material such as oral interviews. The video oral history of dancers and the dance adds a dimension to how people "speak" class with their body, often in dialogue or tension with what they are verbalizing. In the video oral history (which, ironically, here can only be described in words!), the historian can hear and see people speak, embody, and enact class (and gender and ethnicity).

Middle-Class Folk Today

The homogeneity of the American ECD community today is hard to miss: aside from a few people of Indian and Japanese descent, and the rare African American, everyone at dances is white.[21] Of course, the meaning of whiteness changed over the course of the twentieth century, as Northern and Eastern European ethnic groups, as Mathew Jacobson has demonstrated, became "white" in American culture and immigration policy after the Second World War.[22] The class background of the dancers has not changed profoundly since Cecil Sharp's visits, though: the class composition has become a tad less elite, but it has remained preeminently bourgeois and urbane, from affluent suburbs and urban areas. These folk were professional-technical workers or in the arts—the majority (56.3 percent) were (and are today) professors, teachers, librarians, social workers, nurses, and doctors, but there was also a fair representation (14.3 percent) of theatrical and musical people. Most recently, reflecting the changing character of work in the late twentieth century, a substantial number (10.1 percent) work in the computer world.[23] Not surprisingly, this professional-technical group is older, well-established, and highly educated. Reporting an average household income of over $80,000, virtually all are college educated (88.3 percent), and more than half (60.2 percent) have graduate degrees. This class fraction is also a cultural slice defined by age: if youth is to be served, it is not by ECD, where the average age is in the low fifties. The ease of the dance on the knees partially explains its attraction for older people, but, as we shall see below, the ECD community has also embraced a distinctive culture with class signifiers that stand in opposition to central elements of a more lusty cross-class and intra-ethnic alternative youth culture.

The last half-century saw two important shifts in the composition of the modern ECD community. The first reflects the gender politics of many who came to the dance community out of the 1960s counterculture. The dance community has always been heterosexual (93.3 percent of my survey identified themselves as "heterosexual," and about two-thirds listed themselves as partnered), but, coincident with rise of second-wave feminism and the gay liberation movement, the last few decades have seen the emergence of occasional gender-free dances. Although the percentage is lower for men than women, almost all (82.5 percent) of the respondents describe themselves as moderately or strongly influenced by feminism. But gender balance in admission to special dance events—such as balls and dance weekends—that require advance registration, although a subject of great debate, is still largely enforced. Yet there is an increasing willingness to break with gender roles, especially among the women (who also tend to be in the majority). Men have always been less comfortable partnering other men, but even this taboo has begun to break down in the last decade. Christine Helwig, a retired ECD leader who has focused on the reconstruction of historical dances, remembers that the SDS activist and gay rights pioneer Carl Whittman "belonged to a community that never, never segregated by sex. The way they started dances was in a big circle, and the people were scattered all around the circle. Then he would select a couple and you lined up. You might be a woman on the man's side or a man on the woman's side. It didn't make any difference as far as he was concerned."[24] Although such practices are unusual, at least three communities—Boston, the Bay Area, and Durham, North Carolina—held regular gender-free dances at the end of the twentieth century.

The second shift is in the ethnic composition of the dance community. For the first half of the twentieth century, the ECD community was decidedly Waspish, with what some recall as a veneer of anti-Semitism. Helwig, for instance, recalls that the New York City group she joined in the 1960s was "sort of an elite group." Gene Murrow—one of the premier ECD teachers and musicians, and a serious student of the dance's history who began dancing while in college in the 1960s—feels that the community's ethnic composition has changed over the past thirty or forty years. Before the 1960s, it was an elite activity with a prudish Victorian tone that was probably consistent with the values of an older generation of upper-class women. Thus, several long-time dancers remember—albeit with a fond chuckle—that Sharp's appointed successor, May Gadd, beat the bushes at night at Pinewoods Camp, in Plymouth, Massachusetts, to make sure there was no hanky-panky. Although he had no firsthand experience of its narrowness, Murrow sums up the elite social tone of the early dance community this way: "There was some anti-Semitism prior to when I started dancing in the sixties. In this country, English Country Dancing in the thirties and forties and fifties was definitely an American upper-class snooty activity. It was done at the Metropolitan Club in New York, things like that . . . It did loosen up in the sixties, as many other things did."[25] But as a participant and observer looking at all these bourgeois city folk teaching and dancing folk dances in the twenty-first century, and—in the case of the English country dances—doing reels, jigs, and longways set dances with indeterminate, varied, and multiple historical origins among villagers and gentry, I wondered what was the attraction of these village or country dances for these urban professionals.

Ironically, the dancing bodies of the working class were both the objects and subjects of a political project of and for the New Middle Class at the beginning of the twentieth century, which was at the root of the folk revival in the United States and elsewhere.[26] The culture of containment and the culture of liberalism were embedded in Progressives' political culture—in their concern with respectable bodies in space—and in motion in streets, factories, and dance halls. The reformers' focus on immigrant workers and concern with space come together in folk dance, where the immigrant "problem" was to be solved in the celebration of immigrant culture. At the same time, English country dance in America, like other folk dances, was celebrated by revivalists as expressions of the pure folk traditions of a simpler past that peasant peoples had left behind, but that could now be revived to build an inclusive American identity. Jane Addams caught the essentially conservative spirit of this urban liberalism exactly in her 1909 *Spirit of Youth and City Streets*: "These old forms of dancing, which have been worked out in many lands and through long experiences, safeguard unwary and dangerous expression and yet afford a vehicle through which the gaiety of youth may flow. Their forms are indeed those which lie at the basis of all good breeding, forms which at once express and restrain, urge forward and set limits."[27]

When Sharp founded the American branch of the English Folk Dance Society in March 1915 in New York City, he did so against a backdrop of elite reformers' fears that young girls would lose their moral compass in any of the more than 500 new unchaperoned dance halls in the city. ECD, with its gay simplicity and disciplined bodies, was at once an alternative to the wild gyrations and dangerous loss of sense (vertigo) in the tango and animal dance crazes. In contrast, ECD was a healthy exercise regime for confined urban bodies that would not injure young girls' reproductive organs.

But how does ECD function at the beginning of the twenty-first century? Who and what bodily politics, for instance, do contemporary dancers embody as they move through space? For the twin roots of the English country dance—the medieval village circle dances and the gentry dances of the seventeenth century—allow contemporary dancers to develop different stories about the folk they emulate. Thus, Thom Yarnal, a Wisconsin-based community theater manager, invokes both the country bumpkin and the aristocrat; a fifty-something Southern journalist, Mary Alison (a pseudonym) envisions herself as a shepherdess; and a fifty-two-year-old book indexer from Palmya,Virginia, Pat Ruggiero, sees herself as a gentlewoman at one of Jane Austen's balls. But if interviews express a range of voices with these multiple referents, how do dancers speak with their bodies? On the dance floor, tens of bodies—at times, over a hundred—speak, each telling a story with class signifiers in their dress and carriage. The historian has only to try to hear what the body means to express.

Before turning to the dancing body, let me begin with the interviews, for what people express with their bodies is in uneven relationship with what they say about class and identity in interviews. One element of how they imagine themselves is suggested from the antimodern theme that interviewees repeat again and again. For Yarnal, "It's otherworldly, you know. It doesn't have anything to do with the twentieth century, as far as I'm concerned. It takes you to a different place and it takes you mentally and physically . . . People not answering cellphones and running around."[28] The music is a case in point. Glenn Fulbright, a retired "dance gypsy" who taught music at the University of Kentucky, describes the music as the "most transporting experience I have." He characterizes his typical feeling after doing a dance as "like I've been to church."[29] Invoking a sacred place, such attitudes suggest that the music's associations with high-brow culture—tunes by Corelli, Purcell, and other classical and baroque composers—function as a signifier of the distinctiveness and status of the dancers' particular class fraction. The music, as others were quick to note, contrasted with the driving beat of popular music often rooted in working-class and minority-group cultures. Pat Ruggiero says: "Popular music has a very strong beat underneath, and a lot of sexual overtones. And, you know, [ECD] is not hip-hop." Similarly, Thom Yarnal compares ECD movements and music with that of the more aerobic popular music: "The [popular] music is way too loud, number one. And the movements tend to be really violent; it's very staccato kind of stuff. And our—you know, the kind of dancing we do here is aerobic, but it doesn't have that kind of jarring. I think it's more centered on a heartbeat than the driving rhythms of a machine, which is what I think drives modern music."[30]

The antimodern theme translates for many into a celebration of community —an antimaterialist refuge in which people can be "with their own kind."[31] According to Murrow, ECD fulfills the "need for a more gracious time" as a "haven" from "the twenty-first-century American speed-and-greed culture, . . . from what many of us would agree is an increasingly depersonalized, stressful, high-speed world."[32] Sharon Green, a sixty-year-old leader of the New York country dance community, sees the haven as a return to the "innocence and simplicity of childhood." And for Mary Alison, "This is a refuge from the rest of the world. . . . And people here are among their tribe. And out in the real world, you often are not. You're trying to find your way among a lot of people with different values, and people that don't necessarily share your interests and share your common history . . . [Here] they're entering into a community that's accepting of them and that basically wants them here."[33]

Alison's invocation of the dance community speaks, albeit somewhat obliquely, to my abiding interest in the relatively elite social composition of this would-be folk community and how it imagines itself on the dance floor and more generally in relation to the historical dance tradition. They are only a relative elite, however, neither upper crust nor independently wealthy. As Murrow observes, fewer than one in ten (8.9 percent) are managers, and most of these are white-collar managers rather than corporate executives; in fact, most are a peculiar social cut below. Part bohemian, part bourgeois, they resemble Brooks's "bobos."[34] With one foot—perhaps only a large toe—back in the counterculture, they are the ones, as Jenny Beer observes, "who've dropped out of the achievement races and just want to hang out and dance and make music."[35]

The ECD community's embrace of these country dances as an alternative to the feared licentiousness of rough dancing and music-hall culture at the beginning of the last century is reminiscent of what Christopher Lasch called the search for a haven in a heartless world.[36] Those dancers and reformers who advanced dance for the working class occupied a class "middle." But a century later, the group's sense of itself has changed: the contemporary antimodernists use their movement neither to retrain the working class nor to invoke a nationalizing folk, and the ECD community might better be characterized as a haven in an overly wrought world.

Turning to the dance floor, however, one "hears" a more mixed message. To begin with, dances and dancers differ—in tempo, stepping, exuberance, carriage, and more. Some dances are sappy waltzes; others are exuberant—even aerobic—with chase patterns, reels, and jigs. The music, drawn from highbrow, classical composers, also signifies class: that of the Northern European white bourgeoisie and court. And although the dance form, especially in the United States, where eye contact is stressed, encourages sociability and flirtation, the unwritten rules of the dance culture, form, and music send structured messages that speak more to middle-class propriety than tussles in the country hay. Some women do wear garlands in their hair, but they accompany ball dresses or designer "peasant" dresses à la Laura Ashley—the commodified alternative culture. Although most men simply wear white, ruffled shirts with knickers at balls, some put on tuxedos or elaborate eighteenth-century aristocratic costumes. And although marriages within the dance community are not uncommon, they come from community sociability and the intimacy of eye contact, not from intimate physical contact on the dance floor.

Dancers, then, relish the English country dance and the dance community as a temporal and spatial escape from the present. They escape, however, very much as modern folks to embrace a dance form resonant with contemporary social and political meaning. In a world where increasing numbers of older women are single and wary of the sexualized dating scene, the unwritten rule in the ECD community, and particularly in the United States, is that you do not reserve dances with someone and that you change partners after every dance. Indeed, dancing with any partner more than once an evening (except perhaps for the final waltz) is frowned on.

Equally important, ECD's dance form limits physical contact to holding hands, generally at arm's length. Dignified carriage is the predominant body language (at least of those who are more than beginners). In her interview, Ruggiero captures the constrained sexual narrative in ECD dancing that makes it a safe place for her in an imagined earlier time:

> I start with a dignified demeanor, arms quiet at the side, economy of motion, move through the space without any flailing of arms, without any embellishment to the figures, without any unnecessary gestures. Oh, and in body motion, I try to eliminate from my own motion, dancing or not, a lot of twentieth-century ways of conducting ourselves that I no longer care for. Either [the] smarmy sort of gliding across the floor, or

jiggles or thrusts, or little coy affectations of the head, and I try to eliminate all of those so I don't look like a twentieth-century person dancing. I don't like it.

Q: Why? What don't you like about it?

A: . . . It's very overtly physical, and I prefer a reticence in my interactions with people. And so rather than thrust some limb or do some coy or flirtatious thing that would draw someone toward me—that's not what I want in my interactions, so I want to be honest in my interactions with people, and I prefer a certain aloofness, a certain reticence—so I keep my body tight. So I hold my body in reticence.[37]

Most others were less explicit than Ruggiero about the dance style and its sexual meanings in their interviews, but on the dance floor, and in their informal body gestures, tilts of the head, colloquialisms, and flowing dresses one can see them speaking a modern language. Indeed, in video footage. a smiling Ruggiero—dancing in a simple, flowing, blue polka-dot dress—is neither aloof nor of the past: she is very much a sociable, twenty-first-century woman, albeit in a country dance, not at an urban dance club rave.

One dancer, who is unusually articulate and vocal about the related sexual and class meanings of the dance, appreciates the disjunction between the imagined and the expressed. Jenny Beer, a forty-five-year-old self-employed mediator from the Philadelphia area, spoke from an unusually privileged position: she had run the Swarthmore College ECD group and has folk danced for twenty-seven years; she also has a PhD from Berkeley in cultural anthropology. Confirming Ruggiero's views on styling, Beer places the body language in its class context: "There's a certain containment in the way you handle your body all the time that is definitely a class mark . . . [I]t's a structure that allows sexuality, but in a very middle-class, contained kind of way, a safe way." Then, in a particularly prescient observation, she adds: "You don't show off your butt or your breasts the way you might in, say, in African dance, where you let it all hang out."[38]

Although not meant to be about race per se, Beer's comment highlights another fundamental element of the ECD community's sense of itself as a class. All interviewees agree that the dance community is "middle class," but most are also more specific. Ruggiero and Yarnal's appraisals are typical: "We're just educated professionals," notes Ruggiero, and "Caucasian heterosexuals"; Yarnal says, "We're a pretty affluent group of people, [and] we're pretty white." Murrow puts it succinctly: "We are a group of lily-white, middle-class, urbanized Americans." Indeed, various interviewees, echoing the widespread talk about the need for more diversity in the dance community, note the absence of blue-collar workers and African Americans and Hispanics in the dance community.[39] The lack of minorities in their community, which both puzzles and disappoints interviewees, brings us back to the liberal problematic in contemporary middle-class identity. Indeed, the ECD community generally holds countercultural progressive political views on race and class and consistently welcomes African Americans, Asians, and Hispanics on the few occasions when they do appear at a dance. No group makes systematic attempts to reach out to those communities, however, and, not surprisingly, few members of minority groups who come ever return. Reflecting on why they do not come back, Ruggiero candidly admits: "I don't think much about it." Others do think about it, but Bourdieu's lessons on the potential for class dominance in cultural forms are lost on them. Beer notes: "It's pretty esoteric, what we do." And Murrow follows this logic in noting that "I don't think it speaks to [black people]." Alison agrees: "I guess this kind of dancing is not part of their particular traditions."[40]

Yet a cursory review of the Country Dance and Song Society's membership lists or enrollees at Pinewoods Camp discloses a preponderance of ethnic Irish, Italian, and Jewish names in the dance community who seemingly have little ancestral connection to England. The changing history of the ECD community is but another lesson in the history of whiteness in twentieth-century America. Recall that until the middle of the twentieth century, the ECD community had never been especially welcoming to members of such ethnic groups, even if that lack of welcome had been visible only in the subtle demeanor and attitudes of its members. Since the 1960s, second- and third-generation ethnic folks—such as Gene Murrow, Pat Ruggiero, Sharon Weiner Green, and me—have become integral members of the community.[41] Only 36.9 percent of my respondents claimed British ancestry; Jews, who were largely absent a half-century earlier, now made up 27.5 percent of the group.

Historians have demonstrated how Anglo-American tradition has been transformed to incorporate Jews and other white ethnics.[42] At the same time as their inclusion changed the meaning of tradition, the expansion of whiteness to include ethnic Americans coincided with a changed sense of the folk in ECD.[43] The folk early in the twentieth century were part of the imagining of a national Anglo-American identity; at the end of the century, the imagining of the past had come to define an urban subjectivity as white, heterosexual, and antimodern. True, the preponderance of the dancers today may live in suburbs, but it is important to remember that the "burbs" themselves have been constructed as white spaces in relation to cities.[44]

Vestiges of the political impulses from 1930s and 1960s folk traditions can be seen in the ECD community today, especially in the way its members view it as a haven for those who reject the dominant cultural rhythms—the modern "speed-and-greed culture." The contemporary movement, then, is also a countercultural form, but as a site, not as a political or cultural movement. These dancers are urbane, educated, urban professionals; but theirs is an elite distancing itself, not engaging with the city, by creating dance spaces as antimodern refuges.

However, they are antimodern with a difference—they are not technophobes. As noted above, there are disproportionate numbers of computer programmers and scientists in the community. Although some of the more intricately patterned dances seem to appeal to those who are mathematically inclined, the Harvard biochemistry professor George Whitesides expresses the views of another group when he notes that for him, ECD "serves to provide some humanity in the overall [scientific] enterprise" that is his professional life.[45] The "humanity," however, is found in imagining the pastness of the present. In this way, the ECD community's imagining of itself as a gentry folk may be another commentary on the crisis of modern liberalism, one that is not so removed from Sharp's Fabian worldview (though the late-twentieth-century community is not committed to Sharp's imperial vision). As we have seen, the contemporary ECD movement is Anglo-American, but with lots of second- and third-generation ethnic Americans—at least Jewish, Irish, and Italian Americans—who have become "white." That this urban folk identity has no blacks or Hispanics should not be so surprising. The ECD community is in conscious escape from the rap and hip-hop music and rhythms of the dominant urban culture (and the young people who embrace it)—even if those stand only as a metaphor for fast-paced modern life. This makes the past in which the ECD community lives a cultural form with unintended political consequences that are integral to the present failure of liberalism and its imbrication in the constitution of middle-class identity in urban America as white, heterosexual, and isolated from the working people and racial minorities who make up the majority of America's cities. The ECD community's counterculture remains antimaterialist. A majority of my respondents claim no religious affiliation, but a surprising number go out of their way to add how "spiritual" they are. Their hobbies are disproportionately crafts and gardening, rather than competitive sports or activities such as bowling, which is marked as working class. The dancers' preferred sports activities are hiking and biking, both distinct middle-class signifiers. What passes for social activism is a kind of civic associational environmentalism—membership in the Sierra Club, for example, a largely white, middle-income advocacy group with class markers congenial to those in the ECD community. Feminists, environmentalists, and "spiritual" folk, these leftists and liberals inhabit a distinctive class sector. Affluent yet not quite elite, alternative but also bourgeois, the world of the ECD community has little resonance with the working class or racial minorities whose absence on the dance floor they miss. In fact, their cultural messages signify to those they miss how much the absent groups do not fit. In such ways, the history of the modern folkies of English Country Dance suggests the extent to which the liberal political project to right inequity and injustice must engage with the contrary messages of modern liberal culture.

The ECD fraction illustrates a larger problem with the language of class that we have inherited: it has little bearing on the present. Class has become a consumer identity, with classes demarcated by the status of commodities and distinct political cultures much as they are presented in "Class Matters" or "Social Class in America." Oppositional elements are present, but they are delineated more by racial or ethnic difference and cultural style than as oppositional social classes. In an era in which downsizing, outsourcing, and global flows of capital have had profound impact on professional-technical workers more than at any time in the history of that group, it is striking how little the language of class bears on these structural changes or the workplace. The problem for social analysts today is that the contemporary middle class occupies a discursive terrain that has little resemblance to its historical precedents. Today there are multiple middle classes, and they are each other's "other." The consuming classes ignore the forces of production, except perhaps as cocktail party fundraisers for fair trade coffee or some other cause du jour. Capital gets a free ride.

Notes

1. Joan W. Scott, "Gender: A Useful Category of Historical Analysis."

2. Loïc J. D. Wacquant's theorizing of the relationship between class as a discursive site and as a set of concrete material conditions is most helpful. See Wacquant, "Making Class."

3. D. Walkowitz, *Working with Class*. See also D. Walkowitz, "The Cultural Turn and a New Social History."

4. PBS, "People Like Us: Social Class in America," produced and directed by Louis Alvarez and Andrew Kolker, January 5, 2006, http://www.pbs.org/peoplelikeus/.

5. David Leonhardt, "The College Dropout Boom: Working Class and Staying that Way," *New York Times*, May 24, 2005; Timothy Egan, "No Degree, and No Way Back to the Middle," *New York Times*, May 24, 2005.

6. P. Johnson, *The Shopkeepers Millennium*; Ryan, *Cradle of the Middle Class.*

7. Wells, *The Origins of the Southern Middle Class*; Rice, *Minding the Machine.*

8. E. Thompson, *The Making of the English Working Class*, 9–10.

9. D. Walkowitz, *Worker City, Company Town*, 260.

10. D. Walkowitz, *Working with Class*. xi.

11. Harvey, *The Condition of Postmodernity*, 347. See also 285–86, 327–28, 347–48.

12. Halle, *America's Working Man*. See also Zussman, *Mechanics of the Middle Class.*

13. D. Walkowitz, "The Cultural Turn and a New Social History."

14. Joyce, *The Rule of Freedom*, 1–20; J. Stein, *Running Steel, Running America.*

15. D. Walkowitz, *City Folk.*

16. My national survey found 107 of 150 respondents, who in almost equal numbers had done American Country or International Folk Dance—most for many years—before discovering ECD. International was mostly an urban dance movement, but contradance was popular in both urban and rural back-to-the-land communities.

17. George Wein, *Newport Folk Festival*, 1967, Gadd papers, University of New Hampshire, Milne Collection. The Country Song and Dance Society had appeared at the 1959 festival, and the director may have simply been referring to the increased attention being given to folk dance over two days.

18. Cook, *The Arts of Deception*, 160. See also Bourdieu, *Distinction.*

19. George Lipsitz, "Who'll Stop the Rain," 214. See also 221–23.

20. The civil rights and counterculture movements had reshaped the liberalism that the core of the ECD community embraced. On the one hand, the discourse of liberalism shifted during the 1960s from class to rights consciousness; on the other hand, the new liberalism focused less on economic conditions for the good life (for example, the "square meal") to "moral growth and self-fulfillment" and the quality of life (such as the environment). My argument draws heavily here on Collins, "Growth Liberalism in the Sixties," 25–26.

21. My survey found one person who listed herself as mixed race, and she was dancing for only the second time.

22. Jacobson, *Whiteness of a Different Color.*

23. The occupational profile is based on my observations and regular comments on the ECD list serve. Although some have since retired, only one of the people I interviewed had an occupation outside this profile: Christine Helwig had been a town manager in Westchester County, New York.

24. Christine Helwig, interview with me and Stephanie Smith, June 11, 1999, New Haven, Connecticut. My interviews were part of the ECD Documentation Project, a joint activity of the Smithsonian Institution and the Country Dance and Song Society (hereafter referred to as "ECD Doc."). See also Carl Whittman, "Refugees from Amerika: A Gay Rights Manifesto," *San Francisco Free Press*, 1970.

25. Gene Murrow, interview with me, August 29, 2000, Pinewoods Camp, Plymouth, Massachusetts. ECD Doc. The stories about May Gadd were told by several people in informal discussions with me at Pinewoods in August 1999, and in my and Stephanie Smith's interview with Brad Foster, director of the society, August 26, 1999, Pinewoods Camp, Plymouth, Massachusetts, ECD Doc.

26. See D. Walkowitz, *City Folk*.

27. Quoted in a wonderful dissertation by Mirjana Lausevic, "A Different Village," 30.

28. Thom Yarnal, interview with me, August 29, 2000, Pinewoods Camp, Plymouth, Massachusetts, ECD Doc.

29. Glenn Fulbright, interview with me and Stephanie Smith, June 13, 1999, Lenox, Massachusetts, ECD Doc.

30. Pat Ruggiero, interview with me, August 28, 2000, Pinewoods Camp, Plymouth, Massachusetts, ECD Doc., and Yarnal interview.

31. Mary Alison (pseudonym), interview with me, August 29, 2000, Pinewoods Camp, ECD Doc.

32. Murrow interview.

33. Sharon Green, interview with me, August 28, 2000, Pinewoods Camp, Plymouth, Massachusetts, ECD Doc.; Alison interview.

34. Brooks, *Bobos in Paradise*.

35. Jenny Beer, e-mail to me, December 11, 2000.

36. Lasch, *Haven in a Heartless World*. See also Peiss, *Cheap Amusements*.

37. Ruggiero interview.

38. Jenny Beer, interview with me, August 30, 2000, Pinewoods Camp, Plymouth, Massachusetts, ECD Doc.

39. Yarnal, Ruggiero, Green, Murrow, Alison, and Beer interviews.

40. Ruggiero, Beer, Murrow, and Alison interviews.

41. See *Country Dance and Song Society 2000–2001 Members List* (Haydenville, MA: Country Song and Dance Society, 2000). The society lists about 3,600 individual and family members, spread over every US state and Canadian province. It also has members in fifteen other countries, mostly in England and Denmark.

42. Roediger, *The Wages of Whiteness*; Lipsitz, *The Possessive Investment in Whiteness*; Jacobson, *Whiteness of a Different Color*; and Brodkin, *How Jews Became White Folks*.

43. See Roediger, *Wages of Whiteness*; Jacobson, *Whiteness of a Different Color*.

44. See Walkowitz, *Working with Class*.

45. George Whitesides, interview with me and Stephanie Smith, June 14, 1999, Lenox, Massachusetts.

Becoming Middle Class

THE LOCAL HISTORY OF A GLOBAL STORY—COLONIAL BOMBAY, 1890–1940

Prashant Kidambi

Long neglected by historians, the Indian middle class has suddenly become the object of scholarly inquiry. A significant body of writing has emerged in recent years on different aspects of the social history of the middle class in British India. Two themes have been prominent in these works. First, scholars have shown that the idea of respectability was a central feature of middle-class politics and its interventions within the public sphere. Constructing "a new moral, cultural, and political code" based on notions of "self-respect" was "an important part of the activities of the middle class" within this domain. It was through such activities, as Sanjay Joshi has argued, that "a hitherto politically insignificant group of men from 'service communities' was able to emerge as the new arbiters of appropriate social conduct and to establish new modes of political activity that empowered them at the expense of the traditional elites of the city, less powerful social groups, and ultimately also the British rulers."[1] Second, historians have also drawn attention to the "politics of anxiety" that shaped middle-class identity.[2] On the one hand, the self-definition of the Indian middle class and its claims to public leadership were based on "assertions of moral superiority that were connected to the cultural dimensions of modernization." On the other hand, "the identity of the colonial middle class was defined as much by its ambivalences as by its attachments to colonial modernity." Indeed, as Leela Fernades notes, "modernity was experienced as a series of deprivations that invoked a fundamental sense of anxiety in the middle class in the nineteenth century."[3]

This chapter draws on these insights in exploring some aspects of the social history of the Indian middle class in colonial Bombay in the period between 1890 and 1940. Bombay's middle class, unlike its counterparts in Bengal and northern India, has not attracted much scholarly attention. This chapter redresses this neglect and focuses on two key themes. First, it highlights the importance of activities within the public sphere in defining the middle class in Bombay. In particular, it shows how various initiatives to improve and civilize the poor in Bombay served to consolidate the public identity of the city's emerging middle class. Second, the chapter seeks to extend to the late colonial period arguments about the "politics of anxiety" that underpinned middle-class lives. It shows how the volatile economic conditions of the decades between the two world wars inflected public discourse about the middle class. In particular, it argues that in a period characterized simultaneously by economic flux and the availability of a growing range of consumer goods, anxieties about consumption came to occupy an important place in debates about the quotidian practices of middle-class life.

The Middle Class in Bombay

In the course of the late nineteenth century and the early twentieth, there emerged in Bombay an intermediate group of English-educated Indians—lawyers, doctors, engineers, businessmen, journalists, teachers, and clerks—who began to identify themselves in public discourse as "middle class." This social group was a product of colonial policies that dated back to the second quarter of the nineteenth century. The process had commenced in 1822, when the Native School Book and School Society, which had been set up by the Bombay Education Society, began to provide education in the vernacular languages to Indian students. This institution was replaced in 1827 by the Bombay Native Education Society, which sought to improve the existing educational infrastructure. In 1834 college education became available at the newly founded Elphinstone College, which had emerged out of the Elphinstone Institution. The activities of the existing school and college institutions were amalgamated in 1840 and renamed the Elphinstone Native Education Institution. The new institution was placed under a Board of Education that became responsible for administering all educational institutions in the Bombay Presidency.

The expansion of the educational system under the aegis of the Board of Education paved the way for the establishment of the University of Bombay in 1857. This led to a further formalization of the educational network, with the university standing at the apex of the tiers of colleges and secondary schools throughout the presidency, the whole system being supervised by the Department of Public Instruction, which had replaced the Board of Education in 1855. By 1900, the Bombay Presidency possessed thirteen institutions of higher learning (including arts and professional colleges), with 2,662 students enrolled, and 481 secondary schools (including both high and middle schools where English was the medium of instruction), with a total of 47,223 students.[4] Bombay City was the principal node in this educational network and the premier center of higher learning in western India. Not only was Bombay's Elphinstone High School "the leading school in the Presidency, both in numbers and in examination results," but the city had "also benefited from the growth of private high schools . . . encouraged by the operation of the Government's grant-in-aid scheme from 1866–67."[5] Moreover, three of the most prestigious arts colleges in the presidency were located in the city, as were the Grant Medical College and the Bombay Law School.[6]

The English-educated Indians who emerged from these institutions were by no means a homogeneous group. In terms of social origins, for instance, the educated middle class in Bombay, unlike in Calcutta, was not drawn principally from the petty landed gentry.[7] Rather, those who took to higher learning in the Bombay Presidency belonged both to scribal castes such as the Brahmins and Pathare Prabhus, which had long traditions of employment in the administration of precolonial regimes, and to communities such as the Parsis and (admittedly to a much lesser degree) the Khojas and Bohras, whose roots lay in the world of commerce.[8]

Nor were those who emerged from English schools and colleges an undifferentiated stratum with regard to their socioeconomic status in urban society. In Bombay, by the 1880s "successful lawyers, doctors and educated businessmen" had begun to be "widely separated in fame and fortune from government clerks and assistant masters in high schools."[9] Those who carved out a successful professional career for themselves could "make an extremely comfortable livelihood, either independently or in association with a *shetia* [wealthy merchant or businessman] who needed his skills." Some members of the new English-educated professional middle class had also acquired wealth and property on account of their social moorings in the world of trade and industry.

By the end of the nineteenth century, the more successful members of this educated middle class, mostly drawn from traditional high-status castes and communities, had begun to match the city's established business elite in terms of their social status and prestige.[10] At public occasions such as the visits of imperial dignitaries, important events associated with the British sovereign and the royal family, the celebration of victories connected with the British Empire, and other civic gatherings, members of the city's professional elite rubbed shoulders with the shetias. Socially, too, the more successful of the educated intelligentsia forged connections with the commercial and industrial elite, and some pursued lifestyles that were not very different from those of the wealthy business magnates.

At the other end of the spectrum, the world of the English-educated middle class also encompassed those who occupied a more humble niche in urban society. This stratum included those who had relatively modest educational attainments and staffed the lower levels of the government and private mercantile offices. Schoolteachers, clerks, peons, and the like constituted an urban petite bourgeoisie whose economic resources and lifestyles were far removed from those of the professional elites and educated businessmen. But, as in Calcutta, the dividing lines within the world of the Bombay middle class "were permeable."[11] Indeed, there were some well-known examples in Bombay of men who had risen from humble clerical ranks to positions of eminence in later life. For instance, Javerilal Umiashankar, a Nagar Brahmin, "began as a clerk in a spinning and weaving company and afterwards became a merchant," and another Brahmin—Raghunath Narayan Khot, a Saraswat who had graduated from Elphinstone College in 1840—"rose from a clerkship in a merchant's office to make a fortune in commerce."[12]

Notwithstanding the internal differentiation in the objective conditions of their existence, a number of processes within the urban context were vital in shaping the collective identity of the new social class that these men claimed to represent. First, their exposure to colonial educational institutions and the new forms of knowledge imparted there set educated middle-class Indians apart from the world of the unlettered, both rich and poor.[13] Second, the emergence of a flourishing print culture in the late nineteenth century further consolidated the distinctive identity of this class.[14] Finally, the public sphere of civil society was central to the making of the middle class. The first two processes have been the staple fare of writings on the middle class and need not detain us here. However, scholars have only recently begun to recognize the importance of the public sphere in the self-fashioning of the middle class. It is to this theme that I now turn.

Recent scholarship has shown how the making of the middle class in colonial India was a cultural project fashioned through decisive interventions in the public sphere, beginning in the late nineteenth century.[15] Braiding together Brahminical and high Islamic notions of spiritual purity and moral piety with Victorian discourses of improvement and self-discipline, a range of intermediate and high-ranking Hindu scribal and trading communities,[16] as well as *ashraf* Muslim service gentry, came to constitute themselves as new arbiters of appropriate social conduct by redefining notions of respectability.[17]

There are three noteworthy features about the middle-class redefinition of "respectability" in the late nineteenth century and the early twentieth. First, it was integral to middle-class projects of "social reform," a term that denoted a desired transformation among high-status castes and communities of cultural practices that were perceived as being both irrational and the root cause of India's decline as a civilization. Second, in their quest for public leadership, middle-class spokesmen also deployed the discourse of respectability against entrenched elites, most notably the traditional Indian aristocracy and moneyed classes. Third, as the new, self-proclaimed leaders of Indian society, the middle class's quest for "social sovereignty" rendered it imperative that educated Indians "obtain the obedience of the poor" to the new norms of bourgeois respectability, and as a consequence, "the mission of social and moral reform was a central element in the relation of the Indian elites to those whom they identified as the poor and the lower classes."[18]

It is the last of these themes that I wish to pursue here. English-educated Indians had internalized both the colonial ethic of improvement as well as modern "governing conventions" regarding the disciplined conduct of the self in the public sphere.[19] Moreover, notwithstanding important differences, they shared with colonial ruling authorities a belief in the need "to make the bazaar, the street, the *mela*—the arenas for collective action in pre-British India—benign, regulated places, clean and healthy, incapable of producing either disease or disorder."[20] Thus, the emerging Indian middle class came to view the public norms and practices of the poor with a mixture of distaste, contempt, and anxiety. The urban poor were frequently characterized in the Indian press as illiterate, ignorant, and backward; they were also regarded as being prone to wanton outbursts of passion and fury that transgressed the norms of civilized public sociability.[21]

Zealous social activists in colonial Bombay attacked all those plebeian practices that they regarded as contravening the norms of respectable public conduct. For instance, middle-class moralists repeatedly targeted alcohol consumption among the city's working classes and called for liquor shops to be closed on occasions such as religious festivals. Frequent allusions were also made in the Indian press to the connection between drinking liquor and the propensity of the lower orders to indulge in degenerate and licentious behavior in public. Nationalist newspapers also criticized the impact of the colonial government's excise policy on public morals. Indeed, in the eyes of some critics, far from minimizing the temptation of alcohol, the government was responsible for allowing a large number of liquor shops to flourish in "the very heart of localities where large ignorant and thriftless labouring populations have their residences."[22] Temperance campaigns were launched to counter the spread of drinking and encourage purity and thrift among the city's laboring poor. The first association for this purpose had been founded in 1887, when the Indian Temperance Association (affiliated with the Anglo-Indian Temperance Association) set to work among the city's millworkers. But it was during the first decade of the twentieth century that the movement really gathered momentum in the city.

Members of Bombay's intelligentsia also sought the suppression of popular modes of observing the Islamic festival of Muharram, which were regarded as being incompatible with the norms of public decency. In particular, the *tolis* or street gangs that roamed the city during Muharram became the target of sustained criticism.[23] For those who claimed to represent the respectable classes, the raucous observance of Muharram increasingly came to epitomize the degeneracy of the plebeian culture of the street.[24] For instance, the *Din Bandhu* directed the attention of the police commissioner to the "disgustingly indecent gestures which are made by those who accompany the *tabuts* in the presence of crowds of people of both sexes who assemble to witness the *tamasha*." "In no other city that we know of, is so much license allowed as in Bombay," it added, while pleading with the police commissioner "in the name of public morals and decency to put a stop to the filthy exhibitions."[25]

Significantly, educated opinion among Muslims and Hindus alike was vociferous in its condemnation of the excesses of the lower orders during the festival. Sections of educated Muslim opinion, for instance, argued that the festival was meant to be a somber ritual of mourning, and that the practices of the lower orders were un-Islamic. They found support for such views among their educated counterparts in other communities. The problem, sections of educated Hindu opinion argued, was that though the festival was a purely Islamic event, the lower orders of Hindu society insisted on participating in it. According to one Hindu newspaper, it was "not so much the Musalmans who are to blame in this respect as the non-Musalman classes, who run riotous on these occasions and who can easily be stopped if an example be made of some of them or if the manager of a *tabut* [model of the tomb of Hussain at Kerbala carried in procession during Muharram] or a *panjia* [a model of a hand with five fingers extended, each representing a member of Prophet Muhammad's family, which was paraded during Muharram] be held responsible for the good behaviour of his following."[26] It was, therefore, not uncommon for educated Hindus to demand that the government prohibit the participation of the Hindu poor in the festival by refusing to grant them licences to make *tabuts*.[27] Educated Hindu opinion often cited the support of the Muslim elites for such police action by arguing, as the *Dnyanodaya* did, that "the better class of Mahomedans would by no means be displeased if the police cleared the streets of all the low exhibitions of painted men and boys, a large proportion of whom are probably not Mahomedans at all, but Hindus of the lower classes, who use the occasion for sport and profit."[28]

Likewise, reform-minded middle-class Hindu spokesmen and politicians found repugnant the popular mode of celebrating the Holi festival (the Hindu spring festival of colors), and the unseemly excesses that characterized it. Although the celebration of the festival among the upper classes was said to be "a tame affair," for the millworkers of the city, Holi was believed to be "one continuous round of hilarity by day and night."[29] During the festival it was the practice among the working classes to organize tamashas in which young boys dressed up in female attire and moved around the city, collecting subscriptions for a final entertainment. "A diversion of a riotous and noisy character," V. A. Talcherkar noted, "is provided by those who besmear their bodies with soot and oil or with glowing colours, and rig themselves up in fantastic nondescript dresses as jesters, tigers and bears, and play comic antics with a trail of street arabs following." As in the case of the Muharram *tolis*, these were said to "levy blackmail on shopkeepers, specially the Marwadis, or money-lenders, and threaten well-dressed people with a rub-down with their greasy or sooty bodies."[30]

Concerns about the excesses associated with the popular mode of celebration prompted the founding of a Hollika Sammelan (sammelan: literally, a formal or informal gathering) in 1911 by some of the city's prominent reform-minded, liberal Hindus, men like Sir Narayanrao Chandavarkar, Gopal Krishna Devadhar, and N. M. Joshi.[31] The aims of the committee that convened this social-purity movement were "to create a strong public opinion against the excesses of Shimga"; "to keep off young boys and persons belonging to the labouring and depressed classes from unhealthy influences and practices"; and "to impress on the minds of the unthinking masses the fact that these unhealthy practices had absolutely nothing to do with religion."[32] In order to attain these objectives, the Hollika Sammelan sought "to divert the attention of these people from the usual filthy practices to healthy amusements and to organize for this purpose counter-attractions." Thus, it organized sports events, *kirtans* and *bhajans* (Hindu devotional songs), and other forms of entertainment to educate workers in place of their more raucous activities during the festival.[33]

At the same time, the middle-class project of social improvement and civic reform had a powerful pedagogic dimension.[34] As putative leaders of Indian society, members of the middle class increasingly saw it as their duty to educate the poor and inculcate in them modern norms of civic life. The terrifying plague epidemic of the late 1890s had sharpened perceptions among the city's educated middle class that the poor needed to be enlightened about modern principles of sanitation and personal hygiene. Western epidemiological theories that attributed the plague to filth and poverty were enormously influential in informing the attitudes of the Indian educated middle class toward the city's poor. Echoing the views of many colonial medical practitioners, the Parsi social reformer Behramji Malabari wrote in 1897 that the plague epidemic in Bombay "was a disease of the poor," caused by "chronic poverty, habitual underfeeding, insanitary surroundings, and want of physical stamina."[35] Many middle-class observers also held that the unhygienic habits and squalid living conditions of the poor were a menace to public health.[36]

Confronted by, and concerned about, the far-reaching economic and social changes of their times—the rapid pace of industrial urbanization, the emergence of a vast proletarian population, and the growing class differentiation in the city—members of Bombay's educated classes adapted to their own ends the ideas and institutional forms deployed by their counterparts in other global contexts. Most notably, in the early twentieth century a new rhetoric and practice of social service emerged. While "social reform" during the late nineteenth century had largely denoted the internal attempts at self-improvement by particular castes and communities, "social service," as articulated and practiced by members of the English-educated intelligentsia, was directed at the destitute, downtrodden, and disadvantaged.

One of the first organizations in colonial Bombay that devoted itself to professional social work was the Seva Sadan Society, which Malabari founded in July 1908. A report in the *Indian Spectator*, which described the aims and activities of the society, stressed the need for "wholesome students of the poor and the distressed, students of their compensations, students of the law of rewards and punishments, students of the Science of Prevention and of the Art of Consolation and Cure." The report also contended that prior to the society's establishment, "there was no indigenous, non-prosleytising, non-sectarian organisation for lovingly serving all the three races, independently of caste and creed." The society—whose trustees included men like Sir Narayanrao Chandavarkar, Sir Bhalchandra Bhatawadekar, Sir Vithaldas Thackersey, and Gokuldas Parekh—primarily devoted its energies to improving the lot of destitute women. Its activities were divided "into four broad departments—healing the sick, protecting the helpless, instructing the ignorant, and teaching some industry which enables poor women to earn their livelihood."[37]

By far the most prominent of such initiatives was the Social Service League, which was established in March 1911 by some of the most prominent professional middle-class men in Bombay's public life.[38] The league was explicitly "founded on a non-sectarian and broad basis, and its membership was thrown open to all persons without distinction of race or creed."[39] Organizers of the league declared that their principal "motive power" was "a sense of the common brotherhood of man and the innate feelings of the universal love for mankind, pity for the sufferings of the miserable, and justice for all."[40]

The league was especially concerned about the problems of the city, which were seen in explicitly organic terms. According to one contributor to its journal, *The Social Service Quarterly*, "a city does not grow merely by more roads and houses, even better roads and higher-rent houses; but with the growth of the health, comfort, and progressive well-being of its citizens, in all matters and in all aspects in which men live together as social beings."[41] "The well-being of the whole," he added, "depends on the well-being and growth of the constituent parts."[42] Looking around him, this writer perceived a number of pressing problems in Bombay's teeming working-class neighborhoods that prevented such a state of well-being from being attained: overcrowding, dirt, disease, drunkenness, and other social vices such as gambling and prostitution. In order to render the city "healthy" and "fitter," he argued, it was necessary not only to eradicate these evils, but also to nurture "various *positive* forms of social life and social work" that would help "to raise the comfort and well-being of the people."[43]

The league set itself a number of objectives in its founding charter. First, it aimed to collect and study "social facts" and to discuss "social theories and social problems with a view to forming public opinion on questions of social service." Second, it was dedicated to the "pursuit of social service generally and specially with a view to ameliorate the physical, moral, mental and economic condition of the people." A third objective was the "training of social workers."

The league's charter also proclaimed the group's intention to undertake measures for the "organization of charities and social work."[44] In the years that followed, the league laid great emphasis on the practical side of its work. It campaigned for mass education, improved sanitation, and social purity; tried to raise public awareness of the importance and value of social service; and conducted relief work among the urban poor during times of distress.

But the league's activities were not free of internal constraints and contradictions. Its financial resources were not only precarious, but also highly dependent on charitable donations from the city's moneyed elites. Such financial constraints undoubtedly played a part in prompting the league to undertake welfare work on behalf of corporate firms that were able to fund such activity. But this, in turn, rendered its motives suspect in the eyes of many workers. It is not surprising that the organization was rapidly marginalized once the Communists established their political supremacy over Bombay's working-class districts in the 1920s.

Equally, while many of the league's activists had genuine sympathy for the plight of the working classes, they nonetheless partook of the dominant elite discourse, which represented the workers as ignorant, irrational, and intemperate. Indeed, the difficulties that the activists encountered in conducting social work among the working classes served at times to confirm their inherent prejudices about the poor. Furthermore, even though the activists agreed that the task of social work was to make workers independent and self-reliant, their own outlook was paternalist and pedagogical. Hence, the rhetoric of service was imbued with conservative impulses.

The Politics of Anxiety

The previous section highlighted the significance of initiatives within the public sphere in constituting the middle class in colonial Bombay. At the same time, there was another side to the social existence of the middle class: those who aspired to inclusion in this category were beset with anxieties of all kinds. Indeed, it has been argued by Leela Fernandes that "culturally based projects of social reform and moral regeneration" were largely aimed at managing middle-class anxieties about their place in the world. This "politics of anxiety," it has been suggested, "unfolded through a set of middle class debates that centred on social distinctions such as gender and religion."[45] Historians pursuing this line of analysis have focused largely on the late nineteenth century. In what follows, I argue that in the decades between the two world wars, the middle-class "politics of anxiety" came increasingly to focus on the material context of everyday life. Notably, issues pertaining to consumption became central to self-representations of the middle class, especially among those sections that felt most insecure about their place in the urban social order.

The period after the First World War was marked by an expansion in the range of goods, services, and mass entertainments available to city dwellers in India. Equally, the deepening of market relations also led to a proliferation in the choices that consumers had. However, during the 1920s and 1930s such choices had to be made in the context of considerable economic uncertainty and financial hardship. Thus, the emergence of an incipient mass culture and new sources of consumption combined with the rising cost of living and growing unemployment to produce a new concern about domestic economy among members of upper-caste service communities that identified themselves as middle class.

The reflections of contemporary observers shed light on the pressures and dilemmas confronting families within the city's service communities as they struggled to negotiate a new climate of economic flux and rapid social change. On the one hand, those who claimed to belong to the middle class were conscious of the fact that consumption had become an essential measure of status in a modernizing urban context where the traditional markers of the caste hierarchy were no longer adequate guarantors of social standing. On the other hand, their insecure economic situation consistently forced these men and women to monitor their daily spending.

The rest of this section illustrates these themes through a discussion of one particular service community in Bombay during the interwar period. The Kanara Saraswats were a Brahmin community whose members had been migrating to Bombay from the Kanara region in southern India since the late nineteenth century.[46] By the early 1920s there were over two thousand Saraswats in Bombay.[47] They were largely employed in white-collar occupations in the city. Indeed, over 90 percent of the adult males in the community worked as clerks in various commercial establishments, law firms, and government offices.

Like others of their profession, the Kanara Saraswats were badly affected both by the rising cost of living and by the fluctuations in Bombay's economic fortunes that resulted in high unemployment among white-collar workers during the 1920s and 1930s. One consequence of these developments was a growing sense of anxiety within the community about the competing demands of status and solvency. The intense debates over these issues were regularly published in the pages of the *Kanara Saraswat*, the monthly journal of the Kanara Saraswat Association in Bombay. The articles contributed to this journal offer an insight into the ways in which the men and women of traditional upper-caste service communities, who explicitly identified themselves as middle class, responded to the pressures and anxieties generated by the onset of the age of mass consumption.

The danger inherent in living beyond one's means was a recurring theme in the articles published in the *Kanara Saraswat* during the interwar years. The "wicked habit of living beyond one's means," one writer argued, had pauperized many well-to-do families, "while exercise of proper economy has made comparatively poor families self-reliant, happy and contented."[48] The ideal family, in this view, was one that adopted a simple lifestyle and abjured all forms of conspicuous consumption.

Some Saraswats argued that the tendency to live beyond one's means was an outcome of the changing urban environment and its many new enticements—such as the cinema—which had caused men of moderate means to lose their self-restraint. Thus, "in spite of themselves the young and the old of Bombay feel themselves inextricably encircled in the general and indiscriminate scramble for the ignoble and vicious pleasures of life, and a considerable number of them is actually stranded in the plague-spots of Bombay misnamed her pleasure-resorts."[49] For others, however, it was the essential psychological characteristics of modern man, rather than the urban environment, that was at the root of the problem. Yet whatever the perceived cause, most contemporaries agreed that rapidly changing social mores had eroded the traditional values of the Saraswat community. A number of observers contrasted the happy Saraswat home of the past with what they clearly regarded as the pernicious trends at work in the present.

The perception that the "wicked habit of living beyond one's means" was one of the most pressing problems facing the community prompted many Bombay Saraswats during the interwar years to emphasize the need for personal thrift. Interestingly, some observers believed that the urban salaried classes, far from being innately thrifty, were naturally prone to be more profligate in their patterns of expenditure.

But what exactly did contemporaries mean when they called for "thrift"? The articles in the community's journal suggest that thrift did not entail abstaining from consumption altogether; rather, it called for judicious discrimination in one's patterns of expenditure. Central to the cultivation of thrift, writers argued, was the need to distinguish between necessities and luxuries. According to one contributor, "Luxury is said to be practiced when we demand a thing which is not quite indispensable while in the case of necessity one can't do without the thing required."[50] The problem, as some Saraswats saw it, was that the desire for a comfortable lifestyle and the demands of middle-class status were increasingly blurring the traditional distinctions between necessities and luxuries. In other words, "ideas of comfort have reached a higher level, and that fine line of demarcation between what is a necessity and what is a luxury is fast disappearing. The consequence is that several young men become despondent when they do not get what they think they ought to possess."[51]

Contemporary Saraswats also regarded the elimination of waste and excess in patterns of consumption as being integral to the cultivation of thrift. One observer wrote in 1928: "The greatest hindrance to thrift is waste. Extravagance as such as may fall to the share of only a few. But there are numerous abuses leading to waste which the generality of us care little to stop, either through ignorance or carelessness, leading later on to a habit."[52]

Significantly, their reflections on the topic of thrift point to the tensions experienced by Saraswats seeking to negotiate the competing demands of two parallel systems of social hierarchy. On the one hand, they were obliged to perform rituals and ceremonies that were essential to the maintenance of their upper-caste status and identity. On the other hand, the cost of these traditional practices constrained their ability to engage in forms of consumption that were an important marker of urban middle-class status. Indeed, ceremonial rituals increasingly came to be perceived by many middle-class Saraswats as needless expenditures. However, some Saraswats argued that it was anxieties about their status within the modern social order, rather than an adherence to the old way of life, that impelled middle-class men and women to engage in ostentatious festivities. In other words, the expenditure on traditional ceremonies was being driven increasingly by a shallow desire to keep up appearances.

Contributors to the *Kanara Saraswat* in the 1920s and 1930s dwelt frequently on the need for efficient domestic economy. Indeed, following the inquiry into middle-class family budgets published by the newly established Bombay Labour Office, some Saraswats urged their brethren to practice diligent household budgeting, rationalize their patterns of consumption, and use their scarce financial resources with discretion and discipline.[53]

The most sustained and systematic attempt in this regard was by H. Shankar Rau, a prominent member of the Saraswat community in Bombay, who expounded the virtues of sound budgetary management in a series of articles published between March and September 1934.[54] In order to illustrate the benefits of proper household management, Rau constructed the family budget of an average "*Bombay middle class family* of three adults and two children, a family with a gross monthly income of Rs. [rupees] 175."[55] If this family was careful in balancing its budget, he conjectured, it would probably spend its income as follows: sixty rupees for food; eight for fuel and lighting; twelve for clothing; three for bedding; thirty-five for rent; and fifty-seven for miscellaneous expenditures. The scope for domestic thrift for such a typical middle-class household was, he admitted, decidedly limited. In particular, the first five items "do not admit of much curtailment," since any retrenchment might "tell on the health of the family and increase medical charges."[56]

Rau's typical middle-class family could not afford to have a cook. Moreover, in his view, at six annas per head, the amount spent on food "happens to be no more than twice the cost of the daily rations allowed to the C class prisoner in an Indian Jail!" In these circumstances, he argued, it was "not possible for an ordinary middle class family to reduce this scale without impairing health or upsetting convention." But, he suggested, a careful middle-class family ought nonetheless to consider measures that might bring about small economies. This could be effected by buying household items through cooperative schemes, reducing prices by buying in bulk; minimizing needless expenditures on visitors; stopping "altogether the habit of taking tea, coffee etc, either in the house or out of it," given that it was "a habit of comparatively recent growth which does a great deal of harm when repeated too often"; "the gradual elimination of salt, spices and condiments from our dietary"; undertaking steam cooking instead of "ordinary boiling and frying," which, in turn, by avoiding "over-boiling of rice or boiling over of milk" would eliminate the "untidy cook" and the "elaborate kitchen"; and, finally, not serving "what is not at all needed, or more than is needed."[57]

Rau buttressed his case for greater economy in food consumption in the middle-class Saraswat household by pointing to practices in Europe that he regarded as exemplary. For instance, "the European would not think of dining, lunching or taking tea with a friend unless the friend invited him, usually several days beforehand. And then, he is at liberty to take just what he wants and is seldom pressed, if ever. It is such conventions as these that we must copy from the West with advantage."[58]

At the same time, he drew on indigenous Brahminical ideas that embodied "the wisdom of the East." In particular, invoking Hindu notions of bodily humors, Rau argued that food that was "bitter, sour, saline, over-hot, pungent, dry and burning, and which produces pain, grief and sickness," or that which was "stale and flat, putrid and corrupt" was to be avoided at all costs. Adhering to these suggestions, he contended, was "desirable not only from the higher point of view of ethics, but also from the practical point of view of health, and . . . from the lower one of thrift."[59]

Rau also suggested various ways in which the average middle-class family could trim its expenditure on those non-food items that could not be eliminated without triggering serious status repercussions. For instance, he advised Saraswat householders that fuel and lighting costs could be reduced by restricting the number of visitors; "accustoming themselves to the use of tepid or cold water for the bath in preference to hot water"; and "suitably regulating the use of electric light." Likewise, expenditure on clothing could be reduced if, like Europeans, one relied "on regular washing and ironing and on personal gait and posture rather than on the expensive nature of the material"; avoided "the use of separate collars, neck-ties and waistcoats, if possible"; and did "not omit to mend clothing at the right moment: a stitch in time saves nine." One could also save money on bedding, utensils, and other household necessities by eschewing "the prevailing tendency to stuff little rooms with disproportionate quantities of furniture and knick-knacks which not only drain the purse but also give the rooms a cramped appearance and hinder what little free movement is otherwise possible."[60] On the other hand, there was no chance of economizing on rent. The middle-class family in Bombay faced special difficulties because it spent a higher proportion of its income on rent than people living elsewhere in India.

Given the limited scope for savings in the first five categories, Rau discerned greater possibilities for the exercise of thrift in the category of miscellaneous expenditures. "Unlike the other groups," he observed, "it contains a variety of items which may be classed as necessaries, conveniences or luxuries according to one's taste." He listed the following items in this category: income tax; servant's wages; payments to the barber and washerman; "tram or train fares between residence and office of earning member"; "postage, stationery, soap and other toilet requisites"; children's education; medical charges; amusements ("mainly visits to the cinema"); tobacco; and speculation ("competitions, lotteries, satta or races").[61]

Yet closer scrutiny revealed that here, too, many expenditures were unavoidable, given the status requirements of a middle-class household. For instance, for the majority of salaried employees there was "no getting away" from paying income tax. Rau continued:

> The servant cleans the vessels, washes the clothes and sweeps the rooms, and would strike if you reduced his wages; the ladies in our middle-class families are not accustomed to this sort of work. Even in these days of self-shaving, the barber of the saloon or of the visiting fraternity, is required to rear the only crop of which most of us are now the proud possessors; and so

is the washerman who must needs split the recalcitrant stone with the humble shirt. The earning member has perforce to get his season ticket to go to work and cannot walk it out. Postage, stationery, soap and toilet requisites offer little scope for the retrenchment axe. These items thus represent charges which are more or less fixed and obligatory.[62]

Nor was it easy to reduce expenditures on education, which " 'is as expensive as it is necessary." Although reforms were needed in this area, there was very little prospect of a reduction in the cost of education. Likewise, medical charges, "generally a very fluctuating quantity," did not permit of any savings either.[63]

Finally, the miscellaneous category also included expenditures incurred on account of personal vices or the urge to sample the mass entertainments available to the modern city dweller. Rau observed:

> In a place like Bombay, you find temptations at every corner—inviting cinemas which have the most insidious influence on character and a very perceptible one on eye-sight; and countless opportunities for dissipation of every kind, including gambling which begins innocently with cards, "competitions" and lotteries, masquerades as business in cotton and shares, and ends ignominiously at the races. The chief causes are increasing lack of parental control which breeds false notions of independence, and the deplorable absence of a moral and religious background to school education which leaves youth an easy prey to temptation.[64]

However, unlike the other items of miscellaneous expenditure, which did not permit of any major reduction on account of their status connotations, Rau argued that the inducements of urban mass culture could be avoided by adopting a purer lifestyle. In other words, the remedy lay in the "healthy occupation of leisure hours—good company, wholesome reading, useful honorary work, a determined attempt, through devotional exercises in particular, to attain purity of thought, word and deed." Thus, he suggested, by avoiding the urge to give into the temptations of urban mass culture and adopting a more spiritual way of life, the middle-class household could "enjoy better health and truer happiness."[65]

Rau viewed consumption with ambivalence. His account recognized that consumption was a key marker of social worth in the modern world. Indeed, he took it for granted that the demands of middle-class status made certain forms of expenditure inescapable for the average Sarawsat household. At the same time, Rau exalted the values of purity and simplicity and was sharply critical of the hedonistic logic of modern consumer culture. He regarded the unrestrained pursuit of material possessions and pleasures as being inimical not only to the physical and moral well-being of individuals, but also to the values of sociality within the community.

Conclusion

This chapter has tried to highlight some aspects of the making of the middle class in colonial Bombay. How do these specific episodes in a local story relate to the global history of the middle class? I think they do so in two ways. First, the evidence from Bombay bears out the insight of a number of recent studies, both in India and elsewhere, that have suggested that the middle class is best understood not as an objective, sociological entity, but as a project constantly in the making. In particular, it was through activities and interventions in the public sphere that the collective identity of the middle class was forged. These initiatives took a variety of forms, but a common thread running through them was the redefinition of respectability in keeping with the new moral code fashioned by the middle class.

Second, the findings of this chapter also resonate with recent historical accounts of other parts of the modern world, which have stressed the importance of material concerns and status anxieties in the construction of middle-class identity. British historians, for instance, have highlighted the role of the so-called new consumerism of the early twentieth century in defining middle-class identity.[66] Likewise, a study of Japanese bourgeois culture in the early twentieth century has shown that material factors, especially consumption, were integral to the status aspirations of a growing class of white-collar workers in cities like Tokyo.[67] Similar themes have also figured prominently in recent work on Latin America.[68] Notably, in a delicately etched study, Brian Owensby has drawn attention to the centrality of market relations and the material context of everyday life in the fashioning of middle-class social identities in Brazil during the early twentieth century. Patterns of consumption became both a crucial marker of status that enabled Brazilian middle-class men and women to distinguish themselves from those below in a culture that remained hierarchical, and a source of perennial domestic anxiety as they confronted the pressures of a society increasingly ordered along class lines.[69] It was a predicament that their counterparts in late colonial Bombay would have well recognized.

Notes

I am grateful to the University of Leicester for granting a period of study leave that enabled me to carry out the research on which this chapter is based. I also wish to thank A. Ricardo López for his help in preparing the chapter for publication.

1. Joshi, *Fractured Modernity*, 2.

2. Fernandes, *India's New Middle Class*, 12.

3. Ibid.

4. *Report of the Director of Public Instruction in the Bombay Presidency for the Year* [hereafter *RDPI*], *1899–1900* (Bombay: Government of Bombay. 1900), 1. The numbers of those appearing for university examinations rose fairly rapidly during the late nineteenth century. Although in 1865 there were only 166 candidates for the various degrees, by 1900 the number was 4,178. Tikekar, *The Cloister's Pale*, 47.

5. Dobbin, *Urban Leadership*, 161.

6. In 1900, 1,556 students were enrolled in these five institutions of higher learning collectively. *RDPI, 1899–1900*, appendix, xiv.

7. Sarkar, *Writing Social History*, 169.

8. McDonald, "English Education and Social Reform in Late Nineteenth Century Bombay," 454; Dobbin, *Urban Leadership*, 31–36, 160–63.

9. Ibid., *Urban Leadership*, 172.

10. Cashman, *The Myth of the Lokmanya*.

11. Sarkar, *Writing Social History*, 228.

12. Dobbin, *Urban Leadership*, 50.

13. See, for instance, Kumar, *Political Agenda of Education*.

14. Sarkar, *Writing Social History*, 173–74.

15. Joshi, *Fractured Modernity*.

16. For a summary, see O'Hanlon, *A Comparison between Women and Men*, 1–62.

17. Joshi, *Fractured Modernity*, 1–58. Gail Minault's recent study on the movements for social reform among the Muslims in the late nineteenth century shows this process at work in the creation of ashraf identity. See Minault, *Secluded Scholars*.

18. Gooptu, *The Politics of the Urban Poor*, 14.

19. Kaviraj, " 'Filth and Public Sphere,' " 92–93. For a general treatment of the role of the ideology of improvement and its indigenous analogue, dharma, in structuring relations of elite domination and subaltern subordination in the context of colonial India, see Guha, *Dominance without Hegemony*. However, Guha views these ideologies as a manifestation of a structural logic immanent in the state and the dominant proprietary classes in Indian society. Consequently, his account tends to gloss over the specificities of historical context.

20. Chakrabarty, *Habitations of Modernity*, 77.

21. See Gooptu, *The Politics of the Urban Poor*.

22. *Indu*, October 11, 1910, *Report on Native Newspapers in the Bombay Presidency* (RNNBP), no. 42, 1910 (Bombay: Government of Bombay).

23. The most prominent of these traditions was that of the *tamasha*, a theatrical form whose combination of risqué humor and bawdy sexual innuendoes was extremely popular among the city's laboring poor. Arguably, the tamashas enabled the urban poor to contest their subordinate status in everyday life through innuendo and satire directed at those who exercised domination over them. It was generally the practice in such performances to lampoon figures such as the *banias* (an occupational caste of traders, shopkeepers and money-lenders) and the *marwaris* (traders from Rajasthan, well-known throughout India for their money-lending and mercantile activities), who were the creditors of the poor. See, for instance, *Din Bandhu*, September 7, 1890, RNNBP, no. 37, 1890.

24. *Dnyanodaya*, September 5, 1889, RNNBP, no. 36, 1889.

25. *Din Bandhu*, September 6, 1890, RNNBP, no. 36, 1890.

26. Ibid.

27. See *Din Bandhu*, July 8, 1893, RNNBP, no. 27, 1893. See also *Subodh Patrika*, June 17, 1894, RNNBP, 25, 1894.

28. *Dnyanodaya*, July 28, 1892, RNNBP, no. 31, 1892.

29. Talcherkar, "'The Shimga or Holi Festival and the Bombay Mill-Hands,'" 176.

30. Ibid., 177.

31. Kunzru, *Gopal Krishna Devadhar*, 103.

32. Ibid., 104.

33. Karnik, *N. M. Joshi: Servant of India*, 27–28.

34. In this context, see Naregal, "Figuring the Political," 18.

35. Malabari, *India in 1897*, 10.

36. On middle-class representations of the poor in this context, see Arnold, "Touching the Body."

37. "Sisters of India," *Indian Spectator*, August 24, 1912, 665.

38. Karnik, *N. M. Joshi*, 36–49.

39. Chandavarkar, *A Wrestling Soul: A Story of the Life of Sir Narayan Chandavarkar*, 163. The league had five classes of members based on the extent of monetary contribution. These ranged from life members, who had made donations of over five hundred rupees, to those in the lowest class who generally paid anything between one rupee and four rupees a year.

40. "The Social Service League, Bombay: A Brief Record of Four Years' Work," *The Social Service Quarterly* 1, no. 1 (1915): 21–25.

41. Muzumdar, "The Social Problems of a City," 27.

42. Ibid.

43. Ibid., 28–29.

44. The Social Service League's charter was usually published at the end of all its reports and publications.

45. Fernandes, *India's New Middle Class*, 12.

46. For the history of this caste, see Conlon, *A Caste in a Changing World*.

47. Talmaki, "Census of Kanara Saraswats in Bombay and Suburbs, 1922."

48. "What Is the Most Pressing Need of the Saraswats at the Present Day? A Symposium of Opinions of Some of Our Respected Leaders," *Saraswat Quarterly* (here-

after *SQ*), April 1919, 24. The journal was renamed the *Kanara Saraswat* in January 1922.

49. Karnad Sadashiv Rao, "The Future of the Kanara Saraswat," *KS*, October 1925, 8.

50. Vatsala Nath, "Luxuries and Necessities in Saraswat Homes," *KS*, September 1929, 8. Adopting "the standard of a middle class Saraswat family," this writer set out to enumerate the necessities and luxuries in such a household. Her list of necessities included a drawing room, a kitchen, a small library, a daily newspaper, a medicine chest, and interestingly, an "elderly person" who could "guide the younger generation in their life." The list of luxuries comprised cooks ("more a curse . . . than a necessity"), tailors, and, significantly, children. "Pious god-fearing people might be shocked to know that such a question is raised at all," she wrote about having children. "In these hard times," she added by way of justification, "when the addition of a soul into the family means so much more strain on the purse, they might be a luxury. At any rate they are not a necessity when they come in plenty." Ibid., 8–9.

51. "What Is the Most Pressing Need of the Saraswats at the Present Day?," 2.

52. A Faddist, "Stray Thoughts on Thrift," *KS*, April 1928, 4, 7.

53. Of course, middle-class discourses about domestic economy were by no means a new development. As scholars have shown, the need for thrift was a common theme in the modern didactic literature that emerged in the subcontinent in the second half of the nineteenth century. See Joshi, *Fractured Modernity*, 70.

54. Rau, "Family Budgets," 15–31.

55. Ibid., 16. In estimating the size of the typical middle-class Saraswat family in Bombay, Rau drew on two existing reports. In its enquiry into middle-class family budgets published in 1928, the Bombay Labour Office had suggested that the average household size was 5.09. And the community census conducted by the Kanara Saraswat Association in Bombay in 1932 had established that "the average Chitrapur Saraswat family consists of 5.4 members, and the average income per head per month is Rs. 31." Ibid., 15.

56. Ibid., 16–17.

57. Ibid., 19–20.

58. Ibid.

59. Ibid.

60. Ibid, 22–23.

61. Ibid.

62. Ibid., 24.

63. Ibid.

64. Ibid.

65. Ibid.

66. Gunn, "The Public Sphere, Consumption and Modernity," 20–23.

67. Garon and Maclachlan, *The Ambivalent Consumer*, 191–92.

68. Parker, "Middle-Class Mobilization and the Language of Orders in Urban Latin America," 376–77.

69. Owensby, *Intimate Ironies*.

Conscripts of Democracy

THE FORMATION OF A PROFESSIONAL MIDDLE CLASS IN BOGOTÁ DURING THE 1950S AND EARLY 1960S

A. Ricardo López

> We need a professional . . . capable of reconstructing true understandings between capital and labor . . . All we need is a true professional to instill in the society as a whole the desire for progress . . . the desire to live in democracy . . . a professional capable of accomplishing peace . . . to modernize our society by closing the gap between those who have everything and those who have nothing . . . then peace, political stability and a true democracy will necessarily follow . . . This is the task of the twentieth century . . . this is all we need to do[!]
>
> ALBERTO LLERAS CAMARGO[1]

In 1954, the Colombian architect Alberto Valencia took a short trip to the small town of Anolaima, two hours from Bogotá, which he later wrote about to his mother. As an architect at the Inter-American Housing and Planning Center—a joint project of the Organization of American States and the US Office for Technical Assistance—Valencia was excited to arrive in a "remote but attractive place" because "a middle-class guy like [him]" could use this trip to find "the reality of social life." After some days in the field, Valencia resolved to leave his books and the city behind. Instead, he would return to Anolaima to teach local people "how to build houses, how to live in a community . . . how to live in democracy." He wanted to "know the Colombian peasants *in person* . . . their families . . . their lives . . . their souls, their activities." Indeed, he wanted to transform those peasants into "modern citizens of the Colombian nation." Yet he complained that it was "the cultured Colombian elites" who would be the major obstacle in such an important task. Valencia hoped that his fellow professionals would be "committed to work for a democratic society . . . to be fully involved with those who [were] oppressed." In a moment of self-consciousness, Valencia defined himself as a privileged man who had been born "in a beautiful class . . . a class that makes democracy irresistible."[2] His concerns, complaints, and self-definitions raise critical questions about the formation of the middle class in Bogotá during the late 1950s and 1960s. What were the historical circumstances and discursive conditions that enabled Valencia to classify himself as a "middle-class guy"? During those very political years in the Americas, what did it mean to be middle class? Why did the peasants as well as the working class and the "cultured elites" play such as important role in Valencia's self-understanding as a middle-class guy? In the late 1950s—a crucial moment in Colombia's Cold War history, when traditional Liberal and Conservative parties entered into a political coalition for national reconciliation, peace, and democracy—why did he find it so important to be committed to living in a democratic society? What role could he play in creating such a democratic society?

Recent studies repeatedly underline the historical process after the Second World War through which the United States tried to push other societies in the Americas toward a liberal, democratic, and capitalist modernity by promoting the creation of a stable, prosperous middle class inoculated against Communism. These historical narratives have operated under the shared assumption that a domestic "American way of life"—embodied in the so-called middle-class nation—was transparently ready to be exported to the rest of the Western Hemisphere as a central part of development programs such as the Alliance for Progress. If the whole process failed, some argue, it was because, due to certain political and social conditions, Latin America was not ready for a democracy built around a middle class. More recent studies have criticized these development programs by arguing that these policies were only part of a wishful thinking that never became a reality. Some scholars contend that the goal of "improving" the people of "the third world" by making them middle class was a failure precisely because policymakers did not put into practice the social policies they promoted.[3] Had these policymakers accurately implemented their noble intentions to forge a middle class, a truly democratic society could have been created in the Americas. Instead, and contrary to what the policymakers endorsed in theory, US foreign policy during the Cold War in practice weakened the democratic processes in the region as it only "fortified illiberal forces, militarized societies," and limited the social definitions of democracy.[4] As a result, these narratives not only move us away from a more complicated historical analysis of the development programs but also condition us to understand the middle class in the Americas either as a distorted variant of the putative US middle class ideal or as a failed implementation of otherwise well-intentioned or benevolent US policy.[5]

In light of these narratives, historians and social scientists alike have organized their historical inquiries by asking whether the Latin American middle class could become a democratic force—that is, become more like the US middle class. In scholarly works as well as foreign-policy studies, the strength of the middle class has always been regarded as the barometer of modern democracies. Consequently, some scholars have argued quite strongly that the middle class has historically played a democratizing role, while others have been equally determined to show that this class has historically been an antidemocratic force in Latin America. Still others have argued that the middle class has indeed been both democratic and antidemocratic in different contexts. These scholarly debates have left the historical definitions and practices of democracy largely unquestioned because we take for granted the very historical relationship between these practices and meanings and the political consolidation of a middle class.[6]

In this chapter I argue that the power of this ideal of a middle class fundamentally associated with the workings of democracy cannot be diminished merely by presenting counternarratives of what it meant to be middle class in Latin America, which challenge a political model associated with the United States or Europe. Furthermore, this chapter looks specifically at the crucial juncture of the late 1950s and 1960s in Colombia, when the consolidation of the National Front—a bipartisan coalition—sought to usher in a new era of political reconciliation, democracy, and peace by systematically implementing a series of social, political, and economic programs. Rather than ask whether these policies and programs succeeded in resolving the political conflicts known as *la violencia*, the question posed by a number of Colombian historians, I instead explore how the concept and practice of "middle-class professional" became embedded in a new form of democratic rule in the context of US imperial expansion.[7] In so doing, I seek to shift the register of the historical analysis away from questions about where, whether, or to what extent the middle class has been an obstacle to or a promoter of democracy. Instead, I attempt to critically interrogate the historical practices and political rationalities through which a professional middle class became inserted in US imperial rule after the Second World War—why, as vehemently suggested by the chapter's epigraph, did it become so important to create a middle class as a political requirement for achieving a specific notion of progress, peace, and democracy? In short, why did people like Alberto Valencia think that his role as a middle-class professional man would make democracy irresistible?

Toward an Imperial Humanist Governance

During the late 1940s and early 1950s, a new geopolitical order was emerging, characterized by conflicting camps aligned with the United States and the Soviet Union as well as by renewed challenges to the legitimacy of European colonial rule. New political questions, answers, forms, and methods figured in the conceptualization of how governing should be accomplished. In 1939, the US government had set up its first organized and systematic technical cooperation program with Latin America as a part of President Franklin D. Roosevelt's Good Neighbor Policy. The new program was intended to give technical advice, on request, to the government of any American nation. With the potential involvement of the nations of the Western Hemisphere in the Second World War in mind, an executive order from President Roosevelt established the Office of the Coordinator of Inter-American Affairs. Nelson Rockefeller was appointed to this position and shortly thereafter established the Institute for Inter-American Affairs, a government-owned corporation that was authorized to carry out cooperative programs with Latin America governments to promote public health, housing, economic development, public administration, and agricultural development. In 1944, a similar corporation, the Inter-American Educational Foundation, was organized to provide hemispheric cooperation in support of elementary and secondary schools. These Latin American experiences prepared the United States to undertake the Point Four Program of technical cooperation on a transnational basis that, following President Harry Truman's inaugural address of 1949—known as the Four Point Speech—initiated a major program to promote technical assistance, modern technology, knowledge exchange, and capital investment. The International Development Act, approved by Congress in 1950, supplied financial assistance to carry out many technical cooperation programs. In the same year, the Office of Technical Cooperation Administration was established as part of the Department of State. Simultaneously, several recently established international and transnational institutions—the Organization of the American States, the United Nations, the International Bank for Reconstruction and Development—inaugurated an integrated set of liberal economic development policies, technical assistance plans, social welfare activities, population improvement programs, and cultural management agendas.

These reforms, technical programs, and social policies constituted a reconfiguration and reconceptualization of the legitimate forms and methods through which to exercise imperial rule. More specifically, policymakers, institutional experts, consultants, intellectuals, and politicians engaged in a debate about how to overcome what Truman had called "the old imperialism" in 1949.[8] Economic insecurity, fear of anticolonial unrest, and real and imagined concerns for the spread of Communism provoked—or accelerated—debates regarding how imperial rule should be accomplished and made it a central political question.[9] Intellectuals, experts, and policymakers in Colombia and the United States asked what they considered crucial questions: What were the most effective ways to govern in what was seen as a new political context? What methods were appropriate and adequate? What sort of person had the ability to govern effectively? Who should govern whom? What sort of training produced effective leaders? What governance methodologies were most productive in ruling political relationships in society?

According to many documents from this era, traditional imperialism was no longer considered an adequate basis for overseas expansion and influence. In contrast to colonial rule, the new US political agenda in the world was to promote democracy, spread freedom, and invite people in underdeveloped areas into a process of self-governance. As Truman put it when he announced the Point Four Program in 1949:

> The old imperialism—exploitation for foreign profit—has no place in our plans. What we envisage is a program of development based on the concepts of democratic fair dealing . . . Only by helping the least fortunate of its members to help themselves can the human family achieve the decent, satisfying life that is the right of all people. Democracy alone can supply the vitalizing force to stir the peoples of the world into triumphant action, not only against their human oppressors, but also against their ancient enemies—hunger, misery and despair . . . Slowly but surely we are weaving a world fabric of international and growing prosperity . . . We are aided by all who desire self-government and a voice in their own affairs. We are aided by all who long for economic security—for the security and abundance that men in free societies can enjoy . . . [10]

William W. Beatty, an educational consultant for community development programs, went further. In 1958 he wrote a lengthy letter to the United Nations Technical Assistant program in community development in Colombia, insisting on the need for different practices when "approaching the underdeveloped world."[11] History, he wrote, had not allowed the United States to have a period of preparation before its assumption of "international leadership responsibility," as Britain and Europe had had. And precisely because it was unprepared, the United States had made "terrible mistakes" in its foreign relations with the rest of the world.

It was this very same history, however, that would indeed prepare the United States to assume a "leadership role in world affairs." By drawing a specific parallel between the American War of Independence and the mid-twentieth-century process of decolonization, for instance, a State Department report in 1954 portrayed the United States as the model to emulate in what was considered a universal struggle against tyranny. As the first colony liberated through democratic revolution and industrial capitalism, this report went on, the United States could instinctively relate to the historical situation of "dependent and colonial peoples." As a result, the United States could potentially be ready to help, rather than hinder, the spread of democracy and liberty. History, the report concluded, would be the background against which the country could sponsor the development of political independence across the world.[12]

History, however, was not enough. It was necessary to depart from what was considered the practices of "old imperialism." If Truman believed that US involvement in Latin America, because of its lack of interest in profit, could be distinguished from European colonial rule, several policymakers argued otherwise. Ward Hunt Goodenough, a professor of anthropology at the University of Pennsylvania and an active writer on programs for community development, contended in 1957 that US foreign programs in the first half of the twentieth century had primarily been geared to what he called "economicism."[13] Like former European colonizers, Goodenough argued, the United States had offered, at worst, only bread and roads, and, at best, agricultural technology, too.[14] Furthermore, this old imperialism was based on practices of "domination, imposition and subjugation." These practices assumed that people in the underdeveloped countries were, first of all, passive recipients of economic aid; second, victims of their own situations; and third, unable to "think . . . act . . . feel and desire by themselves."[15] In contrast to both European colonial rule and earlier US economicism, America now would use "more imagination and implement multiform approaches" when exercising its "new leadership role." If old imperialism—and its inherent economicism—was a manifestation of domination, America would now develop an international role which would depend on "negotiation . . . engagements . . . social contracts, compromises, exchanges of interests, meaningful encounters, and understandings." Furthermore, if the old imperialism was based on imposition, the United States would approach other regions "by being sensitive" to their "cultural differences." And if the old imperialism worked by subjugating and marginalizing the people of the underdeveloped world, the United States, as self-designated leader, would now inquire as to what the people wanted, desired, and thought. Furthermore, America would fight subjugation by restoring the people's participation, giving them a voice, and promoting "the real possibility that underdeveloped countries [had] interests . . . [and] autonomy to shape their own destiny."[16] Above all, Beatty argued, the United States would seek to develop a role that could break from the practices and understandings of the old imperialism, in which underdeveloped countries were able to do only what "powerful countries commanded" them to do. Instead, the United States would foster the "active participation" and "constant consultation and representation" of underdeveloped countries. In doing so, the United States would be promoting the "development [of] human welfare."[17] This concern for human welfare, Nelson B. Henry—a professor at the University of Chicago—argued, was at the very center of American democracy, which had been built on the proposition that each "human being in himself is significant." As a nation, Henry continued, the United States was being challenged to develop the maturity to conceive of a large "democratic plan" with other nations, which, he said, was actuated by the desire to help meet the needs of people in communities everywhere because "human beings are involved."[18]

What was at stake in all this political determination to get away from these practices that were categorized as old imperialism at the very moment when US foreign power was invigorating Latin American militaries, orchestrating military interventions (such as the coup of 1954 in Guatemala through which a democratically elected president was overthrown), and supporting centralized intelligence agencies? These discussions could be dismissed as empty rhetoric meant to mystify or to mask or even justify imperial activities.[19] In fact, many scholars understand these discourses as a false ideology intended to obscure the realpolitik of empire, as a denial of US imperialism, or as the manifestation of US imperial exceptionalism. I want to argue that by carefully studying these discourses, we can critically interrogate one practice of rule—in my view, a very important one that has not received critical assessment—in the large inventory of US practices of domination during the second half of the twentieth century. These political preoccupations constituted the formation of a new problematic of rule—a new process of governing through which an imperial project could become central to the formation of the US nation during the second half of the twentieth century.

During the 1950s and 1960s, the US government, along with several international institutions, would set in motion new practices of governance as well as a new political rationality underlying them. One of the major specific effects of these practices was the consolidation of community development programs in different parts of the world.[20] Moreover, these programs accelerated an imperial project of rule working within a transnational framework that was every bit as powerful as the better-known programs of US military and economic imperialism. Although in operation since the aftermath of the Second World War, these community development programs were consolidated during the 1950s and more forcefully implemented with the launching of the Alliance for Progress in 1961. Despite the discourse critiquing the old imperialism, the very first attempts at community development drew heavily on the experiences of the British colonial administration with rural social projects in India, as well as community-based organizing prototypes in Mexico, Bolivia, and the Tennessee Valley during the first half of the twentieth century.[21] Significantly, the Cold War versions of these programs appeared in Puerto Rico and the Philippines during the late 1940s. By the early 1950s, the US government, together with international institutions, was consolidating a variety of community development programs to then institutionalize these programs as state policies throughout Latin America under the auspices of the Alliance for Progress.

These programs, I would argue, activated a political rationality that usually was oriented toward several interrelated projects of economic development, human welfare, and proper political preparation for what policymakers and experts both in Colombia and the United States constantly referred to as modern democracies. In seeking to distinguish themselves from an imagined old imperialism, these programs were shaped by a political rationality—mediated by the production of knowledge in the social science disciplines of cultural anthropology, psychology, and rural sociology—that promoted rule through the capacities and productivities of the human body. Older social development programs, it was argued, were centered only on, at best, financial and technical problems, and at worst, "coercively imposing, destroying or disempowering and marginalizing people's participation."[22] In contrast, these new community development programs would incorporate a "culturally and socially sensitive approach" that would take into account how people in the underdeveloped areas of the world were "socially and culturally embedded human subjects." In so doing, it was argued, the US leadership role would depend on constant encounters leading to social arrangements that would allow the communities of the underdeveloped world, through proper economic, political, and cultural guidance, to "best utilize the *human capital* and natural resources available in promoting the interests of their own communities."[23]

Thus the "poor populations of the world" could "learn to understand their own current situation, the disastrous effects of poverty for them, their families, and their countries."[24] Furthermore, this "new mentality" would enable the emergence of a "society [where] human beings" would be able to "take care of themselves and others."[25] Indeed, it would mean a consolidation of what I want to call a society of governors, in which the poor could be guided according to their own interests, so they would learn to govern themselves by first contributing to their own economic progress and development, and, second, and perhaps more important, by living "in freedom and democracy."

This transnational society of governors would be possible if the social, political, and economic agency of the people of the underdeveloped world could be reshaped.[26] For so long, the conceptualizers of these programs in Colombia and the United States argued, an "authoritative approach" had merely used a top-down relationship to deposit ideas and knowledge on passive recipients who had no active role in shaping their society. In stark contrast, the new community development paradigm would work within a "democratic framework." The new programs would promote "bottom-up social approaches" to create truly participatory and "democratic spaces" where the people would be able to develop their own ideas and cultures, enhance their own capabilities, become aware of their own problems, evaluate their own conditions, and, above all, understand what goals they could reach.[27] Furthermore, by stimulating, comprehending, and adapting to the ideas, activities, cultural limitations, social conditions, and sentiments of the poor, community development programs would transform passive subjects into active ones—indeed, the programs would alter "submissive[,] socially constrained" subjects into "fully self-determined" people, capable of acting according to their own self-interest so they would behave as they should in a democratic environment.[28]

By gaining a voice and participating in their own betterment, the poor people of the Third World would become conscious of their oppressed position. And precisely for this reason, it was imperative to know how to guide the energies, political capital, and human potentialities of the poor in their "imminent awakening." People had to be democratically trained—by letting them speak, taking care of them, and promoting their participation—so that they could be politically awakened and taught how to govern themselves. Only then would the people of the Third World be able to exercise their "power of decision, intelligence, their freedom and their autonomy" and enter into a society of self-governors where they would be "responsible, complete and free" to recognize, understand, and, above all, resolve their own problems.[29]

Imperial governance, then, was to take place not by coercion, imposition, or destruction, or by marginalizing people or educating them so they could do nothing but consent. Rather, it would happen through a process of conducting, schooling, guiding, and encouraging proper forms of self-government, self-discipline, and self-guidance that targeted "people's talents . . . human abilities, people's actions, human aspirations, interests, desires, feelings, and beliefs."[30] In short, the new imperial project was to target what policymakers, intellectuals, and politicians constantly came to refer to as human capital. As Caroline Ware, a professor at Howard University, put it in one of several studies sponsored by the Organization of American States during the 1950s, community development programs "will lead to a sense of social human solidarity . . . a concept of conscious, willful and enthusiastic participation of the underdeveloped people. The programs assume the recognition of the natural existence of the latent potentialities of the community, of the human dignity. It recognizes the people's power of decision, their autonomy and their freedom . . . [and] restores their active role in society . . . It is based on the real belief that people are able to live in democracies . . . [and] exercise their role in shaping societies."[31] This process would consolidate a new form of rule—a governmentality—that I will refer to as imperial humanist government.[32] During the 1950s and 1960s, this "govern mentality" was based on a political rationality that promoted human welfare, economic development, and political training so that the people of the underdeveloped world could participate profitably and democratically in their own rule. This mentality was integrated with new technologies of government that sought not to subjugate people or impose authority, but rather to guide human capabilities and productivities, thus enabling social actors to become self-governing. In short, this imperial humanist governance was constantly seeking to make the Third World a society of governors—that is, to make them capable of governing themselves.

The Role of the Middle Class in the Imperial Humanist Project

Central to this imperial humanist project was the formation of a professional middle class. If it was crucial to engage the people of Latin America in the process of improving their own human welfare, economic development, and political training, the simultaneous—if contradictory—process of schooling and guiding a professional middle class was also imperative. Furthermore, imperial humanist governance would take place not in opposition to or in support of, but through democratic middle-class professionals, who would be properly educated, oriented toward, and led to the transformation of the democratic relations between different social groups. That is, the conduct of the professional middle class had to be guided so they could become competent and capable of organizing, distributing, stimulating, and creating the necessary human capital for "national democracies to emerge."[33]

This democratic middle-class professional, conceived of as an agent of transformation and a social catalyst, was to labor not only by helping the poor but, more important, by helping the people to help themselves. The democratic middle-class professionals were to create new "attitudes . . . desires . . . feelings, [and] social climates."[34] Indeed, they would develop new paths for the poor to follow, new lights for the people to see, new aspirations for underdeveloped people to adopt, and new ways of life for the people to understand. They would be professionals skilled in the art of stimulating and helping people at the local level, in guiding them along a path of planned progress for change. They would be friends and brothers of the community who could bring democracy in specific ways to the peasants, so the people would be able—through the professionals' guidance—to become self-governors.

Policymakers, intellectuals, and experts both in Colombia and the United States spent quite some time crafting and producing knowledge about the importance of this democratic middle class. According to several studies carried out by the United Nations, the Organization of American States, and the Rockefeller Foundation, it was necessary to rationalize the tasks of nation-states by training these middle-class professionals, without whom no governmental system could function effectively. The Inter-American Socio-Economic Council of the Organization of the American States, for example, argued that for democracy to work, it was essential to have "intelligent [and] prestigious professionals" who would give themselves—their minds, bodies, and souls—to the tasks of the state and the national ideals of "justice, freedom, progress, social change, democracy and community development."[35] Furthermore, the mission was to create a "human [and] democratic middle class" by putting to work a new class of political professionals who would develop the human capacities to relate to "all social classes in society" and to "freely" recognize the "value [and] worth of another social group," and set up the conditions of "self-understanding."[36]

Those middle-class professionals would work for the state by teaching the poor how to fight "ignorance, ill-health, and low productivity," how to be aware of their "qualities and conditions," and, above all, how to think by—and certainly of—themselves so they were able to participate in democracy. As members of the Inter-American Socio-Economic Council argued in a meeting in 1955: "A society that is full of middle class professionals promoting the use of intelligence and the capabilities of the American man for the benefit, interests and aspirations of the American community . . . professionals who can break the inertia and put the essence of the poor in action . . . professionals that can fight the social isolation of the elites . . . they would put a *human face to capitalism*."[37] And it is in this process that the formation of the middle class became inserted into the new methodology of imperial democratic rule. This specific process of forming middle-class professionals became so integrated with technologies of democratic government precisely because of a political rationality that promoted the creation of a society of governors who could develop themselves into "autonomous selves, capable of actively acting" in the process of democracy, according to their own desires. The new practices of rule had to be based on the formation of a class of professionals who worked for nation-states and who could guide the desires, interests, and, above all, the human capital of the different social groups—in contrast to an imagined "class of experts" who "forced upon individuals and groups what they [knew] was good."[38]

Thus this imperial humanist governance sought to create a hierarchical redistribution of tasks in which democratically capable professionals were able to guide what was considered certain inherent responsibilities and obligations of those who were not yet able to do so themselves. For democracy to work effectively required a distinction yet also a close relation between those considered competent to discover the so-called poor's human capital and those who needed such democratic professionals to discover their own human capital and political potentialities for progress and development. This view assumed an asymmetrical relationship between the two groups, with a hierarchical allocation of specific roles. It was a hierarchical division between those who had the capability to awaken the "dormant attitudes, democratic potentialities . . . and sentiments for change" of the society as a whole and those who needed the knowledge or sentiments of others to become aware of their own potentialities, sentiments, and attitudes.

In sum, the United States, along with several international institutions, promoted a form of democratic government to be achieved by constantly constructing a class rule that rested on hierarchical distinctions between those who were guided to govern others and those who were expected to be governed by others. In the process, I would argue, this new form of imperial rule produced a constant need to define and redefine who could become the best governors in a society of governors. In turn, this constant need provoked endless transnational discussions on how to select and educate these professionals, who would not only make "harmonious societies" but also, and equally important, create "national democratic states."[39]

The Middle Class as a "Center of Attraction"

Perhaps the most important episode precipitating the introduction of community development programs in Colombia was the spurt of *la violencia* during the late 1940s and early 1950s. Erupting a full decade prior to the Cuban Revolution, this process greatly concerned the US government, which had come to see ongoing social unrest in Latin America as a potentially serious problem. The programs and policies on community development, however, went well beyond the concern about containing Communism. Rather, these new initiatives were part of a transnational preoccupation with creating a new form of democratic rule. Specifically, during the late 1940s and early 1950s, the Technical Cooperation Administration, developed as part of the Point Four Program, and the US Agency for International Development, not only provided funding to different programs but also coordinated several activities promoted by other international institutions. And working within an inter-American framework, the United States began to send economic missions to the Third World as part of the process of formulating a program of development for Latin American countries. These missions, along with international development institutions and private US organizations, founded or sponsored technical centers, vocational schools, training centers, universities, and other institutions to train professionals in different areas of technical knowledge and social sciences.[40] Soon after the announcement of the Point Four Program by President Truman in 1949, and specifically after the US-sponsored Colombia IV and Colombia XXV Programs were formalized during the late 1940s and 1950s, the government of President Mariano Ospina (1946–50) invited a mission organized by the International Bank for Reconstruction and Development to visit Colombia. It was the first mission of this kind that the bank sent to Latin America. Formulating a general development program for the country, the mission held discussions about foreign exchange; the transportation, industrial, and service sectors; and health and welfare. The mission's final report repeatedly insisted on the "vital import" of the "assessment of middle class values and middle class participation in development" and the "training of talented professionals" as a crucial part of the renewal of the Colombian state.[41] The government of Laureano Gómez would embrace these policies by supporting the creation of the Colombian Social Security Institute and the Colombian Institute for Technical Education during the early 1950s.[42] The following administration, of Gustavo Rojas Pinilla, sponsored additional social programs that were expanded during the caretaker military regime that held power for fifteen months after Rojas's overthrow.[43] The National Front was a power-sharing arrangement between the Liberal and Conservative Parties that lasted from 1958 to 1974. Alberto Lleras Camargo and Guillermo Leon Valencia, the first two presidents of the National Front, constantly argued for a professionalization of the relationships between social groups in order to overcome Colombia's turbulent recent past—that is, to avoid a return to *la violencia* and create the conditions for democracy and peace to emerge. Alberto Lleras Camargo constantly extolled the community development programs as state policy and founded the Division of Community Action in 1959. These transnational programs and activities for community development, and their concomitant middle-class labor force, were further consolidated (but not initiated as some have believed) in 1961 when the United States launched the Alliance for Progress. As a clear response to the Cuban Revolution of 1959, the Kennedy administration intensified, multiplied, and expanded already existing programs of community development that the United States hoped would deter the rise of Communist insurgencies elsewhere in Latin America. In this context, the first two administrations of the National Front launched several more programs through national private organizations such as the Federación Nacional de Cafeteros (FEDECAFE), together with international institutions such as the United Nations, the Organization of the American States, the World Health Organization, and the Cooperative for American Relief Everywhere (CARE), all of which promoted or sponsored educational institutions, training centers, and universities in Colombia.

The proliferation of these entities worked to expand everyday practices of state rule. As part of their effort to create conditions in which democracy could flourish, the National Front administrations envisioned the possibility to overcome *la violencia* as a political conflict, pacify the different social and political sectors involved in such conflict, and "rehabilitate" the nation economically so Colombia could become part of the charmed circle of the "developed nations." In so doing, I want to argue, the first two National Front Administrations actively sought to consolidate a new form of rule and domination through which the state could become concerned with the promotion of a "new meaningful community life." The purpose, furthermore, was to guide Colombia to "reach social peace and economic justice, physical well-being and democracy." In order to do so, President Alberto Lleras Camargo argued, it was necessary to "create a new Colombian state . . . a new Colombian nation . . . fervently developing its resources and enriching the lives of its people where the great bulk of its population lives and where development really counts most: the local community [and] a local community with hope and ready for self-determination."[44]

As part of this national process of pacification and rehabilitation during the late 1950s and early 1960s, the ideas and practices of community action worked in tandem with the growing interest in *la violencia*, which was increasingly becoming an object of epistemological contemplation. In response to it, not only were Colombian experts, governmental institutions, and policymakers pondering new containment policies informed by sentiments concerning the real and imagined Communist threat, but also, and perhaps more important, they were considering how rule should be accomplished—that is, as Lleras Camargo put it in 1959, how "to *make social relations right*."[45]

A year before the launching of the Alliance for Progress, for example, the international agency CARE signed a contract with the Colombian government to provide support, training, and advice in community development. As part of this program, the Colombian government sent several experts to participate in the US-sponsored programs on community development in the Philippines and Puerto Rico. After these trips, Richard W. Poston—a professor at Southern Illinois University, a prominent writer on community development, and a special consultant in Colombia on behalf of the US government and CARE—wrote several letters to Lleras Camargo describing the major problems that Colombia was facing, as well the first changes that needed to be implemented in order to "enter into [a] meaningful democracy." According to Poston, the problem was not the absence of a middle class in Colombia but, rather, the persistence of one characterized by what Poston called an "anti-human consciousness." To wit: a middle class, on the one hand, "set off from the lower classes . . . expressing disdain for the peasants and the working classes," and, on the other hand, constantly aspiring "to copy the way of life of the elites." This antihumanistic middle class, Poston continued, did not have a productive relationship with either the elites or the poor. And precisely because Colombia was facing new challenges and changes, it was necessary to redefine the specific roles of the classes in society. In order for a "democratic relationship to happen," Poston proclaimed, what was needed was a "new intelligent and feeling middle class . . . A responsible middle class . . . a human middle class . . . a middle class who would care for others . . . A truly professional middle class whose members become the pivot of development, democracy, peace and social justice."[46]

In a reply, Lleras Camargo acknowledged that in Colombia "there [had] not been a middle ground between the upper and the lower classes," but he said he was certain that a "democratic middle class [was] needed." Drawing on ideas of community development, the president contended that a "democratic horizon . . . beyond violence" could become a reality as long as social relations would pivot around the middle class—that is to say, if Colombia became a society in which a democratic middle class was constantly "*the center of attraction.*"[47] Middle-class professionals would become, he argued, a humanistic force to create "lasting relationships among different groups in society." This humanistic class would help the oligarchies to undergo a process of "self-renewal" and, above all, "transform their own social principles." Furthermore, a professional middle class—by developing a solid knowledge of those "at the bottom of the society"—could "make the elites sensible of [their] role in society," could "place new social concerns" for the well-being of others at the very center of an "elite ethos," and, perhaps most important, give the elites the capacity for "sympathiz[ing]" with "the problems of poverty."[48] In a word, a professional middle class could transform the oligarchies into modern elites.

On the other hand, the professional middle class, as a humanistic force, would also "channel the energies, capacities and capabilities of the poor." In doing so, this democratic middle class would prepare the people to "develop stronger relationships with the elites." In a context in which the people had become aware of the oppressive role of the elite and their tendency to isolate themselves from society, place their well-being above that of other groups, and manifest neither interest in nor sympathy for Colombia's social problems, continued Lleras Camargo, middle-class professionals could be the path to a democratic horizon by "go[ing] down to the level of the peasants . . . or workers" to be "sympathizers," while at the same time they could "travel" to the "upper classes" to become "well-informed [and] knowledgeable counselors for the elites."[49]

What was at stake in this discussion was a political question about how to create new social subjects by means of which a democratic state could be created. As "sympathizers" with the lower classes and as "counselors" of the elites, democratic middle-class professionals could be hierarchically ordered as a "center of attraction" so they would be able to govern social relations in a society in need of peace and democracy. The professional middle class became associated with the possibility of abandoning a confrontational style of politics and warding off Communism. A middle class could put Colombian society above and beyond *la violencia* by creating the conditions that would lead to a hierarchical social harmony and political peace.

In a fluid transnational dialogue, this goal of creating a middle class as a center of attraction was appropriated by several advisors to the Kennedy administration and the experts engaged with the Alliance for Progress. Closely replicating the discussion between Lleras Camargo and Richard Poston, Arthur Schlesinger Jr., a Harvard historian and advisor to Kennedy, wrote to the president that, above all else, the Alliance for Progress should engineer "a middle class revolution where the processes of economic modernization carry the new urban middle class into power and produce, along with it, such necessities of modern technical society as a constitutional government, honest public administration, [and] a responsible party system."[50] It is important to emphasize that these political conceptualizations did not merely seek to establish a clear distinction between the middle class and the Colombian elite or working classes.[51] Neither did they envision the middle class as an antipolitical force, as many have argued.[52] Rather, as is clear in these uneven transnational dialogues, at issue was a reformulation of a proper, indeed democratic, hierarchical class rule to guide and conduct social relations in a modern form in the hope of overcoming *la violencia*.

Selecting Middle-Class Professionals

In recent years there has been an increase of scholarly interest in the formation of the modern state. New approaches have convincingly demonstrated both how state practices shaped local communities and how those local communities shaped the practices of the state. An important thread running through these new historical and anthropological arguments is that the state is not a monolithic, all-powerful entity or a homogeneous and efficient manipulator of subaltern groups. Rather, state projects are the result of a set of culturally and politically heterogeneous negotiations between society and the state. In this very important historical work, middle-class professionals appear as representatives of the state, through which local communities and subaltern groups are able to experience—and negotiate—the heterogeneous political and cultural practices of the state. Although my argument has been greatly influenced by this recent literature, I would nonetheless argue that these historical approaches have naturalized the relationship between state rule and the role of professionals. It is imperative to historicize how the state became classed and gendered as a result of a detailed process of selection and education in the methodologies and practices of rule. By looking at the Colombian case, I want to show in the last part of this chapter the process through which these professionals became imagined as part of the workings of state rule. In doing so, I think we can denaturalize the taken-for-granted vertical encompassment of the state by examining the hierarchical class placement of those professionals who were to work as representatives of state rule and those nonprofessionals who were imagined to be in need of being governed.[53]

During the 1950s a number of United Nations missions to Colombia requested the first National Front administration to found the National Civil

Service Office. The main task of this agency—institutionalized as a state office in 1958 and working closely with major international and national private sources of capital such as FEDECAFE and CARE, as well as with the technical support of US universities and the United Nations—was to put in place what was usually referred to as a democratic state for a democratic society. To do so, it was necessary to implement what was considered an impartial, rational, and scientific system of recruitment, selection, and training for those who would be working for the state.[54] In 1959, for example, Seamus Gaffney, director of the United Nations Mission on Public Administration in Colombia, wrote an extensive letter to Bruno Leuschner, director of the Technical Assistance Bureau of the United Nations. According to Gaffney, the future of a democratic state would depend in large measure on the selection of the "most valuable members of the society" as civil servants.[55] Gaffney mentioned repeatedly in the letter that the selection process would have to discover "apolitical professionals"—that is, professionals who could transcend the political party rivalries that had caused *la violencia*, professionals who could place themselves above the Liberal-Conservative divide—with specific qualities and attributes so they could guide "national human capital . . . resources and ethos embracing different social groups in society."[56] Furthermore, other studies and discussions argued that it was necessary to identify these most valuable middle-class professionals, who embodied certain "democratic senses, attitudes and wills."[57] The characteristics and traits necessary to govern the poor as well as the elites were thought to be part of the "nature of the [middle-class] bodies" who only needed to be educated so that a "truly competent [and] capable" professional could "emerge."[58]

It is crucial to emphasize that these seemingly abstract discussions were at the very center of the question of who could be seen and defined as a middle-class professional. Contrary to what some historians would argue, these conversations about consolidating a professional middle class were not abstractions, metaphors, or mere rhetorical devices. Quite the contrary, these practices of selection constituted the very subjectivities of those professionals who, by virtue of being chosen, could consider themselves middle class. In fact, these putatively abstract discussions of how—and who had the right—to rule were often about precisely what was at stake in middle-class professionals' daily lives.

The detailed process of selection taking place in several state institutions and private organizations during the late 1950s and early 1960s—mediated through letters of recommendation, curriculum vitae, interviews, personal essays, evaluations, exams, tests, and questions—speaks to the never-ending search for the right democratic governor to work for the state. Indeed, this process of selection structured—as much as it was constituted by—the constant need to define who could be classified as rulers and who could be categorized as ruled. Rafael Samper (the director of the Socio-Economic Division at FEDECAFE, who also worked with CARE and the Rockefeller Foundation) and Gabriel Kaplan (a sociologist and lawyer from New York who was very much involved in the community programs in the Philippines and then in Colombia during the Lleras Camargo administration) continually emphasized the need to recognize that, contrary to common wisdom, not all human beings were "cut out for the same type of identity, work, obligation or profession."[59] Indeed, in order to be practical, it was "naïve" to think that the "future professional workers" were "made." Quite the contrary, they argued, professional workers were "born." Because these professionals could be found naturally, Samper and Kaplan proposed a careful and meticulously implemented program of recruitment to discover those "necessary, indefinable, and indescribable"—and, above all, "intangible"—aptitudes, democratic attitudes, personal interests, wills, feelings, desires, wants, beliefs, and physical traits that the professional needed to manifest when exercising the arts of governance.[60] These selection processes would be sufficiently effective to reveal a clear idea of what Samper called the "anatomy of qualities."[61] This would hierarchically arrange certain innate democratic dispositions within professional middle-class bodies, a constellation of political orientations, gendered distinctions, and class categories that would ensure that the professional in question would be capable of appropriate self-conduct in ruling other social groups.

Although assumed to be inherent characteristics, these qualities still needed carefully training and education to be cultivated—that is, according to Samper, the professional middle class was not only "born" but also "made." Only then, he argued, would these qualities truly become an essential part of the professional's "habitual nature."[62]

To obtain a preliminary view of the professional candidate, it was necessary to look carefully at the person's curriculum vitae and letters of recommendation. These were used as evidence to be read along with—and against—those qualities needed by a professional working in a range of state social programs. More specifically, the letters of recommendation, usually written by those considered prestigious members of society, listed the personal properties, habits, and attributes that a professional should possess and that were imagined to be necessary in order to work for the state. Letters of recommendation were meticulously read for evidence of professional productivity, composure, intelligence, trustworthiness, and reserve. At the same time, those letters were expected to speak of the professional's passion for the "welfare of society."[63]

Candidates needed to possess a natural disposition for constant interaction with all social classes. Armed with a careful balance between idealism and realism—that is, between the belief in progress and the knowledge of the "limitations of reality"—these professional men were ready to exercise their "obligations and duties with the society at large." Confident, passionate, and responsible for resolving social problems, these men would be able to create lasting relations with the poor. Indeed, the poor themselves would be able to appreciate those personal attributes when "getting close to them."[64] And yet, precisely because these men were uniquely aware of their role in society, they could simultaneously be humble about their "intelligence, culture, education, feelings and professional preparation."[65]

A comparison of two letters of recommendation clearly illustrates the hierarchical evaluation of dispositions, the unequal indexing of properties, and the asymmetrical fragmentation of attributes thought of as necessary for the work of a middle-class professional. In a 1956 letter written by an influential member of Bogotá society to the personnel office of the Instituto de Crédito Territorial (ICT) on behalf of Manuel Mora, Jaime Sánchez said that Mora, a hard worker, would fit nicely into a professional position.[66] Sánchez argued that not only was Mora a very intelligent, cultured, and educated young man but also—and, according to Sánchez, even more important—he had the ability to learn from others. This attribute, Sánchez remarked, was not easy "to find in every other professional."[67] The report from the office of personnel at the ICT expressed excitement at the possibility of hiring somebody like Mora.[68] Mora was different from "common professionals," the hiring report argued, because he was intelligent as well as strong-minded and engaged in a constant process of self-education by interacting with others. Mora was intelligent enough to recognize the partiality and the limitations of his knowledge. These limitations and partialities, however, would be overcome by his eagerness to learn. And precisely because of this disposition, with proper training and education, he could learn to realize that "no one completely lacks intelligence." The possibility of instilling this understanding was significant, the hiring report argued, because it would eventually be valuable when Mora came in contact with "poor people who [were] not remotely as intelligent as [he was]."[69]

There is an illuminating contrast between the material on Mora and a letter submitted in 1955 by Alfonso Guevara, the director of the office of social programs in a municipal company, on behalf of Miguel Pérez, an applicant for a position at the ICT. According to Guevara, Pérez was an outstanding professional who possessed innumerable personal qualities. Like Mora, this applicant was a confident and self-conscious man. He was a well-educated individual, ready to work "for a better society."[70] Indeed, Pérez was very aware of his "unparalleled qualities" and "unmatched intelligence." Guevara argued that Pérez could also be very productive, even if the "environment around [him]" was not entirely favorable. He was a committed man who would be able to focus on his professional obligations and, if necessary, get the work done all by himself. Contrary to what Guevara expected, the report issued by the office of personnel argued that, despite outstanding qualities and attributes, the letter of recommendation revealed the lack of qualities essential for professional work. The problem, it seems, was that Pérez came across as lacking the modest nature that such "prestigious . . . professionals" needed to possess.[71] The evaluation argued, furthermore, that the letter of recommendation gave the impression that Pérez was a "*profesional del montón*"—someone who, because he had had a formal education, thinks he knows everything. This was a serious problem, the report went on, because Pérez would have a tendency to assume that he had "nothing to learn from anybody else." This tendency would have not posed a problem if Pérez were to work only with people like himself, according to the report. For the particular position in question, however, it was a liability because he was expected to be in close contact with poor people who would lack "any intellectual [or] cultural preparation," and their "intellectual differences" would be "too evident" when he came "face to face" with such people.[72] State personnel offices and similar hiring venues produced other statements, evaluations, and reports praising and encouraging the hiring of those who were categorized as "gifted men" willing to take risks in life to "change things," prestigious professionals eager to sacrifice "any privilege [they] might have" to be in "genuine engagement" with the "society around [them]." Such men embodied "unbreakable integrity" and "clear moral judgment."[73]

Each letter of recommendation was also mined for evidence of the social antecedents of the candidate. It was necessary to be generally aware of the "social origins and background" of the potential professionals.[74] This social background, furthermore, was constantly associated with—or evaluated against—"necessary virtues [and] incomparable traits" that professionals would need when performing the arts of government for the Colombian state. In 1956, for instance, Alfonso Ortíz wrote a letter of recommendation on behalf of Juan Granados to work as a professional in the housing project run jointly by the Popular Housing Fund and the ICT.[75] Granados, noted Ortiz, was an admirable example of achievement and advancement. Under very difficult social constraints, Granados had overcome his social background and been able to acquire an education, in order to "be somebody in life." If only for that reason, Ortiz argued, Granados could be a fine example of a prestigious professional man who possessed "perseverance, humility, awareness of life [and] concern for social problems."[76]

However, the evaluation of this recommendation by the office of personnel at the Popular Housing Fund drew a very different association between so-called social background and the qualities, sentiments, and attachments needed by professionals. The evaluation seemed to respond positively to Ortiz's recommendation. There was no doubt, stated the report, that Granados would be an excellent professional who would show perseverance, confidence, determination, and enthusiasm when working with his professional colleagues in different "social aspects" of the housing programs being implemented in Bogotá during the 1950s.[77] At the same time, however, the evaluation stated that Granados's social background could become a problem given the type of work he would be expected to perform. Since he would work "in an environment of poverty," his social background could conflict with—indeed, could be an obstacle to—his achievements as a "prestigious professional." Precisely because he came from the same social environment, the report assumed that he would probably have trouble doing this job. Although the difference in social origins, might not be noticeable among his professional colleagues, the personnel office staff suspected that when working with poor people, he might lack the "necessary distance and objectivity." According to the report, an essential characteristic for a professional was to embody the "capacity to tell the truth about themselves and the others around them." And in order to do so, the professional should "show strong attachment toward the poor." Granados's social background, however, would make him too close to "the people themselves," and thus he might not differentiate—that is, "tell the truth"—about what he had become and about the members of his former class. Furthermore, he would not be likely to develop a "strong social attachment" to—and, more specifically, a bond with—the poor precisely because his social constraints had shaped him as necessarily belonging to "the poor." Neither too close to belong to the poor, nor too distant to be detached toward them, professionals were expected to embody a balance, a disposition to "objectivity," as well as a hierarchical "sentiment of closeness" so they could dedicate themselves to speaking "the truth about themselves and *others* around them."[78] That is to say, in order to govern, it was necessary to calibrate not only social distinctions (as Pierre Bourdieu has argued) but also to establish hierarchical—if temporary—bonds between those who were supposed to be guided to rule and those who were supposed to be ruled.[79]

Yet, after discussing, evaluating, and pondering the letters of recommendation, different selection committees in state offices, transnational private organizations, and various training institutions generally argued that these narratives were too superficial and did not allow them to develop a more elaborated concept of the middle-class professional. Moreover, the overall conclusion was that these letters merely offered a narrow window on who was a "truly democratic professional."[80] During the late 1950s and 1960s, informed by discourses and knowledge of social psychology, cultural anthropology, rural sociology, human relations, and scientific management, these institutions began refining their entrance exams, job orientations, evaluations, interviews, hiring reports, and training sessions to carefully discover—and develop—what was understood as the "professional's second nature."[81]

Interviews were thought to make it possible to go further into the discovery of the anatomy of qualities of democratic middle-class governors. Working with four interlocking narrative forms—questions about social background, cultural descriptions, family biographical anecdotes, and accounts of personal advancement—the interviews sought to elicit a very clear perspective on the context in which the professional candidate had been immersed and had developed. It was imperative to discern the "social view of the individual," or the complex combination of values, desires, beliefs, sensibilities, convictions, aspirations, preoccupations, and interests—all the factors that went into the essential "social composition [and] makeup of the professional."[82] In a word, it was necessary to discover what was called the "human ecology of the professional."[83]

In 1955, Rubén Forero, along with several others who were applying for jobs as professionals in state offices or private companies, was interviewed for a position as an architect in the ICT's housing projects. The report issued by the committee and the office of personnel a few weeks after he was interviewed argued that Forero's responses, among other things, had faithfully shown his "commitment as a true professional man."[84] By closely connecting his self-evident "middle-class background . . . outstanding family history . . . exceptional cultural environment and noticeable personal achievement," the evaluation report asserted that these factors and conditions suggested that Forero had the innate capacity to develop the skills to work with different social groups and embody democratic attitudes when creating "close relationships with the poor." The report noted that Forero's father was an accountant, while his mother was a housewife. His parents had been married for many years, and their marriage was "ideal and harmonious." This meant, the report argued, that Forero had grown up in a family environment that valued sincerity, dialogue, calm, self-control, and honesty.[85]

More importantly, his heterosexual gendered family history had immersed —and shaped—him in a social context and cultural environment that was concerned with "service, knowledge, education, and cultural development."[86] Specifically, the report concluded that Forero amply appreciated the privilege of having a stay-at-home mother. Because of this, he had developed a "democratic sense of himself." That is, he had been able to learn "to be sensitive" about social problems, to be concerned for the complicated situations of others, and to look beyond his personal interests. Indeed, his mother had "transmitted . . . a legacy in service." Forero could embody this democratic sense, feeling of freedom, and legacy in service because his mother had always created an "integrated family environment . . . a sentiment of sacrifice and unselfishness service" that had put no social constraints on the development of Forero's bright future. Above all, Forero's mother had set an incomparable example of service by making anonymous sacrifices: in doing so, his mother had passed on to him an "inborn interest" in helping others.[87]

In addition, Forero's father had taught him "the important things in life" and had been an example of "professionalism, personal commitment in life, perseverance and cultural improvement." Indeed, his father had passed on to Forero a concern about social problems, as well as an interest in education and knowledge. This interest, argued the report, had been the most valuable legacy for Forero since it had shaped him to believe that he could find education and knowledge within himself.[88]

During the late 1950s and 1960s, state agencies and private organizations assumed that what professionals could be and do was the result of their "cultural immersion" in a hierarchically understood social background and cultural environment, with particular family histories and personal development. By essentially categorizing and classifying these social backgrounds in gender and class terms, these agencies tried to identify democratic middle-class professionals to work for the state and exercise its rule. Indeed, what was at stake was the gendered and class hierarchy between those who had the democratic right to rule others and those who had the democratic right to be ruled by others.

When women applied for jobs, especially as social workers, for instance, their interviews were equally concerned with the "social influences [and] the social milieu" to which women had been exposed. In 1958, for example, Celmira Burgos, a recent graduate of the School of Social Work, was interviewed for an ICT community development program being carried out in a Bogotá neighborhood called Quiroga. The report of this interview detailed her family history, social background, cultural description, and personal development and concluded that she had grown up "within a proper social environment."[89] Her family was considered to be middle class: she had professional parents and siblings who were students. In contrast to the evaluation of Rubén Forero's interview, which discussed both parents, Burgos's report focused mainly on her mother's role. The mother had worked as a secretary in a private firm, and the report noted how Burgos had been influenced by these social conditions. She had been immersed in a context of family support and had been educated in the "necessities and sacrifices." Her mother had taught her the most important things for a woman. Indeed, the report contended that Burgos was very aware of the "feminine tasks." Contrary to someone "driven by interest" to work, in order to achieve "material satisfaction," Burgos had been taught to view work as a means of finding a "larger social meaning." Furthermore, the balanced environment she came from had developed in her a "sentiment" to help others. For her—and the report assumed this was a consequence of her social background and family story—to work meant to resonate with the suffering of others, to be concerned with the misery of the poor, to promote the welfare of the people. This "larger meaning" would help Burgos engage with the poor, make them trust her, allow her to understand the social situation of those "unprivileged women" and, no less important, instill in others the desire to "improve themselves."[90]

Although there are comparatively few reports or evaluations on applicants who were rejected, there are elaborations on the reasons why certain candidates might have some difficulties in working as professionals. For example, the reports and evaluations of less successful candidates argued that their family environments tended to have "numerous members, consensual unions, violence, disharmony, [and] disintegration."[91] Furthermore, troubled families with complicated social backgrounds and serious "social constraints," several reports argued, translated into cultural environments devoid of proper parenting—with single mothers or, in some cases, no parental guidance at all. These families had been influenced by cultural conditions in which the "abandonment of women and children by men was normal routine." On the one hand, these "wrong cultural conditions" and social constraints would inherently shape women into those with "few feminine tendencies," no interest other than "material satisfaction," no "maternal sentiment" to help others, and a "strong self-interest" to remain in the "poor social position" where they "found themselves." On the other hand, these same cultural conditions would form innately "weak men" who were hostile, weak-willed, unmotivated, aggressive, and insecure, who expressed "contempt and rejection toward others" as well as "hateful and pessimistic sentiments [about] life."[92]

A comparison of the evaluations of two applicants in 1959, although brief, shows the problems two male candidates were expected to present if they were hired as middle-class democratic governors. According to the report of the ICT office of personnel, Roberto Bonilla's interview began with no "good signs." He was poorly dressed—not wearing a suit or a tie—and unshaven, and his overall presentation "left much to be desired about who he really [was]."[93] These problems clearly reflected his lack of motivation to work as a "true professional." These first impressions were corroborated by an evaluation of Bonilla's cultural environment, social background, and family history. There was an association between the "poor social background" from which Bonilla came, the cultural environment in which he had been "immersed," and the effects of previous conditions and social constraints on his family. Bonilla had had no "proper fathering."[94] Bonilla's father had abandoned his mother and his two siblings several years before the interview, and the applicant had grown up without paternal guidance. Bonilla thus had never acquired what was considered the masculine aspirations for knowledge, culture, and education. Furthermore, the lack of proper fathering had had some effects on Bonilla's inner self. Like others who were categorized as "people from a bad class," he could not develop or possess either the masculine spirit of competition or the capacity to take risks to improve who he was. And if this was not enough for Bonilla, the report noted that his mother had also failed to set a good example for him and his siblings precisely because she had "always been of the same social background." Bonilla had nothing to emulate or aspire to, nothing to be educated for.[95] His gendered cultural environment and social background and, even more important, the inherent characteristics of the Bonilla family history had produced a "weak man . . . afraid of change . . . with no aspirations for education [or] knowledge . . . no desire to better himself." In other words, the evaluation tersely argued, it was difficult to see Bonilla working for the state as a true professional man.[96]

Gabriel Colmenares, a lawyer who was interviewed for a job as a professional in social programs in the ICT in 1959, provides an interesting contrast. The report on his candidacy argued that his privileged social background and complicated family biography had affected who he was. Coming from a social background of "extensive economic means," the report noted, Colmenares had not had any experience with the real problems of life.[97] The cultural environment in which he had been "immersed" had produced a "weak man" who manifested only what were considered improper aspirations because he was not inclined to form attachments with the poor and, instead, would be satisfied merely with his own "professional status." Since he had not had to struggle in life, social problems were neither in his mind nor in his interests. More important, he was not conscious of the poverty of Colombia—he did not possess a cultivated awareness about the role a professional could play in helping people to help themselves. Since he was from "old money," he had not developed personally and was preoccupied with self-interested knowledge. The report argued that he had everything in life. Given this privileged family biography, how would he be able to face the social problems and "rough social situations" involved in working closely with the poor? Predictably, the report argued, his social atmosphere, cultural environment, and family history had had specific effects within him. He was a weak man who would easily be scared, not only of the reality of life but also, and perhaps more important, of the people themselves. Indeed, these cultural and social conditions provoked an innate and "peculiar absence" of feelings, sympathies, and attachments toward the poor. As a weak man, he could not adapt to different social and cultural contexts. The report repeatedly warned that, if hired, he would demonstrate to the people his lack of interest by "look[ing] away"—or excusing himself—from the "situation of the poor." It was inconceivable, the report concluded, that this privileged man, with neither experience with the poor nor "appreciation/understanding" for the "problems of society," could produce any "needed changes" in the "people who suffer the most."[98]

This meticulous, if mundane, process of selection and evaluation was paramount to the constitution of democratic middle-class professionals and their concomitant role in the formation of a gendered and classed state rule. Those selected would be neither from what was considered a poor social background nor from what was conceived of as extensive wealth. The detailed process of selection involved a constant need to hierarchically define and classify who was best suited to work for the state.

Conclusion

In this chapter I have sought to offer a historical interrogation of the political rationalities and methodologies of rule through which a professional middle class became intelligible as a foundational democratic force after the Second World War. Despite what some historians would contend, the professional middle class—as an idea and a practice—was not merely a product of the United States that other parts of the world imported wholesale, partially appropriated, or fully resisted. As part of an uneven transnational dialogue, the consolidation of a middle class, I argue, became foundational in a new form of transnational rule precisely because professionals were hierarchically constituted as the best governors, who would be able to manage social and political relations in what was considered to be a democratic and peaceful society. In the Colombian context of the late 1950s and 1960s in which one of the main political projects was to overcome *la violencia*, the National Front administrations shaped these transnational discourses by promoting middle-class professionals as new practitioners of a democratic state rule. Thus, transnational consultants, university professors, policymakers, and experts in Colombia and the United States argued that, in order to achieve democracy and peace, neither the elites nor the laboring classes should practice state rule. Rather, a middle-class professional was imagined as the foundational democratic figure who could exercise state rule by educating and preparing both the elites and the laboring classes to coexist harmoniously—and hierarchically—in peace. In the process, an idea of a professional middle class became associated with a "proper"—that is, hierarchical—democratic rule through which some specific historical actors were conscripted to exercise the right to dominate others while others were defined as possessing the democratic right to be ruled. During the 1960s and 1970s, however, middle-class women and men would become not only the representation of state legitimacy and hegemonic rule but also the very political class—as middle class—that would question such hegemony and legitimacy by structuring new forms of a democratic state and society. By exercising their cultural and political capital as "proper" governors of state rule, these professionals would radically reconfigure some of the fundamental categories, practices, meanings, and institutions of democracy throughout the Americas, and they would go from being celebrated as "representatives of the state" to being categorized as "enemies of the state." Thus, the goal should not be to evaluate if—or where—the middle class could be more or less democratic but, instead, to critically reconsider the role middle-class people played in the consolidation of US imperial rule in the Americas, and in the formation of revolutionary projects that challenged such imperial rule during the second half of the twentieth century.

Notes

All translations are mine unless otherwise noted. There is no convention for citing primary sources from Colombian archives. Most of them do not have a standardized organization, if any organization at all. And given that the archives used in this chapter are for the most part bureaucratic state productions, they usually do not specify authors or dates. When possible, I use a citation that follows a bureaucratic structure of the different state agencies. I have reviewed the organizational charts during the 1950s and early 1960s to see where specific documents were located. Thus, I roughly employ the following system: title of the document, number of the folder (if available), dates (if available), sección (the specific office where document was produced), serie (the higher office/level in the organization to which "sección" belonged), fondo, archive, and city. Elsewhere, I elaborate how these "obstacles"—the disorganization of state archives and the anonymous documents—invite a more sustained historical analysis on how classed state rule is legitimized. See A. Ricardo López *Makers of Democracy*.

1. Alberto Lleras Camargo to Orlando Fals Borda, February 21, 1960, Despacho Señor Presidente, 1958–60, comité de relaciones laborales, Presidential Archive, Bogotá. (In subsequent references, this archival collection will be designated "PA.") This letter is part of an exchange between Alberto Lleras Camargo, Louis Joseph Lebret, and Orlando Fals Borda, Despacho Señor Presidente, comité de relaciones laborales, 1958–60, PA.

2. Alberto Valencia to his mother, February 1955, Alberto Valencia Personal Archive, Bogotá. See also, "Apuntes de clase, asignaturas, discusión y entrenamiento," December 1954 and July 1955, Folder: material de trabajo de campo, Inter-American Housing and Planning Center, Archive, Universidad Nacional de Colombia, Bogotá.

3. See, for example, Rabe, *The Most Dangerous Area in the World*; Latham, *Modernization as Ideology*; Tafett, *Foreign Aid as Foreign Policy*. In framing development as unified, single, and coherent discourse, I believe that Arturo Escobar (*Encountering Development*) misses the crucial role played by the middle class.

4. See Grandin, *The Last Colonial Massacre*, xiv. See also G. Joseph and Spenser, eds., *In from the Cold*.

5. Here I have found inspiration in Wilder, *The French Imperial Nation-State*. For a history of the Alliance for Progress and the role of the middle class in Colombia, see A. Ricardo López, *Makers of Democracy*. See also Karl, "State Formation, Violence and Cold War in Colombia."

6. This argument has been influenced by recent studies on the anthropology of democracy. See Paley, ed., *Democracy: Anthropological Approaches*.

7. Hartlyn, *The Politics of Coalition Rule in Colombia*; Archila, *Idas y venidas, vueltas y revueltas*; Pecaut, *Order and Violence;* Palacios, *Between Legitimacy and Violence*; Ayala, *Nacionalismo y populismo*.

8. Truman, "Inaugural Address," 254. See also Saldaña Portillo, *The Revolutionary Imagination in the Americas and the Age of Development*.

9. A. Goldstein, "The Attributes of Sovereignty."

10. Truman "Inaugural Address," 254–55.

11. William W. Beatty, National Technical Assistant to Colombia, July 5, 1958, TE 322/1col-s0175-0310-06, United Nations Archive, New York City, New York. (In subsequent references, this archival collection will be designated "UNA.")

12. Quoted in S. Lucas, *Freedom's War*, 224.

13. Ward Hunt Goodenough, Department of State, record relating to Colombia,

International Technical Assistance, 250/63 104 12–3 (1951–1959), Record Group 59, United States National Archives, College Park, Maryland. (In subsequent references, this archival collection will be designated "NARA 59.")

14. Ibid.

15. Ibid. For similar arguments, see also IAS, Box 17, Department of State, Office of Inter-American Regional Economic Affairs, 1950–1963, Health and Sanitation, NARA 59.

16. Ward Hunt Goodenough, Department of State, record relating to Colombia, International Technical Assistance, 250/63 104 12–3 (1951–59), NARA 59.

17. William W. Beatty, reports, Mission to Colombia, Miscellaneous, Subject files, September 15, 1959, United States Mission to Colombia, United States Foreign Assistance Agencies, (1948–61), Record Group 469, United States National Archives, College Park, Maryland. (In subsequent references, this archival collection will be designated "NARA 469.")

18. Nelson B. Henry, mission to Colombia, miscellaneous, subject files, June 16, 1958, United States Mission to Colombia, United States Foreign Assistance Agencies, 1948–61, NARA 469.

19. See Grandin, *Last Colonial Massacre*, 10. For Colombia, see Hylton, *Evil Hour in Colombia*.

20. There has been a growing literature on development as a historical configuration of knowledge and power. See, for example, Ferguson, *The Anti-Politics Machine*; Mitchell, *Rule of Experts*; Gupta, *Post Colonial Development*.

21. M. Ross, *Community Organization*; British Information Services, *Community Development*. For Colombia, see Orlando Fals Borda, "Acción Comunal en una vereda colombiana" in *Monografías Sociológicas*, no 4: 1–96; United States, Team number II, *Report on Community Development Programs in Jamaica, Puerto Rico, Bolivia and Peru* (Washington, DC: International Cooperation Administration, 1955).

22. "Consideraciones de la importancia de los programas de desarrollo de la comunidad en varios países de America Latina, 1956/Informe del Grupo de Expertos sobre la Planificacion del Desarrllo Economico y Social de America Latina," documents attached to Minutes of Inter-America Economic and Social Council of the Organization of the American States (Reuniones Extraordinarias), May 1, 1958, X 1 V1, *documentos* 0–49, Organization of American States Columbus Library and Archives, Washington, DC. (In subsequent references, this archival collection will be designated "OASAR").

23. Technical Assistant to Colombia, 1956, TE 322/1col-s0175-0310-06, UNA (my emphasis). For similar arguments see: "Consideraciones de la importancia de los programas de desarrollo de la comunidad en varios países de America Latina, 1956/ Informe del Grupo de Expertos sobre la Planificacion del Desarrllo Economico y Social de America Latina. Documents attached to Minutes of Inter-America Economic and Social Council of the Organization of the American States (Reuniones Extraordinarias), May 1, 1958, X 1 V1, *documentos* 0–49, OASAR.

24. Community Organization and Development, Colombia, (Colo, 250), 1956, S-0175-03334-02, UNA.

25. Ibid.

26. William H. Olson to José Ricaute García, August 5, 1959, Programas Rurales y

Desarrollo de la Comunidad, Fomento, Project Colombia IV and Colombia XXV, Minister of Agriculture, Colombian-American Cooperative Technical Service in Agriculture Archive, Bogotá.

27. Housing Programs, project IV and Colombia XXV, Office of the Chief Subject Files (1952–59), Mission to Colombia, Records of the US Foreign Assistance Agencies, NARA 469.

28. Ibid.

29. Ibid.

30. Ibid.

31. Ware, *Organizacion de la comunidad para el bienestar social*, 35. See among several others studies about community development, UNESCO, *La educación para el desarrollo de la comunidad* (Paris: UNESCO, Centro de Intercambios de Educacion,1954). Caroline Ware, Orlando Fals Borda, Camilo Torres, Virginia Gutierrez de Pineda, Héctor Abad Gómez, and Roberto Pineda Giraldo would play a pivotal role in promoting community development programs and educating middle-class professionals in Colombia.

32. Gary Wilder, for example, has shown how a "colonial humanism," as rationality of rule, shaped the contradictory role of the French imperial state in Africa between the two world wars. I have found his notion of colonial humanism quite helpful in developing what I call imperial humanist government. I argue that at the center of these rationalities was the idea of a professional middle class, which played a pivotal role in concretizing these forms of democratic rule. See Wilder, *The French Imperial Nation-State*, 43–145. Foucault also argued that, along with the need to historicize the political economy of domination, it was necessary to decipher the political rationality of rule. This rationality could be defined as follows. First, as the plural logics of rule an imperial state produces in order to be seen as an imperial legitimate state and, second, how rule should be fashioned and accomplished. See Foucault, *Security, Territory and Population* and *The Birth of Biopolitics*; D. Scott, "Colonial Govermentality" and "Political Rationalities of the Jamaican Modern."

33. "Notificaciones para la Comisión Nacional para la Reforma Pública en Colombia," Community Organization and Development, Bogotá, 13 December, 1956, Colombia Technical Assistance Program, (250) S-0175–03334–02, UNA.

34. Minutes of Inter-American Socio-Economic Council, April, 12, 1955, OASAR.

35. Ibid.

36. Ibid.

37. Ibid. (my emphasis).

38. Ibid. See also "Propuesta para el establecimieto de un departamento de seleccion y una comision de reclutamiento para profesionales al servicio del estado," February 9, 1959, Community Organization and Development, Colombia, Colom, Technical Assistance Program (250), S-0175–03334–02, UNA.

39. *Propuesta para el establecimieto de un departamento de seleccion y una comision de reclutamiento para profesionales al servicio del estado*, February 9, 1959, Community Organization and Development, Colombia, Colombia Technical Assistance Program (250), S-0175–03334–02, UNA.

40. "Summary of Point IV in Colombia, Program Planning" (1952–59), Office of the

Chief Subject Files, Record of U.S. Foreign Assistance Agencies (1948–61), NARA 469. See also Currie, *Reorganización de la Rama Ejecutiva del Gobierno de Colombia.*

41. Currie, *The Basis of a Development Program for Colombia*, 241, 496–98, 543–49.

42. J. Henderson, *Modernization in Colombia*, 323–47; Palacios, *Between Legitimacy and Violence.*

43. J. Henderson, *Modernization in Colombia*, 323–47.

44. Alberto Lleras Camargo to Richard W. Poston, December 12, 1960, Despacho Señor Presidente, 1960–61, Folder: comercio exterior, PA.

45. Ibid. (my emphasis). Similar arguments were made on the first study on *la violencia* published in 1962—a publication that can be seen as the first truth commission report. Sponsored by the state, and written by three major intellectuals, the study promoted the need to have a different, that is modern, class of professionals so that peace could be finally reached. See Fals-Borda, Guzmán, and Umaña Luna, *La violencia en Colombia.*

46. Richard Poston to Alberto Lleras Camargo, January 19, 1960. Despacho Señor Presidente, 1960–61, Folder: comercio exterior, PA. The Lebret Mission—suggestively called *Economy and Humanism*—sponsored by the United Nations Technical Assistance and the United States Program XXV, argues that the main problem in Colombia was the development of a "sociological morbidity." This consisted of a middle class unable to organize "the human capital of the nation" so both the elite and popular classes could live in harmony. See the Lebret Mision, *Misión economia y humanismo*, 211–59.

47. Letter from Lleras Camargo to Poston, April 12, 1960, Despacho Señor Presidente, 1960–61, Folder: comercio exterior, PA (my emphasis).

48. Ibid.

49. Ibid.

50. Arthur Schlesinger Jr. to John F. Kennedy, "Latin America, Report 3/10/61," Schlesinger Papers, box WH-14, John F. Kennedy Library, Boston.

51. See Owensby, *Intimate Ironies*; D. Parker, *The Idea of the Middle Class.*

52. Influenced by the argument put forward by James Ferguson, many studies have argued that development policies sought to create an antipolitical bureaucratic machine. The middle class would be then seen as an antipolitical force. I want to argue that the middle class was seen as practicing proper politics, rather than antipolitics. It was this proper politics that allowed this class to radicalize some practices and notions of democracy during the late 1960s and 1970s. See J. Ferguson, *The Anti-Politics Machine.* For Colombia, see Palacios, *Between Legitimacy and Violence*, 170–213.

53. These arguments have been influenced by Ferguson and Gupta, "Spatializing States." See also Sharma and Gupta, *The Anthropology of the State.* For recent studies that take the role of the middle class for granted, see Joseph and Nugent, eds., *Everyday of State Formation*; Stepan, *The Hour of Eugenics*; Besse, *Restructuring Patriarchy*; Weinstein, *For Social Peace in Brazil*; Mary Kay Vaughan, *Cultural Politics in Revolution*; Klubock, *Contested Comunities*; Rosemblatt, *Gendered Compromises*; Bliss, *Compromised Positions*; Tinsman, *Partners in Conflict.*

54. Recent studies of the National Front criticize these polices as wishful thinking and say that they were bound to fail. Such critique is highly conditioned by a tendency to

evaluate what is conceived as the policy, on the one hand, versus what are understood as real practices, on the other. In this hypothesis, the National Front policies were, at best, empty rhetoric meant to legitimize its lack of interest for the "social question" of the popular classes. Thus, all the social policies failed precisely because these were never realized in reality. They were, as Maurico Archila argues, "empty rhetoric with good intentions." See, among many others, Archila, *Idas y venidas,* 346–47.

55. Seamus Gaffney to Bruno Leuschner, June 17, 1959, Technical Assistance, mission to Colombia, TE 322/1col S-0175-0310-06, UNA.

56. Ibid.

57. Rafael Samper and Gabriel Kaplan, "Un plan para la integración del sector público y privado en un programa del desarrollo de la comunidad destinado al mejoramiento socio-económico de las veredas y los barrios de Colombia," 1, 7, Despacho Señor Presidente, 1959, comercio exterior, PA.

58. Ibid., 2.

59. Ibid,, 5

60. Ibid,, 2

61. Rafael Samper, "Material de talleres de adiestramiento" (1957–59), Sección: departamento de personal, Serie: gabinete del subgerente general, Fondo: subgerencia general, Instituto de Credito Territorial Archive, Bogotá. (In subsequent references, this archival collection will be designated as "ICTA.")

62. Ibid.

63. "Selección de personal/cartas de recomendación," Folder 43, 1956–59, Sección: departamento de personal, Serie: gabinete del subgerente general, Fondo: subgerencia general, ICTA.

64. Ibid.

65. "Selección de personal/cartas de recomendación," Folder 25, 1956–58, Sección: departamento de personal, Serie: gabinete del subgerente general, Fondo: subgerencia general, ICTA.

66. Jaime Sánchez to oficina de Personal, 1956, "Selección de personal/cartas de recomendación." Contenido: cartas de recomendación y evaluacion de Manuel Mora, Folder 43, 1956–58, Sección: departamento de personal, Serie: gabinete del subgerente general, Fondo: subgerencia general, ICTA.

67. Ibid.

68. "Informes de selección de personal, reportes y evaluaciones de procesos de selección de personal profesional, evaluacion de solicitud de trabajo de Manuel Mora," Folder 73, 1956–58, Sección: departamento de personal, Serie: gabinete del subgerente general, Fondo: ubgerencia general, ICTA.

69. Ibid.

70. Alfonso Guevara to Oficina de Personal, 1955, "Informes de seleccion de personal, contenido: reportes y evaluaciones de procesos de selección de personal profesional, evaluación de solicitud de trabajo de Miguel Pérez," Folder 43, 1956–58, Sección: departamento de personal, Serie: gabinete del subgerente general, Fondo: subgerencia general, ICTA.

71. "Informes de seleccion de personal, contenido: reportes y evaluaciones de pro-

cesos de selección de personal profesional, evaluación de solicitud de trabajo de Miguel Pérez," Folder 89, 1955–57, Sección: departamento de personal, Serie: gabinete del subgerente general, Fondo: subgerencia general, ICTA.

72. Ibid.

73. "Informes y evaluaciones de procesos de selección de personal professional y solicitudes de trabajo," Folder 125, 1956–58, Sección: departamento de personal, Serie: gabinete del subgerente general, Fondo: subgerencia general, ICTA.

74. "Informes de personal, evaluacion y sugerencias," Folder 111, 1954–59, Sección: departamento de personal, Serie: gabinete del subgerente general, Fondo: subgerencia general, ICTA.

75. Alfonso Ortíz to Oficina de Personal, 1956, "Evaluación de solicitud de trabajo de Juan Grandos," Folder 48, 1955–57, reportes de selección de personal, informes y evaluaciones de procesos de selección de personal professional, Sección: departamento de personal, Serie: gabinete del subgerente general, Fondo: subgerencia general, ICTA.

76. Ibid.

77. "Cartas de recomendacion y evaluaciones de trabajo de Juan Granados," Folder 58, 1956–51, Sección: departamento de personal, Serie: gabinete del subgerente general, Fondo: subgerencia general, ICTA.

78. Ibid. (my emphasis).

79. Pierre Bourdieu, *Distinction*.

80. "Comite de selección de personal/solicitudes y respuestas" (no number of folder available), 1957–59, Sección: políticas de personal y adiestramiento, Serie: gabinte del subgerente general, Fondo: subgerencia general, ICTA.

81. Ibid.

82. "Políticas de personal y adiestramiento" (no number of folder available), Sección: actas de comité de personal, 1958–60, Serie: actas, Fondo: secretaría general, ICTA. See also "Políticas de personal," Folder 54, 1956–58, Serie: gabinete de subgerente general, Fondo: subgerencia general, ICTA.

83. "Políticas de personal y adiestramiento" (no number of folder available), 1958–60, Sección: actas de comité de personal, Serie: actas, Fondo: secretaría general, ICTA.

84. "Informes de personal," Folder 23, 1955–57, Sección: departamento de personal, Serie: gabinete del subgerente general, Fondo: secretaría general, ICTA.

85. Ibid.

86. Ibid.

87. Ibid.

88. Ibid.

89. "Informes de personal y evaluaciones de personal activo" (no number of folder available), 1955–57, Sección: departamento de personal, Serie: gabinete del subgerente general, Fondo: subgerencia general, ICTA. See also "Comité de personal/Celmira Burgos" (no number of folder available), 1955–57, Sección: departamento de personal, Serie: gabinete del subgerente general, Fondo: subgerencia general, ICTA.

90. "Informes de personal y evaluaciones de personal activo" (no number of folder available), 1955–57, Sección: departamento de personal, Serie: gabinete del subgerente general, Fondo: subgerencia general, ICTA.

91. "Comité de Personal," Folder 67, 195457, Sección: departamento de personal, Serie: gabinete del subgerente general, Fondo: subgerencia general, ICTA.

92. Ibid.

93. "Informes de solicitudes de trabajo/Roberto Bonilla" (no number of folder available), 1957–59, Sección: departamento de personal, Serie: gabinete del subgerente general, Fondo: subgerencia general, ICTA.

94. Ibid. See also "Evaluación de solicitudes de trabajo" (no number of folder available), 1955–57, Sección: departamento de personal, Serie: gabinete del subgerente genera, Fondo: subgerencia general, ICTA.

95. "Informes de solicitudes de trabajo/Roberto Bonilla" (no number of folder available), 1957–59, Sección: departamento de personal, Serie: gabinete del sub-gerente general, Fondo: subgerencia general, ICTA.

96. Ibid.

97. "Comite de selección y evaluación de personal, reportes de solicitudes de trabajo/ Gabriel Colmenares" (no number of folder available), 1957–59, Sección: departamento de personal, Serie: gabinete del sub-gerente general, Fondo: subgerencia general, ICTA.

98. Ibid.

The Formation of the Revolutionary Middle Class during the Mexican Revolution

Michael A. Ervin

From 1907 to 1910, hundreds of middle-class male adolescents entered Mexico's National School of Agriculture (the Escuela Nacional de Agricultura, or ENA) in search of professional degrees to secure their futures in the age of the dictator, Porfirio Díaz. In November 1910, the start of the Mexican Revolution changed agronomists' careers forever. The ENA's Porfirian curriculum instilled in students a desire to modernize and expand agricultural production, but their encounter with the countryside during the 1910s committed them to agrarian reform. From 1920 to 1940, ENA graduates worked to reconcile productivity and redistribution, a project they called "redemption." The effort to unite agronomists, persuade political elites to redistribute land, and convince *campesinos* to increase yields comprise the middle politics of Mexico's agrarian revolution.

In 1921, agronomists celebrated the centennial of independence by creating a National Agronomic Society (the Sociedad Agronómica Nacional, or SAN) to realize redemption through middle politics. The SAN's first duty was "to unite and channel all agronomic forces" to achieve their goals. Agronomists sought to pressure "the Public Powers, as advisors or as initiators, so that agriculture and its connected interests [would] be promoted and developed in accord with the nation's social and economic capacities." Finally, ENA graduates wanted the "cooperation" and "solidarity" of farmers to make the SAN's work "effective and lasting."[1] By uniting political elites, professionals, and popular groups, agronomists believed the revolution's goals could be achieved and sustained over time.

This chapter tells the story of the SAN's failure to unify agronomists during the Obregón (1920–24) and Calles (1924–28) administrations. In 1921, agronomists believed that Mexico's redemption was close at hand. "The redemption of the world is in us," Juan de Dios Bojórquez proclaimed, "The new Jesus Christ is work."[2] Many issues divided the profession and destroyed the early optimism, however. ENA graduates continued to work to reconcile production and redistribution in the years ahead, but by 1927 the SAN had collapsed, as material realities set agronomists against one another in the struggle to get by and get ahead in revolutionary Mexico.

Unity and Division under Obregón

Immediately after the 1921 centennial, agronomists enthusiastically organized the SAN. Jesús M. "Chucho" Garza, an ENA student who had saved General Obregón's life on the battlefield in 1915 and served the president in many capacities, obtained funding to open offices in Mexico City. Agronomists approved the SAN's statutes and published a message about the new organization to the Mexican people. They collected dues, distributed membership cards, and formed committees in ten states. They searched for a second location to house a library and meeting room. And they published *Germinal*, the periodical whose purpose was to promote a "militant politics."[3] "We will keep alive . . . the postulates of the First National Agronomic Congress," Bojórquez wrote. "We will offer opinions about everything important to human, national, and professional interest . . . We will aspire to be a force in such debates within our specialized social function. And if our work is healthy, if our doctrines are good, if our principles are solid, perhaps we will succeed in elevating ourselves above popular currents like a lighthouse that dominates them by virtue of the truth enclosed within."[4] Agronomists compared *Germinal*'s work with that of the *campesino*. Paper was to the journalist as land to the farmer. Agronomists' letters were the seeds, and their fingers the oxen that took up the pen, their plough. And their ideas would carve furrows and germinate into an enlightened readership.[5]

The group's early unity stemmed from a shared critique of large landowners who challenged agrarian reform based upon two principles: production and the protection of private property. Hacendados maintained that the *campesinos* lacked the capital necessary to modernize and expand production. And no amount of capital could overcome *campesino* backwardness and lack of initiative, they said. The *ejidos* (redistributed communal plots) were being given "to individuals without preparation as farmers, without capital, without tools, without morality." Moreover, *ejidatarios* "wasted their parcels because they are not committed to them. That which costs nothing is worth nothing, and to them the received land has cost them nothing." Landowners also looked to the 1917 Constitution, which protected "small private landownership" and required indemnification for expropriated lands.[6] As a result, landowners had many means of counteracting expropriation in the early years, from seeking a court injunction to dividing estates into smaller plots. Landowner unity culminated in October 1921 with the formation of the Sindicato Nacional de Agricultores just weeks after agronomists had formed the SAN.

Agronomists criticized hacendados, using the slogan "the land belongs to those who cultivate it." Eustacio Contreras referred to the hacendado as a "vampire" who "sucks the energies" of *campesinos*.[7] One youngster—or recent graduate of the ENA—called landowners "parasites" living off the work of others. Ignacio Figueroa noted that hacendado complaints were "not produced in any way for the defense of national agriculture, because it does not exist nor has it ever existed based on today's rational and scientific bases." The "obstinate resistance of the *latifundio*'s defenders," he said, was meant "to conserve privilege, against the reconquest of the land by those who work it."[8] More than words, the ENA graduates' work of land redistribution for the National Agrarian Commission (the Comisión Nacional Agraria, or CNA) and the state-level Local Agrarian Commissions (the Comisiones Locales Agrarias or CLAs) provided their best critique of hacendados.

The landowners responded to the agronomists with threats and violence. In Puebla, hacendados singled out Ignacio Figueroa, the CLA president, for having overturned the original rejection of land reform claims. Noting that public functionaries were not "our caciques, but our servants," landowners demanded justice. In Campeche, they resorted to blacklisting—denying jobs to agronomists for their agrarian reform work. Marte Gómez appeared on one such list in 1922, when Guillermo Pous, the director of the landowners' national Sindicato, declared that his company would "deny work on its lands to those agricultural engineers" who served the revolution. In Yucatán, landowners threatened Francisco Pérez Sierra, a delegate to the CNA, saying that he would not "make old bones in the delegation, cost what it may." Threats also turned into violence. Jesús Guzmán was killed in the line of duty in Veracruz in 1924. In Nayarit, agronomists confronted the Aguirre family, the owners of cotton, tobacco, sugar, and cattle estates who had dominated the region during the Porfirian period.[9]

The agronomists retaliated with threats of their own. Marte Gómez wrote to one landowner who had complained about agrarian reform. "The hacendado who does not seek good harmony with neighboring pueblos is lost," he claimed, because "each day the situation of he who has everything is more difficult faced with the many who want everything." Gómez scoffed at being blacklisted. "What do we lose by appearing on such lists?" he asked. "Mr. Pous, your devilishness moves us to laughter . . . with your black lists you offer to deny us work THAT WE HAVE NEVER HAD." Although that was a slight exaggeration, he challenged the Sindicato to "publish the white list on which appear agronomists or agricultural engineers whom your associates have hired in the past thirty years," adding that "if I had to count them on my extremities, I would not have to take off my shoes to count them all." The youngsters called the Sindicato Nacional de Agricultores the Cinicato Irracional de Agricultores. In one cartoon (see figure 1), Pous is pictured reading about agrarian reform. On reflection, he takes a rope from a dresser and hangs himself from a tree "with the blessing of all the world."[10]

Although unified by a common enemy, agronomists were divided by geography. Some of them came to Mexico City for a short period for the centennial conference, but they then dispersed across Mexico to carry out their work. Unifying the actions of agronomists working in the country's far corners was a difficult task. Agrarian ideology also divided agronomists. One group stressed the need to promote production over redistribution. For example, Juan Ballesteros believed that "the agrarian problem will have to be resolved by taking as a base the productivity of the land." If land reform beneficiaries, or ejidatarios, could not expand production, then "the land grants are a panacea that will delay the true solution" to Mexico's agrarian problem, and the land should be taken from the "clumsy and lazy" and given "to the skilled and laborious." Adding that "there is not just reason to take the land away from a hacendado who works it well," Ballesteros wanted to use indirect methods like tax policy to place land in the hands of productive farmers.[11] Antonio Vera agreed, suggesting that the *ejidos* "should be recovered" by hacendados with the resources to make the land more productive.[12] Carlos Fernández wrote of turning his family's 25,000-hectare farm on the Colima-Jalisco border into "a true agricultural enterprise that satisfies me and fills the social function with which it is charged, that is, to be a source of well-being and progress." By modernizing his family's hacienda, Fernández sought redemption through higher production:

FIGURE 1: "The Beginning of the End." Mysager, "El principio del fin," *Germinal*, February 1, 1922, 24. The caption reads: "Mr. Pous, after coming to his senses [*cuerdamente*] for the first time in his life, proceeds to make a good and prudent decision. [Hanging from a tree,] Mr. Pous, with his *cuerda* resolution [in his right mind], executes it with the blessing of all the world."

> There exists an indestructible religion: that of the LAND. Who knows if the happiness that they say has to come from heaven to earth does not go from earth to heaven, because from [the earth] metals are extracted, plants are born and grow, and feelings sprout as well . . . At the same time that [the land] carries us through sidereal fields [and] shows us new stars and worlds, we learn through work to obtain the greatest yield from it; and thus as we pray Our Father, if we pray at all, to ask for the bread of each day, we should pray the prayer of the Mother Earth to ask for those that work it and make it produce.[13]

A second group sought redemption through private ownership of small parcels of land. These individualists believed in "the need to destroy the *lati-*

fundio" and replace it with a middle class of modern farmers. Ignacio Figueroa further defined "small private landownership":

> [It] should contain the amount of land that in each case a farmer can cultivate directly with the help of his family, utilizing some work animals and a small number of laborers, who will form part of the business or will be hired principally in the most intense agricultural periods. In this way, the intermediaries will disappear, the owner will be worker and businessman . . . On this property the *FARMER* will be formed, the free settler who with his inventiveness, his knowledge, and his effort will know how to extract from the land all of its riches and enjoy them.[14]

Figueroa called on his colleagues to emulate the example of smaller farms in the US Midwest to achieve "agricultural advancement" and "the expansion of national production."[15] Only the small, private, productive, and free farmer could redeem *campesinos*. "If we resolve the problem of small private landownership," Alfredo Valle argued, "we will have taken one great step toward the salvation of the country."[16]

Many means existed for promoting small private landownership. The individualists preferred dividing haciendas into smaller parcels, called *fraccionamientos*. Alejandro Brambila Jr. pointed to such voluntary divisions of estates, along with irrigation and other policies, as possible ways to develop modern small farmers. In Congress, Gilberto Fabila spearheaded the campaign to place fraccionamientos at the heart of revolutionary policy. Genaro Arzave looked instead to colonization—distributing unused national lands to new settlers—as "the best means" of arriving at the small private landowner ideal, "to make all revolutionary men useful to their fatherland, by irrigating the piece of land put at their disposal by the government not with blood, but with the sweat of their brow." The final way to develop small farms was agrarian reform. "The end result that is pursued by" land distribution, wrote Ismael Reyes Retana, "is the formation of small private landownership at the same time as a war on the latifundio."[17]

While the *ejido* was one means of achieving the small farmer ideal, the individualists doubted the ejidatarios' productive potential. Figueroa differentiated the land reform beneficiary from the small private landowner: "The difference stems from the fact that . . . the ejido property . . . is reserved for a family almost exclusively for its subsistence and not for its definitive advancement and improvement." Luis León shared this lack of confidence in the *ejido*.

"The ejido parcel will be . . . a refuge to which [*campesinos*] may return in case of disappointment or failure," he said, "but all of those of restless spirits or higher ambitions will leave the ejido and seek to better their condition outside of it." As head of the Agriculture Ministry (the Secretaría de Agricultura y Fomento, or SAF), in 1925 León advocated dividing *ejidos* into inalienable family-owned parcels. That way, the individualists believed, the *ejido* would become a training ground for small private farmers, or a "bridge" between communal and individual property.[18] Only the small private farmer, not the ejidatario (nor the hacendado, for that matter), could redeem rural Mexicans.

A final group of agronomists believed that Mexico's salvation lay in cooperativism. Embracing the need to protect efficient large estates for fear of disrupting production, many cooperativists envisioned a balanced agricultural sector, divided among large landowners, small farmers, and ejidatarios. Ramón Corral Soto spoke of doing "what is realizable currently without producing great imbalances." He believed that technical studies were needed to "discover to what extent the conservation or division [of the haciendas] is possible."[19] The cooperativists also recognized the value and need to promote small private landownership. Modern small farmers not only were constitutionally protected and had to be respected, but they could also help expand production through cooperative organizations just like ejidatarios.

The cooperativists placed agrarian reform and the *ejido* at the center of their project, however. Marte Gómez, the most vocal cooperativist, noted the failure of Europe's small farmers and demanded that agronomists unite in support of the "socialization of the land." The first step had to be observance of agrarian laws. By 1922 in Morelos, that process was well under way: about 240,000 acres had been redistributed already, and 375,000 remained in hacendados' hands. But in Mexico State, redistribution had barely begun. Ramón Monroy reported that of 332 requests, only 33 villages had received *ejidos*. The victims of a great "deception," the rural poor were "pariahs who live worse than animals." It was time to "strictly comply with the agrarian laws and regulations to uplift our Fatherland in compliance with one of the offerings of the revolution now crystallized in constitutional government." Cooperativists believed that "while the agrarian problem [was] not resolved," redemption would remain elusive.[20]

Second only to compliance with agrarian laws, the cooperativists sought to organize the production of all farmers, especially ejidatarios. Gabriel Itié, a French agronomist and ENA teacher, hailed "the cooperative principle, a true social religion" that "is breathing new life into the social body," and rejected "individualist sentiments" as the source of *campesino* misery. European experience had taught the cooperativists that "isolated, the farmer did not have credit; cooperating, he is member of banks that distribute millions of pesos per year." Alone, the farmer "had no other alternative than to pray, if he believed in God, or to blaspheme if he did not believe in anything." But united in cooperatives, farmers could expect "cheap credit, advantageous purchase and sale of products, [and] all kinds of insurance [that] have suddenly appeared from the magic wand of cooperation, like flowers from a daydream to the call of a beneficent fairy." Ernesto Benavides spoke of "awakening" the "ambitious spirit" of cooperation "to make fruitful the distribution of *ejidos*." Davíd Ibarra considered "urgent the cooperative organization" of Mexico's *campesinos*. Gómez pointed to the Jojutla, Morelos, ejidatarios, who had purchased their own tractor through cooperative work. Cooperatives would allow farmers "to feel the stimulus of competition and to harvest in an equitable way the results of their efforts." Cooperativism combined with agrarianism sought "the realization of the economic liberty" of all *campesinos*.[21]

For the cooperativists, the *ejido* provided the perfect arena in which to reconcile redistribution with production. On October 11, 1922, Gómez elaborated the cooperativist perspective in CNA Circular 51, whose publication initiated the first state-led effort to organize *ejido* production. Worried that "the evolution of agricultural technology tends to abolish small-scale agriculture" due to "an insurmountable incompatibility between [it] and mechanization," Gómez called on agronomists to "organize cooperatives in all the population centers" and collect a fund, based on fifteen percent of *ejido* harvests, to help modernize and expand production. Not content with using *ejidos* for subsistence agriculture alone, the cooperativists sought to incorporate *ejido* produce into local, regional, national, and even international markets. Ramón Monroy spoke of getting the *ejidos* "to produce as much as they can," not merely for subsistence, but to expand national production.[22]

In addition to ideology, procedural issues also divided agronomists. To expand redistribution, some youngsters felt that the law of January 6, 1915, the basis for agrarian reform, had to be modified to confront anti-*agrarista* governors whose powers to appoint CLA personnel placed enormous obstacles in *agrarismo*'s path. Lauro Caloca criticized "all governors, with the exception of one or two, for having systematically opposed" agrarianism in their states. Francisco García Robledo agreed, saying that "the bureaucratic machine" had to be "simplified." Only by centralizing agrarian policy in the CNA—he called for "federalizing" the CLAs—would agrarian reform expand. Puebla's CLA President Ignacio Figueroa disagreed, claiming that centralization was not the solution. Rather, *campesinos* needed to organize and force state governors and the

CLAs to do their constitutional duty. Gómez concurred with the individualist Figueroa. What would happen, Gómez asked, if they centralized agrarianism and then the presidency "came into the hands of a reactionary"? The solution was a balance of power between state and federation, and between political elites and *campesinos*, to expand the agrarian program.[23]

Before confronting the divisions, though, the SAN had to support itself. With Chucho Garza's connections, the agronomists received federal funds to get the society off the ground. In 1922, Miguel Yépez pulled strings for federal financing of SAN activities. In 1923, Bojórquez mentioned the possibility that, if elected, then-presidential candidate Plutarco Elías Calles would provide funds for the SAN. But agronomists could not depend solely on their bosses and the state. They had to find private resources if they were to sustain their society. Membership dues fell far short of hopes. As a result, the burden fell on the most committed agronomists and those with money to invest in SAN activities. From 1921 to 1922, Yépez took the lead, with his ardent dedication to publishing *Germinal* and maintaining the SAN's Mexico City offices. But his heroic efforts were not enough. After five months, *Germinal* ceased publication due to a lack of funds.[24]

Compounding the money problems was the loss of Chucho Garza, the SAN's undisputed leader. On February 11, 1923, Garza—then a shoo-in candidate for the governorship of Nuevo León—committed suicide in a Monterrey hotel room. When he had arrived in his home state's capital a week before, Garza had been unprepared for the frenzy he encountered. The morning he shot himself, he wrote to his wife of being "extremely busy" and of not having had "even one moment of rest." He despaired: "It is so [bad] that I am thinking of returning to Mexico City and, if possible, of rescinding my candidacy, [to] dedicate myself to living in peace."[25] Shortly after signing messages to his wife and son, Garza killed himself.[26] The death of Chucho Garza traumatized many agronomists, who had lost their leader and most important link to the president. In the years following Garza's loss, the youngsters struggled to find a figure who could unite the profession again. Gómez wrote that Garza's death "has left us completely disoriented." Eight months later, he wrote to Bojórquez: "We have or we believe we have a flag, but we lack the standard bearer. Each one of us wants to, but cannot, direct the profession. We suffer from something that I would dare qualify as leader anarchy. The seat of Chucho Garza, still empty, has not succeeded in imposing on us respect for his memory."[27]

Garza's loss sparked professional rivalries, especially in Congress. After elections for San Luis Potosí's governorship in 1923, Jorge Prieto Laurens, leader of the majority Cooperatist Party (the Partido Cooperatista Nacional, or PCN), claimed victory over the Agrarista Party candidate, Aurelio Manrique, who established his own state government in protest. Some ENA graduates supported Prieto Laurens, but most congressional agronomists sided with Manrique due to the Agraristas' commitment to redistribution. The rivalry worsened when the PCN split over the selection of Obregón's presidential successor. Early on, a majority of the cooperatists supported Treasury Minister Adolfo de la Huerta, although others, along with the minority Agraristas and members of the Laborista Party, chose Obregón's candidate, Interior Minister Plutarco Elías Calles. Most agronomists sided with Calles, partly out of the personal connections cultivated by Garza, Bojórquez, and León, and partly because they viewed him as the more radical candidate. At the SAN's October 1923 conference, PCN deputies Fabila, Yépez, and Apolonio Guzmán tried to unite agronomists behind Calles. The effort was "interpreted by some as self-interested," however, and "charges of wanting to take advantage of the profession for personal ends were launched."[28]

Worse than sparking rivalries, Garza's death and the presidential succession dispute allowed some agronomists to await the unfolding of events before expressing their opinions. The failed attempt to unify behind Calles led Gómez to criticize his colleagues' "indecisiveness."[29] But what appeared to be uncertainty to Gómez was merely caution to others. At the time, nobody could have known the outcome of the dispute between the contenders to Obregón's throne. De la Huerta had the support of a majority of the PCN and the military, and he was initially considered to be just as radical as Calles on agrarian matters.[30] Without Chucho Garza to impose discipline, the ENA graduates chose their own courses of action. For some, neutrality appeared to be the most intelligent choice. "How it disheartens one," Gómez mourned, "to see that the bourgeoisie is beginning to appear! Many who have placed themselves in a good bureaucratic position reduce their aspirations to lying in wait now that the brawl is approaching, peacefully awaiting the new master. They believe with childish naiveté that in order to conserve their posts, being bland or changing colors when the candidate appears will suffice."[31]

The notion of adapting oneself to political circumstances even undermined the agronomists' attack on the hacendados. In July 1923, Francisco García Robledo asked SAN members if the society should respond to the landowner Sindicato's efforts to organize farmers against agrarian reform. Some feared that by challenging the Sindicato, agronomists could be accused of meddling in politics rather than carrying out the technical aspects of Mexico's agrarian revolution. Incredulous, Gómez declared to a colleague that the SAN "should by no means remain indifferent to the activities of the Sindicato . . . in spite of the bad interpretations that can result from our attitude." Agronomists had to take up "an intense and frank struggle as corresponds to a profession whose activities are plainly defined and whose high aims require neither hypocrisy nor timidity." He suggested attacking the Sindicato in speeches and editorials to "make known the significance of the fight we undertake." In vain, he hoped that "the duty of raising the flag of the socialization of the land pushed by Jesús M. Garza and bequeathed to us as immediate inspiration" could spark unity of purpose among his colleagues.[32]

By 1924, the agronomists' euphoria had dissipated. In February, Yépez reported feeling "immensely sad, depressed, and . . . desperate" since Garza's death. That month the ENA graduates commemorated Garza's suicide with a public ceremony, remembering him as a "tender brother" and the SAN's "irreplaceable sustainer." Their deep sadness was palpable. In April, Apolonio Guzmán, a PCN deputy, was shot in his car after an altercation at a Mexico City intersection. Later reports claimed a possible connection to Nayarit landowners. Guzmán had served in the state's third district, and his father, Regino, had worked with the agronomists who had challenged the Aguirre clan three years earlier. The youngsters lamented their plight. "Our society is dying," Gómez wrote to Bojórquez, adding that "Guzmán's burial, which should have united us in support of [his wife] . . . , has not as yet awakened any generous impulse. That Fabila asked for 2,000 pesos from the Chamber? That Yépez asked for something from Treasury and took her to the hospital and to an intensely sad gathering afterwards? That I arranged that the [SAF] cover her costs at least temporarily? That five or six of us attended the burial? That is nothing!"[33]

A New ENA: Temple of Knowledge, Cathedral of Agriculture, Altar of the Revolution

Further cause for the divisions among agronomists during the Obregón years was the reorganization of the ENA. Discussions of moving the school from its antiquated Mexico City facilities at San Jacinto to its present-day location at Chapingo (just south of Texcoco, in Mexico State) had preceded the civil war, when Porfirian officials chose the site, an estate formerly owned by President Manuel González. The youngsters eagerly awaited the opportunity to reform their alma mater and to implant a revolutionary spirit in its curriculum, guided by the slogan, "teach the exploitation of the land, not of man."

The first step in the ENA's transformation was the recruitment of a new generation of students. Congressional agronomists successfully lobbied the

Obregón administration to increase ENA funding to train more experts, and in 1922, between 700 and 1,200 freshmen descended upon San Jacinto's facilities.[34] With origins similar to those of their predecessors (middle-class to lower-middle-class), the new students were born and raised in small towns and villages around Mexico. Emilio Alanís Patiño, a 1928 ENA graduate born in Taximaroa, Michoacán, was typical. He grew up in the county seat of Villa Hidalgo, where one-fifth of the municipality's 20,000 residents lived without a public school or electricity. To educate his young son, Emilio's father paid private tutors. In 1913, amid the disruptions of the civil war, Emilio's father died, leaving his wife and four children in the care of Emilio's grandfather and uncles. His uncle Pancho introduced young Emilio to Mexico City, where "the movement of the 'big city' seemed feverish to me," he wrote, "compared with the silent peace of my pueblo."[35] More important, Pancho's associates secured an ENA grant for his nephew. Whether through contacts or merely the result of good grades, the new students came from across Mexico due to the allocation of resources to revive and move the ENA from Mexico City to Chapingo.

The 1922 freshman class overwhelmed the school's facilities and allowed agronomists to pressure for change. According to Ramón Fernández, "the dorms were stuffed to the max" and "the authorities were impotent to contain" the "unbridled multitude" of youngsters. When beds ran out, students were forced to sleep on the floor. Discipline did not exist, and each day became a lesson in survival, not agricultural education. Lunchtime particularly taxed the school's facilities, as scores of unruly students awaited their meals. All those who lived in the capital city were sent to live at home to avert a crisis, but the disorder did not end. One *Germinal* article blamed "the mess in San Jacinto" on the "the orders given to admit students, as many as they wanted, without calculating if there was a way of attending to them." An editorialist urged "that measures be taken to remedy the current conditions." By mid-year José Mares, a youngster committed to ENA reform, had replaced the elder Justino Martínez as director. Mares's greatest contribution came at year's end, when a series of brutal exams eliminated many students. Only the best and brightest survived the seven-year program.[36]

The agronomists' pressure paid off. In 1922, the resources allocated for the Chapingo project expanded (see table 1).[37] The next year, Agriculture Minister Ramón de Negri hired Marte Gómez as the ENA's director. Twenty-six years old at the time, Gómez attended tirelessly to the ENA's move and transformed the school both physically (with its new location and modern facilities) and ideologically. He linked the ENA to the agrarian program, first by inviting Diego Rivera, who had just completed frescoes for Education Minister José Vasconcelos, to paint Chapingo's walls and chapel. Looking back on it, Gómez noted that Rivera's focus on *campesino* forms made him the "right person to perpetuate a message, in the vestibule, in . . . the stairwell of the principal building and in the chapel, converted into a temple of knowledge," to "establish the climate and saturate the atmosphere that we wished to make the new generations of agronomists breathe." It apparently worked. One ENA student, Edmundo Flores, later remembered the profound impact of having been "taught Diego Rivera's ideology." Ramón Fernández remarked that Gómez and Rivera's chapel had "converted Chapingo into an altar of the revolution," adding that the students "heard from the lips of Diego himself the explanation of the concepts converted here into monumental artwork." Each week from 1924 to 1927, Rivera walked the ENA campus, chatted with students and teachers, and painted his brilliant murals.[38]

Gómez also transformed Chapingo's curriculum by inviting radical intellectuals to teach. The agronomists Gilberto Fabila, Gaspar Garza Lara, and Eustacio Contreras, along with other professionals like Gilberto Loyo, Jesús Silva Herzog, Eduardo Villaseñor, and Daniel Cosío Villegas, brought doctrines of social justice into ENA course work. In 1923, Loyo taught Universal History; in 1924, Villaseñor offered Logic and Psychology; in 1925, Loyo teamed up with Fabila and Silva Herzog to teach Political Economy; in 1926, Herzog taught Mexican Agricultural Social Evolution to emphasize agrarismo's righteousness; in 1927, Loyo and Fabila joined forces for Rural Economy and Agricultural Associations; and in 1928, ENA students received another dose of revolutionary inoculation, when Loyo and Wintilo Caloca taught Agrarian Social Evolution and Herzog offered Rural Sociology.[39]

Led by Silva Herzog, the professors challenged students to find solutions for rural Mexico's problems. The focus was on everything new and modern. What had maintained Mexico's backwardness, according to this view, was *rutina* (routine)—code for the antiquated approaches to production in the fields and policymaking in the SAF. Silva Herzog was particularly well remembered by students. "The only thing that does not change," one graduate recalled him saying with his exaggerated lecture style, "is that everything changes!" Some considered the lessons to be "pure demagoguery," but they signaled a sea change in the ideas taught at the ENA. The curriculum focused on cooperativism, and the school taught a new generation to organize *ejido* production according to the CNA's Circular 51.[40] Eduardo Morillo reported to Gómez that the new education "did to us what you wanted it to do. It taught us to love the countryside." Ramón Fernández agreed. "We heard the professors condemn the outdated and imagine a more just future," he wrote. "We received an

1

National School of Agriculture's Budget (in pesos), 1920–29

Year	Budget
1920	109,876
1921	125,570
1922	809,073
1923	723,351
1924	1,381,259
1925	828,761
1926	928,145
1927	276,455
1928	281,514
1929	395,717

Sources: Fernández, *Chapingo hace 50 años*; Manuel Mesa, "La inscripción de alumnos en la Escuela Nacional de Agricultura."

imperishable wealth [of knowledge] that none of this generation has forgotten. Chapingo was our revolutionary alma mater. We were not going to betray her."[41]

A final change wrought by Gómez would lead to his demise as ENA director: discipline. With hundreds of new students descending on San Jacinto's facilities in 1922, the need for discipline became obvious, forcing administrators to respond. Some agronomists empathized with the students. "And after those poor [students] wait their turn to eat, to sleep, to study, . . . to let loose, they want them docile and as manageable as silk!" one *Germinal* editorial declared. Adding that militarization would not solve the problem, the editorialist asked the directors to admit only capable students who committed themselves to careers as agronomists. Gómez agreed, but he also believed that discipline was a prerequisite of ENA success given the need to safeguard Chapingo's expensive new facilities. His first move was to raise academic standards to weed out weak students, sparking immediate protests from parents. Federal Deputy Tereso Reyes complained to Agriculture Minister de Negri of Gómez's "irrational conduct," claiming that "the 800 students that the school had at the end of [1922] has been reduced to less than half." Passing rates at the ENA plummeted to 10 percent. Another parent warned de Negri against hiring agronomists like Gómez: "With those people, even from the Sociedad Agronómica, your ministry will do nothing significant. The result will be that the disrepute in which you find yourself will be augmented more each day, and your office, like all that you have passed through, will wind up in the most resounding failure."[42]

Gómez then militarized Chapingo's campus. Fernández remembered it as "a ferocious discipline that was a violent contrast with the anarchy of the previous years." Marcelino Murrieta, a student leader, wrote Gómez in March 1924. "Informed of your last accord to immediately implant the military regimen," he said, "we the antimilitarists have felt it to be something of a coup d'état." In October, the ENA erupted in student demonstrations, demanding that certain punishments be reversed. Gómez refused repeatedly. On November 3, the ENA students went on strike in response to a colleague's expulsion for disorderly conduct, with all but thirty joining the walkout. They walked all night to Mexico City, where they held "red hot" discussions. "We all remember the proposition of compañero Escopeta," Fernández reported, "to place a bomb of dynamite in" Gómez's home. They marched through the capital's streets, screaming "Death to Marte Gómez!" and "Down with the kaiser of *Petate*!" They demanded his resignation. At one point, they even fired pistols inside the main administration building that housed Gómez's offices, "with the purpose perhaps of terrifying me or pushing me to violence," he wrote. His resignation came a few weeks later, although not officially as a result of the student strike.[43]

The strike was both cause and consequence of professional divisions. Most infuriating to Gómez was the participation of Fabila and Yépez, his close collaborators in the SAN, as the politicians behind the student strike that led to his resignation. Both colleagues had opposed the ENA militarization from the beginning and had provided aid to Murrieta and the students in the year prior to Gómez's tenure as ENA director. But as members of a Callista congressional block, the two radicals were also attacking Agrarista Minister de Negri through his trusted disciple, Gómez.[44] Frustrated and incensed, Gómez decided to leave the ENA and the SAN behind. After four years of struggle, as the SAN's outspoken "Robespierre," *Germinal*'s indefatigable editor, and the ENA's energetic director, Gómez's only recompense was the "hostility of *compañeros*" for whom he had shown nothing but respect in the past.[45] He decided to turn his back on Mexico City politics, because with Calles's election came that of Emilio Portes Gil as governor of Gómez's home state of Tamaulipas. It was time for him to tie his star to that of another, far away from the center of intrigue that Mexico City had become.

The Death of the SAN under Calles

During the Obregón years, the early euphoria and unity among agronomists had dissipated. Although the youngsters remained active after Chucho Garza's death with *Germinal*'s renewed publication, the divisions of 1923–24 took their toll. The October 1923 third annual convention was the last of its kind. And *Germinal* ended its second run in late 1924.

During the Calles administration, agronomists struggled to keep the SAN afloat. In 1925, nearly sixty professionals reorganized the SAN so that it "might serve something." By May, organizers had collected nearly 3,000 pesos to form the Fomentadora Agrícola Mexicana, a joint-stock company that sought "to propel National Agriculture" by providing resources to farmers. Manuel Mesa reported to Gómez (by then in Tamaulipas) on the reorganization's difficulties due to the personal rancor that had spread in recent years. In a meeting at the Café Colón, the lack of unity, even within the group attempting to unify, was evident. García Robledo grumbled about professional divisions and Gómez's editorial policies for *Germinal*. Wintilo Caloca rejected García Robledo's complaints. Mesa and Alberto García Teruel kept their mouths shut, seeing that unity had been the purpose of the meeting in the first place. Ernesto Martínez de Alva referred to the whole reorganization as a "coup d'état" anyway.[46]

The unification effort suffered from the absence of three youngsters who had energized the SAN early on: Fabila, Yépez, and Gómez. The new Agriculture Minister, Luis León, provided some support, but the divisions, particularly the events surrounding the 1924 ENA student strike, discouraged the participation of the profession's most talented members. The SAN's chief officer, José Carrera, begged Gómez to get involved. He spoke of needing a "man of character" with a "virile voice" who could "breathe life into '*los de abajo*' and make observations to '*los de arriba*,' because notwithstanding your recent fall [as ENA director], your prestige among everyone is more firm than ever." Gaspar Garza Lara struck a similar note. "If there was someone here [in Mexico City], like you," he wrote to Gómez, "who not only has more vision of the future but also a great influence over the gremio, the situation would be different . . . , [but] as you are many leagues of distance" away, Garza Lara saw little chance for change. Neither Garza Lara nor Carrera could convince Gómez to get involved. His "determination" to stay "on the margin" of SAN activity was, he said, "well-meditated and serious."[47]

Continued bickering at the ENA did not help the cause of unity. ENA personnel squabbled over whether to celebrate the one-year anniversary of the student strike.[48] Most important, some agronomists began to worry that their colleagues seemed little interested in making a revolution. In 1925, ENA Director Juan Ballesteros attempted to enhance the ENA's practical education by sending students to haciendas for six months of studies. Lamenting the effort to link the school with hacendados, who were "always conservative and bandits," Eduardo Morillo reported that the students, "guided by ideals of redemption," would fight the move. Mesa noted to Gómez that some ENA officials did not "dream like us of the redemption of the humble, of the *campesinos*." Instead, they seemed only interested in securing jobs. Gómez tried to lift the spirits of his friends who had stayed behind. "We can still give them a little bit of war," he wrote to Eustacio Contreras, and victory would be won "because our path is honest and theirs is tortuous; because we want the good for all, and they only want personal benefit."[49]

The SAN also suffered political setbacks. In 1925, the society joined the Partido Jesús M. Garza to spearhead Bojórquez's electoral campaign for Federal District municipal president. After four years as Obregón's ambassador in Guatemala, Bojórquez returned to Mexico City to challenge Luis Morones's Laboristas, and the SAN helped raise funds for the fight. But the "ugly" and "corrupt" campaign that left many "dead, wounded, raped, [and] strangled" led some in the SAN to wonder whether their colleague had lost his way. Bojórquez's loss was a defeat for the SAN as well. In March 1926, Mesa wrote to Gómez about not being sure where to send his letter, "and when I thought about [the SAN] I feared that not even the office existed any more as a consequence of the blow that our society received with the defeat of Bojórquez."[50]

The end came in 1926–27, as the alienation of key members and a dependence on the fortunes of a few leaders impeded any sustained SAN activity. In March 1926, Manuel Fitzmaurice and Wintilo Caloca led a self-labeled Action Group to breathe life into the SAN by fulfilling the society's "radical mission." They approached SAN members, received the financial support of sixty, and prepared for a national conference the next year. Gómez remained skeptical. By early 1927, it appeared that unity might finally prevail, however. In an attempt to mend fences, Gómez revised the ENA's curriculum with Martínez de Alva and even Waldo Soberón, his enemy at the ENA in 1925. Mesa sent Gómez a paper to present at the conference and hoped his colleague had cured himself "of the skepticism with which you recently judged the actions of our *compañeros*." The conference never took place. In April, León resigned as agriculture minister, and any chance of funding for SAN activities disappeared with him. Marcelino Murrieta, leader of the 1924 ENA strike, made a final attempt to salvage at least a mutualist society, but such a divisive personality was in no position to unify agronomists.[51]

Underlying the issues dividing agronomists were material realities that ultimately explain the SAN's collapse by 1927. In part, the disputes stemmed from agronomists' need to link themselves with bosses to make livings in revolutionary Mexico, a requirement that determined agronomists' employment opportunities, compensation, and life expectations in the 1920s. ENA graduates anticipated a great deal from their degrees and professional titles, beginning with security for themselves and their families. This expectation was related to a second: state employment. Most youngsters expected to work in a bureaucratic post carrying out agrarian policy. Although some agronomists hoped for a future that was "independent of the contingencies of politics" that "even poisons itself," efforts to carve out careers in private contracting failed quickly. Others tried to use state employment and its perks to purchase land and long-term security. Gaspar Garza Lara wrote of his "hopes in a *ranchito*" with such a goal in mind.[52] The majority of agronomists could not afford it, though. Luis León's Chihuahua ranch placed him among the minority who had attained independence and security in the 1920s.

Within the bureaucracy, agronomists expected security to come from promotion and the salary increases that accompanied it. Hard work often resulted in an employee's being noticed by his superiors and promoted to positions of ever-increasing power, responsibility, and remuneration. After the difficult work of CNA surveying, Manuel Mesa wrote of not wanting to "return to those fields of God with a theodolite across my back."[53] He was rewarded with a job organizing *ejido* production. Equally important for advancement were contacts that agronomists cultivated with key political figures. Much success depended on the early connections established by Garza, Bojórquez, and León with Obregón and Calles. Others chose to link up with governors in the hopes that their bosses' stars would rise in the future. Salvador de Gortari's work for Veracruz Governor Adalberto Tejeda was one example. And by choosing to work for Tamaulipas Governor Emilio Portes Gil in 1925, Gómez unwittingly allied himself with a future president of Mexico. That is, sometimes good luck came into the mix as well.

The ENA graduates also depended on one another, especially during times of uncertain employment. Correspondence among agronomists is littered with recommendations, the grease of Mexico's revolutionary bureaucracy. After providing temporary work for José Atamoros, "our old *compañero*" who found himself out of work in 1923, León asked Gómez, then the ENA's director, to do the same. Gómez gave Atamoros part-time employment as an instructor until Atamoros could find something more permanent. Following his dismissal as ENA secretary, Mesa counted on colleagues' recommendations to land him a spot on Veracruz's CLA. When unemployment threatened Eustacio Contreras in 1925, Gómez informed him that he could count on friends for interesting work, should he be replaced. Even after resigning as agriculture minister and retiring to his 40,000-hectare ranch, León attempted to secure state loans from his colleagues. Decades later, as retirement threatened financial ruin for many older agronomists, former colleagues helped obtain pensions for *compañeros* who had served the revolution and agrarismo.[54]

When contacts, hard work, and good luck failed, one avenue at least for monetary gain remained: corruption. Minister León was believed to have stolen SAF funds to finance the lavish lifestyle of his mistress, Celia Padilla. Antonio Hidalgo claimed that "Chela" Padilla had walked off with 10,000 pesos from the postal tax (used to fund the campaign against the locust), or from the SAF directly. José Lorenzo Sepúlveda referred to León as the "Minister of Celia Padilla." In one study on corruption, Stephen Niblo cited two cases of agronomists, Gómez and Bojórquez, supposedly guilty of peddling influence in the 1940s. Agronomists, along with numerous other professionals, were constantly criticized for corruption.[55]

Most ENA agronomists viewed corruption as a plague to be eliminated from the bureaucracy, however. The majority of corruption charges were leveled at so-called agronomists who actually had little or no training but were employed due to a shortage of expert professionals. The vast majority of ENA graduates spoke out against and sought to uproot corruption from the SAF. ENA agronomists removed officials who charged *campesinos* for services that were supposed to be provided free of charge. In 1926, Minister León prohibited CNA employees from receiving "gifts or recompense from the public for any service" provided. That same year, Ernesto Benavides suggested that corruption could be eradicated only by hiring ENA-trained agronomists. Leonardo Robles was sickened by the opportunities for graft in the Veracruz and Tamaulipas CLAs in the 1920s. Gómez earned himself the monicker "unhappy nobody" when he rejected the offer of Aaron Sáenz, a crooked Calles crony, to give the young agronomist a car and some land if he would spare Sáenz's Tamaulipas hacienda from expropriation. And after helping Laredo residents obtain a US-made irrigation pump, Eduardo Morillo was offered a commission for his efforts. The local municipal president earned 700 pesos on the deal. Morillo refused, remarking to Gómez how he understood "with what rapidity one makes money" when "in the end it leaves one lacking five cents of dignity."[56]

The case of Eduardo Morillo illuminates the expectations and material realities of an agronomist in the 1920s. An ENA student in his final year of studies in 1925, Morillo went to work in agrarian policy the following year. One result of the 1924 ENA strike had been the creation of alliances between professional agronomists and agronomy students. Marcelino Murrieta and the strikers had allied with Fabila and Yépez in the undoing of ENA Director Gómez, who had his own followers, led by Pascual Gutiérrez Roldán, Gustavo Segura, and Eduardo Morillo, among others.[57] Gómez was to the youngsters what de Negri and Portes Gil were to Gómez: a mentor, a man with connections who could open doors. Morillo referred once to Gómez as "the man who loves us, who opens our eyes, who teaches us the path and how to follow it."[58]

Morillo's career had a number of possible trajectories. One hope of ENA students, like those of Gómez's generation, was to make a living independent of state budgets, or, as Gutiérrez Roldán put it, "to realize independence, our golden dream." On many occasions, Gómez advised the students to seek a government loan to purchase land and establish their own private agricultural enterprise. Another plan involved providing them with plots in the Santa Engracia *ejido* to serve as "useful mentors" to the surrounding ejidatarios. Ultimately, the students decided to work by Gómez's side in Tamaulipas for a time, to save the money to make such a project feasible. Their starting salaries were set at 450 pesos per month, with the hope of combining federal and state contributions to increase the salary over time.[59]

How well agronomists could live on 450 pesos per month depended on their expectations. For Morillo, the salary was never enough, and he constantly barraged Gómez with letters and complaints of not being able to make ends meet. Whether he was building roads, establishing credit societies, valuing Ciudad Victoria properties, or organizing *ejidos*, Morillo repeatedly turned to his mentor and friends to cover expenses he could not afford on his salary alone. His desperation stemmed in part from the irregularity of state pay. Agronomists often waited weeks, if not months, to be paid, forcing them to scramble to keep their creditors happy. Because two-thirds of Morillo's salary was paid by the federal government and one-third by the state of Tamaulipas, his financial stress was especially great. At one point, it was his federal, rather than his state, pay that was in arrears. Morillo pleaded with Gómez to help: "I beg you, maestro, to take special interest in advancing us some money. Understand that the 150 pesos from the state are not enough, and it's been three months since the federation has paid us a single cent. Now the landlord, milkman, baker, pharmacists, and doctors are all over me for lack of payment." The money problems also stemmed from Morillo himself, who admitted to being very bad at personal finances and to spending large sums on liquor. Most onerous, however, were his family obligations. In 1927, Morillo spent one-third of his salary paying off a debt to a friend, and the rest was not enough to cover his costs. The amenities of middle-class life, including his wife's costly medical bills, were too much to afford on his basic salary. In July 1927, he stated that without Licha's medicines, he would be rolling in "abundance," or at least "comfort." The same could be said of most agronomists. One expense or another, especially those associated with illness, always seemed to undercut any semblance of family financial security.[60]

Middle-class life was clearly more expensive than that of the *campesinos*. Mario Bandala noted that "our social class" accumulated costs that were "higher than those of an ejidatario." In his Tamaulipas work, Morillo took great pride in paying laborers one and a half pesos per day, more than the going rate of a peso, leading local hacendados to criticize the youngster. But while proudly paying his workers 45 pesos per month, Morillo could barely survive on his own 450-peso salary. The contradiction seemed not to bother him. At one point, in order to save a little money, Morillo gave up a comfort the *campesinos* he sought to redeem could never have afforded. "I have reached such a point" of financial strain, he wrote Gómez, "that in order to save a little and be able to leave money for my family—which is not a day laborer's family—so that they might eat a little more, I am now traveling in second class."[61]

The problems that most agronomists experienced in meeting expectations and achieving financial security impeded the SAN's work, as the effort to make a living precluded participation in and payment for SAN activities. As early as 1923, the SAN sent members on societal rescue missions. Ramón Corral Soto headed north to convince his colleagues in Chihuahua, Coahuila, and Nuevo León to subsidize the SAN. A handful agreed to join him, but many youngsters could not afford the cost of a *Germinal* subscription, let alone SAN dues. Manuel Rincón Gómez struck a typical chord when he noted that he could not pay SAN dues until receiving 1,500 pesos of back pay. Two months later, he was out of a job altogether. Of course, as agronomists climbed higher in the bureaucratic ranks, their salaries rose. CNA delegates and employees earned enough to help pay for the SAN's activities but were so overworked that they had little time to participate. Office directors earned more than agrarian reform foot soldiers. As a SAF office director, Gonzalo Robles earned twenty-eight pesos per day, almost double Morillo's pay. The salary certainly satisfied Robles's needs, even if those needs expanded with wages.[62] It also meant that the agronomists most able to pay for SAN activities resided in Mexico City. As directors of the ENA, and even as cabinet ministers by 1925, some young agronomists earned enough to subsidize SAN activities.

Higher salaries could not overcome the SAN's difficulties, however. Some agronomists with high salaries still experienced financial distress. As an ambassador, Bojórquez earned more than most agronomists, but even he pleaded with the president to provide him with resources due to the "economic disaster" of having to support two households, in Mexico City and Guatemala City. Those earning good salaries in Mexico City were divided into factions. Generational differences split the profession into Porfirian elders; San Jacinto graduates like Gómez, León, and Bojórquez; and Chapingo graduates like Morillo, Gutiérrez Roldán, and Alanís Patiño, with all the groups competing for jobs. Politics and personal rancor, particularly after Garza's death, also divided the profession. "Instead of helping the one above rise even higher, so he can in turn help us from above," Gómez lamented to Mesa, "we hang ourselves from the feet of the one who ascends." The SAF had become, he said, "the worst place to meet and gossip that you can imagine." Some ENA graduates seemed more devoted to their jobs and bosses than to redemption, as the "magisterial monotony" of bureaucratic life sapped the SAN's strength and early euphoria.[63] Just as the struggle to make ends meet in the countryside prohibited agronomists from a unified and sustained professional activity, so did the material realities of middle-class life in Mexico City.

Conclusion

Founded in 1921, the National Agronomic Society survived for six years. United in optimism against large landowners, agronomists were ultimately divided over a number of issues. On the surface, the SAN's principal problems were financial and political. The divided youngsters never did develop a resource base from which to subsidize SAN activities. Beneath the surface, the financial difficulties and political divisions stemmed from the material realities of being agronomists in revolutionary Mexico, as the demands of middle-class life set the youngsters against each other in a battle to get by and get ahead.

Notes

All translations in the chapter are mine. When sources for multiple quotes are included in one note, the source of the last quote appears first, then the sources that follow start with the first quote in the paragraph, in order of their appearance.

1. Sociedad Agronómica Nacional, "Acta Constitutiva y Estatutos de la Sociedad Agronómica Nacional," (México: Linotip. Artística, 1921), Colección Marte R. Gómez, Biblioteca del Colegio de Postgraduados, Chapingo, 11, 17. (In subsequent references, this archival collection will be designated "CMRG.")

2. Juan de Dios Bojórquez, "Momento decisivo para el gremio agronómico," in Trabajos presentados al Segundo Congreso Agronómico," 2, CMRG.

3. "Voluntad colectiva, lo que hizo la Sociedad Agronómica Nacional durante el mes de octubre," *Germinal*, November 1, 1921, 22.

4. Juan de Dios Bojórquez to Marte R. Gómez, September 26, 1923, 1923 Cartas, Archivo Marte R. Gómez. (In subsequent references, this archival collection will be designated "AMRG.")

5. "Cordial Saludo," *Germinal*, November 1 1921, 1–2.

6. "Fantasias agraristas," *Excélsior*, November 9, 1922, section 1, page 3; Marte R. Gómez, "Ideas: La iglesia y la cuestión social," *Germinal*, February 22 1922, 21.

7. Eustacio L. Contreras, "Notas sobre el Segundo Congreso Agronómico Nacional," *Germinal*, November 1, 1921, 5/69 (Box 5, File 69), 5–6, Archivo Ramón Fernández y Fernández, Zamora, Michoacan. (In subsequent references, this archival collection will be designated "ARFF.")

8. "Alerta, Campesinos," *Germinal*, September 14, 1923, 2; Ignacio L. Figueroa, "Agrarismo, Nuestro Viejo Sistema Agrario, sus Vicios y su Repercusión en el Adelanto de la Agricultura," *Germinal*, November 1, 1921, 16, and "¿Por Fin . . . En Qué Quedamos?," *Germinal*, November 1, 1921, 5.

9. Quoted in Francisco Pérez Sierra to Marte R. Gómez, July 6, 1925, 1925 Cartas, section 2, pages 6–7, AMRG. See also "El Sindicato de Agricultores de Puebla ha presentado una queja al Gobernador," *Excélsior*, July 5, 1922; Marte R. Gómez, "Listas negras," *Germinal*, February 1, 1922, 14; Alvaro Obregón, "CNA Acuerdo," August 28, 1924, and "SAF Acuerdo," September 11, 1924, Group 182, Ramo Presidencial Obregón-Calles, 50/121-A-G-23, Archivo General de la Nación, Mexico City. (In subsequent references, this archival collection will be designated "AGN-O/C.")

10. Marte R. Gómez to Eduardo Hurtado, March 16, 1923, 1923 Cartas, 2, AMRG; Gómez, "Listas negras," *Germinal*, February 1, 1922, 14; and "Cordiales Embestidas," *Germinal*, November 1, 1921, 20; Mysager, "El principio del fin," *Germinal*, February 1, 1922, 24.

11. Juan Ballesteros, "La Tierra Restauratriz," *Germinal*, March 15, 1922, 4; and "Están muy atrasados los campesinos de Michoacán," *Excélsior*, October 15, 1922, section 1, page 1.

12. Quoted in Fabila, "Notas históricas sobre el Primer Congreso Nacional Agronómico," in *Los agrónomos mexicanos: Información histórica* (México: Ediciones Atenagro, 1954), 123.

13. Fernández, "Explotación de una hacienda," 2, 32, 40.

14. Ibid., 5–6, 23.

15. Ignacio Figueroa, "La pequeña propiedad," *Germinal*, February 1, 1922, 5–6, 23. See also Genaro Arzave H., "Colonización Agrícola en el País," 1921, ENA Thesis; Ignacio Velásquez, *Parvifundio, o pequeña propiedad rural de la familia mexicana* (México: Libreria Universal, 1925), CMRG.

16. Alfredo Valle, "Discutió ayer . . . ," *El Universal* (Mexico City), September 9, 1921.

17. Alejandro Brambila Jr., "Trabajo presentado," "Trabajos presentados," 2, CMRG; Gilberto Fabila and Francisco A. Ursúa, "Fraccionamiento de latifundios. Bases para la ley federal sobre esta materia," pamphlet (México: Cámara de Diputados, 1925); Arzave, "Colonización Agrícola en el País," 1; Ismael Reyes Retana, "Causas principales," "Trabajos presentados," 5, CMRG.

18. Ignacio Figueroa, "La pequeña propiedad," *Germinal*, February 1, 1922, 6; Luis León, quoted in Simpson, *The Ejido*, 323, 334 (translations by Simpson).

19. Ramón Corral Soto, "Algunas indicaciones," "Trabajos presentados," 2, 12, CMRG.

20. Marte R. Gómez, "Estudio sobre las condiciones sociales agrícolas y económicas del Estado de Morelos y programa general para su reconstrucción," August 30, 1922, "Trabajos presentados," 42–63, CMRG; Ramón Monroy, "El problema agrario," "Trabajos Presentados," 1–2, 4, 16, CMRG. See also "Los trabajos del Tercer Congreso Agronómico Nacional," *El Universal* (Mexico City), October 11, 1923.

21. Gabriel Itié, "La cooperación en México," *La Revista Agrícola*, February 1, 1919, 430–31; Ernesto Benavides, "Observaciones hechas en el municipio de Nazas, Dgo. sobre unos campos en los cuales se ha practicado la dotación de ejidos," July 22, 1922, "Trabjajos presentados," 3, CMRG; Davíd Ibarra, "La irrigación en el Valle de Actopam, Hgo. y su agricultura," August 1922, "Trabajos presentados," 6, CMRG; Gómez, "Estudio," 19–25; Corral Soto, "Algunas indicaciones," 2. See also Quintin Ochoa, "Iniciativa que propone el establecimiento de una cooperativa en La Barca, Jalisco," November 7, 1922, "Trabajos presentados," CMRG.

22. On Gómez, see Simpson, *The Ejido*, 318–21; Córdova, *La Ideología*, 284; Monroy, "El problema agrario," 17.

23. "El Congreso Agronómico no quiere que las Comisiones Agrarias dependen de los Gobernadores," *El Universal* (Mexico City), October 10, 1923, section 1, page 9.

24. See *Germinal*, April 1, 1922, the last issue of the publication's first run. See also Obregón to Secretaría de Hacienda y Crédito Público, December 11, 1922, 55/121-H-A-24, AGN-O/C; Marte R. Gómez, "Los primeros tiempos de la SAM," 1–2, "Ing. Marte R. Gómez: Datos Biográficos, etc.," AMRG; Bojórquez to Gómez, Oct. 1923, in Antonio Carrillo Flores, ed., *Vida Política Contemporánea: Cartas de Marte R. Gómez* (México: FCE, 1978), 1:24–25; and Ramón Corral Soto to Gómez, November 24, 1923, 1923 Cartas, 1, AMRG.

25. Quoted in *Los agrónomos mexicanos*, 171.

26. For more on the suicide, see "Trágicamente murió ayer el General don Jesús M. Garza," *El Universal* (Mexico City), February 12, 1923, section 1, page 1; Bojórquez, "Jesús M. Garza," in *Los agrónomos mexicanos*, 165; and "Primer Aniversario," *Germinal*, February 15, 1924, 1.

27. Marte R. Gómez to Gustavo Correa Correa, February 20, 1923, 1923 Cartas, 1, AMRG; and Marte R. Gómez to Juan de Dios Bojórquez, October 23, 1923, in Carrillo Flores, ed., *Cartas*, 1:25.

28. Gómez to Bojórquez, October 23, 1923, in Carrillo Flores, ed., *Cartas*, 1:25–26.

29. Ibid.

30. Portes Gil, *Autobiografía*, 334; Luis L. León, *Crónica del poder: En los recuerdos de un político en el México revolucionario* (México: FCE, 1987), 145.

31. Gómez to Bojórquez, October 23, 1923, in Carrillo Flores, ed., *Cartas*, 1:26.

32. Gómez to García Robledo, July 24, 1923, in ibid., 1:21.

33. Miguel Yépez, "En memoria del General J. M. Garza," *Germinal*, February 15, 1924, 3; Gómez to Bojórquez, May 9, 1924, in Carrillo Flores, ed., *Cartas*, 1:4. See also "Sentidas honras fúnebres al malogrado General Jesús María Garza," *Germinal*, February 15, 1924; "Fue muerto por un tiro el Dip. Apolonio R. Guzmán," *El Universal* (Mexico City), April 24, 1924, section 1, page 1; "El que mató al Dip. Apolonio R. Guzmán, Quedará sin Castigo," *El Universal* (Mexico City), April 25, 1924; "El asesinato del Dip. A. Guzmán," *El Universal* (Mexico City), May 6, 1924; and Gómez, *Biografías de agrónomos* (Chapingo, Mexico: Colegio de Postgraduados, 1976), 439, 450.

34. Alanís Patiño, *Vivir entre dos siglos*, 54; Fraternidad Chapingo, *Cuarenta años de ejercicio profesional: Generaciones 1922–1928, 1923–1928* (México, Nov. 1968), 7. The smaller figure appears in "El problema de la Escuela de San Jacinto," *Germinal*, April 1, 1922, 11.

35. Alanís Patiño, *Vivir entre dos siglos*, 49–50.

36. Ramón Fernández y Fernández, "Aniversario de plata: La generación del año de 1928 de la ENA," Box 72, 00362-00369, ARFF, Archivo Ramón Fernández y Fernández, Colegio de Michoacan in Zamora, Michoacan.

2; "El problema de la Escuela de San Jacinto," *Germinal*, April 1, 1922), 11; Gilberto Fabila, "Existe una nueva época aciaga para la Escuela de San Jacinto?," *Germinal*, March 15, 1922; M. M. Grvs, "Per me si va nella citá dolente," *Germinal*, April 1, 1922, 17.

37. See also Fernández, *Chapingo hace 50 años*, 79–80; and Juan de Dios Bojórquez to Marte R. Gómez, May 26, 1924, in Carrillo Flores, ed., *Cartas*, 1:35.

38. Gómez, *Episodios de la vida de la Escuela Nacional de Agricultura*, 277; Edmundo Flores, interview with the author, Mexico City, February 6, 1998; and Ramón Fernández, untitled document, Box 72, 00292 (1), ARFF.

39. For course listings, see Fraternidad Chapingo, *Cuarenta años de ejercicio profesional*, 39–45.

40. Gómez, "Discurso pronunciado en la sesión de clausura del Segundo Consejo Nacional Directivo de la Sociedad Agronómica Nacional, abril 19 de 1941," "Ing. Marte R. Gómez: Datos biográficos, etc.," 4, AMRG. For training in cooperativism, see Pascual Gutiérrez Roldán to Marte R. Gómez, October 21, 1925, 1925 Cartas, AMRG.

41. Edmundo Flores, interview with author; Fernández, *Chapingo hace 50 años*, 103; Eduardo Morillo to Marte R. Gómez, March 7, 1925, 1925 Cartas, AMRG; Fernández, untitled document, Box 72, 00292–3 (1–2), ARFF.

42. "El problema de la Escuela de San Jacinto," *Germinal*, April 1, 1922, 11; Tereso Reyes et al. to Ramón de Negri, July 12, 1923, ENA 1923–1944, AMRG; Pablo López to de Negri, March 7, 1923, ENA 1923–1944, 2, AMRG. See also Alfonso González Gallardo to Marte R. Gómez, May 14, 1925, 1925 Cartas, 2, AMRG.

43. Ramón Fernández y Fernández, "Aniversario de plata: La generación del año de 1928 de la ENA," Box 72, 00362-00369, ARFF, Archivo Ramón Fernández y Fernández, Colegio de Michoacan in Zamora, Michoacan; Marcelino Murrieta to Gómez, March 19, 1924, in Carrillo Flores, ed., *Cartas*, 1:29; Fernández, *Chapingo hace 50 años*, 104; Marte R. Gómez to Bojórquez, November 15, 1924, in Carrillo Flores, ed., *Cartas*, 1:43.

The resignation officially stemmed from a *Germinal* editorial that criticized the opulent new ministry of foreign relations building, but the ENA strike forced Gómez to resign to escape damaging his bosses. See "La Huelga de Alumnos de Agricultura no se ha solucionado," *El Universal* (Mexico City), November 6, 1924; "Los alumnos de Agricultura Acuden al Senado Denunciando Irregularidades Escandolosas," *El Universal* (Mexico City), November 7, 1924.

44. Marte R. Gómez to Bojórquez, November 15, 1924, in Carrillo Flores, ed., *Cartas*, 1:42.

45. Marte R. Gómez to Eustacio Contreras, November 10, 1925, 1925 Cartas, 1, AMRG. The Robespierre reference appears in "Vibraciones," *Germinal*, November 1, 1921, 8.

46. José Carrera to Marte R. Gómez, March 6 and 24, 1925; Jose Mares to Gómez, May 20, 1925; "Fomentadora Agrícola Mexicana, S.A. en Formación," March 25, 1925; Manuel Mesa to Gómez, February 24, 1925, all 1925 Cartas, AMRG; Ernesto Martínez de Alva to Gómez, February 22, 1925, 1, 1925 Cartas, AMRG.

47. José Carrera to Marte R. Gómez, March 24, 1925; Gaspar Garza Lara to Gómez, June 25, 1925; Gómez to Carrera, April 24, 1925, all 1925 Cartas, AMRG.

48. Eustacio Contreras to Marte R. Gómez, November 9, 1925, 1925 Cartas, 2, AMRG.

49. Eduardo Morillo to Marte R. Gómez, November 16, 1925, 2; Manuel Mesa to Gómez, November 17, 1925, 6, all from 1925 Cartas, AMRG; Gómez to Eustacio Contreras, November 10, 1925, 1, 1925 Cartas, AMRG.

50. Manuel Mesa to Marte R. Gómez, March 10, 1926, 1926 Cartas, 1, AMRG. See also Wintilo R. Caloca to Gómez, September 19, 1925, 1925 Cartas, 1, AMRG; Gómez to Mesa, December 13, 1925, 1926 Cartas, AMRG; Gaspar Garza Lara to Gómez, October 24, 1925, 1925 Cartas, 2, AMRG.

51. Gómez/Fitzmaurice exchange, November 15, and December 15, 1926, 1926 Cartas, AMRG; "Dimitió el Sr. Ministro de Agricultura y Fomento," *El Universal*, April 30, 1927; Gómez to Mesa, March 11, 1927; Mesa to Gómez, February 17, 1927, 2; and León to Gómez, July 24, 1927, all 1927 Cartas, AMRG.

52. Gaspar Garza Lara to Marta R. Gómez, January 19, 1923, 1923 Cartas, AMRG. See also Manuel Mesa to Gómez, February 24, 1925, 1925 Cartas, AMRG; AMRG, 1926 Cartas; Mario Bandala to Gómez, March 17, 1926, and Rafael Batiz Paredes to Gómez, April 3, 1926.

53. Manuel Mesa to Marte R. Gómez, February 24, 1925, 1925 Cartas, AMRG.

54. Gómez, "Memorándum confidencial al Señor Presidente de la República Licenciado don Gustavo Díaz Ordaz," "Cartas, AMRG." See also Garza Lara to Gómez, September 7, 1925, 1925 Cartas, AMRG; León/Gómez exchange, March 20 and 27, 1923, 1923 Cartas AMRG; Mesa to Gómez, February 24, 1925, 1925 Cartas, AMRG; Gómez to Contreras, October 29, 1925, 1925 Cartas, AMRG; and León to Gómez, June 22, 1927, 1–2, 1927 Cartas, AMRG.

55. Antonio Hidalgo to Marte R. Gómez, June 22, 1925, 1, 1925 Cartas, AMRG; José Lorenzo Sepúlveda to Gómez, June 24, 1925, 2, and October 17, 1925, 2, 1925 Cartas, AMRG; Obregón to Santana Almada, April 1, 1922, 90/239-L-8, AGN/O-C. See also Gómez to Alfonso González Gallardo, June 20, 1925, 2, 1925 Cartas, AMRG; "Informe

de los trabajos . . . junio actual," July 1, 1927, AGN, Group 215, Secretaría de Agricultura y Recursos Hidráulicos (hereafter AGN-SAF), 5/12G-108–1: Gómez Camacho, 1.

56. Eduardo Morillo to Marte R. Gómez, May 28, 1927, 1, 1927 Cartas, AMRG. See also Corral Soto to Marte R. Gómez, June 15, 1925, 1925 Cartas, AMRG; Fernández, "Los agrónomos y la reglamentación de profesiones," *Crisol* 6/11/63 (1 March 1934), 134; Aguirre, *Cuestiones agrarias*, 216–17; Eustacio Contreras to Gómez, November 9, 1925, 1, 1925 Cartas, AMRG; "Circular Num. AE 141," March 10, 1925; Circulares. Comisión Nacional Agraria, 1, CMRG; "Reglamento interior de la Comisión Nacional Agraria" (México: Imprenta Escallada, 1926), 23; Ernesto Benavides to Gómez, April 29, 1926, 1926 Cartas, AMRG; Gonzalo Robles to Manuel Mesa, December 8, 1933, 1933 Carta, AMRG; Gómez to Alfonso González Gallardo, June 20, 1925, 1925 Cartas, 1, AMRG.

57. For Gómez's student allies, see Ramón de Negri to Alvaro Obregón, November 12, 1924, 92/241-A-E-23, AGN-O/C.

58. Eduardo Morillo to Marte R. Gómez, June 12, 1925, 2, 1925 Cartas, AMRG.

59. P. Gutiérrez Roldán to Marte R. Gómez, October 12, 1925, 2; Gómez to Eduardo Morillo, May 15 and June 19, 1925; Morillo to Gómez, June 12, 1925; Gustavo Segura to Gómez, May 2, 1925; Gómez to P. Gutiérrez Roldán, November 2, 1925, all from 1925 Cartas, AMRG.

60. Marte R. Gómez to Eduardo Morillo, September 8, 1925; Morillo to Gómez, October 3, 1927, 1925 Cartas, AMRG; Morillo to Gómez, November 7, 1926, and March 6, July 1 and 8, 1927, 1927 Cartas, AMRG; Gaspar Garza Lara to Gómez, January 19, and June 29, 1923, 1923 Cartas, AMRG; de Negri to Obregón, February 9, 1924, 109/242-C1-C-6 AGN-O/C; "Circular Num. 62 A.C.," 1 June 1926, Circulares de la CNA, vol. 1, CMRG; Morillo to Gómez, March 17, 1927, 1927 Cartas, 2, AMRG; Garza Lara to Gómez, January 19 and June 29, 1923, 1923 Cartas, AMRG; Jesús Fernández to Gómez, June 5, 1926, 1926 Cartas, AMRG; Adrian Cordero to Jefe Depto de Propaganda Agrícola, March 20, 1926, 3/12C-113–1: Adrián Cordero, 1, AGN-SAF; and CNA Circular Num. 45 T.E.P., March 23, 1926; Ignacio Velázquez Sr., Circular Num. 57 O.M., 18 May 1926; Francisco de P. Rodríguez, Circular Num. 104 T.E.P., November 30, 1926; "Circulares de la CNA," vol. 1, CMRG; Morillo to Gómez, May 27, 1926, 1926 Cartas, AMRG; Morillo to Gómez, October 3, 1927, 1927 Cartas, AMRG; Gómez to Garza Lara, 15 June 1923, 1923 Cartas, AMRG; P. Gutiérrez Roldán to Gómez, October 21, 1925, 1925 Cartas, 1, AMRG; Morillo to Gómez, 26 July 1927, 1927 Cartas, AMRG.

61. Maria Bandala to Marte R. Gómez, March 17, 1926, 2; Eduardo Morillo to Gómez, May 8, 1926, 1, both 1926 Cartas, AMRG. See also Morillo to Gómez, December 5, 1927, 1927 Cartas, 5, AMRG.

62. Ramón Corral Soto to Marte R. Gómez, November 24, 1923, 1923 Cartas, 1, AMRG; Manuel Rincón Gómez to Gómez, January 14 and March 11, 1923, 1923 Cartas, AMRG; Carlos Ramírez to Gómez, November 21, 1926, 1926 Cartas, AMRG; "Circular Num. 17," 12 Feb. 1926, Circulares de la CNA, vol. 1, 1–2, CMRG; Agustín Méndez Macías to SAF Pagador General, August 14, 1925, 1/12A-94: Pablo Aragón, AGN-SAF.

63. Juan de Dios Bojórquez to Alvaro Obregón, September 14, 1923, 59/121-R-B-3, AGN-O/C; and Marte R. Gómez to Manuel Mesa, March 11, 1927, 1927 Cartas, AMRG. See also Federico Berumen to Gómez, July 2, 1925, 1925 Cartas, AMRG.

Commentary on Part II

LABOR PROFESSIONALIZATION, CLASS FORMATION, AND STATE RULE

Mary Kay Vaughan

Each chapter in this part deals with a dimension of middle-class identity, agency, and function much elaborated on in recent historiography. The Hindu reformers of colonial Bombay, the agronomists of revolutionary Mexico, the Colombian development workers, the administrators who selected them, and the US policymakers who defined their mission all form part of a historical social sector that defined itself as "in between" what they understood to be backward upper and lower social groups. Although Daniel Walkowitz's contemporary US English Country Dancers fall outside this definition, their predecessors, the social reformers who taught the same primly contained dances to immigrants in US settlement houses in the 1920s, certainly fit into this sector. They were all convinced that through their own behavior and what they prescribed for others, they would transform society in progressive, modernizing, and civilizing directions. They sought to remake society in their own image.

They forged their identity around a core set of values—thrift, sobriety, self-discipline, order, hygiene, work, responsible patriarchy, and empathy. They believed these to be lacking or deficient in those above and below them in the social hierarchy. They nurtured their identity in their service to others, particularly the subaltern, although at times they tried to reform their social superiors, as is the case here with the Mexican agronomists and was so for generations of headmistresses and teachers in women's boarding schools in the United States. Although some of their service—as in the case of the Hindu reformers in colonial Bombay—took the form of charity, charity was generally a concept they associated contemptuously with aristocracy. They were instead professionals, engineering a modern society. Their identity and cohesion emerged from education. They were not primarily distinguished by their role as merchants, traders, or businessmen, but as the recipients of higher education and degrees that ranged from accounting to medicine, teaching to social work. Although spread here across a wide geographical range from Mexico and India to the United States and Colombia, and a broad span of time from the late nineteenth century to 1960, these actors propagated and appropriated a cultural project that was transnational in nature, diffused, and easily recognizable anywhere it took root. We tend to associate its origins with Enlightenment notions of instrumental reason, market and imperial expansion, urbanization and the sanitary revolution, all of which accelerated in the late eighteenth century. We have tended to demonize these project makers for their single-minded moral certainty and their condescension. But as Robert Wiebe wrote long ago, we should recognize that they responded creatively to new conditions and opportunities for self-expression and self-definition invested in service to society, and in most instances, they had considerable impact. Certainly, the three authors here—Prashant Kidambi, Michael A. Ervin, and A. Ricardo López—celebrate their seizing of opportunity and their commitment to serve. The authors are less interested in the impact.

Much has been written about this social sector, varyingly referred to as missionaries of progress, moral crusaders, social engineers, and conscripts of democracy, as López calls them here.[1] What began for most of us as a literature about English and US experiences now embraces case studies from most parts of the globe. So what new or interesting insights can we glean about this sector by looking at these four fine chapters together? To begin, how are the experiences similar or different? The colonial Bombay reformers and the US settlement house workers, both operating around the same period in history, shuddered at the street behavior of the poor—unruly, unwashed, sexually subversive and overly explicit, physically threatening. As part of the sanitary revolution that targeted burgeoning cities, they sought to discipline bodies. On the surface, the Mexican agronomists were very different. Unlike any of the other projects explored here, the Mexicans actually proposed a radical restructuring of society and a redistribution of wealth and power. They could hardly do otherwise, as workers and peasants in revolution had already set the process in motion. The most forward-looking of the agronomists seized on the broad-based peasant demand for land to propose the transformation of the landed estate system into one that would benefit the small farmer. One might argue that in a revolutionary situation propelled by the very subalterns whom the Hindu reformers and US settlement-house workers sought to contain, the Mexican reformers were less constrained by colonial or transnational models. In any case, these are not mentioned in the chapter. In fact, the agronomists valued efficiency, productivity, and, usually, the small farmer, whose capacities could be enhanced through cooperativism but whose individuality was sacrosanct. That is, the agronomists were no more interested in the rationale of on-the-ground subaltern practices or values than were their counterparts in colonial Bombay and New York. Instead, they advocated their own values and practices as universally correct. Not discussed in the chapter is the educational project that complemented the agrarian reform: one that proposed a transformation of peasant conduct very much in line with the notions of Hindu reformers or US settlement workers, and not one with any respect for or curiosity about subaltern communities.[2] A somewhat greater respect and empathy for peasant culture came through the process of social revolution and the implementation of reform. These forced the reformers' hand and made negotiation imperative. Peasants were just as feisty agents as the reformers. Even without social revolution, wherever reformers met masses, some form of negotiation ensued.

Although the US-Colombian project discussed by López is organized around the same core values of self-discipline, sobriety, thrift, and hard work, it differs in significant ways from the others. The most clearly transnational and imperial project of the four, it took place in a different time period after the Second World War. It was a US-dominated Cold War project opposed to totalitarianisms of the Left or Right. It had wrongly analyzed Latin American societies as feudal. It hypothesized that unless socially engineered into American-style democracies, Latin American nations would succumb to Communist revolution. Unlike the other reform projects, the goal of democracy seemed central, and the language of mobilization and prescription distinct. The project would fall under the heading of development, not moral reform. Rather than repress the behavior and desires of the poor, social reformers proposed to cultivate their human and social capital for purposes of democratization. As López makes abundantly clear, the democracy envisioned was to be tightly controlled: it would both create and depend on individuals shaped in the image of the middle class, practicing the very conduct advocated by the earlier reformers but, allegedly, with more generous promotion of self-help, civic action, and cooperation. "Self-help" for the reformers is a concept resting on a predefined program for action: one would help oneself in particular directions, not others.

Let's be clear. The architects, as described by López, were not the Colombians but the Americans, a conjunctural coming together of Roosevelt New Dealers with modernization theorists, economists, sociologists, and urban planners. They were the relatives and colleagues of the settlement-house reformers who taught immigrants the dances of the English gentry. What is sad here is that if they were familiar with a non-US society, it was most likely England—certainly not the Latin American countries they so aggressively sought to transform. However, López notes the transnational dimensions of the project. US policymakers borrowed from the more radical social programs emanating from the Mexican and Bolivian Revolutions. Survivors and heirs of Ervin's agronomists served as consultants. An influential sector of the Colombian political elites and professionals signed on to the project. They shared some of the same values and goals as the Americans, at a vulnerable but hopeful moment after many years of devastating political violence. The chapter does not tell us to what extent they might have differed in values and goals, particularly in practice, and it does not discuss mutual transformations that probably occurred at the point of implementation.

This leads to a second point: the relationship of the reformers to power. What power did they have to implement their plans, and to what degree did power compromise their plan and themselves? The Hindu reformers appeared to have limited power within a society under foreign rule. They were not even the native economic upper class. They did have their social service organizations, educational institutions, and, above all, their active intervention in the public sphere, an important forum for persuasion despite the constraints within which it functioned. I wonder if Kidambi is suggesting that our understanding of public sphere activity ought to be expanded beyond the Habermasian notion of exchanging political opinion to include the dissemination of a middle-class project of improvement.[3] By disseminating the project within the public sphere, reformers at once defined, expanded, and educated their own social sector while attempting to shape the boundaries of the public sphere and proper conduct within it. That is, they would exclude the practices and pleas of the unruly, the degenerate, and the poor until those groups internalized the reform project. Later they would find that their power to impose boundaries and conduct was somewhat limited.

The Mexican agronomists sought to organize themselves and articulate their project within parameters used by the Hindu reformers: a professional society functioning according to bylaws, with dues-paying members, meetings, and the use of print media to enlighten public opinion and influence the state. But the agronomists found themselves in the midst of a revolution and the collapse of the state. They seized the opportunities opened by the power vacuum to struggle for the actual implementation of their ideas—not just their public circulation. They did so through affiliating with nascent political parties, military strongmen, populist leaders, and fledgling state bureaucracies. In the process of allying with a rapidly forming authoritarian state, they compromised many of their values of fair play and meritocracy, of respect for open discussion and deliberation, of autonomous professional organization and opinion making. They moved from participation in a vital, open, and chaotic public sphere in the early 1920s to participation in one significantly dominated and controlled by the state. Those not associated with the government lost out economically and professionally. The successful agronomists became policymakers and brokers for a corrupt authoritarian regime, but one with a strong populist commitment to social improvement.

From the evidence provided by López, the Colombian professionals hired to implement an externally driven democraticization project probably agreed with its aims. Alberto Valencia delighted in joining a "beautiful class," and the broader cohort found the project compatible with a national need to move beyond years of devastating violence. But in relation to power, these professionals seem to have been minions at various levels—of the Colombian government agencies that hired them; of the political elite that spawned the agencies; and of the US government that supported them. We have no idea what power the Colombian reformers had within the context of their own jobs and projects. As López's argument centers on the formation of a particular sector through an imperial project, perhaps the critical actors were the US foreign policy strategists and agency workers. They had less power than they imagined. They could not socially engineer various steps removed from context, with no understanding of the cultures they wanted to transform. In the end, they were probably not very powerful in the politics of their own or their host states. Realpolitik would push the well-meaning reformers aside. In the process, many of the professionals involved—Colombian, US, and Latin American—became radicalized critics of their own projects and governments. The US government proved more interested at the time in assisting military dictatorships than in fostering dangerous democracies.

Other commentaries in this volume examine how different chapters touch on questions of gender, race, and ethnicity. With the exception of Daniel Walkowitz's analysis of the post-1960s English Country Dance movement in the United States, these themes are surprising absent from the chapters in this part of the volume. For societies like the Indian, Colombian, and Mexican so strongly marked by differences in race and ethnicity, class and caste, a lack of focus on these seems odd until we recognize that these reformers approached their projects as universal, applicable to everyone. Their race, ethnic, class, and caste prejudices were embedded in their practices and even their prose—Prashant Kidambi's descriptions of the Bombay reformers' concerns are most explicit in this respect. As the literature on middle-class reform movements from 1880 to 1930 overflows with women's activities in the promotion of temperance and middle-class domesticity, and in the rescue of prostitutes and wayward girls, one has to ask if Kidambi's exclusive focus on male Hindu reformers is illustrative of an exceedingly patriarchal society or his own predilections. Were there no women in this reform movement, or did they have spaces for participation distinct from the press? The unconsciously masculinist analysis that Michael Ervin provides of the Mexican agronomists, an apparently all-male fraternity, also raises questions. The agronomists enacted the dichotomy of male/production versus female/reproduction. One wants to know how their particular notion of patriarchy influenced their conceptualization and implementation of agrarian reform. Current literature emphasizes how the agrarian reform deepened a patriarchal politics, promoted the male producer, and overlooked the complexity of the *campesino* family as a productive unit.[4] It would be interesting to understand the agronomists' role in this process. How did they perceive *campesino* family organization, production, and consumption?

For the period and the reform movement examined by A. Ricardo López, we have as yet few gendered studies. López himself does not focus on the question. However, from the criteria he describes for selecting professional personnel, we understand the enduring importance of the modern heterosexual patriarchal norms linked to the nuclear family: applicants raised by women or from broken or conflictive households lose points. The one detailed gender study we have of this US-influenced reform movement in Latin America is Heidi Tinsman's study on Chile.[5] The US government strongly backed and helped to shape this program, particularly under Christian Democratic regimes. Although Tinsman documents the important role women had played in prereform agriculture and political struggles, she argues that the paradigm shaping the reform came directly from professionals who promoted a modernized notion of patriarchy that emphasized male authority in politics, production, and family life, while urging respect for wives and complementarity between the imagined domestic and productive spheres.

Prashant Kidambi and Daniel Walkowitz permit us a rare and very welcome view into the intimate spaces of social reproduction in the professional middle class. Each raises issues critical to modernity, class, self, and community in global context. First, Kidambi shows that despite pretensions to universality in the middle-class project, modernity as we have known it has been a hybrid fusing of the project's core tenets with local practices, convictions, and inventions. The latter may pertain to morality and religion, health and medicine, familial and economic organization, or hierarchy and status, but they also embrace, as Dipesh Chakrabarty has written, a particular society's sense of the good life, of enjoyment and pleasure.[6] What has traditionally been enjoyed as the good life will persist for greater or shorter periods of time, often modified to meet changing needs and tastes, often shaping the ever-new forms of pleasure intrinsic to modernity's dependence on market-based consumption, or deployed as a foil or reaction against these new forms. Second, modernity everywhere breeds anxiety. Michael Ervin tells us a student at the National Agricultural School remembered the words of the distinguished Mexican economist, Jesús Silva Herzog: "The only thing that does not change is that everything changes!" He may have been paraphrasing his hero Karl Marx, but the observation is obvious, promising, and tormenting. Who would not be anxious before the constant incineration of things and beliefs, the constant flux of social destiny, the prospect of life with no guarantees? Given these existential conditions, the philosopher Charles Taylor defines critical reflection as integral to modernity.[7] A critical posture is indispensable to negotiating the modern condition. We are no longer—if we ever were—parts of small face-to-face collectives in which decisions and their consequences are taken and assumed in common: we are alone in our negotiation of an unstable, constantly changing terrain and must personally create the real or virtual communities in which we function. These communities are not given to us; we are not automatic heirs to anything. The anxieties that prompt a critical posture derive not just from the challenges of everyday life or an aesthetic sensibility that abhors the wreckage around it. Rather, anxieties derive from the sense that modernity cannot entirely meet our emotional needs. The challenges of modernity will fortify—at least for some time—traditional ways of doing or thinking things that enable survival and mobility in a rapidly changing world, and they will be transformed in the process. At the same time, the sense of loss and lack of fulfillment that accompany modernity at every step create nostalgia: a longing for return felt and imagined in ways that soothe the pain and create community. Some of this longing may be life-giving and life-enriching; it can also become highly destructive to self, to targeted enemies, even to whole societies.

I am not thinking of invented traditions that help modern states to rule through shared symbols and practices. Rather, I am referring to intimate experiences described here for the colonial Bombay middle class and English Country Dance enthusiasts in the contemporary United States as both negotiate terrains of changing configurations of class. In the period between the two world wars, a sense of being overtaken by events—by "modernity"—fueled the anxieties of male Hindu reformers in Bombay. Their ministering to the poor of the city had been eclipsed by the organizing activities of the Communist Party: the poor were transforming themselves into an active working class. A growing economy led to the expansion of both the working class and the sector claiming middle-class status. At the same time, employment became less secure for the traditional middle class. They encountered a burgeoning consumer market that threatened them on several counts. They had to decide what to consume on reduced incomes in order to maintain "distinction" vis-à-vis unacceptable newcomers and their traditional inferiors. The proliferation of radio, movies, dancing, sports, and education threatened their control over women and children. The prescriptions of the Brahmin Shankar Rau almost suggested the obliteration of the once sacred, but now transformed, public sphere. He recommended shunning new sites of entertainment and minimizing visits and visitors. He prescribed, presumably for Brahmin men, spiritual and reading exercises and a diet informed by ancient Hindu science. By all means, servants were to be kept on. The big opening onto the future was budgeting for the children's education.

Daniel Walkowitz does not emphasize anxiety to the same degree in his discussion of the professionals who join the contemporary English Country Dance (ECD) movement in the United States. He emphasizes their search for distinction in a vastly expanded middle class. He also describes their search for the good life and community. These professionals appear to have lost their sense of service or at least any singular zeal for it, although they may relish their personal work in knowledge industries. They are enmeshed in the enormously complex, sprawling, and interlocking bureaucracies that constitute US society today. Walkowitz does not even call them professionals. He refers to them as professional-technical workers. They have abandoned the project of their forebears to recover "traditional" dance to civilize, contain, and "set limits" on immigrant youth otherwise prone to gyrate in urban dance halls. However, Walkowitz argues that they have chosen specific dance and musical forms to distinguish themselves from distasteful others—particularly the more sexually suggestive or explicit music and dance styles they associate with mass-media markets and black and Latino minorities. He notes that they have created a past they can enjoy—white, bucolic, aristocratic, meticulously patterned, without improvisation, sexually contained, and high brow (indeed, Purcell's music is more "high brow" than Beethoven's, as it is less heard). He explains that the group is predominantly white and conventionally heterosexual: its membership does not reflect the growing diversity of the wider society. He describes the contemporary ECD movement as an outgrowth of the countercultural movements of the 1960s. The dancers form a community of refuge, seeking haven from an "overly wrought" world of "speed and greed." Walkowitz uses these markers to reflect on the dancers as indicative of the failure of the liberal project. But could they be a mark of its success? ECD enthusiasts respect the fundamental rules and principles of contemporary liberal, pluralistic society and politics, one of which is, in the words of Seyla Benhabib, "the rightful coexistence of different groups each with its different conceptions of the good [life]."[8] The development of individual identities, she writes, is " increasingly dependent on the reflexive and critical attitudes of individuals in weaving together a coherent life story beyond conventional role and gender definitions. Self-definitions become increasingly autonomous vis-a-vis established social practices and fluid in comparison to rigid role understandings."[9]

Shankar Rau recommended the creative appropriation of tradition to his cohorts in crisis in Bombay in the 1930s. ECD enthusiasts so appropriate in the United States today. They construct communities of "distinction," as do hip-hoppers. The key issue is tolerance as a necessary rule of the game for achieving consensus. Evidence seems to point to growing tolerance for diversity within the United States—perhaps because certain circumscribing rules of the game and cultural norms have been accepted. Respect for otherness has been achieved in the United States but has become a consensually endorsed goal and a principle of intellectual, legal, institutional, social, and political advocacy. The bigger problem for the United States and its middle class is US use of power abroad. As a global hegemon, the United States continues to missionize the same project that López has analyzed here—one hatched over a half-century ago out of entirely ethnocentric principles and experiences. So conceived, the project is as much a failure as the force of arms that has wreaked so much destruction in defense of the liberal project at home. These are challenging issues for the "global middle class" as an idea and a practice.

Notes

1. The bibliography is enormous. Among so many others in addition to Wiebe, see Rodgers, *Atlantic Crossings*; Michel and Koven, *Mothers of a New World*; J. Walko-

witz, *Prostitution and Victorian Society*; O'Connor, *Poverty Knowledge*; Koven, *Slumming*; Stromquist, *Reinventing "The People"*; James Scott, *Seeing Like a State*; Mitchell, *Rule of Experts*; Ferguson, *The Anti-Politics Machine*.

2. Mary Kay Vaughan, *The State, Education, and Social Class in Mexico*.

3. Habermas, *The Philosophical Discourse of Modernity* and *The Structural Transformation of the Public Sphere*.

4. See, among others, the essays in Salamini and Vaughan, *Creating Spaces, Shaping Transitions*.

5. Tinsman, *Partners in Conflict*.

6. Chakrabarty, "Postcoloniality and the Artifice of History," 21, as cited by Sanjay Joshi in this volume.

7. C. Taylor, "Two Theories of Modernity," 172–196.

8. Benhabib, "Models of Public Space," 83.

9. Ibid., 85–86.

PART III

Middle-Class Politics in Revolution

A Middle-Class Revolution

THE APRA PARTY AND MIDDLE-CLASS IDENTITY IN PERU, 1931–1956

Iñigo García-Bryce

On August 23, 1931, in the colonial bullring of the city of Lima, Víctor Raúl Haya de la Torre, the presidential candidate of the Peruvian Aprista Party (PAP), addressed a crowd of thousands, one of the largest rallies Peru had ever seen. The young student leader and labor organizer had returned to his country only a month earlier, after seven years of exile. Now he promised to lead Peru along a revolutionary path by wresting control of the country from its oligarchy, and creating a national state to represent all social classes. An impressive political orator, Haya spoke for two hours, explaining the principles of *aprismo*, the political doctrine of a movement he had founded while exiled from Peru, the American Popular Revolutionary Alliance (APRA).[1] In the story of transformation told by Haya that day, the middle class would lead an "alliance of manual and intellectual workers" in a revolution that sought not only political but also moral renewal: "The best foundation for our Party, is, therefore, our desire to become a moral force in the country signaling the way toward a new dignified and humane politics . . . What Aprismo demands of its members is honesty, sincerity and a firm desire for sacrifice."[2]

The revolutionary role of the middle class emerged from Haya's broader economic argument on the threat of imperialism—particularly US imperialism—in Latin America. Turning Lenin's dictum around, Haya argued that in

Latin America, imperialism in fact represented the first rather than the last stage of capitalist transformation. As the class most affected by imperialism, the middle class would pave the way for the creation of a new nationalist, anti-imperialist state to curb the power of foreign enterprises and promote economic development. Yet the middle class needed a political party to guide it: "We must free the small property holder who hands over his property to the large companies that buy it; the small miner who must do the same; and the entire middle class that suffers as a result of the lack of a scientific organization on the purely national order of things."[3] APRA would be the party providing the organization not only for the working and peasant classes, but also for the middle class that, according to Haya, "perhaps makes up the majority of the country."[4]

Haya had grown up in a region where these dynamics were visibly at play. Around the city of Trujillo in northern Peru, during the early twentieth century, small property holders had gradually lost their lands to expanding sugar estates. Haya's mother's family had owned land and remained socially prominent, although they were no longer wealthy.[5] In many ways, Haya was himself an example of a middle-class intellectual. His father worked as an accountant for a sugar plantation, and during his student years in Peru, Haya held various jobs, including part-time clerk for a law firm and teacher at the Colegio Anglo-Peruano, a secondary school in Lima. At the school he met an American woman, Anna Melissa Graves, who would give him financial support during his years of exile, prior to his first presidential run in 1931.

Although Haya de la Torre did not win the election that year (in fact, the presidency of Peru would elude him his entire life) over the course of the next decades, APRA became Peru's most powerful political force. APRA members succeeded in building one of Latin America's most enduring multiclass political parties. The feat seems all the more remarkable considering that the party was declared illegal and forced to operate underground from 1932 to 1945 (with a brief hiatus in 1934) and then again from 1948 to 1956 by governments that feared a violent revolution. The fears were not unfounded, as APRA staged two major uprisings in 1932 and 1948, as well as dozens of insurgencies. Haya remained in hiding for most of the next thirty years and was forbidden to run for president until 1962, when his narrow victory triggered a military coup. Nevertheless he remained a major power broker in Peruvian politics. The winning presidential candidates in the 1945 and 1956 elections both needed APRA's support, and during its periods of legality, the party was a strong presence in Congress.

Scholars studying the middle class and APRA have invariably linked the rise of this party to the expansion of this social class. Some scholars have identified support for APRA among certain social groups that can be considered part of the middle class. For example, Lewis Taylor includes schoolteachers, judges, and lawyers among APRA's middle-class supporters.[6] In his study of the Peruvian middle class, David Parker identifies APRA as an important part of the process of spreading the idea of a middle-class identity: "APRA did more than any other political movement in Peruvian history to promote and diffuse the emerging idea of the middle class, part of a new and radical political discourse."[7] Beyond Peru, Aprismo also influenced the development of other political parties throughout Latin America associated with middle-class reform, including Acción Democrática in Venezuela, the Partido de Liberación Nacional in Costa Rica, and the Partido Auténtico in Cuba.[8]

Yet the connection between these two interrelated social and political processes—the rise of a political party and that of a new social class—has not been explored in sufficient detail.[9] In what sense can APRA be considered a middle-class party? How did Aprista ideas and the building of the party contribute to the development of a middle-class identity in Peru from the 1930s to the 1950s? By speaking the language of a multiclass alliance (between manual and intellectual workers), APRA helped to forge a new political identity—one that, uncomfortably for some, sought to integrate Peru's indigenous and mestizo masses into a national society. Contact with the party had a strong impact on a person's life, and the values that the party sought to impart to its members made the party itself a vehicle of class mobility.

This is not to say that all members of the middle class were affiliated with APRA. Rather, belonging to APRA became one of many identity markers that could make an individual middle class. Following Parker's approach, this chapter presents APRA not so much as a party that represented a preexisting middle class, but rather as a party that itself helped reinforce a new middle-class identity, both through its political rhetoric and its practices. To the teachers, lawyers, judges, peasants, artisans, and students who joined the party, APRA offered a unifying discourse that placed the middle class squarely at the heart of the political process. APRA was the first political party in Peru to recruit women. The party itself thus acted as a mechanism for incorporating new sectors of the population into a national organization that allowed them to aspire to a middle-class identity.

A purely discursive analysis of Aprismo would fail to establish a correlation between Aprismo and middle-classness, since Aprista political rhetoric reflected the fact that the party sought to represent not only the middle class, but all classes in Peru. APRA was not the party of any particular class. Yet by examining Aprismo more broadly as a set of cultural and social practices, we can see the way in which the party itself functioned to confer a middle-class status on many of its members. In defining social class, I rely on E. P. Thompson's classic definition of the making of class identity: "Class happens when some men, as a result of common experiences (inherited or shared) feel and articulate the identity of their interests as between themselves and as against other men whose interests are different from (and usually opposed to) theirs."[10] Aprismo constituted a common experience for tens of thousands of both men and women, an experience that was more than just political in that it transformed the social lives of the members of the party.[11]

The relationship between Aprismo and middle-class formation in Peru calls for an expansion of the definition of "middle class" to take into account new social groups. Arno Mayer provides a useful direction to follow in his analysis of the lower middle class. He challenges the Marxist notion that the lower middle class was conservative—Marx wrote that "they are reactionary, for they try to roll back the wheel of history."[12] Mayer claims that "the lower middle class generates and keeps generating a separate culture, ethos, life-style, and world view. Even if at first sight it seems to have no apparent class consciousness—except in times of acute crisis—it does have a sharply defined class awareness."[13] He further characterizes this sector as one that is acutely aware of its precarious situation and of the possibilities of downward mobility, and he observes that this awareness leads to an intense level of politicization: "In their struggle for survival they establish or bolster economic and professional organizations; they form political lobbies, pressure groups, or factions; they join or support political organizations, such as leagues, parties, or movements; and, ultimately, when cornered, they take to the streets and to the piazzas."[14]

The lower middle class in Peru lay outside the usual middle-class professions such as white-collar workers and professionals, who first identified themselves as middle class. In the 1920s and 1930s, and more so after the 1940s, population growth, the expansion of education, incipient industrialization, and a growing public administration led to the growth of the middle class. In particular, migration from the countryside to the city brought a growing number of mestizos or cholos—people of mixed race—to the cities, particularly to Lima. The term "cholo," which refers to rural migrants of indigenous descent, has traditionally had a derogatory connotation. In his analysis of Peruvian society, François Bourricaud includes cholos as part of the middle class—mestizos seeking social mobility by moving to the cities, where they had to confront the social and psychological barriers of racism.[15] Earlier, in his 1941 thesis on the Peruvian middle class, Hector Cornejo Chavez had identified mestizos or cholos as middle class: "The privileged class is primarily white in its coloring, with a lesser degree of mestizo appearance; the middle class is half white, half mestizo; and the proletarian class presents a primarily indigenous and mestizo appearance."[16]

Although *indigenismo* became a fixture of political rhetoric after the 1920s, the mestizo or cholo rarely appeared as a political referent. A rare, but telling, mention of the cholo can be found in a 1944 article on the Peruvian political situation by Haya de la Torre, in which he identifies APRA as the party of cholos. Probably written for a Chilean audience, the article contrasts Peruvian conservatism unfavorably with its Chilean counterpart and identifies a cultural and racial divide between Peru's elites and its people: "The hatred and contempt of our oligarchies for the people, for the 'cholo' . . . and for the Indian, becomes evident in the way these oligarchies have always treated the docile and defenseless popular majority of Peruvians. The men of Lima's plutocracy have never dared to engage politically with the poor citizenry in a clean and honest democratic joust . . . But the 'cholos' and the Indians have formed their great Party. And the only one there is—which is not a lap dog of the plutocracy—is Aprismo."[17] Despite the lack of a political rhetoric of *mestizaje*, APRA as a mass party in Peru, with its social and racial makeup, clearly drew its political strength from the country's majority mestizo population.

As several authors have argued, the Latin American middle class has received very little scholarly attention. From modernization theories to dependency analysis, "the middle classes are identified as social actors, . . . but remain largely unproblematized in the interstices between labor, capital, and the state, absent of any interests, culture, politics, or ideologies of their own."[18] More recently, influenced by cultural studies, a few scholars have broken this pattern and begun to correct the oversight by examining the formation of middle-class identities in specific national contexts.[19] As part of this new historiographical trend, David Parker has studied the emergence in Lima at the beginning of the twentieth century of a politically conscious white-collar movement that identified itself as middle class in the fight for its labor rights.[20] The middle class described by Parker sought to emulate the lives of their social superiors and distinguish themselves from manual laborers. Yet in upholding their labor rights, Lima's white-collar workers were at the forefront of creating a middle-class identity in Peru. One of the features of this identity was its exclusionary nature, in that it set *empleados* (white-collar workers) aside from and above *obreros* (blue-collar workers). Thanks to empleado mobilization, this separation was legally enshrined in Law 4916, which granted special benefits to empleados—the law was based on the assumption that the middle-class empleados deserved greater protection than workers. Thus this middle class was both aggressive in pursuing its political rights and exclusive in seeking to differentiate itself from those below, pursuing special privileges in order to safeguard its precarious hold on respectability. Lima's empleados thus reinforced their own sense of middle-class respectability as compared to those whom they considered their social inferiors. This barrier between the working class and the middle class would come under assault with the rise of APRA during the 1930s.[21]

Haya de la Torre, Aprismo, and the Middle Class

One of the radical changes brought about by Aprismo in Peruvian politics was the rhetorical positioning of the middle class as a central agent in the transformation of society. Haya's analysis of the role of the middle class grew out of the process of developing an Aprista ideology distinct from Marxism. Like many Latin American thinkers of his time, Haya wrestled with the problem of applying Marxism to Latin American societies. Like his contemporary, and eventual rival, José Carlos Mariátegui, founder of the Peruvian Socialist Party, Haya realized that with its small industrial labor force that lacked class consciousness, Peru could not follow the path of revolution outlined by Marx in his writings about Western Europe. The driving engine of Marxist revolution, the opposition of capital and labor, was absent in this predominantly agrarian Latin American society. Although Mariátegui turned to Peru's indigenous peasantry as the revolutionary class, Haya placed the middle class squarely at the heart of his political program.[22] In doing so, he was going against the writings of Marx and Lenin, with which he was undoubtedly familiar.[23] A 1933 pamphlet titled "4 aspectos importantes del Aprismo" (Four important features of Aprismo) about Aprismo attempted to disseminate these ideas more broadly. It claimed that "Communism does not accept within its ranks the so-called middle classes, which it calls 'petite bourgeoisie.' Aprismo is the united front of manual and intellectual workers. In other words, it is the Peruvian political party that brings together workers, students, peasants, employees, small capitalists, professionals, sailors and military men."[24]

Haya's designation of the middle class as revolutionary hinged on his analysis of Latin American economies. Because Latin America still had not fully entered the capitalist stage, foreign capital would be necessary for national development. In 1931 he stated in a public speech: "I have said that we consider foreign capital to be necessary in countries with an incipient level of economic development such as our own."[25] Yet in order for this foreign capital to benefit the countries of Latin America, Haya saw the need for the rise of a national middle class.

Although he visited Russia in 1924 and was approached by the leaders of the Comintern, Haya considered Peru to have a greater affinity with China than with Russia. He drew a parallel with the Guomindang, China's nationalist party, which had been founded not as a class-based party put rather as a united front that included workers, peasants, and members of the middle class. Like China, Peru was a primarily agrarian society where the working class had not reached the size and level of organization typical of working classes in industrialized nations; hence the need to include the middle class in the political process. Haya mentioned this parallel not only in his writings, but also at a political rally of thousands where he referred to the Guomindang as APRA's "distant brother."[26]

Haya's interest in the middle class as a political agent probably dates back to his early years as a student leader. León Bieber has argued that Haya's theory of a nationalist, middle-class revolution was influenced by his youthful visits to Uruguay and Argentina, as well as his subsequent visit to Mexico.[27] In 1922 he had attended a congress organized in Uruguay and visited Buenos Aires, where he met leaders of the Radical Party of Argentina. In both Uruguay and Argentina reformist, middle-class movements had succeeded in taking power: in Uruguay under Batlle y Ordoñez, and in Argentina under Yrigoyen. In Mexico in 1924, Haya worked as a secretary to José Vasconcelos, then the minister of education.

Haya's ideas on the middle class developed rapidly between 1926 and 1928—an extremely fertile period, during which Haya studied at Oxford University, visited the United States, and then returned to Mexico, where he founded an APRA cell.[28] In an article titled "What Is the APRA?"—published in London's *Labour Monthly* in 1926—Haya had not yet formulated the notion of a revolutionary middle class. Rather, he described the middle class in more traditional Marxist terms and lumped it together with the ruling classes of Latin America as an ally of imperialism: "1) The governing classes of the Latin American countries—landowners, middle class or merchants—are allies of North American imperialism. 2) These classes have the political power in our countries."[29] This article synthesized Aprismo in five main points, the first of which was "action against Yankee imperialism." In a somewhat Marxist vein, this early article identified the revolutionary classes as the "united front of the toiling masses (workers, peasants, natives of the soil) united with students, intellectuals, revolutionaries, etc."[30]

By the following year, Haya had identified the middle class as a victim of imperialism. In his 1927 article on the role of the middle classes," published in Mariátegui's famous journal *Amauta*, Haya equated the plight of the middle classes with that of the working classes exploited by foreign capitalist enterprises. Companies such as Standard Oil paid lower wages in Peru than they did in the United States. "That firm," he wrote, "exploits both workers and employees equally."[31] Standard Oil had been extracting oil from northern Peru since the early 1900s. The oil fields were nationalized by the military government of General Juán Velasco Alvarado in 1968.

In 1928, Haya wrote *El antimperialismo y el APRA*, which would be published in Chile in 1936. Here he fully developed his argument that the middle class suffered more than others with the advance of imperialist foreign enterprises and would therefore be called on to play a revolutionary role. Workers would get better wages from foreign firms, as would indigenous *campesinos*, although the benefits would be only temporary: "They exchange their miserable salary of a few centavos or of payment in kind, for the higher wage that the foreign master, who is always more powerful and wealthier than the national one, is able to pay."[32] In the case of Indoamerica (his term for Latin America), Haya claimed, imperialism represented not the last but the first stage of capitalism. In response to imperialism, the countries of Indoamerica needed to forge a political alliance and develop a strong anti-imperialist state. In an example with some present-day relevance, Haya claimed that "the famous North American monopolies of small commerce—the so-called 'five and ten cent' stores of which the famous Woolworth is a formidable representative—implies the destruction of the small competitor . . . In the face of a branch of Woolworth's, there is no small shop or store able to compete."[33] As mentioned earlier, Haya's native Trujillo had experienced this process with the growth of large sugar estates.

Haya even suggested that in developing nations, the middle class played a more advanced role than in industrialized countries. In the latter, he claimed, although the middle classes form a large part of the consumer market, they are locked into what he terms a "vicious cycle" in which they are unable to get much further ahead economically and become a "bourgeois class." In developing nations, on the other hand, "the middle classes have a greater field of action."[34] But for the obstacle of imperialism itself, the middle classes would become a national bourgeoisie—hence the motivation for the middle classes to combat imperialism in order to guarantee their own ascendancy.

A key component of Haya's theory was the existence of a vanguard of middle-class intellectuals (like him) who would be agents of political change, particularly in "backward countries," where he considered the working classes to be ignorant because they operate within agrarian or feudal structures. "In the countries of Indoamerica," Haya claimed, "the function of intellectuals has been and definitively is the anti-imperialist struggle."[35] He listed a number of Latin American middle-class intellectuals whom he considered precursors of the APRA movement, including José Enrique Rodó, the Uruguayan intellectual who wrote the influential essay "Ariel" (1900) warning of North American influence in Latin America, and José Vasconcelos, the Mexican author of *La Raza Cósmica* (1925) celebrating Mexico's mestizo heritage.

Haya de la Torre's ideas were echoed by other Aprista exiles whose writings and lectures had an impact in various parts of the continent during the 1920s and 1930s. During her 1929 lecture tour of various Caribbean countries—including the Dominican Republic, Cuba, and Puerto Rico—the Aprista Magda Portal called for the creation of a new consciousness "to make the middle classes—small farmers and merchants, employees, schoolteachers, intellectuals—understand the need to group together in a united front to cooperate in the anti-imperialist fight in defense of their interests as a class destined to disappear in the face of the avalanche of foreign capital, and keeping in mind that our middle classes, which are proletarian from an economic standpoint, nonetheless have a bourgeois mentality that has not yet adapted to the new principles."[36] Also exiled from Peru, Portal had joined the Aprista cell in Mexico in 1928. She would become the highest ranking woman in the party in Peru.

After the fall of the Leguía government in 1930, when Haya began to seek the presidency of Peru, he softened the party's anti-imperialist rhetoric. The shift was also conditioned by events in Peru where, after years of persecution of their party, Apristas put forth a more conciliatory and prodemocratic political discourse. When APRA finally attained legal status in 1945, Haya publicly reassured the business community that their holdings would not be nationalized and emphasized the importance of both economic growth and redistribution. On the international side, Haya began to emphasize a more harmonious relationship with the United States and saw fascism as a worse threat than the United States to Latin America. Yet it is telling that in a speech to workers at the Lima party headquarters the following year, he continued to insist on the importance of the Latin American middle class, as having a "progressive mission."[37]

During the 1940s and 1950s, the party struggled to distance itself from a long legacy of armed insurgencies and attempted to gain respectability and acceptance within the Peruvian political establishment.[38] After the 1945–48 hiatus under the presidency of José Luis Bustamante y Rivero, during which the party held several ministries and was represented in Congress, a failed insurrection in October 1948 sent APRA underground for another eight years. When the party surfaced once more in 1956, it did so by striking a compromise with President Manuel Prado, who had persecuted the Apristas during the early 1940s. The period from 1956 to 1962 known as the *convivencia* alienated some Apristas, who considered that their party had moved too far to the right and betrayed its original ideals. Nonetheless, APRA retained its strength, with a third of the Peruvian electorate consistently supporting it. Although the Aprista rhetoric may have lost some of its youthful fire, the party itself continued to thrive as Peru's strongest political institution, and to integrate new social groups into national politics.

Aprismo as Middle-Class Identity

The Peruvian Aprista Party contributed to the rise of a middle-class identity in ways not anticipated in Haya de la Torre's early writings. By creating a national organization that incorporated large numbers of people into political life, the party itself became a marker of middle-class identity by promoting civic engagement and reinforcing a series of values, including self-improvement through education, that would place its members above the illiterate masses. That this identity was not directly expressed in class terms has to do with the fact that Aprista political discourse sought to blur class differences and emphasize national unity. APRA, the alliance of manual and intellectual workers, would eventually be renamed El Partido del Pueblo, translated as the People's Party. The main reason for this change was to dispel accusations that APRA was an international party. Although the party soon developed a hierarchical structure, with Haya at the top of the pyramid, the myth of equality within the party was a powerful one. Party members refer to each other as *compañero*. Although the party's national leaders clearly belonged to the middle class, the rank and file, with a more liminal class identity, might improve their social status by belonging to the party.

Aprismo was designed as much more than a political doctrine—it was intended to be a moral system that would transform Peruvian society by creating a new engaged and disciplined citizenry. In an article published in the party newspaper, *La Tribuna*, Manuel Seoane—one of the party's national leaders—pointed to this transformative ideal, which involved radically changing both society and the individual: "We Apristas will always be new in the human sense—that is, men free of all inferior passion, open to all suggestions, decisive optimists. That is, we will build a vigorous fraternity that will strike new virile notes in the sickly atmosphere of our country. Our renewal will be not only political. It will also be a spiritual renewal."[39] Numerous scholars have compared Aprismo to a secular religion that generated symbols that resonated with the popular Catholicism of its followers.[40] Haya in particular was aware of the power of religion and incorporated it into his political rhetoric.[41] In a speech to workers on June 6, 1946, for example, he cast the relationship between party and followers in clearly religious terms: "This calling goes through you, delegate *compañeros* of the entire republic, to the worker, the farmer, the tenant farmer, the employee, the artisan, all of whom keep in their hearts the faith of Aprismo, creator of a new Peru, but which sometimes, like the votive lamp that needs new drops of oil, needs our love, our faith, our forgiveness, and a cry that like a bright discharge illuminates the fatherland saying: 'Aprista, be proud of your great party, and continue to prepare to overcome obstacles.'"[42] The years of political persecution fostered a cult of martyrdom within the party.

Party membership became a strong identity marker, and to some degree it has remained so until this day. Julio Cotler has referred to APRA as a "total organization" in the sense that it permeated all areas of a person's life, including the family, the neighborhood, and the workplace.[43] Steve Stein points out that party leaders "strove to provide their followers with a system of values and behavior that touched on every aspect of their lives. The moralistic and familistic fervor of APRA led many outside observers to believe that the loyalty of Apristas to their party far surpassed all other loyalties including those, for instance, to the nation, to a geographical region, or to a particular city."[44] As Jeffrey Klaiber points out, its followers saw APRA "not as a mere political party but as a combination of neighborhood family club, civic reform group, cultural circle, fraternity and charitable organization. For many Apristas the party fulfilled many of the functions of an active neighborhood church."[45]

Apristas could be recognized for, in theory, adhering to a strict code of discipline that included punctuality in a society where people are notoriously late and a desire for education, and by such small but distinctive external traits as a particular way of clapping with three consecutive staccato claps. In fact, APRA has often been accused of fostering sectarian tendencies. The Federación Aprista Juvenil (FAJ), the Aprista youth group, is a good example of the mechanisms that existed within the party to both recruit and transmit a new system of values. The FAJ recruited young Apristas into the party and had a written "Code of Action," with forty-eight points intended to mold the behavior of young Apristas. The first of these was: "Young Aprista: prepare yourself for action and not for pleasure—that is your duty."[46] The code was designed to foster discipline and self-improvement, and it urged young Apristas to always study, learn, and be humble. It included a command not to look down on workers.[47]

The Aprista revolutionary doctrine also involved a new view of women—in fact, APRA was the first party in Peru to recruit female members. When the Peruvian Aprista Party was founded in 1930, it included a Sección Femenina (headed by Magda Portal) intended to incorporate women into the party. Following the years when the party was illegal, Apristas held their first women's national convention in 1946. According to Elsa Chaney, "at the time, a feminine training command was inaugurated as a transition measure to educate politically a group of Aprista women. From this command, the women were to be graduated to whatever party brigades could make use of their services."[48] Despite the disappointment of leaders like Portal at the fact that women were not given the same voting status as men within the party, women continued to join APRA. By 1967, 40 percent of the party's members were women. For many of these women, the PAP offered an opportunity to lead a political life. Besides Portal, the highest ranking female leader, many other women joined the party—some at high levels, such as Julia Jaramillo de Phillips, who ran for Congress in 1962.[49]

Aprista national leadership was clearly middle class. In 1931, 77 percent of Aprista leaders had a professional background, whereas only 8 percent were in business, and only 15 percent were workers.[50] An examination of the class background of just a handful of the party's main leaders reveals their middle-class status. Haya de la Torre himself, as mentioned earlier, had a middle-class background, as did Portal, who was able to study at a national university (San Marcos) and who gained recognition among Peru's intellectual circles for her literary work. Manuel Seoane (the second most important leader after Haya) was the son of literature professor who held important political positions such as diplomat and attorney general. Seoane studied law at San Marcos University. Luis Alberto Sanchez made a career as a well-known literary critic. The rest of the party's most prominent leaders follow the same pattern. By the 1940s, as the party's relationship with the US government improved, some of these leaders traveled to the United States on official visits.

Party leadership itself may have acted as a channel of social mobility, the prestige associated with leadership boosting an individual's class status. The best example of this is Arturo Sabroso, a textile worker who became an important party union leader. Sabroso corresponded directly with Haya, traveled to international labor congresses, and held high positions within the party. Although his high leadership position makes Sabroso atypical of the mass of workers, leadership positions existed at a number of levels nationwide. At the regional level, for example, the number of professionals in leadership positions decreased dramatically and the number of those considered to be working class increased: Giesecke calculates that 52 percent of regional leaders belonged to the working class.[51] A study of individual cases may reveal a similar pattern at the lower levels of leadership.

Various economic and social trends during the 1930s and 1940s suggest that the boundary between the working and middle classes was becoming more porous. On the one hand, population growth and the expansion of education had led white-collar professions to expand and increasingly incorporate mestizos and people of working-class origin.[52] On the other hand, improvements in the lives of workers could lead some of them to consider themselves middle class. Beginning with the winning of the eight-hour work day in 1919—a battle in which Haya de la Torre played a prominent role—the Peruvian labor movement won a series of rights for workers. In a lecture given at the Escuela Técnica de Comercio, on November 30, 1940, the journalist Carlos Miró Quesada Lagos alluded to these improvements for workers and contrasted them with the lack of attention the national state gave to the middle class: "In Peru, workers' hospitals and people's restaurants have been built . . . as well as workers' neighborhoods."[53] In 1936, Peru's president, General Oscar Benavides, signed the Social Security Law. Benavides also promoted government restaurants that, according to Paulo Drinot, afforded workers a degree of respectability.[54] This would suggest that the working class had begun to receive certain benefits that would allow its members to aspire to middle-class status, and perhaps even to think of themselves as middle class.

Cornejo Chavez had alluded to the fact that the border between classes was a porous one. He expressed this idea quite poetically by claming that "the same thing occurs with social classes as with the colors of the rainbow: one cannot establish their limits exactly."[55] Because of class mobility, which he also recognized, individuals might be moving in or out of a particular class and, "therefore, have characteristics of both classes, without belonging definitively to either of them."[56] In *Treinta años de Aprismo*, Haya de la Torre made a telling remark along these lines. He pointed out that certain workers may have had a claim to middle-class identity: "Also belonging to that middle because of their consciousness and tradition are a significant sector of our most skilled proletariat or of our oldest artisanry—who are eventually displaced toward innovative sectors of work with better remuneration."[57]

APRA played a central role in organizing some of Peru's most important labor unions. In 1944, APRA gained control of the largest union, the Confederación de Trabajadores del Perú (CTP). By 1946, during the brief period between 1945 and 1948 when the party was legal and participated in the Bustamante government, the CTP grew to include over two hundred other unions, both white- and blue-collar.[58] The CTP established links to international labor organizations such as the Organización Regional Interamericana de Trabajadores and the AFL-CIO in the United States. This expansion represented a move toward greater inclusion on the part of the middle class, which was becoming willing to associate itself politically with worker's unions. Parker writes: "In effect, the aprista unionists had jettisoned the identification of 'empleado' with 'middle class,' underscoring the extent to which their ideas marked a departure from tradition."[59] By seeking to minimize the difference between white- and blue-collar workers, APRA was working against long-standing prejudices in Peru against manual labor.[60]

This attempt by APRA was met with uneasiness in some sectors of the traditional white-collar middle class. The relationship between white-collar workers and APRA unraveled over time. Although the white-collar middle class originally supported APRA, Parker argues that during the 1930s, as the party became more radicalized, it began to lose its support among Lima's white-collar workers. The loss of APRA control over the Asociación de Empleados del Perú in 1947 signaled this change.[61]

Another sector for which APRA may have represented a vehicle of social mobility was the rural migrants who began to arrive in Lima in increasing numbers after the 1930s. Most research on APRA has focused on its ties to student and labor organizations, and migrants from the countryside to the city have received less attention. María Teresa Quiroz argues that APRA sought to incorporate these migrants: "This relation of socialization that the party established with the migrant sector was intended to progressively integrate these provincial sectors living in Lima into national political life."[62] These migrants were referred to as cholos by those who considered themselves their social superiors in Lima. The APRA party structure included residential cells, or "urban associations of migrants with common regional origins, arising from the massive new influx to the towns."[63] Migration to Lima increased dramatically from the 1930s to the 1960s. The 1950s saw the creation of the first large *barriadas*, or shantytowns, as the number of migrants to the city increased. Without specific data on their self-identification, it is hard to make definitive statements about whether these new migrants joined the middle class. However, to the degree that APRA afforded respectability, membership in the party can be seen as contributing to a middle-class identity.

A Lima taxi driver once commented to me that in the most remote town of Peru you could always find two things: a police station and the local headquarters of the Peruvian Aprista Party (PAP). His comment points to the importance of Aprismo, not only as an ideology with resonance throughout Peru and Latin America, but also as a national political party of remarkable strength and endurance. In fact, the PAP, now eight decades old, won Peru's presidential election in 2006. Although the party was never able to control the state directly prior to 1985 (although it did participate in democratically elected governments during the periods 1945–48 and 1956–68), it undoubtedly became Peru's most important national political party during the twentieth century.

With its call for an "alliance of manual and intellectual workers," APRA sought to eliminate class differences that were deeply rooted in Peruvian culture and to build a new and more just society. Although the middle-class vanguard envisioned by Haya in his early writings ended up spending much of its time in jail, in hiding, or in exile between 1930 and 1956, Aprismo nonetheless had an impact on the formation of a middle-class identity in Peru during this period, as the party became Peru's most important political force. More research is needed on class self-identification among Apristas, but it seems clear that the party's revolutionary rhetoric, combined with its tight-knit organization, challenged long-established class and racial hierarchies. In many cases, the party itself served as a vehicle for social mobility for mestizo migrants and for unionized workers aspiring to middle-class status. This new middle class departed from the traditional middle-class ethos of defining respectability by mimicking the norms of the upper classes and sought to redefine it according to new and revolutionary norms. In some cases, members of APRA were even willing to resort to violence to defend these ideals. The shift toward a more radical middle class was lamented in a 1959 speech by José Luís Bustamante y Rivero, the former president of Peru, when he claimed: "There are sectors of the middle class that have begun to lose their respect for the principle of authority. They seem intent on confronting the power of the state with the power of the union; and there is a tendency for unions to impose a social orientation to legislation."[64]

The Aprista attempt to collapse class boundaries with its political movement of manual and intellectual workers faced many obstacles. The persistence of class and racial differences in Peruvian society and the hierarchical organization of the party itself worked against the realization of Aprista ideals.

During the 1940s and 1950s, the party sought to distance itself from its early radical rhetoric and its history of armed violence, seeking legality and respectability as its ticket into the formal political arena. Yet despite its failure to gain the presidency during these decades, and despite the long periods of political persecution, APRA remained Peru's most important political force. Although its attempts at transforming Peruvian society moved in fits and starts, the party contributed to the emergence of Peru's middle class during the middle decades of the twentieth century.

Notes

1. Throughout the chapter, I use the term "APRA" to refer to the Partido Aprista Peruano (PAP), following colloquial usage in Peru. Originally the PAP had been envisioned as only a branch of what was to be a broader Latin American party. The claim that the party was founded by Haya de la Torre on May 7, 1924, at a ceremony of the Mexican Student Federation seems to belong to the realm of myth rather than that of reality. Pedro Planas points to Haya's presence in Paris and London during 1925 and 1926 as the more diffuse foundational moment that included the 1926 publication of the article "What Is APRA?" in the *Labour Monthly*, a journal associated with the British Labour Party. See Planas, *Mito y realidad*, 35–44.

2. Haya de la Torre, "El Programa, 23.8.31," in *Revolución sin balas*, 48, 50. (All translations are mine unless otherwise noted.)

3. Ibid., 37.

4. Ibid.

5. Del Pomar, *Haya de la Torre*, 22.

6. L. Taylor, "The Origins of APRA in Cajamarca," 449.

7. D. Parker, *The Idea of the Middle Class*, 153.

8. Alexander, "The Latin American Aprista Parties."

9. See Klaren, *Peru*, 292; Davies Jr., "Haya de la Torre y el APRA," 71. In his study of APRA's emergence in the context of modernization, Peter Klaren (*Modernization, Dislocation and Aprismo*) points to the middle-class backing for APRA in Trujillo.

10. E. Thompson, *The Making of the English Working Class*, 9.

11. I have found no exact figures for party membership, and considering the party's history of persecution, it is unlikely that these exist. In 1934, Haya de la Torre claimed that the party had 600,000 members, although as David Werlich points out, this was probably an exaggeration. See Werlich, *Peru*, 204.

12. Marx and Engels, *The Communist Manifesto*, 482. However, Marx also acknowledged that downwardly mobile members of this class about to enter the proletariat could be revolutionary.

13. Mayer, "The Lower Middle Class as Historical Problem," 411.

14. Ibid., 434.

15. Bourricaud, *Power and Society in Contemporary Peru*.

16. Cornejo Chavez, *La clase media en el Perú*, 46.

17. Haya de la Torre, "La situación política peruana," *Obras Completas*, 6:147.

18. See, for example, Jimenez, "The Elision of the Middle Classes and Beyond," 214.

19. See D. Parker, *The Idea of the Middle Class*; Owensby, *Intimate Ironies*; Loaeza, *Clases medias y política en México*; Adamovsky, *Historia de la clase media en Argentina*.

20. As I have shown elsewhere, an early version of such middle-class politics can be found among nineteenth-century artisans in Lima. See García-Bryce, *Crafting the Republic*.

21. David Parker points to this change in *The Idea of the Middle Class*, 156.

22. Mariátegui was also well aware of the value of attracting middle-class support, and he founded a Socialist rather than a Communist party on the assumption that members of the middle class would reject Communism. See Chavarría, *José Carlos Mariátegui and the Rise of Modern Peru*, 159.

23. For Lenin's definition of the role of the middle class, see Robert C. Tucker ed., "'Left Wing' Communism—An Infantile Disorder" in *The Lenin Anthology*, 559.

24. Partido Aprista Peruano, "4 aspectos importantes del Aprismo," 6.

25. Haya de la Torre, "El Programa, 23.8.31," in *Revolución sin balas*, 45.

26. Haya de la Torre, "El Reencuentro, 20.5.45," in *Revolución sin balas*, 67.

27. See Bieber, *En torno al origen histórico ideológico del ideario nacionalista populista latinoamericano*.

28. Soto Rivera, *Víctor Raúl*, 90.

29. Haya de la Torre, "What Is the APRA?," 98.

30. Ibid., 100.

31. Haya de la Torre, "Sobre el papel de las clases medias," *Obras Completas*, 1:172.

32. Haya de la Torre, *El antimperialismo y el APRA*, *Obras Completas*, 4:100.

33. Quoted in Alexander, *Aprismo*, 175–76.

34. Haya de la Torre, *El antimperialismo y el APRA*, *Obras Completas*, 4:102.

35. Ibid., 102.

36. Portal, *América Latina frente al Imperialismo*, 49–50.

37. Haya de la Torre, "A la clase obrera, 6.6.46," in *Revolución sin balas*, 79.

38. See García-Bryce, "A Revolution Remembered, a Revolution Forgotten."

39. Manuel Seoane, "El Aprismo como espíritu," *La Tribuna* (Lima), August 5, 1931.

40. Vega Centeno, *Aprismo popular*, 79–80; Klaiber, *Religion and Revolution in Peru*, 146; S. Stein, *Populism in Peru*, 175.

41. Mackay, *The Other Spanish Christ*.

42. Haya de la Torre, "A la clase obrera, 6.6.46," in *Revolución sin balas*, 88–89.

43. Quoted by Pizarro Guerrero, *Los desafíos del Aprismo*, 46.

44. S. Stein, "Populism in Peru: APRA, the Formative Years," 128.

45. Klaiber, *Religion and Revolution*, 146.

46. Quoted in Soto Rivera, *Víctor Raúl*, 301.

47. The name of the FAJ was eventually changed to Juventud Aprista del Perú (JAP), partly because of the similarity between the names "Fajista" and "Fascista." Kantor, *The Ideology and Program of the Peruvian Aprista Movement*, 63.

48. Chaney, *Supermadre*, 92.

49. She was elected to Congress in 1962, only to lose her seat together with the party's other elected representatives as a result of the military coup that year to prevent Haya de la Torre from becoming president.

50. Giesecke, "The Trujillo Insurrection, the APRA Party and the Making of Modern Peruvian Politics," 115.

51. Ibid., 116.

52. D. Parker, *The Idea of the Middle Class*, 185.

53. Quesada Laos, "Problemas de la clase media," 159.

54. Drinot, "Food, Race and Working-Class Identity."

55. Cornejo Chavez, *La clase media*, 3.

56. Ibid.

57. Haya de la Torre, *Treinta años de Aprismo*, 133.

58. For example, the CTP included the Drivers' Federation of Peru and the Employees' Association. It also included workers' organization from the provinces, such as the Federación de Trabajadores del Cuzco and the Federación de Trabajadores de Puno. This can be seen from the CTP stationary listing the member organizations, for example Oficio No. 257-G.E. Lima, April 21, 1947, CI 1816 (27/64), Archivo Sabroso, Pontificia Universidad Católica del Perú, Lima, Perú.

59. D. Parker, *The Idea of the Middle Class*, 219–20.

60. Some of these class divisions had been consolidated during the nineteenth century. See García-Bryce, *Crafting the Republic*.

61. Parker cites a chart from Victor Villanueva's *El APRA en busca del poder, 1930–1940* (Lima: Horizonte, 1975) that indicates white-collar support for APRA declining from 63.2 percent to 28.9 percent between 1931 and 1945. See D. Parker, *The Idea of the Middle Class*, 177.

62. Quiroz, "La relación partido-pueblo en el recorrido histórico del APRA," 120.

63. Giesecke, "The Trujillo Insurrection, the APRA Party and the Making of Modern Peruvian Politics," 114.

64. Bustamante y Rivero, "Las clases sociales en el Perú," 66.

Revolutionary Promises Encounter Urban Realities for Mexico City's Middle Class, 1915–1928

Susanne Eineigel

When the armed conflict of the Mexican Revolution entered the streets of the country's capital city in 1913, the order and progress of the Porfirian dream came to an end. Among the many victims who suffered hunger and uncertainty were residents who had joined the ranks of the nascent middle class under the relatively stable dictatorship of Porfirio Díaz (1877–1911). This chapter tells the story of this sector, forgotten in the histories of the revolution, and brings to light the centrality of the middle class in the promises made by the first postrevolutionary governments. Influenced by a transnational discourse on the importance of a middle class to national progress, Mexican politicians and intellectuals heralded this sector as the future of the nation's development and stability. But economic and social conflicts continued to plague the capital city, hindering efforts to make these promises a reality for its middle sector. In the continuing chaos of the 1920s, different factions of the middle class mobilized as tram users, renters, and neighborhood residents in the hope of having these promises fulfilled. In contrast to traditional characterizations of the middle class as a passive and apathetic sector of Mexican society, this chapter demonstrates how self-identified members of the middle class took an active part in establishing themselves within an enlarged political, social, and cultural public sphere.

Although scholarship has devoted far more attention to peasants and the formation of the working class than to the middle class in Mexico, recent literature encourages a focus on the latter. This new scholarship on cultural nationalism and national identity—and on how these intersect with class, gender, and racial identity, as well as political and religious affiliation—requires a better understanding of the twentieth-century formation of the middle class. This chapter looks at a very small part of the various forces and influences that shaped conceptions of Mexico's middle class in the aftermath of the Revolution of 1910. In the wake of the revolutionary destruction, government projects economically supported members of the middle sector in order to build an ideal middle class, worthy of its European and American counterparts. This official conception of the middle class both coincided and conflicted with the real lives and desires of self-identified members of the middle class. In the new social and political climate of Mexico in the 1920s, a growing number of discourses contributed to the complex process of fashioning a middle-class identity.

The Porfirian Belle Epoque

After decades of conflict and foreign interventions, Porfirio Díaz's long-standing regime provided a stable period for middle-class growth. Mexico City, Díaz's Parisian-inspired capital, offered white-collar employment in its expanding commercial and government sectors. Although liberal professionals (such as lawyers and doctors) had traditionally occupied the middle strata of society, a burgeoning number of office employees (clerks, typists, telegraphers, and accountants) now occupied the bottom rungs of the middle class. Other members included highly skilled artisans patronized by the capital city's wealthy, who sought ornate craftsmanship. Many members of the middle class moved into new suburban neighborhoods, like Santa María la Ribera, on the west side of the city as improved transportation facilitated urban expansion. New department stores, cafes, theaters, and boulevards provided fashionable places for conspicuous consumption and self-display. In Santa María, residents organized cultural events in the pavilion in the neighborhood's park, including classical music concerts and dances.[1] Although in many ways the residents imitated the lifestyles of the rich, they disdained upper-class Francophile pretensions and took pride in dressing their children as Mexican cowboys for the weekly Sunday stroll through the city's central park.[2] In other words, Mexico City provided the perfect stage for the members of the middle class to engage in self-fashioning a distinct identity, aided by popular etiquette manuals.[3]

Revolutionary Promises for the Suffering Middle Class

When the Carrancista troops entered Mexico City, "we individuals of the middle class stayed in our houses. Entering the city were men of the proletariat class, brown *campesinos*, some dressed in multicolored clothes and some almost with no clothes. Our dreams of a cultured Mexico had been in vain. This that marched before our eyes was Mexico, the truth in all its terrible reality, the one that demanded justice, education and bread."[4] In 1914 and 1915, revolutionary factions fought to control Mexico City and the nation, only two years after the *decena trágica*, which had brought armed conflict to the streets of the nation's capital for the first time. A severe shortage of basic food products caused by fighting in the countryside, with the resulting loss of harvests and massive expulsion of rural workers, made hunger a daily reality for many of Mexico City's residents. Disease and death hovered over the city: carts made daily rounds to pick up dead bodies, and the city's biggest department store offered special prices on mourning clothes. Confusion surrounded the circulation of multiple types of paper money issued by the various revolutionary factions, and shortages produced long lines everywhere, including in front of pawnshops. One lawyer, who had worked in Díaz's administration but in 1915 sold tripe on the streets, commented that the middle class "had to throw to the devil 'what people would say' " and give up its "ridiculous egoism." As a result, he had found a deep appreciation for the poorer classes and admired their virtues, such as humility. Nonetheless, he realized that for many residents, the sight of peasant revolutionaries followed by a steady stream of refugees entering the city and taking over houses and churches added to fears of urban chaos.[5]

Along with the working class and the poor, self-identified members of the middle class suffered from unemployment and shortages of basic necessities. Inflation and stagnant wages meant that many of them could not feed their families. Government workers petitioned for a raise in salaries or for simply their pay, when lack of public funds repeatedly delayed the payment of salaries. Despite the insecure nature of government paychecks, many educated men and women anxiously solicited work in government offices as accountants and typists. They demonstrated their loyalty to the revolution's winning army, claiming that they "identified perfectly with the ideals of Constitutionalism and had lent their services to the cause."[6] These men and women competed for jobs against people from provincial towns seeking refuge and job security in the capital city. Political instability also disrupted urban services and maintenance. For example, the kiosk in the park of the middle-class neighborhood of

Santa María la Ribera, which had been the heart of the cultural life of the *colonia* before the revolution, fell into disrepair, and residents complained about unhealthy and insanitary conditions in the theaters.[7]

Luckily for the middle class, the eventual winners of the revolutionary struggle promised relief and compensation. On August 30, 1915, when the Constitutionalist army occupied the city for the fourth and last time, General Pablo González issued his first decree. Addressing specifically "the great difficulties that confront especially the middle class in providing the most indispensable [things] for living," the general condemned the commercial sector for the excessive prices of basic necessities. The decree's second and third points concerned white-collar labor issues, such as the excessive work demanded of employees and the injustice of the firing of "honorable and long-time *empleados* . . . without compensation and without cause, hurling many families into desperation and misery." The general promised to make Sunday an obligatory day of rest, to provide an eight-hour work day, and to end firing without just cause and without notice.[8]

In order to gain the further support of the city's residents, particularly those belonging to the middle class, the Carrancista administration created municipal government stores that sold basic goods at regulated prices. The government issued cards granting permission to shop at the stores to people who sought relief from high prices. Letters to the municipal government in 1915 and 1916 petitioning for the cards testify to the difficulties that self-identified members of the middle class experienced. Perhaps because the *expendios municipales* (municipal shops) explicitly favored the middle class, many of the letters begin with the authors identifying themselves as members of this sector. "I belong to the middle class and have few resources to feed my family," begins one such letter, before proceeding to ask for a government-issued card.[9] Employees often wrote as a group on the letterhead of their company or government office, while others had their boss petition on their behalf. In 1916 E. Perusquia wrote asking for store cards for the "two employees in my charge . . . that find themselves in the same circumstances as the rest of the people of the middle class."[10] Professionals also wrote requesting help. For example, Dr. Manuel Ortiz, a medical surgeon, complained about the difficulties he and his colleagues faced as "poor professional members of the middle class."[11] Many expressed their gratitude for the *expendios*, praising the government for helping to "alleviate generously the precarious situation that the middle class of this city is going through."[12] A city newspaper reported on the success of the *expendios* in 1915 and announced the opening of four more stores for the middle-class residents of the *colonia* of Santa María la Ribera.[13]

According to one account, 30,000 cards had been issued by January 1916.[14] By that year, most petitioners were asking for expendio cards in order to buy material for clothing, which may indicate that the worst food shortages had passed. Empleados (both male and female) made up the large majority of the writers, and they asked for cards to buy material like calico and cashmere as well as stockings and shoes. Individual residents also wrote. For example, Viriginia J. de Sánchez, a resident of the Santa María la Ribera neighborhood, lamented that "in view of the fabulous prices that all commercial articles have reached and knowing your noble desires to favor the middle class [and] not being able to present myself in public due to the scarcity of clothing, and being one of those elements of the unhappy middle class, I find myself obligated by the pressing circumstances to attract your attention with the objective of being favored with a card to buy clothes."[15] Expendio cards, as employees in one government office explained, will allow us "to obtain a wardrobe to decently present ourselves."[16] The equation of the lack of "proper" clothing to suffering may seem exaggerated, but for members of the middle class, the inability to appear "decently" in public signaled the loss of social and class distinction.

The general's decree and the expendios municipales point to the importance of the middle-class sector for political consolidation within the city. Moreover, it shows a shift in the conception of the middle class from one that had traditionally encompassed liberal professionals and high-end artisans during the Porfiriato to one largely dominated by employees, both private and public, after the revolution. With the increase in the number of office workers in the last few decades of the Porfiriato, these new members of the middle class were now considered key to political stability. This was especially true in the case of government employees, whose loyalty was crucial to the restoration of government services that would in turn bring order to the city.

Creating Thrifty and Cooperative Members of the Middle Class in the 1920s

In the decade that followed, the postrevolutionary governments of Alvaro Obregón (1920–24) and Plutarco Calles (1924–28) continued to consider the middle class a vital component to the strength of the nation. Political leaders followed in the footsteps of Porfirio Díaz, who considered the middle class to be the basis of the nation's progress, attributing the development of countries like England and the United States to the strength of their middle classes. In his famous 1908 interview with the American journalist James Creelman, President Díaz had described the middle class as "the active element of society [that] sustained true democratic institutions."[17] In a series of articles published in the weekly newspaper, the *Boletín municipal* (Municipal bulletin), in the early 1920s, the Mexico City government similarly proclaimed the importance of the middle class to national progress and democratic advancement.[18] The author of one article, titled "La fuerza de los pueblos está en la clase media" (The strength of the people is in the middle class), insisted that the development of Mexico depended on the middle class in the same way that England had developed into a first-rate nation because of the hard work and energy of its middle class. Quoting the popular British essayist Samuel Smiles, the editorial explained that the middle class had succeeded on the basis of being the most ready to organize, cooperate, and unify itself.[19] Mexican officials and intellectuals lamented the lack of these values within their nation's middle class. In response, the Mexico City municipal authorities created several projects to inculcate notions of thrift and cooperation into one sector of the middle class: the public employee.

In 1919 the municipal government announced the creation of a savings account for its employees.[20] The authorities hoped that this would help workers develop the habits of saving and thrift. One *Boletín municipal* article titled "El ahorro es dignificación y es libertad" (Saving is dignity and freedom) proclaimed "that although the employee, the worker of the middle class, possesses true wisdom, true morality, and true aspiration he also has a vice destructive to all these great and undeniable virtues, even greater than its work ethic, given that . . . his tendencies toward the pleasures of luxury and toward squandering are great . . . and as a consequence removes him from the habit of saving."[21] Complaints about the frivolous spending habits of the middle class were not new. Throughout the late nineteenth century, writers had criticized wastefulness and other defects considered particular to the middle class. Even Díaz in his interview with Creelman disparagingly depicted members of the middle class as endlessly entertaining themselves, spending more than they earned, and "drugging themselves with usury."[22] In the 1920s newspaper articles similarly condemned the middle class for extravagance to acquire a lifestyle beyond their means: "The middle class does not economize . . . in its crazy wish to be equal with those with a fortune higher than them, [and] in spite that their earnings are sufficient [for] a modest life, they put themselves in debt."[23] Although a growing consumer culture in the 1920s pushed women's role as consumers, a simultaneous emphasis on teaching women household economy continued an older discourse of condemning middle-class female profligacy. Writers called on mothers to set an example and practice the habit of thrift for their children to learn: "Mothers of families should solve these problems [and] incorporate into the heart of her husband and her children the virtue of economy [and] the virtue of order that should reign in all homes."[24]

Along with the habit of saving, postrevolutionary governments also heavily promoted the creation of cooperative societies to solve economic difficulties among the middle and lower classes. The decade's political and social instability exacerbated local and national economic crises and particularly the financially precarious members of the middle class. In 1923 the Alvaro Obregón administration established a consumer cooperative for Mexico City municipal employees. The government hoped they would take part with "real enthusiasm," since they would join the civilized world in which similar associations existed to prevent abuses by businessmen.[25] According to government officials, the cooperative was the first definitive step on "the road to . . . spiritual and economic liberation of the employee that we have for a long time been preaching and trying to correct."[26] But a report on cooperative societies in Mexico City reveals that the administration considered these associations as an answer to a much older problem of inequality: it is "possible that the greatest benefits of the Cooperative Associations will be that in the short and long term they will constitute an important means to considerably alleviate the condition of the middle class and the proletariat, which have justly complained of the misery and oppression under plutocracy that they have been subjected to since the time of conquest."[27]

For the government, cooperatives and thrift helped citizens in the lower middle class and a certain sector of the working class achieve the goal of home ownership. A house represented financial security as well as social and familial stability, an image mirrored in advertisements by development companies selling lots and houses in the rapidly growing number of new neighborhoods around the city center. President Obregón decided in late 1922 to divide the land around the old racetrack of Peralvillo at the north end of the city in order to establish a neighborhood where government employees and other workers could buy homes. With a low price of 1.50 pesos per square meter, to be paid off in five yearly installments, the lots sold quickly: by the middle of 1923, no properties were left.[28] Land cooperatives were espoused as a way forward for "persons of the lower middle class [as well as] a considerable part of the practical and thrifty men of the working class."[29] After 1926, housing issues came under the newly created Department of Social Security, inaugurated by President Plutarch Calles. The state initiative was the only one of its kind to help finance housing by awarding credits to state workers for the construction and acquisition of a house.[30] Such government efforts helped struggling members of the middle class, specifically public employees, to reestablish themselves socioeconomically. In return, the state hoped to strengthen bureaucrats' political loyalty.

The Calles administration praised cooperatives for not only solving economic problems but also for instilling the values of cooperation supposedly lacking in members of the middle class. Through cooperation, the middle class could help resolve the decade's ongoing social question about the struggle between labor and capital. The idea of cooperatives built on a long history of mutual aid societies, in which workers organized to uplift themselves materially as well as culturally. But Mexico's promotion of cooperative societies was also influenced by a transnational discussion on the value of cooperatives. Mexico's establishment of a cooperative for public employees followed similar projects in countries like Spain and Germany in the early 1920s.[31] The Calles administration looked to Europe for further help in resolving social questions. The author of a government publication titled *¿Estamos capacitados para la cooperación?* (Do we have the ability to cooperate?) explained that cooperatives in Europe taught the value of unity and working together, crucial for solving the problems of labor struggles and class conflict. Mexicans lacked these characteristics, and according to the publication, this was the fault not of "the race" but rather of a lack of discipline, method, and hygiene at work, all which could be corrected through cooperation.[32] According to Mexican writers citing European economists, cooperatives were especially important for members of the middle class, who needed to learn how to unify and work toward a common cause, in order to build a strong nation. As a member of the middle class, one writer in the *Boletín municipal* claimed that cooperatives would "affirm our solidarity and strong (*prepotente*) action; because . . . in our class . . . the strength of the people lies, and today and tomorrow and at all times we must sacrifice ourselves for these ideals and fight for them without rest, breaking once and for all the long-time indifference our educated middle class has had toward civic matters, of which public employees form a small part."[33]

Middle-Class Organizing: Protests and Neighborhood Action in the 1920s

The promises of the postrevolutionary governments could not erase the economic and political problems of the decade that plagued the city and its self-identified middle-class residents. By April 1924, the fiscal crisis at both the local and national levels resulted in the public employees' salaries not being paid. One newspaper article lamented the state of "our suffering bureaucracy," noting that the delay in pay had caused "hunger [to make] its appearance in the homes of this important section of our middle classes."[34] A month later public employees staged a protest in the El Toreo plaza, demanding their pay and discussing efforts to find other quick and effective means to make money until the federal government could cover their salaries.[35]

Other issues besides overdue paychecks mobilized Mexico City's self-identified middle-class residents. Contemporary politicians and intellectuals criticized members of the middle class as passive and uninterested citizens. However, men and women of the class actively participated in the tumultuous politics of the 1920s, a period complicated by the emergence of new social groups (such as unions, workers, and migrants) who demanded the fulfillment of revolutionary promises and competed for government resources. Although studies have emphasized the emergence of new actors, debates, and negotiations with the state in relation to the working or popular classes, members of the middle class also formed part of this expanding public sphere. Here, I will discuss very briefly three ways in which disruptions to services and rising rents threatened the precarious economic position of the middle class and rallied its members to add their voice to an enlarged sphere of public opinion and popular politics.

More than any other element in the city, political struggles over the allocation of urban services became key to the redefinition of social and political order in Mexico City in the 1920s.[36] Decisions about where in the city to direct much-needed urban services such as lighting, paving, and housing had important social and political implications in the volatile climate, as postrevolutionary governments attempted to consolidate their power in Mexico's important political and commercial center. Acting on constituents' complaints about urban services that operated at a minimal or nonexistent level was not an easy task, however.[37] Throughout the 1920s municipal-level political struggles, combined with large deficits, shortage of funds, and disorderly government offices, hindered progress. Furthermore, the city's population grew at unprecedented rates as rural migrants continued to flood into a city disrupted almost daily with protests and strikes. New, often unofficial, neighborhoods competed with older ones that still had not been properly urbanized after decades of existence. For example, the *colonia* of Santa María la Ribera, founded in the 1860s, still lacked paved streets and proper lighting. It was also one of the fastest growing *colonias*, which strained its resources even further. Luckily for its residents, two municipal councilors who lived in the *colonia* petitioned the government for improvements. In 1922, they lobbied for the construction of a new market in the neighborhood to serve a growing population and to replace the numerous "unhygienic" and "unofficial" stalls on the streets.[38] But it was not until three years later that the *colonia* finally received a new modern market befitting its middle-class residents. A year later, most of the major streets of the *colonia* were finally paved.[39] Residents also petitioned for improvements through neighborhood committees called Juntas de mejoras,[40] which sprang up in every type of neighborhood in the city. Middle- and upper-class *colonias* also used these organizations to raise money within the community to improve their residential areas. In Santa María, the Junta de mejoras organized neighborhood parties to collect funds to improve lighting, plant trees, and construct a social and sports center, among other projects.[41]

Housing and rents were among the principal issues that mobilized a large number of lower- and middle-class people. Massive rural migration into the city produced housing shortages, rising rents, unplanned growth, land speculation, and the concentration of urban property in fewer and fewer hands. The results affected the vast majority of the members of the middle class who rented rather than owned property.[42] In 1921, only 4 percent to 6 percent of the population owned property in the city.[43] In the seventh district of the city, where Santa María was located, 0.29 percent of the residents owned property. In comparison, in the second district, the poorest in the city, 0.12 percent of the residents owned property. In the eighth district, the wealthiest in the city, 0.84 percent of the residents owned property. These high numbers of renters expressed the political failure of the earliest postrevolutionary governments, whose redistributive projects were often more rhetoric than reality. Even the projects to construct *colonias* destined for employees and workers with the goal of making them property owners did not have the expected success. One of the problems was the continuing increase in land prices. After three years, land prices in the government-created neighborhood of Peralvillo jumped to six pesos per square meter, four times its initial value.[44] In 1916, a group of mainly middle-class small businessmen had formed the Renters' League of the Federal District, demanding reasonable rents. By 1922 working-class renters had joined the movement, although newspaper articles continued to comment on the participation by renters who lived in "two- or three-room houses for the middle class," and not in working-class tenement housing. Marching in the streets and sending petitions to various levels of government, the movement demonstrates how the middle class mobilized around the notion of a new moral economy in which they appealed to the revolutionary state for help.[45]

Transportation issues also mobilized working members of the middle class who depended on the tramway system to commute to numerous parts of the city for work. The nearly yearly tram strikes (first in 1911, and then in 1921, 1922, 1923, and 1925) produced a city where "all the commercial, bureaucratic, industrial and social activities are slowed down . . . [and] the shops, the theaters, the factories and the schools function at half speed."[46] It left middle-class employees stranded in the streets of the city center, unable to get home. In 1922 the government suggested closing two-thirds of schools when teachers could not reach their workplaces.[47] The middle class appeared in these conflicts not only as a victim but also as the consumer, a new actor in the public sphere. Unlike protests over housing, rents, and other types of urban services, in this case grievances were directed toward the foreign owners of the privately owned tramway company. Many users of the tram supported the strikers, which reflected less their labor solidarity and more their dissatisfaction with the tram service, including prices, access, schedules, safety, and behavior of other passengers in the trams.[48] For the first time, self-identified members of the middle class formed part of a new public opinion, reflected in the press, which supported striking workers' grievances and demands.

After suffering material deprivations during the height of the armed revolution, members of the middle class took an active role in the politics of urban reconstruction. The class had much at stake, trying to reposition itself in the new revolutionary society that expanded the public sphere to incorporate the traditionally marginalized pueblo. In letters to the new postrevolutionary government, writers reveal how they identified themselves as middle class partly through their ability to conspicuously display class standing through "decent" clothing. The petitions also make clear that requesting government help did not threaten their class position. In fact, the middle class quickly took part in the postrevolutionary moral economy, in which citizens demanded rights and goods.

In the decades following the revolution, the governments of Obregón and Calles directed much of their attention and financial support to the middle class. These efforts point to the importance of this sector of society, which grew significantly in the last decades of the Porfiriato, for state consolidation and a revolutionary leadership whose own origins were middle class. Moreover, as part of a larger transnational discussion, the postrevolutionary governments considered the middle class to be crucial for the development of the country. Cooperative and housing projects reveal the type of middle class that the administrations hoped to shape, one that valued thrift, cooperation, the heterosexual family, home ownership, and engagement in the national rebuilding effort. Despite the governments' promises, continued disruptions in the city and shortage of funds forced members of the middle class to organize in order to regain their material well-being and status. Middle-class citizens, like the residents of Santa María, mobilized at a neighborhood level in order to restore their *colonias*, which formed part of their class identity. They also demanded urban services and affordable rents as part of the revolution's promise of social justice. These efforts formed part of a larger endeavor to reposition themselves in a new society and within a larger discourse about the role of the middle class in modern Mexico.

Notes

1. Vol. 1608, exp. 54 (1903), vol. 1609, exp. 154 (1907), vol. 1612, exp. 274 (1900), festividades, gobierno del distrito, Archivo Histórico del Distrito Federal, Mexico City. (In subsequent references, this archival collection will be designated "AHDF.")

2. Beteta, *Jarano*, 8–9, 16–17.

3. Eineigel, "Visualizing the Self." See also Macías-González, "Hombres de mundo."

4. Genaro Fernández MacGregor, *El río de mi sangre*, 243. All translations are mine unless otherwise noted.

5. Ramírez Plancarte, "La ciudad de México durante la revolución constitucionalista," 398.

6. Untitled document, vol. 911, exp. 138 (May 14, 1915), AHDF.

7. Vol. 1398, exp. 1236, and vol. 1399, exp. 1254 (1913), diversiones, gobierno del distrito, AHDF.

8. Ramírez Plancarte,"La ciudad de México durante la revolución constitucionalista," 561–62.

9. Vol. 3860, exp. 6 (October 30, 1916), reguladora de comercio, ayuntamiento, AHDF.

10. E. Perusquia to President Carranza, January 15, 1916, vol. 3861, exp. 1 (January 15, 1916), reguladora de comerico, ayuntamiento, AHDF.

11. Manuel Ortiz, vol. 3860, exp. 6 (October 1, 1915), reguladora de comerico, ayuntamiento, AHDF. In his autobiography, Ramón Beteta describes how his home lacked even basic necessities when the revolution arrived and his father lost his job as a lawyer in a government office. They survived on credit, owing shopkeepers, the milkman, and the Spanish baker. See Beteta, *Jarano*, 54.

12. Employees of the Oficina de la Direccion General de la Ensañana Técnica to President Carranza, January 12, 1916, vol. 3856, exp. 19 (January 12, 1916), reguladora de comercio, ayuntamiento, AHDF.

13. "Habrá cuatro nuevos expendios para la clase media," *El Mexicano*, October 27, 1915.

14. Vol. 3861, exp. 7 (January 25, 1916), reguladora de comerico; ayuntamiento, AHDF.

15. Viriginia J. de Sánchez to President Carranza, March 10, 1916, vol. 3860, exp. 4 (March 10, 1916), reguladora de comercio, ayuntamiento, AHDF.

16. Vol. 3856, exp. 1 (January 18, 1916), reguladora de comercio, ayuntemiento, AHDF.

17. Quoted in González Navarro, *Historia moderna de México*, 389.

18. The government publication was published weekly and sold for 15 centavos.

19. "La fuerza de los pueblos está en la clase media," *Boletín municipal*, 26 October 1923.

20. "Hay que realiza la gran idea," *Boletín municipal*, August 1, 1919.

21. "El ahorro es dignificación y es libertad," *Boletín municipal*, October 12, 1923.

22. Quoted in González Navarro, *Historia moderna de México*, 388–89.

23. *Revista de revistas*, March 9, 1924.

24. Ibid. Savings accounts were also instituted at the level of public schools, teaching schoolchildren the fundamentals of putting away money and therefore instilling the value of thrift early into future workers and housewives. See the section "Caja de ahorros" in *Memorias de Secretaría de Educación Pública* throughout the 1920s.

25. *Boletín municipal*, August 1, 1919.

26. *Boletín municipal*, October 19, 1923.

27. Informe de Sociedades Cooperativas, caja 320, exp. 15; ramo trabajo, Archivo General de la Nación, Mexico City.

28. Berra Stoppa, "La expansión de la Ciudad de México y los conflictos urbanos," 149.

29. "Otra fase el cooperativismo," *Boletín municipal*, November 9, 1923.

30. María Soledad Cruz Rodríguez, *Crecimiento urbano y procesos sociales in el Distrito Federal*, 144–45.

31. Müffelmann, *Orientacion de la clase media*.

32. *¿Estamos capacitados para la cooperación?*, 9–11.

33. "La fuerza de los pueblos está en la clase media," *Boletín municipal*, October 26, 1923.

34. "Las decenas de los empleados," *Revista de revistas*, April 13, 1924, 3.

35. *Revista de revistas*, May 18, 1924.

36. For a similar argument, see Leidenberger, "Las huelgas tranviarias como rupturas del ordern urbano"; Davis, *Urban Leviathan*.

37. Lack of progress was also blamed on employee corruption, the latter a recurring topic in the *Boletín municipal*. See, for example, "La moralización de los empleados municipales," October 31, 1915.

38. *Boletín municipal*, February 24, 1922.

39. Many public works were finally completed when the Partido Laborista Mexicano was in power, from 1925 to 1928.

40. "Las juntas vecinales," *Buletín municipal*, September 12, 1919. The first Juntas de mejoras were created in the late nineteenth century, but they probably stopped functioning during the armed conflict and most chaotic period. See vol. 352, exp. 317 (1872), alumbrado, ayuntamiento, and vol. 388, exp. 4 (February 4, 1902), asociaciones, ayuntamiento, AHDF.

41. *Boletín municipal*, August 31, 1925.

42. Monthly rents increased from an average of 6.50 pesos to 14.00 pesos between 1916 and 1920. See Berra Stoppa, "La expansión de la Ciudad de México y los conflictos urbanos," 456.

43. For rent figures and homeownership in the city, see Lear, *Workers, Neighbors, and Citizens*, 481–82.

44. Massive migration into the city also resulted in neighborhood overcrowding, leading long-time residents to complain of *paracaidismo* (literally, parachuting), in which migrants illegally occupied empty property lots. See Berra Stoppa, "La expansión de la Ciudad de México y los conflictos urbanos," 149.

45. In 1922 the leadership of the renters' league was taken over by the Mexican Communist Party, created in the same year, which provoked major tensions that led to the expulsion and resignation of many of the league's middle-class members. See ibid., chapters 12–14. See also Vázquez Ramírez, *Oganización y resistencia popular en la ciudad de México durante el crisis de 1929–1932*, 86–93.

46. "El servicio de las tranvías se paralizó ayer a las 24," *El Excelsior*, January 21, 1923; see also "Tranvías quieren que los caminones suspenden el tráfico inmediamente," *El Excelsior*, January 22, 1923.

47. See Leidenberger, "Las huelgas tranviarias como rupturas del orden urbano. Ciudad de México, de 1911 a 1925," 150.

48. Leidenberger, "Habermas en el zócalo," 187.

Being Middle Class and Being Arab

SECTARIAN DILEMMAS AND MIDDLE-CLASS MODERNITY IN THE ARAB MIDDLE EAST, 1908–1936

Keith David Watenpaugh

Edmond Rabbath (1901–91), a Sorbonne-educated Arab lawyer in Aleppo, Syria, one of the eastern Mediterranean's most populous cities, argued in a lengthy essay for the winter 1926 issue of the Arabic-language journal *al-Hadith* (The modern) that the middle class, a term he translated directly into Arabic as *al-tabaqa al-wusta*, had played the pivotal role in the emergence of democracy in Europe.[1] Questions about the middle class and democracy were common topics for articles in *al-Hadith*. A kind of cross between *Esquire* and the *Atlantic Monthly*, it was one of the most stable magazines in Syria, continually published with few breaks through the 1950s, and it enjoyed a wide readership among the educated middle class throughout the Arab eastern Mediterranean. Alongside the dry political prose, it also published original short stories and poetry and covered Cairo's vibrant literary scene and developments in republican Turkey. Although regularly including photographs and engravings of scantily clad young Western women on its final pages, it nonetheless championed Arab women's rights, including the right to vote, and featured articles about men's and women's European fashions and proper middle-class manners. Most memorable, though, were the political essays written by Rabbath and other young foreign-educated, middle-class intellectuals that would, among other things, lay the intellectual groundwork for the ideological contours of interwar Arab nationalism.

"The democracy of the nineteenth century," Rabbath explained, "had sprung forth from the efforts of the middle class—the class of the age (*al-tabaqa min al-zaman*) . . . It is the class made up of those who were industrious and built their wealth on trade and invented the tools of modern life." According to Rabbath, this class articulated democracy first in Holland and England; later, in the early 1800s, in France; and by the second half of the nineteenth century in Germany. Central to each case was a middle-class effort to "monopolize capital and gain political power." Rabbath warned that various political strategies could subvert the middle class's hold on power. The most threatening, the "Teutonic form," appeared in Prussia, where it became impossible to "distinguish between nationalism and conservatism, between absolutist power and political action, and between king and religion." "Ultimately," he concluded, "this led to the outbreak of the world war."[2]

Although the essay was ostensibly about Europe's middle class as foil for an evolving anticolonial Arab nationalist discourse, it was also a manifesto of sorts for the Syrian—and, more broadly, Arab—middle class, which had likewise emerged over the course of the late nineteenth century and the early twentieth and whose members had begun to regard themselves as a class similar to, if not indistinct from, their European and American cognates. And like those cognates, this middle class saw itself as entitled to both democratic participation and bourgeois citizenship. Rabbath's writings in *al-Hadith* and his later *L'évolution politique de la Syrie sous mandat* (1928) provide a glimpse into the shape of Arab middle-class identity in the first decades of the last century, but more telling is what Rabbath left out of "The Decline of Democracy": any mention of the preeminent role that non-Muslim Arabs—including Greek Orthodox Christians, like him—had played in the formation of the middle class and the project of modernity in the eastern Mediterranean. A decade later he would find himself addressing this issue head on, as sectarian difference within the middle class would become a dominant issue not just in the electoral politics of the 1930s, but in the definition of society itself.

This chapter draws on Rabbath's life and the experience of the diverse and cosmopolitan middle class of Aleppo to examine a key and to some extent exemplary element in the formation of the Arab middle class in the period 1908–36—a period encompassing the Young Turk Revolution (1908), the First World War, and the establishment of the French Mandate for Syria (1920–46)—the sectarian bifurcation of the Arab middle class. And although this Muslim–non-Muslim dimension to the Arab middle class is somewhat unique in middle-class history, it has reinforced two features common to most middle classes: their tremendous ability to create institutions of civil society and their relative inability to translate those forms of sociability and horizontal solidarity into real political power. Tying these two elemental features together points to a way to use the history of the middle class to conceptualize in both a regional and transnational context the issue of what it means to be modern, thus contributing to a greater understanding of modernity itself as a lived historical experience, as well as theorizing further the concept of middle-class modernity.

The link between the ideational and epistemological foundations of modernity with definitive middle-class cultural and political praxis is a phenomenon that I term "middle-class modernity." This describes a mutually reinforced calculus in which to be modern means to be not like, but just as modern as, the imagined, idealized middle class and, in a transitive sense, the bourgeoisie of Europe. By the same token, being middle class—here almost exclusively in a cultural sense—is the best evidence of being modern. Middle-class modernity suggests a specific kind of experiential phenomenon of modernity distinguished in part by the fact that its "surface momentum conceals its inner sameness, its increasing reproduction of the safe limits of the bourgeois world."[3] And although that sameness is precisely what led Charles Baudelaire, Karl Marx, and others to label this a "false modernity," its association with Europe and its dominant class exercised an immense magnetic attraction on aspiring middle classes throughout the non-West. The open question is, how safe do these limits actually remain as aspects of the bourgeois world are introduced and adopted outside of the West?

As a consequence of technological changes in communication and transportation, the growth of print capitalism, and the introduction of modernist literary forms, a consensual language of social practice that used the perceived behavior of the Western middle class as a standard was available in the eastern Mediterranean and could serve to make distinctions within that society by the second half of the nineteenth century. When examples of middle-class modernity gained currency in the Ottoman eastern Mediterranean through media, literature (novels and self-help books), and later film and radio, education, bureaucratization, travel, and colonial encounters, it contributed both to the emergence and to definitive aspects of the middle class. Middle-class modernity provided at once a ladder and an objective for indigenous middle-class aspirations, although the underlying motives for wanting to incorporate that praxis and those ideas remain as complex as the class itself. Variables including education, wealth, and religion controlled the manner in which middle-class modernity was understood and employed at any given moment; nevertheless, it formed a stable matrix of ineffable specificity that had the power to shape this stratum politically and socially and provide members of the middle class, in turn, with a warrant and a guide with which to seek to shape their own society. To paraphrase Supreme Court Justice Potter Stewart, one knew middle-class modernity when one saw it, without necessarily being able to explain exactly why. Likewise, the adoption of middle-class manners, patterns of consumption, and ways of thought perceived as inherently modern was by definition a cultural necessity, and their implementation a social imperative.

It is crucial to note that, thus conceived, middle-class modernity is not a phenomenon unique to the non-West, and echoes of it resound throughout the social history of contemporary Europe and the Americas. Thinking about the Arab eastern Mediterranean's middle class in terms of a globalized middle-class modernity, it is possible to place the regional experiences of class dynamics and struggle into a larger transnational frame. At the same time, one should be prepared to underscore the hegemonic power of high capitalism and colonialism to shape social, sectarian, and ethnic relations on the most local and intimate levels of society.

Class and Sectarian Dilemmas at the End of Empire

Like other cities of the eastern Mediterranean, including Trieste, Salonica, Izmir, and Alexandria, Aleppo fit uncomfortably into modernist structures of nation and ethnicity. A tremendous ethnic, religious, and linguistic diversity marked the life of these cities. From the perspective of the twenty-first century, such differences are remarkable, but before the First World War, inhabitants of places like Aleppo would have expected such diversity to exist, perhaps considering it proof of their city's prominence. Like these other cities, Aleppo sat astride global trade routes and served in the early modern period as a center of long-distance commerce in luxury goods, attracting merchants from all around the Mediterranean, Northern Europe, and South and Central Asia. Jewish traders, in particular the Sassoon family, came to the city from India, augmenting an already large indigenous Jewish community. Armenian silk merchants and weavers arrived from Anatolia or Shah Abbas's imperial capital, Isfahan. European nations dispatched merchant adventurers to the city. Once there, they established trading houses in any one of the grand urban caravansaries located in and around Aleppo's massive central business district. The Venetians called theirs *fondacos*; the French, *échelles*; and the English, factories. The basic modalities of this Western economic penetration of the region both exploited and enhanced the diverse nature of the city. Each of the foreign merchant groups, known in the parlance of the day as "trading nations," maintained privileged relations with its preferred local religious community. The French favored the Uniate Catholic sects (Melkites and Maronites); the English, the Jews, primarily Arabic and Ladino-speaking Sephardim. These relationships created deep bonds between Europeans and local people—primarily non-Sunni Muslims—that transcended culture and language. These relationships persisted even as Aleppo's international economic importance waned in the nineteenth century. Nevertheless, Aleppo remained a vibrant and cosmopolitan crossroad of the Old World well into the 1900s.

Muslims in the city, and in the rest of the Ottoman Empire, tended to participate in international commerce as superior legal partners. Unlike their non-Muslim counterparts, they enjoyed positions in the military, government, and Islamic religious establishment. As the Ottoman state expanded its bureaucratic, military, and educational systems along European lines over the course of the nineteenth century in a series of modernization programs known collectively as the Tanzimat, knowledge of foreign languages, new technologies, and European forms of political and social organization penetrated into the Muslim community of the city and facilitated a transition to modern middle-class ways of knowing for Muslims. Muslims in Aleppine society derived their comprehension of things modern less from direct contact with Westerners or their metropoles and more through the lens of the imperial capital of Istanbul.

Critically, as Fatma Müge Göçek observes, one of the "unintended consequences" of the Tanzimat was the transformation of "three Ottoman social groups—merchants, officials, and intellectuals—into an emergent bourgeoisie segmented along religious and ethnic lines."[4] The segmentation along religious lines evolved from the basic terms of the customary relationship between the Muslim ruling majority of the empire and its non-Muslim minorities. Already encapsulated into quasi-autonomous administrative units called *millets*, religious minorities in Ottoman society served as a template for the formation of separate classes. The higher degree of access to Western education and forms of socialization and organization helped some people in these already self-contained groups move into the middle class. The cultural origins of this part of the middle class support the argument that the notion of middle class hinges less on objective standards of wealth than on a systematic adherence to patterns of behavior and presentations of self.

Also crucial to this sectarian bifurcation of the class was the Ottoman Land Law of 1858. Before the mid-nineteenth century, real property was not owned per se, but rather held by individuals for use, often in perpetuity, while the land itself belonged to the state. As a feature of economic liberalization, the Ottoman state promulgated a series of land registration and purchasing laws. Used primarily by members of the urban elite to secure their position by recording vast amounts of land in their names, it also opened the door for smaller agricultural entrepreneurs and land speculators. Growing wealth among these smaller landholders created an economic basis for their movement into the middle class, primarily through the vehicle of state education and white-collar bureaucratic jobs. Legally, non-Muslims could own land; in practice, however, state bureaucrats tended to obstruct the purchase of real estate by Christians and Jews in favor of Muslims.[5] This solidified the position of non-Muslims in the retail and banking sectors and resulting forms of cultural capital, but it also strengthened their sense of alienation from the larger Ottoman community.

Despite the existence of these divisions by the start of the twentieth century, the cities of the Arab eastern Mediterranean like Beirut, Aleppo, Baghdad, and Damascus were home to a new social category made up of Western and Western-style educated state bureaucrats and indigenous colonial officials, medical doctors, lawyers, military officers, middle-man agents, bankers, journalists, teachers in state high schools, college students, and similar professionals and white-collar employees. This stratum was drawn primarily from previous generations of the urban merchant class, absentee landowners, the corps of dragomans, Muslim and non-Muslim clerics and scholars, and, in disproportionate numbers, members of the region's ethnic, religious, and linguistic minorities. The social roles and expectations, forms of cultural capital and wealth, and training and education that made one an element of this stratum were novel to the region and can be traced to individual ambition, reform efforts of the Ottoman state, and the growing presence of the West in multiple manifestations from missionary education to economic penetration and outright military occupation.

Moreover, this new social category was distinguished not just by what it had in terms of wealth and property but also by the fact that it had something else as a consequence of its extensive contact with the West, in the form of commercial and trade relations and from educational training in Western and Western-style institutions: knowledge of modern forms of organization, journalism, commercial law, banking, and investment tools, and access—in the broadest sense of the term—to an ascendant world beyond the Arab eastern Mediterranean. This knowledge could be capitalized on in the commercial sphere, but also more generally in civic life. Although this knowledge and capital was by no means exclusive to the non-Muslim minority of the city, it nevertheless contributed to the distance—which increased in the next century—between the Muslim and non-Muslim wings of the middle class.

With the Ottoman Revolution of 1908, more commonly known in the West as the Young Turk Revolution, a diverse group of reform-minded military officers, bureaucrats, and intellectuals who formed the semisecret Ottoman Committee for Union and Progress forced the restoration of the relatively liberal Ottoman Constitution of 1872. Hüseyin Saʿd an Istanbul-educated medical doctor and the inspector of health for the province of Damascus, expressed his sense of the new in a poem published in the bilingual Ottoman and Arabic Aleppine newspaper *Sedâ -yı Shehbâ / Sada' al-Shahba'* (Echo of the gray [city]). In the poem, "The Melody of Freedom," written in Ottoman Turkish, he embraced the change with an unreserved optimism:

> A new world, a new heaven
> A drunken dream of a new land just over the horizon
> We people of the nation resemble a new man of
> Noah's Ark touching land
> O the joy for our nation's youth[6]

Longworth, the long-time British consul in the city, noted in a dispatch to his ambassador in Istanbul that, on the public announcement of the reinstatement of the constitution, "addresses were delivered by different Military officers, by the Director of Public Instruction and several prominent local men, the speeches being in Turkish, Arabic and French, children also delivered declamations. Frequent references were made to liberty, justice, and equal rights, each time receiving vociferous applause, mingled with cries of 'long live liberty,' 'long live freedom,' . . . Moslems, Christians and Jews mingled together, with brotherly feeling, and strong men of all sects wept with joy."[7] This period of relative openness and intersectarian comity was short-lived: it could survive neither the empire's move to a military dictatorship in 1913, nor its entrance into the First World War in the following year.

Nevertheless, it was in this brief revolutionary period that the Arab middle class first defined its sense of itself and its social position by means of the social space created by voluntary organizations. It employed journalism and operated as a group or party in formal and informal politics, using new communication technologies to bypass the traditional elite in the exercise of power. In the months before the First World War, it faced its most serious challenge as forces in the center of the government, bowing to the political demands of the the *aʿyan*, a tenacious political class of landed notables and religious officials, altered the functional definition of the citizen and adapted the tools of modernism to center Islam in political discourse. A majority of the middle class who sought to articulate a substantive role for themselves in the politics of their society came from the region's large commercial middle class; as a class dominated by religious minorities, their exclusion and activism added an inescapable dimension to the form of conflict and change: the traditional patterns of hegemony had at their most fundamental basis Sunni Muslim religious authority and legally upheld superiority because Sunni Muslims were the *millet-i hakime*, the ideologically sanctioned dominant group. The mere act of being modern in this time of revolution challenged this sanction and rendered the bases of power of the old social elite unintelligible in the idiom of emergent middle-class society.

Critically, the manifestation of these challenges in civil society and partisan politics is evidence that being modern did not necessarily lead to the large-scale replacement of sectarian identification with middle-class notions of the secular. It also shows that these institutional forms enhanced and transformed the very nature of sectarian difference and separateness within the wings of the Arab eastern Mediterranean's middle class. This was especially the case when these phenomena became increasingly interconnected with the formal reintegration of Islamic political theory into the definition of both the state and the citizen, and the forms of civil society (voluntary civic organizations, political parties, sports clubs) and the technologies of the public sphere (rational discourse, mass media, public opinion) were reshaped—though rarely explicitly so—to fit within preexisting communal and sectarian boundaries.

Parliamentary Elections and Aleppo's Mutual Aid Society

This question about the role of Islam in the politics of revolution became most acute during the last significant elections in the prewar period. Held in 1913 against the backdrop of the Ottoman Empire's worsening diplomatic and political position in the Balkans, these elections were seen by many as a referendum on the entire ethos of the 1908 revolution. Throughout the empire, the elections occasioned an often fierce exchange of ideas, the use of public forums, and the formation and reformation of constellations of religious, class-based, and even ethnic alliances. Although the Young Turks (the Committee for Union and Progress) ultimately rigged the elections, an ideological shift took place at the time that distanced them from the views on which much of their middle-class support had been based. At that moment, the Young Turks sought to recast their claim to power on a religious and ethnic basis. In part this reflected the rapid transformation during the previous century of the empire's demography—a process that accelerated after the 1908 Revolution—from a multireligious, multiethnic polity to a primarily Muslim state dominated by Turkish and Arabic speakers, which forced a deep reappraisal of the usefulness of the revolution's more secular and modern ideals. This reappraisal manifested itself most visibly in the various language and administrative reforms that would enhance Arab-Muslim religious prestige to the disadvantage of non-Muslims, especially in terms of access to positions in the bureaucracy and politics. Additional measures, especially the suspension of economic privileges that accrued from unequal treaties with Western states and the extension of the draft to non-Muslim men contributed further to this shift and bespoke the underlying divergence in social expectations polarizing the region's middle class. "Muslim patriots," Fatma Müge Göçek concludes, "envisioned sharing equality with all, but only under the rules they themselves determined. The minorities wanted equality to erase all social differences among them and the Muslims [and] were frustrated when this did not occur."[8] Unable to solve Göçek's dilemma, the region's middle class, primarily its Christian middle class, was forced to doubt the Young Turks' commitment to liberalism and secular citizenship.

The constitution also affirmed the liberalization of laws pertaining to the establishment of social clubs. Despite the long history of these organizations, the exponential growth of the European-style voluntary associations in the revolutionary period constituted a fundamental shift in civil society and the form of political and cultural activities within it. Critically, these voluntary associations sought to cut across professional lines (unlike early guild-style *esnaf*) to become sites of proper urban middle-class social interaction, and to provide a blueprint for the broader participation of the middle class in all elements of society. As Geoff Eley has observed of nineteenth-century Germany, "such associational initiatives were fundamental to the formation of bourgeois civil society . . . Put simply, voluntary association was in principle the logical form of bourgeois emancipation and bourgeois self-affirmation." Eley notes that the populist, egalitarian, and benevolent motives in the rhetorical pronouncements of the clubs resulted in charitable work and to some extent laid the foundation for the possible broader liberalization of the Arab eastern Mediterranean.[9] But most of all, they provided the middle class with a venue within which to maintain its distinction from other social classes, resituate gender difference along modern lines, and otherwise create models of embourgeoisement.

The quintessential voluntary association from this era is Aleppo's Nadi al-

Taʿddud, the Aleppo Mutual Aid Society. The association of the leadership of the club with the editorial board of the newspaper *al-Shaʿb* (The people) reveals the club's inner workings and presents a way to trace the collective vision of the club's members of what it meant to be modern, as well as how those members demarcated themselves from larger society. Founded in January 1910, the club clearly borrowed its name from contemporary French General Associations for Mutual Aid.

Like comparable associations in the West, the Aleppo Mutual Aid Society assured the universality and legitimacy of middle-class modernity by the conceit of teaching its key concepts and practices to the lower classes, while at the same time assuming the elite practice of patronage. Though the entire edifice of relief, charity, and elite patronage was undergoing a rapid transformation in the late Ottoman period, the intensely middle-class form of assistance envisioned by the leaders of the Mutual Aid Society marked it as a distinctive and novel feature of the transforming social milieu as it focused on cultural pursuits, education, and urban behavior as much as on economic improvement.

These cultural pursuits included choral singing, poetry writing, and team sports, but they were primarily quasi-educational lectures, the bulk of which were reproduced in *al-Shaʿb*. The Mutual Aid Society created a space in which middle-class men (women were only occasionally part of club activities) could be modern, and these lectures were part of a process by which those similarly included could be trained to recognize their mutual modernity, as well as enforcing it. The lectures provide evidence of the formation of a refined homosociability that translated into possible male solidarity in politics and commerce.

The talks and speeches covered a variety of topics, including history, new agricultural technologies, archaeology, literature, and women's emancipation and the education of girls. Left unsaid in the speeches was the role of religious difference and categories of religious distinction. That said, the lectures and other activities of the Mutual Aid Society lack any clear evidence of Muslim participation: there were no Muslims in the group's leadership, nor did any speak at its podium. The majority of the club's members and its leaders were drawn from the city's large and thriving community of Melkite Catholics, many of whom had been educated in the local French missionary schools. Nevertheless, the members scrupulously avoided any reference to religion in the present, whereas they often made historical allusions to it, in references that invariably came from the Old or New Testament. Of note is the fact that this religious universe was more in keeping with Western European exemplars, as the more exotic and local attributes of Eastern Christianity seem equally absent. The members of the society identified modernity with nonsectarianism, but an insistence on equality and cooperation bereft of religious distinction held little appeal for members of the Muslim elite or even portions of the Muslim middle class, as for them equality represented the surrender of privileges and customary patriarchy. Secularism held out the promise of empowerment only for non-Muslims.

Moreover, the physical location of the society, in a majority Christian middle-class neighborhood, ʿAziziyya; the day and time of the club's meetings, Sunday evening after supper; the occasional use of alcohol during social gatherings; and the public attendance of chaperoned women at the meetings coded the society as non-Muslim and, in particular, Christian. For a middle-class Muslim to cooperate fully with the society, he would have been required to move into a social environment in which Christians and Jews no longer occupied inferior positions; indeed, it was a space in which fluency in bourgeois styles of sociability and horizontal egalitarianism in the universe of voluntary associations was the price of admission.

Participation in clubs such as the Mutual Aid Society hinged on an acknowledgment of the superiority of Western forms of cultural capital acquired by the minority middle class over the preceding generation. In many cases, access to those forms was predicated on their Catholicism, foreign contacts, and ability to be modern with greater fluency than many of their Muslim counterparts. Furthermore, the challenge posed by the opening of public spaces of sociability to women and minorities as part of the project of modernity hardened the intimate boundaries between, on the one hand, Christians and Jews, and, on the other hand, the Muslim community, writ large. Although this time of revolution witnessed moments of intersectarian comity in political and professional spheres, such connections were less evident or absent altogether in the more closed domains of education, sports, and leisure.

After the closure of *al-Shaʿb* in 1913 by the state, there is little information about the Mutual Aid Society. However, it did survive the First World War and reemerged as the Aleppo Club. The transformation of the Mutual Aid Society into the Aleppo Club accompanied the maturation of its constituency and foreshadowed a conscious retreat from overt political activism by the middle class of the city. Although the Aleppo Club has survived into the twenty-first century and still hosts lectures, sponsors sports teams, and aids the poor, its chief function is as a middle-class social club that self-consciously mirrors styles of European bourgeois sociability; it has no overt political presence in the politics of contemporary Syria. In the 1940s and 1950s it was the site of debutante balls and bridge tournaments, and it now hosts gala wedding receptions, karaoke nights, and cocktail parties. On paper, the Aleppo Club has maintained a strict nonsectarianism, but in practice it is still the domain of the city's Francophone Catholic middle class.

The Arab Middle-Class Citizen in French Mandate Syria

For much of the interwar period, Edmond Rabbath was a member of the Aleppo Club. He enjoyed taking his friends and acquaintances there, especially Saʿallah al-Jabiri, a member of Aleppo's most powerful Sunni Muslim family and a leader of the elite-dominated National Bloc, the primary political opposition to French colonial rule in Syria. For Jabiri, these were extraordinary occasions, during which he seemed at once obsessed and repelled by the sexual allure of unveiled Jewish and Christian women and jealous of the apparent ease with which middle-class non-Muslim men and women mixed in public. He noted wistfully in his diary on May 12, 1929: "There was a soireé [at the Aleppo Club] and Christian men came with their women and I flirted with some of them with my eyes. Especially pleasant were the Jewish girls who were eyeing me and I was looking at them."[10]

The very association of these two individuals seems at odds with prewar notions about the distinct and bounded religious, social, intellectual, and educational spheres of a city where connections were often based on class and religion and became solidified through economic cooperation, alliances by marriage, and school ties. Although both men would acknowledge these differences later, for a time the two became closely linked in the urban politics of French Mandate Syria, and their association is understandable within that context.

Jabiri was exemplary of a political dynamic in the early modern and modern eastern Mediterranean that was called the "Politics of Notables" by the leading Middle Eastern historian of the previous generation, Albert Hourani.[11] Although that may be an accurate description of the calculus of power during the French Mandate for most of Syrian society, many in the emerging urban middle class of lawyers, doctors, schoolteachers, bureaucrats, international merchants, bankers, and their families—both in the Muslim and non-Muslim wings of the class—continued to question the claims of the traditional elite to a position of hegemony in the city. Journalism, history writing, and modern forms of social and political organization had enabled the middle class to contest the architectures of community in the cities of the eastern Mediterranean, beginning with the Revolution of 1908 and continuing with the establishment of the French Mandate for Syria and Lebanon in 1920. Throughout this period, this process brought the middle class into conflict with the notables. In the postcolonial period, political parties—primarily on the Left like the Syrian Communist Party and, later, the Arab Socialist Renaissance Party (al-Baʿth)—would eventually become the fiercest opponents of the "Politics of Notables," and populist programs of land reform and wealth redistribution would contribute to its complete elimination. Yet in the interwar period, opposition equally found voice in the liberal political discourse emanating from institutions of middle-class civil society. Furthermore, French support and ever-increasing contacts with the West gave the middle class of the region—especially its Christian and Jewish components—even greater power in the fledgling state, adding a new dimension to the politics by intensifying the hostility between non-Muslims and the elite, and ultimately inflecting the conflict with sectarian overtones.

Rabbath's relationship with Jabiri unfolded in the context of the attempt by the notables of Syria to use a cadre of young, Western-educated, middle-class intellectuals to recast their hold on power—or their collective desire to regain a measure of hegemony—in the language of Wilsonian self-determination and nationalism. Tellingly, the process by which the notables of the cities of the Levant sought to contain the political activity of the urban middle class closely parallels the methods by which the ancien régime of Europe retained so much of its authority and power despite the rapid transformation of that continent's class structure in the period before the First World War. Arno Mayer has argued that "inveterate nobles firmly occupied and controlled access to the high social, cultural, and political terrain to which the bourgeoisie aspired. With characteristic flexibility and adaptability, and capitalizing on the bourgeois elements craving for social status and advancement the grand notables admitted individual postulants from business and the professions into their midst. Rather than yield institutional ground, they opted for this selective co-optation, confident of their ability to contain and defuse its attendant ideological and cultural contamination."[12] Although these young, foreign-educated intellectuals fit into the notables' broader hegemonic project in the interwar period, they were by no means the only tactic by which the elite intended to contain and control the potential threat of middle-class dissent; the ultimate failure of these young men to deliver the complete compliance of their class led the notables to call on a reserve of customary urban violence to finish the task of ensuring middle-class quiescence.

This is not to cast Rabbath as a passive actor in this relationship, drawn into it solely on the basis of ambition or the cultural and religious prestige of the elite. Rather, beginning in the late 1920s and along with other young men in Aleppo and elsewhere in the eastern Mediterranean, who had been born within a few years of the turn of the century and come of age after the war, he asserted the modernity of an Arab Syria.

Based in two worlds, men like Rabbath were mediating figures capable of comprehending both the basic terms of the "Politics of Notables" and the organizing principles and modes of political activity of middle-class civil society; likewise, they could serve as interlocutors in the kinds of discussions and negotiations that typified the style of interwar elite colonial resistance in Syria. Critically, they contributed to the transformation of Ottoman-era customary authority into a recognizably modern vernacular of power. Rabbath went even further and was among the first to elaborate on the idea that a positivist view of a religion, in this case Islam, could be welded with a modern national identity, the Arab, and then serve as a legitimate basis for rule. In this he prefigured other Christian or non–Sunni Muslim Arab nationalist intellectuals of the interwar and postwar period who sought to secularize and historicize Islam as a definitive cultural practice of the Arabs. Among these were Michel ʿAflaq and Zaki al-Arsuzi,the founders of the Baʿth movement. Ironically, in their case, this connection of Islam to the conception of a broader Arab nation would serve as a basis for their dissent from the elite and often parochial nationalism of the old notables.[13]

The full contours of the contradictory and ultimately unstable relationship between Jabiri and Rabbath became visible during the most important political events of the early 1930s: the constituent assembly elections of December 1931 and January 1932, the delegation to France of 1936, and the elections that took place in that year. Similarly, a clearer picture of the way the middle class sought to contest the city's politics emerged in this period, as did the full extent of the sectarian gulf that Rabbath intended to bridge. The form of Syrian elections during most of the mandate, which were modeled on the old Ottoman system of tiered representation, contributed in no small way to the shape of that discursive environment. Such a system was calculated both to help maintain the status quo and to facilitate official manipulation. Voting took place at public places around the city, such as mosques, schools, churches, synagogues, and cafes. Individuals voted for electors rather than for any specific party although, like a caucus-style vote, the electors were generally identified with a certain faction or individual. These electors then met and chose the final delegates from among themselves. Corruption of the process could occur at any step—most easily at the level of registration.

Mandate-era elections resembled pre-1908 Ottoman elections in an additional way: confessional representation was guaranteed. In other words, on the basis of preliminary calculation, and regardless of the eventual vote totals, religious communities were awarded representatives. In 1932 the electors filled six seats with "Muslims" (conceived of as a monolithic group); two other seats were "Armenian Orthodox," one "Armenian Catholic," one "Greek Catholic," and one "Syrian Catholic." In subsequent elections a seat would be reserved for "Aleppo's minorities"—that is Jews, Chaldeans, and Greek and Syrian Orthodox. For example, Rabbath ran as a "Greek Catholic" and lost in that category to Latif al-Ghanima by 174 to 293 votes.[14]

The French Mandate authorities juggled such allotments throughout the mandate period. Direct vote rigging was usually unnecessary to gain an outcome favorable to those who were least antagonistic to the mandate; rather, French efforts indicate that they had identified, supported, and protected a crossconfessional constituency—Muslim, Christian, and Jewish—within Aleppine society that was unwilling to support notables like Jabiri.

The elections of 1931–32 also proved the National Bloc's organizational weakness in the Christian community. Rabbath reflected on this problem in an unpublished manuscript, "Courte histoire du mandat en Syrie et au Liban." In his recollections of the period, he came to the conclusion that the French had persuaded his coreligionists that they were involved in a sectarian conflict of "cross versus crescent" rather than resistance to colonialism. And were they to support the bloc, they risked immersion in a "sea of Islam."[15] A recurring complaint in the bloc's statement addressed to the League of Nations voiced a similar concern, primarily that the French Mandate authority had conspired to manipulate the vote through appeals to sectarian fears.

The bloc's failure could also be explained by its "rather complacent attitude toward the Christian vote, which it all but ignored."[16] For Rabbath, a French colonial policy that emphasized communalism and the protection of minorities had implications beyond electoral politics. In his estimation, such a policy undermined the long-term goal of creating a national identity for Syria. Rather than protecting members of minority groups like him, such a policy condemned Syria to continue as a *régime de cloisons étanches*, a system of watertight compartments of religious communities in which the state was officially Muslim and Muslims and non-Muslims alike lived within their own bounded religious and legal fictions rather than in the same state, all as its citizens. Rabbath had first explored this idea in *L'évolution*, writing: "The absolute liberty of conscience is incompatible with the existence of a state religion." Likewise, "freedom of conscience . . . cannot find its total application under the Syrian communitarian régime. [Such] freedom is indirectly reduced to the liberty of believing in an official religion and precludes either adhesion to an unofficial faith or the freeing of oneself from any confessional group."[17]

Establishing society on the basis of secular citizenship could ensure equality more readily than the status quo and no doubt appealed to those in the middle class like Rabbath. Conversely, it could have had little appeal to someone like Jabiri, whose natural leadership derived in general from the institutional domination of society by Sunni Muslims and was legitimized by his clan's claim to descent from the family of the Prophet Muhammad. Similarly, what Rabbath considered to be a colonialist-inspired division of society made improbable the formation of a Syrian national identity. "Does this mean," he asked, "there do not exist collective sentiments other than those which follow from this very regime [communalism]? Such a conclusion would singularly support the thesis of those who declared that there does not exist in Syria anything but confessions that act in the place of national sentiment and fatherland and that the Syrians are still far from conceiving and realizing the national sovereignty and liberty to which their leaders lay claim."[18] Election results broadly reflecting an unwillingness of much of the Aleppine middle class, especially its Christian wing, to support the notables of the National Bloc and their nationalism reinforced such a conclusion. Creating nationalist sentiment, a key moment in the claiming of modernity, was therefore blocked by the perpetuation of a confessional division by the French imperialists and those whom Rabbath would label collaborators. He had come to believe that the French had vested in the local Christian population a false consciousness of the centrality and essential nature of sectarianism in Syria. In reaction, his writings reveal that by the mid-1920s he had imagined a type of Syrian citizenship that was at variance with both colonial policy and the dominant conception of Ottoman-style institutionalized Muslim dominance of the state. Such a secular interpretation of citizenship was an expression of both his middle-class origins and his intellectual training. However, in Rabbath's estimation, the Sunni notables who opposed the French represented the best means to the desired end of the formation of a national identity in Syria; hence, association with the elite bloc represented a short-term concession on his part in order to serve a more important long-term goal.

An effort to reconcile such contradictions—the persistence of class and sectarian distinction alongside the assertion of the irrelevance of such differences—motivated Rabbath to write a series of newspaper articles on the subject in the spring of 1936. Appearing in the "Tribune Libre" section of the Lebanese French-language *Le Jour*, the series both outlined the bloc's public interpretation of the French policy toward minorities and employed an Orientalist argument that true Islam, and a state dominated by Muslims, would tolerate Christians who would prosper as long as they willingly cooperated with it. Writing in French and using almost exclusively French Orientalist and legal sources, Rabbath inflected his argument in a way that pandered to the cultural snobbery of the Levant's Francophone Christian middle class. For many, French was nearly a native tongue, defining those who spoke it as members of a separate community within a non-French milieu. It did not define them as French per se but gave them an identity opposed to that of Arab or Syrian advocated by Rabbath. His central aim in the articles was to leave the Christian middle class in no doubt that a nationalist government would—while protecting their rights as fellow citizens—deny to them access to this alternative identity. He sought to show that this identity had no basis in the historical past, nor would it have any meaning in the politics of the postcolonial future.

Entitled "Les Minorités," the articles ran from March 6 through March 10, 1936. Rabbath began the first, subtitled "Muslim Tolerance," by arguing that the Christians of the Levant had always viewed the Arab Muslim conquerors as just rulers: "We can honestly say that . . . [French] prejudice against majoritarian Islam is profoundly unjust."[19] Things only began to fall apart, the history lesson continued, on the accession to the throne of the Abbasid Caliph al-Mutawakkil (847–61), when "a phenomenon similar to Hitlerian anti-Semitism arose" and "persecution became more generalized because Islam was no longer well understood by its adherents." Moving swiftly from the medieval to the modern period, Rabbath assigned the blame for various massacres of Christians by Muslims in the mid-nineteenth century to outsiders—that is, non-Arabs. The son of the Albanian Mehmet Ali, Ibrahim Pasha, the Janissaries, and rapacious and corrupt "Turkish" governors all came under indictment: "In 1860 what has been called massacres were merely . . . revolts of a popular and agrarian nature that pitted feudal lords against exasperated serfs and that were encouraged, as if for fun, by the Turkish pashas."[20] Nevertheless, the late Ottoman reforms, presaged by "the habit of the Great Powers to insert themselves in the relationships of the Ottoman Empire with its non-Muslim subjects," assisted the cause of the Christians in the empire. "They [the Christians and Jews] triumphed in commerce and banking, their privileged domain," he wrote of the period after 1878—adopting the dominant historiographical prejudices about the position of Christians and Jews in Ottoman society. "In the great cities they lived in the best quarters and in the most beautiful buildings . . . Many Christians became ministers, senators, magistrates, and members of official bodies. They exerted a definite political influence; their patriarchs were treated as the equals of viziers." In the waning days of the empire, "rights, conscription, [and] taxes were equally imposed on all."

Similarly, the Young Turk general, Cemal Pasha, executed both Christian and Muslim "nationalists" in 1915: "The gibbet was set up for everyone, without distinction of religion." The First World War, concluded Rabbath, ushered in an era when the "conflict of races and that of religions seemed a thing of the past." As Syria was a "racially homogeneous" state under King Faysal, the question of minorities was not an issue: "The Damascus cabinet [included] four Christians out of eight ministers." And "public spirit was steering itself toward Arabism and unity." This final thought is an explicit criticism of the French presence, which he saw as both a disruption in the natural evolution of an Arab Syria and a return to the period in which outsiders employed sectarianism to deter the modernization of his nation. Paraphrasing a passage from Ernest Renan's 1882 Sorbonne lecture "Qu'est-ce qu'une nation?"—"the essence of a nation is that all individuals have many things in common and thus they have forgotten many things"—Rabbath argued that a kind of conscious amnesia and an enlightened censorship would be the final act that would return Syria to the correct historical trajectory.

This necessary "forgetfulness" segued into the final article, "The 'Protection' of Minorities," and Rabbath's chilling warning to his fellow Syrian Christians.[21] Following a complex and pedantic argument about the role of the League of Nations in protecting minorities, Rabbath shifted into the first person and addressed his coreligionists directly: "The future is not in Europe . . . but in Islam in which we are immersed." A Bible verse ends the series: the Old Testament prophet "Jeremiah's words remain meaningful: 'But seek the welfare of the city where I have sent you into exile, and pray to the Lord on its behalf, for in its welfare you will find your welfare.' "[22]

In this sweeping history, Rabbath bound the Orientalist—and, ironically, Salafist—trope of an essential Islamic community to the nationalist construct of a timeless Arab race, thereby making a striking historicist argument. Further developed in his last overtly political text, *Unité syrienne et devenir arabe*, a gloss of this argument unfolds as follows: Arab history is a history of intersectarian comity, where the responsibility for provoking sectarianism rested on non-Arabs. Since Islam by definition is a tolerant religion, if there were no outside interference, then Arabs would live in harmony together. Christians had nothing to fear because historical strife has its origins in the lands beyond the Arab-Islamic world. Regardless, the violence of the past, and the trepidation of survivors of the massacres, should be forgotten because that forgetting is the basis of the nation, a nation within which one's condition as a minority would have no standing; rather, the law would protect the legitimate rights of all. Minorities would not be allowed any special status and would have no appeal to an outside power because they would not need such protection. Nevertheless, with the implications of the Prophet Jeremiah's words in mind, Syrian minorities—like the Hebrews during the Babylonian captivity—would remain in a subordinate condition as not quite Syrians, still exiles in their own land.

In return for the support of the minorities and their middle class, the bloc then would also protect their access to civil society. Consequently, key components of the civil society sphere—free association, speech, and religion—were enshrined in their statements and promises to the French dating from this period. It is unlikely that the bloc would have made such promises in the absence of the growing power of the Syrian middle class, especially its Christian wing, whose fears Rabbath had sought to assuage in these articles.

Despite the promises and public devotion to these ideals, the events of the 1936 election showed that Rabbath's arguments had little resonance in his own community and that ultimately, in lieu of persuasion, the bloc would resort to much less subtle means. The fact that the bloc abandoned such ideals may have caused Rabbath's eventual disenchantment with its leadership and led to his distancing himself from Jabiri. In the end, his system of belief was based on the rule of law and the logos of modernity; he was ill prepared for the grim realities of Syrian urban politics of the late 1930s.

By 1946, when Jabiri became the first prime minister of independent Syria (he would die in 1947), Rabbath had emigrated to Lebanon, where he became that country's premier constitutional scholar. He remained in Lebanon as Syria was turned into an old-fashioned police state by successive coups d'état and the rise of the Baath movement. On the eve of the 1975 Lebanese civil war, he completed the hauntingly prescient *La formation historique du Liban politique et constitutionne* (1973), and he finished his career with the multivolume *Les Chrétiens dans l'Islam des premiers temps* (1980–85). He never returned to live in Aleppo.

Ultimately Edmond Rabbath was something more than a middle-class Syrian mimic man, in Homi Bhabha's sense of the term;[23] his ambivalence toward both the colonial state and the bases of the notables' power points to a double act of subversion. His commitment to a positivist and progressivist program of middle-class modernity was inconsistent not only with French colonialism but also, ultimately, with notable hegemony. Still he understood the value of a strategic, though presumably temporary, alliance with the notables; the fact that he had something to offer Jabiri also reflects the changing function of the intellectual in the interwar eastern Mediterranean. The establishment of a French colonial presence in Syria had empowered men who, like Rabbath, could translate, formulate, or adapt modern conceptions of the nation and citizen into that moment's epistemic lingua franca. Rabbath's self-imposed exile in Lebanon is emblematic of the larger failure of middle-class modernity to create strong secular (or at least nonsectarian) institutions that could challenge the centrifugal attractions of sectarian interests. Lebanon's constitution establishes the nonsectarian nature of Lebanese citizenship, but the practice of Lebanese politics is the very definition of confessional politics, euphemistically called consociationalism—in which positions in the government and parliament are doled out on the basis of religious affiliation and are derived from a 1930s-era census, now wholly out of date.

The weakness of such a system points to a conceptual axiom that I propose as both a conclusion of this chapter and a starting point for the future comparative study of the history of the middle class as a social and cultural phenomenon in the West and non-West. The middle class was expert at forming institutions of civil society, bringing to these institutional forms shared expectations of participation, equality, and accountability. Although these forms were a template for larger participation in society, the bonds that the middle class created in the universe of voluntary associations were weak. Other bonds of religion, ethnicity, and family were stronger, so the bonds made in civil society were not strong enough to challenge the state or withstand hostile interference by it, and they rarely translated directly into political ascendance. This weakness made the individual members of the middle class vulnerable to forms of cultural and economic cooptation by colonialist, conservative, and authoritarian elites.

Notes

This chapter is drawn in part from my *Being Modern in the Middle East*. All translations are mine unless otherwise noted.

1. Idmun al-Rabbat (Edmond Rabbath), "The Decline of Democracy [in Arabic]," *al-Hadith* 2 (February 1926).
2. Ibid., 100–101.
3. Nicolls, *Modernisms*, 7.
4. Göçek, *Rise of the Bourgeoisie, Demise of Empire*, 109–10.
5. Karpat, *The Politicization of Islam*, 93–98; Sluglett and Farouk-Sluglett, "The Application of the 1858 Land Code in Greater Syria."
6. Hüseyin Sa'd, (Melody of freedom), *Sedâ-yı Shehbâ/Sada' al-Shahba',* December 16, 1908.
7. Longworth (Aleppo) to Lowther (Constantinople), August 10, 1908, Public Record Office, Foreign Office, 195/2272, Kew, United Kingdom.

8. Göçek, *Rise of the Bourgeoisie, Demise of Empire*, 136.

9. Eley, "Nations, Publics and Political Cultures," 298. See also 289–339.

10. Saʿallah al-Jabiri, entry for May 12, 1929, Folder 95: "Private Papers of Saʿdallah al-Jabiri," Syrian State Archives, Damascus. Jabiri was apparently sitting in the area of the Aleppo Club reserved for single men. Men accompanied by female family members or girlfriends could sit in the mixed-sex area. This practice of segregating males unaccompanied by women in public places was prevalent in the 1930s, as it is in Syria today. It might have been more difficult for Jabiri to come to the club accompanied by female members of his family because of the practice of seclusion imposed on Muslim women of the highest social status.

11. The term was developed by Hourani in his seminal "Ottoman Reform and the Politics of Notables," 41–68. Philip Khoury has suggested further that the middle class is the missing piece. See Khoury, "The Urban Notables Paradigm Revisited," 226.

12. Mayer, *The Persistence of the Old Regime*, 81.

13. Michel ʻAflaq, a Greek Orthodox Christian born in Damascus in 1910, attended the Sorbonne in the 1930s. In a speech delivered at the Syrian National University in 1943 titled "In Remembrance of the Arab Prophet," he argued: "To the Arabs, the Islamic movement embodied in the life of [Muhammad] is not merely a historical occurrence . . . rather, it is at the very depths . . . and bound fiercely into the life of the Arab." Furthermore, he concluded that "Islam has renewed Arabism and completed it." Mishil [Michel] ʻAflaq, *Fi sabil al-ba'th* [For the cause of the Baath], 8th ed. (Beirut: Dar al-tali'a lil-tiba'a wa al-nashr, 1972), 127. See also Watenpaugh, "Creating Phantoms."

14. Assistant Delegate (Aleppo) to High Commissioner (Beirut), no. 61/13, January 9, 1932; High Commissioner (Damascus) to Minister of Foreign Affairs, no. 87, January 29, 1932, Cabinet Politique 399, Fonds Beyrouth,Centre des archives diplomatiques Nantes Ministére des affair etrangéeres, For discussion of the Aleppine electoral politics, see Peter Sluglett, "Urban Dissidence in Mandatory Syria: Aleppo 1918–1936," 301–16.

15. Quoted in Khoury, *Syria and the French Mandate*, 362.

16. Ibid., 372.

17. Rabbath, *L'evolution*, 19.

18. Ibid., 20.

19. *Le Jour* (Beirut), March 6, 1936, Rabbath's initial paragraph was a refutation of Édouard Daladier's widely quoted statement to the French Chamber of Deputies on March 30, 1929: "Why . . . must we maintain troops in Syria? . . . [B]ecause the day when you recall these forces you will risk seeing these different races attacking each other, as it has happened very regularly in their history."

20. Ibid.

21. *Le Jour* (Beirut), March 10, 1936.

22. Ibid.

23. Bhabha, *The Location of Culture*, 85–92.

Commentary on Part III

MIDDLE-CLASS POLITICS IN REVOLUTION

Brian Owensby

The middle class will always have to exist, just as will the rich and the poor classes. They are all necessary and can never disappear. It would be utopian to affirm otherwise.
DEMOCRITO DE CASTRO SILVA, *Middle Class*

One might hear in the statement above a strong and secure affirmation of middle-class identity. Yet consider. Just before uttering these words, Torquato, a traveling shoe salesman, had been wondering whether he was any different from the factory workers who manufactured the shoes he spent his life peddling from town to town in the modernizing Brazil of the 1940s. They too were exploited by the factory's owner and denied any share of the profits, even though together the salesmen and the workers were the real authors of progress. And although this flash of class solidarity is gone after a moment, its afterimage remains, for Torquato senses that middle-class identity is especially vulnerable to the realities of class struggle, since the pressure to choose sides tends to negate a clear class position. In short, middle-class people live fully exposed to and simultaneously in self-denial about the categorical and existential instability of that to which they appeal for a class identity—the idea of the middle class as denying the very class divisions on which it is premised.

In different ways, each of the three chapters in this part testifies to this dilemma. The fact that it appears in such disparate geographical and historical circumstances—Mexico, Peru, and Syria—suggests that a deeper truth regarding the idea of the middle class may be lurking here, one that can be revealed only through a comparative and transnational approach. In this commentary, I shall discuss the chapters as exemplars of this approach and conclude with a broader reflection on the problems of identity and power in thinking about the middle class beyond the North Atlantic.

In her chapter, Susanne Eineigel peers into postrevolutionary Mexican society and finds a vibrant middle-class discourse beginning as early as 1915. Individual Mexicans, chiefly in larger cities, began to use the term "middle class" to describe themselves and their situation, just as those in political power started to use the same term to describe a politically relevant social grouping above the working class and the poor. Eineigel is clear that this language emerged in relation to a transnational discourse that alerted middle-class Mexicans, and others, to their existence as a class and offered them a model against which to measure their own circumstances and calibrate their aspirations. Eineigel's larger point is that a nascent middle class played a crucial role in enlarging the sphere of public opinion and popular politics. Even as the revolution raged, middle-class Mexicans were far from the "passive and apathetic sector" they have often been made out to be. Through their claims making, concludes Eineigel, Mexico City's middle class "expanded the public sphere to incorporate the traditionally marginalized pueblo," and in doing so "took part in the postrevolutionary moral economy, in which citizens demanded rights and goods."

These arguments bespeak a nuanced historical understanding of a tumultuous postrevolutionary situation that encouraged disparate social groups to make themselves heard. They also raise critical questions. Although it is true that middle-class claims making helped expand the public sphere, the role of middle-class Mexicans themselves in this expansion remains to be fleshed out. Many social groups also learned to express themselves during the decades following 1920, including unions, workers, migrants, peasants, and others galvanized by revolutionary promises of social justice. It is not entirely clear from Eineigel's argument how far middle-class Mexicans were willing to go in "incorporating" the "pueblo" into political discourse, and on what terms. What Eineigel's argument does make clear is how much more we must know to understand the collision and convergence of competing claims and the way their articulation enlarged the public sphere after 1920 or so, when the bullets had stopped flying so thickly. This may be especially crucial for Eineigel's emerging middle class, since conventional accounts tend to assume that middle-class agency follows naturally from processes of modernization. It would seem important, thus, to know which middle-class demands complemented, and which were in tension with, the demands of other groups. For instance, while urban services such as lighting, paving, housing, markets, and trams seem to affect broader, citywide interests, it is likely that middle-class efforts to obtain the services were oriented to neighborhoods in the process of becoming middle class, rather than at working-class or poor *colonias*. How, then, did middle-class demands for modern city services—in many ways a normal and natural part of middle-class engagement with the public sphere—relate to demands made by groups underserved by those same services? Do demands for these services by the middle class necessarily mean they sought to incorporate marginal sectors more fully into the life of the nation?

This question, in turn, raises others. Just how was the public sphere being broadened? Was it chiefly discursive? Was it simply additive—in the sense that the sphere expanded as the clamor for benefits grew—or was a more intricate mechanism at work? In this regard, it is worth noting that in Eineigel's account, middle-class claims makers almost invariably limited themselves to asking for what "modernity" entitled them to—paved streets, public lighting, efficient trams, modern markets, and properly staffed schools. This suggests that those who were advancing middle-class interests were able to make their case more easily than workers seeking certain social goods rather than others, precisely because as a "modern" class they could appeal to the transnational discourse of modernity more readily than poor workers could. Claims to better wages and working conditions, and better access to state mediation, can also be seen as modern. Yet compared to the technological and infrastructural manifestations of modernity, which supposedly benefited all, such demands could seem narrow and self-serving. Middle-class politicking doubtless pushed the revolutionary Mexican state to make good on a narrow modernizing agenda. But we are left to wonder whether such claims, bolstered by the transnational discourse on which middle-class people drew to articulate their claims, were but a stand-in for the common good mediated by state-driven modernization. If so, middle-class politics may not only have broadened the public sphere but also have limited, channeled, and shaped it, by reinforcing the state's ability to delegitimize and absorb a more combative, confrontational working-class politics.

Iñigo García-Bryce's chapter on Peru suggests that Víctor Raúl Haya de la Torre understood this dilemma and sought to confront it by combining the rhetorics of anti-imperialism and modernity to connect the middle and working classes politically and ideologically through the American Popular Revolutionary Alliance (APRA). For a time, Haya succeeded in leading important elements of the middle class along this path by insisting that through APRA middle-class Peruvians might play an even more influential, and more conciliatory, role in their country than the middle classes had in the United States or

Europe. In those places, claimed Haya, the middle classes had been locked into a lower position by the "bourgeois class." In Peru, which had no such class to speak of, the middle class would have a greater field of action. Indeed, but for imperialism, concluded Haya, the Peruvian middle class could have become a national bourgeoisie in its own right. The struggle against imperialism was tantamount to a struggle for upward mobility that was simultaneously a bid for class harmony: although in Europe class politics had produced only conflict, in Peru it would produce harmony, enabling the country to modernize more quickly—an interesting reinterpretation of the middle class as the flywheel of capitalist societies always threatened by social imbalances.

It is hard to know what to make of Haya's argument, and harder still to guess what middle-class Apristas and others thought of it. There is no denying its superficial appeal: a class politics that allowed reformism against the rich, producing a national bourgeoisie linked to rather than alienated from a beset working class. Yet middle-class Limeños in particular may have been more ambivalent than García-Bryce suggests. Many benefited from an imperial corporate presence, as employees of foreign firms, or in private and public bureaucracies crucial to the functioning of a dependent national economy. Others may not have shared Haya's confidence in reformist measures. Still others may have recoiled from being likened to manual workers. To make better sense of what was happening in mid-twentieth-century Peru, we would need to know more about how these tensions played themselves out in everyday lives and politics.

Though García-Bryce does not address this issue directly, his conclusion makes a crucial point. As David Parker has noted, when in the late 1940s APRA sought to play down class differences between white-collar workers and manual laborers, the middle-class relationship to APRA began to unravel. Members bolted flagship organizations, unwilling to be reduced to working-class status for political purposes. The irony, as García-Bryce notes, is that by the 1950s, APRA's appeal focused on a "new middle class" identified rhetorically as upwardly mobile mestizos and unionized workers. Ideologically and strategically, this made a certain sense. By the late 1930s, as Parker has shown, "the idea of the middle class had become an overtly political idea." As such, it was open to manipulation and to struggle over the boundaries of the category.[1] Nor could it any longer be appealed to, or believed in, as a transnational idea apart from or even above the workings of local class politics.

This brings key issues into stark relief. García-Bryce says little about whether working-class people really took up APRA's offer of middle-class status or, if they did, whether they retained a working-class identity at the same time. Without some understanding of this, it is hard to judge the political effects of the rhetorical change. We have to recall as well that APRA's redefinition of the middle class to include manual workers meant that "traditional" white-collar and professional employees who had made up the Aprista middle class during earlier decades were losing control of their own class discourse and its connection to politics and ideology. Many of these people could not find themselves in the new rhetoric and left the organization. Did they simply cede the term "middle class," seek other means to reclaim it, or try harder to assimilate to the upper classes? Although these are open questions, one thing is beyond doubt: APRA's ideological appropriation of the middle-class discourse demonstrated for all to see just how rhetorically unstable the label could be.

In a very different way, the instability of the middle-class label is at the heart of Keith Watenpaugh's chapter on non-Muslim elements of the Syrian middle class in the 1920s and 1930s. Watenpaugh refers to "middle-class modernity" as the condition of Aleppo's non-Muslim middle class, people who lived by the idea that "to be modern means to be not like, but just as modern as, the imagined, idealized middle class." This is no less true of middle-class Mexicans or Peruvians, but there is a particular twist in Syria: Aleppo was a place divided along sharp sectarian lines, between Muslims and non-Muslims. The core of Watenpaugh's analysis is his discussion of Edmond Rabbath, a non-Muslim Arab who sought to combine middle-class modernity with Syrian national identity during the 1930s. Rabbath appealed to Muslims by arguing that non-Muslims could accept a religious state, and to non-Muslims by offering them a place in a Syrian nationality that could free itself from the French Mandate. Rabbath charged that the French had overdrawn sectarian divisions in order to facilitate their rule, and he insisted that a modern Arab identity shared by Muslims and non-Muslims could create the basis for a national community rooted in Islam's natural religious tolerance. Ultimately, says Watenpaugh, this project failed. Rabbath's middle-class ideas, anchored in "the rule of law and the logos of modernity," came up against the "politics of notables," organized around notions of clan and descent from the Prophet Muhammad. Rabbath could neither persuade Sunnis to accept limitations on religion's role in the polity, nor non-Muslims to accept Islam's cultural dominance in society—the only way, he argued, for Syria to confront French colonialism.

From his understanding of Rabbath's political impasse, Watenpaugh derives what he calls a "conceptual axiom" regarding the middle class. Middle-class people like Rabbath have been expert in forming and sustaining, or at least imagining, the institutions of civil society—whether in Europe, Peru, Mexico, or Syria. What differs are the circumstances in which the performance of that expertise is expressed. In Syria, the bonds of religion, ethnicity, and family were stronger than the attractions of an abstract "middle-class modernity." For Rabbath and other middle-class non-Muslims, modernity represented a place of discursive power from which to challenge their marginalization in a society of religious divisions. But they did not control the state, and for those who did, the modernizing idea, far from an objective fact of progress, seemed little more than politics from a particular perspective. This "weakness," concludes Watenpaugh, "made the individual members of the middle class vulnerable to forms of cultural and economic cooptation by colonialist, conservative, and authoritarian elites."

Watenpaugh is on to something here, though it is unclear how non-Muslim middle-class Syrians faced their situation. With the collapse of his project, Rabbath left for Lebanon, never returning to Syria. Most non-Muslim middle-class Aleppans would not have been able to do the same. How did they cope with the failure that Watenpaugh describes? Did they close ranks and cling to a secular middle-class identity through the Aleppo Club? Did they bemoan Rabbath's failure, or see his effort as idiosyncratic and doomed to failure? Watenpaugh's conclusion also poses questions regarding a Muslim middle class, represented by Saallah al-Jabiri. Did they uniformly oppose Rabbath's ideas, or did some see virtues in his approach? Did they think of themselves as Muslims and as middle class, or were these labels thought to be irreconcilable? Was there no space for compromise? Was there, finally, any middle-class role on a political stage where dominant notions of identity tended to cut across the appeal of modernity from a sectarian, rather than class, perspective?

At the end of the day, these questions beg the larger riddle that has dogged the study of the middle class for much of its history: to what extent has the middle class been "real," and to what extent only a discursive construction serving particular and concrete political purposes in class-divided (or class-dividing) societies? This was the point raised years ago by Dror Wahrman in his study of English middle-class discourse in the late eighteenth century and the early nineteenth.[2] Although Wahrman gave up too much to discourse in his analysis, his point regarding the interplay between language and social reality is a sharp reminder of just how complex the historical analysis of middle-class lives can be.

Indeed, the tension between discourse and experience signals a central issue in scholarly efforts to understand middle-classness. In terms of social class, perhaps no other social group has been as dependent on self-referential language for a conception of itself as the middle class has. Without any particular need for a rhetoric of their own existence in capitalist societies, the rich can easily relate their experience to their position in a social order organized around money and its circulation. For their part, the working industrial poor, such as Torquato's shoe factory workers, could understand intuitively that they occupied a subordinate position in a capitalist society (though they did not necessarily draw any particular political conclusions from this fact). Both groups can ultimately accept, or at least recognize, class labels for what appeared to them to be certain hard facts of social reality (which is not to say that they always spoke of themselves in such terms). There is no denying that the idea and discourse of the middle class contributed to the identities of those above and those below through the period of intense modernization in the nineteenth and twentieth centuries. And although middle-class people have been obsessed with money and work, their place in capitalist societies has been chiefly a matter of the ideological and structural role they have played as the balance wheel of social orders fractured by class differences.

In different ways, the three chapters here demonstrate this fact, even as they reveal how tenuous a proposition the middle class has been in political, ideological, and methodological terms. Members of Mexico City's middle class expanded the public sphere but limited their claims to what modernity's script prescribed for them. Elements of the Peruvian middle class initially accepted APRA's linking them to the working class, only to find at the end that they had lost control of their own name. In Syria, Rabbath struggled to articulate a position for a non-Muslim middle class but ran up against a political power with no interest in "middle-class modernity." At every turn, the middle class is most fragile where social identity intersects with political power.

One aspect of this insight is to realize that the middle class has represented modernity's best account of itself, an account in constant tension with the experience of those whose lives have unfolded amid the competition, mobility, large systems, and inequality of capitalist modernity. From this vantage, the middle class has embodied and expressed a discourse that was drawn into being by the very fact of a class politics that could not acknowledge its own existence. The middle class took on social and sociological reality from the depths of this politics of implicit negation.[3] And capitalist societies, like all other societies aspiring to long-term stability, demand adherence to a principle of harmony, or at least of social peace, lest they succumb to their own excesses. The middle class is that principle transformed into lived reality.

So it is, as Torquato notes, that the middle class is the class that must always exist. Without it, the politics of modernity, lacking a clear theory of the common good, might reveal itself for little more than a naked play of interests, and no system can long survive the revelation of its own worst self. This hints at a deep truth about the "middle class," one that was present at its birth: the idea of the middle class has always obscured the operations of power in capitalist modernity. This may be why middle-class people have so often found themselves brought up short by politics.[4] As these chapters show, middle-class people have felt the tug of confrontational politics. More tightly than has been the case with other groups, arguably, their very identity constrained them to act in ways that limited political conflict to the sphere of what modernity could allow without disrupting its own operations. In this view, middle-class "politics" has been less about a specific ideology than about the tension at the very core of how modern societies should govern themselves. "Democratic," or at least some notion of inclusive participation, represented the main fault line of political struggle in places like Mexico and Peru (and elsewhere in the West) throughout the twentieth century precisely because the fractures of class produced by competitive social orders undermined social peace, making political inclusion dangerous.[5] The alternative was a discourse rooted in some principle of order beyond politics itself, the case Watenpaugh describes for Aleppo.

Such a view requires no vast conspiracy by way of explanation. Nor do we have to attribute agency to modernity. Rather, as these chapters and others in this volume argue, we must recognize the complex ways modern societies have reproduced and sustained themselves through the actions and utterances of middle-class people, who—perhaps more nakedly than others—have stood at the volatile point of encounter between highly localized politics and the discourses and realities of transnational modernity.

Notes

1. D. Parker, *The Idea of the Middle Class*, 183.

2. Wahrman, *Imagining the Middle Class.*

3. The middle class, in other words, is a socially constructed object: the idea of the thing, the discourse about the thing, and the thing itself are ontologically inseparable. This is a qualification of the point that the middle class is, at bottom, nothing more than a discursive construct. In this view, discourse is constitutive of social reality.

4. Through bureaucracies and policymaking, middle-class people have often had a deep influence on the conditions of political debate in modernizing societies, even as they often thought of themselves as acting apolitically, or politically in way that rose above the cruder politics of sectoral interest. See Mehrtens, *Urban Space and National Identity in Early Twentieth Century São Paulo, Brazil*; López, *Makers of Democracy*; Owensby, *Intimate Ironies*.

5. This has been true even when openness and democracy have been denied. Consider, for instance, the lengths to which the Brazilian military regimes of the 1970s and 1980s went to maintain a facade of democratic process.

PART IV

Middle-Class Politics and the Making of the Public Sphere

The City as a Field of Female Civic Action

WOMEN AND MIDDLE-CLASS FORMATION IN NINETEENTH-CENTURY GERMANY

Gisela Mettele

On December 26, 1867, Therese Schaaffhausen died in Cologne at the age of ninety. The obituary published by her descendants has the following to say about her: "It was those truly rare qualities of heart and mind, the upright and religious life she led, her unflagging, considerate and strongly supportive dedication to all that was beneficial and to the common good that earned our dear departed one the undivided affection and respect of all those circles with whom she came into contact during her long and active life."[1]

The circles with which Therese Schaaffhausen had been associated all her life were quite obviously not limited to the family. Her descendants particularly emphasize her commitment to the "common good," which had earned her such distinction as a good citizen of her city. In 1800, Therese deMaes had moved from the Dutch town of Roermond to Cologne, where she married Abraham Schaaffhausen, a banker and merchant. In 1814, she first took an active part in Cologne's civic affairs, joining the patriotic women's association. Ten years later, she collected money for the Greek War of Liberation. She became one of the founders of the Cologne Association for Poor Girls' Schools and served as its chair until 1859. She had also belonged to the city's Arts Society, beginning at its foundation in 1838. And as a widow, she was a financial benefactor of Cologne's new theater.[2]

The impressive range of her public activities is not typical of all women of her time, but neither was Therese Schaaffhausen an isolated case. Indeed, the scope of her activities exemplifies the spectrum of the public involvement of German middle-class women during the nineteenth century. This chapter will examine the role that these female public activities played within the general context of an emerging civil society that was itself unfolding first and foremost as an increasingly tight-knit network of voluntary associations. In particular, I argue that the women's associations, through their specific forms of interaction, contributed to an essentially democratic civic activism.[3]

The activities of middle-class women were significant because the project of civil society in Germany, until the end of the nineteenth century, was closely connected to the culture and aspirations of the middle class. The reality of women's lives in other social classes was quite different, both as far as their specific social background was concerned and with regard to the opportunities women had to express themselves in public. The class bias of civil society remained intact for a long time during the nineteenth century, and this holds true even for a gender-sensitive notion of civil society.

The City and Civil Society

For several reasons, this chapter uses a local—more specifically, an urban—perspective. First, it was in the cities that those new forms of communication and interaction that led to the development of a civil society were initially established. In nineteenth-century Germany, citizens' primary field of action was the city. The middle class was for the most part not involved in the governmental decision-making processes, yet its members did not withdraw into private domestic life. It was in the domain of the city that they took their affairs into their own hands. Indeed, for liberals, the city even became the prototype for civil society as a whole. Within a local framework, the middle class demanded the right of cultural and political self-determination and in the process gained the self-confidence to demand a voice in structuring the state and the wider society as well. Hence activities on the local level were not necessarily parochial but rather served as local manifestations of issues of national significance.[4] Second, the shift of perspective from the nation to the city is significant precisely with regard to women, since they were primarily active on a local level.[5] And third, a perspective on civil society that refers back to the community may be more adaptable than a national perspective to current questions concerning the transnational or global significance of civil society. Since this perspective puts the focus on agency and active participation rather than on institutions, it points toward the possibility of a multi-layered conceptualization of citizenship that loosens its ties with the nation-state.

Citizenship and Personal Independence

According to Immanuel Kant's famous definition, a citizen is "he who has been enfranchised." The "sole" prerequisite for this, "aside from the natural one (that he not be a child, nor a woman)," was "that he be his own lord and master . . . , which is to say, own some form of property . . . which provides for his subsistence."[6] Explicitly, this is a deeply gendered notion of citizenship. For Kant as for his contemporaries, personal independence was the decisive criterion for participation with other citizens in self-government. It established the middle-class male as a mature individual and responsible political subject. Since women were economically and legally dependent, they were—"naturally," as Kant put it—excluded from political participation and the institutional nexus. The German liberal constitutional movement believed in a broad integration of politically and socially disadvantaged lower-class men into what Lothar Gall calls a future "classless society of middle-income bracket citizens"—of course not instantly, but by improving their conditions up to the point where they could meet the requirements of independent heads of households.[7] As far as women were concerned, however, there was no comparable anticipation of eventual emancipation and integration. Enfranchising women was not even included on the long-term liberal agenda.[8] Citizenship and civil society were not universal projects in the first place; the referent for the "free and individual actor" was always the independent paterfamilias, and this was not a hidden agenda but taken for granted by Kant and his contemporaries.[9] Thus, at the core of the concept of civil society in nineteenth-century Germany was the abstract notion not of single males, but of families whose male heads represented the entire household in the political sphere.[10]

In middle-class political ideology, men's and women's worlds constituted two separate spheres, but in the everyday reality of city life, women's experience did not necessarily conform to this conceptual model. Actual relations between the sexes deviated from the normative ideals of liberal middle-class theorists. The lack of formal, political rights by no means prevented women from becoming involved in the emerging middle-class public sphere.[11] Indeed, one might argue that women's actions helped to create this sphere. Thus I want to propose a broader concept of personal independence, based on agency and the autonomy that derives from it. In accordance with Ruth Lister and others, I want to conceptualize citizenship not only as a status but also as a practice that considers the interests of the wider community.[12] Full citizenship would have to include both status and practice. But since status can develop out of practice, it seems justifiable to focus on practice first, especially in an attempt to create a more inclusive notion of citizenship.

Free Association and Civic Spirit

In the nineteenth century, the idea of "civic spirit" stood at the center of German discourse on civil society. This key slogan referred not only to political self-determination but also, in a practical sense, to the commitment to supra-individual goals and tasks—in other words, to a sense of civic duty. This meant a concept of life that was not limited to professional or materialistic interests but that also found its expression in participation in society and orientation toward the "common good," which was always defined within the confines of a middle-class perspective on reality. Only thus was it possible to prove one's citizenship in relation to what was understood by the notion at the time.

The concept of "civic spirit" had strong roots in a tradition of civic republicanism in German cities that was marked by a cooperative spirit. It was based on the self-government and self-regulation of a political community composed of independent heads of households with equal rights.[13] In the nineteenth century the concept became a byword for those traditions, reinterpreted in an emancipatory manner. In particular, activities in voluntary associations became a characteristic of true civic spirit.[14] The principle behind the concept of association was the notion of self-organization, and hence self-determination. Through its emphasis on voluntary participation, the concept of civic spirit directly opposed both the paternalistic or bureaucratic state and the traditional corporate structure of society. Society, according to the new middle-class ideal, should be formed by the free association of (male) equals, without regard to their social status, origin, or occupation. This was obviously a somewhat idealistic notion, but it nevertheless represented a powerful mental concept that held huge potential for dynamism and adaptability.

In the nineteenth century, associations became a main structural principle of society and the crucial arenas where the middle class's claim to social emancipation unfolded and new forms of social interaction were developed. As Thomas Nipperdey has noted, "all middle-class activity was organized in voluntary associations."[15] Concert associations held regular musical performances; municipal theaters were often financed and run by theater societies; art societies organized exhibitions and supported artists by purchasing their works.

Important art galleries and museums, orchestras, and theaters emerged from these activities of the urban middle class. Numerous social, economic, and political reform initiatives were carried out by associations, or at least initiated and partly financed by them, creating institutions such as hospitals and institutes for the deaf and dumb.[16]

The activities of the individual associations were not isolated from one another, but formed a kind of network. Members of different associations in a city formed tight-knit personal connections and frequently interacted with one another in a variety of associational and social contexts. This close social contact guaranteed middle-class cohesion and made the abstract term "civil society" something that citizens could experience firsthand in their daily lives, which underlined their right to social emancipation. Even if the associations did not pursue any clear political goals, their structure alone—with internal elections, set rules of procedure for speaking at meetings; and the postulated openness to members regardless of social status—served as the model of a future society.[17]

Women in "General" Associations

In contrast to the female-dominated informal sociability in private middle-class homes, the more formal associations, clubs, and societies were formed to a large extent as part of male culture. Even though the practice of open houses continued to a certain extent in the nineteenth century, it ceded its dominant role in the building of a civil society to the associations.[18] Women were granted limited membership in some theater and art societies, and also in some choral societies, where female participation was desirable if only for purely musical reasons—to increase, as one source says, the "diversity" of the singing.[19] As a rule, however, the female members did not possess the same rights to vote as the men did, nor did the women have any direct influence in matters relating to the associations themselves. With respect to women's participation, the "general" associations can be divided into two groups: those intended to promote moral and aesthetic refinement and the ennoblement of life, which allowed women to be involved to a certain degree; and those seen as a place for informal social interaction free from social constraints, a counterbalance to an increasingly formal and more refined middle-class life, which would not accept the presence of women. Here the "fraternal bonds underpinning civil society"[20] become most apparent. The same was true with Masonic sociability, where male friendship and bonding were at the center of the members' activities.[21]

Another reason for women's limited participation in the "general" associations was that the activities of these groups were always connected with money. The establishment of a club, the purchase of a piano, or the cost of construction of a theater was mostly financed by the members of the association. But married women had very limited opportunity to own any property in the nineteenth century. For that reason alone, the participation of women was mostly restricted to some wealthy widows and single women. Thus the "general" associations remained, in most cases, men's clubs.[22]

Women were also absent when things turned political, because in the eyes of the middle class in the nineteenth century, politics was a matter for men. This can be seen in the case of most of the liberal and middle-class democratic associations that arose during and after the 1848 Revolution, all of which barred female members.[23] Only the republican-socialist associations and some dissenting religious groups opened their doors to full female membership.[24] After the revolution, public female political activity was often banned, as for example in Prussia by the 1850 association law. It was not until 1908 that German law permitted female membership in political associations.

Women's Associations

At an early date, women began organizing themselves in their own voluntary associations. The work of women's organizations was usually associated with charity. In the area of social welfare in particular, women developed a broad spectrum of activities in the nineteenth century, beginning in 1813–14, with patriotic women's associations, maternal care associations, poor girls' schools, and the like.[25] Charity work is a classic example of the tasks assigned to women, but in the nineteenth century it was also a main concern of the emerging civil society. Throughout the century, care for the poor was an important part of local self-government. In some cities poor-law administration even formed the largest municipal department. The urban welfare system had its roots in the traditions of the early modern city. In the nineteenth century, charity became regarded as an expression of "civic spirit" and of the middle-class capacity to organize civil society independent of the state. The state's influence was seen as an infringement on citizens' freedom, and until the state took over welfare responsibilities around the end of the nineteenth century, poor-law administration in Germany remained largely within the purview of local authorities.[26] Through their specific welfare activities, middle-class women not only participated in the building of civil society, but by adding the needs of women and children to the agenda of communal charity, and by generating and implementing specific welfare policies, they also expanded and transformed the way it looked.[27]

Voluntary social work by female citizens was not linked, as it was for male citizens, to any political rights or positions within institutions of local self-government, yet in the charitable societies, women acquired public influence that they otherwise would not have had in the middle-class public sphere. In this way, the boundaries between private and public became blurred. Moreover, through their associations, middle-class women often acquired social power over women of the lower classes. Indeed, it can even be said that women's charity was an important and constituent part of middle-class domination in the cities.[28] If civil society is both a sphere of emancipation and, as Antonio Gramsci has argued, the arena in which cultural and social hegemony is contested, women's charitable associations are a prime example of the middle-class struggle for emancipation and domination—acted out in the language of the "common good."

Being active for the common good of the community—as the members of the middle class understood it—was the ultimate goal of the women's associations. They were organized along the same lines as the "general" associations of the time, with statutes, internal elections, and set rules of procedure for meetings. In the Cologne's Poor Girls School Association (CPGSA), which I take here as an example of women's multifaceted charity activities, women who wished to join had to be nominated by two members and accepted on the basis of a simple majority vote. The president and executive committee were elected for two-year terms. Each member was authorized to enter proposals and motions, and resolutions were passed by a majority vote.[29]

The statutes of most women's associations were cast in broadly inclusive terms, commonly welcoming "all well-intentioned fellow lady citizens" to participate. However, the social openness of the women's associations existed in theory more often than in practice. Just like most "general" associations, the women's associations were characterized by a considerable measure of social exclusivity.[30] The social spectrum of the members remained limited, with most usually from the upper middle class or (to a lesser extent) the educated middle class. This combination of inclusive rhetoric and exclusive reality, which was so typical of civil society in the nineteenth century, had its reflection in the women's associations as well. In merchant cities like Cologne, for example, women from the wealthiest merchant families dominated the associations,[31] and, not surprisingly, the women acted primarily as members of their class, not on the basis of universal female solidarity.[32]

Within their associations, these women defined their own goals and were responsible for all aspects of associational life. In the CPGSA, for example, the women oversaw all aspects of the schools' organization and handled inspections, bookkeeping and accounting. They saw to the maintenance and renewal of furniture, equipment and materials as well as procurement of clothing for the girls. In addition, they took the liberty of making personal visits to parents, claiming the right, "in the event of recurring mistakes by children or negligence on the part of the parents the association . . . [to] summon the children and the parents to the monthly association meetings."[33] This is but one example of the ways in which middle-class women exercised social power over lower-class women (and men).

The CPGSA depended on private donations to keep up the schools. Since most women owned no property, there was no provision for membership fees, but members were bound by the statutes to support the association's work through voluntary contributions.[34] Therese Schaaffhausen, for example, donated a thousand thalers to the CPGSA in 1841 and left the same amount to the association in her will.[35] To secure the continuous inflow of funds, women's associations actively sought money from outside sources and thus developed a new form of civic fundraising culture. Members of the CPGSA, for example, collected money from friends and acquaintances and organized benefit concerts, charity balls, and raffles of women's handicraft work.[36] They launched calls for donations in the city's newspapers, which usually met with considerable success. In addition to donations from private individuals, they often also received contributions from other associations, such as the Cologne Freemason's Lodge and the music lovers society, which donated the proceeds from a concert.[37] These exchanges reveal how closely women worked together with their male fellow citizens and the extent to which the men acknowledged their work. This in turn calls into question some historians' assumptions of a separate women's political culture arising from women's public activities.[38] Indeed, the women's success depended on their close integration into a network of personal relations, friendships, and kinship within the middle classes. Far from trying to create a separate female counterculture, these women collaborated with their male counterparts in establishing a common civic culture.

Women's methods of financing their own work had been tried and proven since 1813–14, the first time they took sides by establishing associations of "Patriotic Women and Maidens." Associations by this name were founded in many German cities in the course of the so-called Wars of Liberation in order to ensure that volunteers had the necessary equipment to care for wounded soldiers. Records indicate that there were 258 such associations in Prussia alone.[39] It was not until the 1830s that the number of newly founded "general" associations reached a similar peak.

Women's work within the patriotic associations expanded the horizons of individual women well beyond the city walls. Although the projects were local, in outlook they were national. Women spoke the language of charity but often shared the anti-French tone of the German nationalist movement, a tone that was becoming increasingly aggressive. One published announcement of the Cologne Association of Patriotic Women and Maidens from October 1813 stated: "In the battle for Freedom and Fatherland . . . the unruly, perfidious and notorious French people shall be trodden underfoot once and for all by obedience, loyalty and steadfast courage."[40] Here the women were speaking in a clearly politicized language; they saw themselves as part of the German nationalist movement, and the women's associations of 1813–14 can be regarded as among its first organizations. Women were also involved in the aggressive anti-French course taken by this movement and in the close linking of the idea of a German nation and war, a linkage that would continue to play a role in German history.

Only a few years later, the organizational experiences that women had acquired in the Wars of Liberation led to renewed sociopolitical commitment. When the liberal Leipzig University Professor Wilhelm Traugott Krug launched the first public appeal for support for the Greek cause in 1821, the response was overwhelming. In August 1821, the *Augsburger Allgemeine* reported the great success of the campaign, noting that women in particular had quickly organized themselves in groups "after the model of those who saw the birth of the German war of liberation."[41] The philhellenic movement was to become the broadest social movement in Germany in the period between the Carlsbad Decrees (1819) and the French July Revolution (1830).[42] As the historian Christoph Hauser has pointed out, German support for the Greek struggle for freedom against the Ottoman Empire was also an expression of the Germans' own aspirations for freedom, which—under the repressive conditions of the *Vormärz*—could only be expressed covertly with regard to a situation outside Germany.[43] The philhellenic movement, like support for the Polish liberation struggles that followed in 1830–31, relied heavily on women, and through their associations women continued to play an active role in liberal politics.[44] To the extent that scholars acknowledge female participation at all, they usually regard women's philhellenic associations as having purely humanitarian motives and thus exclude them from the political context. Although closer examination reveals that the arguments advanced by men were not much more "political" than those of women, historians attribute the lack of explicitly political arguments in the men's philhellenic associations—but not in the women's—to the conditions of censorship.[45] Here clearly the argument becomes somewhat tautological. In applying a double standard to male and female actions, scholars define women out of the political context. As Jean Quataert points out, "only male actions are considered as political and through this prism, nationalism indeed becomes a debate among German men."[46] Thus scholars fail to analyze women's role in shaping civic identity.

But regardless of how one wishes to assess the fact that women's work was "limited" to providing humanitarian aid, their involvement meant taking a stand—and a public one at that—on a contemporary political event. Before becoming actively involved in a cause as far removed from their own lives as the Greek or Polish struggle for freedom seemed to be, these women had to participate in the middle-class public sphere by, for example, reading the newspaper. It can therefore be assumed that the women were just as (well or poorly) informed about the overall context of solidarity with Greece as were their male contemporaries. The activities of Cologne's philhellenic women met with considerable financial success. Several Cologne associations made donations to the cause, and the painter Katz put the earnings from an art exhibition at their disposal. In addition, donations came from nearby communities, funds were raised by private individuals, and the net proceeds from a concert organized by a singing club were donated as well. The largest share of the funds received came from the proceeds of the raffle of women's handicraft work.[47]

German involvement ultimately had no impact on the outcome of the struggle for liberation in Greece or in Poland, but it was significant as the expression of middle-class self-organization vis-à-vis the state: "Overshadowed by the bans . . . in the crypto- and semipolitical sphere," Nipperdey has noted, "the middle-class movement and public sphere nevertheless managed to establish themselves."[48] What Wolfgang Hardtwig terms the "latent politicization" of society that was generated by philhellenism consisted for the most part of the experiences that were acquired in the organizations themselves.[49] To a large extent, it was women who had these experiences.

In Cologne many of the women who were active in the Association of Patriotic Women and Maidens in 1813–14 also participated in the philhellenic movement some years later. Women's civic engagement was thus too diverse to warrant the general conclusion, articulated by Nancy Reagin and others, that the middle-class women's movement in nineteenth-century Germany was politically conservative.[50] This assessment does not do justice to the complex mix of traditional and modern elements in women's activities, and in German civil society more generally, during the nineteenth century.

Conclusion: Associational Culture and Female Civic Virtues

If we take as a given the fact that civil society presents itself through the context of the actions of such social constellations, the women's associations are a prime example of the process through which civil society constituted itself. For women and men alike, sociability was an important catalyst in the process of developing civic awareness. Through their associations, women learned the civil society's grammar of conduct: self-organization, self-determination, orientation toward the common good. And they attached great value to the forms of social interaction associated with civil society: a democratic internal organization, refined discourse, and the purported openness of doors and activities to all classes of society.

Women's associations were not inward-turning circles that simply adopted a self-satisfied attitude; instead, they brought their influence to bear in strong measure on the society in which their members lived. Women's public activities profoundly influenced their cities in many ways, whether through the sociopolitical impact of the activities themselves or the events that were necessary to finance these activities, such as raffles, concerts, and balls. Women accumulated organizational experience and experience in dealing with the public. They confidently inserted themselves into a framework of public action and had no qualms about regularly launching public appeals. However, as the annual reports they published in local newspapers reveal, their self-confidence in demanding the support of their fellow citizens was matched by the sense of responsibility they felt toward them. The women's associations were integrated into the social network that constituted the city's public life, and with their work the women gained the recognition of their fellow citizens. They understood themselves to be participating in the establishment of a common civic culture, not creating a separate female counterculture.

Women's activities usually met with broad-based support, and criticism was rare. Thus it was unusual when, in 1815, the *Westfälischer Anzeiger*, the daily newspaper of Westphalia, denounced women's patriotic involvement on the grounds that "it is only appropriate for German women to work for the good cause quietly, modestly and unassumingly."[51] The women defended themselves with spirit:

> Would it be disgraceful to do good only in order to conceal it? Should the better of us consort with those who work in the shadows? . . . No, when the house is on fire we are not afraid to pull out the hoses in public, and to climb on the roof for everyone to see; and when the fatherland is in danger, we have no reservations about taking our place shoulder to shoulder with others to save the day under the eye of our fellow citizens. Soldier with soldier in the field, men's federation with men's federation at home, women's association with women's association.[52]

Both women and men did their civic duty in a specific way, according to their own understanding of themselves and their roles. Thus I would like to propose a concept of civil society that is based on a plurality of families in which patresfamilias and matresfamilias both had public duties to fulfill. As male householders' sense of community expanded in the course of the unfolding civil society, so did that of women, who transformed their identity as housewives into a concept of civic motherhood.[53] This is not to say that there were no gender differences; indeed, these were deeply inscribed into the associational culture of nineteenth-century civil society. But within, and through, their own associations, women nevertheless participated in shaping civil society. Their associations were important in the processes of collective and individual identity formation as citizens, and in the associations, women built up reservoirs of social capital—shared beliefs and values. Moreover, we should understand civil society not only as social practice but also as the process of learning a particular form of social behavior. By taking part in the associational life, women developed the habit of working together for common purposes and learned to see with a collective vision. And they learned to take for granted the citizen's right to participate in the polity. The social attachments, the codes of conduct, and the public distinction that the associations provided supported the self-respect that gave rise to a strong sense of individual agency. Women might not have had the legal status of citizens, but they acted as citizens and thus fulfilled the potential of that status: personal independence.[54]

As the historian Nancy Isenberg reminds us, middle-class women did not encounter difficulties in becoming publicly active; rather, they had to contend with a political culture that defined their public activities as essentially and necessarily nonpolitical. Although their significant contributions to civil society through charitable associations were widely recognized by their male fellow citizens, women could not assume that this would turn them into political agents.[55] Nevertheless, the lines between charity and rights of citizenship began to blur, and by the end of the nineteenth century, women were making political demands based on their activities. Middle-class feminists argued that women's work in welfare associations gave them the right to vote and hold municipal posts; indeed, they argued, honorary activity in the local welfare system qualified women as citizens with independent political rights. In 1904, the feminist and politician Helene Lange asked: "Why [is] the topic 'the woman as a citizen' . . . of practical interest today[?] The answer would be: because today the woman actually is a citizen; because the woman . . . has already begun in the area of social work to take on board those tasks that officially fall to society as a whole . . . If this development is to be a blessing for herself and society at large, then the system of laws for public life must also acknowledge her as a citizen."[56] Lange's argument sums up what the concept of citizenship meant to her contemporaries even at the beginning of the twentieth century: independence in a material, but also in a figurative, sense that is proved by honorary work for the common good and that bestows the right to a voice in the political decision-making processes. In other words, since women were already performing the duties of citizens, they deserved the formal status of citizenship.

Notes

1. Document 1296, number of file, C 10, Family archives Schaaffhausen Best, Historical Archives of the City of Cologne, Cologne, Germany. (This archive will be designated as "HASTK.") All translations are mine unless otherwise noted.

2. Ibid.

3. An extensive review of the literature on women's associations in the nineteenth century can be found in Huber-Sperl, *Organisiert und engagiert.*

4. The importance of the local level for the self-mobilization of German civil society is commonly assumed by scholars of the German middle classes. See, for example, Nolte, *Gemeindebürgertum und Liberalismus in Baden 1800–1850*; Kaschuba, "Zwischen deutscher Nation und deutscher Provinz."

5. For a recent overview of women's history, see von Saldern, "Die Stadt und ihre Frauen." See also Wolff, *"Stadtmütter."* For an examination of the patterns of German women's publicly taking sides in the different political framework of American society, see Ortlepp, *"Auf denn, Ihr Schwestern!"*

6. Kant, *Vom Verhältnis der Theorie zur Praxis im Staatsrecht*, 7:295. See also, for example, Walzer, *Toward a Global Civil Society*; Pettman, "Globalisation and the Gendered Politics of Citizenship"; Christidoulidis, *Communitarianism and Citizenship.*

7. Gall, *Liberalismus und "bürgerliche Gesellschaft,"* 176. See also 162–86.

8. See Andrea Löther, *Unpolitische Bürgerin*, 239–73; and Spree, *Die verhinderte "Bürgerin"?* 274–308; Opitz, Weckel, and Kleinau, *Tugend, Vernunft und Gefühl*; Ursula Vogel, "Patriarchale Herrschaft, bürgerliches Recht, bürgerliche Utopie."

9. See Appelt, *Geschlecht, Staatsbürgerschaft, Nation*, 61–72; Pateman, *The Sexual Contract*; Elshtain, *Public Man, Private Woman*, chapter 3. On the gendered notions of citizenship in the twentieth century, see the special issue by Kathleen Canning and Sonya O. Rose, eds., "Gender, Citizenship and Subjectivities," in *Gender & History* 13, no. 3 (2001).

10. Gall, *Liberalismus und "bürgerliche Gesellschaft,"* 176.

11. The separation of public and private spheres has a long orthodoxy in nineteenth-century women's history, which has been questioned and considerably qualified in recent years. References to this literature can be found in Rennhak and Richter, *Revolution und Emanzipation*.

12. Lister, *Citizenship*. See also Kymlicka and Norman, "Return of the Citizen," 283–322.

13. Nolte, among others, points out that the distinctions between liberal theory and civic republicanism were not clear-cut in nineteenth-century political theory or practice. See Nolte, *Bürgerideal, Gemeinde und Republik*, 609–56.

14. Nipperdey, "Verein als soziale Struktur in Deutschland im späten 18 und frühen 19." See also Dann, *Vereinswesen und bürgerliche Gesellschaft in Deutschland*; François, *Sociabilité et Société Bourgeoise en France*.

15. Nipperdey, *Verein als soziale Struktur*, 17.

16. Ibid. See also Lothar Gall, *Der hiesigen Stadt zu einer wahren Zierde und deren Bürgerschaft nützlich: Städel und sein* (Frankfurt: Kunst-Institut, 1992), 13.

17. Many scholars of civil society also regard voluntary associations as the "cement" of civil society. According to them, associations enhance social connectedness and make it possible for members to form deep interpersonal bonds, an important prerequisite for the democratic process. See, for example, Putnam, *Making Democracy Work* and *Bowling Alone*; Walzer, "The Civil Society Argument."

18. See Mettele, "Der private Raum als öffentlicher Ort"; Brigitte Schnegg, "Soireen, Salons, Sozietäten."

19. Lipp, "Frauen auf der Straüe," 22.

20. Canning and Rose, "Gender, Citizenship and Subjectivity," 429.

21. Stefan-Ludwig Hoffmann has pointed out the significance of male friendship as an important presupposition for civility and a "brotherhood of man." Masonic secrecy made possible a form of sociability that allowed men to experience intimate relations with each other. Hoffmann, "Civility, Male Friendship, and Masonic Sociability in Nineteenth-Century Germany."

22. Vogel, "Patriarchale Herrschaft," 167–96.

23. See, for example, Langewiesche, "Die schwäbische Sängerbewegung in der Gesellschaft des 19."

24. Paletschek, *Frauen und Dissens*; Prelinger, *Charity, Challenge, and Change*.

25. The history of female welfare activities has been a vital field of research since the 1990s. See, for example, Bock and Thane, *Maternity and Gender Policies*; Meyer-Renschhausen, *Weibliche Kultur und Sozialarbeit*.

26. See Jürgen Reulecke, "Formen bürgerlich-sozialen Engagements in Deutschland und England im 19, Jahrhundert," 261–85. The welfare system in the German cities

was modernized in the nineteenth century, with systematic and preventive measures such as schools for the poor and improvements to the infrastructure introduced as an alternative to simply helping in situations of acute need. But this new concept was still connected to the traditions of the old burghers. See Langewiesche, "Staat" und "Kommune," 621–35; Reulecke, "Die Armenfürsorge als Teil der kommunalen Leistungsverwaltung und Daseinsvorsorge im 19 Jahrhundert," 71–80. See also Scarpa, *Gemeinwohl und lokale Macht*; Küster, *Alte Armut und neues Bürgertum*.

27. See Michel and Koven, "Womanly Duties."

28. Hüchtker, *"Elende Mütter" und "liederliche Weibspersonen."*

29. Document 403, Volume, XX, 1–732, Statutes §§ 14, 17, HASTK, u. 17.

30. Kill, *Das Bürgertum in Münster 1770–1870*; Schulz, *Vormundschaft und Protektion*; Möller, *Bürgerliche Herrschaft in Augsburg 1790–1880*; Zerback, *München und sein Stadtbürgertum*; Schambach, *Stadtbürgertum und industrieller Aufbruch*; Mettele, *Bürgertum in Köln*.

31. See Mettele, *Bürgerliche Frauen und das Vereinswesen im Vormärz*. What was true in Cologne was also the case in other German merchant cities. See, for example, Schulz, *Vormundschaft und Protektion*; Roth, *Stadt und Bürgertum in Frankfurt am Main*.

32. See Reagin, *A German Women's Movement*.

33. Document: 403, Volume, XII-1–735, HASTK.

34. "Chroniken und Darstellungen 219–227 (1834–1836)," Document: 403, Volume: XII-1–735 (1846–1852), HASTK. See also, Document: 403-Volume: XII-1–732 (1853–1859), HASTK.

35. Document: 1296, File: 2 and 9, Family archives Schaaffhausen Best, HASTK.

36. Document: 403, Volume, XII-1–735, HASTK.

37. Document, Volume III-24, File: 1, HASTK.

38. See, for example, Kirsten Heinsohn, *Politik und Geschlecht*.

39. Luise Scheffen-Döring, *Frauenbewegung und christliche Liebestätigkeit*, 12. For the German female patriotic associations, see Quataert, *Staging Philanthropy*; Daniel, "Die Vaterländischen Frauenvereine in Westfalen"; Reder, *Frauenbewegung und Nation*.

40. Document, Volume III-24, File: 1, HASTK.

41. Quoted in Hauser, *Anfänge bürgerlicher Organisation*. For the philhellenic movement, see Natalie Klein, *"L'humanité, le Christianisme, et la liberté."*

42. Resolutions adopted by the ministers of the German states at a conference in Carlsbad 1819, the Carlsbad Decrees provided for uniform press censorship, with the goal of suppressing all liberal agitation against the conservative governments of the German Confederation. The resolutions remained in force until 1848. The period between the Carlsbad Decrees and the Revolution of March 1848 is also called *Vormärz* (literally, "pre-March").

43. Hauser, *Anfänge bürgerlicher Organisation*.

44. See Lipp, *Frauen und Öffentlichkeit*, 284.

45. See, for example, Tischler, *Die Philhellenische Bewegung*, 42. The double standard in his argument also shows on 229, 233, 285, 327.

46. Quataert, *Staging Philanthropy*, 294.

47. Tischler, *Die Philhellenische Bewegung*, 231ff.

48. Nipperdey, *Deutsche Geschichte 1800–1866*, 401.

49. Hardtwig, "Strukturmerkmale und Entwicklungstendenzen des Vereinswesens in Deutschland 1789–1848," 29.

50. Reagin, *A German Women's Movement*; Quataert, *Staging Philanthropy*, 6. In general, see Streubel, "Literaturbericht." Streubel counts even the confessional associations working for parochial welfare as being on the political right.

51. Quoted in Reder, " 'Im Felde Soldat mit Soldat, daheim Männerbund mit Männerbund, Frauenverein mit Frauenverein'—Der Patriotische Frauenverein Köln in Krieg und Armenpflege 1813–1826," in *Geschichte in Köln* 32, 1992, 76.

52. Quoted in ibid.

53. For the significance of the concept of public motherhood for the German feminist movement, see Sachsse, "*Social Mother*" and *Mütterlichkeit als Beruf*; Stoehr, "Organisierte Mütterlichkeit," 221–49.

54. See Kymlicka and Norman, "Return of the Citizen."

55. Isenberg, *Sex and Citizenship in Antebellum America*, 66.

56. Quoted in Schröder, "Soziale Frauenarbeit als bürgerliches Projekt," 224. See also Schröder, *Arbeiten für eine bessere Welt*.

Putting Faith in the Middle Class

THE BOURGEOISIE, CATHOLICISM, AND POSTREVOLUTIONARY FRANCE

Carol E. Harrison

Religious faith and bourgeois identity make an uneasy pairing for historians, particularly historians of France who are accustomed to locating religiosity and class society on opposite sides of the division marked by the French Revolution and the advent of modernity. Under the ancien régime, a subject's relationship to the Roman Catholic Church was one of the markers that defined his or her estate. The revolution, in contrast, ushered in the secular principle of equality before the law and the dechristianized fluidity of class society. In classic studies of the emergence of class in France, "Voltairean" is the adjective that naturally modifies "bourgeoisie," suggesting an urbane materialism and a purely instrumental attitude toward religion. Bourgeois society, the "Voltairean" label suggests, had moved beyond the religious dogma of the ancient regime but continued to recognize religion as a useful tool of social order to be imposed on classes who had yet to reach a similar degree of intellectual sophistication. This demystified religion was an instrument for the manipulation of others, not a mirror for the understanding of the self. In the development of the post-Enlightenment West, "religion" and "class" appear as sequential identities, class replacing religion as a means of locating oneself in the world.

In this chapter I propose that we think about religiosity and the bourgeoisie simultaneously.[1] I begin with the historiography of the French bourgeoisie, focusing particularly on the challenge that women's history posed to ideas about class. Locating women within categories of class has reintroduced religiosity to the study of bourgeois life, although in peripheral and troubling ways. "Domesticity" has come to define the bourgeoisie, but the role of religion in forming bourgeois domestic spheres has had little impact on class as a secular category. In the second half of the chapter, I turn to the domestic life of the postrevolutionary French bourgeoisie, examining the role of religion in the particular organization of family that has become a hallmark of recent studies of class. In particular I focus on the children—both male and female—of bourgeois families. Catholicism was part of the moral and social foundations for many bourgeois children, and their belief and practice, I argue, in turn anchored the Catholic identity of many bourgeois families. Children's literature of the first half of the nineteenth century is a source that can teach us—as it taught its original readers—how to navigate the postrevolutionary social world. Children's stories imagined Catholic rituals and charity as giving class society a stability and coherence that many in postrevolutionary France felt it sorely lacked. When children performed charitable acts, generosity and compassion brought together rich and poor and allowed bourgeois parents to imagine society as a space of shared values and of solidarity that transcended economic interest. Both class hierarchy and religious sentiment structured the French social imaginary, producing a version of modern society in which status difference did not imply conflict.

Class Society and Gendered Dichotomies of Belief

Like many of the analytical categories by which we understand the emergence of modernity, class locates itself in a narrative of secularization. In the 1840s, Marx's writing on history explicitly drew religion into the revolutionary moment; religion's decline marked the end of the ancien régime and the emergence of the bourgeoisie. Thus the French Revolution occurred when "feudal society fought its death battle with the then revolutionary bourgeoisie" and when "Christian ideas succumbed . . . to [the] rationalist ideas" of the Enlightenment. What emerged was bourgeois Voltaireanism: "ideas of religious liberty and freedom of conscience" reproduced bourgeois economic competition in the spiritual domain.[2] Instead of a foundation for a feudal community, religion became a tool of capitalist oppression, the opiate of the masses, with the bourgeoisie as its pushers. Because the churches and the religious belief they promoted served bourgeois interests, the "criticism of religion," Marx believed, was in fact political and legal criticism in another guise, and it was a vital step in the dismantling of bourgeois society. Crucially, Marx believed that this critique of religious belief was "in essence complete"; the vacuity of bourgeois religiosity had already been revealed for all to see, and its strictures could no longer inhibit working-class organization.[3] The abandonment of religious mysteries in the eighteenth century was thus constitutive of the modern bourgeoisie; what remained was less a matter of belief than of convenience, the Voltairean sense that faith was an appropriate accompaniment to social inferiority.

The French social history tradition, which produced massive studies of the French bourgeoisie, reflected this Marxist evaluation of religion in its account of the emerging dominant class of the postrevolutionary period. Drawing on marriage contracts, wills and death inventories, voting rolls, and taxation records, French historians of the 1960s produced a series of studies focused on bourgeois property that delineated the boundaries between *grande*, *petite*, and *moyenne* bourgeoisies; sketched out the relationship between industrial, commercial, and landed capital; and examined the political loyalties that derived from economic position.[4] The goal of this research was to model the relationship between economic and political change, an attempt to map the political loyalties of France's contentious and revolutionary nineteenth century onto a bedrock of economic interest. Catholicism, in this treatment, corresponded with noble landowning, legitimist politics, and the desire to restore the Bourbon monarchs and the ancien régime social order.[5] Religiosity had no autonomy in this view of society; rather, it functioned as the rhetorical justification for inherited economic status and monarchical politics.

Although class is an analytical category that historians generally use and explain without recourse to religious sentiment, domesticity is a different story. The domestic sphere, the location where women's history and social history met beginning in the 1970s, brought religion into the study of class, but in problematic ways. In particular, research on middle-class women has produced the concept of a "feminization of religion" that has proven remarkably resilient in a variety of different national settings. The classic study of French bourgeois women, Bonnie Smith's 1981 *Ladies of the Leisure Class*, pointed out that standard French discussions of class left women located in a sort of classless limbo, since bourgeois married women, in particular, did not share their husbands' or fathers' relationship to the means of production. Instead of building class on economic foundations, then, Smith argued for a cultural definition of class that would be broad enough to include women as well as men. In Smith's view, domesticity and separate spheres were the cultural practices that made the bourgeoisie, and Catholicism, crucially, was what kept male and female spheres separate. Catholicism remained at the center of the "preindustrial" lives of the womenfolk of France's bourgeoisie "for reproduction predisposed them to a religious world view." In sharp contrast, "the commitment to business rather than the quest for salvation determined the course of male life among the Northern bourgeoisie."[6]

Bringing religion back to the study of class via women's history was hardly an exclusively French phenomenon. Barbara Welter similarly argued that female piety compensated for the religious indifference and the economic sins of middle-class men.[7] Leonora Davidoff and Catherine Hall did not draw as stark a religious division between men and women but nonetheless argued that early-nineteenth-century evangelicalism shaped the English middle class by establishing "home" as a sacred feminine space, protected from the godless market in which men risked their souls.[8] In the influential *History of Women in the West*, edited by Geneviève Fraisse and Michelle Perrot, the Italian historian Michela de Giorgio maintained that "the nineteenth century's estrangement from the Church, its militant or passive anti-clericalism, were exclusively masculine phenomena . . . Catholicism of the nineteenth century was expressed in the feminine gender."[9] The domestic sphere, undergirded by female religiosity and compensating for male disbelief, is a trope of studies of the nineteenth-century middle class, both in Europe and in America, and it is a remarkably durable notion, since it crosses both national and confessional boundaries.[10]

The saturation of the nineteenth-century domestic sphere with religious sentiment does not, however, suggest to historians that the religiosity of bourgeois women truly belonged in the modern world. Female religiosity is often cast in terms of "persistence"; in embracing faith, women were demonstrating either their reluctance to engage with modernity or the ways in which their limited options held them at a distance from the modern world.[11] Moreover, nineteenth-century women's devotions are implicitly part of a world we have lost, a world that contemporary feminism has left behind. Lynn Abrams's synthesis, *The Making of Modern Woman*, like the work of Bonnie Smith and other historians of middle-class women, presents religion as a key component of the lives of nineteenth-century women, but also as a phase through which they passed as they followed men toward a secular society, albeit at a slower pace.[12] A variety of studies of women's reform activism and charitable work suggests that religiosity was the path that women took from domestic questions to social ones, and that religious imperatives licensed women's departure from their own domestic sphere.[13] These studies read women's religion as protofeminist—but only proto, because eventually these women would recognize that the appropriate arguments for the modern world are rights-based and secular. Feminism, like class society, appears to be an ideology that accompanies secularization; it steps in to structure our understanding of society as religiosity declines.

This tendency to position devout women in the early stages of a developmental narrative leading toward feminism and secular society is an example of what Phyllis Mack has described as feminist scholarship's failure to understand female religiosity.[14] This failure has serious consequences for contemporary feminism, and it obscures the historical development of gender and class identities. The concept of a feminized religiosity buttressing bourgeois domesticity should raise serious concerns among historians, particularly historians of women. The precise nature of the relationship between domesticity and religiosity remains murky, since it is not clear if women embraced the domestic sphere because their religious beliefs encouraged them to do so, or if, rather, they embraced faith because the domestic limits of their world pushed them toward religious outlets. Moreover, the association of women with the "persistence" of premodern and traditional worldviews should offer historians an easy target. The broad generalizations of the "feminization of religion" thesis raise the possibility that scholars are dealing with something they find disruptive—the persistence of religious faith in an allegedly secular modern world—by feminizing it.

Arguments about bourgeois women, religious faith, and the delayed path to secular society are also troubling because they echo nineteenth-century misogynist anticlericalism. French anticlericals certainly believed that female religiosity was an atavistic phenomenon by which many, perhaps even most, women resolutely turned their backs on modernity. The republican tradition assumed that women had to give up their attachment to their church before they could reasonably expect to enjoy full participation in the modern world, for instance by exercising the rights of citizens. In 1845 Jules Michelet's *Priests, Women, and Families* famously warned bourgeois Frenchmen of women's fatal tendency toward a sentimental piety and of priests' willingness to encourage them. In an image that both titillated and frightened readers, Michelet cautioned husbands to beware of wives who, in the marital bed, whispered "lessons learned from another." The slippery priest and the foolishly devout bourgeoise were the stock characters of Michelet's imagination, and the priest's chameleon-like gender and class identity facilitated his insinuation into the bosom of the family. Although the priest was "born male and strong," he "makes himself weak, like a woman." His peasant cunning permitted him to exert a "vulgar attraction" over women of the bourgeoisie.[15]

Michelet's dire warnings of female susceptibility to Catholicism and its priests were the corollary of his celebration of male autonomy and republican citizenship. His polemic, which quickly went through multiple editions and translations, explicitly addressed a bourgeois male audience; it warned its readers against "our adversaries" the priests, who seek to control "our wives" and "our daughters."[16] Michelet made no attempt to address women, to convince them of the error of their ways, or to induce them to choose their husbands over their confessors; the remedy lay entirely in the hands of laymen. Michelet's history of French republicanism—like so many histories of the modern world—featured a narrative of secularization, with republican men in the lead. In fact, Michelet described God as having changed sex—priests' gender ambiguity had a distinguished model. The process had begun in the twelfth century with the castration of Abelard, the "restorer of philosophy," and with the proliferation of the Virgin on church altars—vapid female sentimentality defeating austere male reason.[17] The process culminated in the nineteenth century with the emancipation of male citizens from the authority of both kings and priests, but also with the concomitant strengthening of priests' empire over women and girls. Far from being the tranquil sphere over which men ruled and from which they derived the autonomy that allowed them to participate in the public sphere as equal citizens, domesticity, for Michelet, represented a worrying challenge to men's patriarchal and political authority.

The "feminization of religion" scholarship in France has had a disturbing tendency to echo Michelet. This research had its origins in the tradition of religious sociology; women in the nineteenth century increasingly outnumbered men among communicants, and Claude Langlois's classic work on female religious orders investigated the proliferation of vocations among women that, by the end of the century, had resulted in male religious being significantly outnumbered by female religious.[18] From an argument about numbers, however, historians have slipped with disturbing ease to an argument about culture, and the "feminization of religion" has become, according to Langlois, a sort of "linguistic tic" whose meaning has become increasingly diffuse.[19] A feminized Catholicism in France by the nineteenth century was not only a religion characterized by large numbers of women in pews and in convents, but also one marked by sentimental forms of devotion that rational and autonomous bourgeois men found repellent. An obsession with the Virgin Mary and a host of adolescent girl saints and visionaries, the worship of an androgynous Christ, the cultivation of tears, and a fascination with victimhood, the whole package represented by artists trained in the pretty, but utterly unchallenging,

Sulpician tradition of religious art—this was a church that offered only a profoundly feminized piety.[20]

The slippage from numbers to culture in the scholarship of the feminization of religion tends to maintain Michelet's history, only purged of its overt misogyny. It begs a whole series of questions that historians have only begun to pose: Was the connection between female numbers and devotional culture really that close? Did men need a muscular Christ, and were only women drawn to worship the Virgin and child?[21] How much can we properly conclude about male de-Christianization from patterns of attendance at mass?[22] The historians' "feminized" Catholicism relies on Michelet's trope of a God who has changed sex and on the highly questionable assumption that both nineteenth-century men and women looked for self, rather than other, when they tried to understand the divine. Michelet and the historians agree that Catholicism really was feminized, both in its numbers and in its forms of expression, and that women did persist in their religiosity in defiance of an increasingly secular world. Michelet's explicit contempt for female devotion is missing from contemporary scholarship, but these researchers often understand themselves to be analyzing nineteenth-century bourgeois women from the same postreligious vantage point that Michelet claimed for republican men.

Adopting Michelet's notion of a feminized Catholicism fails to account for the fact that republican anticlericals of the nineteenth century wrote political polemic, not sociological description. A feminized religion served a political purpose for Michelet and later French anticlerical politicians: it protected the masculinity of politics, especially of the republican tradition, and it justified the exclusion of women from full citizenship.[23] Michelet and many of his contemporaries responded to the disturbing persistence of religious devotion in the modern world by feminizing it, a move that contained, if it did not eliminate, the threat. Domesticity's association of bourgeois women with religion in the nineteenth century was not simply descriptive. Rather, it was an argument intended to disenfranchise precisely those women of the educated, property-owning classes who—but for their sex—might easily have fit into liberal notions of citizenship. That Michelet did not call on women to emancipate themselves from their priests was neither accidental nor coincidental, because his purpose was not to create autonomous women but rather to protect and celebrate the autonomy of men.

Finally, the notion that bourgeois women's spiritual life represented a persistence of the premodern social order is difficult to sustain in light of recent scholarship in religious history, particularly on what some historians refer to as the "new Catholicism."[24] The Roman Catholic Church of the nineteenth century appears increasingly like a dynamic, innovative participant in the construction of modernity rather than its recalcitrant opponent. Recent studies highlight the extent to which the church was deeply implicated in, not opposed to, the construction of modern nationalism, the mass media, and consumer culture, for instance.[25] In France, in particular, devout Catholics had little choice but to create anew because the revolution effectively disrupted the institutions of the church and the ritual lives of French Catholics. Catholicism re-created itself in the postrevolutionary period, simultaneously with the construction of class society, and it should be possible for historians to integrate the two and to think in terms of articulations between religious and class identity. Such a project would require us to abandon notions of a secular male public and a religious female private. We would give up the notion of secularization as a condition for the emergence of modernity and its analytical tools, such as class. Instead we would have "bourgeoisie" and "Catholicism" as a pair of concepts, elaborated simultaneously on a social field cleared by the revolution. Class and religion both structured women and men's navigation of nineteenth-century French society and restored order and legibility to that society after revolutionary upheaval.

Learning Class, Practicing Faith: Stories for Children

The project of thinking through religion and class as mutually constitutive rather than historically sequential is a large one, and here I will only touch on one way in which I think it might be accomplished: examining children's literature for evidence of Catholic influence on a bourgeois view of society. Family is clearly an important avenue of inquiry into understanding the place of Catholic faith among the bourgeoisie, although domesticity—with its baggage of separate spheres and its tendency to dichotomize female faith and male disbelief—ought not be the only way to investigate family life. Instead, I suggest that individuals played different roles in anchoring a family's Catholic identity in a sort of division of religious labor that operated among wives, husbands, and their children. Mothers, fathers, sons, and daughters exercised the faith in different ways, each of which contributed to rooting the family's identity in the teachings of the church. There is, for instance, a great deal of evidence to suggest that bourgeois fathers, many of them probably not devout or even regularly practicing, expected their children to receive a grounding in Catholic teaching. The restoration and expansion of Catholic schooling for both boys and girls, especially at the secondary level, suggests that many fathers wanted religious education for their children.[26] First communion was a "nearly universal" experience for nineteenth-century French children; reception into the church remained a crucial marker of progress through youth.[27] Children's religiosity prepared them for later life as individual Catholic adults, but it also kept their families anchored to the church.

The years immediately following the French Revolution saw the expansion and consolidation of literary genres aimed especially at children: publishing houses specialized in the field; overall numbers of books grew dramatically; and tales written especially for girls or for boys gained an important share of the market.[28] Children's literature instructed its young readers in the navigation of postrevolutionary society, and the stories of the period make it clear that Catholic practice structured the social field in which children were imagined to operate.

For the most part, these stories of the postrevolutionary period are strikingly simple: short moral tales in which children personify various elements of virtue and vice. The juvenile novel, with its longer format and more complex characters, did not emerge until the 1850s with the writings of Madame de Ségur. There is nothing particularly surprising about the fact that early-nineteenth-century French children's literature was moralizing. Just as in their Anglo-American counterparts, in French stories, good children obey their parents, study hard at school, and receive their due rewards, while bad children are lazy, defiant, and headed for a comeuppance.

In France, however, explicitly Catholic content filled in the general outlines of these moralistic tales: childish goodness, misbehavior, and their consequences were automatically and almost unreflectingly Catholic. Fictional children led lives punctuated by the rituals of the church, and they absorbed a view of a social order permeated by religious devotion and obligation. First communions structured narratives of growing up as predictably as they marked actual children's lives, and the practice of Catholic charity became the main occasion for lessons in social distinction. The automatic quality of the stories' religious content is particularly important. Despite the revolutionary disruption of the life of the church, it went without saying in postrevolutionary fiction that bourgeois children learned their moral code in the context of Catholic liturgy. We find stories on the far ends of the spectrum of religious morality: tales that go out of their way to push specifically Catholic themes and warn of the dangers of nonobservance, and others that self-consciously present a secular moral code. For the most part, however, Catholic morality appears to have been the default mode of storytelling for bourgeois children.

Children's literature of the postrevolutionary period was profoundly aware of status, although this consciousness often appears suspended between an ancien régime emphasis on birth and estate and a new sense of social fluidity. As far as children are concerned, class is an inherited status, and French stories were clear that children's behavior should follow from their parents' social position. The children in storybooks inherited their lot in life, and the good children accepted their roles and endeavored to fulfill the obligations that derived from their birth. A parent's class was a child's fate, not merely his or her starting point in life. Thus when Madame de Verneuil's children worry that the orphan girl adopted by the silk merchant seems to have a hard life with no one to cuddle her, their mother explains that this lack of affection is really for the best. The girl will grow up having to work for a living and is now receiving "the only suitable education"; she will, in the long run, be far happier than the seamstress's spoiled daughter who hasn't learned not to touch things, and who calls the Verneuil children by their first names.[29] The poor always remain with us in the world of children's fiction, with their inferior status clearly demarcated and offering bourgeois children an object lesson in the inescapable realities of social distinction. Thus in another story, a peasant girl possesses a peasant doll, and both are invited over once a year to play with the bourgeois Céline and her exquisite doll, Merveilleuse.[30] For both little girls the die is cast from the beginning of the story, and even the make-believe world of dolls reflects the harsh realities of the girls' divergent social destinies.

When stories appear to break social rules and open up the possibility of mobility, it very often turns out that the child's birth has been misrepresented. Plots turn on foundlings and the revelation of true social identities. Good or bad behavior may influence a child's social trajectory, leading an obedient girl to an advantageous marriage, but these stories never really doubt that there is such a thing as a "true" social place. Establishing order in the denouement of the story requires not that each character achieve a position suited to his or her character, but that the truth about their birth and status be revealed and acknowledged. Setting the world to rights may require a foundling's adoptive siblings to fade into the background, uncomplainingly pensioned off by a now-complete wealthy family.[31] When a prodigal son, led astray by a taste for gambling, is hauled before a judge for his crimes, the judge fortuitously turns out to be his father, ready to restore his repentant son to his rightful place.[32] For some particularly bad children, foundling stories serve as punishment: at her wits' end, Delphine's mother arranges for her wicked (and nosy) daughter to overhear a staged conversation that reveals that Delphine is, in fact, a peasant child, "fit for nothing but keeping cows."[33] Delphine remains in her mother's house as a chambermaid until her character improves and she is restored to the social position that is rightfully hers. Sadly, Delphine's childish bad habits had irreparably damaged her health, and she dies at sixteen, shortly after being reinstated in her true family.

The story of Delphine—with its shocking harshness in no way attenuated by the charming paper doll accompanying the book, which the reader can dress first in bourgeois finery, then in a maid's sober gown—captures the dramatic possibilities for decline and fall that dominated much of the children's literature of the period. Children and their families had true social identities and places in which they belonged, but they very often found themselves expelled from their rightful positions. Moreover, Delphine's tale is also typical in its unfairness, even the randomness of the child's fate. Certainly Delphine was a naughty child, but pouting, rudeness to servants, smashing birds' nests, and dirtying a dress do not seem to merit the withholding of maternal love or early death, particularly since we learn that her foolish mother spoiled her—and Delphine does repent! Like many storybook characters of the period, Delphine is not entirely innocent, but neither does she fully deserve her fate. People may belong in clearly determined social locations, but reversals of fortune proliferate in these tales, and they strike without warning or justification.

In contrast to Anglo-American children's literature, in which children generally get their just desserts, there is a strong streak of randomness in French stories.[34] Many tales explicitly lay the blame for disrupting families on the French Revolution, and sometimes a childish fault—especially bragging about elevated social position—leads to parents' imprisonment and execution under the Terror.[35] Other stories refer in vague terms to parents' falling on hard times, dying in unspecified circumstances, or simply being away on business trips.[36] The trajectory is not always downward: in one story, a poor family learns of the death of a fabulously wealthy relative from a newspaper that falls out of the handbag of a charitable woman delivering alms. The two families, originally brought together by giving and receiving charity, are finally united by marriage, as the daughter of the charitable lady marries the eldest son of the once-poor family who is now Don Francisco, marquis de Saldagna.[37] Some mobility is difficult to characterize: Dorothée's father, the village schoolmaster, is concerned that his daughter is too much at home at the château, and he fears that she will forget her love for her family. One day her father goes on an errand and never returns. Her mother goes after him and disappears as well. The lady of the château, who already loved Dorothée like a daughter, adopts the child and gives her clothes appropriate to her new station in life.[38] In stories like these, class appears simultaneously fixed by birth and liable to be held hostage by fortune. Class mobility was not the reward for hard work, as promised by the British literature inspired by Samuel Smiles's *Self-Help*, but rather the catastrophic result of revolution or of other mysterious forces well beyond the child's control.[39]

As in the tales of the newly restored marquis de Saldagna or the abandoned Dorothée, an act of charity features as the turning point of the narrative in many stories for children.[40] Charity ranked high among the list of virtues that children's literature sought to transmit, and French stories usually located childish charity within a specifically Catholic framework. Charity was a social glue that guaranteed that class difference did not become class conflict. Bourgeois children learned class and Catholicism simultaneously, as social practices that ought to be combined in the charitable impulse. Charity staged as an activity for children offered bourgeois writers the opportunity to imagine a society in which the differences of class were balanced by a shared religious faith.

Charity practiced among adults has been an important part of the foundation of historians' case for bourgeois Voltaireanism and an instrumental attitude toward religion. We often assume that bourgeois charity, particularly when practiced by men, obeyed a capitalist rather than a Christian logic, with its primary purpose the enforcement of deference. Charitable Frenchmen contributed significantly to this impression by adopting the label "philanthropy" in the revolutionary period in order to proclaim their love of humanity above their loyalty to the institutional church.[41] Charitable giving set the inequalities between rich and poor in high relief and was necessarily fraught with tension and often recriminations. Those anxieties, however, were not exclusively a product of working-class resentment of the bourgeois social order. Scholars have recently observed that nineteenth-century charitable motivations were far more complex than the maintenance of social hierarchy. Bourgeois donors' desires to represent their civic responsibility or their religious devotion might work against economic rationality: instead of producing deferential, dependent workers, charitable schemes prepared poor children for nonexistent careers or invested in training programs that had no graduates because virtually every child was expelled for moral failings. In the practice of charity, bourgeois goals were more complex than profit or social control.[42]

Some tales of childish charity were quite practical about the economics of giving, and they do appear to lend themselves to a Voltairean interpretation of bourgeois generosity. Charity was not to be performed thoughtlessly, and good children were to reflect on the charitable balance sheet of profit and loss. There was no merit to wasted resources, and girls and boys needed to be practical about their charity. Thus two sisters who want to raise money for poor children set about producing goods for sale at a charitable bazaar. Naturally they both sew, but Amaglia chooses to embroider a single dress with great care, while her sister Pulchérie decides to knock off a hundred or so simple purses and garters. Amaglia easily finds a buyer for her beautiful dress among the bazaar's wealthy patrons, but Pulchérie has great difficulty locating a market for her shoddy purses and endless garters.[43] Enforced charitable giving might be a punishment for a child's wastefulness, as when Achille's father makes him put a penny in the parish collection box each time he loses a toy or a school exercise book.[44] Another little girl's mother gives her a savings book, with which the child learns that if she refrains from buying expensive clothing, she may have the pleasure of giving to the poor.[45] Charity and arithmetic were natural companions, as in the word problems from a schoolboy's newspaper that challenged students to divide small sums among various numbers of paupers.[46]

On the whole, however, the purpose of charity was not to provide an object lesson in class inequality and social control so much as it was to discipline childish desire. The stories' main goal in emphasizing that children must think through their charitable practice was not to make their charity more socially effective, but rather to ensure that generosity would shape every aspect of a child's life. The regular practice of charity was part of a process that fostered a bourgeois child's transition from bad to good. Thus although charity begins as a punishment for Achille, it ends up as a reward. Once he learns to stop misplacing his toys and making kites out of his lesson books, his father increases his allowance to five francs, so that the poor of the parish do not suffer for his improving character.[47] Children like Achille might be innocently and endlessly generous, but only after self-control replaces their selfish instincts, and children's books expressed far more anxiety about the cultivation of generosity than satisfaction with a bourgeois social order.

Storybook charity in France ordinarily assumed explicitly Catholic forms, often in automatic, unremarkable ways. Charitable episodes often appear simply in passing, as part of a family's weekly schedule or as events in a story whose main point is quite different. The practice of charity was the clearest possible shorthand indication of a good child, one who had absorbed the lessons that children's stories had to offer. Charitable children had succeeded in moderating their desires and directing them outward toward others. Charity was thus both an end and a means; the purpose of the regular practice of charity was to transform the willful child into a responsible Christian and an individual fit for society. The charitable act was not an isolated moment or a strategic calculation, but a component of a spiritual discipline shaped by the liturgical life of the church. And the authors of children's stories imagined postrevolutionary French society as a field in which a shared religious faith mediated dramatic and often apparently random differences in social status.

Even among the youngest children, charity was in many ways a gendered activity. Little girls, of course, sewed for the poor. Laure, for instance, learns that it is more fun to sew for a real baby orphan than for her dolls, and she looks forward to teaching the child to read as well.[48] The little girls whose lessons frame an abridged children's edition of Josephus's *Jewish War* take a break from their study of the Romans to deliver bonnets they have made for a poor neighbor.[49] Mothers and daughters sew together, and girls learn to visit "our regular paupers" by following their mothers' example.[50] The lithograph for the first issue of the girls' magazine, *Journal des jeunes personnes*, features young ladies' charitable visiting—an appropriate theme for a publication that promised to cultivate "the seeds of piety" sown by "an early Christian education" and "maternal solicitude."[51] Books set in girls' boarding schools depict sewing circles in which pupils work for the poor until the bell rings for evening prayers and bed.[52] Although girls' charity does sometimes involve their giving pennies from little purses, their sewing—either plain items, to be given directly to the poor, or fancy ones, to be sold in charitable raffles—features more prominently. "Little girls," one storybook mother tells us, "don't have very much money, and even their clothes don't really belong to them; the only thing that they can give away is their time. If they dedicate a few hours of their spare time to working for their poor neighbors, . . . that may be the only act of charity within their reach."[53] Self-abnegation, even for the youngest, had gendered variants, and girls' stories reminded their readers that, although they were not poor, they nonetheless lacked property and might need to rely on their own work.

The spiritual disciplining of children could be surprisingly stringent in some tales, exposing girls, in particular, to hard labor, disease, and even death. In a story in one children's paper, a little girl rips up her doll's dress to bandage the diseased limb of a poor old woman.[54] Another little girl wakes at dawn by arranging for the gardener to tap on her window so that she may sew for the poor until the light fails and her wrists and back ache, despite her excellent posture.[55] Failure to achieve a properly charitable outlook may be punished by death, as in the story where a greedy little girl mistakes arsenic for sugar.[56] Even in childhood, girls learned the concept of expiation, by which suffering—offered graciously and without measure—redeemed both one's own sins and those of others.

Boys also perform charity with great regularity in early-nineteenth-century tales, but their charitable practice differed from that of their sisters; boys generally give money, and their stories focus on countering childish greed. In one typical example, boys who are spending their school vacation learning about natural history (the main subject of the book) encounter a nameless poor boy. The bourgeois pupils offer the poor child enough money to call the doctor to his sick father's bedside.[57] Children's tales often paired virtues and vices, contrasting good children with their naughty counterparts; where boys were concerned, the opposite of charity was often gluttony. The trade-off of buying candy or saving money that could be offered to the poor was a common feature of the lives of storybook boys. Good boys manage their allowances carefully to include charitable giving, or they pool the pennies they saved for sweets with their schoolmates in order to help boys in need.[58] Even a book that is all about food—the *Abécédaire des petits gourmands*—includes anecdotes about food refused: *F*—for flan—features the story of three brothers, one of whom chooses to give money to a poor boy rather than purchase the treat for himself. His brothers make themselves sick to their stomachs, and the good little boy's act of charity is reported to his father, who rewards him with a special excursion to the countryside.[59] Not all children were feminized in early-nineteenth-century stories, and charity had distinct male and female variants. While little girls learned to give when they owned nothing, little boys learned of the dangers of excessive attachment to property. Greed rather than vanity was the specific form of self-absorption that threatened boys.

Whether practiced by girls or boys, storybook charity represented spiritual discipline and the child's humble entry into Christian society. *Le Bon Génie*, a newspaper for children published in the 1820s, promised in its prospectus to participate in this spiritual development by printing stories of good deeds—but only unsolicited ones. In the "age of the newspaper," *Le Bon Génie* warns, it is important not to lure children to charity through the promise of publicity. Naughty children, however, may find themselves named and publicly shamed in the pages of the paper.[60] Similarly, the point of charitable visiting was less the transfer of goods than the routine confrontation between misery and ease intended to keep the rich child's conscience alert. Bourgeois families needed "regular paupers" so that their children would be familiar with the spectacle of poverty and their compassion would be fully engaged. Charitable visiting learned as a child remained an element of a Catholic adulthood: girls might grow up to make the rounds with their own children, and young men could join a branch of the Society of Saint Vincent de Paul where visiting the poor was the center of male devotional life. The encounter between rich and poor in the charitable visit, like the unsolicited good deeds published in *Le Bon Génie*, cultivated humility and discouraged flamboyant, self-seeking charitable performances. The best charitable deeds were always those carried out in secret, although in children's stories they were almost always observed and reported to gratified parents. The approval of parents supplemented the omniscient eye of God in these stories of children's self-effacing goodness.

First communion featured in both boys' and girls' stories as the point toward which denial of self and charity toward others tended; virtually all stories assumed that first communion would be the key moment in the life of any child. Serious children might choose to postpone their communion if they recognized that their souls were not adequately prepared; the regular practice of charity and exposure to suffering created this kind of spiritual awareness even in young children.[61] Preparation for communion disciplined children's impulses, both good and bad, and directed them toward the life of the church. Among the most common, and most praiseworthy, elements of that preparation was to provide poor children with a proper dress or suit so that all might approach the altar together for the first time as equals. The story of Eusèbe, brought up in poverty in his grandfather's household under the grasping housekeeper Berthe, reaches its climax when Berthe insists that Eusèbe must make his first communion in shabby hand-me-downs. Patient Eusèbe reaches the end of his rope and confronts Berthe, and the parish priest arrives to set everything to rights. It transpires that Berthe has hidden quite a sizable fortune, so Eusèbe is able to clothe twenty other little boys in suits identical to his own, thus making first communion a joyous experience for all.[62] Similarly the aristocratic Léontine, sent to a convent school to cure her of frivolity and insolence, reveals her changed character when she provides veils for all of the village girls and walks to church with them rather than riding in a carriage. When Léontine later marries well, she offers her childhood savings to dower a poor girl, who turns out to have been a member of that happy first communion class.[63] Léontine and her poorer sister are equally able to marry happily, just as they earlier had donned identical veils to approach the altar as new communicants.

The moral of these stories for children is that class difference matters immensely, but that it calls for charity and respect, not arrogance. Moreover, in an unpredictable world, charity functions not as a tool of bourgeois oppression but as a sort of insurance policy against the next upheaval. Children in a position to offer compassion now might find themselves in need of it later, and the practice of charity brings together individuals who, although currently on different sides of a social divide, might find themselves in the same predicament through some future injustice. In postrevolutionary literature, the charity performed by children fulfilled two functions. First, it prepared children for possible reversals of fortune, teaching them frugality and hard work, familiarizing them with the virtues of the poor, and giving them the spiritual resources on which to draw in adversity. Second, charity acted as a sort of glue that held society together, even as random and revolutionary events attempted to tear it apart. The logic of charity was profoundly conservative, but it was certainly not capitalist.

The young bourgeois audiences who consumed the growing number of children's books and magazines learned about the world's social hierarchies and about their religious duties simultaneously. Although gender difference was key to these stories, families were Catholic. Children's literature did not send its readers along separate paths to devout womanhood or dechristianized manhood, nor, by treating all children as somehow feminized, did it suggest a completely different destiny for men, one that bore no resemblance to the simple Catholic tales contained within its covers. Finally, the stories children read did not suggest that their social position, either in the bourgeois elite or in the protected realm of the home, was comfortable or safe from challenge. The boundaries between rich and poor often seemed random in children's fiction, and the circumstances that sent one child out to work while another child played in the garden did not appear to be divinely ordained. The post-revolutionary social order was fully secular in this sense, but children's stories did not treat this as a matter for self-congratulation. Wise children recognized that they owed charity to those less fortunate. The inequalities between them were the consequences of the world inaugurated by the French Revolution, and the scales might tip at any time, but the shared obligations and devotions of the Catholic Church rendered society both more coherent and more stable.

Notes

Research for this chapter draws on the exceptional collection of the Cotsen Children's Library at Princeton University, and I am grateful to the Friends of the Princeton University Library and to Andrea Immel for her help in navigating the holdings.

1. I use "bourgeoisie" rather than "middle class" because the French term better expresses the French preference for seeing society as a coherent whole. Maza, *The Myth of the French Bourgeoisie*. All translations are mine unless otherwise noted.

2. Marx, "Manifesto of the Communist Party," 225–26. For a classic account of French bourgeois disbelief, see Groethuysen, *Origines de l'esprit bourgeois en France*.

3. Marx, "Introduction to the Critique of Hegel's Philosophy of Right," 115–16.

4. See especially Daumard, *La Bourgeoisie parisienne de 1815 à 1848* and *Les Fortunes françaises au XIXe siècle*. Social historians of the early modern period used similar

sources to examine religious conviction. See especially Vovelle, *Piété baroque et déchristianisation en Provence au XVIIIe siècle*.

5. Tudesq, *Les Grands Notables en France*, offers a particularly good treatment of legitimist Catholicism from a social-history perspective.

6. B. Smith, *Ladies of the Leisure Class*, 95–96.

7. Welter, "The Cult of True Womanhood." See also Fesseden, "Gendering Religion."

8. Davidoff and Hall, *Family Fortunes*.

9. De Giorgio, "The Catholic Model." 169.

10. Carroll, "Give Me That Ol' Time Hormonal Religion"; Steinhoff, "A Feminized Church?"

11. For France, see especially Ford, *Divided Houses*, chapter 1.

12. Abrams, *The Making of Modern Woman*, 34–40.

13. For France, see Curtis, "Charitable Ladies."

14. Mack, "Religion, Feminism, and the Problem of Agency."

15. Michelet, *Du prêtre, de la femme, de la famille*, 12, 237. On anticlericals' manipulation of the language of gender inversion, see Vinken, "Wounds of Love."

16. Michelet, *Du prêtre, de la femme, de la famille*, 7, 43–44.

17. Michelet, *Histoire de France au moyen age*, 1:293.

18. Boulard, Hilaire, and Cholvy, *Matériaux pour l'histoire religieuse du peuple français*; Gibson, *A Social History of French Catholicism*, especially chapter 6; and Langlois, *Le Catholicisme au féminin*.

19. Langlois, "Le Catholicisme au féminin revisité," 141.

20. Ford, *Divided Houses*, chapter 4; R. Burton, *Holy Tears, Holy Blood*; R. Bell and Mazzoni, *The Voices of Gemma Galgani*.

21. Harrison, "Zouave Stories"; Seeley, "O Sainte Mère."

22. Ralph Gibson cautions against interpreting declining numbers at mass as dechristianization. Low levels of practice in the late eighteenth century, he argues, reflected a rural rejection of the austerities of urban-focused Tridentine Catholicism, while male nonattendance in the nineteenth century reflected distaste for the clerical association of limiting family size with male sin. See Gibson, *A Social History of French Catholicism*, 185–86. See also Sevegrand, *Les Enfants du bon Dieu*, chapter 1.

23. Sowerwine, "The Sexual Contract of the Third Republic."

24. Clark, "The New Catholicism and the European Culture Wars," 19–20.

25. D. Bell, *The Cult of the Nation in France*; Kaufman, *Consuming Visions*.

26. Rogers, *From the Salon to the Schoolroom*; Seeley, "Virile Pursuits"; Carol E. Harrison, "Protecting Catholic Boys and Forming Catholic Men at the Collège Stanislas in Restoration Paris."

27. As late as 1890, 85 percent of children in the Paris suburbs, an area with low levels of religious practice, received their first communion. See Gibson, *A Social History of French Catholicism*, 165–66.

28. Havelange, "1650–1830: des livres pour les demoiselles?," 363–76; Renonciat, *Livres d'enfance, livres de France*, 11–17.

29. Renneville, *Les Bons Petits Enfants, ou portraits de mon fils et de ma fille*, 1:113.

30. Hauteville, *Aventures d'une poupée*.

31. See, for example, Anne Marie Beaufort d'Hautpoul, "Pierre et Eugène, ou le jeune mousse," in *Contes et nouvelles de la grand'mère ou le séjour au château pendant la neige*, 2 vols. (Paris, 1823), 1:63–129; Muller, "La Nourrice à Paris," in *Innocence et vertu*, 4–7.

32. Fléché, "Les Suites du jeu."

33. Legrand, *Delphine ou l'enfant gâté*, 17.

34. MacLeod, *American Childhood*, 87–98; Rogers, *From the Salon to the Schoolroom*, 37–43.

35. J. G. Masselin, "La Ménagère," 91–93, and "La Frugalité," 100–104, in *Le Monde en miniature*; M. Allent, "La Fille adoptive," in *Les Sept Péchés capitaux: nouveaux contes moraux* (Paris, 1823), 5–20; and *Le Bon Génie*, August 15 1824, 59–60.

36. See [Mme Van Der Buck], "Le Plaisir de faire le bien: la punition du malfaiteur" and "La Docilité et la désobéissance," in *Nouveaux Contes et conseils à mes enfants à l'usage de l'adolescence* (Paris, 1821), 133–55, 156–95.

37. "Une Visite," *Journal des jeunes personnes*, 1 (1833), 17–28.

38. Muller, "La Dame," in *Innocence et vertu*, 24–27.

39. Smiles, *Self-Help*.

40. Bénédicte Monicat, "Romans pour filles et littérature féminine du dix-neuvième siècle," 207.

41. See, for example, B. Smith, *Ladies of the Leisure Class*, chapter 6; Woolf, *The Poor in Western Europe in the Eighteenth and Nineteenth Centuries*; Price, "Poor Relief and Social Crisis in Mid-Nineteenth-Century France." On the language of philanthropy, see Duprat, *Le Temps des philanthropes*.

42. Seeley, "Catholics and Apprentices"; Harrison, *The Bourgeois Citizen in Nineteenth-Century France*, chapter 6.

43. "La Sensibilité et la susceptibilité," in *Nouveaux Contes et conseils*, 103–35.

44. [Mme Van Der Buck], "Achille ou le petit brouillon," in *Contes et conseils à mes jeunes enfants convenables à la première enfance pour les deux sexes* (Paris, 1822), 19–25.

45. Madame Amable Tastu, "Le Livre des recréations," in *L'Education maternelle: simples leçons d'une mère à ses enfants*, 3d ed. (Paris: Didier, 1849), 42–49.

46. *La Recréation: journal des écoliers* 20 (1834): 251.

47. "Achille ou le petit brouillon," in *Contes et conseils à mes jeunes enfants*, 19–25.

48. Madame Wetzell, "Laure et Geneviève," in *Contes à mes petits élèves* (Paris, 1846), 65–76.

49. *La Guerre des Juifs, pour server à l'éducation et à l'amusement de l'enfance* (Paris, n.d.), 75.

50. Carroy, *La Journée d'une petite fille*, 75. See also *Le Mérite des jeunes mères* (Paris, 1817), 105–6.

51. "A nos jeunes lectrices," *Journal des jeunes personnes* 1 (1833): 2.

52. *Scènes de la vie de pension, ou souvenirs d'une jeune pensionnaire* (Paris, [1835]).

53. Arnaud Berquin, *Lydie de Gersin, ou histoire d'une jeune anglaise de huit ans, pour server à l'instruction et à l'amusement des jeunes françaises du même âge* (Paris, 1812), 60–61. The plot of Carroy, *La Journée d'une petite fille*, turns on whether or not little girls can rightfully dispose of property—in this case, food—to the poor.

54. *Le Bon Génie*, May 23, 1824, 11–12.

55. [Mme Van Der Buck], "La Sensibilité et la susceptibilité," in *Nouveaux Contes et conseils*, 103–35.

56. Allent, "La Mort de Juliette," in *Les Sept Péchés*, 70–71.

57. Jules Clère, *Les Vacances de Noël, ou les jeunes chasseurs* (Paris, 1837), 117.

58. *Le Bon Génie*, July 4, 36, and May 30, 1824, 16.

59. Madame Dufrénoy, *Abécédaire des petits gourmands* (Paris, [c. 1820]), 20–23. See also "Hippolite, ou le petit tétu corrigé" and "Laurence et Rogacien, ou les petits mendians" in *Contes et conseils à mes jeunes enfants*, 77–85, 103–12; *Soirées du père de famille, ou conversations familières d'un père avec ses enfants sur plusieurs sujets de morale et d'instruction*, 2nd ed. (Paris, 1822), 45–46, 55. The pairing of gluttony and charity is much less common in stories about girls, but see Rousseau, "Les Pensionnaires."

60. L. P. de Jussieu, "Prospectus," *Le Bon Génie*, April 10, 1824. Issues of the publication regularly contained anecdotes that purported to report true tales of childish misdeeds. See also [Mme Van Der Buck], "Le Journal des petits enfans," in *Contes et conseils à mes jeunes enfants* in which grandparents fabricate a newspaper which reports the misbehavior of their grandchildren (7–19).

61. *Le Bon Génie*, August 1, 1824. See also Sanon, "Charles et Henri," in which misbehaving boys consider whether or not to postpone communion.

62. "Le Bonheur d'être riche pour faire des heureux et le mauvais emploi des richesses," in *Nouveaux Contes et conseils*, 212–49. In addition to buying a suit for a poor little boy, Adolphe pools his resources with his cousins to place the child in a good apprenticeship. See "Adolphe, ou le jeune bienfaiteur," in *Contes et conseils à mes jeunes enfans*, 175–90.

63. *Les Six Ages de Léontine* (Paris, [1815–30 ?]), 49, 137–41.

Siúticos, Huachafos, Cursis, Arribistas, and *Gente de Medio Pelo*

SOCIAL CLIMBERS AND THE REPRESENTATION OF CLASS IN CHILE AND PERU, 1860–1930

David S. Parker

The middle class, like other social categories, is best considered as an abstraction. No matter how real the materiality of economic inequality, a class comes into being only when people think of themselves as members of that class and act accordingly.[1] If they were instead to speak of society as divided between "the people" and "the oligarchy," or between "decent folk" and "the plebe," then "middle class" would be an impoverished concept devoid of resonance. Social analysts, to be sure, are free to impose whatever taxonomical pigeonholes they like; some may be heuristically useful, others less so. But people's own social imaginary, the labels and definitions that they themselves employ in everyday life, have a special power.

Categories of social description are almost always relational; every identity requires its "other," an outsider against whom the group defines itself. And a middle class requires, by definition, not one set of outsiders but two: those above and those below. Yet the terms "above" and "below" are themselves problematic. Societies value and reward different attributes in an individual: wealth may be one, or education, or family name, or how one earns a living, or how one behaves in public. Even within a shared cultural milieu, people can have deeply conflicting ideas about how society is ordered and what qualities command respect. So while self-professed members of a middle class might define themselves as superior to a "lower class" for reasons *x*, *y*, or *z*, you can be sure that those in the "lower class," engaged in their own enterprise of self-definition, probably see things differently.

By the same logic, how a middle class defines itself cannot help but be influenced by how the upper class defines *it*. After all, every time people attach social labels, they place one another in an imagined hierarchy, and in so doing they negotiate the criteria by which some people claim superiority over others. These battles around categorization are not merely rhetorical. They have a concrete impact on the outcomes of individual and collective struggles over social boundaries, be they attempts to move into "better" circles or to enforce the exclusion of "undesirables." All these acts of inclusion and exclusion, striving and gatekeeping, occur within a sometimes shared, sometimes disputed universe of cultural meaning, a universe constructed by language. The terms that people use to define social categories and to describe social types play no small role in constituting the social order itself.

This chapter therefore examines how words, images, insults, and stereotypes shaped the battle over the boundary separating "upper class" from "middle class" in Chile and Peru between about 1860 and 1930. In particular, the chapter looks at depictions of the social climber. Throughout the late nineteenth century and the early twentieth, Chilean and Peruvian essayists, novelists, playwrights, and memorialists devoted inordinate attention to the social climber, typically portrayed as comic, sinister, pathetic, or all three at once. Contemporaries vilified and ridiculed social climbers for their pretension, bad taste, and lack of social graces. In so doing they created a rich lexicon of epithets—*arribista, medio pelo, cursi* (originally native to Spain), *siútico* (native to Chile), *huachafo* (native to Peru)—and a compendium of vivid anecdotes that have long attracted the interest of literary scholars. More is at work here than simple *costumbrismo*,[2] however: I will argue that these images were weapons in a class struggle waged on symbolic terrain. Because so many writers described the social climber as an illegitimate, unwelcome intruder, this literature offers a unique perspective on how those favored by society fought to preserve the exclusivity of their ranks, how others challenged that exclusivity, and how both sides defined gentility in fast-changing but still hierarchical societies. That Peruvians and Chileans between the 1860s and the 1930s would intensely debate the nature of their social order should not come as a surprise: both nations experienced profound economic and demographic transformations (booming export-led economies, urbanization, and immigration) and equally intense cultural changes (secularization, the "social question," new roles for women, and deepening ties to Europe and the United States). It was a time of upward mobility for many and downward mobility for some, and a time of rapidly changing mores.[3] As middle- and upper-class Chileans and Peruvians began to process mentally the changes happening around them, competing images of the social climber stood in as proxies for competing visions of what a just and proper societal hierarchy should look like.

Debating Essence in an Open Society of Castes

As late as the 1940s, both foreign and local observers overwhelmingly described Latin American social structure in terms of two separate castes, with an impenetrable barrier between them. "I met them on the country road," wrote George McBride in 1936, "Don Fulano and his *mozo* (servant), the latter riding at a respectful distance behind."[4] After describing the appearance of master and servant in intimate detail, McBride explained how the two men provided a metaphor for Chilean society: "Here has existed a new world country with the social organization of old Spain; a twentieth-century people still preserving a feudal society; a republic based on the equality of man, yet with a blue-blood aristocracy and a servile class as distinctly separated as in any of the monarchies of the Old World."[5]

Although succinct, even lyrical, McBride's description was no revelation. In 1849 José Victorino Lastarria had written of a Chilean society divided between "the respectable and the not respectable."[6] Frequently used synonyms included *gente decente*, *gente de familia*, *la sociedad culta*, *hombres de bien*, or *gente sana* for those above the great dividing line, and for those below, *gente de pueblo*, *el bajo pueblo*, *plebe*, *chusma*, and, in Chile, *rotos*. Implicit in all of these terms was the idea that one's place in the social order was innate, not a temporary stopping point on fortune's fluid pathway but an essential moral quality, built on character and blood. The memoirs of Ramón Subercaseaux illustrate this point well. He describes a play put on for charity around 1910, with the participation of some hundred of the "most beautiful and elegant girls of the city": "The theatrical spectacle, as a piece of art, was marvelous; the girls with their consorts [*galanes*], all select, criollo scions of true Basque, Saxon or Andalusian blood; that distinction of birth and education that one feels, sees, and cannot explain . . . No, it is not possible to repeat an event like that one, so filled with elegance and grandeur [*señorío*]."[7] Clearly, the mental world of Subercaseaux was inhabited by superior and inferior beings, not by socioeconomic categories in any modern sense.

Yet this convention of two hermetic castes did not remotely describe Chilean or any other Latin American society. Some surnames survived the centuries, but the extent of elite turnover belies any pretension that "respectable" people could only be born, not made. Some of Chile's "best" oligarchic families of the late nineteenth century—Edwards, Matte, Cousiño, even Subercaseaux—had acquired their fortunes in the not-so-distant past, in mining, commerce, or banking. People who cared made fine distinctions between those families and longer-established ones, but no one would go so far as to question a Matte's or a Cousiño's upper-caste credentials. Despite the belief that social position reflected innate quality, they had parlayed a lucky vein or a string of investment windfalls into a place among Chile's exalted names.[8] Furthermore, the very image of "Don Fulano and his *mozo*" obscures the fact that Chile and Peru had long known people who were neither. Clerks in the public and private sectors, officers in the armed forces, liberal professionals lacking fortune or contacts, and prosperous artisans were also part of Latin American society, and they were treated as Don Fulano's inferiors and his mozo's superiors.[9]

If the two-caste vision failed to acknowledge either the fluidity or the complexity of Latin American urban society, why did the image persist? A simple answer is that persons of wealth and power almost always assert their inherent moral superiority. High culture, etiquette, and the other classic hallmarks of status serve to legitimize an artificial exclusivity, buttressing the myth that some people are the natural betters of others.[10] Dualism—*decente* versus *no-decente*, *de familia* versus *del pueblo*—was a useful corollary to this vision of social position as an inborn trait. To muddy the waters by recognizing additional classes might undermine the whole edifice. Still, that simple answer needs to be complicated somewhat, because every justification of privilege is specific to a place and time. What qualities defined the decent people and disqualified the *chusma*? Family name? Occupation? Education? Whiteness? Wealth? Had turn-of-the-century Chile and Peru been divided between two truly impregnable castes, these questions would have been merely academic. Had the two societies been self-consciously open and mobile, the questions would not have arisen at all. But because they were at the same time objectively open and subjectively divided into castes, because mobility occurred regularly but was not quite legitimate, the answers to these questions took on great importance.

The most basic question was the extent to which wealth defined the social hierarchy. Few people wish to believe that their value as a human being is a function of their accumulated capital, yet this was the message that seemed to be on the rise universally in the later nineteenth century. As a result, some writers began to express openly their worry that money counted for more than it had in the past, and that character and family name no longer carried the weight they should. This, for example, is a central theme of Chile's best-known novel of the nineteenth century, Alberto Blest Gana's *Martín Rivas* (1860). *Martín Rivas* is the story of a poor but talented provincial youth who arrives in Santiago to study law and is accepted into the aristocratic home of Don Dámaso Encina as a debt to the young man's late father. Throughout the novel, Martín is painfully conscious of the social gulf that separates him from the wealthy Encinas, and particularly from the daughter Leonor, with whom he falls—he believes hopelessly—in love. The main plot of the novel revolves around the process by which Martín overcomes barriers to win Leonor's hand. Blest Gana uses this familiar nineteenth-century storyline to deliver a sustained attack on the role of money in defining social position. Noting that Don Dámaso's wealth derived from a lucky mining strike, Blest Gana underscores the artificiality of the great man's prestige, and by extension, the precariousness of the Chilean elite's pretension to superiority:

> [In Europe] there exists what is called an aristocracy of money, whose power and grandeur never succeed in making [people] forget the obscurity of their birth; in Chile, however, we see that wealth is all, and the glitter of silver has conquered the arrogant disdain that once used to be directed at the social parvenu. We very much doubt that this is a step toward democracy, because those who measure their vanity by the blind favor of fortune typically affect an insolence that makes them look down upon those who, unlike them, cannot purchase respectability with luxury or with the fame of their riches.[11]

Blest Gana lampoons the gallicized affectation of the new elite in the figure of Don Dámaso's son, Agustín, a superficial playboy who sprinkles every sentence with expressions picked up in Paris. Similarly he ridicules the crass materialism of Dámaso's brother-in-law, Fidel, whose every decision—even the choice of a suitor for his daughter—is determined by its impact on the profitability of his country estate. Both are comic figures not to be taken seriously. In contrast, the novel's one truly evil character is the social climber Amador Molina, who will stop at nothing to escape his lowly birth. The very picture of the Chilean *siútico* (a word Blest Gana uses), Amador consumes beyond his means, aspires to elegance in dress but fails for lack of taste, and shamelessly resorts to all manner of fraud in the scramble to make money without actually working. Amador's family, described as medio pelo, consists of a scheming, illiterate widow with two attractive daughters, Adeleida and Edelmira. Adeleida has been tragically seduced and abandoned, and Blest Gana makes it clear that her ambition to marry an aristocrat contributed to her downfall.[12] Later, a combination of ambition and revenge lead her to trick Agustín into a sham marriage. Edelmira, nobler in character, harbors a pure but unrequited love for Martín Rivas.

It is not hard to discern authorial intent in this openly didactic novel. On the one hand, Blest Gana argues that inner substance should be valued above money or appearance. Martín, while poor, wins Leonor's hand through the quality of his character. Time and time again, Martín demonstrates his morality, judgment, intelligence, and inner strength, as he administers Don Dámaso's business affairs and extracts the Encina family from various misadventures. On the other hand, Blest Gana's ideal society remains unrepentantly hierarchical. From beginning to end, the book takes a dim view of intimate social relations between the elite and the *gente de medio pelo*. Amador's vices arise from his attempt to enter a world to which he does not belong. Adeleida's disgrace and Agustín's brush with scandal both result from seeking love outside of their proper circle. Why is the relationship between Martín and Leonor different? Because Blest Gana sees Martín as a born member of the superior class, despite his poverty. At the beginning of the novel, Blest Gana points out that Rivas possessed "a certain air of distinction that contrasted with the poverty of his dress,"[13] and later he amplifies this message, using Leonor as a mouthpiece: "Martín, though poor, has a noble soul, high intelligence, and this is enough for me . . . *He is also from a very good family*; thus he lacks nothing except to be rich, and I am sure that with the abilities you recognize he possesses, I will never be poor."[14] Although money for Blest Gana should not bring social distinction, character and bloodline should. The best proof can be seen in the fate of Edelmira Molina. Even though morally she is as noble as Martín, Blest Gana implies that she cannot and perhaps should not escape her humble origins.[15] Her love for Martín is doomed, and she ends up marrying a policeman she does not love, but who shares her station.

Martín Rivas demonstrates the persistence of hierarchical thinking, even by a writer who decried the use of money as a social yardstick. It is telling that liberals like Blest Gana and Lastarria used terms like "gente decente" and "medio pelo," affirming that social position is—or at least should be—a matter of birth and character. Theirs was not a democratic critique of elitism, but an illustrated critique of materialism, something quite different.

"Money Laundering" and *Buen Tono*

Blest Gana wrote *Martín Rivas* in 1860, at a time when Chile's silver and copper boom had just begun to spew forth a new class of millionaire aristocrats, drawn from mine owners and the merchant bankers who financed their operations. Chilean historians point in particular to the 1870s as the decade when this rising class first began to impose its French-style mansions, cosmopolitan tastes, and extravagant lifestyles on what had been a sleepy, austere, devout, and rather provincial colonial capital.[16] Although the fantastic expansion of new wealth sparked growing unease among many, the rising elites desperately sought new ways to promote the fiction of their innate superiority. With an intensity rarely seen before, the newly rich dedicated themselves to converting their fortunes into a respectable family name, an *abolengo*. The methods they employed—metaphorically speaking, a kind of social "money laundering"—have been well described by historians: investment in rural property, education and the cultivation of school ties, philanthropy, involvement in politics, and the forging of family networks through strategic marriages.[17]

Money laundering was also achieved, increasingly, through dress, speech, manner, taste, and lifestyle. "The way he presented himself," wrote Luis Orrego Luco in *Casa Grande* (1908), "his air, the style of his suit and of his person, placed him immediately among Santiago society and in the fashionable circles."[18] Chileans believed they could size up a stranger's social position at a single glance. The cues were subtle and constantly changing with the ebb and flow of fashion, but somehow they were always perceptible to the select who knew what to look for. An entire language of signs and codes, rules and transgressions, separated good society from those who could only aspire. These unspoken standards were known as *buen tono* (roughly, "good taste").[19]

Just as other forms of metaphorical money laundering sought to cloak a recent or precarious fortune in the mantle of timeless tradition, the rules of buen tono preserved the fiction that social superiority was a matter of blood, not money. In theory, at least, buen tono was the visible manifestation of inner refinement; it could not simply be bought, nor was it the exclusive patrimony of the rich. For example, the novelist and essayist Joaquín Edwards Bello recounted the true story of a German immigrant who bought and sold scrap metal. He lived in a small house he built himself, dressed simply, spent modestly, and eschewed the obligatory appearances at the racetrack and the club. So despite accumulating a fortune of four million pesos, he was a social nobody.[20] Meanwhile, in *En familia* (1912), Orrego Luco told the fictional story of a white-collar employee with little money but descended from a notable Santiago family. Following the requirements of buen tono, he wore elegant clothes in the latest style, spent his nights in fashionable cafes and clubs, and gambled the nights away with the cream of the city's bohemian youth. Until he was caught embezzling to finance that lifestyle, he was accepted unconditionally as one of the superior class.[21]

Though theoretically having little to do with wealth, buen tono was obviously for sale. With freer trade and the growing availability of European status goods, cosmopolitan consumption increasingly defined gentility in ways that were ostensibly more democratic (given the abolition of colonial sumptuary laws), but in practice just as exclusionary.[22] Money was the key that allowed one to dine on French haute cuisine in an appropriately elegant restaurant, to wear fashionable imported clothes, to send one's children to the correct private schools, to vacation in Paris, and to pay the membership fees of the Club de la Unión. Only by following these rituals to the letter was buen tono maintained. Not surprisingly, therefore, yet another theme in Latin American literature is the plight of the fallen aristocrat, who understood perfectly the demands of buen tono but could no longer afford them. This was the story of Teresa Iturrigoriaga in Edwards Bello's best-selling novel *La chica del Crillón*, whose greatest fear was to fall out of the circles of buen tono, and thereby lose her status, her name—everything. Teresa expressed her terror that she would come to be seen as siútica, "an illness of humiliation that lasts several generations."[23] "La pared de enfrente" (1903), an acclaimed short story by the Peruvian author Jorge Miota, tells much the same tale.[24]

Finally, men and women of recent fortune could not successfully "launder" their money without the approval of others. At the end of the day, buen tono was in the eye of the beholder, and prestige could not be earned quickly. Social dues had to be paid, sometimes over a generation or more. Indeed, it might be possible for two different people to carry out identical actions—purchasing an estate, running for political office, spending time in Europe, buying the latest English cut of suit—with widely different effects. The first might win the hearts and minds of the "best" families and thereby slip quietly into their ranks, while the second might earn ridicule. The reasons for rejection could be subtle, ranging from some almost imperceptible social faux pas to a slightly premature effort to break into a particular social circle. They could also be arbitrary: one might follow the rules of buen tono impeccably and still be rejected on the basis of family name, politics, or even personality. Potential social climbers had to conquer the difficult terrain of opinion, a battlefield of malicious gossip and disdain. Nevertheless, what should catch our attention is not elite society's resistance to upward mobility as much as its openness to new blood—so long as the practices of money laundering and the rituals of buen tono were followed. As the Chilean historian Gonzalo Vial puts it: "Just as the oyster traps the impurity and turns it into a pearl, so the 'good' family surrounds their *siútico* son-in-law and incorporates him into the aristocracy. One or two generations and those *siútico* roots are for all practical purposes dead and buried, only coming to the surface occasionally as a barb in some vehement discussion."[25] Vial again describes an open society of castes, where the image of impenetrable social barriers prevailed but where channels of controlled upward mobility functioned effectively and were quite well understood.

However, the rules of metaphorical money laundering and buen tono did not go uncontested. As we have already seen, some writers ridiculed the pretensions of buen tono. Just as Blest Gana had denounced the growing belief in money as the measure of man, so early-twentieth-century critics refused to submit to the new tyranny of lifestyle and appearance. Many saw buen tono for what it was: the dignification of new money through conspicuous consumption and the canonization of fashion. While men of fortune imposed ever more elaborate, costly, imported rituals of etiquette and taste, other members of the elite publicly lamented the loss of the old ways—the quiet dignity of the colonial aristocracy, the savor of local cuisine, the paternalism of the rural estate. Several forces fueled this romantic nostalgia. For one thing, some members of traditionally distinguished families lacked the wherewithal to keep up with the latest Continental styles. More than just a literary cliché, downward mobility was as much a part of the landscape as upward mobility, even more so as the new rich pushed the minimum consumption standards of polite society ever upward. The essayist Domingo Melfi recounts the auctioning off of an old Santiago mansion and all its contents in order to ruminate on this contrast between the older aristocracy and the new moneyed elite: "Into the hands of the newly rich, little by little, disappeared tradition, the opulent soul of the founders of the nation, the perfume of the elegance of old."[26]

Starting in the first decade of the twentieth century, most notably in Chile, a new generation of essayists, novelists, and critics began to write about this clash of values as they lamented the nation's moral crisis. Their concerns ranged from economic dependency to political corruption to poverty and social unrest, but they generally agreed on the culpability of an estranged, cosmopolitan elite that had abandoned traditional values.[27] Although some intellectuals found themselves moving toward a denunciation of inequality itself, the majority, like Blest Gana a half-century earlier, continued to accept the ideal of hierarchy as innate and God-given. They called into question the legitimacy of this particular new elite, but not the principle of elitism itself. At the very least, they continued to employ the vocabulary of gente decente and gente del pueblo, with everything that those terms implied.

In essays, memoirs, novels, and daily conversation, Chilean and Peruvian elites obsessively debated the qualities of the siútico and the huachafo, respectively. Both words approximate the Spanish cursi and describe the bad taste and comic pretentiousness of the social climber who unsuccessfully attempts to infiltrate a group to which he does not belong.[28] On closer inspection, however, the words "huachafo" and "siútico," like "cursi," appear in the literature with several distinct and ambiguous meanings, describing significantly different kinds of people. As we will see, how people defined a siútico or a huachafo depended on the qualities they attributed to the "legitimate" elite, thus offering a glimpse of their mental images of class, hierarchy, and gentility.

The complexity of elite images of the social climber can be illustrated by looking at the vocabulary employed to describe them. In general, medio pelo denoted people of modest means and undistinguished family, but not the indigent masses. Although we might be tempted to translate medio pelo as lower middle class, we would miss the point that medio pelo described alleged qualities of birth and character, having nothing to do with "lower middle class" as a socioeconomic concept. Gente de medio pelo were by no means all social climbers, but most social climbers came from the gente de medio pelo.[29] The word "arribista" had the least ambiguous definition, denoting the deliberate bounder, the parvenu (*advenedizo*) openly and aggressively seeking entry into higher circles.[30] Here the connotations of new money and lack of taste were the clearest. An arribista was someone who too prematurely, too energetically, or too transparently engaged in social money laundering, without first mastering the subtleties of buen tono. Examples included the successful Spanish-born importer who had an extravagant coming-out party to introduce his daughters to society, or the immigrant industrialist who spent lavishly in the bar of the Gran Hotel Bolívar but who would find true happiness only when he could drink and mingle in the members-only Club Nacional.

Some Peruvian and Chilean writers used their local terms—huachafo and siútico—with exactly this meaning. The Chilean Tomás Gatica invented the following exchange, supposedly spoken at the opera:

> Look at those siúticas in the orchestra seats, fourth row on the right.
>
> Jesus, look at that hair! How do they dare mix with people [like us]? [*¿Como se atreven a meterse entre la gente?*]
>
> What amazes me is that they were allowed in.[31]

Because this conversation supposedly took place inside Santiago's elegant and pricey Teatro Municipal, we are evidently witnessing a definition of "siútico" as the moneyed but tasteless nouveau riche. Similarly, Domingo Melfi recounted the ordeal of "enriched middle-class families" at the theater: "They feared the stares of the aristocratic women; incisive, penetrating, ironic stares that seemed to say: 'and these gate-crashing siúticas?' "[32]

Perhaps the best example comes from *En familia*, where three of Orrego Luco's fictional female characters argued about which of Chile's political parties contained more siúticos. The year was supposed to be 1886.

> Only the siúticos support the government. The gentlemen, the well-born do not . . .
>
> There are also many caballeros among the Liberals. Without looking any further, you have Don Tulio Fernández, a descendant no less of the counts of Santa Bella.
>
> Don Tulio is nothing but a simple siútico and his title of count . . . [i]s nothing but a purchased title, just like the titles they regularly hand out in Portugal, or like other decorations that are peddled in various countries.[33]

Here, too, the word "siútico" was used by the old aristocracy to disqualify new money. The first speaker railed against "the parvenus, the recently enriched, the champions of the posh society."[34] This was the lament of those for whom tradition and family name took precedence over luxury and buen tono, and it contained a fervent critique of the social, cultural, and political changes brought about by the rise of so many new fortunes. Orrego Luco painted the conversation with humorous brush strokes, but he was trying to capture the spirit of arguments that surely took place in many fashionable Santiago drawing rooms—including his own—at that time.

Somewhat later, in 1942, Federico Schwab constructed a theory of the Peruvian huachafo that built on that same image of the rich but uncultured social climber. Despite the time difference and Schwab's social-science, rather than literary, style, the themes are identical. Schwab argued that in Europe, the historical transition from a closed caste society to a mobile class society had been gradual. As a result, upward mobility went hand in hand with cultural assimilation, so the economically successful rarely stood out as social misfits. In Peru, however, the barriers of a caste system endured well into the twentieth century, as did ethnic heterogeneity and intense cultural differences between classes. At the same time, opportunities for economic advancement increased markedly. Thus, "in Peru it turns out to be much easier for individuals from the lower classes to become economically well-off than for them to acquire a broad and deep culture."[35]

Significantly, however, this is not the only definition of "huachafo" or "siútico" that appears in the literature. Remember that Edwards Bello's character Teresa Iturrigoriaga, in *La chica del Crillón*, used siútico to describe not the uncultured nouveau riche but its opposite: the fallen aristocrat. The Peruvian scholar Hugo Neira gives a similar example of the "*aristócrata venido a menos* who shuts himself up in an old mansion in Barranco, without enough to eat, yet with a butler."[36] But most commonly, huachafo or siútico referred to the person who had neither money nor breeding but tried to feign possession of both. In the words of the Peruvian poet Manuel Velázquez Rojas: "In my consideration, *snob*, literally, is one who possesses money but not nobility. That is to say the bourgeois without civilized refinement, who imitates certain actions without understanding or feeling the values that those actions embody. *Snob* should not be confused with *huachafo* . . . *Huachafo* is one who does not possess money and imitates (in dress, conduct, actions, etc.) those who do."[37] Bad taste remained the central feature of *huachafería* or *siutiquería*, but the words took on a very different meaning when applied not to the wealthy arribista (who ostensibly could afford good taste if he knew what it was), but to the impoverished taste of the struggling medio pelo. Both nouveau riche and medio pelo sought to enter previously inaccessible social circles, and both failed because they could not master the arcane cultural secrets of the superior caste. But on close inspection, the representation of the huachafo or siútico as poor, rather than rich, betrays an entirely different and opposing interpretation of social climbers and social climbing.[38]

In his memoirs, Orrego Luco described an old Santiago Holy Week custom, in which young men would go from house to house wearing the black robe and mask of the *cucurucho*, taking advantage of their carnival disguise in order to steal anonymously into the homes of acquaintances, friends, girlfriends, or girls they hoped to court:

> There was a humorous custom, to defend one's self from the siúticos or cursis of those times. Whenever some cucurucho entered a home, the head of the household would say to him point-blank:
>
> "Let's see the foot . . ."
>
> Then the *cucurucho* was supposed to pull up the robes he was dragging and show his foot. In this way, by instantly assessing his shoe, one knew if he was a *persona bien* or simply a siútico, in which case he was thrown out of the house ignominiously.[39]

This anecdote, which has that authentic, unguarded ring of many early childhood memories, implies that the personas bien viewed poor-quality footwear as a mark of inferiority, reason enough to kick a man out of one's house. Here again it appears to be poverty, not the poor taste of the nouveau riche, that defines the siútico. And coming from Orrego Luco, who so often criticized the Chilean elite for its materialism and superficiality, the passage illustrates how unconscious and ingrained those prejudices could be.

The connotations of poverty are even more dominant in Peru. According to the essayist Sebastian Salazar Bondy, huachafo described the seamstress who copied the latest fashions using cheaper material, the bureaucrat with no higher education who spoke and wrote with an artificially elegant vocabulary, and the shopkeeper who built his modest house in the style of a Greek temple or a French palace.[40] Common to all of these examples was the effort to scale the social ladder not by metaphorical money laundering, but by putting on a show of ostentation in order to conceal limited economic means. Luis Alberto Sánchez placed the classic huachafo, geographically, in the lower-class Lima neighborhoods of Chirimoyo or La Victoria.[41] A few years earlier, the Peruvian essayist Abelardo Gamarra had written: "Poverty of the spirit and poverty of the pocketbook are what engender huachafas. The desire to appear and to be no less than anyone else turns people into huachafas."[42]

When used in this way, with this meaning, huachafería often became a feminine attribute, the stereotype being the poor but attractive girl who spent every last penny on her appearance, hoping that the gamble would pay off in the marriage market and ultimately assure her financial security.[43] José Carlos Mariátegui wrote in 1929 of the *huachafita* as a girl of middle-class origins whose ideal was to marry an American employee of W. R. Grace or the Foundation Company.[44] The place of gender stereotypes in the depiction of social climbers is significant. On the one hand, young women were often described as cunning and creative manipulators of the new consumer culture, who could fool gullible elite men by fashioning attractive public identities that masked their modest circumstances. On the other hand, women were also the ones most likely to fail horribly—either tragically or comically or both—in the effort to appear to be that which they were not.[45] Although siútico, like cursi in Spain, tended to be a more gender-neutral epithet, the alleged behavior of the female siútica in Chile was much the same as that of the Peruvian huachafita.

So here's the key question: Why did Peruvians and Chileans employ identical words to describe entirely different kinds of people? Why did the rich immigrant capitalist earn the same label as the poor girl whose only aspiration was to marry an American clerk? The reason is complex but crucial. For one thing, these very different uses of huachafo and siútico share one common characteristic. Both describe social posturing, the attempt to pass oneself off as something one is not. The stereotypical siútico treated the lower classes with arrogant disdain (something a genuine gentleman would never do), paid excessive attention to the rules of buen tono, and was more class conscious than the aristocracy itself, all in spite of his own humble origins.[46] Writers described him or her as meticulous in dress and personal hygiene, elegant in speech, and obsessively trained in etiquette. As Ricardo Valdés wrote in 1919:

> The siútico speaks with affected pulchritude. He says "my residence" for the house he lives in, "onomastic" and "interment" for what the majority of us mortals simply call birthday and burial . . . The siútico lives for foreign words: *boudoir, chaise longue, comme il faut*. He calls his girlfriend "Mary" [in English], though she's a María quite *criolla* and dark-complexioned like him.
>
> . . . The siútico knows by heart the language of flowers and the meaning of each tiny movement of the fan . . . He wears mourning dress with an amazing strictness; hat of black straw, ebony cane, jet-black collar, black handkerchief. He complains about not finding sufficiently funereal crepe shirts to better exteriorize his soul's bereavement.[47]

What made this behavior siútico and subject to ridicule, at least according to Valdés, was that it was too studied, too wooden, too deliberate, lacking the effortless savoir faire of a man born and bred in the world of buen tono. The racial undertones are also clear: Valdés's siútico was a mestizo or mulatto, whose elegant façade contrasted with his innate inferiority. Neira's discussion of the Peruvian huachafo similarly invokes the memory of a notable and talented attorney who used rice powder to lighten his skin.[48]

For some writers, the distance between appearance and reality did not have to be particularly great for an action to qualify as huachafería or siutiquería. According to the Peruvian writer José Chioino, it took a discerning eye to distinguish genuine elegance from huachafería: "Huachafería is precisely the desire not to appear (*huachafo*), the drive to be elegant at all costs. It is the jewelled tie-clip, the hat, the way of speaking, by which certain people hope to make themselves interesting. Because between originality that is innate elegance, and huachafería . . . , there is but a step (*hay un paso*)."[49] The basis of that step—for Chioino and other writers as well—was authenticity versus imitation.

If huachafería and siutiquería were rooted in the supposed conflict between appearance and reality, then nouveau riche and medio pelo were equally capable of being huachafo, albeit for different reasons. The rich arribista was assumed not to possess the requisite character, breeding, or blood and sought to use wealth and conspicuous consumption in order to infiltrate the ranks of those who did. Poor social climbers also lacked those innate attributes, but to make matters worse, they could not even follow the rituals of buen tono, affecting instead a visibly phony or ill-fitting veneer of sophistication. By either definition, the huachafo or siútico pretended to be what he or she was not, and could not possibly be. "Pretend" is exactly the right term, because both meanings of the Spanish word "pretender" apply: pretend as in "make pretend" and pretend as in a pretender to the throne, an illegitimate usurper. The obsession with inauthenticity, with an appearance out of synch with intrinsic quality, lay at the heart of Peruvian and Chilean definitions of huachafería and siutiquería.

This, too, had long been the classic meaning of the Spanish cursi, going back at least to the 1869 *Diccionario de la Real Academia Española*: "*cursi:* person who presumes himself fine and elegant without being so,"[50] or to an earlier and even better definition in an 1857 dictionary of regional Cádiz slang: "*cursi:* a person who desires to be elegant without having the necessary qualities, *either for lack of money or for lack of good taste*."[51]

This whole idea of authenticity and inauthenticity, however, brings us back to the crux of the matter. If the words "huachafo," "siútico," and "cursi" all denote a gulf between appearance and essence, then there must be an innate hierarchy of essence. But what *is* this alleged essence, if we are talking about social distinctions and hierarchies? Have we not already established that the very idea of essence was a myth, an ideological mystification perpetrated by the elites of the day, whose own exalted position, more often than not, owed a debt to some ancestor's successful money laundering? On closer contemplation, the words themselves make no sense unless one actually believes that social position is a matter of character, not circumstance. And on this point, both definitions of "huachafo" or "siútico"—as nouveau riche or as dissembling poor—were in agreement.

Clearly we are seeing a discursive weapon designed to stigmatize the upwardly mobile and shore up an invented edifice of discrimination built on a fiction.[52] But what were those innate, essential qualities that the huachafo or siútico sought to project but supposedly could never attain? On this point the disagreement returns. Those who attacked the nouveaux riches, like Orrego Luco's matrons in *En familia*, focused on the contrast between the siútico's elegant bearing and undistinguished birth. For them, what made the siútico siútico was the presumptuousness of wealth without bloodline. In contrast, those who stigmatized the medio pelo, as in Orrego Luco's childhood memory of the cucurucho, emphasized the fashion flaws of those unable to afford buen tono. It was vulgarity of taste and poverty of consumption, rather than lowliness of birth, that reflected and supposedly proved the inferiority of the siútico's character.

Because so many social climbers lacked multiple attributes of gentility, it is perhaps unsurprising that writers of the era reified the huachafo or siútico as an identifiable social type and ignored these contradictions. From time to time, however, the tension between blood and money rose to the surface. The Chilean essayist Ricardo Latcham described the furor that arose when "a young man who suffers from the *criollo* malady of geneologism, a Mr. Larrain, referred [in print] to very distinguished [unnamed] girls in disdainful tones. In a word, he 'siúticized' them . . . All of Santiago lived for a week in a tumult of scandal and apology."[53] Why the scandal? Because in this instance the word "siútico" was not an epithet hurled from the social heights against those below, but a weapon in intra-elite debate over the meaning of gentility and the ranking of individuals.[54] Those who focused on surnames and pined for the austerity of patriarchal tradition used the word to ridicule the arrogant pretension of the new Europeanized millionaires. In turn the millionaires, who defined the elite by their elegant style and perfect Continental etiquette, used the word to ridicule the arrogant pretension of those old colonial families, who may once have been of some importance in Trujillo or Talca, but who now (like Teresa Iturrigoriaga) scratched out a pathetic living from the exiguous rents of their run-down estates. Buen tono versus abolengo: in theory they always went together, but when they did not, sparks could fly.

Latcham's use of "siúticize" as a verb underscores the extent to which public name-calling, derision, and words in general played a part in the enforcement of hierarchy. The belief that social position was a matter of inborn character made Peruvian and Chilean elites intensely sensitive to the presence of intruders threatening the exclusivity of their ranks. When the "true" elites discovered such pretenders, they launched epithets like huachafo, siútico, and cursi in order to unmask and ostracize them. Gossip mattered in this style of class struggle. Yet these were not struggles with predetermined outcomes. Many new rich did metaphorically launder their money and marry into the "best" families. Some ancient families fell from grace, and some gente de medio pelo broke into circles their parents could not have imagined. In fact, the multiple controversies over how to define the gente decente created openings for the skillful social climber. It was, after all, simpler to infiltrate a divided, contested elite than it would have been to join a united, undisputed one.[55]

Conclusion

From the late nineteenth century to the mid-twentieth, starting earlier in Chile than in Peru, newspaper columnists, novelists, essayists, and memorialists wrote extensively about the peculiar qualities and characteristics of the social climber—the arribista, the siútico, the huachafo. These writers believed that they were accurately describing a quaint, humorous, often pathetic figure, suffering from a specific character flaw: the misplaced desire to enter the superior class by appearing to be something he or she was not. Many believed that this unique pathology defined their nation's middle class and distinguished it from the middle classes of healthier, wealthier Western nations. Yet this reification of the middle-class social climber as an objective personality type can work only if we accept the false premise on which the image rests: that society is divided between natural superiors and natural inferiors, and that one cannot escape one's born essence. If we agree, however, that people have always moved up and down the social ladder, that the "best" families of today did not always carry blue blood in their veins, that money has always played a role in defining the elite, and that the rules of buen tono are entirely capricious conventions of fashion, then the edifice collapses. Huachafo and siútico, cursi and arribista become not objective portraits of real people, but weapons in a rhetorical class struggle.[56] This is not to say that social climbers never behaved in the manner their critics described. One assumes they often did. But rather than a collective pathology, their actions make more sense as a logical response to the genuine, if scarce, opportunities for advancement that existed in Peru or Chile's open society of castes. Ascent by posturing, by disguise, was perhaps the only viable strategy in nations where elites continued to embrace the fiction that social hierarchy was a matter of intrinsic moral character, while at the same time fighting bitterly over which qualities defined the select.

In *Distinction*, Pierre Bourdieu famously argued that aesthetic tastes in art, music, clothing, and other visible forms of consumption were simultaneously markers of class and learned behaviors that reproduced class divisions from one generation to the next.[57] Bourdieu stressed how difficult it was for people of working-class or lower-middle-class backgrounds to acquire the cultural capital that would enable them to master the predispositions, tastes, and lifestyles (habitus) that defined the elite and fixed its borders.[58] Interestingly, however, though Bourdieu correctly unmasked habitus as learned rather than innate, he never problematized its content. Bourdieu found little conflict over which tastes should be considered highbrow, middle-brow, or lowbrow, most likely because in his own late-twentieth-century Paris, little conflict existed.

The vehemence with which early-twentieth-century Peruvians and Chileans wrote about social climbers reveals a different story. The competing and incompatible constructions of huachafo and siútico—as pretentious nouveau riche, fallen aristocrat, or dissembling medio pelo—were at heart encoded arguments about habitus. Images of social climbers, to be sure, served as rhetorical means to enforce arbitrary standards of gentility, and thereby to police the boundaries of the superior caste. But Peruvian and Chilean images of social climbers equally demonstrate profound disagreement over what those codes and standards should be, and an ongoing struggle to define what made the superior caste inherently superior. Huachafos, siúticos, cursis, arribistas, and gente de medio pelo both embodied and betrayed the contradictions of an arbitrary, invented social order.

Notes

My research in Chile was made possible by a grant from the Advisory Research Council of Queen's University, with funds provided by the Social Sciences and Humanities Research Council of Canada. I thank Sergio Grez Toso, Gonzalo Cáceres Queiro, and José Pablo Silva for their advice and guidance. Arnold Bauer, Charles Walker, Beatriz de Alba-Koch, and the editors of this volume provided valuable comments on earlier drafts of the chapter. All translations are mine unless otherwise noted.

1. Geoff Eley and Keith Neild argue that this constructivist view of class, once controversial, now stands as the new orthodoxy. See Eley and Neild, "Farewell to the Working Class?," 17.

2. *Costumbrismo* is the Spanish term for literature that takes as its subject the depiction of daily life and customs, often but by no means always in rural or provincial contexts.

3. The era was also punctuated by a major war, the War of the Pacific, which left Peru economically and emotionally devastated, while triumphant Chile experienced both accelerated economic change and rising social and political conflict.

4. McBride, *Chile*, 3.

5. Ibid., 14.

6. Lastarria, *El manuscrito del diablo*, 48.

7. R. Subercaseaux, *Memorias de ochenta años*, 231.

8. Vial Correa, *Historia de Chile*, vol. 1, part 2, 628–30; Villalobos, *Orígen y ascenso de la burguesía chilena*, 45–70. Frederick Pike provides a classic analysis of elite openness to new blood. See Pike, "Aspects of Class Relations in Chile." Claudio Véliz makes a contrary case for elite continuity across the generations, but his argument is based more on the lasting prestige of old elites than on the absence of new ones. See Véliz, "La mesa de tres patas," 244.

9. D. León, "Las capas medias en la sociedad chilena del siglo XIX." McBride probably

realized as much, but his point was to describe the essence of social hierarchy as rural Chileans experienced it.

10. Bourdieu, *Distinction*; Kasson, *Rudeness and Civility*, 65–69; Levine, *Highbrow/Lowbrow*.

11. Blest Gana, *Martín Rivas*, 15. Throughout I will use my translation; the Tess O'Dwyer translation (Oxford University Press, 2000), is more concise but loses nuance.

12. Ibid., 65.

13. Ibid., 10.

14. Ibid., 361 (my emphasis).

15. For example, Blest Gana says that while Edelmira is "more cultured than the majority of those of her class," she nevertheless shares the medio pelo's tendency to be overly melodramatic. See ibid., 280.

16. Godoy Urzua, *La cultura chilena*, 381–87.

17. Balmori, Voss, and Wortman, *Notable Family Networks in Latin America*; Brading, *Miners and Merchants in Bourbon Mexico*.

18. Orrego Luco, *Casa grande*, 23.

19. Barros Lezaeta and Vergara Johnson, *El modo de ser aristocrático*, 55–71.

20. Edwards Bello, "Vicho Balmaceda," 10. The story is also cited in Barros Lezaeta and Vergara Johnson, *El modo de ser aristocrático*, 89. The concept of "nobodies" and "somebodies" is also explored in Jayawardena, *Nobodies to Somebodies*, xxiv and chapter 10.

21. Orrego Luco, *En familia*.

22. Bauer, *Goods, Power, History*, chapter 5.

23. Quoted in Edna Coll, *Chile y los chilenos en las novelas de Joaquín Edwards Bello*, 128.

24. On Miota and "La pared de enfrente," see McEvoy Carreras, *Forjando una nación*, 279–80.

25. Vial Correa, *Historia de Chile* vol. 1, part 2, 677.

26. Melfi, "Tiempos de tormenta en el remate de un viejo palacio santiaguino," 105.

27. Some of the best-known figures of this generation of writers are Francisco A. Encina, *Nuestra inferioridad económica* (1912), Alejandro Venegas, *Sinceridad* (1910), Tancredo Pinochet LeBrun, *La conquista de Chile en el siglo XX* (1909), and Nicolas Palacios, *Raza chilena* (1904). For an excellent introduction to their work, see Barr-Melej, *Reforming Chile*, chapters 2–3. See also Contardo, *Siútico*, which I was only able to obtain after completion of this chapter.

28. Spanish discussion of the cursi is even more extensive than the Peruvian and Chilean literature examined here. See Valis, *The Culture of Cursilería*.

29. Arturo Jauretche's *El medio pelo en la sociedad argentina*, originally published in 1966, remains one of the classic explorations into Argentine social psychology.

30. In "An Analysis of 'Arribismo' in Peru," Carlos Delgado O. provides a highly entertaining introduction to the motives and methods of the Peruvian arribista, although his analysis consistently teeters on the edge of falling into an oversimplified "national character" argument.

31. Quoted in Vial Correa, *Historia de Chile* vol. 1, part 2, 707.

32. Melfi, *Sin brújula*, 78.

33. Orrego Luco, *En familia*, 70–71. I have modified the passage to make it read as a dialogue.

34. Ibid. "Los advenedizos, los enriquecidos de ultima hora, los luchadores por la sociedad encopetada."

35. Federico Schwab, "Lo huachafo como fenómeno social," 402–3.

36. Hugo Neira, *Hacia la tercera mitad*, 480.

37. Quoted in Pinto Gamboa, *Lo huachafo*, 28.

38. On the huachafo or huachafa as poor or lower-middle-class, see Neira, *Hacia la tercera mitad*, 471–72. Neira also provides examples of the huachafo as nouveau riche; see 469–70.

39. Orrego Luco, *Memorias del tiempo viejo*, 6.

40. Salazar Bondy, *Lima la horrible*, 117–18. Although Salazar Bondy wrote this famous essay in the 1960s, it reflected his memories of an earlier era.

41. Sánchez, *Peru*, 98. This is also quoted in Pinto Gamboa, *Lo huachafo*, 27.

42. Quoted in Pinto Gamboa, *Lo huachafo*, 39.

43. Neira, *Hacia la tercera mitad*, 472.

44. Mariátegui, "Punto de vista anti-imperialista," 88.

45. See, for example, Moncloa y Covarrubias, *Las Cojinovas*. Moncloa y Covarrubias used the well-established Spanish word "cursis," not the (at that time) still very new Peruvianism, "huachafo."

46. B. Subercaseaux, *Contribución a la realidad*, 163.

47. Valdés, "Sobre el siútico criollo."

48. Neira, *Hacia la tercera mitad*, 469.

49. Quoted in Pinto Gamboa, *Lo huachafo*, 34.

50. Quoted in Santos, *Tropical Kitsch*, 108.

51. Quoted in Valis, *The Culture of Cursilería*, 58 (my translation and emphasis).

52. Neira, *Hacia la tercera mitad*, 474, 482–83.

53. Latcham, "Psicología del caballero chileno," 318.

54. Later, particularly in Peru, the word "huachafo" would also come to be used *by* the poor to stigmatize those who broke ranks of solidarity in their desire to rise socially. See Neira, *Hacia la tercera mitad*, 483.

55. On the ways in which astute social climbers could exploit elite disagreements over the rules of hierarchy in order to scale the social ladder, see D. S. Parker, *The Idea of the Middle Class*, 34–39.

56. Salazar Bondy, *Lima la horrible*, 118.

57. Bourdieu, *Distinction*, 1–2 and chapter 1.

58. Ibid., especially chapters 2 and 4. For the definition of "habitus," see 101.

"Los Argentinos Descendemos de los Barcos"

THE RACIAL ARTICULATION OF MIDDLE-CLASS IDENTITY IN ARGENTINA, 1920–1960

Enrique Garguin

The historical formation of the Argentine middle class is particularly paradoxical. Early-twentieth-century Argentina enjoyed the largest "middle sectors" and the most vigorous capitalist economy of Latin America.[1] Based on the 1936 census, Gino Germani estimated that the middle class constituted 45.9 percent of the economically active population in the city of Buenos Aires.[2] Moreover, between 1916 and 1930, Argentina was ruled by the Unión Cívica Radical (UCR), often considered an "archetypical" middle-class-based political party. However, one finds scant reference to the middle class in primary sources until the 1950s.[3] This is all the more remarkable considering that by 1900, Argentines possessed a clear sense of upward social mobility and a well-established language of (working) class. Indeed, it is hard to talk about the Argentine middle class before the emergence of Peronism as anything other than the kind of heuristic category with which current scholars try to standardize a multifarious reality that had previously resisted reduction to that category.[4]

This chapter is concerned with the time lag between the advance of the process of capitalist development in Argentina and the emergence of the idea of the middle class as a distinctive social and political subject. How can we explain the late popularization of a term—"middle class"—that would later seem so appropriate in characterizing central aspects of Argentine history? I argue that during the first half of the twentieth century, the notion of middle class was constructed on the basis of two key differentiations: one in opposition to the landed bourgeoisie, mainly articulated through the binary contrast of people and oligarchy; and another in opposition to the working class, mainly articulated through racial categories.[5]

Focusing on the realm of representation, this chapter analyzes one particular dimension of the complex process of middle-class historical formation in Argentina: its discursive articulation. It argues that middle-class identity in Argentina crystallized only when it was articulated via a range of racializing discourses accompanying the emergence and entrenchment of Peronism. If such a middle-class identity was not clearly articulated earlier, this was in part because representations of the nation had been defined as the extension of the experiences of the urban middle sectors of Buenos Aires and the littoral. Thus, the nation was constructed as homogeneously white, European (in contrast to the mestizo representation of other Latin American nations), and lacking significant social differences, a representation that did not favor the configuration of a clear notion of a middle class. The emergence of Peronism would stimulate the discovery that such a racialized image did not apply to the whole nation but only to a part of it; and this part would be increasingly identified as the middle class.[6]

The Argentine Middle Class: A Delayed Identity?

By the mid-twentieth century, the middle class was represented in opposition to the working-class-based Peronist movement. Paradoxically, the policies of Juan Perón's government—economic nationalism, social welfare, and democratization—would soon be considered typical goals of Latin American middle classes. Moreover, Perón was probably the first politician to explicitly address a middle-class subject before shifting all his bets toward the unions—a shift due, in part, to the failure of his first appeals to middle-class people.[7] It is not our aim to analyze the failure of that first attempt, but the negative response to it suggests a more fundamental question: was there a middle class already in existence to be mobilized?

There is no doubt that the mass of immigrants arriving from overseas between 1860 and 1930 had a great impact in the shaping of Argentine identities.[8] According to a popular saying, which tries to link Argentine national identity with European immigration, "we, Argentines, descend from ships."

This myth of "Europe in the Río de la Plata" coincides with another myth about the tremendous social mobility offered by Argentina to anyone who wishes to work hard on its generous soil. My first hypothesis is that as a result of these two myths—and the partial truth they express—the very notion of being Argentine became so conflated with socially mobile middle sectors from the littoral cities that the specific idea of a middle class did not carry much meaning, and the idea itself thus remained undeveloped. The identification of ill-defined middle sectors with the nation writ large was reflected and reinforced in the political arena by the UCR, which hardly ever appealed explicitly to a middle-class subject but rather to "the people"—constructed in binary opposition to the "oligarchy" and identified with the entire nation.[9]

The making of such a national identity was never a smooth, linear process. Sectors of the elite challenged it periodically, raising the traditional and Creole gaucho as the national hero.[10] From below, working-class-based ideologies, such as anarchism, offered contested notions of identity. But they lost strength after the first decade of the twentieth century, and a vast—and less conflicted—web of ethnic and neighborhood associations, popular libraries, and political committees gained preeminence during the 1920s.[11] Some authors identify the membership of those voluntary associations as "popular sectors," a descriptive term that is in tune with the dominant interpellation of the time—"the people"—but that blurs the processes of class formation underlying those seemingly consensual popular sectors.[12] I argue that a middle-class identity was not clearly constructed until Peronism eroded the popular public sphere that had been consolidated from the 1920s on.[13] Identifying "the people" with the working class and replacing associations by unions and Unidades Básicas (political committees, mostly led by workers), Peronism deprived that popular public sphere of its mediating role between the state and the people. Thus, Peronism broke the middle sectors' main links with the people—encouraging a new, tripartite image of society (oligarchy, middle class, and people) to compete with the old bipartite one (oligarchy and people).

But Peronism and the working class were not the sole actors in this drama. The middle sectors of the 1940s considered themselves to be not only a central part of the people, but also the heirs of Europe and immigration. Thus, confronted with the disturbing irruption of Peronist workers within *their* space, they sought to differentiate themselves not only from the oligarchy, as in the past, but also from the new Peronist "other." A racialized gaze played a key role in this process. The Peronist masses, with all their plebeian features overtly displayed in public, were almost incomprehensible within previous symbolic and cognitive schemata and were soon identified with new migrants from the interior of the country. The middle sectors increasingly objectified and belittled them through the use of the term *cabecita negra* (little black head), which became tantamount to the Peronist worker.[14]

Such a racist reaction suggests that a deep sense of whiteness played an important role in the process of middle-class formation. Some anthropologists have unveiled the deep sense of whiteness implicit in the dominant national imaginary for contemporary Argentina, some of them even centering their analysis on the middle class.[15] Scholars have noted both the success achieved by the nineteenth-century elite's project of whitening the population, and the appropriation of European racial science by intellectual elites during the first decades of the twentieth century.[16] But what was the bridge between nineteenth-century whitening projects, the explicit racism of early-twentieth-century intellectuals, and the racialized class language of midcentury? I argue that the bridge was the dialectical process of white and middle-class identity formation. I will consider some of the trails connecting both ends of that bridge through an analysis of discourses produced by intellectuals, politicians, and other public figures. Not all of them can be characterized as belonging to the middle sectors, but their ideas and preconceptions have deep roots in public opinion as well as in common sense. This was in part due to their prestige (they wrote mainly from a white, educated, and "civilized" position), which made their work key reading for a range of social sectors, particularly among those that would become middle class. It was also due to the amazing efficacy of public schools in spreading similar values. Finally, the same ideas were dispersed among innumerable voluntary associations and through the mass media.[17]

Thus, I trace the construction of a key element of the national imaginary. I demonstrate how a particular social actor, "the man from Corrientes and Esmeralda" depicted by Raúl Scalabrini Ortiz, created a partial and synthetic image of himself—an image that, extended in both social and geographical senses, became the archetypical figure representing the whole nation.[18] This hegemonic construction, through which the *porteño* who met his friends in downtown coffee shops would be identified with the whole nation, resulted from the displacements inscribed in two key myths. First, the myth of upward social mobility made class differences irrelevant by extending some people's experience of mobility to the whole population. Second, the myth of Europe in the Río de la Plata projected onto the whole population the ethnicity of the overseas immigrants, who were considered to be homogeneously white and European.

Argentines Descend from Ships

Racially [Buenos Aires] is a white city . . . within a mestizo America. A black man in Buenos Aires is as exotic as in London. And the same is true for a gaucho. In that sense, it is whiter (extremely white) than New York. [Buenos Aires] has no Indians or mulattos. Its men and women do not have the same skin and hair color; nevertheless they are white. This does not constitute a privilege, especially from an aesthetic point of view, but it is a good eugenic possibility.
—FLORENCIO ESCARDÓ, *Geografía de Buenos Aires*

The myth of the European origins of the Argentine population is linked to nineteenth-century efforts by the elites to think of Argentina as different from the rest of Latin America—which, according to the ideological tropes of the time, did not fit in the category of civilized societies. Even after independence, the Río de la Plata area exhibited "a more complete consensus than other regions of Spanish America" about the benefits expected from immigration.[19] Together with the success reached by the promotion of immigration during the second half of the nineteenth century, that consensus encouraged the making of a national imaginary in which the European immigrants occupied a central place.

Although the idea of Argentina as a white nation can be traced back to the middle of the nineteenth century, it was during the twentieth century—as an effect of massive immigration—that it crystallized into an undisputable myth of origin and achieved the status of common sense, expressed in the standing joke that Argentines descend from ships. In fact, nineteenth-century intellectuals recognized the dubiousness of the idea, affirming that the white and European character of the Argentine population was a matter of dominance, not total exclusivity. Since they could not deny that nonwhite elements were involved in the making of the so-called Argentine race, they resorted to various devices to try to prove that such elements were minimal or were subsumed under the dominant European ones.

Bartolomé Mitre was probably the first proponent of an organic and coherent image of Argentine history and nationhood, one that proved to be particularly compelling and lasting. The so-called father of Argentine historiography claimed that the Río de la Plata region had been different from the rest of the Spanish colonies since the time of the conquest. In many respects, its history had been closer to that of the English colonies of North America than to that of the rest of Spanish America. In Mitre's view, Mesoamerica and the Andes were regions populated by semicivilized peoples who had been conquered by rapacious and adventurous men representing the most backward parts not just of Europe but also of Spain. The result had been the establishment of feudalism and a hardly desirable racial mixture. By contrast, the Río de la Plata had received the most advanced of the Spanish settlers, "true colonists in the sense of settling and civilizing," "true immigrants" who brought with them a "municipal spirit" and a work ethic. As a result, it was possible to create a "rudimentary democracy" based on scarcity, work, and shared efforts.[20] The nation had begun its history linked to the most advanced notions of Western civilization. It was also better positioned in its racial composition: "Three races converged . . . to create the physical and moral genesis of the [Río de la] Plata's sociability; the European or Caucasian as an active component, the indigenous or American as an auxiliary one, and the Ethiopian as a complement. An original type resulted from their fusion. In this type the European blood prevailed because of its superiority, constantly regenerating itself through immigration. Next to it, another mixed race of the black and the white grew and improved, assimilating the physical and moral qualities of the superior race."[21]

Mitre recognized that the colonial history of the interior of the country was closer to the history of Peru. The resulting feudal backwardness had been a main cause of the long-term conflicts between Buenos Aires and the interior provinces. But in the making of the nation, that dissimilar interior was subsumed to Buenos Aires (which was "the head and soul" of the Argentine provinces), much the same way as the "inferior races" in the Río de la Plata region were subsumed to the superior element of European origin.[22] Mitre's arguments conjured up and then vanquished the ghosts of inferior races and justified his idea of an Argentina born from the seeds of European liberty and democracy. Such an intellectual construction, however, was not enough to place Argentina on the same plane as the advanced societies of Europe. Hence, pro-immigration policies were meant not only to civilize and populate the desert, but also to whiten the population.

The immigration projects that had begun in the mid-nineteenth century were soon considered quite successful as regards to both economic growth and the transformation of the country's ethnic composition—particularly that of its littoral region. These projects were coeval with the expansion of social Darwinism and the biological theories of races, and thus it is not surprising that so many intellectuals glorified the whitening road. Authors such as the late Domingo F. Sarmiento and José Ingenieros (in his most positivist stage) wrote global interpretations of Argentina and Latin America that centered on their racial composition. The authors argued for rigid racial hierarchies, slightly mitigated by the future socializing effects of public education.[23] These authors contributed to the establishment of long-lasting racial stereotypes, but their racial thought was not the most influential aspect of their writings. By the early twentieth century, the problems the elites considered the most serious were related not to the racial inferiority of the population, but to massive immigration (which in turn had ethnic and racial connotations) and its disruptive consequences for the quiet, village-like life that had characterized *criollo* Buenos Aires.

Much has been written about the nationalist reaction surrounding Argentina's centennial, but, as Tulio Halperin Donghi has pointed out, the nationalists neither denied immigrants' contributions to the population nor tried to stop the immigration process at all. On the contrary, nationalists sought to promote national cohesion by accelerating the assimilation of foreigners, revealing at the same time the existence of deeply rooted perceptions about the importance of the immigrants. In this sense, the nation was seen as a project in the making. Indeed, national identity was to be found in the future, and it had to be a project to be fostered by the state.

After the centennial, however, there was a key change in relation to the nineteenth-century liberals' project concerning immigration. Part of what the nineteenth-century advocates of immigration expected it to achieve had already been achieved, while part had been shown to be impossible. The whitening aspect of the project, in particular, seemed to have been successfully achieved on the surface, although it did not seem to be the expected panacea. This situation may have weakened the absolute faith in immigration, but even chauvinist reactions proved to be unable to undermine the nineteenth-century consensus about the generally positive outcomes of European immigration. In any case, the image of the Argentine population as overwhelmingly European was irreversible. The 1914 census reinforced that symbolic construction by showing that one-third of the population had been born in foreign lands—a percentage that rose to 50 percent in the city of Buenos Aires.

A consensus was built around the melting-pot model.[24] Its constitutive elements were already present in the work of nineteenth-century thinkers, but it became widely accepted in the twentieth century, albeit with an important variation. Starting then, the melting pot would accept only European immigrants and *criollos* (allegedly also of European origin). In other words, by the middle of the nineteenth century, the alleged white predominance went hand in hand with the recognition of its incomplete success, the admitted need for a whitening project, and a clear awareness of the differences between Buenos Aires and the interior provinces. By the twentieth century, pro-immigration policies had already produced some of the expected results. At the same time, the interior provinces—already conquered by the federal government—were no longer more political problems and had been replaced in the elite's concerns by a new source of malaise provoked, in part, by the cumulative effects of pro-immigration policies. From Buenos Aires outward, all Argentina was seen as a country of European origins, and the concern was no longer located in a racial "other," but in a population considered as homogeneously white. As the Socialist Representative Enrique Dickman announced to his colleagues in 1924:

> We are a country of immigrants . . . The Argentine country, this vast crucible of a new race, has brought here men of all races, the upper crust of human races. It is enough to look at this arena and to analyze each representative to see that this is something new, singular, unique and exemplary in this world . . . I am part of the Argentine crucible, the Argentine tree deeply rooted in the native race of the country, its robust Iberian trunk, its implanted branches of all the most vigorous and intelligent races, and its blood sprinkled with a touch of Semitic ferment which is, historically and socially, leaven of a healthy and fertile rebellion.[25]

It seems surprising that the idea of the melting pot could coexist with considering some races superior to others. By "the most vigorous and intelligent races," Dickman meant the European races. Twenty-two years later, in 1946, he proclaimed the need "to attract—as in the past—a healthy and large immigration." As in 1924, he did not then always refer explicitly to the European immigrant he had in mind, but occasionally he did, calling for "the arrival and settlement of a large number of industrious Europeans."[26] In fact, he used interchangeably notions such as "all races" and the "immigrants," together with others that made explicit reference to Europe, all of them melted into the common pot of criticism to any kind of racism.[27] Hence, after specifying the different nationalities of European (and only European) immigrants, he concluded: "Such is the ethnic composition of the Argentine country. It is a real and wonderful melting pot! And it is such a monstrous aberration to encourage hatred among races and religious persecution in the social and political Argentine environment!"[28] Notwithstanding the universal character of this antiracist discourse, Dickman considered "European" and "immigrant" to be synonyms, and he dismissed the native peoples almost entirely: "In America, we are all immigrants—with the exception of native Indians who form a minority of the population."[29]

The identification of Argentina with immigration and European whiteness was linked to the contemporary making and expansion of that popular public sphere I mentioned earlier, since the broad web of voluntary associations not only had frequent contacts with the intellectuals analyzed here, but also spread the same ideas that they did. An article published by Asociación de Maestros, an association of thousands of teachers in the Province of Buenos Aires, began: "In a cosmopolitan country like ours."[30] With equal spontaneity, a traveling salesman's wife began a message to her Brazilian peers: "From Rosario de Santa Fe [the second industrial and port city in Argentina], where the assimilation of races, temperaments and cultures is making a uniform, progressive and liberal human type."[31] Is it necessary to speculate about which races were making that "uniform, progressive and liberal human type"?

There were, certainly, some dissenting voices denying immigrants a place in the making of Argentine nationality, but they did not manage to interrupt the formation of a consensus. Moreover, they did not question the immigrants' contribution to the population; they only rejected immigrants' claim to a role in the spiritual formation of the nation. The conservative nationalist Carlos Ibarguren, for example, stated in *La Inquietud de esta hora* in 1934: "The massive avalanche of immigrants . . . has transformed Buenos Aires and the great Littoral into a polyglot and heterogeneous region, a real chaotic ethnic Babel [that] has not promoted the formation of a spiritual unity, a proper Argentine soul. This soul will emerge and will be powerful only when nationalism creates the moral and organic unity of all the social forces amalgamated in one only spirit."[32] In a strictly demographic sense, then, the crucible of races was apparent even to Ibarguren. As Eduardo Archetti points out, Ibarguren did not see the nation as a mixture of races: "The idea of amalgamation so explicitly presented" was "a kind of Renanian conception of the spirit of the nation as an expression of a collective psychology." Hence, the nation was "reduced to a psychological phenomenon, to a collective consciousness that [had to] be created. The question of racial mixing [was] thus avoided."[33] Following this trend, Ibarguren even dared to deny the Argentine origin of the tango, arguing that it was the result of hybridity. This view pushed Ernesto Sábato to reply:

> Although it is certain that the tango is a product of hybridity, it is false to say that it is not Argentine; in any case, there aren't any platonically pure peoples, and today's Argentina is the result . . . of successive invasions, starting from the one headed by the family of Carlos Ibarguren who, undoubtedly, should be regarded by the Cafulcurás as an intruder, and whose opinions should be considered as typical of an improvised Pampean.
>
> Denying the Argentine origin of the tango is a very pathetic self-destructive act; it would be the same as denying the existence of Buenos

> Aires. Ibarguren's autistic thesis would erase in just one move our capital city . . . And there wouldn't be a government either, since our presidents and governors tend to be mere children of Italians or Basques, or hybrid products exactly like the tango. But what am I saying? Not even nationalism would survive the hecatomb, since we would have to sacrifice the Scalabrinis and the Mosconis.[34]

Far from denying the white character of the *criollo* population, right-wing nationalists and Catholic integrists reproduced the same kind of curses against aboriginal peoples and the Afro-Argentine population earlier seen from turn-of-the-century liberal intellectuals. In this regard, many exponents of the reactionary nationalism that began in the 1920s were better followers of the late Sarmiento than those who explicitly vindicated the nineteenth-century liberal tradition, including the Socialists. "Mental and ethnic mulattos" was the formula used by Manuel Gálvez to denigrate his liberal and positivist intellectual enemies—vindicating Catholic and Hispanicist spiritualism in its place.[35] The revisionist historian Ernesto Palacio went even further. He claimed that the Indians' contribution to Argentina had been null in cultural terms and limited in demographical terms. "We are a white nation," he asserted, an extension of Spain, "of its race," in America.[36] And arguing against those who might have thought that there was something positive in the aborigines, he claimed that the rural people who knew the Indians had never held such a mistaken belief. In order to prove this, he invoked the gaucho Martín Fierro, the character of the famous poem written by José Hernández:

> The Indians spend their lives
> stealing or lying on their bellies.
> The law of the spear's point
> is the only one they'll respect,
> and what they're lacking in knowledge
> they make up with suspicion . . .
> They've a mortal hatred for Christians
> and give no quarter when they fight . . .
> All a savage knows how to do
> is how to get drunk and fight.[37]

"He who talks," continues Palacio, "is not a mestizo . . . [like most] men of our pampas. He is white and he is a Christian; he is a Spaniard; and as such, he is fond of the tribes' extermination."[38] In the next section I will elaborate on the significance of such racializing discourses for the articulation of a middle-class identity. Here, I will focus on the building of a national consensus about the European origin of the Argentinian population, paying special attention to another view that incorporated populist tones and was as far from progressive liberalism as it was from conservative nationalism, while it remained attached to the white-nation myth. *El hombre que está solo y espera*, by Raúl Scalabrini Ortiz, is a particularly interesting source. The author was in the process of breaking with the liberal tradition in which he had been raised. Although his book soon became a kind of manifesto for popular nationalism, it also tried to respond to those who questioned that Buenos Aires could embody the national soul because of its hybrid nature, forged in a crucible of immigrants. With six editions in two years, the book was one of Argentina's best-sellers in the 1930s, a time when Argentines were particularly concerned with questions about the national being.

According to Scalabrini, "the porteño is a chemical combination of races," "whose main property is to reject any filial relationship with the ancestors." The creator of that alchemy is "the spirit of the land," represented as an unreachable and "gigantic man." This complicates comprehension, since "the testimony of the porteño circulates within a formal European system," but his "substance" is quite different. "Whoever focuses on physiognomy or habits will think he is in Europe, but who observes the pulse or the inspirations will not."[39] When Scalabrini talks about European physiognomy and habits, he is clearly talking about a white and civilized ideal type, even though he refers to it as the superficial form covering the substance. The one who best incarnates the Argentine substance imposed by the enigmatic giant, by the land, is the "porteño," "the man from Corrientes and Esmeralda, who, to me, will be the Man by antonomasia." "The man from Corrientes and Esmeralda is the center in which the Argentine vortex converges on the most subjugating spiritual frenzy. Whoever is far from him will have a more unmistakable foreign flavor, the most extravagant peculiarities . . . but he will have less spirit of the land."[40] This is particularly significant, since Scalabrini—not a proponent of the liberal view—explicitly argued that the man from the interior provinces is less representative of Argentina than is the Europeanized porteño. He recognized the existence of different peoples in the interior. They were (formally) less European, but they were not more Argentine. Far from questioning the exclusion of the *criollos* made by the hegemonic discourse, Scalabrini reinforced that exclusion by identifying middle-sector porteños with the archetypical Argentine. Like Dickman with his crucible, Scalabrini argued that Argentines "come from four different races," but he never specified which races he meant, and he returned repeatedly to the dominant notion of the European origin. He even claimed that the porteños kept some marks of their origin and, hence, "those who manage to save some money don't lose the opportunity to travel to Europe." Europe is the only origin he constantly considered as making the porteño. Yet, inside the porteño, "the man from Europe is always part of a plurality, something that in himself appears mutilated, incomplete. The porteño is a man of an individualistic society formed by juxtaposed individuals, kept together by just one veneration: the race they are making."[41]

The porteño, archetype of the Argentine, is still in the making; "that is why the porteño son of a European father is not the descendant of his ancestor . . . He is not the son of his father, he is the son of his land."[42] In fact, Scalabrini dealt with the integration of the immigrants' children to Argentina, implicitly accepting and reproducing the myth about the European origin of the country—although that does not make us identical to our immigrant parents. Argentina may not be Europe in the Río de la Plata, but we, Argentines, certainly descend from (European) ships. In fact, his entire book can be read as a constant counterpoint between the porteño and the European with the purpose of showing the peculiarities of the former, which can be found in a more intimate and deeper stratum than his European appearance. In addition, "the man from Corrientes and Esmeralda," the white porteño, belongs to the middle sectors, for his referent could not just be any porteño—it must be one with a certain standard of life, which would allow him to be free of worries about having enough to eat or losing his job, to go to downtown cafes in the evening, and eventually to travel to Europe.

Up to this point I have traced the construction of a discourse about the nation that had many roots in the nineteenth century and crystallized into common sense in the twentieth century. At the center of this construction was the assertion of the European origins of Argentina's population. Some upheld the melting-pot model without hesitation. Others thought that it was necessary to prompt the immigrants' children to absorb the *criollo* national substance. For all of them, however, the search for a national definition during the first half of the twentieth century took for granted the European foundation of Argentina's population. Clearly, none of the writings that I analyze here can be individually taken to represent the whole content of the general notion that I am trying to tease out. Two elements, however, allow me to argue that they reflect a view that was shared by the majority of the urban population of the littoral. The first is the fact that discourses that were very dissimilar in other respects presented a clear consensus on the understanding of national origins. The second is that, typically, such consensus was expressed as something that was taken for granted and tended to appear among the less analytical components of those discourses. This peculiarity tells us that we are dealing with conceptions that are deeply ingrained in a domain lying beyond critical consciousness.

The shared consensus built a myth of origin with numerous exclusions. Africans and indigenous peoples were by and large erased from the representation of the nation, and the identification with Europe was constructed, ignoring the population from the interior and the least privileged social sectors from the littoral. This was done without any significant challenge to a representation of the national community that imagined it as something homogeneous, which could be hybrid but not divided. In addition, many of the advocates of the consensus belonged to ill-defined urban middle sectors of the littoral, particularly the city of Buenos Aires. Retrospectively, and bearing in mind many other features of their social position, it would seem that they could have easily claimed a middle-class identity. But they did not, probably, because they considered such identification unnecessary.

Peronism and Racialization

> There they were, poised to show all their might so that nobody could doubt that they really existed. We watched them from the sidewalk, feeling something similar to compassion. Where were they coming from? Did they exist? And so many? So dissimilar from us? . . . [T]hat day, when the voices burst and columns of anonymous earthen-colored faces started to parade, we felt that something was vacillating, something that until that moment had been unmovable.
> —FELIX LUNA, *El 45*

The rise of Peronism produced a radical rupture within the dominant representation of the nation. The Peronist plebeian masses had no place in a nation imagined as civilized, European, and culturally homogeneous. Confronting their entrance to the center of the political stage, many people, like Felix Luna, felt that "something that until that moment had been unmovable" was then shaking.[43] The result would be the emergence of a new identification: that of the middle class. A middle class would preserve a good deal of what had been previously considered features of the whole nation but were now increasingly perceived as belonging to only a part of it. This shift happened hand in hand with another process by which racializing sensitivities and discourses produced a category that even today continues to denote the Peronist masses: the *cabecita negra* (little black head). Years later, the most famous exponent of popular nationalism in Argentina, Arturo Jauretche, wrote: "The presence of the cabecita negra had a strong impact on the urban physiognomy, and the ideological injury of mental colonialism worsened because of that irruption that changed the physiognomy of the city, flooding the commercial centers, the recreational areas and the means of transportation, even reaching summer resorts."[44]

Compelling as it is, Jauretche's interpretation points to a rupture and an identification of Peronism with the cabecita negra that was much less complete than it seems. The rise of Peronism was first perceived by its opponents within the conceptual frame of the struggle against fascism, while Peronists developed an interpretation based on the old people-oligarchy dichotomy.[45] Neither of these views implied changes in the national self-image. Centered as they were on the political realm, they did not foster clear distinctions in terms of class or ethnicity—although Peronists gave preference to social features, and the incorporation of the civilization-barbarism dichotomy by anti-Peronists opened the possibility of abysses between different cultural and ethnic groups.

The familiar fascism-antifascism dichotomy had pervaded anti-Peronist discourse since its inception. This centered the debate in political terms, although it also had broader cultural tones through its articulation with the civilization-barbarism dichotomy. Thus, an antifascism that considered itself representing both civilization and the whole nation saw the rise of Perón as the rise of totalitarian and barbarian fascism.[46] The consequence was an "other" that was excluded from the national construction; an "other" that would soon reveal itself not only as the popular majority but also as located in the urban littoral that had been the center of much of the national thought.

On October 17, 1945, workers poured into the streets of the main cities and occupied the symbolic center of the country, Plaza de Mayo, demanding the appearance of their new leader, Colonel Juan Perón. The full consequences of such an unexpected event were not immediately clear, but the workers' mobilization caught too many actors unprepared, astonishing the anti-Peronists. Since they really believed they represented the "true" Argentina, this massive support for Perón undermined an essential pillar of the anti-Peronist self-image. The anti-Peronists first processed the shock within the old paradigm built by antifascist struggles, which had proved effective in previous contexts. But new elements appeared that would contribute to the construction of a more radically different "other" than the one emerging from a politically framed dichotomy. It would take time to make a transition from a bipartite model of society (people and oligarchy) to a tripartite one (popular masses, middle class, and oligarchy). In the meantime, however, the anti-Peronists tried to make sense of the new and incomprehensible reality without changing the core of their self-image and identity. Hence, they did not see Perón's followers as belonging to the true nation: "That human scum is not, in fact, the great Argentine people . . . , it is just Perón's people," stated Eugenia Silveyra de Oyuela in *Antinazi*.[47]

The people were not Peronist, and Peronists could not be a legitimate part of the people. Then, who were the Peronists? Why did they support barbarian fascism? The most sympathetic explanations, evoked notions such as heteronomy and demagogic manipulation of inexperienced masses. Phrases such as the lumpenproletariat and *compadrito* (wise guy) reappeared in the political language to contrast the allegedly uncivilized manners of Perón's followers and the previously idealized workers—who were seen as educated and respectful men of labor.

On occasion, the Peronists were relegated to the world of deviance: "Colonel Perón showed his troupe of pimps and gangsters," claimed the official newspaper of the Communist Party in the caption for an allegorical drawing that showed a bunch of prostitutes and delinquents under Perón's control.[48] In other cases, their disdain was framed in aesthetic terms. According to *La Nación*, the "spectacle" had been "unusual and disgraceful"; according to *Crítica*, the demonstrators "offended the good taste and the aesthetics of the city, made ugly by their presence in our streets."[49] Later, Ernesto Sammartino (a UCR representative) would refer to the Peronist voters as a "zoological flood," casting them into the animal realm.[50]

The derogative treatment of the Peronist "other" soon acquired racial tones. The socialist paper considered the Peronist parade to be a "horde," a "masquerade," and a "mob (*balumba*), which sometimes degenerated into *murga* [popular musical theater performed during carnival]."[51] Months later, Américo Ghioldi wrote in an editorial in *La Vanguardia*: "*Romería*, *candombe*, popular dancing, naked dances, spontaneous—if not gracious—relaxation, tricks against this or that . . . [and] all that is proper, in their bodies and their symbolism, to the liberation of native and rudimentary forces."[52] Such writings began to make certain racial figures the subject of derision. *La Vanguardia* frequently repeated the image of candombe,[53] whose racial connotations were as evident as was its metaphorical use—nobody could think that *La Vanguardia* was describing an actual African-Argentine parade. However, such a discursive racialization of the "other" is particularly meaningful because of what it implied in terms of self-representation: implicitly, those who used such a language put themselves in the place of the authentic white or, at least, the nonblack. The counterpoint between the (implicit) whiteness of the speaker and the Peronist masses is seen in an anonymous poem that mocked the promise of fair elections using the metaphor of whiteness: "The day we vote, white will be the act, / the ballot boxes will be white / and white will be the emotion . . . / the day we vote, everything will be so white / as white as the candombes of the revolution are."[54]

Years later, a renowned writer would say about Perón: "He even formed an army of anthropomorphic mulattos, stubborn illiterates, horseback corps that make up his court."[55] Racial stigmatization of the political enemy had many precedents.[56] Scalabrini Ortiz said some time around 1931: "They now talk about the foreign-like rabble (*chusma agringada*), the unrefined plebe, as they talked in the past about the *tapes*, the mulattos, the *zambos*, the Indians, the *chiruzas*."[57] We could think that by 1930, Argentina had replaced a language based on race with another one based on class, but this was not exactly true. Thus, *La Fronda* claimed in 1929 that the electoral triumph of Radicalism was the "mirage of the *malón*," "the essence of a candombe," and had "as its main consequence the predominance of a Negro-like mentality."[58]

Though not a novelty, the racial stigmatization of the political enemy, added to the revival of the civilization-barbarism dichotomy with which anti-Peronists tried to make sense of the new phenomenon, surely facilitated the construction of a racial "other." However, in spite of what an already traditional vision implies, the chain of signifiers linking the Peronist working class with migrants from the interior and the cabecitas negras did not emerge in 1945 but during the Peronist years.[59] Nor does the construction of a racialized Peronist "other" seem to have been a response to the arrival of people from the interior provinces. It is still unclear how many migrants came from the interior provinces and how many from the littoral provinces by 1945, but contemporary accounts did not emphasize ethnic differences. Only a few of them alluded to the migrants from the interior, as Scalabrini Ortiz did in February 1946, while recalling the events of October 17, 1945: "It was the most heterogeneous crowd imagination could conceive. The traces of their origins could be seen in their physiognomy. The descent of the Southern European was together with the blond man of the North and the olive-skinned person where the blood of the native still survived."[60] Scalabrini distinguished the *criollo* from the interior by his physiognomy, but he found *criollos* together with Southern and Northern Europeans, making a "heterogeneous crowd." Similarly, the Communist Party argued that "Peronism managed to deceive some sectors of the working class, small ones, especially women and young men recently incorporated into production and from the interior," but the emphasis was clearly put on the political inexperience of youth and not on their ethnic or regional origins.[61]

For most contemporaries, the use of disparaging and sometimes racist adjectives did not evoke explicit ethnic or racial differences as a social category. The evidence suggests that, at the beginning, the anti-Peronist discourse put in motion an old battery of derogatory terms—including racist ones—used earlier against other political enemies. The antifascist frame within which Peronism was first analyzed had already reenacted the traditional opposition between civilization and barbarism, an opposition that was never free of racial connotations.[62] Both processes—the political stigmatization of the popular masses and the reenactment of the opposition between civilization and barbarism—helped to consolidate some disparaging chains of signifiers, such as the one that began with Carnival and went through candombe to ignorant Negros or malón, savages and unrefined Indians. It is clear that in Argentine society poverty darkens just as a dark skin signifies poverty—if not atavistic backwardness or perversion. It seems that the chain of signifiers linking the Peronist masses with the ethnic or racial "other" crystallized in the term "cabecita negra," during the early 1950s, when the discursive processes analyzed here had led to the perception of a racialized "other" as an invader of the sacred spaces previously occupied by a society that had seen itself as white and European.

The rise of Peronism made visible two absences in a national identity built from the society of Buenos Aires: the excluded working class and the people from the interior provinces. The figure of the cabecita negra, the synthesis of an "other" radically opposed to the respectable, white, and civilized man, would later include everyone who had been rejected from the spaces and welfare of modern urban civilization. And it would be at that moment that a whole range of urban occupations, lifestyles, and levels of education would be articulated and unified under one concept: the middle class. It is a double process through which some social groups defined a social and ethnic "other" and, in so doing, constituted themselves as white and middle class.

Conclusion

I will conclude by revisiting Scalabrini Ortiz's work, not only because of what he wrote but also because of the ways in which his work was read after Perón's fall. A good example is the revisionist historian José María Rosa's prologue in the 1964 edition of *El hombre que está solo y espera*. The strong identification between (European) immigration and the nation was not limited to progressive liberals and socialists. Those who questioned the liberal melting pot also recognized the profound impact of immigration, although, like Scalabrini, they tried to reduce it to the visual surface of an erstwhile, deeper essence. Rosa was evidently aware of this when he remarked: "Scalabrini analyzed the Argentine of the 1930s and early 1940s. To him, the Argentine is a 'multi-gene,' a product of the clash of many races, but not a hybrid at all; Adán Buenos Aires cannot be explained by the matter that constitutes him, or by the education he received."[63] Moreover, what in the 1930s was intended to represent the Argentine—a porteño somehow located above the inferior layers of society—appeared more clearly defined in the 1960s: "Adán Buenos Aires, the middle-class man of Argentina." The gap that separated the porteño from the "the middle-class man" seems difficult to bridge, yet Rosa took the risk. It is true that he used "Adán Buenos Aires" to talk about Scalabrini, the author; yet "Adán Buenos Aires" was also the man from Corrientes and Esmeralda and "a little part of us all," added Rosa. In short, "Adán Buenos Aires" is the porteño, the Argentine (and, as such, the immigrants' child): "Adán Buenos Aires . . . is the middle-class man trapped by the feeling of nationhood, . . . [The] identification with the land and the dead has reached today the middle class to which Adán Buenos Aires belongs to, [a man who is] possibly a child of gringos brought by Alberdi and a student in the schools of Sarmiento, but also a man who after stepping onto this land is absorbed by a spirit stronger than blood or education."[64]

It is worth noting that four times in six pages, Rosa used the expression "middle class" to refer to "Adán Buenos Aires" who was Scalabrini Ortiz, as well as Rosa himself, the porteño, the Argentine. And Rosa did this in the prologue to a book of 140 pages that uses the expression only once, to refer to the porteño.[65] This isolated reference shows that the concept did exist and that it was understood. Yet, at the same time, it also shows an almost intuitive refusal to use it—in clear opposition to Rosa's abundant use of it thirty years later. Concepts such as "the man from Corrientes and Esmeralda" or simply "the porteño" (which Scalabrini used repeatedly to mean the same) seemed more appropriate, especially because of their general nature and lesser precision. To him, as to the porteño, "words are dangerous toys," and he "does not use them to classify his equals."[66]

Although the category of middle class classifies people, Scalabrini refused to do so. Still, the fact that he employed the category at least once shows us that his reluctance to use it was not caused by doubts about its applicability but by the unnecessary use of a terminology that excluded many people who should not be excluded. That is why "middle class" was used as a synonym for "the man from Corrientes and Esmeralda," equal to "porteño," and identical to Argentine—and descending from ships. During the 1930s, the concept of middle class was employed on few occasions, and it served not to identify a clearly defined or differentiated class, but to refer to a group that more often than not was considered part of "the people," or even a synonym of "the people"—and thus equal to the nation. This way of imagining the social world was far removed from the one predominant after the overthrow of Perón, when in a plurality of writings—many of them evoking the relationship between Peronism and the cabecita negra—the middle class appeared not only different from but also opposed to "the people." The gap is the racial articulation of a middle-class identity constructed during the Peronist years.

During the first half of the twentieth century, the symbolic construction of a civilized Argentina, homogeneously white and open to upward social mobility, allowed social and political conflicts to be represented through a bipartite model; a model in which the only opposition to "the people" was an oligarchy whose incredible accumulation of power did not prevent the rest of the nation from achieving a respectable and modern life. The emergence of Peronism did not erase this people-oligarchy dichotomy. What it did was to add another element, by drawing a new class line that also implied a racial and cultural division. The people could no longer be one after the "discovery" of a Peronist working class that was considered neither civilized nor descended from the ships. Hence, the possibility of a tripartite image of society appeared. Only then would a highly heterogeneous group of occupations be unified under the notion of middle class—a notion that maintained the cultural and racial features previously thought to characterize the entire nation.

Notes

I would like to thank Paul Gootenberg, Brooke Larson, Ana Julia Ramírez, Silvia Cristelli, Ana Barletta, and León Zamosc for their helpful comments on previous versions of this chapter. Liliana Kuguel helped me with the English version. Finally, I would like to acknowledge the Social Sciences Research Council for an International Dissertation Field Research Fellowship. An earlier version of this chapter appeared in *Latin American and Caribbean Ethnic Studies* 2, no. 2 (2007): 161–84. All translations are mine unless otherwise noted.

1. J. Johnson, *Political Change in Latin America*.
2. Germani, "La clase media en la ciudad de Buenos Aires," 119.
3. P. Romero, "La clase media urbana en la literatura nacional"; Garguin, "The Discov-

ery of the Middle Class as a Political Agent"; Adamovsky, "Acerca de la relación entre el Radicalismo argentino y la 'clase media' (una vez más)."

4. The troublesome nature of the concept of middle class is well known. For a discussion, see the introduction to this volume.

5. Processes of class differentiation based on unequal distribution and appropriation of cultural or economic capital underlied those social constructions.

6. By "articulation," I mean the process by which the diversity inherent in any group is subsumed by an "equivalential logic" that, through the exclusion of an "other," produces some closure (even though a precarious one), allowing the differential ensemble to be constructed as a totality. See Laclau, *On Populist Reason*, 69–70. I define "racial articulation" in the Argentine middle-class identity as the differential and the equivalential logics that worked through "the formation of othered groups on the basis of selectively racialized and ethnicized marks" (Briones, "Formaciones de alteridad," 17; see also Wade, *Race and Ethnicity in Latin America*, 5–24).

7. Perón, *El pueblo quiere saber de qué se trata*, 120–37; J. Horowitz, "Populism and Its Legacies in Argentina."

8. J. Romero, *Las ideas políticas en Argentina*; Halperin Donghi, "¿Para qué la inmigración?"; Archetti, *Masculinities*.

9. J. Romero, *Las ideas políticas en Argentina*; Adamovsky, "Acerca de la relación entre el Radicalismo argentino y la 'clase media' (una vez más)"; Rock, *El radicalismo argentino*.

10. Rock, "Intellectual Precursors of Conservative Nationalism in Argentina"; Halperin Donghi, "¿Para qué la inmigración?"; Joseph, "Taking Race Seriously"; Svampa, *El dilema argentino*.

11. Rock, *El radicalismo argentino*; del Campo, *Sindicalismo y peronismo*.

12. Gutiérrez and Romero, *Sectores populares*. I find Miguez's argument on the role of civic association and middle-class formation quite insightful. See Eduardo Miguez, "Tensiones de identidad: reflexiones sobre la experiencia italiana en la Argentina," 354–58.

13. I prefer the concept of "popular public sphere" to that of "popular sectors" to emphasize the idea of a contested field in which different subjects are being made and remade through their practices. See Eley, "Nation, Publics and Political Cultures"; Laclau, *Populist and Ideology in Marxist Theory*.

14. Jauretche, *El medio pelo en la sociedad argentina*; Ratier, *El cabecita negra*; D. James, *Resistance and Integration*.

15. Briones, *(Meta)cultura del estado-nación y estado de la (meta)cultura*, 244, and "Formaciones de alteridad"; Segato, *Alteridades históricas/identidades políticas*; Grimson, "Nuevas xenofobias, nuevas políticas étnicas en Argentina"; Joseph, "Taking Race Seriously"; Guano, "A Color for the Modern Nation" and "The Denial of Citizenship."

16. Halperin Donghi, "¿Para qué la inmigración?"; Andrews, *Los afro-argentinos de Buenos Aires*; Wade, *Race and Ethnicity in Latin America*; Helg, "Race in Argentina and Cuba"; Stepan, *The Hour of Eugenics*; Svampa, *El dilema argentino*.

17. See Joseph, "Taking Race Seriously"; Guano, "A Color for the Modern Nation"; Briones, "Formaciones de alteridad."

18. Scalabrini Ortiz, *El hombre que está solo y espera*.

19. Halperin Donghi, "¿Para qué la inmigración?," 191

20. Mitre, *Historia de Belgramo y de la independencia Argentina*, 20–25.

21. Ibid., 31.

22. Ibid., 42–43.

23. See Helg, "Race in Argentina and Cuba," 45–47; Svampa, *El dilema argentino*, 115–28; Terán, *En busca de la ideología argentina*, 51–84.

24. Eduardo Archetti rightly points out that the melting-pot model implies a notion of mixture, and that nonliberal sectors of the Argentine intelligentsia created different models to characterize the national spirit. In most cases they stated that the unique Argentine character could not be the product of a mixture but had to have been produced by the infusion of some previous and immutable substance. But this did not affect their recognition (most of the time implicit) that the population was hybrid, though predominantly European. See Archetti, *Masculinities*, 102–9.

25. Dickman, *Población e inmigración*, 154–55.

26. Ibid., 152.

27. Ibid., 152–57.

28. Ibid., 154.

29. Ibid.

30. Asociación de maestros de la provincial de Buenos Aires, Boletín, 1–2 (1931): 19.

31. *Clarín. Revista del sindicato de Viajantes de Comercio*, 109, Septiembre, 1940.

32. Quoted in Archetti, *Masculinities*, 31.

33. Ibid.

34. Sábato, *Tango: discusión y clave*, 11–12.

35. Quattrocci-Woisson, *Los males de la memoria*, 92. Some nationalists believed indigenous peoples deserved a place in Argentina, but the natives they had in mind were usually those belonging to the past: the surviving indigenous peoples were rarely (if ever) welcomed.

36. Palacio, *La historia falsificada*, 62.

37. Ibid., 64.

38. Ibid., 64.

39. Raúl Scalabrini Ortiz, *El hombre que está solo y espera*, 29.

40. Ibid., 34.

41. Ibid., 38.

42. Ibid.

43. Luna, *El 45*, 321.

44. Jauretche, *El medio pelo en la sociedad argentina*, 298–99. See also Ratier, *El cabecita negra*; J. Taylor, *Eva Perón*, 27–28.

45. For an analysis of the role of the workers in the consolidation of Peronism, see Luna, *El 45*; del Campo, *Sindicalismo y peronismo*; James, *Resistance and Integration*; Bisso, *Acción Argentina*.

46. Bisso, *Acción Argentina*.

47. Quoted in ibid., 312.

48. Quoted in Luna, *El 45*, 306.

49. Quoted in ibid., 309; James, *Resistance and Integration*, 126.

50. Quoted in García Sebastiani, *Los antiperonistas en la Argentina peronista.*

51. Quoted in del Campo, *Sindicalismo y peronismo*, 230.

52. Ibid., 241.

53. *La Vanguardia*, December 4, 1945, and February 24, 1946 (I thank Andrés Bisso for lending me his notes on *La Vanguardia*). A flyer of the Communist Party preferred to talk about the "Peronist *malón*." (Quoted in Luna, *El 45*, 305.)

54. *La Vanguardia*, February 24, 1946.

55. Martínez Estrada, *¿Qué es esto?*, 21

56. See J. Taylor, *Eva Perón*, 120–26; Jauretche, *El medio pelo en la sociedad argentina*, 358–59.

57. Scalabrini Ortiz, *El hombre que está solo y espera*, 144.

58. Quoted in Svampa, *El dilemma argentino*, 153.

59. Jauretche, *El medio pelo en la sociedad argentina*; Ratier, *El cabecita negra*; Briones, "Formaciones de alteridad." The relationship between the cabecita negra and Peronism became a central topic in the sociopolitical literature of the 1960s, particularly that written from a pro-Peronist point of view. See Altamirano, "La pequeña burguesia."

60. Scalabrini Ortiz, "Emoción para ayudar a comprender," in Fermín Chávez, *La jornada del 17 de octubre por cuarenta y cinco autores*, 29–30. See also Halperin Donghi, "Algunas observaciones sobre Germani"; Svampa, *El dilema argentino*, 211–21.

61. Quoted in del Campo, *Sindicalismo y peronismo*, 230. See also V. Codovilla, *Batir el nazi-peronismo*, 140–43; Altamirano, *Bajo el signo de las masas*, 181–82.

62. J. Taylor, *Eva Perón*, 112–22; Svampa, *El dilemma argentino*; Joseph, "Taking Race Seriously."

63. Rosa, "Prólogo," 11. *Adan Buenosayres* is a 1948 novel by Leopoldo Marechal. Its main character, a porteño writer, represents both the author's alter ego and the Argentine archetype. For Rosa, Adan is "the middle-class man" as well.

64. Ibid., 12–14.

65. Scalabrini, *El hombre que está solo y espera*, 108.

66. Ibid., 113.

Commentary on Part IV

MIDDLE-CLASS POLITICS AND THE MAKING OF A PUBLIC SPHERE: WORKING TOWARD A TRANSNATIONAL HISTORY OF THE MIDDLE CLASSES

Robyn Muncy

Taken together, the chapters in this part of the volume bring home the substantial amount of social, cultural, and political work it has taken to bring middle classes into existence and to hold them there. The chapters reveal middle-class aspirants organizing voluntary associations and dispensing charity, educating their children, forming political parties, and writing popular literature for both adults and children—all in the service of establishing their place in between. According to the analyses in this part, the formation of middle classes has occurred in multiple arenas and registers; the process of formation and reformation has been exhausting; and still, some achievers of middle-class status have tried to escape. Accepting a constructivist view of class formation, the chapters awaken readers to the realization that much had to be perceived to be at stake in order to motivate all that work and, moreover, that other dimensions of social relationship—gender, religion, and race, for instance—have routinely been bound up in the creative and unending processes that produced the middle classes.

Voluntary associations proved one especially effective instrument used by hodgepodges of people to identify themselves as a distinct class. In Gisela Mettele's chapter on women's civic activism in nineteenth-century Germany, we watch as German women in the emerging middle class organize a wide variety of voluntary associations devoted especially to philanthropy and patriotism and—through their participation in local, civic life—not only create a self-conscious middle class but also lay a foundation for women's own fuller citizenship in the future. We come to understand through this chapter that middle classes constituted themselves in part through civic activism that established the new class in a particular relation to the nation, the state, and the poor.

In fact, by arguing that civil society was itself a largely middle-class project in nineteenth-century Germany, and by focusing on patriotic and philanthropic voluntary associations, Mettele identifies a German middle class that defined itself in contrast to the state on the one hand and the poor on the other hand. That is, the layers that these middle-class civic activists imagined as above and below them were not a simultaneously emerging working class and capitalist ownership class. Locating a middle class in this particular way assumed, interestingly, that the middle class was the only dynamic unit of society at the time. Likewise, Carol Harrison's nineteenth-century French bourgeoisie identified itself as above "the poor" rather than above an industrial working class, while David Parker's nineteenth-century Peruvian and Chilean writers seem to mush wage earners and the destitute into an indistinguishable blur as they were concerned overwhelmingly about patrolling the borders between the middle and upper classes. Indeed, among the populations considered in this part, only Enrique Garguin's Argentinian middle class identified itself in contrast to an organized and politicized working class, that process occurring in the mid-twentieth century rather than the nineteenth.

One of the many variables, then, in the emergence and maintenance of middle classes around the globe has been the precise way that middle-class subjects identified who their social superiors and inferiors were. For instance, if the state, an imperfect institutionalization of an upper class rooted in precapitalist forms of wealth in the nineteenth-century German case, and "the poor" were the outside layers of the class sandwich, then the middle class could imagine itself as the only representative of modernity. Both the state and the poor were ancient categories of humanity unassociated with liberalism, nationality, or fully capitalist modes of production. The mission of such a middle class would seem to be quite different from one in which the other classes, too, represented new social relations, values, and forces of production. Moreover, if "the poor" rather than a working class were imagined as the lower layer of society, then the possibility of conflict may have been muted—in ideology if not actuality. As Harrison's chapter argues for the French case, the bourgeois relation to the poor was imagined as one not of overt conflict but of charitable obligation. If the poor rather than increasingly alienated workers constituted the lower orders of society, then it was possible to perceive an unconflicted interrelationship between the middle and lower strata in which the poor actually embodied an opportunity for the middle class, an opportunity to demonstrate commitment to the "common good" through charitable donations, institution building, and voluntary organizations. Harrison helps us to see that by identifying the lower layer as the poor, bourgeois folk obscured social and economic divisions in favor of a vision of social cohesion. The kind of work that Mettele's chapter investigates, civic work in voluntary associations, and that she identifies as a class project, comes up in Garguin's discussion of a popular public sphere in Argentina during the late nineteenth century and the early twentieth. There, he argues, voluntary associations in the popular public sphere often pulled together members of groups that would later identify themselves as middle or working class. In the voluntary associations of this earlier period, those who would later self-identify as middle class served as an elite group of officers and public spokesmen, but before the 1940s they formed cohesive bodies with wage earners who would only later unionize and join Colonel Juan Perón's party. In these Argentine voluntary organizations, clerks and shopkeepers along with workers identified themselves as "the people," a group that defined itself vis-à-vis only one other: the oligarchy. In such a situation, voluntary organizations could not be construed as strictly middle-class projects, the way they were in nineteenth-century Germany. Voluntary associations, then, seem a useful component of our histories of the middle classes, as they reveal how groups of people sorted themselves out.

Voluntary associations may also prove fruitful sites for studying the multiple ways that individuals imagined their class position at any one time and for studying the transnational interconnections in middle-class formation. For instance, in the United States during the late nineteenth century and the early twentieth, many people belonged to voluntary associations that would seem to proclaim their middle-class position quite explicitly—for instance, professional associations or local chambers of commerce—but at the same time also belonged to political parties or religious organizations that included both workers and professionals that might well speak in the language of "the people" versus the rich, or, as some did in the early twentieth century, the classes versus the masses. In the latter dichotomy, the masses included wage earners, professionals, and owners of small businesses, while the classes embraced only those of extreme wealth, the US counterparts of Garguin's oligarchy. In addition to revealing the several ways that people imagined their social positions at any one time, these same voluntary associations often participated in international conferences or even were chapters of international organizations. Such women's associations as the Women's Christian Temperance Union, for instance, various social science and professional associations, and chambers of commerce organized internationally. As a result, they promise a useful focus for studying many different questions driving our global study of middle classes. They allow us to do both comparative analyses and studies of the transnational circuits of exchange that helped to produce, identify, and maintain middle classes.

Popular literature also played an important role. David Parker's chapter goes a long way toward showing just how confusing a process was the one by which class society emerged from a society of legal orders. His Peruvian and Chilean writers in the nineteenth century and the early twentieth were trying to figure out what constituted a legitimate upper class or political or economic elite in a world where money seemed to overshadow family name and character in establishing social power. Although Parker has elsewhere argued compellingly that a middle class emerged in Peru in the early twentieth century, the writers he analyzes here see Peru and Chile in the way that Garguin sees Argentina: they represent Peru and Chile as having no self-conscious middle class in the late nineteenth century or the early twentieth; they see their countries as being "open societies of castes." Just as voluntary associations may reveal multiple ways that people self-identified at any one time, so popular literature may prove illuminating of that dynamic. Both civic associations and popular literature certainly represent the hard work undertaken to produce and maintain the modern middle class.

Likewise, gender and religion often figured directly in the constructions of emerging classes. Harrison argues that charity toward the poor was a significant component of the education of the nineteenth-century French bourgeoisie. But while Mettele sees philanthropy in Germany as a special obligation of middle-class women, Harrison insists that charity was taught to boys and girls alike in the French case, and as an expression of Catholic Christianity. Middle-class formation was not the strictly secular process that it has often seemed to be in France; religion and class were mutually constitutive rather than sequential.

Harrison's evidence that religion was constitutive of the French bourgeoisie lies in children's literature in the first half of the nineteenth century and thus reveals both writing for children and overseeing their education as other aspects of the work involved in creating middle classes. In the stories that middle-class French parents read to their male and female children alike, Catholicism was assumed. Its rituals—especially first communion—were represented as a frame on which the rest of life was built. According to these stories, Catholic formation crucially involved the development of a generous spirit, a sincere sense of obligation toward the poor. Although Protestantism has long been construed as part of the modernizing project and the creation of middle classes in Christian countries, Catholicism has not until recently been implicated in those processes. Indeed, in the French case, as Harrison points out, Catholicism has been identified as a drag on the progressive historical movement toward modernity.

Harrison's special contribution in this chapter is to insist that Catholicism among the French bourgeoisie was not confined to women. In earlier analyses of the nineteenth century, secularizing men were the heroes of historical narratives that ushered in the modern bourgeois republics. Feminized religion —and women themselves—were often seen as enemies of this political progress. Harrison argues persuasively that Catholicism, although assigning different charitable roles to boys and girls, and to men and women, enveloped both middle-class men and women in its culture of bourgeois generosity toward the poor.

In their chapters, both Harrison and Mettele are struggling toward a new conception of the ways that gender structured the nineteenth-century middle classes. In earlier treatments of the issue, historians have argued that a particular set of relations between women and men helped to constitute the middle classes—that is, that one of the ways that emerging middle-class families in the nineteenth century differentiated themselves from the upper and lower classes was by embodying particular versions of manhood and womanhood. In at least some of those characterizations, the attributes associated peculiarly with middle-class womanhood included piety and self-sacrifice, while middle-class men were assumed to eschew religion for the self-assertiveness of business and politics. In some versions, the political cultures that grew from the separation of women and men into public and private spheres proved oppositional. Indeed, Mettele points out that women's political culture, as that of the subordinate gender, has sometimes been represented as countercultural. In contrast, she and Harrison are trying to help us see that middle-class women and men in nineteenth-century France and Germany, while observing a gender division of labor, nevertheless shared a political and religious culture and were pushing toward common ends. The gender system that constituted these middle classes did not, of course, assume that women and men were identical or equal, but it drew women and men into political and religious cultures that they shared in a more meaningful way that some earlier historical understandings of the middle classes have suggested.

Moreover, Mettele argues that the particular gender system that constituted the mid-nineteenth-century German middle class did not define that group forever. In her account, middle-class formation in Germany had liberatory effects for some women, eventually empowering them to claim not only informal public voice through voluntary associations but also formal political power. Mettele thus reminds us that we have to ask the question of how gender structured intra- and inter-class relations over and over again, because those relations changed over time. Indeed, one way of tracking shifts from one era of middle-class history to another is by charting how gender relations changed within and between classes.

Among the chapters in this part, Garguin's especially calls our attention to the significance of race in creating a middle class, in this case in Argentina during the twentieth century. Contrary to expectation, Garguin argues that in a country whose national identity in the early twentieth century was settled on the middle sectors of society, no fixed notion of a middle class existed. Instead, Garguin argues, Argentines—especially in Buenos Aires—imagined themselves as a socially mobile crew of mixed-race people in whom the superior European blood had subdued inferior strains, producing a nation of European-descended masses or "people" distinguished only from an oligarchy.

Not until the 1940s, when Perón identified the working class as his particular political constituency and the unions as their special associational location did the remainder of "the people" have to find a way to identify themselves not only against the oligarchy above them but also now the working class below them. The work of creating a self-conscious middle class here originated in the political arena, and the group that was left by a Peronist secession of the working class from the category of "the people" managed to hold on to its association with Europe, and with whiteness. This remainder then overtly associated Perón's working class with the country's interior—that is, with a racial "other-than-European." Thus, whiteness and middle-classness came to be mutually constitutive in mid-twentieth-century Argentina.

Certainly, Argentina was not the only country where race was implicated in middle-class identity, but the processes through which class and race were constantly renegotiated in different places and at different times need the kind of careful historical attention that Garguin has given it in the Argentine case. We will need to investigate when and how race became significant, for instance, to the German middle class and the French bourgeoisie. How did imperial ventures, decolonization movements, and more recent immigrations racialize middle classes in Europe? In those efforts, we will have to be attentive not only to the ways that race was made a marker of class difference but also to intra-class difference. As Daniel Walkowitz has argued in this volume, for instance, racially specific middle classes have to be part of our understanding of the United States—and perhaps elsewhere.

The point is worth elaborating. In the mid-twentieth-century United States, for instance, we can identify two very different relations between middle-classness and race. On the one hand, certain policies of the federal government, especially those connected with housing, promoted the association of whiteness with middle-class position. As the historian David Freund has recently demonstrated in *Colored Property*, federal housing policy racialized homeownership and simultaneously suggested homeownership as a marker of middle-class identity. Here, as in Argentina, whiteness was integral to middle-classness. But at the same time, many black people identified themselves as middle class, just as white people did. Our histories of the middle class will need to see the variable ways that race and class intersected at any one time, and how those relationships changed over time.

In general, the chapters in this part confirm that since the early nineteenth century, middle classes have been in a continual process of change. One result has been that some of the very income groups and occupations that might have set a person firmly in the working class at one point in history make her eligible for middle-class status at another. Consequently, as we imagine writing transnational histories of the middle class, it will be essential to include, as both Garguin and Parker did in their chapters, some material indicators of the people about whom we are writing. Although I hate to admit what seems a primitive desire for knowledge of the occupation and income of the subjects under study, I was brought up against the need to know more about those economic markers when Harrison identified the French bourgeoisie as the middle class and Enrique Garguin saw the Argentine middle class as identified in opposition to the bourgeoisie. The apparent contradiction is easily resolved by reference to the particular moment about which each author was writing; the middle and upper classes included different people over time. But this example suggests that any transnational history of the middle classes will need to identify the kinds of work that self-identified middle-class people did, and the relative standards of living they enjoyed (or regretted). Analyzing the changing material conditions of our middle classes does not in any way undermine our commitment to constructivist understandings of class; rather, it confirms that class has been created not only by changing relations to the means of production but also by vigorous cultural, political, and social work.

In the end, the histories in this part demonstrate some of the ways that other social categories were implicated in middle-class formation and reformation over the course of the nineteenth and twentieth centuries. Religion, gender systems, constructions of race, and older social identities such as caste or rank all served as materials for distinguishing one class from another. Economic difference alone did not do the trick. These chapters also suggest the dynamism of class formation over the course of the last two centuries, and in this way especially help us to make sense of our current world. Middle classes, once formed, were not static entities. They had to be maintained by continual work. We understand, then, that in the current phase of economic globalization, class identities from an earlier era will play a role in organizing new social identities and hierarchies, as will religion, race, and gender. We know to look to popular literature and voluntary associations, as well as politics and statistics on income and occupation, to learn how people might recategorize themselves. With this understanding, we might even intervene in the process to urge social groupings of greater equality, justice, and international reach.

Afterword

Mrinalini Sinha

This volume, as A. Ricardo López announces in the introduction, is meant as an intervention in, and a provocation to, the recent outpouring of both academic and popular writing that is already coalescing around the rubric of global middle-class studies. This efflorescence in recent years, of course, is connected precisely to the centrality of the middle class to current discussions about globalization. Take the following example. In February 2009, the *Economist* heralded an important global milestone: for the first time in history, apparently, as a result of the exponential economic growth in countries like China and India, the majority of the world's population could now be declared middle class.[1] The growing middle class of Asia had allegedly already outnumbered the middle class of Europe and North America somewhere around 2007 or 2008. The article, while recognizing the difficulty of defining who is middle class, arrives at a definition based on having a percentage—starting at roughly a third—of one's income available for discretionary spending after paying for basic food and shelter.

The article also recognizes that it may be best to speak of middle classes rather than a single middle class. This middle class is plural because it is comprised of both a creamy layer of a properly global middle class, whose members' income levels would put them at home in any part of the world, and a far thicker section containing many more people who would not qualify as middle class in the "developed" world on the basis of their income but would on the basis of the percentage of it that is discretionary. This bloated middle class, despite its different temporal and spatial dynamics, is expected, as the *Economist*'s John Parker has it, to inherit the role that once belonged to the "original" middle class in Britain and the United States of America: that is, the role of creating and consolidating democracies as well as of serving as the backbone of a currently teetering market economy. This contradictory accounting for the middle class within a global context is symptomatic precisely of larger historical and historiographical cruxes of our times.

Let us stay a little longer with this article from the *Economist*. There is no doubt that experts will challenge both the statistical particulars, as well as the sociological foundation, on which the article rests: its definition of the middle class. To bracket these concerns for now, however, let us note that the article still raises certain critical questions for historical scholarship. The economic transformations to which it alludes, for example, need to be situated within a global-historical perspective that is also sensitive to their implications for class formations. To be sure, especially in the wake of the "linguistic turn," and more specifically after the impact of cultural history, few scholars are likely to find evidence for class either in economic positions or political interests themselves. And to be fair, the article does not end its claims for a new middle class here. In fact, not unlike a dominant trend in the contemporary scholarship on the middle class, it considers the middle class in relationship neither to the means of production nor to the body politic, but through its access to widely available consumer goods. The explosive consumer revolution of the turn of this century, more than anything else, undergirds the article's claim of a new era characterized by a worldwide mass middle-class formation.

By this limited measure, at least, the article cannot be considered entirely out of step with certain current academic fashions, whether in the understanding of class or in the recognition of a shifting cast of characters thrown up by the forces of globalization. Even while making much ado about the changing composition of the middle class worldwide, however, the article subscribes to a relatively outmoded script, a European-diffusionist model, of the history of modernity: first in the West and then in the Rest.[2] The assumption that the North Atlantic predecessors of the Asian middle laid down a path that all subsequent middle classes must follow demonstrates a surprising level of ignorance of the by-now several decades of scholarship that has been challenging such Eurocentrism, in the very specific sense of the belief that the modern developments in Europe are universal and, at the same time, uniquely European.[3] Why, then, the persistence of this blindness, of which the article in the *Economist* is scarcely the only exemple, even in writings that on other fronts are sometimes surprisingly au courant?[4]

The contributions in this volume, taken together, tackle this issue head on. They do this sometimes explicitly, but mainly by the very nature of the collective and comparative project. The volume consists of richly contextualized accounts of multiple middle-class formations from the mid-nineteenth century onward, in a variety of different geographical locations—from the North Atlantic to Continental Europe, and from Latin America to South Asia, as well as in what are now Zimbabwe and Syria. By the very fact of bringing together different geographical and temporal histories of the middle class in a single frame, the book as a whole ends up being much more than variations on a historical theme. The chapters work together to drive home two crucial relativizing points: that middle classes everywhere draw, implicitly or explicitly, for their consolidation on a transnational repertoire of resources; and that middle classes are inherently unstable social formations, with no middle class anywhere ever living up to its mythic construction as the agent of a pure modernity. The volume successfully demolishes the view of the singularity of a middle class that sprang fully formed only in certain sites and in particular moments; it also puts paid to the belief in the uniqueness of North Atlantic middle classes against which they themselves and all other middle classes are measured. When individual chapters on their own cannot make these points, the brilliant commentaries at the end of each part not only help draw out the connecting thread between the chapters, but also point to their broader implications for reconceiving the history of the middle class globally. The end result, reinforced in the individual contributions as well as by the structure of the volume, is unmistakable and overwhelming. There are, to be sure, differences—sometimes minor and sometimes more substantial—between individual contributors; but, as far as such collective projects go, this is a remarkably cohesive volume. Each chapter demonstrates from its patch of the earth the particular manifestation of a phenomenon that, from the perspective of the whole, appears inescapably enmeshed in larger connections and linkages.

This relentless message of "connected histories," which constitutes the substantive contribution of the volume, is reinforced by certain analytical maneuvers at the center of which lies the focus on the middle class.[5] The volume starts out by signaling a desire to put forth a more capacious understanding of the middle class, as, say, both concept and practice, than is often the case. Furthermore, the book makes a ground-clearing gesture for a truce between unnecessarily polarized discursive and materialist understandings of class.

Apart from one or two holdouts, the majority of the contributors seem to share Barbara Weinstein's observation that the discursive formation of class serves only as the starting point, but not necessarily as the end point, of the analysis. The result is that the volume pushes in at least three ways against the contours of the now-routine conception of class in discursive terms.

First, the chapters provide a wider range of discourses, beyond the overtly political, in which middle-class identities are constituted.[6] These range from considerations of the languages of social reform, thrift, and charity to that of the revolutionary discourse of Michael Ervin's professional agronomists during the Mexican Revolution or, as in A. Ricardo López's chapter, the meticulous professionalism that conscripted Colombian development workers as democratic middle-class professionals in US imperial rule. Second, most chapters also go beyond the discursive construction of identities to consider the impact of embodied practices on middle-class formation. The emphasis on the practices of women's associational culture in nineteenth-century Germany, for example, allows Gisela Mettele to draw attention to the public lives of women in middle-class formation. Print culture, voluntary associations, and a range of public-sphere activities, as well as the processes of social reproduction, the passing down of different forms of "capital," receive the attention of the contributors. From a purely discursive analysis, as Iñigo García-Bryce argues, it would be difficult to establish the correspondence between *Aprismo* in Peru and the middle class; when he extends the scope of analysis to the cultural practices of the American Popular Revolutionary Alliance (APRA), however, he can demonstrate the party's role in constructing middle-classness. Third, and, perhaps, less explicitly, the chapters here also lead, as Robyn Muncy seems to suggest, to a recognition that a discursive conception of class need not preclude consideration of the impact of such social-structural questions as income, education, profession, and domicile. Enrique Garguin, for example, makes a convincing case that middle-class identity as a distinct political subject does not enter in Argentine national politics until after the eruption of a plebian Peronism in the public sphere; his descriptions of the social typology of the ill-defined "middle sector," which was part of a broad pre-Perón coalition before it bifurcated to constitute itself as an avowed middle class, no less than the subsequent racial articulation of a European whiteness, allow us to understand the delay that characterized the political articulation of middle-classness in Argentina. In expanding the contours of currently dominant conceptions of class, this volume adds to an ongoing scholarly conversation that wishes to replace the now-discarded Marxist definition of class—that included both something that approximated a linguistic dimension in the idea of class consciousness, a class-for-itself, and a more objective" socioeconomic formation in class-in itself—with a new understanding that is "at least as rich and embracing as the one left behind."[7]

The ubiquitous drum roll that surrounds contemporary talk of the middle class serves as a reminder that our conceptions of class cannot ignore the implications of changing material conditions on class formations. This is the kind of opening that is, indeed, initiated by this volume. Consider, for example, Daniel Walkowitz's argument about the inapplicability of nineteenth-century categories of class under the changed work and labor conditions of the late twentieth century. The class identity of the professional-technical workers he studies, for example, is demarcated more by racial or ethnic difference and cultural style than by oppositional social class. Ultimately, however, the real contribution of putting a relatively robust conception of class to work is that it provides an opening for the connected histories of the world that could dislodge the insidious Eurocentrism that persists in histories of modernity.

The stronger conception of class, alongside the "fuzziness" at the heart of the category of the middle class, provides a suitably flexible framework for the historical revisionism that is the ambition of this volume: it offers a way to highlight the transnational linkages between different histories without collapsing them into a singular, centripetally driven narrative.[8] López conceives of the middle class in appropriately minimalist terms as an "integrated and connected formation, historically unfolding in the same temporal frame on a transnational terrain"; and it is precisely as such that it becomes the pivot for the crucial positioning of the volume's particular critique of Eurocentric accounts of the world. This approach rejects, not unsurprisingly, the defanged pluralizing response that consists of positing multiple autonomous histories of modernity and of middle-class identities. But it also resists the temptation of an alternative approach, associated with certain modes of postcolonial and subaltern-studies scholarship, whose dual registers of modernity allow for a different non-Western modernity as parallel to another modernity associated with a hyperreal Europe.[9] By proposing a transnational history of middle-class formation, this volume positions its critique of Eurocentrism differently: one that proceeds, in fact, by deliberately tracing the story of modernity as the effects of a globally connected history.

This challenge plays out in the volume in a few different registers. It does so, first of all, by gesturing toward a connected history in the linkages that it traces across different formations of the middle class. The point is not necessarily to dislocate the accounts of middle-class formations from the national or subnational contexts in which they operate but, rather, to underscore and denaturalize these boundaries in the first place as being porous and constructed. This is done both in individual chapters as well as via the commentaries that round off each of the parts of the book. We thus learn not just of the repertoire of ideas and institutions that form part of the common stock on which middle classes in different parts of the world draw freely, but also of the more self-conscious "anxiety of influence" that shadows these formations.[10] We learn in Susanne Eineigel's chapter, for example, of the extent to which the shadow of the English middle class haunted the postrevolutionary projects directed on behalf of a middle class in Mexico City. As we learn also, in Keith David Watenpaugh's contribution, of an Arab middle-class identity in the period between the two world wars that was constructed not merely in the likeness of but, rather, just as modern as an idealized Euro-American middle class. The Chilean and Peruvian writings that David Parker explores defend their respective nation's middle classes from the supposedly healthier and wealthier middle classes of Western nations. Yet there are also different models—like that of the Soviets and the Chinese, alluded to in García-Bryce's chapter on Peru, or, say, the Japanese—that have likewise animated the imagination of particular middle-class formations.

Even the North Atlantic middle classes, furthermore, were not immune from anxieties that bedeviled other European as well as non-European middle classes. As Simon Gunn shows us, the discourses of "backwardness" that haunted even the classic nineteenth-century English middle class were, in fact, only the other side of the coin of the discourses that vaunted its pioneering modernity. There is, moreover, a further lesson to be learned about what Watenpaugh calls "middle-class modernity": that is, its inevitably fragile and contradictory nature. Sanjay Joshi argues that a "fractured modernity" characterizes not only the allegedly incompletely modern middle class of colonial Lucknow, but also the metropolitan European middle classes themselves. And, indeed, Carol Harrison's chapter demonstrates that Catholicism in postrevolutionary France cannot be relegated to a safely "feminized" domain that apparently left untouched an otherwise secular bourgeoisie. Modernity, by this reckoning, has a history that is far more connected and far more fraught throughout the world than we have been led to believe.

This book goes a considerable way—precisely because it places the question of the middle class at its center—in demonstrating what the contours of an alternative history of modernity might look like. There are, however, a few directions in which the volume's contributions could be pushed further. One logical direction points to rethinking the periodicization of the history of modernity and of the middle class. There is, indeed, much interesting work on this question that is suggestive for the kind of critique of Eurocentric narratives that is inaugurated here. Take, for example, the implications of the concept of "first modernity" (pioneered by Spain and Portugal) or the now-thriving study of "early modernities."[11] The latter, especially, has "shed new light on modernity by detaching its origins from Europe" and, further, has demonstrated that "early modernity was not modernity's logical precursor or inchoate immanence."[12] The North Atlantic's path to modernity, in fact, was not only contingent and derivative, but it was also conditioned by its emergence at a particular juncture in world history. The view that all modernities, indeed, may be "derivative" does much to reframe the paradigmatic place that the North Atlantic assumes in the history of modernity.

The exploration of early modernities could lead to new thinking about the emergence of the concept of the middle class itself. In British and English history, for example, the shift from a language of "middling sorts" in the eighteenth century to that of the middle class in early nineteenth century is typically also reflected in the historiography; it may be more interesting, however, to consider longer longitudinal studies across the two centuries from the perspective of people in the middle.[13] Such a reorientation could help make the category of the middle class less tied to the moment of a certain European modernity. Its possibilities are anticipated, for example, by Nelly Hanna's book *In Praise of Books: A Cultural History of Cairo's Middle Class, Sixteenth to the Eighteenth Century*, which sets out to establish that a middle class, with its own distinctive culture, existed in early modern Egypt.[14]

Another fruitful line worth pursuing is in the direction of the "indigenization" of modernity, in the sense invoked by Susan Stanford Friedman, in different social formations.[15] Some of the most interesting work in this vein has come from the Caribbean, in the work of scholars from C. L. R. James to Sidney Mintz and Laurent Dubois. The Caribbean, which Mintz studies, not unlike the "Black Atlantic" explored by Paul Gilroy, is the site for a precocious modernity that prefigured in many substantial ways the later modern developments of Europe.[16] The story of the Caribbean modernity that James and Dubois tell is, likewise, not a derivative or belated one: instead, the Caribbean is where some of the fundamental categories of European modernity are reinvigorated and returned, transformed, to Europe.[17] These works offer a possibility for reconsidering the contributions—in the strong sense of the word—that middle classes around the world have made to the repertoire of ideas and institutions of modernity still seen in terms of the class's "original" European provenance. For example, as some scholars are beginning to suggest, the middle class's engagement with liberalism in colonial India could provide us with a picture of liberalism very different, in fact, from its history in Europe.[18]

Finally, I would like to suggest, perhaps somewhat more tentatively, that there may be a case to be made for the return to some sort of a "grand narrative" to underpin a global history that will be adequate for our times.[19] The pitfalls of constructing such a narrative, of course, are enormous. But it is still worth doing. There could be no better model to follow in constructing such a narrative than the connected history of middle-class formations inaugurated by this volume.[20] And it is a tribute to the achievement of this intellectually invigorating volume that it has already provoked a host of questions that, I suspect, will probably be debated for some time to come.

Notes

1. J. Parker, "Burgeoning Bourgeoisie."

2. Blaut, *The Colonizer's Model of the World*.

3. Amin, *Eurocentrism*.

4. See, for example, the discussion in the introduction of this volume of even some recent scholarly works on the middle class that are unable to free themselves of this Eurocentric premise.

5. The phrase is meant to allude to the argument made by Sanjay Subrahmanyam. See his "Connected Histories."

6. The reference here, of course, is to the two most cited discursive analyses of the middle classes that focus on the language of the political: Dror Wahrman's *Imagining the Middle Class* and Sara Maza's *The Myth of the French Bourgeoisie*. I am indebted to Jan Goldstein's discussion of an expanded understanding of class for identifying the contribution of this volume; see his "Of Marksmanship and Marx."

7. Goldstein, "Of Marksmanship and Marx," 107. Marx discusses this distinction in *Eighteenth Brumaire of Louis Bonaparte*.

8. The reference here is to the excesses associated with the unidirectionality of particular elaborations of the world-systems approach. See Wallerstein, *The Modern World-System*.

9. The most influential argument here is made in Chakrabarty, *Provincializing Europe*.

10. The reference here is to Bloom, *The Anxiety of Influence*.

11. For a discussion of a "first modernity," see Dussel, "World-System and 'Trans'-Modernity." For the concept of "early modernities," see Eisenstadt and Schluchter, eds., "early modernities."

12. Ludden, "Modern Inequality and Early Modernity," 471.

13. For the emergence of the concept of the middle class, see Briggs, "The Language

of Class in Early 19th Century England." For the transition, see Seed, "From 'Middling Sort' to Middle Class." My argument for reexamining this narrative of transition is indebted to Barry, "Review."

14. N. Hanna, *In Praise of Books*.

15. Friedman, "Periodizing Modernity." Barbara Weinstein has described this move as going beyond the "diffusionist model of intellectual history." See Weinstein, "History without a Cause?"

16. See Mintz, *Sweetness and Power*. See also D. Scott, "Modernity that Predated the Modern." For Gilroy, see his *The Black Atlantic*.

17. See C. James, *The Black Jacobins*; and Dubois, *Avengers of the New World* and *A Colony of Citizens*.

18. See, for example, T. Sarkar, "Enfranchised Selves"; Sinha, *Specters of Mother India*; Bayly, "Rammohun Roy and the Advent of Constitutional Liberalism in India."

19. For a discussion somewhat sympathetic to this point of view, see Weinstein, "History without a Cause?" The editors of this volume, however, have chosen to situate their project in the context of a transnational rather than a global history. It is sometimes argued that transnational history defines itself as a rejection of "grand narratives." See the "Conversation on Transnational History with CA Bayly, Sven Beckert, Matthew Connelly, Isabel Hofmeyer, Wendy Kozol and Patricia Seed." *American Historical Review* 111, no. 5 (December 2006), 1441–64. For one attempt to bring back something like a "grand narrative" to structure global history, see Bayly, *The Birth of the Modern World*.

20. I am thinking especially of the suppleness of the organizing principle for such a narrative that a history of the middle class affords. Similarly supple structuring devices for such a narrative might help address some of the valid points raised in sympathetic critiques that Bayly's ambitious attempt (cited in the previous note) has nevertheless provoked. See Ballantyne, "Putting the Nation in Its Place?"; Megan Vaughan, "Africa and the Birth of the Modern World."

BIBLIOGRAPHY

Abel, Mary Hinman, "Community and Personal Standards." In *American Standards and Planes of Living: Readings in the Social Economics of Consumption*, edited by Thomas Dawes Elitot, 185–98. Boston: Ginn & Co., 1931.

Abrams, Lynn. *The Making of Modern Woman, Europe 1789–1918*. New York: Longman, 2002.

Abu-Lughod, Lila. *Remaking Women: Feminism and Modernity in the Middle East*. Princeton: Princeton University Press, 1998.

Acemoglu, Daron, and James A. Robinson. *Economic Origins of Dictatorship and Democracy*. New York: Cambridge University Press, 2005.

Adamovsky, Ezequiel. "Acerca de la relación entre el Radicalismo argentino y la 'clase media' (una vez más)." *Hispanic American Historical Review* 89, no. 2 (2009): 209–51.

——. *Historia de la clase media en Argentina. Apogeo y decadencia de una ilusón, 1919–2003*. Buenos Aires: Planeta, 2009.

Adams, Mary Louise. *The Trouble with Normal: Postwar Youth and the Making of Heterosexuality*. Toronto: University of Toronto Press, 1997.

'Aflaq, Mishil [Michel]. *Fi sabil al-ba'th* [For the cause of the Baath]. 8th ed. Beirut: Dar al-tali'a lil-tiba'a wa al-nashr, 1972.

Aguirre, Norberto. *Cuestiones agrarias*. México City: Joaquín Mortiz, 1977.

Alanís Patiño, Emilio. *Vivir entre dos siglos*. México City: Edamex, 1990.

Alexander, Robert J. "The Latin American Aprista Parties." *Political Quarterly* 20, no. 3 (July 1949): 236–47.

Altamirano, Carlos. *Bajo el signo de las masas*. Buenos Aires: Editorial Planeta/Aries, 2001.
——. "La pequeña burguesía: una clase en el purgatorio." *Prismas* 1 (1997): 105–23.
Amin, Samir. *Eurocentrism*. Translated by Russell Moore. New York: Monthly Review, 1989.
Anderson, Perry. "The Figures of Descent." *New Left Review* 1, no. 161 (1987), 20–77.
——. "The Origins of the Present Crisis." *New Left Review* 1, no. 23 (1964): 26–53.
Anderson, Sherwood. *Sherwood Anderson's Love Letters to Eleanor Copenhaver*. Edited by Charles E. Modlin. Athens: University of Georgia Press, 1989.
Andrews, George Reid. *Los Afroargentinos de Buenos Aires*. Buenos Aires: De la Flor, 1990.
Appadurai, Arjun. "Putting Hierarchy in Its Place." *Cultural Anthropology* 3, no. 1 (1996): 36–49.
Appelt, Erna. *Geschlecht, Staatsbürgerschaft, Nation: Politische Konstruktionen des Geschlechterverhältnisses in Europa*. Frankfurt: Campus, 1999.
Archetti, Eduardo. *Masculinities: Football, Polo, and the Tango in Argentina*. Oxford: Berg, 1999.
Archila, Mauricio. *Idas y venidas, vueltas y revueltas; Protestas sociales en Colombia, 1958–1990*. Bogotá: Centro de Investigación Popular, Instituto Colombiano de Antropología e Historia, 2003.
Arendt, Hannah. *The Origins of Totalitarism*. 1948. New York: Schocken, 2004.
Arnold, David. "Touching the Body: Perspectives on the Indian Plague, 1896–1900." In *Writings on South Asian History and Society*, edited by Ranajit Guha, 55–90. Delhi: Oxford University Press, 1987.
Asad, Talal. *Genealogies of Religion: Discipline and Reasons of Power in Christianity and Islam*. Baltimore: Johns Hopkins University Press, 1993.
Ascheson, Neal. "The English Bourgeoisie." In *Games with Shadows*, 31–35. London: Radius Books, 1989.
Auret, Michael. *From Liberator to Dictator: An Insider's Account of Robert Mugabe's Descent into Tyranny*. Cape Town: David Philip, 2009.
Ayala, César. *Nacionalismo y populismo: Anapo y el discúso político de la oposición en Colombia: 1960–1966*. Bogotá: Universidad Nacional de Colombia, 1995.
Baines Junior, Edward. *On the Social, Educational and Religious State of the Manufacturing Districts*. London: Marshall and Co., 1843.
Baldwin, F. Spencer. "Some Aspects of Luxury." *North American Review*, February 1899, 154–62.
Ballantyne, Tony. "Putting the Nation in Its Place? World History and C. A. Bayly's *The Birth of the Modern World*." In *Connected Worlds: History in Transnational Perspective*, edited by Tony Curthoys and Marilyn Lake, 23–43. Canberra: The Australian National University E Press, 2005.
Balmori, Diana, Stuart F. Voss, and Miles L. Wortman, eds. *Notable Family Networks in Latin America*. Chicago: University of Chicago Press, 1984.
Banks, Joseph Ambrose. *Prosperity and Parenthood: A Study of Family Planning among the Victorian Middle Classes*. London: Routledge, 1954.

Barnes, Teresa. *"We Women Worked So Hard": Gender, Urbanization and Social Reproduction in Colonial Harare, Zimbabwe, 1930–1956*. Portsmouth, UK: Heinemann, 1999.
Barnett, Corelli. *The Audit of War: The Illusion and Reality of Britain as a Great Nation*. London: Pan, 1986.
Barr-Melej, Patrick. *Reforming Chile: Cultural Politics, Nationalism, and the Rise of the Middle Class*. Chapel Hill: University of North Carolina Press, 2001.
Barros Lezaeta, Luis, and Ximena Vergara Johnson. *El modo de ser aristocrático: el caso de la oligarquía chilena hacia 1900*. Santiago: Aconcagua, 1978.
Barry, Jonathan. "Review: The Making of the Middle Class?" *Past and Present* 145, no. 1 (1994): 194–208.
——. "Introduction." In *The Middling Sort of People: Culture, Society and Politics in England, 1550–1800*, edited by Jonathan Barry and Christopher Brooks, 1–27. New York: St. Martin's, 1994.
Bauer, Arnold J. *Goods, Power, History: Latin America's Material Culture*. Cambridge: Cambridge University Press, 2001.
Bayly, C. A. *The Birth of the Modern World, 1790–1914: Global Connections and Comparisons*. Malden, MA: Blackwell Publications, 2004.
——. "Rammohun Roy and the Advent of Constitutional Liberalism in India, 1800–1830." *Modern Intellectual History* 4, no. 1 (2007): 25–41.
Beban, Paul. "India Rising: Globalization and the Middle Class." PBS video, 26:39. June 20, 2008. http://www.pbs.org/now/shows/425/index.html.
Beckert, Sven. "Review of *Social Contracts under Stress: The Middle Classes of America, Europe, and Japan at the Turn of the Century*." *Journal of American History* 90, no. 3 (2003): 1116–17.
Bederman, Gail. *Manliness & Civilization: A Cultural History of Gender and Race in the United States, 1880–1917*. Chicago: University of Chicago Press, 1995.
Bell, David A. *The Cult of the Nation in France: Inventing Nationalism, 1680–1800*. Cambridge: Harvard University Press, 2001.
Bell, Rudolph, and Cristina Mazzoni. *The Voices of Gemma Galgani: The Life and Afterlife of a Modern Saint*. Chicago: University of Chicago Press, 2003.
Belmonte, Laura A. "Mr and Mrs America: Images of Gender and the Family in Cold War Propaganda." Paper presented at the Berkshire Conference on the History of Women, Chapel Hill, NC, June 1996.
Benhabib, Seyla. "Models of Public Space: Hannah Arendt, the Liberal Tradition, and Jurgen Habermas." In *Habermas and the Public Sphere*, edited by Craig Calhoun, 73–98. Boston: MIT Press, 1992.
Benwell Community Project. *The Making of a Ruling Class: Two Centuries of Capitalist Development on Tyneside*. Benwell, England: Newcastle upon Tyne Publications, 1978.
Berghoff, Hartmut. "Public Schools and the Decline of the British Economy, 1870–1914." *Past and Present* 129, no.1 (1990): 148–67.
Berman, Marshall. *All That Is Solid Melts into Air: The Experience of Modernity*. London: Penguin, 1982.
Berra Stoppa, Erica. "La expansión de la Ciudad de México y los conflictos urbanos: 1900–1930." PhD diss., El Colegio de México, 1982.

Beteta, Ramón. *Jarano*. Translated by John Upton. Austin: University of Texas Press, 1970.
Besse, Susan. *Restructuring Patriarchy: The Modernization of Gender Inequality in Brazil, 1914–1940*. Chapel Hill: University of North Carolina Press, 1996.
Bhabha, Homi K. *The Location of Culture*. New York: Routledge, 1994.
Bhambra, Gurminder K. *Rethinking Modernity: Postcolonialism and the Sociological Imagination*. Basingstoke, UK: Palgrave, 2007.
Bieber, León. *En torno al origen histórico ideológico del ideario nacionalista populista latinoamericano: gestación, elaboración y vigencia de la concepción aprista de Haya de la Torre*. Berlin: Colloquium, 1982.
Binfield, Clyde. *So down to Prayers*. London: J. M. Dent, 1977.
Bingham, Alfred. *Insurgent America: Revolt of the Middle Classes*. New York: Harper and Brothers, 1935.
Bisso, Andrés. *Acción Argentina: un Antifascismo nacional en tiempos de guerra mundial*. Buenos Aires: Prometeo, 2005.
Blackbourn, David, and Geoff Eley. *The Peculiarities of German History*. Oxford: Oxford University Press, 1984.
Blaut, J. M. *The Colonizer's Model of the World: Geographical Diffusionism and Eurocentric History*. New York: Guilford, 1993.
Bledstein, Burton J., and Robert D. Johnston. *The Middling Sorts: Explorations in the History of the American Middle Class*. New York: Routledge, 2001.
Blest Gana, Alberto. *Martín Rivas*. 9th ed. Santiago: Zig-Zag, 1963.
Bliss, Katherine Elaine. *Compromised Positions: Prostitution, Public Health, and Gender Politics in Revolutionary Mexico City*. University Park: Pennsylvania State University Press, 2001.
Bloom, Harold. *The Anxiety of Influence: A Theory of Poetry*. New York: Oxford University Press, 1973.
Bock, Gisela, and Pat Thane. *Maternity and Gender Policies: Women and the Rise of the European Welfare States, 1880s–1950s*. London: Routledge, 1991.
Boulard, Fernand, Yves Marie Hilaires and Gérard Cholvy, eds. *Matériaux pour l'histoire religieuse du peuple français*. 4 vols. Paris: Editions de l'Ecole des hautes études en sciences socials, 1982–2011.
Bourdieu, Pierre. *Distinction: A Social Critique of the Judgement of Taste*. Translated by Richard Nice. Cambridge: Harvard University Press, 1984.
Bourricaud, François. *Power and Society in Contemporary Peru*. Translated by Paul Stevenson. New York: Praeger, 1970.
Brading, David A. *Miners and Merchants in Bourbon Mexico, 1763–1818*. Cambridge: Cambridge University Press, 1971.
Briggs, Asa. *The Age of Improvement*. London: Longmans, 1959.
——. "The Language of 'Class' in Early Nineteenth-Century England." In *Essays in Labour History*, edited by Asa Briggs and John Saville, 43–73. London: Macmillan, 1960.
Briones, Claudia. "Formaciones de alteridad: contextos globales, procesos nacionales y provinciales." In *Cartografías Argentinas: Políticas Indigenistas y Formaciones*

Provinciales de Alteridad, edited by Claudia Briones, 11–43. Buenos Aires: Antropofagia, 2005.
——. *(Meta)Cultura del estado-nación y estado de la (meta)cultura*. Brasilia: Departamento de Antropología. Universidad de Brasilia, 1998.
British Information Services. *Community Development*. London: Central Office of Information, 1962.
Brodkin, Karen. *How Jews Became White Folks and What That Says about Race in America*. New Brunswick, NJ: Rutgers University Press, 1998.
Brooks, David. *Bobos in Paradise: The New Upper Class in America*. New York: Simon and Schuster, 2000.
Bulmer, Martin, Kevin Bales, and Kathryn Kish Sklar, eds. *The Social Survey in Historical Perspective, 1880–1940*. Cambridge: Cambridge University Press, 1991.
Burton, Antoinette. *Burdens of History: British Feminists, Indian Women and Imperial Culture, 1865–1915*. Chapel Hill: University of North Carolina Press, 1994.
——. "Introduction: The Unfinished Business of Colonial Modernities." In *Gender, Sexuality and Colonial Modernities*, edited by Antoinette Burton, 1–16. New York: Routledge, 1999.
Burton, Richard D. E. *Holy Tears, Holy Blood: Women, Catholicism, and the Culture of Suffering in France, 1840–1870*. Ithaca: Cornell University Press, 2004.
Bustamante y Rivero, José Luís. "Las clases sociales en el Perú." In *Exigencias sociales del catolicismo en el Perú: Primera semana social del Perú*, 64–129. Lima: Secretaría Genaral del Episocpado del Perú, 1959.
Butler, Tim, and Mike Savage, eds. *Social Change and the Middle Classes*. London: Routledge, 1995.
Cain, P. J., and A. G. Hopkins. *British Imperialism: Innovation and Expansion, 1688–1914*. London: Longman, 1993.
Calder, Lendol. *Financing the American Dream*. Princeton: Princeton University Press, 1999.
Calhoun, Craig. "Postmodernism as Pseudohistory." *Theory, Culture and Society* 10, no. 1 (1993): 75–96.
Campbell, Helen. *Prisoners of Poverty: Women Wage Workers, Their Trades and Their Lives*. 1887. Westport, CT: Greenwood, 1970.
Campbell, Horace. *Reclaiming Zimbabwe: The Exhaustion of the Patriarchal Model of Liberation*. Cape Town: David Philip, 2003.
Cannadine, David. *Class in Britain*. New Haven: Yale University Press, 1998.
Canning, Kathleen, and Sonya O. Rose. "Gender, Citizenship and Subjectivity: Some Historical and Theoretical Considerations." *Gender & History* 13, no. 3 (2001): 427–43.
Carnes, Mark C., and Clyde Griffen. *Meanings for Manhood: Constructions of Masculinity in Victorian America*. Chicago: University of Chicago Press, 1990.
Carroll, Michael P. "Give Me That Ol' Time Hormonal Religion." *Journal for the Scientific Study of Religion* 43, no. 2 (2004): 275–78.
Carroy, Madame. *La Journée d'une petite fille*. Paris, [c. 1840].
Casanova, José. *Public Religions in the Modern World*. Chicago: University of Chicago Press, 1994.

Cashman, Richard I. *The Myth of the Lokmanya: Tilak and Mass Politics in Maharashtra*. Berkeley: University of California Press, 1975.

Cavell, Richard, ed. *Love, Hate, and Fear in Canada's Cold War*. Toronto: University of Toronto Press, 2004.

Chakrabarty, Dipesh, "The Difference-Deferral of a Colonial Modernity: Public Debates on Domesticity in British India." In *Subaltern Studies, vol. 8: Writings on South Asian History and Society*, edited by David Arnold and David Hardiman, 50–88. Delhi: Oxford University Press, 1994.

——. *Habitations of Modernity: Essays in the Wake of Subaltern Studies*. Chicago: University of Chicago Press, 2002.

——. "Postcoloniality and the Artifice of History: Who Speaks for 'Indian' Pasts?" *Representations* 37 (Winter 1992): 1–26.

——. *Provincializing Europe: Postcolonial Thought and Historical Difference*. Princeton: Princeton University Press, 2000.

Chamunorwa Mutambirwa, James A. *The Rise of Settler Power in Southern Rhodesia (Zimbabwe), 1898–1923*. Rutherford, NJ: Farleigh Dickinson University Press, 1980.

Chandavarkar G. L. *A Wrestling Soul: A Story of the Life of Sir Narayan Chandavarkar*. Bombay: Popular Book Depot, 1955.

Chaney, Elsa. *Supermadre: Women in Politics in Latin America*. Austin: University of Texas Press, 1979.

Chapin, Robert. *The Standard of Living of Workingmen's Families in New York*. New York: Charities Publication Committee, 1909.

——. "The Influence of Income on Standards of Life." *American Journal of Sociology* 14, no. 5 (1909): 638–42.

Chatterjee, Partha. *Our Modernity*. Rotterdam, the Netherlands: South-South Exchange for the History of Development, 1997.

——. *The Politics of the Governed: Reflections on Popular Politics in Most of the World*. New York: Columbia University Press, 2004.

Chavarría, Jesús. *José Carlos Mariátegui and the Rise of Modern Peru, 1890–1930*. Albuquerque: University of New Mexico Press, 1979.

Christidoulidis, Emilios A., ed. *Communitarianism and Citizenship*. Aldershot, UK: Brookfield, 1998.

Clark, Christopher. "The New Catholicism and the European Culture Wars." In *Culture Wars: Secular—Catholic Conflict in Nineteenth-Century Europe*, edited by Christopher Clark and Wolfram Kaiser, 11–46. New York: Cambridge University Press, 2003.

Clarke, Alison J. *Tupperware: The Promise of Plastic in 1950s America*. Washington: Smithsonian, 1999.

Cobb, Jonathan, and Sennett, Richard. *The Hidden Injuries of Class*. New York: Vintage, 1972.

Codovilla, Victorio. *Batir al nazi-peronismo para abrir una era de libertad y progreso*. Buenos Aires: Editorial Anteo, 1946.

Cohen, Shana. *Searching for a Different Future: The Rise of a Global Middle Class in Morocco*. Durham: Duke University Press, 2004.

Coll, Edna. *Chile y los chilenos en las novelas de Joaquín Edwards Bello*. 2nd ed. San Juan, Puerto Rico: Juan Ponce de Leon, 1965.
Collins, Robert M. "Growth Liberalism in the Sixties: Great Societies at Home and Grand Designs Abroad." In *The Sixties: From Memory to History*, edited by David Farber, 11–44. Chapel Hill: University of North Carolina Press, 1964.
Combs, Margaret. "Wives and Household Wealth: The Impact of the 1870 Married Women's Property Act on Wealth-Holding and Share of Household Resources." *Continuity and Change* 19, no. 1 (2004): 141–63.
Compagnon, Daniel. *Robert Mugabe and the Destruction of Zimbabwe*. Philadelphia: University of Pennsylvania Press, 2010.
Conlon, Frank F. *A Caste in a Changing World: The Chitrapur Saraswat Brahmans, 1700–1935*. Berkeley: University of California Press, 1977.
Contardo, Oscar. *Siútico: Arribismo, abajismo y vida social en Chile*. Santiago: Ed. Vergara, 2008.
Cook, James W. *The Arts of Deception: Playing with Fraud in the Age of Barnum*. Cambridge: Harvard University Press, 2001.
Cooper, Frederick. *Decolonization and African Society: The Labor Question in French and British Africa*. New York: Cambridge University Press, 1996.
Cooper, Frederick, and Ann Laura Stoler, "Between Metropole and Colony: Rethinking a Research Agenda." In *Tensions of Empire: Colonial Cultures in a Bourgeois World*, edited by Frederick Cooper and Ann Laura Stoler, 1–56. Berkeley: University of California Press, 1997.
Córdova, Arnaldo. *La ideología de la Revolución Mexicana; la formación del nuevo régimen*. México City: Ediciones Era, 1973.
Corfield, Penelope J. "Class by Name and Number in Eighteenth-Century Britain." In *Language, History, and Class*, edited by Penelope J. Corfield, 101–30. Oxford: Basil Blackwell, 1991.
Cornejo Chavez, Hector. *La clase media en el Perú*. Lima: Tipografía Cornejo, 1941.
Currie, Lauchlin. *The Basis of a Development Program. Report of a Mission*. International Bank for Reconstruction and Development. Baltimore: Johns Hopkins University Press, 1950.
——. *Reorganización de la rama ejecutiva del gobierno de Colombia*. Bogotá: Imprenta Nacional, 1952.
Curtis, Sarah. "Charitable Ladies: Gender, Class and Religion in Mid-Nineteenth-Century Paris." *Past and Present* 177 (2002): 121–56.
Daniel, Ute. "Die Vaterländischen Frauenvereine in Westfalen." *Westfälische Forschungen* 39 (1989): 158–79.
Dann, Otto. *Vereinswesen und bürgerliche Gesellschaft in Deutschland*. Munich: R. Oldenbourg, 1984.
Daumard, Adéline. *La Bourgeoisie parisienne de 1815 à 1848*. Paris: Ecole des Hautes Etudes, 1963.
——. *Les Fortunes françaises au XIXe siècle*. Paris: La Haye, 1973.
Davidoff, Leonore. *The Best Circles: Women and Society in Victorian England*. Totowa, NJ: Rowman and Littlefield, 1973.

Davidoff, Leonore, and Catherine Hall. *Family Fortunes: Men and Women of the English Middle Class, 1780–1850*. Chicago: University of Chicago Press, 1991.

Davies, Thomas, Jr. "Haya de la Torre y el APRA: La política de la ideología," In *El APRA de la ideología a la praxis*, edited by Heraclio Bonilla and Paul Drake, 52–82. Lima: Editorial y Productora Gráfica Nuevo Mundo, 1989.

Davis, Diane. *Discipline and Development: Middle Class and Prosperity in South Asia and Latin America*. Cambridge: Cambridge University Press, 2005.

——. *Urban Leviathan: Mexico City in the Twentieth Century*. Philadelphia: Temple University Press, 1994.

Dawisha, Adeed I., and Dawisha, Karen. "How to Build a Democratic Iraq." *Foreign Affairs*, May–June 2003, 36–50.

De Giorgio, Michela. "The Catholic Model." Translated by Joan Bond Sax. In *Emerging Feminism from Revolution to the Great War*, vol. 4 of *A History of Women in the West*, edited by Geneviève Fraisse and Michelle Perrot, 166–97. Cambridge: Harvard University Press, 1993.

De Grazia, Victoria. *Irresistible Empire: America's Advance through Twentieth-Century Europe*. Cambridge: Harvard University Press, 2005.

del Campo, Hugo. *Sindicalismo y Peronismo: los comienzos de un vínculo perdurable*. Buenos Aires: Consejo Latinoamericano de Ciencias Sociales, 1983.

Delgado O., Carlos "An Analysis of 'Arribismo' in Peru." *Human Organization* 28, no. 2 (1969): 133–39.

De León, César A. "Las capas medias en la sociedad chilena del siglo XIX." *Anales de la Universidad de Chile* 132 (October–December 1964), 51–91.

Del Pomar, F. Cossio. *Haya de la Torre: El Indoamericano*. Lima: Nuevo Dia, 1946.

Dintenfass, Michael. *The Decline of Industrial Britain, 1870–1980*. London: Routledge, 1992.

Dirks, Nicholas. "Castes of Mind." *Representations* 37 (Winter 1992): 56–78.

Dobbin, Christine. *Urban Leadership in Western India: Politics and Communities in Bombay City, 1840–1885*. Oxford: Oxford University Press, 1972.

Donham, Agnes. "Conscious Standards." In *American Standards and Planes of Living: Readings in the Social Economics of Consumption*, edited by Thomas Eliot, 477–78. Boston: Ginn & Co., 1931.

Drinot, Paulo. "Food, Race and Working-Class Identity: *Restaurantes Populares* and Populism in 1930s Peru." *Americas* 62, no. 2 (2005): 245–70.

Dubois, Laurent. *Avengers of the New World: The Story of the Haitian Revolution*. Cambridge: Harvard University Press, 2004.

——. *A Colony of Citizens: Revolution and Slave Emancipation in the French Caribbean, 1787–1804*. Chapel Hill: University of North Carolina Press, 2004.

Dumont, Louis. *Homo Hierarchicus: An Essay on the Caste System*. Translated by Mark Sainsbury. Chicago: University of Chicago Press, 1970.

Duprat, Catherine. *Le Temps des philanthropes: la philanthropie parisienne des lumières à la monarchie de Juillet*. Paris: Editions du Mémoires et documents, Ministère de l'éducation nationale et de la culture, 1993.

Dussel, Enrique. "World-System and 'Trans'-Modernity." *Nepantla* 3, no. 2 (2002): 221–24.

Earle, Peter. *The Making of the English Middle Class: Business, Society, and Family Life in London, 1660–1730*. Berkeley: University of California Press, 1989.

Easterly, William. "The Middle Class Consensus and Economic Development." *Journal of Economic Growth* 6, no. 4 (2001): 317–35.

Edwards Bello, Joaquín. *La chica del Crillón*. 2nd ed. Santiago: Ercilla, 1940.

——. "Vicho Balmaceda." In *Crónicas del centenario*, 1–15. Santiago: Zig-Zag, 1968.

Eineigel, Susanne. "Visualizing the Self: Modernity, Identity, and the *Gente Decente* in Porfirian Mexico." MA thesis, University of British Columbia, 2003.

Eisenstadt, Shmuel N., and Wolfgang Schluchter, eds. "Early Modernities." *Daedalus* 127, no. 3 (1998).

Eley, Geoff. "The British Model and the German Road: Rethinking the Course of German History before 1914." In *The Peculiarities of German History: Bourgeois Society and Politics in Nineteenth-Century Germany*, edited by David Blackbourn and Geoff Eley, 18–55. New York: Oxford University Press, 1984.

——. *A Crooked Line: From Cultural History to History of Society*. Ann Arbor: University of Michigan Press, 2005.

——. "Nations, Publics, and Political Cultures. Placing Habermas in the Nineteenth Century." In *Culture/Power/History: A Reader in Contemporary Social Theory*, edited by Nicholas B. Dirks, Geoff Eley, and Sherry B. Ortner, 289–339. Princeton: Princeton University Press, 1993.

Eley, Geoff, and Keith Nield. "Farewell to the Working Class?" *International Labor and Working-Class History* 57 (April 2000): 1–30.

——. *The Future of Class in History*. Ann Arbor: University of Michigan Press, 2007.

Elshtain, Jean Bethke. *Public Man, Private Woman: Women in Social and Political Thought*. Princeton: Princeton University Press, 1981.

Enke, Anne. *Finding the Movement: Sexuality, Contested Space, and Feminist Activism*. Durham: Duke University Press, 2007.

Ervin, Michael. "The 1930s Agrarian Census in Mexico: Agronomists, Middle Politics and the Negotiation of Data Collection." *Hispanic American Historical Review* 87, no. 3 (2007): 537–70.

Escardó, F. *Geografía de Buenos Aires*. 1945. Buenos Aires: Goncourt, 1968.

Escobar, Arturo. *Encountering Development: The Making and Unmaking of the Third World*. Princeton: Princeton University Press, 1997.

——. *Territories of Difference: Place, Movements, Life*, Redes. Durham: Duke University Press, 2008.

Estache, Antonio, and Danny Leipziger, eds. *Stuck in the Middle: Is Fiscal Policy Failing the Middle Class?* Washington: Brookings, 2009.

¿Estamos capacitados para la cooperación? Propaganda Cooperativa V. Mexico City: Publicaciones de la Secretaría de Educación Púbica, 1925.

Fals-Borda, Orlando. *Acción comunal en una vereda colombiana: su aplicación, sus resultados y su interpretación*. Bogotá: Universidad Nacional de Colombia, Departamento de Sociología, 1960.

Fanon, Frantz. *The Wretched of the Earth*. New York: Grove, 1968.

Farhni, Magda. *Household Politics: Montreal Families and Postwar Reconstruction*. Toronto: University of Toronto Press, 2005.
Ferber, Edna. *Fanny Herself*. New York: Frederick A. Stokes Co., 1917.
Ferguson, James. *The Anti-Politics Machine: "Development," Depolitization, and Bureaucratic Power in Lesotho*. Minneapolis: University of Minnesota Press, 1994.
——. "Decomposing Modernity: History and Hierarchy after Development." In *Postcolonial Studies and Beyond*, edited by Ania Loomba et al., 166–81. Durham: Duke University Press, 2005.
Ferguson, James, and Akhil Gupta. "Spatializing States: Toward an Ethnography of Neoliberal Govermentality." *American Ethnologist* 29, no. 4 (2002): 981–1002.
Fernandes, Leela. *India's New Middle Class: Democratic Politics in an Era of Economic Reform*. Minneapolis: University of Minnesota Press, 2006.
Fernández, Carlos. *Chapingo hace 50 años*. Chapingo, Mexico: Colegio de Postgraduados, 1991.
——."Explotación de una hacienda." Escuela Nacional de Agricultura, Thesis, Biblioteca de Chapingo, Escuela de Postgrados, 1919.
Fernández MacGregor, Genaro. *El río de mi sangre; memorias*. México: Fondo de Cultura Económica, 1969.
Fesseden, Tracy. "Gendering Religion." *Journal of Women's History* 14, no. 1 (2002): 163–69.
Fléché, M. "Les suites du jeu." In *Les douze contes, ou la morale en estampes*, 119–29. Paris, 1825.
Ford, Caroline. *Divided Houses: Religion and Gender in Modern France*. Ithaca: Cornell University Press, 2005.
Foucault, Michel. *The Birth of Biopolitics: Lectures at the Collège de France, 1978–1979*. Translated by Graham Burchell. New York: Palgrave Macmillan, 2008.
——. *Discipline and Punishment: The Birth of the Prison*. Translated by Aln Sheridan. New York: Vintage, 1995.
——. *Security, Territory and Population: Lectures at the* Collège *de France, 1977–1978*. Translated by Graham Burchell. New York: Palgrave Macmillan, 2007.
François, Etienne. *Sociabilité et société bourgeoise en France, en Allemagne et en Suisse, 1750–1850*. Paris: Recherche sur les Civilisations, 1987.
Frederick, Christine. "New Wealth, New Standards of Living and Changed Family Budgets." *Annals of the American Academy of Political and Social Science*, 115 (September 1924): 74–82.
Freund, David M. P. *Colored Property: State Policy and White Racial Politics in Suburban America*. Chicago: University of Chicago Press, 2007.
Fridenson, Patrick. "Could Postwar France Become a Middle Class Society?" In *Social Contract under Stress*, edited by Olivier Zunz, Leonard Schoppa, and Nobuhiro Hiwatari, 89–107. New York: Russell Sage Foundation, 2002.
Friedman, Susan Stanford. "Periodizing Modernity: Postcolonial Modernity and the Space/Time Borders of Modernity Studies." *Modernism/Modernity* 13, no. 3 (2006): 425–43.
Gall, Lothar. *Liberalismus und "bürgerliche Gesellschaft."* Cologne: Kiepenheuer und Witsch, 1976.

Gamble, Andrew. *Britain in Decline: Economic Policy, Political Strategy and the British State*. Basingstoke, UK: Palgrave, 1991.
García-Bryce, Iñigo. *Crafting the Republic: Lima's Artisans and Nation Building in Peru, 1821–1879*. Albuquerque: University of New Mexico Press, 2004.
——. "A Revolution Remembered, a Revolution Forgotten: The Aprista Insurrection." *A Contracorriente* 7, no. 3 (2010): 277–322.
García Canclini, Nestor. *Hybrid Cultures: Strategies for Entering and Leaving Modernity*. Minneapolis: University of Minnesota Press, 1995.
García Sebastiani, Marcela. *Los antiperonistas en la Argentina peronista: radicales y socialistas en la política argentina entre 1943 y 1951*. Buenos Aires: Prometeo Libros, 2005.
Garon, Sheldon M., and Patricia L. Maclachlan. *The Ambivalent Consumer: Questioning Consumption in East Asia and the West*. Ithaca, N.Y.: Cornell University Press, 2006.
Gay, Peter. *The Naked Heart*. London: W. W. Norton, 1998.
——. *Pleasure Wars*. London: W. W. Norton, 1998.
——. *Schnitzler's Century: The Making of a Middle Class Culture, 1815–1914*. New York: Norton, 2002.
Germani, Gino. *Política y Sociedad en una epoca de transición*. Buenos Aires: Paidós, 1962.
——. "La clase media en la ciudad de Buenos Aires: estudio preliminar." *Boletín del Instituto de Sociología* 1 (1942): 105–26.
Ghosh, Kaushik. "A Market for Aboriginality: Primitivism and Race Classification in the Indentured Labour Market of Colonial India." In *Subaltern Studies*, vol. 10, edited by Gautam Bhadra, Gyan Prakash, and Susie Tharu, 8–48. Delhi: Oxford University Press, 1999.
Gibson, Ralph. *A Social History of French Catholicism*. London: Routledge, 1989.
Giesecke, Margarita. "The Trujillo Insurrection, the APRA Party and the Making of Modern Peruvian Politics." PhD diss., London University, 1993.
Gilbert, Dennis. *Mexico's Middle Class in the Neo-Liberal Era*. Tucson: University of Arizona Press, 2007.
Gilkeson, John S., Jr. *Middle-Class Providence, 1820–1940*. Princeton: Princeton University Press, 1986.
Gilroy, Paul. *The Black Atlantic: Modernity and Double Consciousness*. Cambridge: Harvard University Press, 1993.
Glassman, Robak M. *The New Middle Class and Democracy in Global Perspective*. New York: St. Martin's, 2002.
Gleason, Mona. *Normalizing the Ideal: Psychology, Schooling, and the Family in Postwar Canada*. Toronto: University of Toronto Press, 1999.
Göçek, Fatma Müge. *Rise of the Bourgeoisie, Demise of Empire: Ottoman Westernization and Social Change*. Oxford: Oxford University Press, 1996.
Godoy Urzua, Hernán. *La cultura chilena*. Santiago: Universitaria, 1982.
Goldstein, Alyosha. "The Attributes of Sovereignty: The Cold War, Colonialism and Community Education in Puerto Rico." In *Imagining Our Americas: Toward a*

Transnational Frame, edited by Sandhya Shukla and Heidi Tinsman, 313–37. Durham: Duke University Press, 2007.
Goldstein, Jan. "Of Marksmanship and Marx: Reflections on the Linguistic Construction of Class in Some Recent Historical Scholarship." *Modern Intellectual History* 2, no. 1 (2005): 87–107.
Goldstene, Claire. " 'America Was Promises': The Ideology of Equal Opportunity, 1877–1905." PhD diss., University of Maryland, 2009.
Gómez, Marte R. *Episodios de la vida de la Escuela Nacional de Agricultura*. Chapingo, Mexico: Colegio de Postgraduados, 1976.
González Navarro, Moises. *Historia moderna de México: La vida social*. México City: Hermes, 1974.
Gooptu, Nandini. *The Politics of the Urban Poor in Early Twentieth-Century India*. Cambridge: Cambridge University Press, 2005.
Gordon, Andrew. "The Short Happy Life of the Japanese Middle Class." In *Social Contracts under Stress*, edited by Olivier Zunz, Leonard Schoppa, and Nobuhiro Hiwatari, 108–29. New York: Russell Sage Foundation, 2002.
Gordon, Eleanor, and Gwyneth Nair. *Public Lives: Women, Family, and Society in Victorian Britain*. New Haven: Yale University Press, 2003.
Goswami, Manu. "Remembering the Future." *American Historical Review* 113, no. 2 (2008): 417–24.
Gramsci, Antonio. *Letters from Prison*. Translated by Raymond Rosenthal. New York: Columbia University Press, 1993.
Grandin, Greg. *The Last Colonial Massacre: Latin America in the Cold War*. Chicago: University of Chicago Press, 2004.
Greenwald, Maurine, and Margo Anderson, eds. *Pittsburgh Surveyed: Social Science and Social Reform in the Early Twentieth Century*. Pittsburgh: University of Pittsburgh Press, 1996.
Grimson, Alejandro. "Nuevas xenofobias, nuevas políticas étnicas en Argentina." Seminario-Taller: Migración Intrafronteriza en América Central, 2005 (http://ccp.ucr.ac.cr/noticias/migraif/pdf/grimson.pdf).
Groethuysen, Bernard. *Origines de l'esprit bourgeois en France*. Paris: Gallimard, 1927.
Guano, Emanuela. "A Color for the Modern Nation: The Discourse on Class, Race, and Education in the Porteño Middle Class." *Journal of Latin American Anthropology* 8, no. 1 (2003): 148–71.
——. "The Denial of Citizenship: 'Barbaric' Buenos Aires and the Middle Class 'Imaginary.' " *City and Society* 16, no. 1 (2005) 69–97.
Guha, Ranajit. "Discipline and Mobilize." In *Subaltern Studies*, vol. 7, edited by Partha Chatterjee and Gyanendra Pandey, 69–120. Delhi: Oxford University Press, 1992.
——. *Dominance without Hegemony: History and Power in Colonial India*. Cambridge: Harvard University Press, 1997.
——. *History at the Limit of World History*. New York: Columbia University Press, 2002.
Gunn, Simon. "Class, Identity and the Urban: The Middle Class in England, *c.*1790–1950." *Urban History* 31, no. 1 (2004): 29–47.
——. "The 'Failure' of the Victorian Middle Class: A Critique." In *The Culture of Capital*,

edited by John Seed, and Janet Wolff, 17–43. Manchester, UK: Manchester University Press, 1988.
——. "The Manchester Middle Class, 1850–80." PhD diss., University of Manchester, 1992.
——. *The Public Culture of the Victorian Middle Class: Ritual and Authority in the English Industrial City 1840–1914*. Manchester, UK: Manchester University Press, 2000.
——. "The Public Sphere, Modernity and Consumption: New Perspectives on the History of the English Middle Class." In *Gender, Civic Culture and Consumerism: Middle-Class Identity in Britain 1800–1940*, edited by Alan Kidd and David Nicholls, 12–30. Manchester, UK: Manchester University Press, 1999.
——. "Translating Bourdieu: Cultural Capital and the English Middle Class in Historical Perspective." *Journal of British Sociology* 56, no. 1 (2005): 49–64.
Gunn, Simon, and Rachel Bell. *Middle Classes: Their Rise and Sprawl*. London: Weidenfeld and Nicolson, 2002.
Gupta, Akhil. *Postcolonial Development: Agriculture in the Making of Modern India*. Durham: Duke University Press, 1998.
Gupta, Sannulal. *Strīsubodhin*. Lakhanau: Tejakumara Press, 1970.
Gutiérrez, Leandro, and Luis Alberto Romero. *Sectores populares, cultura y política*. Buenos Aires: Sudamericana, 1995.
Guzmán Campos, Germán, Orlando Fals-Borda, and Eduardo Umaña Luna. *La violencia en Colombia*. 2 vols. Bogotá: Taurus, 2005.
Habermas, Jürgen. *The Philosophical Discourse of Modernity*. Cambridge: MIT Press, 1987.
——. *The Structural Transformation of the Public Sphere*. Cambridge: Cambridge University Press, 1992.
Hacker, Jacob S. *The Great Risk Shift: The Assault on American Jobs, Families, Health Care, and Retirement and How You Can Fight Back*. New York: Oxford University Press, 2006.
Hall, Catherine. *Civilising Subjects: Metropole and Colony in the English Imagination 1830–1867*. Chicago: University of Chicago Press, 2002.
——. *White, Male and Middle Class: Explorations in Feminism and History*. New York: Routledge, 1992.
Hall, John R. *Reworking Class*. Ithaca: Cornell University Press, 1997.
Halle, David. *America's Working Man: Work, Home, and Politics among Blue Collar Property Owners*. Chicago: University of Chicago Press, 1984.
Halperin Donghi, Tulio. "Algunas observaciones sobre Germani, el surgimiento del peronismo y los migrantes internos." *Desarrollo Económico* 13, no. 51 (1973): 765–81.
——. "¿Para qué la inmigración? Ideología y política inmigratoria en la Argentina (1810–1914)." In *El espejo de la historia: Problemas argentinos y perspectivas hispanoamericanas*, edited by Tulio Halperin Donghi, 189–238. Buenos Aires: Sudamericana, 1987.
Halsey, A. H., A. F. Heath, and J. M. Ridge. *Origins and Destinations: Family, Class and Education in Modern Britain*. Oxford: Oxford University Press, 1980.

Hancock, Ian. *White Liberals, Moderates, and Radicals in Rhodesia, 1953–1980*. New York: St. Martin's, 1984.
Hanna, Archibald. *Mirror for the Nation: An Annotated Bibliography of American Social Fiction, 1901–1950*. New York: Garland, 1985.
Hanna, Nelly. *In Praise of Books: A Cultural History of Cairo's Middle Class, Sixteenth to the Eighteenth Century*. Syracuse, NY: Syracuse University Press, 2003.
Hardtwig, Wolfgang. "Strukturmerkmale und Entwicklungstendenzen des Vereinswesens in Deutschland 1789–1848." In *Vereinswesen und bürgerliche Gesellschaft*, edited by Otto Dann, 11–50. Munich: R. Oldenbourg, 1984.
Harlan, Louis R. *Booker T. Washington: The Making of a Black Leader, 1856–1901*. New York: Oxford University Press, 1972.
——. *Booker T. Washington: The Wizard of Tuskegee, 1901–1915*. New York: Oxford University Press, 1983.
Harootunian, Harry. "Some Thoughts on Comparability and the Space-Time Problem." *Boundary* 32, no. 2 (2005): 23–52.
Harrison, Carol E. *The Bourgeois Citizen in Nineteenth-Century France: Gender, Sociability, and the Uses of Emulation*. Oxford: Oxford University Press, 1999.
——. "Protecting Catholic Boys and Forming Catholic Men at the Collège Stanislas in Restoration Paris." *French Culture and Civilization: Papers from the George Rudé Seminar* 1 (2005): 160–71.
——. "Zouave Stories: Gender, Catholic Spirituality and French Responses to the Roman Question." *Journal of Modern History* 79, no. 2 (2007): 274–305.
Hartlyn, Jonathan. *The Politics of Coalition Rule in Colombia*. Cambridge: Cambridge University Press, 1988.
Hartmann, Thom. *Screwed: The Undeclared War against the Middle Class—and What We Can Do about It*. San Francisco: Berrett-Koehler, 2006.
Harvey, David. *The Condition of Postmodernity: An Enquiry into the Origins of Cultural Change*. Cambridge: Blackwell, 1990.
Harzig, Christiane. "MacNamara's DP Domestics: Immigration Policy Makers Negotiate Class, Race, and Gender in the Aftermath of World War Two." *Social Politics* 10, no. 1 (2003): 23–48.
Hauser, Christoph. *Anfänge bürgerlicher Organisation: Philhellenismus und Frühliberalismus in Südwestdeutschland*. Göttingen, Germany: Vandenhoeck und Ruprecht, 1990.
Hauteville, Madame de. *Aventures d'une poupée ou histoire de Merveilleuse*. Paris, [1850s].
Havelange, Isabelle. "1650–1830: des livres pour les demoiselles?" *Cahiers de la recherché en éducation* 3 (1996): 363–76.
Haya de la Torre, Víctor Raúl. "El Programa, 23.8.31." In *Revolución sin balas: 15 discursos de Haya de la Torre*, 48–50. Lima: Okura Editores, 1984.
——. *Obras Completas*. Vol. 6. Lima: Mejía Baca, 1976.
——. *Treinta años de aprismo*. México: Fondo de Cultura Económica, 1956.
——. "What Is the APRA?" In *Aprismo: The Ideas and Doctrines of Víctor Raúl Haya de la*

Torre, edited by Robert Alexander, 97–101. Kent, OH: Kent State University Press, 1973.

Haya de la Torre, Víctor Raúl, and Robert J. Alexander. *Aprismo: The Ideas and Doctrines of Victor Raúl Haya De La Torre*. Kent, OH: Kent State University Press, 1973.

Hayes, Dereck. *Historical Atlas of Canada*. Edmonton: Douglas and McIntyre, 1988.

Haynes, Douglas. *Rhetoric and Ritual in Colonial India: The Shaping of a Public Culture in Surat City, 1852–1928*. Berkeley: University of California Press, 1991.

Heinsohn, Kirsten. *Politik und Geschlecht: Zur politischen Kultur bürgerlicher Frauenvereine in Hamburg*. Hamburg: Verein für Hamburgische Geschichte, 1997.

Helg, Aline. "Race in Argentina and Cuba, 1880–1930: Theory, Policies, and Popular Reaction." In *The Idea of Race in Latin America*, edited by R. Graham, 37–69. Austin: University of Texas Press, 1990.

Henderson, James. *Modernization in Colombia: The Laureano Gómez Years, 1889–1965*. Gainesville: University of Florida Press, 2001.

Henderson, Yandell, and Maurice Davie, eds. *Incomes and Living Costs of a University Faculty*. New Haven: Yale University Press, 1928.

Hilton, Matthew. *Consumerism in Twentieth-Century Britain*. Cambridge: Cambridge University Press, 2003.

Hinsley, Curtis, and David Wilcox, eds. *The Southwest in the American Imagination: The Writings of Sylvester Baxter, 1881–1889*. Tucson: University of Arizona Press, 1996.

Hobsbawm, Eric J. *The Age of Capital, 1848–1875*. London: Cardinal, 1989.

——. "The Example of the English Middle Class." In *Bourgeois Society in Nineteenth-Century Europe*, edited by Jürgen Kocka and Allan Mitchell, 127–50. Oxford: Berg, 1993.

Hoffmann, Stefan-Ludwig. "Civility, Male Friendship, and Masonic Sociability in Nineteenth-Century Germany." *Gender & History* 13, no. 2 (2001): 224–48.

Hofstadter, Richard. *The Age of Reform*. New York: Vintage, 1955.

hooks, bell. *Where We Stand: Class Matters*. New York: Routledge, 2000.

Horne, Gerald. *From the Barrel of a Gun: The United States and the War against Zimbabwe, 1965–1980*. Chapel Hill: University of North Carolina Press, 2001.

Hornstein, Jeffrey M. *A Nation of Realtors: A Cultural History of the Twentieth-Century American Middle Class*. Durham: Duke University Press, 2005.

Horowitz, Daniel. *The Morality of Spending: Attitudes toward the Consumer Society in America, 1875–1940*. Baltimore: Johns Hopkins University Press, 1985.

Horowitz, Joel. "Populism and Its Legacies in Argentina." In *Populism in Latin America*, edited by Michael L. Conniff, 22–42. Tuscaloosa: University of Alabama Press, 1999.

Hourani, Albert. "Ottoman Reform and the Politics of Notables." In *Beginnings of Modernization in the Middle East*, edited by William R. Polk and Richard L. Chambers, 41–68. Chicago: University of Chicago Press, 1968.

Huber-Sperl, Rita, ed. *Organisiert und engagiert: Vereinskultur bürgerlicher Frauen im 19. Jahrhundert in Westeuropa und den USA*. Königstein im Taunus, Germany: Helmer, 2002.

Hüchtker, Dietlind. *"Elende Mütter" und "liederliche Weibspersonen": Geschlechterverhältnisse und Armenpolitik 1770–1850 in Berlin*. Münster: Dampfboot, 1999.

Huffington, Arianna. *Third World America: How Our Politicians Are Abandoning the Middle Class and Betraying the American Dream*. New York: Crown Publishers, 2010.

Hunt, Margaret R. *The Middling Sort: Commerce, Gender and the Family in England, 1680–1780*. Berkeley: University of California Press, 1996.

Hutber, Patrick. *The Decline and Fall of the Middle Class—and How It Can Fight Back*. London: Associated Business Programmes, 1976.

Hylton, Forrest. *Evil Hour in Colombia*. New York: Verso, 2006.

Iacovetta, Franca. *Gatekeepers: Reshaping Immigrant Lives in Cold War Canada*. Toronto: Between the Lines, 2006.

——. " 'Making New Canadians': Social Workers Women and the Reshaping of Immigrant Families." In *A Nation of Immigrants: Women, Workers and Communities in Canadian History, 1840s–1960s*, edited by Franca Iacovetta, Paula Draper, and Robert Ventresca, 482–513. Toronto: University of Toronoto, 2002.

Iacovetta, Franca, and Valerie Korinek, "Jello Salads, One Stop Shopping and Maria the Homemaker: The Gender Politics of Food." In *Sisters or Strangers: Immigrant, Ethnic and Racialized Women in Canadian History*, edited by Franca Iacovetta, Frances Swyripa, and Marlene Epp, 190–230. Toronto: University of Toronto Press, 2004.

Igo, Sarah. *The Averaged American: Surveys, Citizens, and the Making of a Mass Public*. Cambridge: Harvard University Press, 2008.

Ingham, Geoffrey. *Capitalism Divided? The City and Industry in British Social Development*. London: Palgrave Macmillan, 1984.

Inglehandt, Ronald, and Welzel, Christian. *Modernization, Cultural Change and Democracy: The Human Development Sequence*. Cambridge: Cambridge University Press, 2005.

Isenberg, Nancy. *Sex and Citizenship in Antebellum America*. Chapel Hill: University of North Carolina Press, 1998.

Itié, Gabriel. "La cooperación en México." *La Revista agrícola*, February 1, 1919, 430–31.

Jacobs, Joseph. "The Middle American." *American Magazine* 63, March 1907, 526–28.

Jacobson, Matthew Frye. *Whiteness of a Different Color: European Immigration and the Alchemy of Race*. Cambridge: Harvard University Press, 1998.

James, C. L. R. *The Black Jacobins: Toussaint L'Ouverture and the San Domingo Revolution*. 1938. New York: Vintage, 1989.

James, Daniel. *Resistance and Integration: Peronism and the Argentine Working Class, 1946–1976*. New York: Cambridge University Press, 1988.

Jauretche, Arturo. *El medio pelo en la sociedad argentina*. Buenos Aires: Corregidor, 1966.

Jayawardena, Kumari. *Nobodies to Somebodies: The Rise of the Colonial Bourgeoisie in Sri Lanka*. London: Zed, 2000.

Jimenez, Michael. "The Elision of the Middle Classes and Beyond: History, Politics and Development Studies in Latin America's 'Short Twentieth Century.' " In *Colonial*

Legacies: The Problem of Persistence in Latin American History, edited by Jeremy Adelman, 199–238. New York: Routledge, 1999.
Johnson, David. *World War II and the Scramble for Labour in Colonial Zimbabwe, 1939–1948*. Harare: University of Zimbabwe Publications, 2000.
Johnson, John J. *Political Change in Latin America: The Emergence of the Middle Sectors*. Stanford: Stanford University Press, 1958.
Johnson, Paul. *The Shopkeepers: Society and Revivals in Rochester, New York, 1815–1837*. New York: Hill and Wang, 2004.
Johnston, Robert. *A Radical Middle Class: Populist Democracy and the Question of Capitalism in Progressive Era Portland, Oregon*. Princeton: Princeton University Press, 2003.
Joseph, Galen. "Taking Race Seriously: Whiteness in Argentina's National and Transnational Imaginary." *Identities* 7, no. 3 (2000): 333–71.
Joseph, Gilbert, Catherine LeGrand, and Ricardo Salvatore, eds. *Close Encounters of Empire: Writing the Cultural History of U.S.–Latin American Relations*. Durham: Duke University Press, 1998.
Joseph, Gilbert, and Daniel Nugent, eds. *Everyday Forms of State Formation: Revolution and the Negotiation of Rule in Modern Mexico*. Durham: Duke University Press, 1993.
Joseph, Gilbert, and Daniel Spenser, eds. *In from the Cold: Latin America's New Encounter with the Cold War*. Durham: Duke University Press, 2008.
Joseph, Keith. "Is Beckerman among the Sociologists?" *New Statesman*, April 18, 1975, 501.
Joshi, Sanjay. *Fractured Modernity: Making of a Middle Class in Colonial India*. Oxford: Oxford University Press, 2001.
Joyce, Patrick, ed. *Class*. Oxford: Oxford University Press, 1995.
——. *Democratic Subjects: The Self and the Social in Nineteenth-Century England*. Cambridge: Cambridge University Press. 1994.
——. *The Rule of Freedom: Liberalism and the Modern City*. London: Verso, 2003.
——. *Work, Society and Politics: The Culture of the Factory in Later Victorian England*. Brighton, UK: Ashgate, 1980.
Kant, Immanuel. *Vom Verhältnis der Theorie zur Praxis im Staatsrecht*. 1793. 15 vols. Berlin: Reimer, 1923.
Kantor, Harry. *The Ideology and Program of the Peruvian Aprista Movement*. New York: Octagon Books, 1966.
Kaplan, Amy. *The Anarchy of Empire and the Making of U.S. Culture*. Cambridge: Harvard University Press, 2002.
Kaplan, Amy, and Donald Pease, eds. *Cultures of U.S. Imperialism*. Durham: Duke University Press, 1993.
Karl, Robert. "State Formation, Violence and Cold War in Colombia." PhD diss., Harvard University, 2009.
Karnik, V. B. *N.M. Joshi: Servant of India*. Bombay: United Asia of Publications, 1972.
Karpat, Kemal. *The Politicization of Islam: Reconstructing Identity, State, Faith, and Community in the Late-Ottoman State*. Oxford: Oxford University Press, 2001.
Kaschuba, Wolfgang. "Zwischen deutscher Nation und deutscher Provinz: Politische Horizonte und soziale Milieus im frühen Liberalismus." In *Liberalismus im 19.*

Jahrhundert: Deutschland im europäischen Vergleich, edited by Dieter Langewiesche, 83–108. Göttingen, Germany: Vandenhock und Ruprecht, 1988.
———. "German Bürgerlichkeit after 1800: Culture as Symbolic Practice." In *Bourgeois Society in Nineteenth-Century Europe*, edited by Jürgen Kocka and Allan Mitchell, 392–422. Brigend, 1993.
Kasson, John F. *Rudeness and Civility: Manners in Nineteenth-Century Urban America*. New York: Hill and Wang, 1990.
Katz, Sidney. "How Mental Health Is Attacking Our Immigrants." *Maclean's*, January 4, 1958.
Kaufman, Suzanne K. *Consuming Visions: Mass Culture and the Lourdes Shrine*. Ithaca: Cornell University Press, 2005.
Kaviraj, Sudipta. "'Filth and Public Sphere': Concepts and Practices about Space in Calcutta." *Public Culture* 10, no. 1 (1997): 83–113.
Kelley, Ninette, and Michael Trebilcock. *The Making of the Mosaic: A History of Canadian Immigration Policy*. Toronto: Toronto University Press, 1998.
Khoury. Philip S. *Syria and the French Mandate: The Politics of Arab Nationalism, 1920–1945*. Princeton: Princeton University Press, 1987.
———. "The Urban Notables Paradigm Revisited." *Revue du Monde Musulman et de la Méditerranée* 55–56, nos. 1–2 (1990): 215–30.
Kidd, Alan, and David Nicholls, eds. *Gender, Civic Culture and Consumerism: Middle-Class Identity in Britain 1800–1940*. Manchester, UK: Manchester University Press, 1999.
———, eds. *The Making of the British Middle Class? Studies of Regional and Cultural Diversity since the Eighteenth Century*. Stroud, Gloucestershire: Sutton, 1999.
Kill, Susanne. *Das Bürgertum in Münster 1770–1870*. Munich: Oldenbourg, 2001.
Killingray, David, with Martin Plaut. *Fighting for Britain: African Soldiers in the Second World War*. Woodbridge, UK: James Currey, 2010.
Kinsman, Gary, Dieter K. Buse, and Mercedes Steedman, eds. *Whose National Security? Canadian State Surveillance and the Creation of Enemies*. Toronto: Between the Lines, 2000.
Kirkpatrick, Ellis Lore. *The Farmer's Standard of Living*. New York: Century and Co., 1929.
Klaiber, Jeffrey. *Religion and Revolution in Peru, 1824–1976*. Notre Dame, IN: University of Notre Dame Press, 1977.
Klaren, Peter. *Modernization, Dislocation and Aprismo: Origins of the Peruvian Aprista Party, 1870–1932*. Austin: University of Texas Press, 1973.
———. *Peru: Society and Nationhood in the Andes*. New York: Oxford University Press, 2000.
Klein, Natalie. *"L'humanité, le christianisme, et la liberté": Die internationale philhellenische Vereinsbewegung der 1820er Jahre*. Mainz, Germany: Philipp Von Zabern, 2000.
Klubock, Thomas. *Contested Communities: Class, Gender, and Politics in Chile's El Teniente Copper Mine, 1904–1951*. Durham: Duke University Press, 1999.

Kocka, Jürgen. "The Middle Class in Europe." *Journal of Modern History* 67 (December, 1995): 783–810.
Koditschek, Theodore. *Class Formation and Urban Industrial Society*. Cambridge: Cambridge University Press, 1990.
Korinek, Valerie J. *Roughing It in the Suburbs: Reading Chatelaine Magazine in the Fifties and Sixties*. Toronto: University of Toronto Press, 2000.
Koven, Seth. *Slumming: Sexual and Social Politics in Victorian London*. Princeton: Princeton University Press, 2006.
Kriger, Norma J. *Zimbabwe's Guerrilla War: Peasant Voices*. Cambridge: Cambridge University Press, 1992.
Krishnaswamy, Revathi, and John C. Hawley, eds. *The Postcolonial and the Global*. Minneapolis: University of Minnesota Press, 2008.
Krugman, Paul. *The Return of Depression Economics*. New York: W. W. Norton, 2008.
Kumar, K. *Political Agenda of Education: A Study of Colonialist and Nationalist Ideas*. New Delhi: Sage, 1991.
Kunzru, Hirday Nath. *Gopal Krishna Devadhar*. Poona: Servants of India Society, 1939.
Küster, Thomas. *Alte Armut und neues Bürgertum*. Münster: Aschendorff, 1995.
Kymlicka, Will, and Wayne Norman, "Return of the Citizen: A Survey of Recent Work on Citizenship Theory." In *Theorizing Citizenship*, edited by Ronald Beiner, 283–322. Albany: State University of New York, 1995.
Kyrk, Hazel. *Economic Problems of the Family*. New York: Harper & Bros., 1929.
Laclau, Ernesto. *On Populist Reason*. London: Verso, 2005.
——. *Politics and Ideology in Marxist Theory: Capitalism, Fascism, Populism*. London: Verso, 1977.
Lake, Marilyn, and Henry Reynolds. *Drawing the Global Colour Line: White Men's Countries and the Question of Racial Equality*. Cambridge: Cambridge University Press, 2008.
Landes, Joan. *Women and the Public Sphere in the Age of the French Revolution*. Ithaca: Cornell University Press, 1988.
Langewiesche, Dieter. "Die schwäbische Sängerbewegung in der Gesellschaft des 19. Jahrhunderts—ein Beitrag zur kulturellen Nationsbildung." *Zeitschrift für württembergische Landesgeschichte* 52 (1993): 257–301.
——. "'Staat' und 'Kommune': Zum Wandel der Staatsaufgaben in Deutschland im 19. Jahrhundert." *Historische Zeitschrift* 248 (1989): 621–35.
Langlois, Claude. *Le Catholicisme au féminin: les congrégations à supérieure générale au XIXe siècle*. Paris: Les Editions du cerf, 1984.
Lasch, Christopher. *Haven in a Heartless World*. New York: W. W. Norton & Company, 1995.
Lastarria, José Victorino. 1849. *El manuscrito del Diablo*. Santiago: Ercilla, 1941.
Latcham, Ricardo. "Psicología del caballero chileno." In *Páginas escogidas*, edited by Hernán Godoy, 310–92. Santiago: Andrés Bello, 1969.
Latham, Michael E. *Modernization as Ideology: American Social Science and "Nation Building" in the Kennedy Era*. Chapel Hill: University of North Carolina Press, 2000.

Latour, Bruno. *We Have Never Been Modern*. Cambridge: Harvard University Press, 1993.

Lausevic, Mirjana. "A Different Village: International Folk Dance and Balkan Music and Dance in the United States." PhD diss., Wesleyan University, 1998.

La Vopa, Anthony. "Conceiving a Public: Ideas and Society in Eighteenth-Century Europe." *Journal of Modern History* 64, no. 1 (1992): 79–116.

Lear, John. *Workers, Neighbors, and Citizens: The Revolution in Mexico City*. Lincoln: University of Nebraska Press, 2001.

Lears, T. J. Jackson. *No Place of Grace: Antimodernism and the Transformation of American Culture*. Chicago: University of Chicago Press, 1994.

Lebret Mision, Comité Nacional de Planeación. *Misión economia y humanismo: estudios sobre el desarrollo de Colombia*. Bogotá: Cromos, 1958.

Lee, C. H. "Regional Growth and Structural Change in Victorian Britain." *Economic History Review* 34, no. 3 (1981): 438–52.

Legrand, Augustin. *Delphine ou l'enfant gatée*. Vol. 2 of *Contes pour les enfants avec gravures découpées*. Paris, [1840s].

Leidenberger, Georg. "Habermas en el Zócalo: La Transformación de la Esfera Pública y la Política del transporte público en la Ciudad de México, 1900–1947." In *Actores, espacios y debates en la historia de la esfera pública en la ciudad de México*, edited by Cristina Sacristán and Pablo Piccato, 178–98. Mexico City: Instituto de Investigaciones Históricas, Universidad Autonoma de México; Instituto Mora, 2006.

———. "Las huelgas tranviarias como rupturas del orden urbano. Ciudad de México, de 1911 a 1925." In *Formas de descontento y movimientos socials, siglos XIX y XX*, edited by José A. Ronzón León y Carmen Valdez Vega, 139–66. México City: Universidad Autonoma Metropolitana, 2005.

Lemke, Thomas. "'The Birth of Bio-Politics'—Michel Foucault's Lecture at the Collège de France on Neo-Liberal Governmentality." *Economy and Society* 30, no. 2 (2001): 130–207.

Levine, Lawrence W. *Highbrow/Lowbrow: The Emergence of Cultural Hierarchy in America*. Cambridge: Harvard University Press, 1988.

Lewis, Brian. *The Middlemost and the Mill Towns*. Stanford: Stanford University Press, 2001.

Lewis, Roy, and Angus Maude. *The English Middle Classes*. New York: Alfred A. Knopf, 1949.

Lietchty, Mark. *Suitably Modern: Making Middle Class Culture in a New Consumer City*. Princeton: Princeton University Press, 2002.

Light, Alison. *Forever England: Femininity, Literature and Conservatism between the Wars*. London: Routledge, 1991.

Lincoln, Bruce. *Holy Terrors: Thinking about Religion after September 11*. Chicago: University of Chicago Press, 2003.

Lind, Michael. *The American Way of Strategy: U.S. Foreign Policy and the American Way of Life*. Oxford: Oxford University Press, 2006.

———. "Are We Still a Middle-Class Nation?" *Atlantic Monthly*, January/February 2004, 120–28.

Lipp, Carola. "Frauen auf der Straüe. Strukturen weiblicher Öffentlichkeit im Unterschichtsmilieu." In *Schimpfende Weiber und patriotische Jungfrauen. Frauen im Vormärz und in der Revolution 1848*, edited by Caroa Lipp, 16–24. Bühl-Moos, 1986.

Lipsitz, George. *The Possessive Investment in Whiteness: How White People Profit from Identity Politics*. Philadelphia: Temple University Press, 1998.

——. "Who'll Stop the Rain: Youth Culture, Rock 'n Roll, and Social Crises." In *The Sixties: From Memory to History*, edited by David Farber, 206–34. Chapel Hill: University of North Carolina Press, 1964.

Lister, Ruth. *Citizenship: Feminist Perspectives*. Basingstoke, Hampshire: Palgrave Macmillan, 2003.

Loaeza, Soleda. *Clases medias y política en México: la querella escolar, 1959–1963*. México City: El Colegio de México, 1988.

López, A. Ricardo. *Makers of Democracy: The Transnational Formation of the Middle Class in Colombia, 1958–1982*. Forthcoming.

Löther, Andrea, "Unpolitische Bürger. Frauen und Partizipation in der vormodernen praktischen Philosophie." In *Bürgerschaft. Rezeption und Innovation der Begrifflichkeit vom Hohen Mittelalter bis ins 19*, edited by R. K. Koselleck, 239–73. Jahrhundert, Klett-Cotta: Stuttgart, 1994.

Ludden, David. "Modern Inequality and Early Modernity: A Comment for the *AHR* on Articles by R. Bin Wong and Kenneth Pomeranz." *American Historical Review* 107, no. 2 (2002): 470–80.

Lukas, J. Anthony. *Big Trouble: A Murder in a Small Western Town Sets Off a Struggle for the Soul of America*. New York: Simon and Schuster, 1997.

Luna, Felix. *El 45: Crónica de un año decisico*. S.l.: J. Alvarez S. A, 1900.

Lynd, Robert S., and Helen Merrell Lynd. *Middletown: A Study in Modern American Culture*. New York: Harcourt, Brace, 1929.

Macaulay, George. *History of England*. Garden City, N.Y.: Doubleday, 1953.

Macías-González, Victor M. "Hombres de mundo: la masculinidad, el consumo, y los manuales de urbanidad y buenas maneras." In *Orden social e identidad de género: México, siglos XIX y XX*, edited by María Teresa Fernández Aceves, Carmen Ramos Escandón, and Susie Porter, 267–97. Guadalajara, México: Centro de Investigación y Estudios Superiores en Antropología Social and Universidad de Guadalajara, 2006.

Mack, Phyllis. "Religion, Feminism, and the Problem of Agency: Reflections on Eighteenth-Century Quakerism." *Signs* 29, no. 1 (2003): 149–77.

Mackay, John. *The Other Spanish Christ*. New York: MacMillan, 1932.

MacLeod, Anne Scott. *American Childhood: Essays on Children's Literature of the Nineteenth and Twentieth Centuries*. Athens: University of Georgia Press, 1994.

Majumdar, N. M. "The Social Problems of a City." *The Social Service Quarterly* 2, no. 1 (1916): 27–35.

Malabari, Behramji Maharbanji. *India in 1897*. Bombay: A. J. Combridge, 1898.

Mallon, Florencia. *Peasant and Nation: The Making of Postcolonial Peru and Mexico*. Berkeley: University of California Press, 1995.

Mandler, Peter. "The Consciousness of Modernity? Liberalism and the English

National Character, 1870–1940." In *Meanings of Modernity: Britain from the Late-Victorian Era to World War II*, edited by Martin Daunton and Bernhard Rieger, 119–35. London: Berg, 2001.
Mariátegui, José Carlos. "Punto de vista anti-imperialista." In *Ideología y política*, 83–91. Lima: Amauta, 1969.
Marshall, Gordon, Adam Swift, and Stephen Roberts. *Against the Odds? Social Class and Social Justice in Industrial Societies*. Oxford: Oxford University Press, 1997.
Martin, David, and Phyllis Johnson. *The Struggle for Zimbabwe*. New York: Monthly Review, 1981.
Marx, Karl. *Eighteenth Brumaire of Louis Bonaparte*. 1852. New York: International Publishers, 1963.
——. "The English Middle Class." In Karl Marx and Friedrich Engels, *Collected Works*, vol. 12, 664–65. Translated by Joan Walmsley and Trevor Walmsley. London: Lawrence & Wishart, 1980.
——. "Introduction to the Critique of Hegel's Philosophy of Right." In *The Portable Karl Marx*, edited by Eugene Kamenka, 115–24. New York: Penguin, 1983.
——. "Manifesto of the Communist Party." In *The Portable Karl Marx*, edited by Eugene Kamenka, 203–87. New York: Penguin, 1983.
Marx, Karl, and Friedrich Engels. *The Communist Manifesto*. London: Penguin Books, 1967.
Martz, Fraidie. *Open Your Hearts: The Story of the Jewish War Orphans in Canada*. Montreal: Vehicle Press, 1996.
Masselin, J. G. *Le Monde en miniature ou les contrastes de la vie humaine*. Paris, n.d.
Masterman, Charles F. G. *The Condition of England*. London, 1911.
——. *England after the War*. London, 1922.
Mayer, Arno. "The Lower Middle Class as Historical Problem." *Journal of Modern History* 47, no. 3 (1975): 409–36.
——. *The Persistence of the Old Régime*. London: Pantheon, 1981.
Maza, Sarah. *The Myth of the French Bourgeoisie*. Cambridge: Harvard University Press, 2003.
McBride, George McCutchen. *Chile: Land and Society*. New York: American Geographical Society, 1936.
McCord, Norman. *The Anti-Corn Law League*. London: Routledge, 1958.
McDonald, Ellen E. "English Education and Social Change in Late Nineteenth Century Bombay, 1858–1898." PhD diss., University of California, 1972.
McEvoy Carreras, Carmen. *Forjando una nación: ensayos de historia republicana*. Lima: Pontificia Universidad Católica, 1999.
McKibbin, Ross. *Classes and Cultures: England 1918–1951*. Oxford: Oxford University Press, 1998.
McNeely, John H. *Salaries in Land-Grant Universities and Colleges*. Washington: Government Printing Office, 1932.
Mead, Walter Russell, and Sherle R. Schwenninger, eds. *The Bridge to a Global Middle Class: Development, Trade, and International Finance*. Boston: Kluwer, 2003.

Mehrtens, Cristina. *Urban Space and National Identity in Early Twentieth Century São Paulo, Brazil: Crafting Modernity*. New York: Palgrave Macmillan, 2010.
Mehta, Uday Singh. *Liberalism and Empire: A Study in Nineteenth-Century British Liberal Thought*. Chicago: University of Chicago Press, 1999.
——. "Liberal Strategies of Exclusion." In *Tensions of Empire: Colonia Cultures in a Bourgeois World*, edited by Frederick Cooper and Ann Laura Stoler, 59–86. Berkeley: University of California Press, 1997.
Melfi, Domingo. *Sin brújula*. Santiago: Ercilla, 1932.
——. "Tiempos de tormenta en el remate de un viejo palacio santiaguino." In *Páginas escogidas*, 1–156. Santiago: Dirección de Bibliotecas Archivos y Museos, Centro de Investigación Diego Barros Arana, 1993.
Mendieta, Eduardo. "The Liberation of Politics: Alterity, Solidarity, and Liberation." In Enrique Dussel, *Twenty Theses on Politics*, translated by George Ciccariello-Maher, vii–xvi. Durham: Duke University Press, 2008.
Mesa Manuel, A. "La inscripción de alumnos en la Escuela Nacional de Agricultura." *Crisol* 2, no. 4 (1930): 104–5.
Mettele, Gisela. *Bürgertum in Köln: Gemeinsinn und freie Association*. Munich: Oldenbourg, 1998.
——. "Der private Raum als öffentlicher Ort: Geselligkeit im bürgerlichen Haus." In *Bürgerkultur im 19. Jahrhundert*, edited by Dieter Hein and Andreas Schulz, 155–69. Munich: C. H. Beck, 1996.
Meyer-Renschhausen, Elisabeth. *Weibliche Kultur und Sozialarbeit: Eine Geschichte der Frauenbewegung am Beispiel Bremens 1810–1927*. Cologne: Böhlau, 1989.
Michel, Sonya, and Seth Koven, eds. *Mothers of a New World: Maternalist Politics and the Origins of Welfare States*. London: Routledge, 1993.
——. "Womanly Duties: Maternalist Politics and the Origins of Welfare States in France, Germany, Great Britain, and the United States, 1880–1920." *American Historical Review* 95, no. 4 (1990): 1076–108.
Michelet, Jules. *Du Prêtre, de la femme, de la famille*. 4th ed. Paris, 1845.
——. *Histoire de France au moyen age*. Paris: Calmann-Lévy, 1833.
Michelguglielmo, Torri. "'Westernized Middle Class': Intellectuals and Society in Late Colonial India." In *The Congress and Indian Nationalism: Historical Perspectives*, edited by John L. Hill, 18–38. London: Curzon, 1991.
Mignolo, Walter. *Local Histories/Global Designs: Coloniality, Subaltern Knowledge and Border Thinking*. Princeton: Princeton University Press, 2000.
Miguez, Eduardo. "Tensiones de identidad: reflexiones sobre la experiencia italiana en la Argentina." In *Asociacionismo, trabajo e identidad étnica*, edited by Fernando Devoto and Eduardo Miguez, 337–58. Buenos Aires: Centro de Estudios Migratorios Latinoamericanos, 1992.
Minault, Gail. *Secluded Scholars: Women's Education and Muslim School Reform in Colonial India*. Delhi: Oxford University Press, 1998.
Minter, David. *A Cultural History of the American Novel*. New York: Cambridge University Press, 1994.

Mintz, Sidney. *Sweetness and Power: The Place of Sugar in Modern History*. New York: Viking, 1985.
Misra, Bankey Bihari. *The Indian Middle Classes: Their Growth in Modern Times*. Delhi: Oxford University Press, 1961.
Mitchell, Timothy. *Rule of Experts: Egypt, Techno-Politics, Modernity*. Berkeley: University of California Press, 2002.
Mitre, Bartolomé. *Historia de Belgramo y de la independencia Argentina*. 1857. Buenos Aires: Anaconda, 1950.
Möller, Frank. *Bürgerliche Herrschaft in Augsburg 1790–1880*. Munich: R. Oldenbourg, 1998.
Moncloa y Covarrubias, Manuel. *Las Cojinovas: costumbres limeñas cursis*. Lima: Badiola y Berrio, 1905.
Monicat, Bénédicte. "Romans pour filles et littérature féminine du dix-neuvième siècle." *French Literature Series* 31 (2004): 197–208.
Moran, Thomas Francis. "The Ethics of Wealth." *American Journal of Sociology* 6, no. 6 (May 1901): 823–38.
Morley, John. *The Life of Richard Cobden*. Vol. 1. London: Chapman and Hall, 1880.
Morris, R. J. *Class, Sect and Party: The Making of the British Middle Class: Leeds, 1820–50*. Manchester, UK: Manchester University Press, 1990.
——. *Men, Women and Property in England, 1780–1870: A Social and Economic History of Family Strategies amongst the Leeds Middle Class*. Cambridge: Cambridge University Press, 2004.
Moskowitz, Marina. *Standard of Living: The Measure of the Middle Class in Modern America*. Baltimore: Johns Hopkins University Press, 2004.
Müffelmann, Leo. *Orientacion de la Clase Media*. Barcelona-Buenos Aires: Labor, 1926.
Muller, Henry. *Innocence et vertu: Historiettes pour les adolescens des deux sexes*. Paris, 1834.
Muzumdar, N. M. "The Social Problems of a City." *Social Service Quarterly* 2, no. 1 (1916): 27–35.
Naregal, Veena. "Figuring the Political as Pedagogy: Colonial Intellectuals, Mediation and Modernity in Western India." *Studies in History* 17, no. 1 (2001): 17–55.
Neira, Hugo. *Hacia la tercera mitad: Perú XVI–XX, ensayos de relectura herética*. Lima: SIDEA, 1996.
Nicolls, Peter. *Modernisms: A Literary Guide:* London: Macmillan, 1995.
Nipperdey, Thomas. *Deutsche Geschichte 1800–1866: Bürgerwelt und starker Staat*. Munich: C. H. Beck, 1989.
——. "Verein als soziale Struktur in Deutschland im späten 18 und frühen 19. Jahrhundert" In *Geschichtswissenschaft und Vereinswesen im 19. Jahrhundert*, edited by Hermann Heimpel, 1–44. Göttingen, Germany, 1972.
Nkrumah, Kwame. *Ghana: The Autobiography of Kwame Nkrumah*. New York: Nelson, 1957.
Nolte, Paul. "Bürgerideal, Gemeinde und Republik, Klassischer Republikanismus im frühen deutschen Liberalismus." *Historische Zeitschrift*, no. 254 (1992): 609–56.

——. *Gemeindebürgertum und Liberalismus in Baden 1800–1850*. Göttingen, Germany: Vandenhock und Ruprecht, 1994.
Oberoi, Harjot. *The Construction of Religious Boundaries: Culture, Identity and Diversity in the Sikh Tradition*. Chicago: University of Chicago Press, 1994.
O'Connor, Alice. *Poverty Knowledge: Social Science, Social Policy and the Poor in Twentieth-Century U.S. History*. Princeton: Princeton University Press, 2002.
O'Dougherty, Maureen. *Consumption Intensified: The Politics of Middle-Class Daily Life in Brazil*. Durham: Duke University Press, 2002.
O'Hanlon, Rosalind. *A Comparison between Women and Men: Tarabai Shinde and the Critique of Gender Relations in Colonial India*. Oxford: Oxford University Press, 2000.
Olcott, Jocelyn, Mary Kay Vaughan, and Gabriela Cano, eds. *Sex in Revolution: Gender, Politics, and Power in Modern Mexico*. Durham: Duke University Press, 2006.
Oldenburg, Veena Talwar. *The Making of Colonial Lucknow, 1856–1877*. Princeton: Princeton University Press, 1984.
Olney, Martha. *Buy Now, Pay Later: Advertising, Credit, and Consumer Durables in the 1920s*. Chapel Hill: University of North Carolina Press, 1991.
Omi, Michael, and Howard Winant. *Racial Formation in the United States: From the 1960s to the 1990s*. New York: Routledge, 1994.
Opitz, Claudia, Ulrike Weckel, and Elke Kleinau, eds. *Tugend, Vernunft und Gefühl: Geschlechterdiskurse der Aufklärung und weibliche Lebenswelten*. Münster: Waxmann, 2000.
Orrego Luco, Luis. *Casa grande: escenas de la vida en Chile*. 3rd ed. Santiago: Nascimento, 1934.
——. *En familia: recuerdos del tiempo viejo (1886)*. Santiago: Zig-Zag, 1912.
——. *Memorias del tiempo viejo*. Santiago: Ediciones de la Universidad de Chile, 1984.
Ortlepp, Anke. *"Auf denn, ihr Schwestern!" Deutschamerikanische Frauenvereine in Milwaukee, Wisconsin, 1844–1914*. Stuttgart: F. Steiner, 2004.
Owensby, Brian. *Intimate Ironies: Modernity and the Making of Middle-Class Lives in Brazil*. Stanford: Stanford University Press, 1999.
Palacio, Ernesto. *La historia falsificada*. Buenos Aires: Difusion, 1945.
Palacios, Marco. *Between Legitimacy and Violence: A History of Colombia, 1875–2002*. Durham: Duke University Press, 2006.
Paletschek, Sylvia. *Frauen und Dissens: Frauen im Deutschkatholizismus und in den freien Gemeinden 1841–1852*. Göttingen, Germany: Vandenhoeck und Ruprech, 1990.
Paley, Julia, ed. *Democracy: Anthropological Approaches*. Santa Fe, NM: School of Advanced Research Press, 2009.
Palmer, Robin. *Land and Racial Discrimination in Rhodesia*. Berkeley: University of California Press, 1977.
Palmié, Stephan. *Wizards and Scientists: Explorations in Afro-Cuban Modernity and Tradition*. Durham: Duke University Press, 2002.
Panayi, Panakos. *German Immigrants in Britain during the Nineteenth Century, 1815–1914*. Oxford: Berg, 1995.
——. *Immigrants, Ethnicity and Racism in Britain, 1815–1945*. Manchester, UK: Manchester University Press, 1994.

Parker, David S. *The Idea of the Middle Class: White-Collar Workers and Peruvian Society*. University Park: Penn State University Press, 1998.

——. "Middle-Class Mobilization and the Language of Orders in Urban Latin America: From Caste to Category in Early Twentieth-Century Lima." *Journal of Urban History* 31, no. 3 (2005): 367–81.

Parker, David S., and Louise Walker, eds. *Latin America's Middle Class: Unsettled Questions and New Histories*. Lexington, 2012.

Parker, John. "Burgeoning Bourgeoisie." *Economist*, February 12, 2009 (http://www.economist.com/specialreports/displaystory.cfm?story_id=13063298).

Partido Aprista Peruano. *4 Aspectos importantes del Aprismo: preguntas y respuestas Apristas*. Manco Capac, 1933.

Pateman, Carole. *The Sexual Contract*. Stanford: Stanford University Press, 1988.

Patten, Simon. "The Standardization of Family Life." In *American Standards and Planes of Living: Readings in the Social Economics of Consumption*, edited by Thomas Eliot. Boston: Ginn & Co, 1931.

Pécaut, Daniel. *Orden y violencia: evolución socio-política de Colombia entre 1930 y 1953*. Bogotá: Grupo Editorial Norma, 2001.

Peiss, Kathy. *Cheap Amusements: Working Women and Leisure in Turn-of-the-Century New York*. Philadelphia: Temple University Press, 1986.

Peixotto, Jessica B. *Getting and Spending at the Professional Standard of Living: A Study of the Costs of Living an Academic Life*. New York: Macmillan, 1927.

Perkin, Harold. *The Origins of Modern English Society, 1780–1880*. London: Routledge and K. Paul, 1969.

——. *The Rise of Professional Society*. London: Routledge, 1989.

Perón, Juan Domingo. *El pueblo quiere saber de qué se trata*. Buenos Aires, 1944.

Pettman, Jan Jindy. "Globalisation and the Gendered Politics of Citizenship." In *Women, Citizenship and Difference*, edited by Nira Yuval-Davis and Pnina Werbner, 207–20. London: St. Martin's, 1999.

Piccato, Pablo. "Public Sphere in Latin America: A Map of the Historiography." *Social History* 35, no. 2 (2010): 165–92.

Pieper, Antje. "The Making of a Middle-Class Cultural Identity: A Comparative History of Leipzig's Gewandhaus and Birmingham's Triennial Festival, c. 1780–1914." PhD diss., University of Birmingham, 2005.

Pike, Frederick B. "Aspects of Class Relations in Chile, 1850–1960." *Hispanic American Historical Review* 43, no. 1 (1963): 14–33.

Pinto Gamboa, Willy. *Lo huachafo: trama y perfil (Jorge Miota, vida y obra)*. Lima: Cibeles, 1981.

Pizarro Guerrero, Miguel. *Los desafíos del aprismo: Ensayo sobre la formación de cuadros*. Lima, 1988.

Planas, Pedro. *Mito y realidad: Haya de la Torre (Orígenes del APRA)*. Lima: Centro de Documentación e Información, 1985.

Portal, Magda. *América Latina frente al Imperialismo*. Lima: Cahuide, 1931.

Portes Gil, Emilio. *Autobiografiía de la Revolución Mexicana; un tratado de interpretación histórica*. México City: Instituto Mexicano de Cultura, 1964.

Prakash, Gyan. "Subaltern Studies as Postcolonial Criticism." *American Historical Review* 99, no. 5 (December 1994): 1475–90.
Prelinger, Catherine M. *Charity, Challenge, and Change: Religious Dimensions of the Mid-Nineteenth-Century Women's Movement in Germany*. New York: Greenwood, 1987.
Price, Roger. "Poor Relief and Social Crisis in Mid-Nineteenth-Century France." *European Studies Review* 13, no. 4 (1983): 423–54.
Putman, Robert D. *Bowling Alone: The Collapse and Revival of American Community*. New York: Simon and Schuster, 2000.
——. *Making Democracy Work: Civic Traditions in Modern Italy*. Princeton: Princeton University Press, 1993.
Quataert, Jean. *Staging Philanthropy: Patriotic Women and the National Imagination in Dynastic Germany, 1813–1916*. Ann Arbor: University of Michigan Press, 2001.
Quattrocci-Woisson, Diana. *Los males de la memoria*. Buenos Aires: Emece, 1995.
Quesada Laos, Carlos Miró. "Problemas de la clase media." In Carlos Miró Quesada Laos, *Ficción y realidad del Ecuador y otras cinco conferencias*, 156–68. Lima: Tipografía Peruana S.A., 1942.
Quiroz, María Teresa. "La relación partido-pueblo en el recorrido histórico del APRA." In *Comunicación y cultura política: entre públicos y ciudadanos*, edited by Alfaro Moreno, Rosa María, José Joaquín Brunner, Carlos Franco, Arturo Granados, Sandro Macassi Lavander, and Jesús Martín Barbero, 115–35. Lima: Calandria, Asociación de Comunicadores Sociales, 1994.
al-Rabbat, Idmun [Edmond Rabbath]. "The Decline of Democracy [in Arabic]." *al-Hadith* 2 (February 1927): 100–198.
Rabe, Stephen C. *The Most Dangerous Area in the World: John F. Kennedy Confronts Communist Revolution in Latin America*. Chapel Hill: University of North Carolina Press, 1999.
Raftopoulos, Brian, and Tyrone Savage, eds. *Zimbabwe: Injustice and Political Reconciliation*. Cape Town: Institute for Justice and Reconciliation, 2004.
Ranger, Terence O. *Revolt in Southern Rhodesia, 1896–97: A Study in African Resistance*. Evanston, IL: Northwestern University Press, 1967.
Ratier, Hugo. *El Cabecita negra*. Buenos Aires: Centro Editor de America Latina, 1971.
Rau, Shankar, "Family Budgets." In *A Chitrapur Saraswat Miscellany*, edited and compiled by H. Shankar Rau, 15–31. Bombay, 1938.
Ravallion, Martin. *The Developing World's Bulging (but Vulnerable) "Middle Class."* Washington: World Bank Development Research Group, 2009.
Reagin, Nancy R. *A German Women's Movement: Class and Gender in Hanover, 1880–1933*. Chapel Hill: University of North Carolina Press, 1995.
Reder, Dirk. *Frauenbewegung und Nation: Patriotische Frauenvereine in Deutschland im frühen 19. Jahrhundert (1813–1830)*. Cologne: SH-Verlag, 1998.
Renneville, Madame de. *Les Bons Petits Enfants, ou portraits de mon fils et de ma fille*. 2 vols. Paris, 1827.
Rennhak, Katharina, and Virginia Richter, eds. *Revolution und Emanzipation: Geschlechterordnungen in Europa um 1800*. Cologne: Böhlau, 2004.
Renonciat, Annie, Viviane Ezratty, and Geneviève Patte. *Livres d'enfance, livres de France*. Paris: Hachette jeunesse, 1998.

Reulecke, Jürgen. "Die Armenfürsorge als Teil der kommunalen Leistungsverwaltung und Daseinsvorsorge im 19. Jahrhundert. " In *Kommunale Leistungsverwaltung und Stadtentwicklung vom Vormärz bis zur Weimarer Republik*, edited by Hans Heinrich Blotevogel, 71–80. Cologne: Böhlau, 1990.

——. "Formen bürgerlich-sozialen Engagements in Deutschland und England im 19. Jahrhundert." In *Arbeiter und Bürger im 19. Jahrhundert*, edited by Jürgen Kocka, 71–80. München: R. Oldenbourg, 1986.

Rice, Stephen P. *Minding the Machine: Languages of Class in Early Industrial America*. Berkeley: University of California Press, 2004.

Rich, Rachel. "Bourgeois Consumption: Food, Space and Identity in London and Paris, 1850–1914." PhD diss., University of Essex, 2004.

Riley, Denise. *"Am I That Name?" Feminism and the Category of "Women" in History*. Minneapolis: University of Minnesota Press, 1988.

Rock, David. "Intellectual Precursors of Conservative Nationalism in Argentina, 1900–1927." *Hispanic American Historical Review* 67, no. 2 (1987): 271–300.

——. *El radicalismo argentino: 1890–1930*. Buenos Aires: Amorrortu, 1977.

Rodgers, Daniel T. *Atlantic Crossings: Social Politics in a Progressive Age*. Cambridge: Harvard University Press, 2000.

Roediger, David R. *The Wages of Whiteness: Race and the Making of the American Working Class*. London: Verso, 1991.

Rogers, Rebecca. *From the Salon to the Schoolroom: Educating Bourgeois Girls in Nineteenth-Century France*. University Park: Penn State University Press, 2005.

Romer, Patricia. "La clase media urbana en la literatura nacional, 1880–1930." Senior thesis, Universidad de Buenos Aires, 1998.

Romero, José. Luis. *Las ideas políticas en Argentina*. Buenos Aires: Fondo de Cultura Económica, 1946.

Rosa, José María. "Prólogo." In Raúl Scalabrini Ortiz, *El hombre que está solo y espera*, 11–14. Buenos Aires: Librerías Anaconda, 1932.

Rose, Nikolas. *Power of Freedom: Reframing Political Thought*. Cambridge: Cambridge University Press, 1999.

Rosemblatt, Karin Alejandra. *Gendered Compromises: Political Cultures and the State in Chile, 1920–1950*. Chapel Hill: University of North Carolina Press, 2000.

Ross, Dorothy. *The Origins of American Social Science*. Cambridge: Cambridge University Press, 1991.

Ross, Murray G. *Community Organization: Theory, Principles and Practice*. New York: Harper & Row, 1955.

Roth, Ralf. *Stadt und Bürgertum in Frankfurt am Main: ein besonderer Weg von der ständischen zur modernen Bürgergesellschaft, 1760–1914*. München: Oldenbourg, 1996.

Rousseau, M. V. "Les Pensionnaires." In *Cotes de la jeune tante*, 304–58. Paris, [c. 1830].

Rubin, Joan Shelley. *The Making of Middlebrow Culture*. Chapel Hill: University of North Carolina Press, 1992.

Rubinstein, W. D. *Capitalism, Culture and Decline in Britain*. London: Routledge, 1993.

——. *Men of Property: The Very Wealthy in Britain since the Industrial Revolution*. New Brunswick, N.J.: Rutgers University Press, 1981.

Rubinstein, W. D., and Martin Daunton. "Debate: 'Gentlemanly Capitalism' and British Industry 1820–1914." *Past and Present*, no. 132 (1991): 150–70.

Ryan, Mary P. *Cradle of the Middle Class: The Family in Oneida County, New York, 1790–1865*. Cambridge: Cambridge University Press, 1983.

Sábato, Ernesto. *Tango: discusión y clave*. Buenos Aires: Losada, 1963.

Sachsse, Christoph. *Mütterlichkeit als Beruf: Sozialarbeit, Sozialreform und Frauenbewegung 1871–1929*. Opladen, Germany: Westdeutscher, 1994.

——. "Social Mothers: The Bourgeois Women's Movement and German Welfare-State Formation, 1890–1929." In *Mothers of a New World*, edited by Seth Koven and Sonya. Michel, 136–58. New York: Routledge, 1993.

Sadavish Rao, Karnad. "The Future of the Kanara Saraswat." *Kanara Saraswat* 9 (1925): 4–9.

Sahai, Indu. *Family Structure and Partition: A Study of the Rastogi Community of Lucknow*. Lucknow, India: Ethnographic and Folk Culture Society, 1973.

Salamini, Heather Fowler, and Mary Kay Vaughan, eds. *Creating Spaces, Shaping Transitions: Women of the Mexican Countryside, 1850–1990*. Tucson: University of Arizona Press, 1994.

Salazar Bondy, Sebastian. *Lima la horrible*. Lima: Ediciones Peisa, 1974. Reprint edition.

Saldaña Portillo, Maria José. *The Revolutionary Imagination in the Americas and the Age of Development*. Durham: Duke University Press, 2003.

Scarpa, Ludovica. *Gemeinwohl und lokale Macht: Honoratioren und Armenwesen in der Berliner Luisenstadt im 19. Jahrhundert*. München: Saur, 1995.

Samkange, Stanlake. *Origins of Rhodesia*. London: Heinemann, 1968.

Samuel, Raphael. "The Middle Class between the Wars," parts 1 and 2. *New Socialist*, nos. 9–11 (January–February 1983): 30–36 and (March–April 1983): 28–32.

Sánchez, Luis Alberto. *Peru: retrato de un país adolescente*. 3rd ed. Lima: Ediciones Peisa, 1973.

Sanon, A. J. "Charles et Henri." In *La Petite morale en action, dédiée à la jeunesse*, 75–78. 3rd ed. Paris, [1815–30].

Santos, Lidia. *Tropical Kitsch: Mass Media in Latin American Art and Literature*. Princeton: Markus Wiener, 2006.

Sarkar, Sumit. *Writing Social History*. Delhi: Oxford University Press 1997.

Sarkar, Tanika. "Enfranchised Selves: Women, Culture, and Rights in Nineteenth-Century Bengal." *Gender and History* 13, no. 3 (2001): 546–65.

Savage, Mike. "Individuality and Class: The Rise and Fall of Gentlemanly Social Contract in Britain." In *Social Contracts under Stress*, edited by Olivier Zunz, Leonard Schoppa, and Nobuhiro Hiwatari, 47–65. New York: Russell Sage Foundation, 2002.

Scalabrini Ortiz, Raúl. *El hombre que está solo y espera*. Buenos Aires: Librerías Anaconda, 1932.

——. "Emoción para ayudar a comprender." In *La jornada del 17 de octubre por cuarenta y cinco autores*, edited by Fermin Chavéz, 29–35. Buenos Aires: Corregidor, 1996.

Schambach, Karin. *Stadtbürgertum und industrieller Aufbruch: Dortmund 1780–1870*. Munich: Oldenbourg, 1996.
Schmidt, Elizabeth. *Peasants, Traders, and Wives: Shona Women in the History of Zimbabwe, 1870–1939*. Portsmouth, UK: Heinemann, 1992.
Schnegg, Brigitte. "Soireen, Salons, Sozietäten: Gechlechtsspezifische Aspekte des Wandels städtischer Öffentlichkeit im Ancien Régime am Beispiel Berns." In *Frauen in der Stadt. Les femmes dans la ville*, edited by Anne-Lise Head-König and Albert Tanner, 163–84. Zurich: Chronos, 1993.
Schröder, Iris. *Arbeiten für eine bessere Welt: Frauenbewegung und Sozialreform 1890–1914*. Frankfurt: Campus, 2001.
——. "Soziale Frauenarbeit als bürgerliches Projekt: Differenz, Gleichheit und weiblicher Bürgersinn in der Frauenbewegung um 1900." In *Wege zur Geschichte des Bürgertums*, edited by Klaus Tenfelde and Hans-Ulrich Wehler. Göttingen, Germany: Vandenhoeck & Ruprecht, 1994.
Schulz, Andreas. *Vormundschaft und Protektion: Eliten und Bürger in Bremen 1750–1880*. Munich: Oldenbourg, 2002.
Schwenninger, Sherle R. "Democratizing Capital." *Nation*, April 7, 2008, 27–28.
——. "Reconnecting to the World." *Nation*, June 18, 2005, 13.
Scott, David. "Colonial Governmentality." *Social Text* 43 (Autumn 1995): 191–220.
——. "Modernity That Predated the Modern: Sidney Mintz's Caribbean." *History Workshop Journal* 58, no. 1 (2004): 191–210.
——. "Political Rationalities of the Jamaican Modern." *Small Axe* 7, no. 2 (September 2003): 1–22.
Scott, James. *Seeing Like a State: How Certain Schemes to Improve the Human Condition Have Failed*. New Haven: Yale University Press, 1998.
Scott, Joan Wallach. *Gender and the Politics of History*. New York: Columbia University Press, 1988.
——. "Gender: A Useful Category of Historical Analysis." *The American Historical Review* 91, no. 5 (December 1986), 1053–75.
Scott, Lucas. *Freedom's War: The American Crusade against the Soviet Union*. New York: New York University Press, 1999.
Schwab, Federico. "Lo huachafo como fenómeno social," *Peruanidad* 2, no. 5 (March 1942): 402–3.
Seed, John. "From 'Middling Sort' to Middle Class in Late Eighteenth and Early Nineteenth-Century England." In *Social Orders and Social Classes in Europe Since 1500*, edited by M. L. Bush, 114–35. Manchester, UK: Manchester University Press, 1992.
Seeley, Paul. "Catholics and Apprentices: An Example of Men's Philanthropy." *Journal of Social History* 25, no. 3 (1992): 531–45.
——. "O Sainte Mère: Liberalism and the Socialization of Catholic Men in Nineteenth-Century France." *Journal of Modern History* 70, no. 4 (1998): 862–91.
——. "Virile Pursuits: Youth, Religion, and Bourgeois Family Politics in Lyon on the Eve of the French Third Republic." PhD diss., University of Michigan, 1995.
Segato, Rita Laura. *Alteridades Históricas/identidades políticas: una crítica a las certezas del pluralismo global*. Universidade de Brasília, 1998.

Seigel, Micol. *Uneven Encounters: Making Race and Nation in Brazil and the United States.* Durham: Duke University Press, 2009.

Sevegrand, Martine. *Les enfants du bon Dieu: les catholiques français et la procréation au XXe siècle*. Paris: Albin Michel, 1995.

Shamuyarira, Nathan. *Crisis in Rhodesia*. London: Andre Deutsch, 1965.

Sharma, Aradhana and Gupta Akhil. *The Anthropology of the State: A Reader*. Oxford: Blackwell, 2006.

Shukla, Sandhya, and Heidi Tinsman, eds. *Imagining Our Americas: Toward a Transnational Frame*. Durham: Duke University Press, 2007.

Simon, Brian. *Education and the Social Order, 1940–1990*. London: Palgrave Macmillan, 1990.

Simpson, Eyler M. *The Ejido: Mexico's Way Out*. Chapel Hill: University of North Carolina, 1937.

Sinha, Mrinalini. *Colonial Masculinity: The "Manly Englishman" and the "Effeminate Bengali" in the Late Nineteenth Century*. Manchester, UK: Manchester University Press, 1995.

——. *Specters of Mother India: The Global Restructuring of an Empire*. Durham: Duke University Press, 2006.

Sisters of India, *Indian Spectator*, August 24, 1912, 665–66.

Sluglett, Peter. "Urban Dissidence in Mandatory Syria: Aleppo 1918–1936." In *Etat, ville et mouvvements sociaux au Maghreb et au Moyen Orient*, edited by Kenneth Brown, 301–16. Paris: L'Hartmattan, 1986.

Sluglett, Peter, and Marion Faraouk-Sluglett, "The Application of the 1858 Land Code in Greater Syria." In *Land Tenure and Social Transformation in the Middle East*, edited by Tarif Khalidi, 409–24. Beirut: American University Beirut, 1984.

Smail, John. *The Origins of Middle-Class Culture: Halifax, Yorkshire, 1660–1780*. Ithaca: Cornell University Press, 1994.

Smiles, Samuel. *Self-Help; With Illustrations of Conduct and Perseverance*. London: J. Murray, 1958.

Smith, Bonnie. *Ladies of the Leisure Class: The Bourgeoises of Northern France in the Nineteenth Century*. Princeton: Princeton University Press, 1981.

Smith, Cheryl. "Stepping Out: A History of the Canadian Ballet." PhD diss., University of Toronto, 2002.

Smith, George Barnett. *The Life and Speeches of John Bright, M.P.* London: Hodder and Stoughton, 1882.

Smith, Paul. *Disraelian Conservatism and Social Reform*. London: Routledge, 1967.

Soto Rivera, Roy. *Víctor Raúl: El hombre del siglo XX*. Lima: Instituto Víctor Raúl Haya de la Torre, 2002.

Sowerwine, Charles. "The Sexual Contract of the Third Republic." *French History and Civilization: Papers from the George Rudé Seminar* 1 (2005): 247–55.

Spiegel, Gabrielle M. "The Task of the Historian." *American Historical Review* 114, no. 1 (2009): 1–15.

Spree, Ulrike. "Die verhinderte 'Bürgerin Ein begriffsge begriffsgeschichtlicher Vergleich zwischen Deutschland, Frankreich und Großbritannien." In *Bürgerschaft:*

Rezeption und Innovation der Begrifflichkeit vom Hohen Mittelalter bis ins 19. Jahrhundert, edited by Reinhart Koselleck and Klaus Schreiner, 274–308. Stuttgart: Klett-Cotta, 1994.

Stein, Judith. *Running Steel, Running America: Race, Economic Policy and the Decline of Liberalism*. Chapel Hill: University of North Carolina Press, 1998.

Stein, Steve. *Populism in Peru: The Emergence of the Masses and the Politics of Social Control*. Madison: University of Wisconsin Press, 1980.

Steingart, Gabor. "A Super Power in Decline: America's Middle Class Has Become Globalization's Loser." *Spiegel Online International*, October 10, 2006 (http://www.spiegel.de/international/0,1518,439766,00.html).

Steinhoff, Anthony J. "A Feminized Church? The Campaign for Women's Suffrage in Alsace-Lorraine's Protestant Churches, 1907–1914." *Central European History* 38, no. 2 (2005): 18–49.

Stepan, Nancy. *"The Hour of Eugenics": Race, Gender and Nation in Latin America*. Ithaca: Cornell University Press, 1991.

Stoehr, Irene. "Organisierte Mütterlichkeit. Zur Politik der deutschen Frauenbewegung um 1900." In *Frauen suchen ihre Geschichte*, edited by Karin Hausen, 221–49. Munich: C. H. Beck. 1983,

Stoler, Ann Laura, ed. *Haunted by Empire: Geographies of Intimacy in North American History*. Durham: Duke University Press, 2006.

——. *Race and the Education of Desire: Foucault's "History of Sexuality" and the Colonial Order of Things*. Durham: Duke University Press, 1995.

Stoler, Ann Laura, Carole McGranahan, and Peter C. Perdue. *Imperial Formations*. Santa Fe, NM: School for Advanced Research, 2008.

Streightoff, Frank Hatch. *The Standard of Living among the Industrial People of America*. Boston: Houghton Mifflin, 1911.

Stromquist, Shelton. *Reinventing "The People": The Progressive Movement, the Class Problem, and the Origins of Modern Liberalism*. Urbana: University of Illinois Press, 2006.

Streubel, Christiane. "Literaturbericht: Frauen der politischen Rechten." *H-Soz-u-Kult*, June 10, 2003 (http://hsozkult.geschichte.hu-berlin.de/rezensionen/2003-2-141).

Subercaseaux, Benjamin. *Contribución a la realidad*. Santiago: Studium, 1939.

Subercaseaux, Ramón. *Memorias de ochenta años*. 2nd ed. Vol 2. Santiago: Nascimento, 1936.

Subrahmanyam, Sanjay. "Connected Histories: Notes towards a Reconfiguration of Early Modern Eurasia." *Modern Asian Studies* 31, no. 3 (1997): 735–62.

Svampa, Maristella. *El dilema argentino: "Civilizacion o Barbarie."* Buenos Aires: El Cielo por Asalto, 1994.

Tafett, Jeffrey. *Foreign Aid as Foreign Policy: The Alliance for Progress in Latin America*. New York: Routledge, 2008.

Talcherkar, V. A. "'The Shimga or Holi Festival and the Bombay Mill-Hands.'" *Indian Textile Journal* 14, no. 162 (1904): 176–78.

Talmaki, S. S. "Census of Kanara Saraswats in Bombay and Suburbs, 1922." *Kanara Saraswat* 4, no. 4 (1922): 107–17.

Taylor, Charles. "Two Theories of Modernity." In *Alternative Modernities*, edited by Dilip Parameshwar Gaonkar, 172–96. Durham: Duke University Press, 2001.
Taylor, J. M. *Eva Perón, the Myths of a Woman*. Chicago: University of Chicago Press, 1979.
Taylor, Lewis. "The Origins of APRA in Cajamarca, 1928–1935." *Bulletin of Latin American Research* 19, no. 4 (2000): 437–59.
Terán, Oscar. *En busca de la ideología Argentina*. Buenos Aires: Catálogos, 1986.
Thompson, Edward P. *The Making of the English Working Class*. New York: Vintage, 1963.
Thompson, F. M. L. *Gentrification and the Enterprise Culture: Britain 1780–1980*. Oxford: Oxford University Press, 2001.
Thompson, Paul, "Family, Myth, Models and Denials in the Shaping of Individual Life-Paths." In *Between Generations: Family Models, Myths, and Memories*, edited by Paul Thompson, 13–38. New York: Oxford University Press, 1993.
Thurner, Mark, and Andrés Guerrero, eds. *After Spanish Rule: Postcolonial Predicaments of the Americas*. Durham: Duke University Press, 2003.
Tikekar, Aruna. *The Cloister's Pale: A Biography of the University of Bombay*. Bombay: University of Bombay, 1984.
Tinsman, Heidi. *Partners in Conflict: The Politics of Gender, Sexuality, and Labor in the Chilean Agrarian Reform, 1950–1973*. Durham: Duke University Press, 2002.
Tischler, Andreas. *Die philhellenische Bewegung der 1820'er Jahre in den preussischen Rheinprovinzen*. Cologne: Forschheim, 1981.
Trevelyan, von George Macaulay. *History of England*. London: Longmans, Green and Co., 1926.
Truman, Harry. "Inaugural Address." In *The Presidents Speak: The Inaugural Addresses of the American Presidents from Washington to Clinton*. Edited by David Newton Lott, 251–25. New York: Henry Holt, 1994.
Tucker, Robert C., ed. *The Lenin Anthology*. New York: W. W. Norton, 1975.
Tudesq, André-Jean. *Les Grands Notables en France (1840–1849) Etude historique d'une psychologie sociale*, 2 vols. Paris, 1964.
Tyrell, Alex, and Paul Pickering. *The People's Bread: A History of the Anti-Corn Law League*. Leicester, UK: Leicester University Press, 2000.
Valdes, Ricardo. "Sobre el siútico criollo." *Pacífico*, January 1919, 63–65.
Valis, Noël. *The Culture of Cursilería: Bad Taste, Kitsch, and Class in Modern Spain*. Durham: Duke University Press, 2002.
Vambe, Lawrence. *From Rhodesia to Zimbabwe*. Pittsburgh: University of Pittsburgh Press, 1972.
Van der Veer, Peter. "The Moral State: Religion, Nation, and Empire in Victorian Britain and British India." In *Nation and Religion: Perspectives on Europe and Asia*, edited by Peter van der Veer and Hartmut Lehmann, 15–43. Princeton: Princeton University Press, 1999.
Van Onselen, Charles. *Chibaro: African Mine Labour in Southern Rhodesia, 1900–1933*. London: Pluto, 1976.
Vatsala, Nath. "Luxuries and Necessities in Saraswat Homes." *Kanara Saraswat*, 9, no. 3 (1925): 4–9.

Vaughan, Mary Kay. *Cultural Politics in Revolution: Teachers, Peasants, and Schools in Mexico*. Tucson: University of Arizona Press, 1997.

——. *The State, Education and Social Class in Mexico, 1880–1928*. DeKalb: Northern Illinois University Press, 1982.

Vaughan, Megan. "Africa and the Birth of the Modern World." *Transactions of the Royal Historical Society* 16, no. 6 (2006): 143–62.

Vaughan, Robert. *The Age of Great Cities; Or, Modern Civilization Viewed in Its Relation to Intelligence, Morals and Religion*. London: Jackson, 1843.

Vázquez Ramírez, Esther Martina. *Oganización y resistencia popular en la ciudad de México durante el crisis de 1929–1932*. México, D.F.: Instituto Nacional de Estudios Históricos de la Revolución Mexicana, 1998.

Vega Centeno, Imelda. *Aprismo popular: mito, cultura e historia*. Lima: Tarea, 1985.

Véliz, Claudio. "La mesa de tres patas," *Desarrollo Económico* 3, nos. 1–2 (1963): 231–47.

Vial Correa, Gonzalo. *Historia de Chile (1891–1973)*. Vol. 1, part 2. Santiago: Santillana, 1981.

Vickery, Amanda. "Shaking the Separate Spheres: Did Women Really Descend into Graceful Indolence?" *Times Literary Supplement*, March 12, 1993, 6–7.

Villalobos, Sergio. *Orígen y ascenso de la burguesía chilena*. Santiago: Universitaria, 1987.

Vinken, Barbara. "Wounds of Love: Modern Devotion According to Michelet." *Clio* 36, no. 2 (2007): 155–75.

Vogel, Ursula. "Patriarchale Herrschaft, bürgerliches Recht, bürgerliche Utopia. Eigentumsrcthte der Frauen in Deutschland and England." In *Bürgertum im 19. Jahrhundert*, edited by Jürguen Kocka, 134–66. Göttingen, Germany: Vandenhoeck & Ruprech, 1995.

von Saldern, Adelheid. "Die Stadt und ihre Frauen: Ein Beitrag zur Gender Geschichtsschreibung." In *Informationen zur modernen Stadtgeschichte, Stadtraum und Geschlechterperspektiven*, 6–17. Deutsches Institut für Urbanistik, 2004.

Vovelle, Michel. *Piété baroque et déchristianisation en Provence au XVIIIe siècle: les attitudes devant la mort d'après les clauses des testaments*. Paris: Plon, 1973.

Wacquant, Loïc J. D. "Making Class: The Middle Class(es) in Social Theory and Social Structure." In *Bringing Class Back In: Contemporary Historical Perspectives*, edited by Scott G. McNall, Rhonda F. Levine, and Rick Fantasia, 39–64. Boulder, CO: Westview, 1991.

Wade, Peter. *Race and Ethnicity in Latin America*. London: Pluto, 1997.

Wahrman, Dror. *Imagining the Middle Class: The Political Representation of Class in Britain, c. 1780–1840*. Cambridge: Cambridge University Press, 1996.

Walkowitz, Daniel J. *City Folk: English Country Dance and the Politics of the Folk in Modern America*. New York: New York University Press, 2010.

——. "The Cultural Turn and a New Social History: Folk Dance and the Renovation of Class in Social History." *Journal of Social History* 39, no. 3 (2006): 781–801.

——. *Worker City, Company Town: Iron and Cotton Worker Protest in Troy and Cohoes, New York, 1855–1884*. Urbana: Illinois University Press, 1978.

——. *Working with Class: Social Workers and the Politics of Middle-Class Identity*. Chapel Hill: University of North Carolina Press, 1999.
Walkowitz, Judith. *City of Dreadful Delight: Narratives of Sexual Danger in Late Victorian London*. Chicago: University of Chicago Press, 1992.
——. *Prostitution and Victorian Society: Women, Class, and the State*. Cambridge: Cambridge University Press, 1980.
Wallech, Steven. "Class Versus Rank: The Transformation of English Social Terms and Theories of Production." *Journal of the History of Ideas* 47, no. 3 (1986): 409–31.
Wallerstein, Immanuel. *The Modern World-System*. New York: Academic Press, 1974.
Walzer, Michael, ed. *Toward a Global Civil Society*. Providence, RI: Berghahn, 1995.
——. "The Civil Society Argument." In *Theorizing Citizenship*, edited by Ronald Beiner, 153–74. Albany: State University of New York Press, 1995.
Warde, Alan, and Mark Tomlinson. "Taste among the Middle Classes, 1968–88." In *Social Change and the Middle Classes*, edited by Tim Butler and Mike Savage, 241–56. London: Routledge, 1995.
Ware, Caroline. *Organizacion de la comunidad para el bienestar social*. Washington: Organization of American States, 1956.
Watenpaugh, Keith David. *Being Modern in the Middle East: Revolution, Nationalism, Colonialism, and the Arab Middle Class*. Princeton: Princeton University Press, 2006.
——. "Creating Phantoms: Zaki al-Arsuzi, the Alexandretta Crisis and the Formation of Modern Arab Nationalism in Syria." *International Journal of Middle East Studies*, 28, no. 3 (1996): 363–89.
Weatherill, Lorna. *Consumer Behaviour and Material Culture in Britain, 1660–1760*. London: Routledge, 1988.
Weinstein, Barbara. "Developing Inequality." *American Historical Review* 113, no. 1 (2008): 1–18.
——. *For Social Peace in Brazil: Industrialists and the Remaking of the Working Class in São Paulo, 1920–1964*. Chapel Hill: University of North Carolina Press, 1996.
——. "History without a Cause? Grand Narrative, World History, and the Postcolonial Dilemma." *International Review of Social History* 50 (2005): 71–93.
Wells, Jonathan Daniel. *The Origins of the Southern Middle Class, 1800–1861*. Chapel Hill: University of North Carolina Press, 2004.
Welter, Barbara. "The Cult of True Womanhood, 1820–1860." *American Quarterly* 18, no. 2 (1966): 151–74.
Werlich, David P. *Peru: A Short History*. Carbondale: Southern Illinois University Press, 1978.
West, James L. W. *American Authors and the Literary Marketplace*. Philadelphia: University of Pennsylvania Press, 1988.
West, Michael O. *The Rise of an African Middle Class: Colonial Zimbabwe, 1898–1965*. Bloomington: Indiana University Press, 2002.
——. "The Struggle for Zimbabwe, Then and Now: Notes toward a Deep History of the Current Crisis." *Safundi* 8, no. 2 (2007): 139–47.
——. "The Tuskegee Model of Development in Africa: Another Dimension of the African/African-American Connection." *Diplomatic History* 16, no. 3 (1992): 371–87.

Whitaker, Reg. *Double Standard: The Secret History of Canadian Immigration*. Toronto: Toronto University Press, 1987.

Whitaker, Reg, and Gary Marcuse. *Cold War Canada: The Making of a National Insecurity State, 1945–1957*. Toronto: University of Toronto Press, 1994.

Wiebe, Robert. *The Search for Order, 1877–1920*. New York: Hill and Wang, 1967.

Wiener, Martin. *English Culture and the Decline of the Industrial Spirit, 1840–1980*. Cambridge: Cambridge University Press, 1980.

Wilder, Gary. *The French Imperial Nation-State: Negritude and Colonial Humanism between the Two World Wars*. Chicago: University of Chicago Press, 2005.

Wile, Ira S. "Standards of Living." *Journal of Home Economics* 5 (December 1913): 412–16.

Williams, Raymond. *Keywords: A Vocabulary of Culture and Society*. London: Fontana, 1983.

Wilson, Kathleen. *The Island Race: Englishness, Empire and Gender in the Eighteenth Century*. London: Routledge, 2003

Wolff, Kerstin. *"Stadtmütter": Bürgerliche Frauen und ihr Einfluss auf die Kommunalpolitik im 19. Jahrhundert (1860–1900)*. Konigstein, Germany: Ulrike Helmer: 2003.

Woolf, Stuart. *The Poor in Western Europe in the Eighteenth and Nineteenth Centuries*. New York: Methuen, 1986.

Wrightson, Keith. "Estates, Degrees and Sorts in Tudor and Stuart England," *History Today*, 37, no. 1 (1987): 17–22.

Wyckoff, Walter. *The Workers: An Experiment in Reality*. New York: Charles Scribner's Sons, 1897.

Young, Hugo. *One of Us: Life of Margaret Thatcher*. London: Macmillan, 1993.

Young, Linda. *Middle Class Culture in the Nineteenth Century: America, Australia and Britain*. New York: Palgrave Macmillan, 2003.

Zerback, Ralf. *München und sein Stadtbürgertum*. Munich: Oldenbourg, 1997.

Zunz, Olivier. *Why the American Century?* Chicago: University of Chicago Press, 1998.

Zunz, Olivier, Leonard Schoppa, and Nobuhiro Hiwatari, eds. *Social Contracts under Stress: The Middle Class of America, Europe and Japan at the Turn of the Century*. New York: Russell Sage Foundation, 2002.

Zussman, Robert. *Mechanics of the Middle Class: Work and Politics among American Engineers*. Berkeley: University of California Press, 1985.

CONTRIBUTORS

SUSANNE EINEIGEL holds a master's degree in history from the University of British Columbia. Currently she is a doctoral candidate at the University of Maryland, College Park, where she is writing a dissertation on the middle class in Mexico City, 1890–1940.

MICHAEL A. ERVIN is a foreign service officer with the US Department of State, serving in Guadalajara, Mexico. Until March 2010, he was an associate professor of history at Central Washington University, where his research focused on agronomists, nation building, and nationalism during the Mexican Revolution. His publications have appeared in the *Hispanic American Historical Review* and *The Americas*.

IÑIGO GARCÍA-BRYCE is an assistant professor of history at New Mexico State University. He is the author of *Crafting the Republic: Lima's Artisans and Nation Building in Peru, 1821–1879* (University of New Mexico Press, 2004).

ENRIQUE GARGUIN teaches history at the Universidad Nacional de La Plata and is a doctoral candidate in the Department of History at the State University of New York at Stony Brook. He has coedited, with Sergio Visacovsky, the reader *Moralidades, economías e identidades de clase media: Estudios históricos y etnográficos* (Antropofagia, 2009).

SIMON GUNN is a professor of urban history at the University of Leicester and the coeditor of the Cambridge University Press journal *Urban History*. His publications include *The Public Culture of the Victorian Middle Class* (Manchester University Press,

2000) and, most recently, *The Peculiarities of Liberal Modernity in Imperial Britain* (University of California Press, 2011), coedited with James Vernon.

CAROL E. HARRISON is an associate professor of history at the University of South Carolina. She is the author of *The Bourgeois Citizen in Nineteenth-Century France: Gender, Sociability, and the Uses of Emulation* (Oxford University Press, 1999) and is currently writing a book about French Catholics after the French Revolution.

FRANCA IACOVETTA is a professor of history at the University of Toronto and the coeditor of the Studies in Gender and History series at the University of Toronto Press. Her most recent book, *Gatekeepers: Reshaping Immigrant Lives in Cold War Canada* (Between the Lines, 2007) won the Canadian Historical Association's John A. Macdonald prize for the best book in Canadian history.

SANJAY JOSHI is a professor of history at Northern Arizona University. He is the author of *Fractured Modernity: Making of a Middle Class in Colonial India* (Oxford University Press, 2001) and recently edited *The Middle Class in Colonial India* for Oxford University Press's Themes in Indian History series.

PRASHANT KIDAMBI is a senior lecturer in colonial urban history at the University of Leicester. He is the author of *The Making of an Indian Metropolis: Colonial Governance and Public Culture in Bombay, 1890–1920* (Aldershot, 2007). He has been awarded a Leverhulme Research Fellowship to work on a project that explores the social and cultural history of the first Indian cricket tour to Britain.

A. RICARDO LÓPEZ is an assistant professor of history at Western Washington University. He is currently completing a manuscript titled *Makers of Democracy: The Transnational Formation of the Middle Class in Colombia, 1958–1982*.

GISELA METTELE is a professor of gender history at Friedrich-Schiller University, in Jena, Germany. She has coedited, with Karen Hagemann and Jane Rendall, *Gender, War and Politics, Transatlantic Perspectives* (Palgrave, 2010). Her research focuses on social and cultural history, with an emphasis on gender, from the eighteenth century to the mid-twentieth, especially the history of urbanization, civil society, and religion and society.

MARINA MOSKOWITZ is reader of history at the University of Glasgow. She is the author of *Standard of Living: The Measure of the Middle Class in Modern America* (Johns Hopkins University Press, 2004). She is currently working on a manuscript titled "Seed Money: The Economies of Horticulture in Nineteenth-Century America," which traces the development of the seed trade in the United States.

ROBYN MUNCY is an associate professor of history at the University of Maryland, College Park. She is the author of *Creating a Female Dominion in American Reform, 1890–1935* (Oxford University Press, 1991) and the coauthor, with Sonya Michel, of *Engendering America* (McGraw-Hill, 1999). She is currently working on a political biography of Josephine Roche, a progressive reformer from the 1910s through the 1960s.

BRIAN OWENSBY is a professor of history at the University of Virginia. He is the author of *Empire of Law and Indian Justice in Colonial Mexico* (Stanford University Press, 2008) and *Intimate Ironies: Modernity and the Making of Middle-Class Lives in Brazil* (Stanford University Press, 1999).

DAVID S. PARKER is an associate professor of history at Queen's University, Kingston, Ontario. He is the author of *The Idea of the Middle Class: White-Collar Workers and Peruvian Society, 1900–1950*, (Penn State University Press, 1998). His current work on the duel in Uruguay tries to explain how dueling shaped the norms of politics and journalism in the nineteenth and twentieth centuries, and explores the tension between elites' embrace of the duel and their goal of establishing a political order based on the rule of law. He is the coeditor, with Louise Walker, of *Latin America's Middle Class: Unsettled Questions and New Histories* (Lexington, 2012).

MRINALINI SINHA is the Alice Freeman Palmer Professor of History at the University of Michigan, Ann Arbor. She is the author of *Specters of Mother India: The Global Restructuring of an Empire* (Duke University Press, 2006).

MARY KAY VAUGHAN is a professor of history at the University of Maryland, College Park. She is the author of *Cultural Politics in Revolution: Teachers, Peasants, and Schools in Mexico, 1930–1940* (University of Arizona Press, 1997). Her most recent publications are *The Eagle and the Virgin: Cultural Revolution and National Identity in Mexico, 1920–1940* (Duke University Press, 2006), coedited with Stephen Lewis, and *Sex in Revolution: Gender, Politics, and Power in Modern Mexico* (Duke University Press, 2006), coedited with Jocelyn Olcott and Gabriela Cano. She is a former editor of the *Hispanic American Historical Review.*

DANIEL J. WALKOWITZ holds a joint appointment as professor in the Department of History and Department of Social and Cultural Analysis at New York University. His most recent publications are *City Folk: English Country Dance and the Politics of the Folk in Modern America* (New York University Press, 2010) and the collection he edited with Donna Haverty-Stacke, *Re-Imagining US Labor History* (Continuum, 2010).

KEITH DAVID WATENPAUGH is an associate professor of modern Islam, human rights, and peace at the University of California, Davis. He is author of *Being Modern in the Middle East: Revolution, Nationalism, Colonialism, and the Arab Middle Class* (Princeton University Press, 2006), and has also published in the *American Historical Review*, the *International Journal of Middle East Studies*, and *Social History*. Watenpaugh is writing a history of mass human rights abuse and the humanitarian response in the eastern Mediterranean, titled *Bread from Stones: The Middle East and the Making of Modern Humanitarianism (1914–1946).*

BARBARA WEINSTEIN is the Silver Professor of History at New York University; she has also taught Latin American history at the University of Maryland, College Park, and Stony Brook University. In 2007, she served as president of the American Historical Association. Her publications include *For Social Peace in Brazil: Industrialists and the Remaking of the Working Class in São Paulo, 1920–1964* (University of North Carolina Press, 1998). She is currently completing a book on race, region, and national identities in twentieth-century Brazil, to be published by Duke University Press.

MICHAEL O. WEST is a professor of sociology and Africana studies at Binghamton University, State University of New York. His publications include *The Rise of an African Middle Class: Colonial Zimbabwe, 1898–1965* (Indiana University Press, 2001). He is the coeditor of *From Toussaint to Tupac: The Black International since the Age of Revolution* (Chapel Hill, University of North Carolina Press, 2009).

INDEX

A. RICARDO LÓPEZ is assistant professor of history,
Western Washington University.

BARBARA WEINSTEIN is professor of history,
New York University.

Library of Congress Cataloging-in-Publication Data
The making of the middle class : toward a transnational history / A. Ricardo López
and Barbara Weinstein, editors.
p. cm.—(Radical perspectives : a radical history review book series)
Includes bibliographical references and index.
ISBN 978-0-8223-5117-7 (cloth : alk. paper)
ISBN 978-0-8223-5129-0 (pbk. : alk. paper)
1. Middle class—History—19th century. 2. Middle class—History—20th century.
3. Middle class—History—21st century. I. López, A. Ricardo, 1974– II. Weinstein,
Barbara. III. Series: Radical perspectives.
HT684.M27 2012
305.5′509—dc23
2011030978